Your **full-circle** solution— from assessment to instru...

McDougal Littell
Assessment System

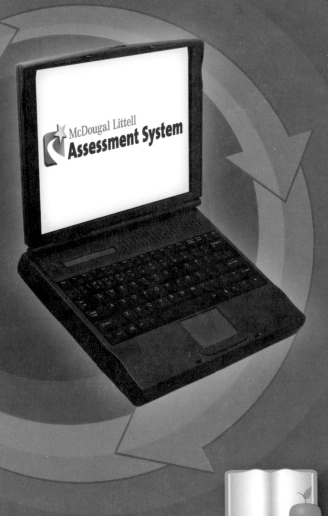

Test

- Access pre-made lesson and benchmark tests correlated to standards
- Create custom tests using the McDougal Littell Test Generator

Score

- Score tests online or use our unique plain-paper scanner system
- Avoid expensive scan cards and other impractical answer sheets

Report

- Generate instant progress reports for individual students or for groups of students
- Track students' performance over time to measure and monitor improvement

Reteach

- Access a complete library of worksheets, study guides, and enrichment exercises tied to standards
- Identify at-risk students and target reteaching based on individual needs

McDougal Littell
Where Great Lessons Begin

1a

McDougal Littell

¡Avancemos!

TEACHER'S EDITION

AUTHORS

Estella Gahala

Patricia Hamilton Carlin

Audrey L. Heining-Boynton

Ricardo Otheguy

Barbara J. Rupert

McDougal Littell

A DIVISION OF HOUGHTON MIFFLIN COMPANY

Evanston, Illinois • Boston • Dallas

* Pre-AP is a registered trademark of the College Entrance Examination Board, which was not involved in
  the production of and does not endorse this product.

* International Baccalaureate is a registered trademark of the International Baccalaureate Organization

ISBN-10: 0-618-68729-7
ISBN-13: 978-0-618-68729-9

3 4 5 6 7 8 9 VHM 10 09 08 07

Internet: www.mcdougallittell.com

Contents

Teacher Reviewers

❈ Teacher's Edition

Sue Arandjelovic
Dobson High School
Mesa, AZ

Shaun A. Bauer
Olympia High School, *retired*
Orlando, FL

Hercilia Bretón
Highlands High School
San Antonio, TX

Maria Fleming Alvarez
The Park School
Brookline, MA

Fatima Hicks
Suncoast High School, *retired*
Riviera Beach, FL

Robin C. Hill
Warrensville Heights High School
Warrensville Heights, OH

Pam Johnson
Stevensville High School
Stevensville, MT

Kristen M. Lombardi
Shenendehowa High School
Clifton Park, NY

Debbe Tomkinson
Madison Middle School
Titusville, FL

Ronie R. Webster
Monson Junior/Senior High School
Monson, MA

❈ Middle School Student Text

Mary Jo Aronica
Lincoln Hall Middle School
Lincolnwood, IL

Suzanne M. Auffray
The Overlake School
Redmond, WA

Elizabeth M. Bossong
Vestal High School
Vestal, NY

Zahava Frymerman
G. W. Carver Middle School
Miami, FL

Ana T. Vázquez-Johnson
Rising Starr Middle School
Fayetteville, GA

Sharon Larracoechea
North Junior High
Boise, ID

Debbe Tomkinson
Madison Middle School
Titusville, FL

Elizabeth L. Torosian
Lowell Community Charter
 Public School
Lowell, MA

Heather T. Walker
Chester Middle School
Chester, VA

Mari Zimmerman
James C. Wright Middle School
Madison, WI

❈ High School Student Text

Susan K. Arbuckle
Mahomet-Seymour High School
Mahomet, IL

Kristi Ashe
Amador Valley High School
Pleasanton, CA

Sheila Bayles
Rogers High School
Rogers, AR

Robert L. Bowbeer
Detroit Country Day Upper School
Beverly Hills, MI

Hercilia Bretón
Highlands High School
San Antonio, TX

Adrienne Chamberlain-Parris
Mariner High School
Everett, WA

Mike Cooperider
Truman High School
Independence, MO

Susan B. Cress
Sheridan High School
Sheridan, IN

Michèle S. de Cruz-Sáenz, Ph.D.
Strath Haven High School
Wallingford, PA

Lizveth Dague
Park Vista Community High School
Lake Worth, FL

Parthena Draggett
Jackson High School
Massillon, OH

Rubén D. Elías
Roosevelt High School
Fresno, CA

Phillip Elkins
Lane Tech College Prep High School
Chicago, IL

Michael Garber
Boston Latin Academy
Boston, MA

Marco García
Derry University Advantage Academy
Chicago, IL

David Gonzalez
Hollywood Hills High School
Hollywood, FL

Raquel R. González
Odessa Senior High School
Odessa, TX

Neyda Gonzalez-Droz
Ridge Community High School
Davenport, FL

Becky Hay de García
James Madison Memorial High School
Madison, WI

Robin C. Hill
Warrensville Heights High School
Warrensville Heights, OH

Gladys V. Horford
William T. Dwyer High School
Palm Beach Gardens, FL

Richard Ladd
Ipswich High School
Ipswich, MA

Patsy Lanigan
Hume Fogg Academic Magnet
  High School
Nashville, TN

Kris Laws
Palm Bay High School
Melbourne, FL

Elizabeth Lupafya
North High School
Worcester, MA

David Malatesta
Niles West High School
Skokie, IL

Patrick Malloy
James B. Conant High School
Hoffman Estates, IL

Brandi Meeks
Starr's Mill High School
Fayetteville, GA

Kathleen L. Michaels
Palm Harbor University High School
Palm Harbor, FL

Linda Nanos
Brook Farm Business Academy
West Roxbury, MA

Nadine F. Olson
School of Teaching and Curriculum
  Leadership
Stillwater, OK

Pam Osthoff
Lakeland Senior High School
Lakeland, FL

Nicholas Patterson
Davenport Central High School
Davenport, IA

Carolyn A. Peck
Genesee Community College
Lakeville, NY

Daniel N. Richardson
Concord High School, *retired*
Concord, NH

Rita E. Risco
Palm Harbor University High School
Palm Harbor, FL

Miguel Roma
Boston Latin Academy
Boston, MA

Nona M. Seaver
New Berlin West Middle/High School
New Berlin, WI

Susan Seraphine-Kimel
Astronaut High School
Titusville, FL

Mary Severo
Thomas Hart Middle School
Pleasanton, CA

Clarette Shelton
WT Woodson High School, *retired*
Fairfax, VA

Maureen Shiland
Saratoga Springs High School
Saratoga Springs, NY

Lauren Schultz
Dover High School
Dover, NH

Irma Sprague
Countryside High School
Clearwater, FL

Mary A. Stimmel
Lincoln High School
Des Moines, IA

Karen Tharrington
Wakefield High School
Raleigh, NC

Alicia Turnier
Countryside High School
Clearwater, FL

Roberto E. del Valle
The Overlake School
Redmond, WA

Todd Wagner
Upper Darby High School, *retired*
Drexel Hill, PA

Ronie R. Webster
Monson Junior/Senior High School
Monson, MA

Cheryl Wellman
Bloomingdale High School
Valrico, FL

Thomasina White
School District of Philadelphia
Philadelphia, PA

Jena Williams
Jonesboro High School
Jonesboro, AR

✿ Program Advisory Council

Louis G. Baskinger
New Hartford High School
New Hartford, NY

Linda M. Bigler
James Madison University
Harrisonburg, VA

Jacquelyn Cinotti-Dirmann
Duval County Public Schools
Jacksonville, FL

Flora Maria Ciccone-Quintanilla
Holly Senior High School
Holly, MI

Desa Dawson
Del City High School
Del City, OK

Robin C. Hill
Warrensville Heights High School
Warrensville Heights, OH

Barbara M. Johnson
Gordon Tech High School, *retired*
Chicago, IL

Ray Maldonado
Houston Independent School District,
  retired
Houston, TX

Karen S. Miller
Friends School of Baltimore
Baltimore, MD

Dr. Robert A. Miller
Woodcreek High School Roseville Joint
  Union High School District
Roseville, CA

Debra M. Morris
Wellington Landings Middle School
Wellington, FL

Maria Nieto Zezas
West Morris Central High School
Chester, NJ

Rita Oleksak
Glastonbury Public Schools
Glastonbury, CT

Sandra Rosenstiel
University of Dallas, *retired*
Grapevine, TX

Emily Serafa Manschot
Northville High School
Northville, MI

¡Avancemos!

Where great lessons begin!

❖ Culture is a Cornerstone

- Celebrates the cultural diversity of the Spanish-speaking world
- Motivates students to think critically with essential questions
- Transports students from the classroom to authentic locations

Language Learning that Lasts

- Presents manageable chunks of material
- Recycles and reviews frequently so students remember
- Spirals content across levels

Practice with a Purpose

- Sets a clear goal
- Provides built-in self-checks
- Offers abundant leveled practice

Time-Saving Teacher Tools

- Simplify your planning with the all-inclusive **easyPlanner DVD-ROM**

- Enliven your presentations with ready-made **POWER PRESENTATIONS**, including **Animated Grammar**

- Test, Score, Report, and Reteach with the comprehensive **McDougal Littell Assessment System**

Easy Articulation

One Complete Program for Middle School through Level 4

or

Levels 1a & 1b are designed with middle school learners in mind. They include more practice, more games and more appropriate visuals for your middle school students. These books prepare students for *¡Avancemos!* level 2.

Level 1 introduces students to the culture and language of the Spanish-speaking world in eight manageable units. To provide flexibility and pacing options, the material taught in units 7 and 8 is fully spiraled in level 2.

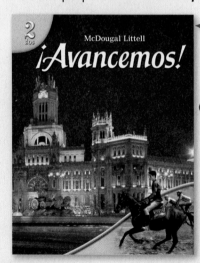

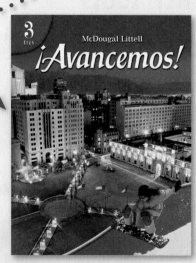

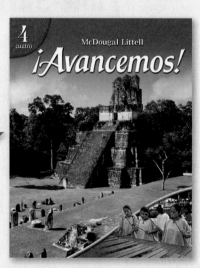

Level 2 begins with a thorough review of core level 1 content. Seamless articulation continues, as material taught in units 7 and 8 of level 2 is spiraled into level 3.

Level 3 reviews core content from levels 1 and 2 before students move on to more advanced language skills.

Level 4 reviews and expands upon the content from the first three levels, as students go on to master more advanced language skills.

1a

	Theme	Vocabulary	Grammar	♻ Recycling
Preliminar	**¡Hola!**	**Nueva York**		
		Greetings; Introductions; Saying where you are from; Numbers from 1 to 10; Exchanging phone numbers; Days of the week; The weather; Classroom phrases	The Spanish alphabet	
Unidad 1	**Un rato con los amigos**	**Estados Unidos**		
	1 ¿Qué te gusta hacer?	After-school activities; Snack foods and beverages	Subject pronouns and **ser**; **Gustar** with an infinitive	Weather expressions
	2 Mis amigos y yo	Describing yourself and others	Definite and indefinite articles; Noun-adjective agreement	**Ser**; Snack foods; **Gustar** with an infinitive; After-school activities
Unidad 2	**¡Vamos a la escuela!**	**México**		
	1 Somos estudiantes	Daily schedules; Telling time; Numbers from 11 to 100	The verb **tener**; Present tense of **-ar** verbs	After-school activities
	2 En la escuela	Describing classes; Describing location; Expressing feelings	The verb **estar**; The verb **ir**	Class subjects; Adjective agreement; Telling time
Unidad 3	**Comer en familia**	**Puerto Rico**		
	1 Mi comida favorita	Meals and food; Asking questions	**Gustar** with nouns; Present tense of **-er** and **-ir** verbs	**Gustar** with an infinitive; Snack foods; The verb **estar**; Telling time
	2 En mi familia	Family; Giving dates; Numbers from 200 to 1,000,000	Possessive adjectives; Comparatives	The verb **tener**; Numbers from 11 to 100; After-school activities; Describing others
Unidad 4	**En el centro**	**España**		
	1 ¡Vamos de compras!	Clothing; Shopping	Stem-changing verbs: e → ie; Direct object pronouns	Numbers from 11 to 100; The verb **tener**; After-school activities
	2 ¿Qué hacemos esta noche?	Places and events; Getting around town; In a restaurant	Stem-changing verbs: o → ue; Stem-changing verbs: e → i	Present tense of **-er** verbs; The verb **ir**; Direct object pronouns; **Tener** expressions

1b

	Theme	Vocabulary	Grammar	♻ Recycling
	Repaso ♻	**Antes de Avanzar**		
		♻ This unit reviews most of the vocabulary in Units 1–4.	♻ This unit reviews most of the grammar in units 1–4.	♻ This unit recycles most of the vocabulary and grammar in units 1–4.
Unidad 5	**Bienvenido a nuestra casa**	**Ecuador**		
	1 Vivimos aquí	Describing a house; Household items; Furniture	**Ser** or **estar**; Ordinal numbers	Stem-changing verbs: o → ue; Location words; Colors; Clothing
	2 Una fiesta en casa	Planning a party; Chores	More irregular verbs; Affirmative **tú** commands	**Tener que**; Interrogative words; Expressions of frequency; Direct object pronouns
Unidad 6	**Mantener un cuerpo sano**	**República Dominicana**		
	1 ¿Cuál es tu deporte favorito?	Sports	The verb **jugar**; **Saber** and **conocer**; The personal **a**	Numbers from 200 to 1,000,000; **Gustar** with nouns; Comparatives
	2 La salud	Staying healthy; Parts of the body	Preterite of regular **-ar** verbs; Preterite of **-car, -gar, -zar** verbs	**Gustar** with nouns; Stem-changing verbs: o → ue; Telling time
Unidad 7	**¡Una semana fenomenal!**	**Argentina**		
	1 En el cibercafé	Sending e-mails; Talking about when events occur	Preterite of regular **-er** and **-ir** verbs; Affirmative and negative words	Affirmative **tú** commands; Telling time; Foods and beverages; Preterite of regular **-ar** verbs;
	2 Un día en el parque de diversiones	Making a phone call; Places of interest	Preterite of **ir, ser,** and **hacer**; Pronouns after prepositions	Noun-adjective agreement; Places around town; Stem-changing verbs: o → ue
Unidad 8	**Una rutina diferente**	**Costa Rica**		
	1 Pensando en las vacaciones	Daily routines; Vacation plans	Reflexive verbs; Present progressive	Preterite of **hacer**; Direct object pronouns; Parts of the body; Chores; Houses; Telling time
	2 ¡Vamos de vacaciones!	Discussing vacation and leisure activities	Indirect object pronouns; Demonstrative adjectives	Family; Numbers from 200 to 1,000,000; **Gustar** with an infinitive; Present progressive; Classroom objects

Scope and Sequence

Theme	Vocabulary	Grammar	♻ Recycling
Preliminar ¡Hola!	**Nueva York**		
	Greetings; Introductions; Saying where you are from; Numbers from 1 to 10; Exchanging phone numbers; Days of the week; The weather; Classroom phrases	The Spanish alphabet	
Unidad 1 Un rato con los amigos	**Estados Unidos**		
1 ¿Qué te gusta hacer?	After-school activities; Snack foods and beverages	Subject pronouns and **ser**; **Gustar** with an infinitive	Weather expressions
2 Mis amigos y yo	Describing yourself and others	Definite and indefinite articles; Noun-adjective agreement	**Ser**; Snack foods; **Gustar** with an infinitive; After-school activities
Unidad 2 ¡Vamos a la escuela!	**México**		
1 Somos estudiantes	Daily schedules; Telling time; Numbers from 11 to 100	The verb **tener**; Present tense of -**ar** verbs	After-school activities
2 En la escuela	Describing classes; Describing location; Expressing feelings	The verb **estar**; The verb **ir**	Class subjects; Adjective agreement; Telling time
Unidad 3 Comer en familia	**Puerto Rico**		
1 Mi comida favorita	Meals and food; Asking questions	**Gustar** with nouns; Present tense of -**er** and -**ir** verbs	**Gustar** with an infinitive; Snack foods; The verb **estar**; Telling time
2 En mi familia	Family; Giving dates; Numbers from 200 to 1,000,000	Possessive adjectives; Comparatives	The verb **tener**; Numbers from 11 to 100; After-school activities; Describing others
Unidad 4 En el centro	**España**		
1 ¡Vamos de compras!	Clothing; Shopping	Stem-changing verbs: **e → ie**; Direct object pronouns	Numbers from 11 to 100; The verb **tener**; After-school activities
2 ¿Qué hacemos esta noche?	Places and events; Getting around town; In a restaurant	Stem-changing verbs: **o → ue**; Stem-changing verbs: **e → i**	Present tense of -**er** verbs; The verb **ir**; Direct object pronouns; **Tener** expressions
Unidad 5 Bienvenido a nuestra casa	**Ecuador**		
1 Vivimos aquí	Describing a house; Household items; Furniture	**Ser** or **estar**; Ordinal numbers	Stem-changing verbs: **o → ue**; Location words; Colors; Clothing
2 Una fiesta en casa	Planning a party; Chores	More irregular verbs; Affirmative **tú** commands	**Tener que**; Interrogative words; Expressions of frequency; Direct object pronouns
Unidad 6 Mantener un cuerpo sano	**República Dominicana**		
1 ¿Cuál es tu deporte favorito?	Sports	The verb **jugar**; **Saber** and **conocer**; The personal **a**	Numbers from 200 to 1,000,000; **Gustar** with nouns; Comparatives
2 La salud	Staying healthy; Parts of the body	Preterite of regular -**ar** verbs; Preterite of -**car**, -**gar**, -**zar** verbs	**Gustar** with nouns; Stem-changing verbs: **o → ue**; Telling time
Unidad 7 ¡Una semana fenomenal!	**Argentina**		
1 En el cibercafé	Sending e-mails; Talking about when events occur	Preterite of regular -**er** and -**ir** verbs; Affirmative and negative words	Affirmative **tú** commands; Telling time; Foods and beverages; Preterite of regular -**ar** verbs;
2 Un día en el parque de diversiones	Making a phone call; Places of interest	Preterite of **ir**, **ser**, and **hacer**; Pronouns after prepositions	Noun-adjective agreement; Places around town; Stem-changing verbs: **o → ue**
Unidad 8 Una rutina diferente	**Costa Rica**		
1 Pensando en las vacaciones	Daily routines; Vacation plans	Reflexive verbs; Present progressive	Preterite of **hacer**; Direct object pronouns; Parts of the body; Chores; Houses; Telling time
2 ¡Vamos de vacaciones!	Discussing vacation and leisure activities	Indirect object pronouns; Demonstrative adjectives	Family; Numbers from 200 to 1,000,000; **Gustar** with an infinitive; Present progressive; Classroom objects

	Theme	Vocabulary	Grammar	♻ Recycling
Preliminar	**Mis amigos y yo**	**Florida**		
		♻ Saying who you are; Personality characteristics; Daily activities and food; Places in school and around town; Saying how you feel; Daily routine; Making plans	♻ Definite and indefinite articles; Subject pronouns and **ser**; Adjectives; The verb **tener**; The verb **gustar**; **Ir + a +** place; **Ser** or **estar**; Regular present-tense verbs; Stem-changing verbs	
Unidad 1	**¡A conocer nuevos lugares!**	**Costa Rica**		
	1 **¡Vamos de viaje!**	Going on a trip	Direct object pronouns; Indirect object pronouns	Possessions; Prepositions of location; Places around town; Daily activities
	2 **Cuéntame de tus vacaciones**	On vacation	Preterite of **-ar** verbs; Preterite of **ir**, **ser, hacer, ver, dar**	Interrogatives; Food; Days of the week; Parties
Unidad 2	**¡Somos saludables!**	**Argentina**		
	1 **La Copa Mundial**	Sports and health	Preterite of **-er** and **-ir** verbs; Demonstrative adjectives and pronouns	Food; Sports equipment; Colors; Clothing; Classroom objects
	2 **¿Qué vamos a hacer?**	Daily routines	Reflexive verbs; Present progressive	**Pensar;** Parts of the body; Telling time; Places in school and around town
Unidad 3	**¡Vamos de compras!**	**Puerto Rico**		
	1 **¿Cómo me queda?**	Clothes and shopping	Present tense of irregular **yo** verbs; Pronouns after prepositions	**Gustar;** Clothing; Expressions of frequency
	2 **¿Filmamos en el mercado?**	At the market	Irregular preterite verbs	Family; Chores; Food
Unidad 4	**Cultura antigua, ciudad moderna**	**México**		
	1 **Una leyenda mexicana**	Legends and stories	The Imperfect tense; Preterite and imperfect	Expressions of frequency; Weather expressions; Daily activities
	2 **México antiguo y moderno**	Past and present	Preterite of **-car, -gar, -zar** verbs; More verbs with irregular preterite stems	Daily activities; Arts and crafts
Unidad 5	**¡A comer!**	**España**		
	1 **¡Qué rico!**	Preparing and describing food	**Usted/ustedes** commands; Pronoun placement with commands	Staying healthy; Chores
	2 **¡Buen provecho!**	Ordering meals in a restaurant	Affirmative and negative words; Double object pronouns	Prepositions of location; Pronoun placement with commands
Unidad 6	**¿Te gusta el cine?**	**Estados Unidos**		
	1 **¡Luces, cámara, acción!**	Making movies	Affirmative **tú** commands; Negative **tú** commands	Daily routines; Telling time
	2 **¡Somos estrellas!**	Invitations to a premiere	Present subjunctive with **ojalá**; More subjunctive verbs with **ojalá**	Spelling changes in the preterite; School subjects; Vacation activities; Sports
Unidad 7	**Soy periodista**	**República Dominicana**		
	1 **Nuestro periódico escolar**	The school newspaper	Subjunctive with impersonal expressions; **Por** and **para**	Present subjunctive; Events around town
	2 **Somos familia**	Family and relationships	Comparatives; Superlatives	Clothing; Family; Classroom objects
Unidad 8	**Nuestro futuro**	**Ecuador**		
	1 **El mundo de hoy**	The environment and conservation	Other impersonal expressions; Future tense of regular verbs	Expressions of frequency; Vacation activities
	2 **En el futuro...**	Careers and professions	Future tense of irregular verbs	Clothing; Telling time; Daily routine

¡Avancemos! Level 3

Scope and Sequence

	Theme	Vocabulary	Grammar	♻ Recycling
Preliminar	**Una vida ocupada** — Estados Unidos			
		♻ Talking about yourself and your friends; Saying what you know how to do; Talking about people and places you know; Describing your daily routine; Making comparisons	♻ Verbs like **gustar**; Present tense of regular verbs; Present tense of irregular verbs; Present tense of **yo** verbs; Stem-changing verbs; The verbs **decir, tener,** and **venir; Saber** or **conocer; Ser** or **estar;** Reflexive verbs	
Unidad 1	**Nos divertimos al aire libre** — México			
	1 Vamos a acampar	Camping; Nature	Preterite tense of regular verbs; Regular preterites	Irregular present tense
	2 Vamos a la playa	Family relationships; At the beach	Imperfect tense; Preterite vs. imperfect	**Saber** and **conocer**
Unidad 2	**¡Es hora de ayudar!** — Estados Unidos			
	1 ¡Todos para uno y uno para todos!	Volunteer activities and projects	**Tú** commands; Other command forms	Irregular preterite; Family relationships; Describing a camping trip; Beach activities; **Ir a** + infinitive
	2 ¿Cómo nos organizamos?	Requests and recommendations; Media	Pronouns with commands	Preterite vs. imperfect; Beach activities; Volunteer activities
Unidad 3	**¡El futuro de nuestro planeta!** — Centroamérica			
	1 ¿Cómo será el futuro?	Environmental concerns	Future tense; **Por** and **para**	**Ustedes** commands; **Ir a** + infinitive; Media vocabulary
	2 Por un futuro mejor	Social awareness; Presenting and supporting opinions	Present subjunctive of regular verbs; More subjunctive verb forms	**Ustedes** commands; Impersonal expressions; Future tense
Unidad 4	**Así quiero ser** — El Caribe			
	1 ¿Quién te inspira?	Describing others; Professions	Future tense; Subjunctive with verbs of influence	**Ser** vs. **estar;** Future tense
	2 ¿Quiénes son los héroes?	Expressing positive and negative emotions; More professions; Supporting opinions	Subjunctive with doubt; Subjunctive with emotion	Describing people; Superlatives; Family relationships; **-ísimo**
Unidad 5	**¿Cómo te entretienes?** — Los países andinos			
	1 Comuniquémonos entre naciones	Travel preparations; Computers; Requirements and conditions	Subjunctive with conjunctions; Subjunctive with the unknown	Commands with **tú;** Professions vocabulary
	2 Nuevos amigos, nuevas oportunidades	Participating in a group discussion; Leisure activities	Conditional tense; Reported speech	Preterite; Computer vocabulary
Unidad 6	**¿Dónde vivimos?** — España			
	1 La vida en la ciudad	Around the neighborhood; An apartment in the city	Past participle as adjectives; Present perfect tense	Preterite; Direct object pronouns
	2 Fuera de la ciudad	Traveling by train; Describing a historical site	Past perfect tense; Future perfect tense	Present perfect; **Tú** commands; Places in the neighborhood; Past participles as adjectives
Unidad 7	**Tu pasado y tu futuro** — Venezuela y Colombia			
	1 Recuerdos	Planning for the future; School activities and events; Part-time jobs	Imperfect subjunctive; Subjunctive of perfect tenses	Present perfect; Subjunctive with doubt; Impersonal expressions
	2 Nuevos principios	Pursuing a career	**Si** clauses; Sequence of tenses	Subjunctive with impersonal expressions; Conditional future; Architectural structures
Unidad 8	**Hablemos de literatura** — Cono Sur			
	1 Cuentos y poesía	Discussing and critiquing literature	Past progressive; Conjunctions	Preterite vs. imperfect; Professions
	2 El drama	Reading and interpreting plays	**Se** for unintentional occurrences; Uses of the subjunctive	**Si** clauses; Literary vocabulary

	Theme	Vocabulary	Grammar	♻ Recycling
Unidad 1	**1 En busca de trabajo**	Office equipment; Insurance and professions; Job interview	**Ser** vs. **estar**; Direct and indirect object pronouns used together	Reflexive constructions; **Ir a** + infinitive; Present progressive; Imperative commands using **usted**
	2 Correo electrónico	E-mail; Talking and writing about work	Use and omission of definite and indefinite articles; **Por** vs. **para**	**Saber** and **conocer**
Unidad 2	**1 Los deportes**	Sports and outdoor activities	Preterite vs. imperfect; Changes in meaning with verbs in the preterite	**Por** vs. **para**; Possessive pronouns; Prepositions; Direct and indirect object pronouns; Interrogative pronouns
	2 Para pasarlo bien	City life; Leisure activities; Entertainment	Comparatives of equality and inequality; Prepositions; Superlatives	Preterite; Imperfect; Reflexive verbs; Present progressive; **Ir a** + infinitive
Unidad 3	**1 ¿Adónde vamos de vacaciones?**	Planning a trip	Past participle; The preterite perfect and pluscuamperfecto	**Ser** vs. **estar**; Present progressive; Adjective endings; **Ir a** + infinitive; Prepositions
	2 De viaje	Air travel	Future and conditional tense to express possibility and conjecture	**Ir a** + infinitive; **Por** vs. **para**; Direct and indirect object pronouns; Present progressive
Unidad 4	**1 Pintura y música**	Art; Music	Future perfect; Conditional perfect; Relative pronouns	Prepositions; **Por** vs. **para**; Imperfect; Preterite; Present perfect; Direct and indirect object pronouns; Possessive pronouns; Reflexive verbs
	2 Escultura y literatura	Sculpture; Literature	Passive voice; Idiomatic expressions	Conditional; Preterite; Present progressive; Relative pronouns; Superlative; Future; Imperfect; **Ir a** + infinitive; Direct and indirect object pronouns
Unidad 5	**1 La familia y los problemas sociales**	Family relationships; Courtship; Marriage; Social problems and solutions	The subjunctive	Preterite; Adjectives; Reflexive verbs
	2 La educación y las finanzas	School and college; Finances	Subjunctive vs. indicative; Command forms	**Ir a** + infinitive; Future tense; Object pronouns; Reflexive pronouns
Unidad 6	**1 La televisión y las noticias**	Television; Politics; Natural disasters	**Tú** commands; **Nosotros** commands	Relative pronouns; **Ser** vs. **estar**; **Por** vs. **para**; Adjectives (form and position); Reflexive verbs; **Ir a** + infinitive; Preterite; Stem-Changing verbs (e → ie, o → ue); Imperfect; Prepositions (a, de, en); Comparatives; Present progressive; Possessive pronouns; Present perfect
	2 La programación y la publicidad	Television programming; Commercial advertising	Imperfect subjunctive; Compound tenses in the subjunctive	**Hace** meaning ago; Direct and indirect object pronouns; Relative pronouns; Imperfect; Adjectives (form and position); **Por** vs. **para**; Reflexive verbs; **Ir a** + infinitive; Adverbs; Demonstrative adjectives; **Ser** vs. **estar**; Prepositions (a, de, en, con); Preterite

Cultural References

Geography, Maps, Flags

History and Politics

early cultures and civilizations

events

people

Holidays and Celebrations

Language

regional variants for

Literature

Monuments and Museums

monuments

museums

Music and Dance

music

Spanish Speakers Around the Globe

Traditions

¡Avanza con celebraciones!

- The *Celebraciones* section of *¡Avancemos!* includes twelve mini cultural lessons about holidays and celebrations, one for each month of the year. *Celebraciones* allows you to teach a special lesson about a holiday when it is relevant and when it fits your schedule!

- The *Celebraciones* mini cultural lessons are also available online. The **online version** gives you the added benefit of *Cultura interactiva*. Just click on any photo and watch the celebration come to life!

febrero

Cultura INTERACTIVA ClassZone.com *See these pages come alive!*

¡Carnaval!

Carnaval marks a period of festivity prior to the beginning of Lent. Lent was, and for some still is, a 40-day period of solemnity and fasting with the removal of meat from the diet being a key feature. You can see the word *carne* (meat) in *Carnaval*; traditionally, this was the last chance to eat meat before the Lenten fast. Today, *Carnaval* often resembles a lively, multi-day party.

Falling in either February or March, *Carnaval* is typically celebrated during the five days that precede Ash Wednesday, the first day of Lent. In some countries, *Carnaval* lasts longer, overlapping other local celebrations. In many regions, traditions such as throwing water and eggs can start over a month before the actual holiday. The planning for the next year's parades, parties, and dance groups often starts as soon as the current *Carnaval* ends!

México

Cascarones Breaking *cascarones* on the heads of friends and other party-goers is a *Carnaval* tradition. The sprinkling of confetti from these hollowed-out eggs is said to bring good luck, as seen here in Mazatlán.

Bolivia

Máscaras are a *Carnaval* tradition dating back to medieval Spain. This masked dancer is from the parade in Oruro, where some 40,000 folkloric dancers and musicians participate.

Bailarines folklóricos Dancers from the Mestizaje dance group perform in Barranquilla. The Colombian government proclaimed this city's *Carnaval* celebration, which combines indigenous, African, and European traditions, a National Cultural Heritage. UNESCO declared it a "Masterpiece" for its cultural uniqueness.

Colombia

Disfraces Elaborate costumes are central to the *Carnaval* celebration. This costume, entitled "África soy yo," appeared in Las Palmas, in the Canary Islands.

España

Carnaval Revelers dance in Encarnación, site of the largest celebration in Paraguay.

Paraguay

Vocabulario para celebrar
los bailarines	dancers
la banda	musical band
Carnaval	Carnival
los cascarones	confetti-filled eggs
el disfraz	costume
las máscaras	masks

Comparación cultural

1. The ways in which *Carnaval* is celebrated in the Spanish-speaking world differ depending on the region. Why do you think the celebrations have evolved differently?
2. Compare the traditions of *Carnaval* to any holiday that you celebrate. Which one(s) are similar? How are they similar?

C14 Celebraciones

Celebraciones C15

- *Celebraciones* online is also available completely in Spanish!

¡Avanza con cultura!

- Each unit includes two thematic lessons that present just the right amount of material for students.

- Each unit is set in a location that provides the **cultural backdrop** for real-life themes.

- Experience **authentic culture** online at ClassZone.com!

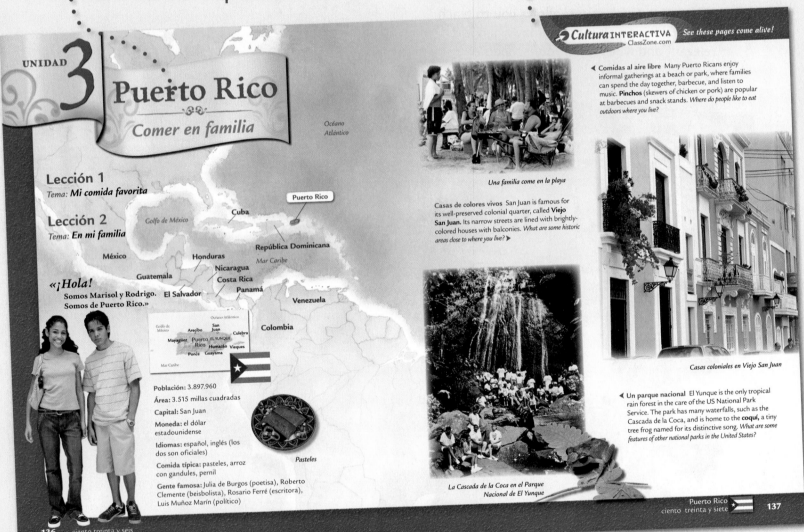

Cultura INTERACTIVA ClassZone.com · *See these pages come alive!*

UNIDAD 3

Puerto Rico
Comer en familia

Lección 1
Tema: **Mi comida favorita**

Lección 2
Tema: **En mi familia**

Océano Atlántico

Puerto Rico

Cuba

Golfo de México

República Dominicana

México
Honduras
Mar Caribe
Guatemala
Nicaragua
Costa Rica
El Salvador
Panamá
Venezuela
Colombia

«¡Hola!
Somos Marisol y Rodrigo.
Somos de Puerto Rico.»

Golfo de México
Océano Atlántico
Arecibo San Juan
Mayagüez Puerto EL YUNQUE Culebra
Rico Humacao Vieques
Ponce Guayama
Mar Caribe

Población: 3.897.960

Área: 3.515 millas cuadradas

Capital: San Juan

Moneda: el dólar estadounidense

Idiomas: español, inglés (los dos son oficiales)

Comida típica: pasteles, arroz con gandules, pernil

Pasteles

Gente famosa: Julia de Burgos (poetisa), Roberto Clemente (beisbolista), Rosario Ferré (escritora), Luis Muñoz Marín (político)

136 ciento treinta y seis

◄ **Comidas al aire libre** Many Puerto Ricans enjoy informal gatherings at a beach or park, where families can spend the day together, barbecue, and listen to music. **Pinchos** (skewers of chicken or pork) are popular at barbecues and snack stands. *Where do people like to eat outdoors where you live?*

Una familia come en la playa

Casas de colores vivos San Juan is famous for its well-preserved colonial quarter, called **Viejo San Juan.** Its narrow streets are lined with brightly-colored houses with balconies. *What are some historic areas close to where you live?* ►

Casas coloniales en Viejo San Juan

◄ **Un parque nacional** El Yunque is the only tropical rain forest in the care of the US National Park Service. The park has many waterfalls, such as the Cascada de la Coca, and is home to the **coquí,** a tiny tree frog named for its distinctive song. *What are some features of other national parks in the United States?*

La Cascada de la Coca en el Parque Nacional de El Yunque

Puerto Rico
ciento treinta y siete **137**

- Students get a quick look at important **facts and figures** about the target country.

- Meet the *Telehistoria* characters who will accompany you and your students through the unit.

Avanza lets your students know what they will learn and why.

Lessons are based on themes that are relevant to students.

Online tools help your students succeed!

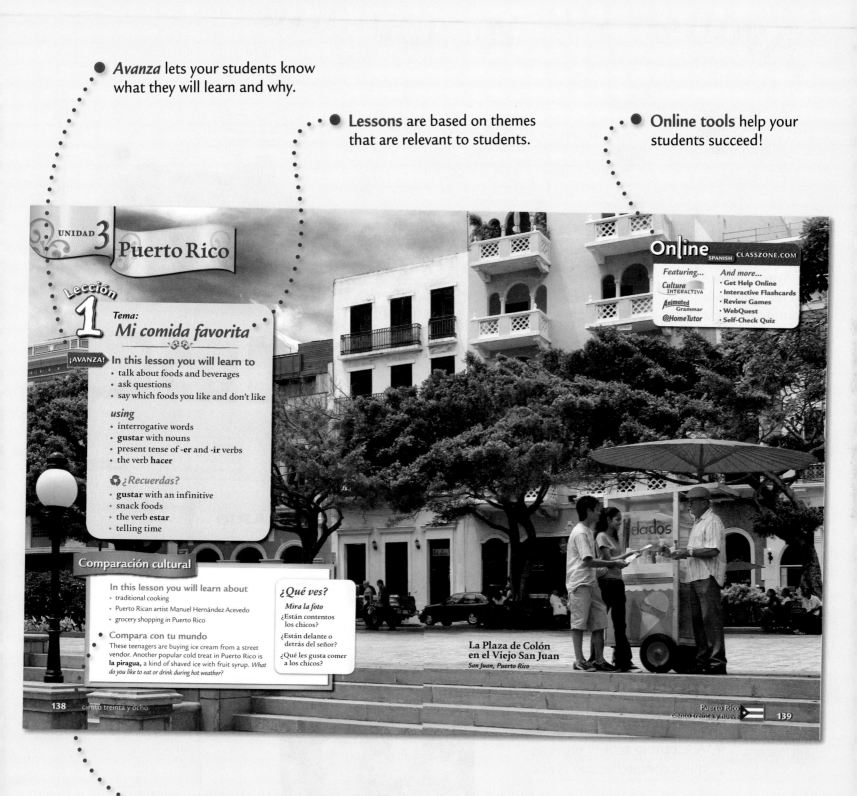

UNIDAD 3

Puerto Rico

Lección **1**

Tema:
Mi comida favorita

¡AVANZA! **In this lesson you will learn to**
- talk about foods and beverages
- ask questions
- say which foods you like and don't like

using
- interrogative words
- **gustar** with nouns
- present tense of **-er** and **-ir** verbs
- the verb **hacer**

♻ *¿Recuerdas?*
- **gustar** with an infinitive
- snack foods
- the verb **estar**
- telling time

Comparación cultural

In this lesson you will learn about
- traditional cooking
- Puerto Rican artist Manuel Hernández Acevedo
- grocery shopping in Puerto Rico

● **Compara con tu mundo**
These teenagers are buying ice cream from a street vendor. Another popular cold treat in Puerto Rico is **la piragua**, a kind of shaved ice with fruit syrup. *What do you like to eat or drink during hot weather?*

¿Qué ves?
Mira la foto
¿Están contentos los chicos?

¿Están delante o detrás del señor?

¿Qué les gusta comer a los chicos?

La Plaza de Colón en el Viejo San Juan
San Juan, Puerto Rico

Online SPANISH CLASSZONE.COM

Featuring...
Cultura INTERACTIVA
Animated Grammar
@HomeTutor

And more...
- Get Help Online
- Interactive Flashcards
- Review Games
- WebQuest
- Self-Check Quiz

138 ciento treinta y ocho

Puerto Rico ➤ ciento treinta y nueve 139

Compara con tu mundo helps students see the relevance of cultural information by asking them to compare the target culture with their own. Look for this feature throughout the unit.

¡Avanza con vocabulario!

● **Vocabulary** is presented in context.

● *Avanza* provides a clear goal to let students know what is new and what is review.

● **Blue words** help students know what to study.

● A **listening** activity provides a quick comprehension check.

● **Additional practice** is available online.

Presentación de VOCABULARIO

¡AVANZA! **Goal:** Learn about what Rodrigo and Marisol eat for breakfast, lunch, and dinner. Then practice what you have learned to talk about foods and beverages. *Actividades 1–2*

¿Recuerdas? **gustar** with an infinitive p. 44

VIDEO DVD / AUDIO

A ¡Hola! Me llamo Rodrigo y ella es Ana. Son las ocho de la mañana. **Es importante comer un desayuno nutritivo** todos los días.

el desayuno

los huevos

el pan

B Cuando **tengo hambre**, me gusta comer **huevos** y **pan**. Cuando **tengo sed**, bebo **jugo de naranja**. Me gusta mucho porque es **rico**. Nunca bebo **café** porque es **horrible**.

el cereal

el yogur

En Puerto Rico se dice... In Puerto Rico the word for *orange juice* is **el jugo de china**.

las bebidas

el jugo de naranja · el café · la leche

Unidad 3 Puerto Rico
156 ciento cincuenta y seis

C Es la una y **ahora** Marisol y yo comemos **el almuerzo**. En la cafetería **venden** muchas **comidas**: **sándwiches, hamburguesas** y **sopa**. También venden **bebidas**: **leche, jugos** y **refrescos**.

el almuerzo

el sándwich de jamón y queso

la hamburguesa

la sopa

Más vocabulario

¿Cómo? *How?*	¿Quién(es)? *Who?*
¿Cuál(es)? *Which?*	compartir *to share*
¿Por qué? *Why?*	otro(a) *other*
¿Qué? *What?*	*Expansión de vocabulario* p. R4

Continuará...

Lección 1
ciento cincuenta y siete **157**

Presentación de VOCABULARIO
(continuación)

D Marisol y yo compramos fruta **para** mi papá: **manzanas, bananas** y **uvas**. **La cena** es a las siete y **tengo ganas de** comer. Siempre como mucho cuando mi mamá prepara la comida.

la manzana

las uvas

la banana

En Puerto Rico se dice... The word for *banana* is **el guineo**.

la cena

¡A responder! Escuchar

Write **desayuno** and **almuerzo** on separate pieces of paper. Listen to the list of foods. Hold up the correct piece or pieces of paper to indicate when you eat each food.

@HomeTutor VideoPlus
Interactive Flashcards
ClassZone.com

Unidad 3 Puerto Rico
158 ciento cincuenta y ocho

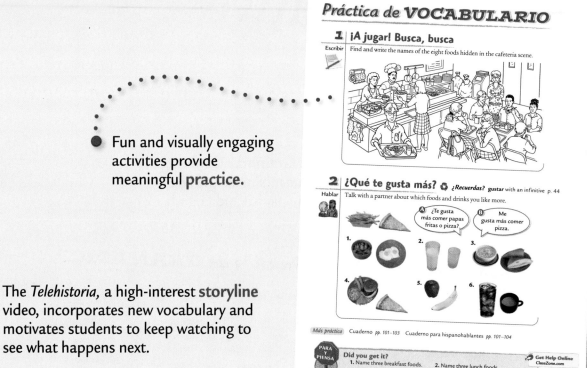

● Fun and visually engaging activities provide meaningful **practice.**

● The *Telehistoria,* a high-interest **storyline** video, incorporates new vocabulary and motivates students to keep watching to see what happens next.

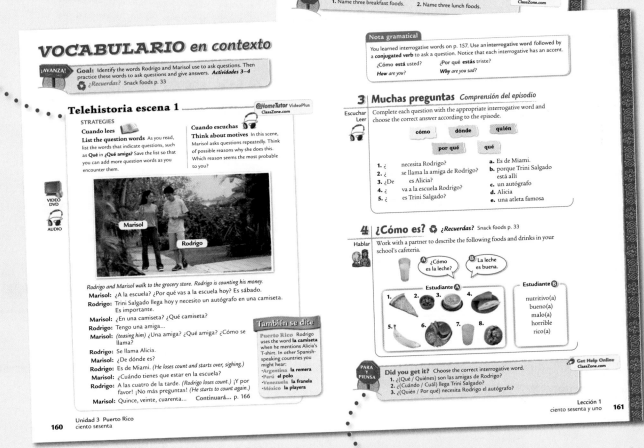

Para y piensa helps students know if they "got it."

¡Avanza con gramática!

- A wide **variety** of practice activities keeps students interested. Careful sequencing builds success.

- **English Grammar Connection** helps students make the link between Spanish and English.

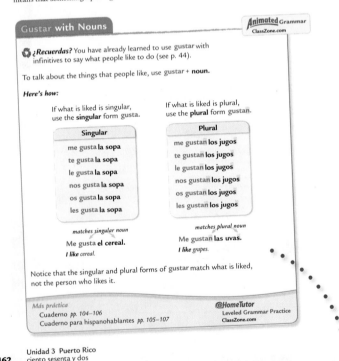

Presentación de GRAMÁTICA

¡AVANZA! **Goal:** Learn how to use **gustar** with nouns. Then practice using this verb to express what foods you like and don't like. **Actividades 5–11**

English Grammar Connection: In English, the phrase *I like* doesn't change. In Spanish, there are two ways to say it, depending on whether what you like is singular or plural. This is because the Spanish phrase **me gusta** literally means that something *is pleasing to me.*

Gustar with Nouns

Animated Grammar
ClassZone.com

🔄 **¿Recuerdas?** You have already learned to use gustar with infinitives to say what people like to do (see p. 44).

To talk about the things that people like, use gustar + **noun.**

Here's how:

If what is liked is singular, use the **singular** form gusta.

If what is liked is plural, use the **plural** form gustan.

Singular
me gusta **la sopa**
te gusta **la sopa**
le gusta **la sopa**
nos gusta **la sopa**
os gusta **la sopa**
les gusta **la sopa**

Plural
me gustan **los jugos**
te gustan **los jugos**
le gustan **los jugos**
nos gustan **los jugos**
os gustan **los jugos**
les gustan **los jugos**

matches singular noun
Me gusta **el cereal.**
I like cereal.

matches plural noun
Me gustan **las uvas.**
I like grapes.

Notice that the singular and plural forms of gustar match what is liked, not the person who likes it.

Más práctica
Cuaderno *pp. 104–106*
Cuaderno para hispanohablantes *pp. 105–107*

@HomeTutor
Leveled Grammar Practice
ClassZone.com

Práctica de GRAMÁTICA

5 ¿Qué les gusta?

Hablar
Escribir

Tell whether the following people like or don't like the following foods and drinks.

modelo: a Luis / el yogur 😊
A Luis le gusta el yogur.

1. a los maestros / el café 😊
2. a nosotros / las papas fritas 😊
3. a Adela / las manzanas 🙁
4. a mí / las hamburguesas 🙁
5. a mis amigos / los sándwiches 😊
6. a ti / las uvas 😊
7. a Jaime y a Rafael / la leche 🙁
8. a usted / el cereal 😊
9. a ellos / las bananas 🙁
10. a ustedes / el jugo 😊

6 En el supermercado

Leer
Escribir

Indicate what these people like and don't like at the supermarket, according to the description.

modelo: El yogur es horrible. (a Rodrigo)
A Rodrigo no le gusta el yogur.

1. Las uvas son ricas. (a ti)
2. La sopa es buena. (a Marisol)
3. El cereal es malo. (a nosotros)
4. Los huevos son horribles. (a mí)
5. El café es muy bueno. (a usted)
6. Los jugos son nutritivos. (a ellos)

Pronunciación   Las letras r y rr

AUDIO

In Spanish, the letter **r** in the middle or the end of a word is pronounced by a single tap of the tongue against the gum above the upper front teeth. The letter **r** at the beginning of a word or **rr** within a word is pronounced by several rapid taps called a trill.

El cereal y el yogur son ricos; no son horribles.

Listen and repeat.

pa**r**a   ce**r**eal   be**b**er   yogu**r**
rico   **r**ubio   ho**rr**ible   piza**rr**ón

- **Grammar presentations** are clear and easy to follow.

Comparación cultural boxes highlight the variety within the Spanish-speaking world. Students personalize what they learn by comparing it with their own world.

Students **activate** newly learned language to talk about culture.

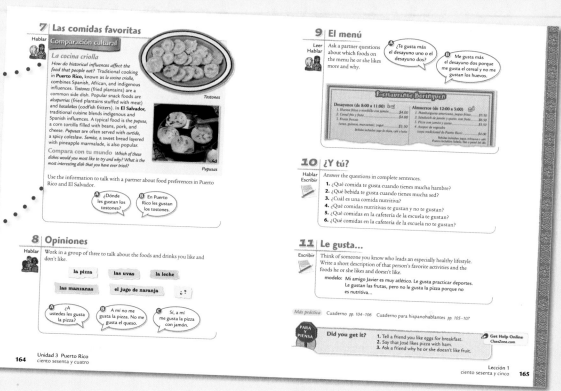

7 | Las comidas favoritas

Hablar

Comparación cultural

La cocina criolla

How do historical influences affect the food that people eat? Traditional cooking in **Puerto Rico**, known as *la cocina criolla*, combines Spanish, African, and indigenous influences. *Tostones* (fried plantains) are a common side dish. Popular snack foods are *alcapurrias* (fried plantains stuffed with meat) and *bacalaitos* (codfish fritters). In **El Salvador**, traditional cuisine blends indigenous and Spanish influences. A typical food is the *pupusa*, a corn tortilla filled with beans, pork, and cheese. *Pupusas* are often served with *curtido*, a spicy coleslaw. *Semita*, a sweet bread layered with pineapple marmalade, is also popular.

Compara con tu mundo Which of these dishes would you most like to try and why? What is the most interesting dish that you have ever tried?

Tostones

Pupusas

Use the information to talk with a partner about food preferences in Puerto Rico and El Salvador.

A ¿Dónde les gustan los tostones?

B En Puerto Rico les gustan los tostones.

8 | Opiniones

Hablar

Work in a group of three to talk about the foods and drinks you like and don't like.

la pizza | las uvas | la leche

las manzanas | el jugo de naranja | ¿ ?

A ¿A ustedes les gusta la pizza?

B A mí no me gusta la pizza. No me gusta el queso.

C Sí, a mí me gusta la pizza con jamón.

9 | El menú

Leer Hablar

Ask a partner questions about which foods on the menu he or she likes more and why.

A ¿Te gusta más el desayuno uno o el desayuno dos?

B Me gusta más el desayuno dos porque me gusta el cereal y no me gustan los huevos.

Restaurante Boriquen

Desayunos (de 8:00 a 11:00)		Almuerzos (de 12:00 a 3:00)	
1. Huevos fritos a revoltillo con jamón $4.00		1. Hamburguesa americana, papas fritas $3.50	
2. Cereal frío y fruta $4.00		2. Sándwich de jamón y queso, con fruta $6.50	
3. Frutas frescas $3.50		3. Pizza con jamón y queso $5.50	
(uvas, guineos, manzanas), yogur		4. Asopao de vegetales	
		(sopa tradicional de Puerto Rico) $4.00	
Bebidas incluidas: jugo de china, café o leche		Bebidas incluidas: limonada, té o panel del día	

10 | ¿Y tú?

Hablar Escribir

Answer the questions in complete sentences.

1. ¿Qué comida te gusta cuando tienes mucha hambre?
2. ¿Qué bebida te gusta cuando tienes mucha sed?
3. ¿Cuál es una comida nutritiva?
4. ¿Qué comidas nutritivas te gustan y no te gustan?
5. ¿Qué comidas en la cafetería de la escuela te gustan?
6. ¿Qué comidas en la cafetería de la escuela no te gustan?

11 | Le gusta...

Escribir

Think of someone you know who leads an especially healthy lifestyle. Write a short description of that person's favorite activities and the foods he or she likes and doesn't like.

modelo: Mi amigo Javier es muy atlético. Le gusta practicar deportes. Le gustan las frutas, pero no le gusta la pizza porque no es nutritiva...

Más práctica Cuaderno pp. 104–106 Cuaderno para hispanohablantes pp. 105–107

PARA Y PIENSA

Did you get it?
1. Tell a friend you like eggs for breakfast.
2. Say that José likes pizza with ham.
3. Ask a friend why he or she doesn't like fruit.

Get Help Online ClassZone.com

Unidad 3 Puerto Rico
ciento sesenta y cuatro **164**

Lección 1
ciento sesenta y cinco **165**

Strategies for reading and listening give you options for presenting the *Telehistoria* and strengthen your students' skills.

The continuing *Telehistoria* motivates students to find out what happens next and reinforces the grammar they have just learned.

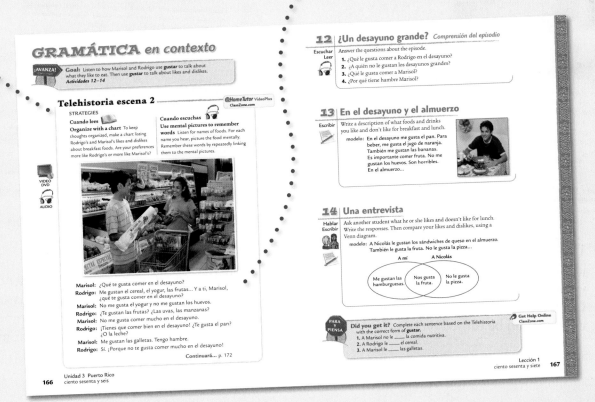

GRAMÁTICA en contexto

¡AVANZA! **Goal:** Listen to how Marisol and Rodrigo use **gustar** to talk about what they like to eat. Then use **gustar** to talk about likes and dislikes. **Actividades 12–14**

Telehistoria escena 2

@HomeTutor VideoPlus ClassZone.com

STRATEGIES

Cuando lees
Organize with a chart To keep thoughts organized, make a chart listing Rodrigo's and Marisol's likes and dislikes about breakfast foods. Are your preferences more like Rodrigo's or more like Marisol's?

Cuando escuchas
Use mental pictures to remember words Listen for names of foods. For each name you hear, picture the food mentally. Remember these words by repeatedly linking them to the mental pictures.

VIDEO
DVD

AUDIO

Marisol: ¿Qué te gusta comer en el desayuno?
Rodrigo: Me gustan el cereal, el yogur, las frutas... Y a ti, Marisol, ¿qué te gusta comer en el desayuno?
Marisol: No me gusta el yogur y no me gustan los huevos.
Rodrigo: ¿Te gustan las frutas? ¿Las uvas, las manzanas?
Marisol: No me gusta comer mucho en el desayuno.
Rodrigo: ¡Tienes que comer bien en el desayuno! ¿Te gusta el pan? ¿O la leche?
Marisol: Me gustan las galletas. Tengo hambre.
Rodrigo: Sí. ¡Porque no te gusta comer mucho en el desayuno!

Continuará... p. 172

12 | ¿Un desayuno grande? *Comprensión del episodio*

Escuchar Leer

Answer the questions about the episode.

1. ¿Qué le gusta comer a Rodrigo en el desayuno?
2. ¿A quién no le gustan los desayunos grandes?
3. ¿Qué le gusta comer a Marisol?
4. ¿Por qué tiene hambre Marisol?

13 | En el desayuno y el almuerzo

Escribir

Write a description of what foods and drinks you like and don't like for breakfast and lunch.

modelo: En el desayuno me gusta el pan. Para beber, me gusta el jugo de naranja. También me gustan las bananas. Es importante comer fruta. No me gustan los huevos. Son horribles. En el almuerzo...

14 | Una entrevista

Hablar Escribir

Ask another student what he or she likes and doesn't like for lunch. Write the responses. Then compare your likes and dislikes, using a Venn diagram.

modelo: A Nicolás le gustan los sándwiches de queso en el almuerzo. También le gusta la fruta. No le gusta la pizza...

A mí — A Nicolás

Me gustan las hamburguesas. | Nos gusta la fruta. | No le gusta la pizza.

PARA Y PIENSA

Did you get it? Complete each sentence based on the Telehistoria with the correct form of **gustar**.
1. A Marisol no le _____ la comida nutritiva.
2. A Rodrigo le _____ el cereal.
3. A Marisol le _____ las galletas.

Get Help Online ClassZone.com

Unidad 3 Puerto Rico
166 ciento sesenta y seis

Lección 1
ciento sesenta y siete **167**

¡Avanza con Todo junto!

- *Todo junto* brings together everything students have learned so they can show what they know.

- Each activity is labeled so you and your students know exactly which **skill** to focus on.

Todo junto

¡AVANZA! **Goal:** *Show what you know* Pay attention to the **-er** and **-ir** verbs Rodrigo and Marisol use to talk about eating healthy food. Then practice these verbs and **gustar** to talk about lunchtime in the cafeteria. *Actividades 21–25*

¿*Recuerdas?* Telling time p. 99

Telehistoria completa

@HomeTutor VideoPlus
ClassZone.com

STRATEGIES

Cuando lees
Find the twist There is sometimes a "twist," or something unexpected, toward the end of a story or scene. Find the twist in this scene. What is it? Why is it unexpected?

Cuando escuchas
Listen for attitude changes To understand the scene fully, notice people's attitudes. At the beginning of the scene, what are Marisol's and Rodrigo's contrasting attitudes? Whose attitude changes during the scene? Why?

Escena 1 **Resumen**

Rodrigo necesita el autógrafo de Trini Salgado para Alicia. Tiene que estar en la escuela a las cuatro de la tarde.

Escena 2 **Resumen**
Rodrigo compra comida. Le gusta la comida nutritiva. Marisol tiene hambre porque no le gusta comer mucho en el desayuno.

VIDEO DVD
AUDIO

Escena 3

Marisol stops to order an ice cream.
Rodrigo: ¿Helado? ¿En el almuerzo?
Marisol: Sí, tengo ganas de comer helado. ¿Compartimos?
Rodrigo: El helado no es nutritivo.
Marisol: ¡Pero es muy rico!
Rodrigo: ¿Qué comes en la cena? ¿Una hamburguesa con papas fritas?

Marisol: ¿Venden papas fritas?
Rodrigo: Tienes que comer comidas buenas.
Marisol: Sí, sí. Yo como comida nutritiva de vez en cuando.
Rodrigo: ¿Sí? ¿Qué comes?
Marisol: Me gusta la sopa.
Rodrigo: La sopa es muy buena.
Marisol: Necesito una bebida.
Marisol walks away. Rodrigo sneaks a taste of her ice cream.
Rodrigo: El helado es muy rico.

Unidad 3 Puerto Rico
ciento setenta y dos
172

---

21 | ¡A completar! *Comprensión de los episodios*

Escuchar Leer

Complete the following sentences, based on the episodes.
1. Rodrigo necesita...
2. La amiga de Miami se llama...
3. En el desayuno Rodrigo come...
4. Marisol tiene hambre porque...
5. Marisol tiene ganas de...
6. Cuando Marisol compra una bebida, Rodrigo...

22 | Organiza la información *Comprensión de los episodios*

Escuchar Leer

Write an article about Marisol or Rodrigo. Copy this map on a piece of paper and use it to organize the information.

¿cuándo? — ¿qué?
¿quién? Marisol
¿cómo? simpática

23 | ¿Qué hacen en la cafetería? ¿*Recuerdas?* Telling time p. 99

Hablar

STRATEGY Hablar
Think and practice in advance First write down words or phrases you want to say. Then practice pronouncing them aloud. Say them in sentences several times and you will be ready for your conversation!

Work in a group of three to talk about what you do in the cafeteria. Include what time you go and what they sell there. Also explain what you eat and drink and why.

A ¿A qué hora van ustedes a la cafetería? ¿Qué hacen?
B Como en la cafetería a la una. Los lunes como pizza y bebo jugo porque no me gusta la leche.
C Yo compro una manzana y leo un libro...

Lección 1
ciento setenta y tres **173**

- The *¡Avancemos!* program on DVD includes Vocabulary Presentation videos, ongoing *Telehistoria*, and *Comparación cultural* videos. Spanish captions can be turned on or off.

- Show the whole *Telehistoria* or simply view scene three!

- Frequent **recycling** helps students remember previously taught material.

Students read, listen, and speak using theme-related prompts. *Integración* prepares students for the new format of the AP Language test.

Juegos y diversiones provides great ideas for active learning to keep your students fully engaged.

24 | Integración

Leer
Escuchar
Hablar

Read the newspaper ad for Supermercado Grande. Then listen to the radio ad for Supermercado Econo. Say what foods you like and where they sell them.

Fuente 1 Anuncio

Fuente 2 Anuncio de radio

Listen and take notes
• ¿Qué comidas venden en el Supermercado Econo?
• ¿Qué venden en la cafetería?

modelo: A mí me gustan las uvas. Venden uvas en el Supermercado Grande...

25 | La cafetería de la escuela

Escribir

Write a letter to your principal about the school cafeteria. What is good and bad there? Why? Do you have any questions about it?

modelo: Sr. Hogan:

¿Cómo está usted? Me gusta la escuela pero no me gusta mucho la cafetería. No es muy grande y hay muchos estudiantes. ¿Por qué no venden...

Writing Criteria	Excellent	Good	Needs Work
Content	Your letter includes a lot of information.	Your letter includes some information.	Your letter includes little information.
Communication	Most of your letter is organized and easy to follow.	Parts of your letter are organized and easy to follow.	Your letter is disorganized and hard to follow.
Accuracy	Your letter has few mistakes in grammar and vocabulary.	Your letter has some mistakes in grammar and vocabulary.	Your letter has many mistakes in grammar and vocabulary.

Más práctica Cuaderno pp. 110–111 Cuaderno para hispanohablantes pp. 112–113

PARA Y PIENSA

Did you get it? Complete the first sentence with a form of **gustar**, and the second sentence with the correct form of **compartir** or **beber**.
1. A Rodrigo le _____ la fruta. Él _____ jugo de naranja.
2. A Rodrigo y a Ana les _____ los sándwiches. Siempre _____ un sándwich.

Get Help Online
ClassZone.com

174 Unidad 3 Puerto Rico
ciento setenta y cuatro

An open-ended writing activity provides a model and a rubric so students know exactly what they have to do to succeed.

Juegos y diversiones

Review food vocabulary by playing a game of Fly Swatter.

MATAMOSCAS

The Setup

Your teacher will tape a number of picture cards on the board and divide the class into two teams.

Playing the Game

The first player from each team will go up to the board. Your teacher will give each player a fly swatter and then say a vocabulary word represented by one of the pictures. The player who "swats" the correct picture first gets a point.

Play continues with new players from each team.

The Winner!

The team with the most points at the end wins.

Materials
• picture cards representing vocabulary words
• two fly swatters
• tape

Lección 1
ciento setenta y cinco **175**

¡Avanza con lecturas!

- **Reading strategies** help students become successful readers.

- **Authentic readings** spark students' interest!

- **Comprehension** questions encourage students to apply the information they have learned from the reading.

- *Lectura cultural* highlights cultural diversity. Each reading presents a topic and compares how practices, products, and perspectives are the same or different in two Spanish-speaking countries.

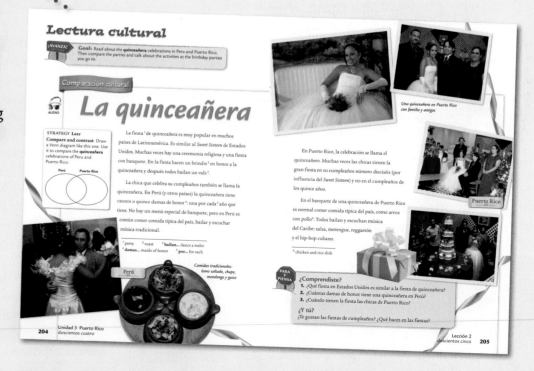

¡Avanza con proyectos!

Fun projects offer a variety of opportunities for students to explore new topics.

Students use Spanish to learn more about other disciplines in *Conexiones*.

Conexiones   *Las ciencias*

Los huracanes

The Caribbean island of Puerto Rico is located in an area prone to hurricanes (**huracanes**). The word *hurricane* comes from the Taino word *hurákan*, which was used by the pre-Columbian inhabitants of the island to describe these storms (**tormentas**). Hurricanes draw energy from the surface of warm tropical waters and from moisture in the air. The extreme winds of 74 miles per hour or more can create storm surges—domes of water up to 20 feet high and 100 miles wide—and can spawn tornadoes, torrential rain, and floods. Research and write about the most severe weather condition where you live. Create a diagram or drawing to illustrate your report.

La ruta del huracán Georges

el 27 de septiembre

el 25 de septiembre

Puerto

el 22 de septiembre

el 20 de septiembre

el 18 de septiembre

el 17 de septiembre

Las etapas del huracán Georges
17/09/98 Tormenta tropical
18/09/98 Huracán – categoría 2
20/09/98 Huracán – categoría 4

Proyecto 1 *Las matemáticas*

Hurricane Georges passed over Puerto Rico at a speed of about 24 kilometers per hour (**kilómetros por hora**). Find the distance from Humacao to Mayagüez in kilometers and calculate the time it took for the storm to move from one city to the other.

Proyecto 2 *La historia*

Research another major hurricane that has hit Puerto Rico in the past century. Draw a map showing the trajectory of the hurricane. Then write a paragraph describing the storm.

Proyecto 3 *La geografía*

Compare this map to the one on page xxxi to name three other countries that were hit by Hurricane Georges. Make a chart in Spanish showing the three countries, the dates of the storm, and the category of the hurricane at the time it hit.

La playa Ocean Park, Puerto Rico, durante el huracán Georges

Proyectos culturales

Comparación cultural

Instrumentos de Puerto Rico y Perú

How do certain instruments and music become associated with a particular region? Percussion instruments that produce strong beats and rhythms are the base of much of the music of **Puerto Rico**. In **Peru**, the **zampoña** is a wind instrument that adds a deep and distinctive sound to traditional Andean music.

Proyecto 1 *Percussion*

Puerto Rico Make your own rhythm on a homemade percussion instrument.

Materials for your own percussion instrument
An object that can be used as a "found" percussion instrument, such as:
• coffee or juice can
• yogurt cup with pebbles, sand or seeds, secured inside with a lid on top
• wooden, plastic, or metal spoons
• pan lid and long-handled brush
• upside-down basket

Instructions
Practice making a rhythm pattern you can repeat on your "found" percussion instrument. Try creating different tones by striking the instrument in different places or with different objects.

Proyecto 2 *Zampoña*

Perú Use these simple materials to create your own **zampoña**.

Materials for zampoña
4 or more plastic or glass bottles, all the same size
Water

Instructions
1. Bring to class four or more bottles (all the same size) and add water so that they all have different amounts, ranging from empty to two thirds full.
2. Put your mouth to the top of each bottle and blow as if playing the flute. Because each bottle contains a different amount of air and water, you should hear various pitches.
3. Add tape so that the bottles are connected in a row. Arrange the bottles according to their pitch, from low to high.

En tu comunidad

You can find Andean music in most large music stores. If there is one in your community, find out what Andean music is sold there and if music from other countries is also available.

En tu comunidad opens the door for students to use Spanish in their community.

¡Ya llegamos!

The **all-inclusive review** page highlights essential vocabulary and grammar from the lesson.

Llegada reminds students exactly what they have accomplished in the lesson.

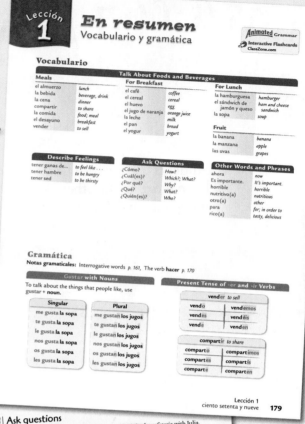

Lección 1

En resumen
Vocabulario y gramática

Animated Grammar
Interactive Flashcards
ClassZone.com

Vocabulario

Talk About Foods and Beverages

Meals

el almuerzo	lunch
la bebida	beverage, drink
la cena	dinner
compartir	to share
la comida	food; meal
el desayuno	breakfast
vender	to sell

For Breakfast

el café	coffee
el cereal	cereal
el huevo	egg
el jugo de naranja	orange juice
la leche	milk
el pan	bread
el yogur	yogurt

For Lunch

la hamburguesa	hamburger
el sándwich de jamón y queso	ham and cheese sandwich
la sopa	soup

Fruit

la banana	banana
la manzana	apple
las uvas	grapes

Describe Feelings

tener ganas de...	to feel like . . .
tener hambre	to be hungry
tener sed	to be thirsty

Ask Questions

¿Cómo?	How?
¿Cuál(es)?	Which?; What?
¿Por qué?	Why?
¿Qué?	What?
¿Quién(es)?	Who?

Other Words and Phrases

ahora	now
Es importante.	It's important.
horrible	horrible
nutritivo(a)	nutritious
otro(a)	other
para	for; in order to
rico(a)	tasty, delicious

Gramática

Notas gramaticales: Interrogative words *p. 161*, The verb **hacer** *p. 170*

Gustar with Nouns

To talk about the things that people like, use gustar + **noun**.

Singular
me gusta **la sopa**
te gusta **la sopa**
le gusta **la sopa**
nos gusta **la sopa**
os gusta **la sopa**
les gusta **la sopa**

Plural
me gustan **los jugos**
te gustan **los jugos**
le gustan **los jugos**
nos gustan **los jugos**
os gustan **los jugos**
les gustan **los jugos**

Present Tense of -er and -ir Verbs

vender	*to sell*
vendo	vendemos
vendes	vendéis
vende	venden

compartir	*to share*
comparto	compartimos
compartes	compartís
comparte	comparten

Lección 1
ciento setenta y nueve **179**

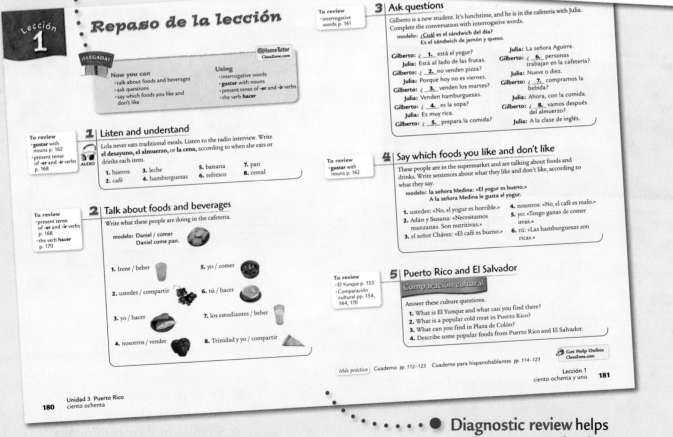

Lección 1

Repaso de la lección

¡LLEGADA!

@HomeTutor
ClassZone.com

Now you can
- talk about foods and beverages
- ask questions
- say which foods you like and don't like

Using
- interrogative words
- **gustar** with nouns
- present tense of **-er** and **-ir** verbs
- the verb **hacer**

To review
- **gustar** with nouns p. 162
- present tense of **-er** and **-ir** verbs p. 168

1 Listen and understand

Lola never eats traditional meals. Listen to the radio interview. Write **el desayuno**, **el almuerzo**, or **la cena**, according to when she eats or drinks each item.

AUDIO

1. huevos
2. café
3. leche
4. hamburguesas
5. banana
6. refresco
7. pan
8. cereal

To review
- present tense of **-er** and **-ir** verbs p. 168
- the verb **hacer** p. 170

2 Talk about foods and beverages

Write what these people are doing in the cafeteria.

modelo: Daniel / comer
Daniel come pan.

1. Irene / beber
2. ustedes / compartir
3. yo / hacer
4. nosotros / vender
5. yo / comer
6. tú / hacer
7. los estudiantes / beber
8. Trinidad y yo / compartir

To review
- interrogative words p. 161

3 Ask questions

Gilberto is a new student. It's lunchtime, and he is in the cafeteria with Julia. Complete the conversation with interrogative words.

modelo: ¿Cuál es el sándwich del día?
Es el sándwich de jamón y queso.

Gilberto: ¿ **1.** está el yogur?
Julia: Está al lado de las frutas.
Gilberto: ¿ **2.** no venden pizza?
Julia: Porque hoy no es viernes.
Gilberto: ¿ **3.** venden los martes?
Julia: Venden hamburguesas.
Gilberto: ¿ **4.** es la sopa?
Julia: Es muy rica.
Gilberto: ¿ **5.** prepara la comida?

Julia: La señora Aguirre.
Gilberto: ¿ **6.** personas trabajan en la cafetería?
Julia: Nueve o diez.
Gilberto: ¿ **7.** compramos la bebida?
Julia: Ahora, con la comida.
Gilberto: ¿ **8.** vamos después del almuerzo?
Julia: A la clase de inglés.

To review
- **gustar** with nouns p. 162

4 Say which foods you like and don't like

These people are in the supermarket and are talking about foods and drinks. Write sentences about what they like and don't like, according to what they say.

modelo: la señora Medina: «El yogur es bueno.»
A la señora Medina le gusta el yogur.

1. ustedes: «No, el yogur es horrible.»
2. Adán y Susana: «Necesitamos manzanas. Son nutritivas.»
3. el señor Chávez: «El café es bueno.»
4. nosotros: «No, el café es malo.»
5. yo: «Tengo ganas de comer uvas.»
6. tú: «Las hamburguesas son ricas.»

To review
- El Yunque p. 153
- Comparación cultural pp. 154, 164, 170

5 Puerto Rico and El Salvador

Comparación cultural

Answer these culture questions.

1. What is El Yunque and what can you find there?
2. What is a popular cold treat in Puerto Rico?
3. What can you find in Plaza de Colón?
4. Describe some popular foods from Puerto Rico and El Salvador.

Get Help Online
ClassZone.com

Más práctica Cuaderno *pp. 112–123* Cuaderno para hispanohablantes *pp. 114–123*

Lección 1
ciento ochenta y uno **181**

Unidad 3 Puerto Rico
180 ciento ochenta

Diagnostic review helps students prepare for the test.

Comparación cultural integrates reading and writing skills with cultural information.

Writing strategies help students organize their ideas.

Repaso inclusivo provides options for cumulative review.

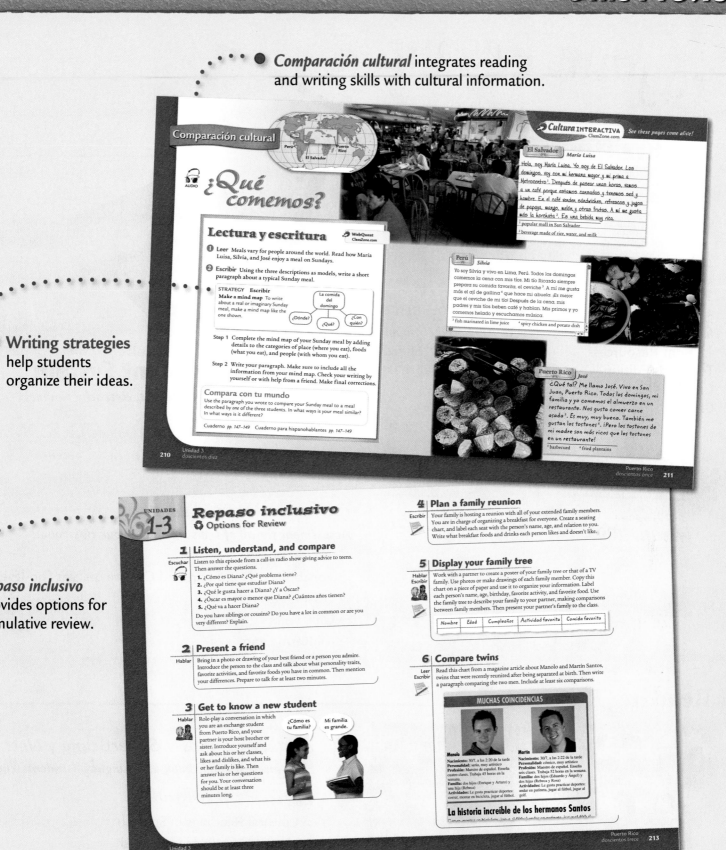

Activities focus on integrating language taught in previous units.

Program Resources

❖ Teacher Time Savers

EasyPlanner
includes audio and video, plus
- All Print Resources
- Teacher's Edition
- Calendar Function
- Clip Art

PowerPresentations
with Animated Grammar!
- PowerPoint™ Slides
- Overhead Transparencies
- Review Games

McDougal Littell Assessment System
Test, Score, Report, Reteach - Online!

Test Generator CD-ROM
with downloadable editable content

Differentiated Assessment Program
Assessment for all of the students in your classroom!
includes
- Vocabulary, Grammar, and Culture quizzes (on-level only)
- Lesson Tests
- Unit Tests
- Midterm Exam
- Final Exam

❖ Reading Resources

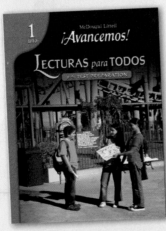

AvanzaCómics   *SuperBruno y Nati*
High-interest comic book uses language students know

Lecturas para todos
- Cultural Readings in Spanish
- Literary Readings in Spanish
- Academic and Informational Readings
- Standardized Test Preparation
- Audio CD available

❖ Authentic Language Comes to Life

¡Avancemos! video program
· Vocabulary Video
· Telehistoria (3 scenes per lesson)
· Cultural Comparison Video

Audio Program
· Student Text Audio
· Workbook Audio
· Assessment Audio
· Heritage Learners Audio
· Lecturas para todos Audio

❖ Personalized Practice with a Purpose

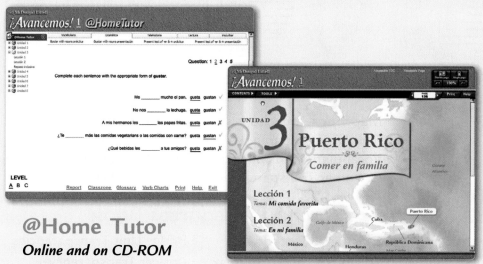

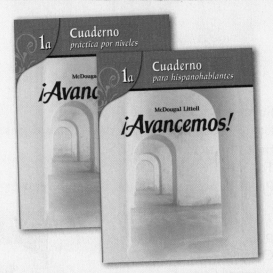

@Home Tutor
Online and on CD-ROM
· Leveled Practice
· Animated Grammar
· Audio
· VideoPlus with
  Interactive Script

eEdition Online
· Cultura interactiva
· Audio
· Video
· Links to Reteaching Copymasters

Cuaderno: práctica por niveles
Cuaderno para hispanohablantes
3 levels of practice — A, B, C

· Vocabulary	· Reading
· Grammar	· Writing
· Integrated skills	· Culture
· Listening	

❈ Resources for Heritage Learners

Lecturas para hispanohablantes

- Cultural Readings in Spanish
- Literary Readings in Spanish
- Academic and Informational Readings
- Standardized Test Preparation
- Audio CD available

Cuaderno para hispanohablantes

- Leveled practice to meet the varied needs of heritage learners
- Additional instruction targeted to heritage learners' unique needs

Heritage Learners Assessment

- Lesson Tests
- Unit Tests
- Midterm Exam
- Final Exam

❈ Teacher Resource Manager

Best Practices Toolkit

- Strategies for Effective Teaching
- Using Technology in the World Languages Classroom
- Best Practices in Middle School
- Tools for Motivation
- Pre-AP and International Baccalaureate*

Unit Resource Books

- Reteaching & Practice Copymasters
- Practice Games
- Video Activities
- Video Scripts
- Audio Scripts
- Map/Culture Activities
- Fine Art Activities
- Family Letters
- Family Involvement Activities
- Absent Student Copymasters

Unit Transparency Books

- Map Transparencies
- Fine Art Transparencies
- Vocabulary Transparencies
- Grammar Transparencies
- Situational Transparencies
- Warm-up Transparencies
- Student Book and Workbook Answer Transparencies

Middle School Resources Book

- Diagnostic Test for 1b
- Vocabulary and Grammar Practice Copymasters for the Bridge Unit
- Bridge Unit Transparencies
- Answer Transparencies
- Audio CD for 1b

Lesson Plans

Teaching Proficiency Through Reading and Storytelling

*International Baccalaureate is a registered trademark of the International Baccalaureate Organization.

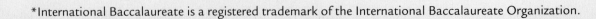

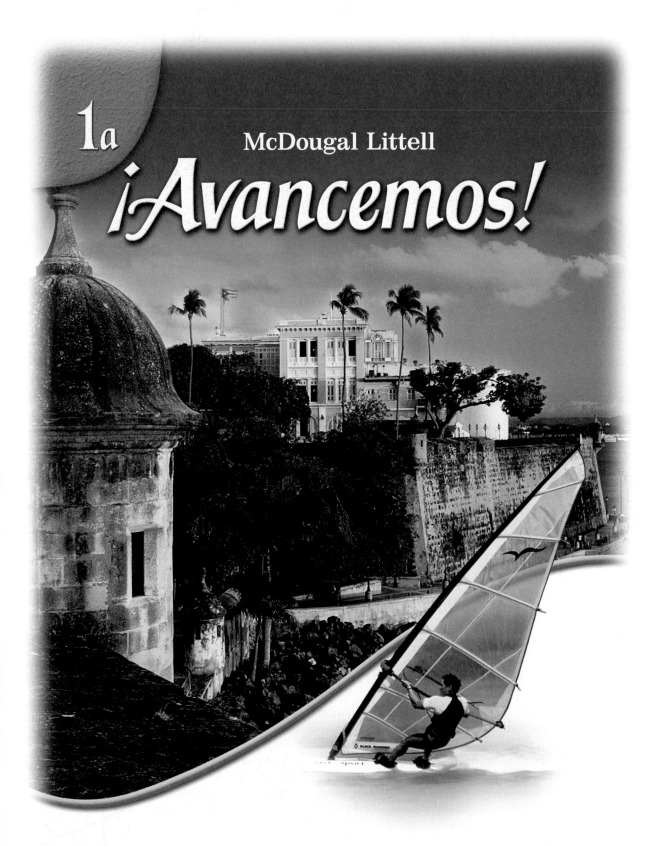

1a

McDougal Littell

¡Avancemos!

McDougal Littell

A DIVISION OF HOUGHTON MIFFLIN COMPANY

Evanston, Illinois • **Boston** • **Dallas**

Cover Photography

Front cover
View toward La Fortaleza, San Juan, Puerto Rico, Steve Dunwell/The Image Bank/
Getty Images
Inset: Windsurfing in Puerto Rico, © Mark Bacon/Latin Focus.com

Back cover
Level 1a: View toward La Fortaleza, San Juan, Puerto Rico, Steve Dunwell/The Image Bank/
Getty Images
Level 1b: View of Buenos Aires through the Puente de la Mujer, Rodriguez Joseph/Gallery
Stock Limited
Level 1:   Monumento a la Independencia on the Paseo de la Reforma at night, Mexico City,
Mexico, Panoramic Images/Getty Images
Level 2:   Cibeles Fountain and Palacio de Comunicaciones at night, Madrid, Spain, Doug
Armand/Getty Images
Level 3:   Plaza de la Constitución at night, Santiago, Chile, David Noton/Masterfile
Level 4:   Templo II, Tikal, Guatemala, P. Pet/zefa/Corbis

ISBN-10: 0-618-61102-9
ISBN-13: 978-0-618-61102-7

2 3 4 5 6 7 8 9 WMW 10 09 08 07 06

Internet: www.mcdougallittell.com

1a

¡Avancemos!

Celebraciones

El Día de los Muertos,
Santiago Sacatepéquez, Guatemala

Online at CLASSZONE.COM

Cultura INTERACTIVA *pp.* C2–C3, C4–C5, C6–C7, C8–C9, C10–C11, C12–C13, C14–C15, C16–C17, C18–C19, C20–C21, C22–C23, C24–C25

New Year's Eve, Madrid, Spain

Nueva York

¡Hola!

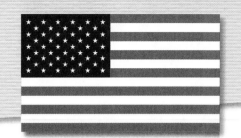

Cultura
- **Un mural del
  metro** *p. 9*

Did you get it?
Student Self-Check
*pp. 5, 9, 11, 15, 17, 19,
21, 24*

A performer wearing the colors of the Puerto Rican Flag

Dominican dancers in colorful costumes

Un rato con los amigos

Cultura
- **Explora Estados
  Unidos** *p. 28*
- **Los Premios Juventud**
  p. 43
- **El arte de Miami**
  p. 45
- **¿Qué te gusta hacer?**
  p. 52

 ¿Recuerdas?
- weather expressions
  p. 37

Did you get it?
Student Self-Check
pp. 35, 37, 41, 43, 47, 50

Online at CLASSZONE.COM

Cultura INTERACTIVA	**Animated** Grammar	**@HomeTutor** VideoPlus
pp. 28–29 86–87	*pp. 38, 44, 55 66, 72, 83*	*pp. 36, 42, 48 64, 70, 76*

Video/DVD
Vocabulario
pp. 32–34, 60–62
Telehistoria
*pp. 36, 42, 48
64, 70, 76*

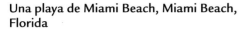

Una playa de Miami Beach, Miami Beach,
Florida

Paseo del Río, San Antonio, Texas

Lección 2

Tema: **Mis amigos y yo** **58**

VOCABULARIO

GRAMÁTICA

TODO JUNTO

Cultura

 ¿Recuerdas?

 Did you get it?

**UNIT 1
WRAP-UP**

Comparación cultural

Cultura
- **Explora México** *p. 90*
- **Uniformes escolares** *p. 102*
- **Los murales en México** *p. 109*
- **Una escuela bilingüe en México** *p. 114*

 ¿Recuerdas?
- after-school activities *p. 103*
- days of the week *p. 105*

 Did you get it?
Student Self-Check
pp. 97, 99, 103, 105, 109, 112

Online at CLASSZONE.COM

Cultura INTERACTIVA	**Animated** Grammar	**@HomeTutor** VideoPlus
pp. 90–91 *148–149*	*pp. 100, 106, 117* *128, 134, 145*	*pp. 98, 104, 110* *126, 132, 138*

 **Video/DVD**
Vocabulario
pp. 94–96, 122–124
Telehistoria
pp. 98, 104, 110
126, 132, 138

La fuente de San Miguel en el Zócalo,
Puebla, México

El patio de una escuela secundaria,
México

Cultura

 ¿Recuerdas?

PARA Y PIENSA **Did you get it?**
Student Self-Check

Puerto Rico
Comer en familia

Online at CLASSZONE.COM

Video/DVD

La Plaza de Colón en el Viejo San Juan,
San Juan, Puerto Rico

Una familia come en casa,
San Juan, Puerto Rico

Lección 2

Tema: **En mi familia** **182**

VOCABULARIO

GRAMÁTICA

TODO JUNTO

Cultura

- **Las elecciones en Puerto Rico** *p. 193*
- **Los retratos** *p. 199*
- **La quinceañera** *p. 204*
- **Instrumentos de Puerto Rico y Perú** *p. 206*
- **¿Qué comemos?** *p. 210*

 ¿Recuerdas?

- the verb **tener** *p. 189*
- numbers from 11 to 100 *p. 189*
- after-school activities *p. 191*
- describing others *p. 192*

 Did you get it?
Student Self-Check
pp. 187, 189, 193, 195, 199, 202

UNIT 3 WRAP-UP

Una tienda de ropa, Madrid, España

El Teatro de la Comedia en la calle
Príncipe, Madrid, España

Lección 2

Tema: ¿Qué hacemos esta noche? 244

VOCABULARIO

GRAMÁTICA

TODO JUNTO

 ¿Recuerdas?
- present tense of **-er** verbs *p. 249*
- the verb **ir** *p. 251*
- direct object pronouns *p. 259*
- **tener** expressions *p. 261*

 PARA Y PIENSA **Did you get it?**
Student Self-Check
pp. 249, 251, 255, 257, 261, 264

UNIT 4 WRAP-UP

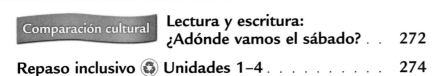 Comparación cultural

España
Contenido **xiii**

Recursos

¡Avancemos!

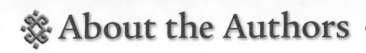 About the Authors

Estella Gahala

Estella Gahala received degrees in Spanish from Wichita State University, French from Middlebury College, and a Ph.D. in Educational Administration and Curriculum from Northwestern University. A career teacher of Spanish and French, she has worked with a wide variety of students at the secondary level. She has also served as foreign language department chair and district director of curriculum and instruction. Her workshops and publications focus on research and practice in a wide range of topics, including culture and language learning, learning strategies, assessment, and the impact of current brain research on curriculum and instruction. She has coauthored twelve basal textbooks. Honors include the Chevalier dans l'Ordre des Palmes Académiques and listings in *Who's Who of American Women, Who's Who in America,* and *Who's Who in the World.*

Patricia Hamilton Carlin

Patricia Hamilton Carlin completed her M.A. in Spanish at the University of California, Davis, where she also taught as a lecturer. Previously she earned a Master of Secondary Education with specialization in foreign languages from the University of Arkansas and taught Spanish and French at the K–12 level. Patricia currently teaches Spanish and foreign language/ESL methodology at the University of Central Arkansas, where she coordinates the second language teacher education program. In addition, Patricia is a frequent presenter at local, regional, and national foreign language conferences. In 2005, she was awarded the Southern Conference on Language Teaching's Outstanding Teaching Award: Post-Secondary. Her professional service has included the presidency of the Arkansas Foreign Language Teachers Association and the presidency of Arkansas's DeSoto Chapter of the AATSP.

Audrey L. Heining-Boynton

Audrey L. Heining-Boynton received her Ph.D. in Curriculum and Instruction from Michigan State University. She is a professor of Education and Romance Languages at The University of North Carolina at Chapel Hill, where she teaches educational methodology classes and Spanish. She has also taught Spanish, French, and ESL at the K–12 level. Dr. Heining-Boynton served as the president of ACTFL and the National Network for Early Language Learning. She has been involved with AATSP, Phi Delta Kappa, and state foreign language associations. In addition, she has presented both nationally and internationally and has published over forty books, articles, and curricula.

Ricardo Otheguy

Ricardo Otheguy received his Ph.D. in Linguistics from the City University of New York, where he is currently professor of Linguistics at the Graduate Center. He is also director of the Research Institute for the Study of Language in Urban Society (RISLUS) and coeditor of the research journal *Spanish in Context.* He has extensive experience with school-based research and has written on topics related to Spanish grammar, bilingual education, and Spanish in the United States. His work has been supported by private and government foundations, including the Rockefeller Brothers Fund and the National Science Foundation. He is coauthor of *Tu mundo: Curso para hispanohablantes,* and *Prueba de ubicación para hispanohablantes.*

Barbara J. Rupert

Barbara Rupert completed her M.A. at Pacific Lutheran University. She has taught Level 1 through A.P. Spanish and has implemented a FLES program in her district. Barbara is the author of CD-ROM activities for the *¡Bravo!* series. She has presented at many local, regional, and national foreign language conferences. She has served as president of both the Pacific Northwest Council for Languages (PNCFL) and the Washington Association for Language Teaching, and was the PNCFL representative to ACTFL. In 1996, Barbara received the Christa McAuliffe Award for Excellence in Education, and in 1999, she was selected Washington's "Spanish Teacher of the Year" by the Juan de Fuca Chapter of the AATSP.

Carl Johnson, Senior Program Advisor

Carl Johnson received degrees from Marietta College (OH), the University of Illinois, Université Laval, and a Ph.D. in Foreign Language Education from The Ohio State University, during which time he studied French, German, Spanish, and Russian. He has been a lifelong foreign language educator, retiring in 2003 after 27 years as a language teacher (secondary and university level), consultant, and Director of Languages Other Than English for the Texas Department of Education. He has completed many publications relating to student and teacher language proficiency development, language textbooks, and nationwide textbook adoption practices. He also served as president of the Texas Foreign Language Association, Chair of the Board of the Southwest Conference on Language Teaching, and president of the National Council of State Supervisors of Foreign Languages. In addition, he was named Chevalier dans l'Ordre des Palmes Académiques by the French government.

Rebecca L. Oxford, Learning Strategy Specialist

Rebecca L. Oxford received her Ph.D. in educational psychology from The University of North Carolina. She also holds two degrees in foreign language from Vanderbilt University and Yale University, and a degree in educational psychology from Boston University. She leads the Second Language Education and Culture Program and is a professor at the University of Maryland. She has directed programs at Teachers College, Columbia University; the University of Alabama; and the Pennsylvania State University. In addition, she initiated and edited *Tapestry*, a series of student textbooks used around the world. Dr. Oxford specializes in language learning strategies and styles.

Contributing Writers

Louis G. Baskinger
New Hartford High School
New Hartford, NY

Jacquelyn Cinotti-Dirmann
Duval County Public Schools
Jacksonville, FL

Consulting Authors

Dan Battisti
Dr. Teresa Carrera-Hanley
Bill Lionetti
Patty Murguía Bohannan
Lorena Richins Layser

✸ Teacher Reviewers

Middle School Reviewers

Mary Jo Aronica
Lincoln Hall Middle School
Lincolnwood, IL

Suzanne M. Auffray
The Overlake School
Redmond, WA

Elizabeth M. Bossong
Vestal High School
Vestal, NY

Zahava Frymerman
G. W. Carver Middle School
Miami, FL

Ana Johnson
Rising Star Middle School
Fayetteville, GA

Sharon Larracoechea
North Junior High
Boise, ID

Deborah Tomkinson
James Madison Middle School
Titusville, FL

Elizabeth L. Torosian
Lowell Community Charter Public
  School
Lowell, MA

Heather T. Walker
Chester Middle School
Chester, VA

Mari Zimmerman
James C. Wright Middle School
Madison, WI

High School Reviewers

Sue Arandjelovic
Dobson High School
Mesa, AZ

Susan K. Arbuckle
Mahomet-Seymour High School
Mahomet, IL

Kristi Ashe
Amador Valley High School
Pleasanton, CA

Shaun A. Bauer
Olympia High School, *retired*
Orlando, FL

Sheila Bayles
Rogers High School
Rogers, AR

Robert L. Bowbeer
Detroit Country Day Upper School
Beverly Hills, MI

Hercilia Bretón
Highlands High School
San Antonio, TX

Adrienne Chamberlain-Parris
Mariner High School
Everett, WA

Mike Cooperider
Truman High School
Independence, MO

Susan B. Cress
Sheridan High School
Sheridan, IN

Michèle S. de Cruz-Sáenz, Ph.D.
Strath Haven High School
Wallingford, PA

Lizveth Dague
Park Vista Community High School
Lake Worth, FL

Parthena Draggett
Jackson High School
Massillon, OH

Rubén D. Elías
Roosevelt High School
Fresno, CA

Phillip Elkins
Lane Tech College Prep High School
Chicago, IL

Maria Fleming Alvarez
The Park School
Brookline, MA

Michael Garber
Boston Latin Academy
Boston, MA

Marco García
Derry University Advantage Academy
Chicago, IL

David Gonzalez
Hollywood Hills High School
Hollywood, FL

Raquel R. González
Odessa Senior High School
Odessa, TX

Neyda Gonzalez-Droz
Ridge Community High School
Davenport, FL

Becky Hay de García
James Madison Memorial
  High School
Madison, WI

Fatima Hicks
Suncoast High School, *retired*
Riviera Beach, FL

Gladys V. Horford
William T. Dwyer High School
Palm Beach Gardens, FL

Pam Johnson
Stevensville High School
Stevensville, MT

Richard Ladd
Ipswich High School
Ipswich, MA

Patsy Lanigan
Hume Fogg Academic Magnet
  High School
Nashville, TN

Kris Laws
Palm Bay High School
Melbourne, FL

Kristen M. Lombardi
Shenendehowa High School
Clifton Park, NY

Elizabeth Lupafya
North High School
Worcester, MA

David Malatesta
Niles West High School
Skokie, IL

Patrick Malloy
James B. Conant High School
Hoffman Estates, IL

Brandi Meeks
Starr's Mill High School
Fayetteville, GA

Kathleen L. Michaels
Palm Harbor University High School
Palm Harbor, FL

Linda Nanos
Brook Farm Business Academy
West Roxbury, MA

Nadine F. Olson
School of Teaching and Curriculum
   Leadership
Stillwater, OK

Pam Osthoff
Lakeland Senior High School
Lakeland, FL

Nicholas Patterson
Davenport Central High School
Davenport, IA

Carolyn A. Peck
Genesee Community College
Lakeville, NY

Daniel N. Richardson
Concord High School, *retired*
Concord, NH

Rita E. Risco
Palm Harbor University High School
Palm Harbor, FL

Miguel Roma
Boston Latin Academy
West Roxbury, MA

Lauren Schultz
Dover High School
Dover, NH

Nona M. Seaver
New Berlin West Middle/High
   School
New Berlin, WI

Susan Seraphine-Kimel
Astronaut High School
Titusville, FL

Mary Severo
Thomas Hart Middle School
Pleasanton, CA

Clarette Shelton
WT Woodson High School, *retired*
Fairfax, VA

Maureen Shiland
Saratoga Springs High School
Saratoga Springs, NY

Irma Sprague
Countryside High School
Clearwater, FL

Mary A. Stimmel
Lincoln High School
Des Moines, IA

Karen Tharrington
Wakefield High School
Raleigh, NC

Alicia Turnier
Countryside High School
Clearwater, FL

Roberto E. del Valle
The Overlake School
Redmond, WA

Todd Wagner
Upper Darby High School, *retired*
Drexel Hill, PA

Ronie R. Webster
Monson Junior/Senior High School
Monson, MA

Cheryl Wellman
Bloomingdale High School
Valrico, FL

Thomasina White
School District of Philadelphia
Philadelphia, PA

Jena Williams
Jonesboro High School
Jonesboro, AR

Program Advisory Council

Louis G. Baskinger
New Hartford High School
New Hartford, NY

Linda M. Bigler
James Madison University
Harrisonburg, VA

Flora Maria Ciccone-Quintanilla
Holly Senior High School
Holly, MI

Jacquelyn Cinotti-Dirmann
Duval County Public Schools
Jacksonville, FL

Desa Dawson
Del City High School
Del City, OK

Robin C. Hill
Warrensville Heights High School
Warrensville Heights, OH

Barbara M. Johnson
Gordon Tech High School, *retired*
Chicago, IL

Ray Maldonado
Houston Independent School
   District
Houston, TX

Karen S. Miller
Friends School of Baltimore
Baltimore, MD

Dr. Robert A. Miller
Woodcreek High School
   Roseville Joint Union High School
   District
Roseville, CA

Debra M. Morris
Wellington Landings Middle School
Wellington, FL

Maria Nieto Zezas
West Morris Central High School
Chester, NJ

Rita Oleksak
Glastonbury Public Schools
Glastonbury, CT

Sandra Rosenstiel
University of Dallas, *retired*
Grapevine, TX

Emily Serafa Manschot
Northville High School
Northville, MI

La Telehistoria

Hi! My name is Alicia. My family and I live in Miami, Florida. My favorite thing to do is play soccer. At the Pan-American Youth Games, my team took second place. I made a lot of great friends from all over the world. I also met Trini Salgado, the best soccer player ever!

I got a T-shirt like hers, but I never got her to autograph it. She is always traveling to different countries, so maybe I can send my shirt to some of my soccer friends to try to get it signed.

Follow along in the ¡Avancemos! Telehistoria to find out what happens to Alicia's T-shirt as it travels from country to country.

Trini Salgado

En Parque de l...

Próximo Sábado, 15 de Jun...

Sandra-San Antonio ✓
Pablo-México
Rodrigo-Puerto Rico ✓
Maribel-España ✓
Manuel-Ecuador ✓
Mario-República
          Dominicana ✓
Florencia-Argentina ✓
Jorge-Costa Rica ✓

Level 1a

1 San Antonio
Sandra

2 Mexico
Pablo

3 Puerto Rico
Rodrigo

4 Spain
Maribel

Level 1b

5 Ecuador
Manuel

6 Dominican Republic
Mario

7 Argentina
Florencia

8 Costa Rica
Jorge

Key Words to Know

el autógrafo autograph

la camiseta T-shirt

el jugador (la jugadora) de fútbol soccer player

Why Study Spanish?

Discover the world

Deciding to learn Spanish is one of the best decisions you can make if you want to travel and see the world.

More than 400 million people around the globe speak Spanish. After Chinese, English and Spanish are tied as the two most frequently spoken languages worldwide. Spanish is now the third most-used language on the Internet. In Europe, Spanish is the most popular foreign language after English. People who speak both Spanish and English can communicate with people from all around the globe, no matter where they find themselves.

Explore your community

Inside the United States, Spanish is by far the most widely spoken language after English.

There are currently about 30 million Spanish-speakers in the U.S. When you start to look and listen for it, you will quickly realize that Spanish is all around you—on the television, on the radio, and in magazines and newspapers. You may even hear your neighbors speaking it. Learning Spanish will help you communicate and interact with the rapidly growing communities of Spanish-speakers around you.

Experience a new perspective

Learning a language is more than just memorizing words and structures.

When you study Spanish, you learn how the people who speak it think, feel, work, and live. Learning a language can open your eyes to a whole new world of ideas and insights. And as you learn about other cultures, you gain a better perspective on your own.

Create career possibilities

Knowing Spanish opens many doors.

If you speak Spanish fluently, you can work for international and multinational companies anywhere in the Spanish-speaking world. You can create a career working as a translator, an interpreter, or a teacher of Spanish. And because the number of Spanish-speakers in the U.S. is growing so rapidly, being able to communicate in Spanish is becoming important in almost every career.

What is Vocabulary?

Building Your Spanish Vocabulary

Vocabulary is a basic building block for learning a foreign language. By learning just a few words, you can start to communicate in Spanish right away! You will probably find that it is easier to understand words you hear or read than it is to use them yourself. But with a little practice, you will start to produce the right words in the right context. Soon you will be able to carry on conversations with other Spanish-speakers.

How Do I Study Vocabulary?

First Steps

· Read all of the new words in **blue** on the Vocabulary presentation page in your textbook.

· Point to each word as you say it out loud.

Be Creative

· Make flashcards with your new vocabulary words. You could also draw pictures of the words on the back of the flashcards.

· Group vocabulary words by theme. Add other words that fit the categories you've learned.

· Imagine a picture of the word.

· Create a rhyme or song to help you remember the words.

Make It Personal

· Use vocabulary words to write original sentences. Make them funny so you'll be sure to remember!

· Label everyday items in Spanish.

· Create reminders for difficult words. Put note cards inside your locker door, or on your mirror at home.

· See it, and say it to yourself! For example, if you are learning colors and clothing words, think of the Spanish word to describe what your friends are wearing.

el cuaderno

Practice Makes Perfect

· Say your vocabulary words out loud and repeat each word several times.

· Write each word five times, keeping its meaning in mind.

· Use Spanish words with your classmates outside of class—if you're having lunch in the cafeteria, use the words you know for food. Greet your classmates in the hallway in Spanish!

Create Your Own System

· Practice a little bit every day. Many short sessions are better than one long one.

· Focus on the words that are the hardest for you.

· Find a buddy. Quiz one another on the vocabulary words.

· Keep a vocabulary notebook and update it regularly.

· Use the study sheets in the back of your workbook to review vocabulary.

What is Grammar?

Some people think of grammar as the rules of a language, rules that tell you the "correct" way to speak a language. For instance, why do you say *big red house,* not *red big house*? Why do you say *how much money do you have* instead of *how many money*? If English is your first language, you probably don't think about the rule. You make the correct choice instinctively because it *sounds right.* Non-native speakers of English have to learn the rules. As you begin your study of Spanish, you will need to learn the grammar rules of Spanish.

Why Should I Study Grammar?

Grammar helps you to communicate.

For instance, using the past tense or future tense makes it clear when something happens (*I did my homework* versus *I will do my homework*.) Using subject pronouns lets you know who is performing the action. (*I gave the book to her* versus *She gave the book to me*.) Using correct grammar when speaking Spanish will help you communicate successfully with native speakers of Spanish.

 # How Do I Study Grammar?

Read the English Grammar Connection before each grammar explanation.

Think about how you use the same type of grammar in English. Understanding your own language will help you to better understand Spanish.

> **English Grammar Connection:** A **verb tense** is the form of the verb that shows *when* an action is happening. The **present tense** shows that an action is happening *now*. The Spanish present-tense verb form **estudiamos** can be expressed in English in three different ways: *we study, we are studying,* or *we do study*.

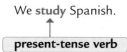

We **study** Spanish.   **Estudiamos** español.

| present-tense verb | | present-tense verb |

Practice the new forms that you are learning.

Completing the practice activities in your student book and workbook will help you to learn the correct way to say things.

Use the Spanish you know as often as you can.

After all, that's how you learned to speak English, by hearing and speaking it every day.

What Is Culture?

To communicate with people from Spanish-speaking countries in a meaningful way, you need to know something about their culture. Vocabulary and grammar will help you learn what words to say and how to put them together, but culture will give you a better understanding of "how, when, and why to say what to whom."

What exactly is culture?

Culture includes . . .

Art
History
Traditions
Relationships
Music
Holidays
Food
Architecture
Pastimes

and more!

How can I learn about another culture?

- Read the **Comparación cultural** information to find out more about the cultures that you are studying.
- Think about the answers to the questions in the **Comparación cultural.**
- Think about the perspectives and practices that shape and influence the culture.
- Compare your own culture with the cultures you are studying.

El mundo

OCÉANO ÁRTICO

Mar de Siberia Oriental

Mar de Beaufort

Bahía de Baffin

GROENLANDIA (DINAMARCA)

RUSIA

Alaska (EE.UU.)

Mar de Bering

Bahía de Hudson

Mar del Labrador

CANADÁ

ESTADOS UNIDOS

OCÉANO ATLÁNTICO

Golfo de México

REP. DOMINICANA

ISLAS BAHAMAS

PUERTO RICO (EE.UU.)

SAN CRISTÓBAL Y NEVIS

HAITÍ

Islas Hawai (EE.UU.)

CUBA

ANTIGUA Y BARBUDA

MÉXICO

JAMAICA

GUADALUPE (FRANCIA)

BELICE

Mar Caribe

DOMINICA

MARTINICA (FRANCIA)

SANTA LUCÍA

SAN VICENTE Y GRANADINAS

ISLAS MARSHALL

GUATEMALA

GRANADA

BARBADOS

EL SALVADOR

PANAMÁ

TRINIDAD Y TOBAGO

OCÉANO PACÍFICO

HONDURAS

NICARAGUA

COSTA RICA

VENEZUELA

COLOMBIA

GUAYANA FRANCESA (FRANCIA)

NAURU

KIRIBATI

Islas Galápagos (Ecuador)

ECUADOR

GUYANA

SURINAM

ISLAS SALOMÓN

ISLAS TUVALU

PERÚ

BRASIL

VANUATÚ

SAMOA

Samoa Americana (EE.UU.)

BOLIVIA

FIDJI

TONGA

NUEVA CALEDONIA (FRANCIA)

PARAGUAY

CHILE

URUGUAY

ARGENTINA

NUEVA ZELANDA

Islas Malvinas (R.U.)

OCÉANO ÁRTICO

Mar de Kara

Mar de Laptev

Mar de Barents

Mar de
Noruega

1 DINAMARCA	9 ESLOVENIA	
2 HOLANDA	10 CROACIA	
3 BÉLGICA	11 BOSNIA Y HERZEGOVINA	
4 LUXEMBURGO	12 SERBIA Y MONTENEGRO	
5 SUIZA	13 ALBANIA	
6 REPÚBLICA CHECA	14 MACEDONIA	
7 ESLOVAQUIA	15 BULGARIA	
8 HUNGRÍA		

RUSIA

SUECIA   FINLANDIA

NORUEGA

ESTONIA
LETONIA
LITUANIA

REINO
UNIDO

Mar del
Norte

Mar Báltico

IRLANDA

BIELORRUSIA

Lago
Baikal

Mar de
Ojotsk

60°N

ALEMANIA POLONIA

UCRANIA

KAZAKSTÁN

MONGOLIA

FRANCIA   AUSTRIA
RUMANIA

MOLDAVIA

ANDORRA

Mar Negro

Mar Caspio

ITALIA

ESPAÑA

UZBEKISTÁN

KIRGUISTÁN

COREA
DEL NORTE

Mar de
Japón

PORTUGAL

GEORGIA

GRECIA

TURQUÍA
ARMENIA

TADJIKISTÁN

COREA
DEL SUR

JAPÓN

(MAR.)

MALTA

CHIPRE
LÍBANO

SIRIA

AZERBAIYÁN

TURKMENISTÁN

CHINA

TÚNEZ   Mar Mediterráneo

MARRUECOS

IRAQ

IRÁN

AFGANISTÁN

BHUTÁN

Canarias

ISRAEL

JORDANIA

KUWAIT
QATAR

PAQUISTÁN

NEPAL

ARGELIA   LIBIA

EGIPTO

BAHREIN

E.Á.U

30°N

SÁHARA
OCCIDENTAL

ARABIA
SAUDITA

OMÁN

INDIA

MYANMAR

TAIWÁN

Trópico de Cáncer

MAURITANIA

MALÍ

NÍGER   CHAD

ERITREA

YEMEN

Mar Rojo

Mar
Arábigo

Golfo
de
Bengala

LAOS

TAILANDIA

VIETNAM

FILIPINAS

GUAM
(EE.UU.)

OCÉANO
PACÍFICO

SENEGAL

BURKINA
FASO

SUDÁN

JIBUTI

CAMBOYA

Mar de
China

GUINEA

BENIN
NIGERIA
TOGÓ

ETIOPÍA

BRUNEI

MICRONESIA

COSTA
DE
MARFIL

GHANA

CAMERÚN

REP. CENTRO-
AFRICANA

SOMALIA

ISLAS
MALDIVAS

SRI
LANKA

MALASIA

PALAU

LIBERIA

GUINEA
ECUATORIAL

UGANDA
KENIA

SINGAPUR

INDONESIA

PAPUASIA
NUEVA GUINEA

SANTO TOMÉ
Y PRÍNCIPE

CONGO

GABÓN

REP. DEM.
DEL CONGO

RUANDA

Ecuador 0°

CABINDA
(ANGOLA)

BURUNDI

TANZANÍA

SEYCHELLES

TIMOR
ORIENTAL

ANGOLA

COMORES

ZAMBIA   MALAWI

NAMIBIA   ZIMBABWE

BOTSWANA

MOZAMBIQUE

MADAGASCAR

MAURICIO

OCÉANO ÍNDICO

Trópico de Capricornio

AUSTRALIA

SUAZILANDIA

SUDÁFRICA   LESOTHO

30°S

0   1,000   2,000 millas

0   1,000   2,000 kilómetros

N

O   E

S

60°S

ANTÁRTIDA

México y Centroamérica

ESTADOS UNIDOS

Washington, D.C.

OCÉANO
ATLÁNTICO

Tijuana
Mexicali

Ciudad Juárez

Hermosillo

Chihuahua

Nuevo
Laredo

ISLAS
BAHAMAS

Golfo de México

Nassau

MÉXICO

Monterrey

Durango

San Luis
Potosí

Tampico

Trópico de Cáncer

La Habana

CUBA

Guadalajara

Mérida

México, D.F.

Veracruz

JAMAICA

Kingston

Puebla

Belice

BELICE

Oaxaca

Belmopan

Acapulco

HONDURAS

Mar Caribe

Guatemala

Tegucigalpa

GUATEMALA

San Salvador

NICARAGUA

EL SALVADOR

Managua

San José

OCÉANO
PACÍFICO

COSTA RICA

Colón

Panamá

PANAMÁ

COLOMBIA

Ecuador

Quito

ECUADOR

Baja California

SIERRA MADRE OCCIDENTAL

SIERRA MADRE ORIENTAL

N
O   E
S

| 0 | 250 | 500 millas |
| 0 | 250 | 500 kilómetros |

PERÚ

40°N

30°N

20°N

10°N

0°

10°S

110°O   100°O   90°O   80°O

El Caribe

ESTADOS
UNIDOS

OCÉANO ATLÁNTICO

Nassau

Estrecho de Florida

ISLAS BAHAMAS

25°N

Trópico de Cáncer

La Habana

Santa Clara

CUBA

Nueva Gerona

ISLAS DE TURCOS
Y CAICOS (R.U.)

Camagüey

Holguín

REPÚBLICA
DOMINICANA

Manzanillo

Guantánamo

20°N

Santiago
de Cuba

HAITÍ

La Española

Arecibo   San Juan

Mayagüez

A N T I L L A S

Puerto
Príncipe

Santo
Domingo

Ponce   Humacao

JAMAICA

Kingston

M A Y O R E S

PUERTO
RICO

HONDURAS

Mar Caribe

15°N

NICARAGUA

Aruba (Hol.)

Curaçao (Hol.)

Bonaire (Hol.)

Caracas

San José

10°N

COSTA
RICA

PANAMÁ

Panamá

VENEZUELA

Golfo
de
Panamá

OCÉANO
PACÍFICO

N

O   E

S

5°N

Bogotá

COLOMBIA

0   150   300 millas

0   150   300 kilómetros

Mapas **xxxiii**

Sudamérica

Mar Caribe

OCÉANO ATLÁNTICO

Barranquilla
Cartagena
Maracaibo
TRINIDAD Y TOBAGO
Puerto España
Lago Maracaibo
Caracas
Río Orinoco
VENEZUELA
Georgetown
Paramaribo
Medellín
GUYANA
Cayena
Manizales
Bogotá
SURINAM
GUAYANA FRANCESA (FRANCIA)
COLOMBIA
Cali

Otavalo
Quito
Ecuador 0°
Río Negro
Río Amazonas
ECUADOR
Guayaquil
Cuenca

PERÚ
Río Madeira
Río Tapajós
Río Xingú
Río Tocantins
Trujillo

BRASIL
10°S
Río São Francisco

Callao
Lima

Lago Titicaca
BOLIVIA
La Paz
Cochabamba
Brasilia
Sucre
Santa Cruz

Salta
GRAN CHACO
PARAGUAY
20°S
San Miguel de Tucumán
Asunción
CHILE
Resistencia
Trópico de Capricornio

Córdoba
30°S
Valparaíso
Mendoza
Rosario
URUGUAY
Santiago
Buenos Aires
Montevideo
ARGENTINA
La Plata
OCÉANO ATLÁNTICO
Concepción
Mar del Plata
OCÉANO PACÍFICO
PAMPAS
Temuco
Bahía Blanca

PATAGONIA
40°S

N
O   E
S

0   250   500 millas
0   250   500 kilómetros

Estrecho de Magallanes
Islas Malvinas (R.U.)
50°S

Tierra del Fuego
Cabo de Hornos

100°O   90°O   80°O   70°O   50°O   40°O   30°O   20°O

Inset map

OCÉANO PACÍFICO
Bogotá
COLOMBIA
Islas Galápagos (Ecuador)
Quito
ECUADOR
0   200   400 millas
0   200   400 kilómetros
PERÚ

España

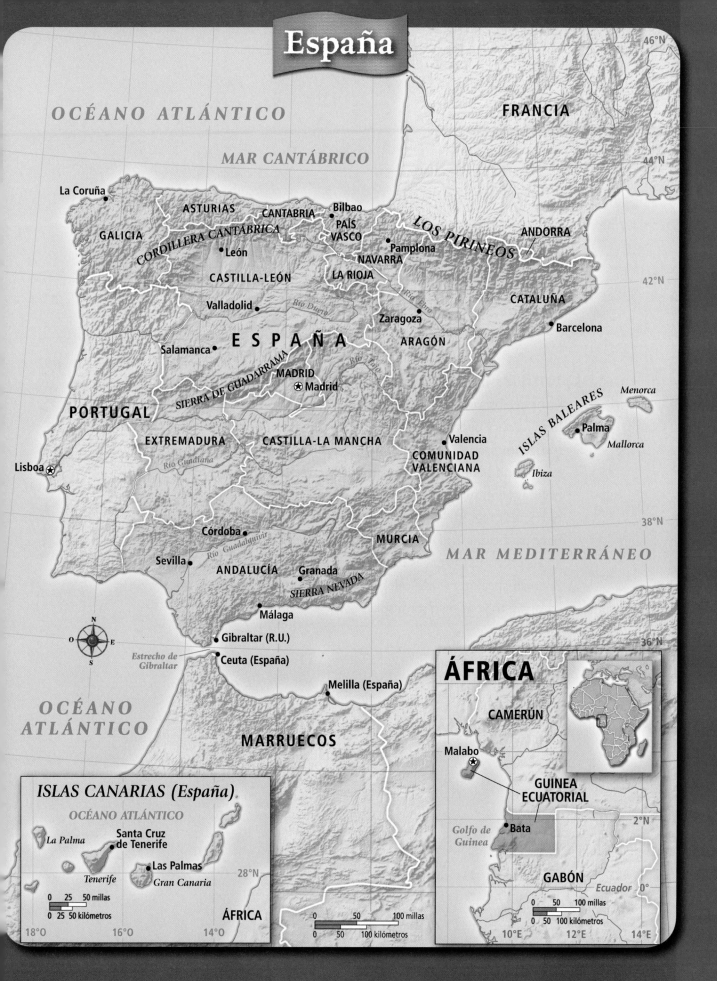

OCÉANO ATLÁNTICO

FRANCIA

MAR CANTÁBRICO

La Coruña

ASTURIAS CANTABRIA Bilbao
GALICIA   PAÍS
         CORDILLERA CANTÁBRICA VASCO
                  León   Pamplona
                              NAVARRA
CASTILLA-LEÓN   LA RIOJA

LOS PIRINEOS ANDORRA

CATALUÑA

Valladolid   Río Duero
                        Zaragoza   Barcelona
E S P A Ñ A   Río Ebro
                        ARAGÓN
Salamanca
         SIERRA DE GUADARRAMA   Río Tajo
                  MADRID
PORTUGAL   ★ Madrid

                                          Menorca
                              ISLAS BALEARES
                                    Palma
EXTREMADURA   CASTILLA-LA MANCHA   Mallorca
                              Valencia
Río Guadiana   COMUNIDAD
Lisboa ★   VALENCIANA   Ibiza

                  Córdoba
              Río Guadalquivir   MURCIA
Sevilla   MAR MEDITERRÁNEO
         ANDALUCÍA   Granada
              SIERRA NEVADA
                              38°N

         Málaga

    N   Gibraltar (R.U.)
O ✦ E   Ceuta (España)
    S
OCÉANO   Estrecho de
ATLÁNTICO Gibraltar   36°N
                        Melilla (España)

MARRUECOS

46°N
44°N
42°N
40°N (implied)
38°N
36°N

ÁFRICA

CAMERÚN

Malabo ★

GUINEA
ECUATORIAL

Golfo de   Bata
Guinea   2°N

GABÓN

10°E   12°E   14°E

0   50   100 millas
0   50   100 kilómetros

ISLAS CANARIAS (España)

OCÉANO ATLÁNTICO

La Palma   Santa Cruz
            de Tenerife
                  Las Palmas
   Tenerife   Gran Canaria   28°N

0 25 50 millas
0 25 50 kilómetros
                              ÁFRICA

18°O   16°O   14°O

0   50   100 millas
0   50   100 kilómetros

Las celebraciones

The following lessons about holidays are provided for your personal enjoyment. You may choose to read them on your own, or your teacher may present them throughout the year.

Countries in the Spanish-speaking world often share the same celebrations and holidays. The celebrations are a result of a long history of traditions that reflect the mix of primarily Spanish, indigenous, and African cultures. Holidays celebrating religious events and beliefs are often similar between countries. Other holidays commemorate events or people that are important to a particular region. Many holidays, though celebrated on the same day, have traditions and customs that differ between countries.

As you read the pages of Celebraciones, you will discover how the Spanish-speaking world celebrates important holidays and how they compare to your own traditions.

Contenido

Feria de Málaga

Objectives
- Provide background for the topic: Feria de Málaga
- Familiarize students with the origin of the Feria de Málaga and its traditions.

Presentation Strategies
20-minute lesson
- Ask students to locate Spain and Málaga on a map.
- Have students read the pages about Feria de Málaga.
- Have small groups discuss the Comparación cultural questions.

50-minute lesson
- Complete 20-minute lesson.
- Have students preview the pictures to identify ways Feria de Málaga is celebrated. (music, food, dancing, rides)
- Introduce the Vocabulario para celebrar and pronounce the English and Spanish terms.
- Ask students to use math to determine how many years ago Ferdinand and Isabella entered Málaga. (Subtract 1487 from the present year.)
- Ask the groups to summarize their discussions for the class.

✿ STANDARDS
2.1 Practices and perspectives
2.2 Products and perspectives
4.2 Compare cultures

Connections
Social Studies

Use a world map or map of the Mediterranean area (pp. xxx–xxxi, xxxv).
- Help students locate the country of Spain and the city of Málaga on the map, pointing out that Málaga is a coastal city on the Mediterranean Sea.
- Tell students that Málaga is the capital city of the province (similar to an American state) also named Málaga.
- Explain that Málaga is an important port city. Encourage students to investigate the goods exported from and imported to the city.

FERIA DE MÁLAGA

La Feria de Málaga celebrates King Ferdinand and Queen Isabella's triumphant entrance into the coastal city of Málaga on August 19, 1487. The pair claimed the city for the crown of Castile, an event this Spanish city has been celebrating for over 500 years. The *Feria de Málaga* now lasts for nine days and takes place in two parts of the city. Each day at noon the downtown fills with fairgoers. In the *Real,* a separate fairground, participants in *flamenco* dress or riding clothes ride on horseback or in horse-drawn carriages, or stroll, in a tradition known as *el paseo.* This daytime *feria* unfolds against a backdrop of music, singing, and dancing and ends at 6:00 p.m., when everyone goes home to rest. The celebration starts again at night in the *Real* and continues into the early morning hours. For this nightly *feria,* people gather in public and private *casetas,* to enjoy concerts, theatrical presentations, music, dance, and food. The last night of the *feria* ends with a city-sponsored concert followed by a spectacular fireworks display.

Feria de caballos More than a thousand riders and over a hundred horse-drawn carriages and carts participate in *el paseo.*

Música callejera Musicians play in the streets during the *feria.* Here a *panda,* or group, plays *verdiales,* traditional music that features guitars, tambourines, and tiny cymbals.

C2 Celebraciones

Bridging Cultures

Heritage Language Learners

Regional Variations Some words in this mini-lesson have multiple or regional meanings. For example, **feria** can mean *small change* in Mexico and *tip* or *gratuity* in Central America. Help students identify the meaning of the word as used in the mini-lesson by providing several context sentences in which they insert the word. Do this for words such as **real** and **feria.**

English Learners

Increase Interaction Many of the English terms in the lesson may be unfamiliar to students. Encourage groups to find or draw pictures to illustrate the terms. Have them post each picture on a card and write the English term it illustrates. Have students work with partners to review the vocabulary using the cards.

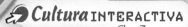

Una caseta offers free samples of *paella*, a rice and seafood dish that is a regional specialty from the coastal cities of Spain.

Bailando flamenco Fairgoers perform folkloric dances such as *flamenco* and *sevillanas* in the streets, plazas, and *casetas*, wherever there is music.

Una entrada a la feria Riders pass in front of one of the decorative entrances to a street in the historic downtown of Málaga.

Vocabulario para celebrar

los caballos	horses
las carretas	horse-drawn carriages
las casetas	small houses or tents
la feria	fair
el paseo	a walk, stroll, or ride

Comparación cultural

1. Does your town or city celebrate its beginnings or inauguration as a community, or is there a special "town day"? What events take place during the celebration?
2. What events in your community or region are similar to those of the *Feria de Málaga*? Describe them and then compare them to the *Feria de Málaga*.

Celebraciones **C3**

Culture

About the Photos

Entranceway Encourage students to analyze the left-hand photograph on page C3. Point out that the entranceway depicts important parts of the culture of Málaga. Encourage students to list soccer ball, fans, guitar, fish, and flowers and relate them to the culture. Point out the name Picasso. If necessary, explain that Picasso was one of the most important artists of the 1900s. Ask students to infer why Picasso would be mentioned on the entranceway and to do research to verify their inference. (Picasso was a native son of Málaga, born on October 25, 1881.)
Gratis Have students read the sign in the top, right-hand photograph and the caption. Have students find, share, and compare recipes for paella. Explain that there are many variations on the recipe but most include seafood and rice.

Comparación cultural

Possible Answers

1. Students' communities may not celebrate their own historical beginnings, but they may have a special community festival each year or celebrate a national holiday. Encourage students to compare these celebrations to the Feria de Málaga. Students are likely to identify music and food as activities common to both celebrations.
2. The events may include parades, street festivals, carnivals, musical performances, and street dances.

Enrichment

Arts and Crafts

Entranceway Decoration Have students examine the photograph of the entranceway on page C3. Tell students to imagine they are on a committee in charge of designing an entranceway for a holiday and a city of their choosing. Have them work in small groups to create the design. Have them post their designs on a bulletin board.

Music

Sevillanas and Flamenco Play traditional sevillanas or flamenco music and have students describe the music. You might arrange for a video demonstration of these folk dances. Encourage students to learn several steps and perform them as you play the music.

C3

Objectives

- Provide background for the topic: Día de la Independencia.
- Familiarize students with Independence Day celebrations in Latin American countries.

Presentation Strategies
20-minute lesson

- Use a map to locate Mexico, the Central American countries, and Chile.
- Have students read aloud the pages about Día de la Independencia.
- Conduct a class discussion of the Comparación cultural questions.

50-minute lesson

- Complete 20-minute lesson.
- Display the national flags or pictures of the flags of the countries identified in the lesson. Encourage students to note similarities and differences in the flags.
- Have students reenact the commemoration activity of the Mexican president. Students might also role-play the president giving an Independence Day speech.

STANDARDS

2.1 Practices and perspectives
3.1 Knowledge of other disciplines
4.2 Compare cultures

DÍA DE LA INDEPENDENCIA

El Día de la Independencia falls in September for many of the Spanish-speaking countries in the Americas. Mexico celebrates on September 15 and 16, with the *Grito de la Independencia,* music, fireworks, and parades. The first *Grito* occurred at dawn on September 16, 1810, when Padre Miguel Hidalgo de Costilla called to the people of Dolores to rise up against the Spanish crown. That rebellion led to the Mexican War of Independence.

Just two days later, on September 18, 1810, Chile declared its independence from Spain. Today Chile celebrates the date during a week of *fiestas patrias* that include parades, rodeos, dance competitions, and special foods.

Eleven years later, on September 15, 1821, a large part of Central America also proclaimed its independence from Spain, becoming El Salvador, Nicaragua, Guatemala, Costa Rica, and Honduras. These countries celebrate their independence on the 14 and 15 with a focus on students: parades, assemblies, and sports competitions.

México

El Grito de la Independencia On the night of September 15, the president of Mexico commemorates *el Grito* by ringing a bell, proclaiming *¡Que viva México!*, and waving the Mexican flag from a balcony above the Zócalo. Crowds gather below to participate in the *Grito*.

C4 Celebraciones

Bridging Cultures

Heritage Language Learners

Support What They Know Students may have participated in independence celebrations themselves or their family members may recall celebrations in their homeland. Encourage students to share their experiences to enrich the cultural understandings of all students. They might share songs, costumes, dance steps, or traditional foods.

English Learners

Increase Interaction Have partners of differing abilities read the mini-lesson together. The more proficient student can read the lesson aloud in English and summarize it in simpler language. A student might also provide a summary in Spanish. He or she might ask the English learner questions about the reading and have him or her answer them in simple English.

Cultura INTERACTIVA *See these pages come alive!*
ClassZone.com

Fiestas patrias Costa Rican schoolchildren, dressed in colors of their country, dance in a parade.

Costa Rica

Guatemala

El recorrido de la antorcha Runners carrying a flaming torch start in Guatemala and end in Costa Rica. All along the route, uniformed schoolchildren wait expectantly for the torch to pass.

Vocabulario para celebrar

la antorcha	torch
la banda	band
las fiestas patrias	patriotic holidays
el grito	shout
el recorrido	run, journey
proclamar	to declare

Culture

About the Photos

Mexico Explain that on the morning of September 16, 1810, Miguel Hidalgo rang the church bell to gather the people of Dolores, Mexico, together. He then called on the people to rebel against the Spanish, who ruled Mexico. Ask students why the president of Mexico rings a bell as part of today's independence celebration.

Guatemala Ask why the torch is carried from Guatemala to Costa Rica as part of the independence celebration.

Costa Rica Have students read the caption and study the picture to help them identify the colors of the national flag of Costa Rica. (red, white, and blue)

Comparación cultural

Possible Answers

1. Students may find more similarities in activities such as parades, dances, and fireworks than differences in activities, such as student competitions or rodeos.

2. Students may suggest family events such as picnics or community events such as parades or fireworks.

Comparación cultural

1. Compare the way your town or city celebrates Independence Day with the celebrations in Mexico and Central America. How are they similar? Are there any differences?

2. How do you celebrate Independence Day? Do you participate in community events or have a special tradition?

Celebraciones   **C5**

Enrichment

Timeline

Sequencing Independence Have students research information about the independence efforts of the countries mentioned in the mini-lesson as well as the United States. They can then make a timeline identifying important dates leading up to independence. For example, Mexico called for independence in 1810 but did not gain it until 1821. Both of these dates would be placed on the timeline.

Music

National Anthem Every nation has a national anthem that reflects the history or culture of the nation. Assign each country to a pair of students. Have students find the lyrics and music for the country's national anthem. Ask them to research the history of the anthem—its origins or what it stands for. Have students present their research and play or sing the national anthem.

Objectives

- Familiarize students with the origin of El 12 de Octubre and the differing ways people celebrate the holiday.
- Trace the route of Columbus' first voyage.

Presentation Strategies
20-minute lesson

- Ask students to locate Spain, the Canary Islands, Cuba, and Hispaniola on a map.
- Have students read the pages about El 12 de Octubre.
- Discuss the Comparación cultural questions as a class.

50-minute lesson

- Complete 20-minute lesson plan.
- Have students note the different names for October 12 celebrations. Discuss why different cultures might view the holiday differently.
- Introduce the Vocabulario para celebrar and pronounce the English and Spanish terms.
- Have students work in groups to develop a map showing Columbus' route, labeling the indigenous groups who lived in each location he visited.

 STANDARDS

2.1 Practices and perspectives
4.2 Compare cultures

Connections

Social Studies

Columbian Exchange Encourage students to research information about the exchange of goods, people, and ideas that resulted from Columbus' arrival in the Americas and Spanish colonization.

- Provide examples of foods found in the Americas that were previously unknown in the rest of the world: chocolate, sweet potatoes, white potatoes, corn, peanuts, hot peppers, and tomatoes.
- Identify examples of plants and animals introduced in the Americas as part of the Columbian Exchange: wheat, rice, cattle, horses, and bees. Talk about how horses changed the lives of some Native Americans on the Plains.

octubre 12

El 12 de Octubre

El 12 de Octubre has many different meanings in the Spanish-speaking world. For some people it is *el Día de Colón,* the day Christopher Columbus arrived in the Americas. For some, it is *el Día de la Hispanidad,* a day to celebrate one's connection with all other Spanish-speaking people, regardless of their country. And for others, it is *el Día de la Raza,* a day when indigenous people come together as a community and celebrate their heritage. Other Spanish speakers celebrate their mixed heritage of indigenous, African, and European cultures. How you celebrate depends very much on you and your family's origin and on the community where you live. For all Spanish-speaking groups, *el 12 de octubre* marks a key turning point in the lives and cultures of the people in Spain and those living in the Americas.

Vocabulario para celebrar

Cristóbal Colón	Christopher Columbus
el Día Nacional	National Day
la hispanidad	the cultural community of Spanish speakers
la raza	race

México

Día de la Raza Indigenous groups gather in Mexico City dressed in their community's traditional outfits, some wearing pre-Columbian clothing and headdresses.

C6 Celebraciones

Bridging Cultures

Heritage Language Learners

Regional Variations Encourage students to consider reasons for the different views of October 12. For many indigenous people, it signaled the end of their traditional way of life. For others, it meant the pursuit of riches and opportunity. Have students identify and list the different names of the holiday in different places. Encourage them to give the English and Spanish translation of the holiday names.

English Learners

Provide Comprehensible Input English terms such as *indigenous* in the lesson may be unfamiliar to many students. Have students skim the lesson for words that are unfamiliar to them. They can make a chart giving the word, a dictionary pronunciation, and a definition. Have students refer to the chart as they read.

Cultura INTERACTIVA *See these pages come alive!*
ClassZone.com

Culture

About the Photos
Have students note the names of the celebrations in each place. All celebrate the same day but focus on different meanings to the communities.

México Ask students which photograph shows someone in pre-Columbian costume.

Nueva York Ask students to identify the nations represented by the flags carried by the students.

Chile Ask why different indigenous groups might meet to celebrate their own identities.

Día de la Raza A woman from the Pehuenche indigenous community gathers with other indigenous groups in downtown Santiago.

Día de la Hispanidad High school students carry flags representing all the American countries as they march in a parade down Fifth Avenue.

España

Día Nacional de España The Spanish government celebrates with a parade in Madrid.

Comparación cultural

Possible Answers
1. Celebrations may depend on students' heritage and cultural identity. Some communities may host parades and festivals; others may not plan any special activities.
2. Students should provide reasons for their preferences, which may be based on their heritage or personal identity. Their renaming of the holiday should reflect their opinion about the Columbian Exchange.

Comparación cultural

1. How do you celebrate October 12 in your community or school? Is it similar to or different from the celebrations in Spanish-speaking countries? How so?
2. What does October 12 mean to you? Which of the Spanish names for the holiday has the most meaning for you? How would you rename the holiday to celebrate your heritage?

Celebraciones **C7**

Enrichment

Language Arts
Columbus Day Poetry Have students locate and read poems about Christopher Columbus and 1492. One classic poem is *In 1492*. Another is Emma Lazarus's poem *1492*. Help students read and summarize the poems. Have them compare and contrast the viewpoints of the poems.

Timeline and Maps
Columbian Voyages Columbus returned to the Americas three times after the first voyage. Ask students to draw a timeline and a map showing events related to Columbus' explorations.

Objectives

- Familiarize students with Día de los Muertos celebrations in Mexico, the United States, Central America, and South America.
- Locate Mexico, the United States, Guatemala, and Ecuador on a map.

Presentation Strategies
20-minute lesson

- Use a map to locate the United States, Mexico, Guatemala, and Ecuador.
- Have students read aloud the pages about Día de los Muertos, including the picture captions.
- Conduct a class discussion of the Comparación cultural questions.

50-minute lesson

- Complete 20-minute lesson.
- Pronounce the Vocabulario para celebrar and ask students to use the terms in sentences about Día de los Muertos.
- Use a Venn diagram to compare and contrast Día de los Muertos celebrations from different nations or to compare and contrast Halloween and Día de los Muertos celebrations.

STANDARDS

2.1 Practices and perspectives
4.2 Compare cultures

Long-term Retention
Critical Thinking

Many Latino families have immigrated to the United States and no longer live close to the cemeteries and gravesites of their deceased family members. Ask students how these families might honor deceased family members if they cannot visit the gravesites to leave flowers.

¡Día de los Muertos!

Estados Unidos

On Día de los Muertos families visit the cemeteries and gravesites of their loved ones. They clean the sites and leave flowers and candles and, in many countries, they bring entire meals with special drinks and traditional breads to share with the deceased. Displays are set up next to the gravesite that include flowers, hand-crafted skeletons, colorful paper cutouts, candy skulls, personal items, and photos. Family members pass the night sharing food and conversation as they keep vigil for their ancestors.

The celebration of *Día de los Muertos* spans two days, November 1 and 2. Also known as *Día de los Difuntos*, the traditions originate in the centuries-old religious holiday *Día de Todos los Santos*. In the Americas, this holiday coincided with pre-Columbian festivals that celebrated the harvest, the new year, and honored the dead. The mix of cultures and traditions resulted in the celebration *Día de los Muertos*.

Las mojigangas People parade through the Pilsen-Little Village neighborhood of Chicago. Some carry *mojigangas*, giant papier-mâché puppets typically carried in Mexican processions.

México

Las calaveras A display of dressed-up skulls and skeletons on a street in Mexico City

C8 Celebraciones

Bridging Cultures

Heritage Language Learners

Support What They Know Some families may associate deep religious meaning with Día de los Muertos whereas others enjoy it as a time for festivities. Encourage students to respect the differences. Suggest that students ask their families how Día de los Muertos was celebrated in their homelands. Discuss the similarities and differences in the way it is celebrated by families here.

English Learners

Provide Comprehensible Input Have a native English-speaking student tape record the lesson. Be sure he or she records the picture captions, vocabulary, and questions, as well as the paragraphs. Play the tape for students, stopping at the end of each paragraph. Ask students to verbally summarize the paragraph.

¡Día de los Muertos!

Ecuador

El pan de muertos This bread is made only for *Día de los Muertos*. In Ecuador, these breads are called *guaguas de pan*. *Guagua* is the Quechua word for "baby" and refers to the bread's shape. The *guaguas* are served with *colada morada,* a warm, purple-colored drink made from blueberries and raspberries.

México

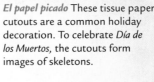

El papel picado These tissue paper cutouts are a common holiday decoration. To celebrate *Día de los Muertos,* the cutouts form images of skeletons.

Guatemala

Los barriletes Guatemalans celebrate by flying *barriletes,* or colorful kites, to which they attach messages for the deceased. The town of Santiago Sacatepéquez celebrates with a *barrilete* contest.

Vocabulario para celebrar

las calaveras	skulls
el cementerio	cemetery
los difuntos	deceased
el esqueleto	skeleton
el pan de muertos	special bread made for *Día de los Muertos*
el papel picado	paper cutouts
los santos	saints

Comparación cultural

1. Does your family or community have a special day or specific traditions to remember the deceased? How are they similar to or different from the traditions of *Día de los Muertos*?
2. Centuries ago in Europe, the night of October 31, before All Saint's Day, was known as "All Hallowed's Eve." According to ancient beliefs, on this night the dead join the world of the living. Today we call this night Halloween. How would you compare the celebrations of Halloween and *Día de los Muertos*?

Celebraciones **C9**

Culture

About the Photos

Estados Unidos Find Chicago on a map of the United States. Point out that the Pilsen-Little Village section of the city has a large immigrant Latino population. Ask students to discuss why immigrants tend to move to the same neighborhoods.

México Encourage students to observe and comment on the fact that the skulls and skeletons shown on page C8 look friendly, rather than frightening.

Ecuador Tell students that Quechua is a native language spoken in Peru, Argentina, Bolivia, Chile, and Ecuador.

Guatemala Point out the city name Santiago Sacatepéquez on the kite in the foreground. Then ask students to identify the other word on the kite and its meaning. (**paz** meaning "peace") Ask why this might be a good word for a Día de los Muertos celebration.

Comparación cultural

Possible Answers

1. The traditions for remembering deceased loved ones may differ from culture to culture or family to family.
2. Students may find that in many places Halloween celebrations no longer relate to the original meaning of the holiday. Many Día de los Muertos celebrations continue to emphasize the traditional meanings and purpose of the holiday.

Enrichment

Arts and Crafts

El pan de muertos Have students use molding clay rather than bread dough to fashion **guaguas de pan**. They can use the handle end of a paintbrush to carve designs into the clay. They can also use paints to draw faces and other details for the **guaguas de pan**. Alternatively, students might make paper cutouts of skeletons.

Projects

Family Have every student choose a deceased ancestor to commemorate. Ask students to write a brief biography of the individual. If photographs are available, a student could include those in the biography. Ask the student to plan a way to remember the individual through a **Día de los Muertos** activity.

Objectives

- Familiarize students with the differing ways people celebrate las Navidades.
- Identify foods enjoyed during the holiday.
- Locate the countries mentioned on a map.

Presentation Strategies
20-minute lesson

- Ask students to locate the countries of Mexico, Panama, Peru, Argentina, Dominican Republic, Paraguay, and Spain.
- Have students read pp. C10–C11.
- Have students discuss the Comparación cultural questions in pairs.

50-minute lesson

- Complete 20-minute lesson plan.
- Have students summarize the content.
- Ask students to find these cities on a map: Panama City, Panama; Oaxaca, Mexico; Buenos Aires, Argentina; Madrid, Spain.
- Introduce the Vocabulario para celebrar and discuss the meaning of the terms.
- Have students list the foods identified in the text. Ask them to describe the foods.
- Ask a member from each pair to summarize their discussion.

STANDARDS

2.1 Practices and perspectives
2.2 Products and perspectives
4.2 Compare cultures

Connections
Language Arts

An **idiom** is a phrase or sentence with a meaning that does not have exactly the same meaning as the individual words. Write the phrase **contar muchas navidades** (to count many Christmases) on the board. Discuss the meaning of the individual words. Then discuss the meaning of the phrase (to be old). Encourage students to keep a log of English and Spanish idioms.

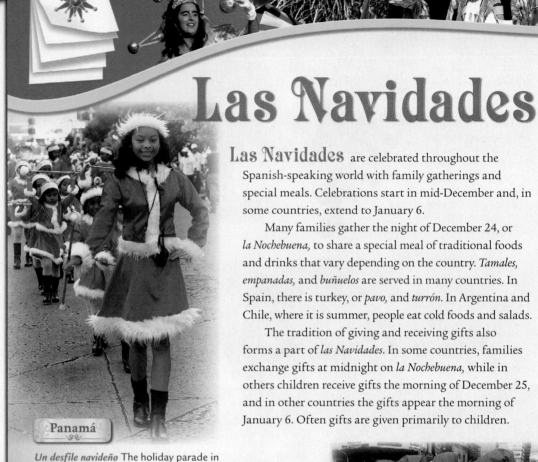

Las Navidades

Las Navidades are celebrated throughout the Spanish-speaking world with family gatherings and special meals. Celebrations start in mid-December and, in some countries, extend to January 6.

Many families gather the night of December 24, or *la Nochebuena,* to share a special meal of traditional foods and drinks that vary depending on the country. *Tamales, empanadas,* and *buñuelos* are served in many countries. In Spain, there is turkey, or *pavo,* and *turrón.* In Argentina and Chile, where it is summer, people eat cold foods and salads.

The tradition of giving and receiving gifts also forms a part of *las Navidades.* In some countries, families exchange gifts at midnight on *la Nochebuena,* while in others children receive gifts the morning of December 25, and in other countries the gifts appear the morning of January 6. Often gifts are given primarily to children.

Panamá

Un desfile navideño The holiday parade in Panama City takes place in mid-December.

México

La noche de rábanos On the night of December 23, elaborate carvings made from radishes, or *rábanos,* are on display in Oaxaca's central plaza. The figures include people, animals, and even entire scenes. This unique tradition has been celebrated for over 100 years.

Argentina

Las empanadas Dancers dress as *empanadas* in Buenos Aires. These meat-filled pies are especially enjoyed during *las Navidades.*

C10   Celebraciones

Bridging Cultures

English Learners

Increase Interaction Have students learning English read the pages with an English-speaking student. Ask the pair to construct several true/false questions that they can use to quiz other students on lesson content. Pairs can take turns asking and answering each other's questions.

Heritage Language Learners

Support What They Know Encourage students to talk about Las Navidades celebrations. Have them ask family or friends whether the way the holidays are celebrated here differ from the way they are celebrated in their country of origin. Talk about reasons why people might adapt their celebrations when they move to a new place.

Cultura INTERACTIVA *See these pages come alive!*
ClassZone.com

Perú

El Día de los Reyes Magos In Peru, Argentina, the Dominican Republic, Paraguay, and Spain, children receive presents on January 6 from *los Reyes Magos*. In anticipation, children leave out a snack for the Three Kings, carrots or grass for the camels, and a pair of empty shoes for the gifts.

España

Un desfile navideño Circus elephants take part in Madrid's holiday parade on January 5. In Spain, parades on January 5 or 6 celebrate the arrival of *los Reyes Magos*.

Vocabulario para celebrar

la Nochebuena	Christmas Eve
los Reyes Magos	Three Kings
la rosca de reyes	sweet bread eaten on January 6
el turrón	almond nougat candy
los villancicos	seasonal children's songs

Comparación cultural

1. Do you and your family celebrate a holiday in December? If so, compare the traditions of your family to the traditions of *las Navidades*.
2. What special meals and foods do you associate with certain holidays? Describe the foods you traditionally enjoy on a holiday you celebrate.
3. What time of the year do you give or receive gifts and for what reason?

Celebraciones **C11**

Culture

About the Photos

Panamá Help students use context to conclude that the Spanish word **desfile** has the same meaning as the English word *parade*.
México Point out that the radishes carved are much larger than the little red radishes found in the grocery store.
Argentina In Argentina, empanadas are pastries that may be filled with ground beef, olives, onions, eggs, and raisins. They might also be filled with other meats, cheese, tuna, corn, or spinach. There are also dessert empanadas.
Perú According to tradition, the Three Kings followed a star to bring gifts to a newborn child. Children receive gifts on January 6 from the kings in memory of this event.
España Children and other onlookers watch a circus elephant perform during the parade that celebrates the arrival of the Three Kings.

Comparación cultural

Possible Answers

1. Many families celebrate religious and nonreligious holidays in December. Christmas is on December 25. Hanukah occurs in December, and Eid al-Adha can fall in December too. Kwanzaa, an African American holiday, begins on December 26.
2. Students may associate specific foods with specific holidays, such as turkey and Thanksgiving. Encourage students to name at least three foods and tell when they enjoy them.
3. Students may exchange gifts on birthdays, at New Year, or on other special days. Some students may not have gift-giving traditions.

Enrichment

Arts and Crafts

Piñatas The tradition of **las posadas** is a strong one in many Mexican communities. Each evening from December 16 through December 24, families gather at a different neighbor's home for a party. Each party ends with the breaking of a piñata. Although traditionally made from pottery, piñatas today may be papier-mâché covered in crepe paper. Have groups of students make piñatas.

Food

Holiday Drinks As part of the holidays, some Mexican families prepare special drinks. These include **rompope** (eggnog), **chocolate caliente** (hot chocolate), and spicy cider. Ask students to find a recipe for Mexican hot chocolate. Work with students to prepare the beverage in class. Provide cups so students can enjoy the tasty drink.

Objectives
- Familiarize students with Año Nuevo celebrations.
- Locate on a map the countries featured in the lesson.

Presentation Strategies
20-minute lesson
- Use a map to locate Peru, Spain, Colombia, and Guatemala.
- Have small groups read pages C12–C13 and respond to the Comparación cultural questions.

50-minute lesson
- Complete 20-minute lesson.
- Review the vocabulary in the Vocabulario para celebrar and ask students to pronounce and define the terms.
- Ask students to present summaries of the group discussion to the class and tally the number of individuals who participate in each kind of celebration mentioned.

STANDARDS
2.1 Practices and perspectives
4.2 Compare cultures

Long-term Retention
Critical Thinking

Different cultures have different traditional calendars. For example, the Chinese calendar is a lunar calendar and the New Year begins sometime between January 19 and February 21. Yet, most Chinese as well as other people celebrate the January 1 New Year holiday. Ask students why it is important for countries around the world to use the same calendar.

¡Año Nuevo!

Perú

La buena suerte In Lima, people believe touching a Chinese Lion brings happiness, good luck, and prosperity in the New Year. Ten percent of Peru's population is of Chinese descent.

España

La medianoche In Madrid, people gather in the Puerta del Sol, holding bags of 12 grapes as they wait for the 12 strokes of midnight from the Puerta del Sol clock, the city's official timekeeper.

El Año Nuevo celebrates the arrival of the New Year and *la Nochevieja* says goodbye to the old. In much of the Spanish-speaking world, traditions include making a toast, exchanging a kiss or hug, or eating twelve grapes—one for each stroke of midnight—to ensure your wishes come true for the New Year. Other good luck traditions include wearing yellow or red, eating a tablespoon of lentils, or carrying a suitcase around the block if you hope to take a trip. To wish someone a happy New Year, say *¡Feliz año nuevo!* or *¡Próspero año nuevo!*

On *Nochevieja,* there are also traditions for saying goodbye to the old year. Some people dress in masks representing *el año viejo.* Others build satirical figures called *los años viejos* that represent famous people or politicians. Adorned with poems or messages that poke fun at *el año viejo,* and filled with shavings and firecrackers, these figures are lit on fire at midnight, to burn and explode on street corners, as a final *despedida,* or farewell, to the old year.

C12 Celebraciones

Bridging Cultures

Heritage Language Learners
Regional Variations Spanish has several ways of saying New Year's Eve. **La noche vieja, la víspera de año nuevo,** and **noche de uvas** all mean *New Year's Eve.* Have students find out from their families their most common way of referring to New Year's Eve.

English Learners
Build Background English learners may find it helpful to record Spanish terms with their English meanings that are not defined in Vocabulario para celebrar. Suggest that they alphabetize the Spanish terms. They can use the log to find the English meaning of Spanish terms easily.

Cultura INTERACTIVA
ClassZone.com *See these pages come alive!*

Colombia

Paseo de los años viejos In Popayán, families and neighbors take their *año viejo* figures out for a final ride before the *Nochevieja* celebration. Later on, at midnight, they will burn the figures.

Guatemala

Baile de los Gigantes In Antigua, people celebrate the New Year with the folkloric "Dance of the Giants." These giant heads, or *cabezudos,* are similar to costumes used since the medieval period in Spain.

Vocabulario para celebrar

el Año Nuevo	New Year
el brindis	toast
las doce uvas	twelve grapes
las lentejas	lentils
la medianoche	midnight
la Nochevieja	New Year's Eve

Comparación cultural

1. How do you celebrate the New Year? Does your family or community have any special traditions? Are any of the traditions similar to the ones in Spanish-speaking countries? How are they similar or different?
2. If you were to build an *año viejo* representing the past year, what figure or event would you portray? Explain your choice.

Celebraciones **C13**

Culture

About the Photos

Perú Lima is Peru's capital city. It is located just inland from the Pacific Coast. Have students locate Lima on a map of Peru.

España Puerta del Sol is in the middle of historic Madrid. Prominently displayed there is a statue of an upright bear eating fruit from a tree.

Colombia Popayán is located south of Cali. Have students find this colonial town on a map of Colombia. An earthquake in the 1980s destroyed much of its historic architecture.

Guatemala For about 200 years until the late 1770s, Antigua served as the seat of Spanish government in Central America. This city sits in the shadow of an extinct volcano, west of the present-day capital city Guatemala City. Have students find the city on a map of Guatemala.

Comparación cultural

Possible Answers

1. Students should identify New Year's celebrations that they have participated in or observed. They might use a Venn diagram to compare and contrast celebrations.
2. Students' responses should identify the figure or event and cite reasons for their choices.

Enrichment

Social Studies

Current Events Have students choose a nation and do research to find out what current events took place in the past year. Have students write a brief description of one of the events. Ask them to draw satirical figures of the people involved in the events. Post their written descriptions and drawings on a bulletin board.

Music

Holiday Songfest Encourage students to find English and Spanish lyrics to the well-known New Year song "Auld Lang Syne." Discuss the meaning of the lyrics. Then help students learn the song in both Spanish and English. They can perform both versions for another class.

Objectives
- Familiarize students with Carnaval and its varied celebrations.
- Identify the traditional meaning of Carnaval and when it is held.

Presentation Strategies
20-minute lesson
- Ask students to find the Canary Islands, Paraguay, Mexico, Bolivia, and Colombia on a map.
- Read pages C14–C15 and discuss the photographs.
- Assign the Comparación cultural questions as homework.

50-minute lesson
- Complete 20-minute lesson.
- Introduce the Vocabulario para celebrar, pronounce the terms, and discuss their meanings.
- Discuss the word origin of **carnaval** and identify words in English and Spanish with the same origin.
- Have groups of students discuss the Comparación cultural questions. Students might use a Venn diagram to compare holidays.

STANDARDS
2.1 Practices and perspectives
2.2 Products and perspectives
4.2 Compare cultures

Connections
Social Studies

Help students find the Canary Islands off the coast of northwestern Africa. Also have students locate the islands in relationship to the mainland of Spain.

febrero

¡Carnaval!

Carnaval marks a period of festivity prior to the beginning of Lent. Lent was, and for some still is, a 40-day period of solemnity and fasting with the removal of meat from the diet being a key feature. You can see the word *carne* (meat) in *Carnaval*; traditionally, this was the last chance to eat meat before the Lenten fast. Today, *Carnaval* often resembles a lively, multi-day party.

Falling in either February or March, *Carnaval* is typically celebrated during the five days that precede Ash Wednesday, the first day of Lent. In some countries, *Carnaval* lasts longer, overlapping other local celebrations. In many regions, traditions such as throwing water and eggs can start over a month before the actual holiday. The planning for the next year's parades, parties, and dance groups often starts as soon as the current *Carnaval* ends!

España

Disfraces Elaborate costumes are central to the *Carnaval* celebration. This costume, entitled "África soy yo," appeared in Las Palmas, in the Canary Islands.

Carnaval Revelers dance in Encarnación, site of the largest celebration in Paraguay.

Paraguay

C14   Celebraciones

Bridging Cultures

Heritage Language Learners
Support What They Know Carnaval is derived from the Latin words meaning removal of meat. Many Spanish and English words include the base *carn-* meaning *flesh* or *meat*. Encourage students to list Spanish and English words with this base. For example, the Spanish word **carnicería** means *butcher shop* and the English word *carnivore* means *an animal that eats meat.*

English Learners
Increase Interaction Many terms in this lesson may be unfamiliar to English learners. Have students work with native English-speaking partners. Together they can identify, pronounce, and define terms such as *solemnity, typically,* and *current,* that may present problems for English learners.

Cultura INTERACTIVA *See these pages come alive!*
ClassZone.com

México

Cascarones Breaking *cascarones* on the heads of friends and other party-goers is a *Carnaval* tradition. The sprinkling of confetti from these hollowed-out eggs is said to bring good luck, as seen here in Mazatlán.

Bolivia

Máscaras are a *Carnaval* tradition dating back to medieval Spain. This masked dancer is from the parade in Oruro, where some 40,000 folkloric dancers and musicians participate.

Bailarines folklóricos Dancers from the Mestizaje dance group perform in Barranquilla. The Colombian government proclaimed this city's *Carnaval* celebration, which combines indigenous, African, and European traditions, a National Cultural Heritage. UNESCO declared it a "Masterpiece" for its cultural uniqueness.

Colombia

Vocabulario para celebrar

los bailarines	dancers
la banda	musical band
Carnaval	Carnival
los cascarones	confetti-filled eggs
el disfraz	costume
las máscaras	masks

Comparación cultural

1. The ways in which *Carnaval* is celebrated in the Spanish-speaking world differ depending on the region. Why do you think the celebrations have evolved differently?
2. Compare the traditions of *Carnaval* to any holiday that you celebrate. Which one(s) are similar? How are they similar?

Celebraciones **C15**

Culture

About the Photos

España Ask students to translate the name of the costume **África soy yo.** Encourage discussion of what these words mean and why the costume was given this name.

Paraguay Encarnación is in southeastern Paraguay. It was founded in the early 1600s as a mission. Its Carnaval features parades, dancing, and a king and queen of the festival.

México Mazatlán is a popular Carnaval destination in Mexico. The celebration there even features a literary contest.

Bolivia In addition to parades, water fights are a popular Carnaval activity in Oruro. Spectators can join the dance groups in the parade.

Colombia Barranquilla in northern Colombia has a Carnaval filled with dancing, music, and theater that displays its diverse cultural heritage.

Comparación cultural

Possible Answers

1. The different ways of celebrating **Carnaval** may have evolved because of the different cultural heritage of the people.
2. Students should name a specific holiday that they or their community celebrates. They might use a chart to identify the celebrations that are similar to and different from **Carnaval** festivities.

Enrichment

Arts and Crafts

Los cascarones Have students make their own cascarones with adult supervision. First they make a hole in an egg, shake out its contents, and use hot water to wash the egg, inside and out. Be sure they wash their hands thoroughly afterwards. They can use paints, wax pencils, glitter, and other supplies to decorate the eggs, fill them with confetti and tissue paper to seal them.

Research

UNESCO UNESCO is an acronym for United Nations Educational, Scientific, and Cultural Organization. Have students do research focused on this agency of the United Nations. Ask them to identify its goals and its history.

Objective
- Familiarize students with an unusual holiday celebration in Valencia, Spain.

Presentation Strategies
20-minute lesson
- Locate Valencia on a map of Spain.
- Have students take turns reading aloud paragraphs in the lesson.
- Discuss the Comparación cultural questions in small groups.

50-minute lesson
- Complete 20-minute lesson.
- Review the vocabulary in the Vocabulario para celebrar, asking students to pronounce and define the terms.
- Discuss the text, photographs, and captions.
- Have a volunteer from each group summarize its discussion for the class.

STANDARDS
2.1 Practices and perspectives
2.2 Products and perspectives
4.2 Compare cultures

Long-term Retention
Critical Thinking

Fireworks, firecrackers, and bonfires are important parts of the **Las Fallas** celebration. This presents serious risks to the city. Ask students how they think the community protects the buildings and people from potential damage. What steps do they think firefighters and other safety personnel take to help protect the people and the buildings of Valencia?

Las Fallas

Las Fallas is a weeklong festival in March that engulfs the city of Valencia, Spain. Tens of thousands of visitors from all over the world come to the city to experience *Las Fallas*, a week of pageants, music, flowers, and creative displays. Each day, the deafening explosions of thousands of firecrackers, *la mascletà*, fills the city at 2:00 p.m. and each night's celebration ends in fireworks.

The main characters of the celebration are the *ninots*, gigantic figures built of wood, plaster, and cardboard. The largest are up to several stories tall. Neighborhood organizations build these enormous figures during the preceding year. Then, during the week of *Las Fallas*, they display them in intersections, parks, and plazas throughout the city. The public visits the more than 400 *fallas* and votes for their favorite one. On the last night at midnight, all but the favorite are burned in enormous bonfires. Then one final, brilliant display of fireworks explodes over the city.

Los ninots These gigantic figures poke fun at well-known people or current events from the preceding year.

Las falleras During the festival, women dress in traditional outfits that include lace dresses, veils, jewelry, and colorful sashes.

C16 Celebraciones

Bridging Cultures

Heritage Language Learners
Support What They Know Although **Las Fallas** is a well-known celebration throughout Spain, it is unique to Valencia. Ask students to discuss with family members any celebrations in their homelands that may be unusual or unique. Provide time for students to give a brief summary of the celebration.

English Learners
Increase Interaction English learners may benefit from reading the lesson in small groups. Encourage group members to read the paragraphs aloud, stopping to summarize sentences or to define terms as they read.

Cultura INTERACTIVA *See these pages come alive!*
ClassZone.com

La Cremà At midnight on the last night, the *fallas* are burned throughout the city. At the same time there are huge displays of colorful fireworks, which include explosions of roman candles and thousands of firecrackers.

Una falla iluminada Thousands of visitors come at night to see the illuminated *fallas*. This display was entered into a special contest, *la Sección Especial*, where a committee judges the *fallas* for creativity, gracefulness and charm, originality, and lighting.

Vocabulario para celebrar

La Cremà	burning of the *fallas*
las fallas	displays of figures
los falleros	celebrants of *Las Fallas*
los fuegos artificiales	fireworks
la mascletà	rhythmic explosion of large and small firecrackers
los ninots	large papier-mâché figures
quemar	to burn

Culture

Expanded Information

Ninots The ninots are built by groups throughout Valencia. Many take up to six months to build and cost thousands of dollars. Most **ninots** are burned on the last day of **Las Fallas.** Those that have won prizes are the last to be burned. Only the favorite ninot is saved from destruction. It is displayed in a museum.

Mascletà The **mascletà** takes place every day at two in the afternoon. Firecrackers of different sizes are exploded in a plaza.

Celebration Las Fallas festivities include processions, concerts, dances, and street vendors.

Comparación cultural

Possible Answers

1. Students may identify holidays such as July 4 and New Year's Day as days in which communities have fireworks displays.
2. Traditions that might be similar to those from **Las Fallas** will vary depending on the celebrations in the students' community.

Comparación cultural

1. Fireworks are a major part of *Las Fallas*. Does your community or region have fireworks displays? When and for what reasons?
2. Are there any other traditions in the festival of *Las Fallas* that are similar to traditions you follow in your community? What are they? Are they part of a specific celebration or season?

Celebraciones   **C17**

Enrichment

Social Studies

Travel Arrangements Valencia, Spain's third largest city, is visited by thousands during the **Las Fallas** festival. Encourage students to find out about hotel accommodations and travel arrangements for a visit to Valencia in March for the festival. Have them prepare a brochure that an agent might use to promote the festival and discuss travel arrangements.

Arts and Crafts

Ninots and Fallas Have small groups of students brainstorm lists of past or present public celebrities. Ask each group to use cardboard and other art materials to make a ninot of one or more of the personalities on their list. They can create a scene in which to place their ninots as well. Have each group present its display to the class.

Semana Santa

Objectives
- Familiarize students with Semana Santa.
- Identify ways people in different countries celebrate Semana Santa.

Presentation Strategies
20-minute lesson
- Ask students to find Mexico, Ecuador, Peru, and El Salvador on a map.
- Have students read pp. C18–C19 together.
- Discuss the Comparación cultural questions.

50-minute lesson
- Complete 20-minute lesson.
- Discuss the photographs on pp. C18-C19.
- Introduce the Vocabulario para celebrar, pronounce the terms, and discuss their meanings.
- Discuss cognates such as **las procesiones** and *processions*.

STANDARDS
2.1 Practices and perspectives
2.2 Products and perspectives
4.2 Compare cultures

Long-term Retention

Critical Thinking

Summarize Have students work in pairs to write brief summaries of the reading and photo captions. Have them include as many Spanish words as possible.

Semana Santa

La Semana Santa is one holiday during the year where in most Spanish-speaking countries entire towns, businesses, schools, and government close for at least four days, Thursday through Sunday. People that have relocated to other places often go back to their hometowns. Others take advantage of the long break to go to the countryside or beach. Entire communities come together for *Semana Santa* celebrations. In some places, religious processions fill the streets each day of the week from Palm Sunday to Easter; in others, Thursday and Friday are the most important days. Most *Semana Santa* traditions are hundreds of years old and originated in Spain, but many now have a unique twist due to the mix of cultures in each country.

México

Vestidos blancos Girls from San Miguel de Allende dress in white for the procession on *Viernes Santo*. In this town, the celebrations extend for two weeks, ending on *el Domingo de Pascua* with an explosion of papier-mâché figures in the center of town.

El Salvador

Alfombras de aserrín Rugs traditionally made of colored sawdust or sand, flowers, and fruits cover the streets where processions will pass in Sonsonate. Artisans also now use modern industrial paints and sprays.

C18   Celebraciones

Bridging Cultures

Heritage Language Learners

Support What They Know For many people, **Semana Santa** is the most important religious holiday of the year. As students discuss their family traditions, remind them of the importance of respecting all religious and nonreligious observances of the week.

English Learners

Build Background The words **procesiones** and **processions** are cognates. Both the Spanish and the English terms are derived from Latin roots. Encourage students to identify any other related cognates. Remind them that knowing cognates can help them understand the meaning of the words in both languages.

Cultura INTERACTIVA *See these pages come alive!*
ClassZone.com

Perú

Decoraciones de flores Flowers fill the city of Tarma for the *Semana Santa* celebrations. In preparation for the processions that begin on Thursday, arches and rugs made of flowers decorate the streets and remain on display until Sunday.

Vocabulario para celebrar

las alfombras	rugs
las flores	flowers
las procesiones	processions
Semana Santa	Holy Week

Ecuador

La fanesca Ecuadorians eat *fanesca*, a bean and grain soup with a fish base, only during *Semana Santa*. The soup is traditionally served with *bolitas de harina* (fritters), *plátano verde* (fried green plantain), fresh cheese, and *ají*, a spicy sauce.

México

Una procesión
Young boys carry streamers during the processions in Cadereyta.

Comparación cultural

1. What holidays do you celebrate with special parades or processions? What kinds of decorations do people use?
2. In what kind of event would most of the people in your community participate? Compare the event to *Semana Santa*.

Celebraciones **C19**

Culture

About the Photos

México Throughout Mexico, girls in white dresses are among those who participate in processions on Good Friday. Boys carry streamers in a street parade as part of the Holy Week celebration.

El Salvador Artisans spend many hours making the detailed sand and flower rugs for the streets of Sonsonate, a city west of the national capital San Salvador.

Perú Tarma is a town northeast of Lima. The carpets of flowers are roped off so that people do not walk on them.

Ecuador Ecuadorian **fanesca** has a cod-based broth and is full of vegetables including corn, cabbage, beans, peas, and squash. It is garnished with hard-boiled eggs and grated cheese.

Comparación cultural

Possible Answers

1. Students may mention a variety of holidays such as Labor Day, Thanksgiving Day, and Fourth of July that include parades. Decorations include flags, banners, and flowers.
2. Different communities have different festivities or community activities. These may include food sampling festivities, carnivals, street sales, heritage days, or national celebrations. Some celebrations may be primarily religious as with Semana Santa and others may be non-religious or neighborhood celebrations.

Enrichment

Arts and Crafts

Carpets of Flowers or Sand Have students examine the sand and flower carpets shown in the pictures. Encourage students to design a pattern for their own sand or flower carpet to reflect a holiday of their choice. They can sketch their design, showing the colors they would use. If they have colored sand or can make paper flowers, they may wish to make a minirug of their design.

Foods

Fried Green Plantains With adult supervision, students can easily make fried green plantains. They simply peel and slice green plantains, which are similar to bananas. They then fry the plantains in a pan until golden; carefully remove and smash the plantains, sprinkle them with salt, and refry them until they are crispy. They should drain the plantains and let them cool before eating.

Objectives
- Familiarize students with Cinco de Mayo.
- Differentiate Cinco de Mayo from Mexican independence celebrations.
- Identify Cinco de Mayo celebrations in the United States.

Presentation Strategies
20-minute lesson
- Remind students that Mexican independence is celebrated in September.
- Locate Puebla, Mexico; Los Angeles; and Washington, D.C., on a map.
- Read the lesson and discuss the holiday.
- Discuss the Comparación cultural questions in small groups.

50-minute lesson
- Complete 20-minute lesson.
- Review the vocabulary in the Vocabulario para celebrar.
- Discuss the text, photographs, and captions.
- Ask groups to summarize their discussions of the Comparación cultural questions for the class.

STANDARDS
2.1 Practices and perspectives
3.1 Knowledge of other disciplines
4.2 Compare cultures

Long-term Retention
Critical Thinking

Discuss reenactments as a means of commemorating events. How do reenactments differ from other kinds of celebrations? How are reenactments like plays? Would people involved in reenactments have to rehearse? Explain.

¡Cinco de Mayo!

Cinco de Mayo has become a popular celebration thoughout the United States. However, not everyone who celebrates this uniquely Mexican holiday knows its origin. To find the reason, you must travel back to the year 1862 in Mexico. On May 5, in the town of Puebla de los Ángeles, the Mexican army, joined by farmers and townspeople, fought against the French and forced them to retreat. The Mexicans were led by General Ignacio Zaragoza and the town was later renamed Puebla de Zaragoza in his honor. Although the French went on to occupy Mexico City and assume a short-lived role in Mexico's government, *Cinco de Mayo* became a national holiday symbolizing Mexican unity.

A *Cinco de Mayo* celebration in Mexico includes dancing, music, and reenactments of the battle. In many parts of the U.S. where there is a large Mexican or Mexican-American community, you will often find *Cinco de Mayo* celebrations.

Los Ángeles

Mariachis y bailarines Folkloric dancers and musicians perform throughout the day in the Plaza Olvera during the *Cinco de Mayo* celebrations.

C20 Celebraciones

Bridging Cultures

Heritage Language Learners

Family Celebrations Encourage students of Mexican descent to discuss Cinco de Mayo celebrations with their families. Is the holiday celebrated in their hometowns in Mexico? If so, how? Students can share their findings with the class. Encourage students to bring in photographs, programs, or costumes of past Cinco de Mayo celebrations to share with the class.

English Learners

Increase Interaction Pair English learners with native English-speaking students. Have them read pp. C20–C21 aloud, alternating after every few sentences. Encourage English learners to correct their own pronunciation and to use their partner's pronunciation as a model.

Cultura INTERACTIVA *See these pages come alive!*
ClassZone.com

México

Reconstrucción de la batalla A reenactment of the historic battle in Puebla commemorates Mexico's victory over the French.

Vocabulario para celebrar

los bailarines	dancers
la batalla	battle
el ejército	army
los franceses	French
los músicos	musicians
la reconstrucción	reenactment

Washington, D.C.

Bailarín folklórico A dancer performs in a traditional Mexican costume at the White House.

Comparación cultural

1. Do you know of a *Cinco de Mayo* celebration in your community or region? If so, how or where is it celebrated?
2. What important battles or historic events are celebrated in your community or state? How are they celebrated? Are they local or national holidays? Compare one of these holiday celebrations with the *Cinco de Mayo* celebrations.

Celebraciones **C21**

Culture

About the Photos

Los Ángeles Los Angeles, California, is the second largest city in the United States. It is home to a large Latino population. Plaza Olvera is part of Olvera Street, a historic section of Los Angeles.

México Puebla is southeast of Mexico City, the national capital. The May 5th celebration commemorates the defeat of the French army by the Mexican army. Despite the victory, the French went on to rule Mexico for a time. The French finally withdrew in 1867.

Washington, D.C. Cinco de Mayo celebrations take place around the United States, which has a large Mexican American population. It is a celebration of freedom that all can enjoy.

Comparación cultural

Possible Answers

1. Cinco de Mayo celebrations include parades and theatrical performances. Large cities and even schools may have Cinco de Mayo events.
2. Celebrations of historic events in much of the United States are celebrated with parades, memorial services, fireworks, concerts, and more. Different communities celebrate community and national events in different ways.

Enrichment

Social Studies

Cinco de Mayo in the News Have students prepare news reports detailing the events of Cinco de Mayo, 1862, in Puebla, Mexico. The news reports should provide background information as well as information about the Mexican victory. Students can present their reports in a modern television documentary format. Encourage them to use drawings and maps to visually support the report.

Arts and Crafts

Folk Dance Invite Mexican folk dancers to perform for the class. If possible, ask a member of the troupe to teach the students a simple dance routine. Students can practice and perform the dance for other classes.

Objectives
- Familiarize students with Inti Raymi.
- Differentiate between summer and winter solstices.

Presentation Strategies
20-minute lesson
- Locate Peru, Ecuador, and Bolivia on a world map or globe. Trace the equator and identify the Northern and Southern hemispheres.
- Have students take turns reading aloud pages C22–C23.
- Have groups of students discuss the Comparación cultural questions.

50-minute lesson
- Complete 20-minute lesson.
- Review the Vocabulario para celebrar.
- Discuss the summer and winter solstices and when they occur in the Northern and Southern hemispheres.
- Ask group representatives to present their group's answers to the class.

STANDARDS
2.1 Practices and perspectives
4.2 Compare cultures

Inti Raymi

Inti Raymi, or the "Festival of the Sun," falls on June 21 or 22, the date of the southern hemisphere's winter solstice, the shortest day of the year. Indigenous communities throughout the Andean highland countries of South America celebrate the winter solstice with ceremonies designed to bring the Sun back and shorten the longest night. Incan in origin, *Inti Raymi* honored the sun as the source of light, heat, and life, and celebrated the start of a new planting season. The name *Inti Raymi* comes from the Quechua language: *inti* means "sun" and *raymi* means "festival." The largest festival takes place in Cuzco, Peru, the ancient capital of the Incan civilization and empire. In Cuzco, *Inti Raymi* has grown into a major tourist attraction. Thousands of people visit the city to enjoy the performances by folkloric groups and to watch the theatrical presentation of the Incan ceremony, the focal point of the celebration.

Perú

Presentación cultural de Inti Raymi
In Cuzco, professional actors and actresses interpret the roles of the Incan emperor and others.
Above: A woman carries offerings.
Right: The Incan emperor passes through the streets of Cuzco to the ruins of the Incan fortress, Sacsayhuaman.

C22   Celebraciones

Bridging Cultures

Heritage Language Learners

Support What They Know The **Inti Raymi** celebration began as an Incan holiday. Have students with family members from South America ask about celebrations of the summer or winter solstice. Together students can make a chart identifying nations that celebrate the solstice and the types of celebrations enjoyed.

Heritage Language Learners

Indigenous Languages Both Spanish and Quechua are official languages of Peru. Although Quechua is spoken in Ecuador, it is not an official language. In Bolivia, Spanish, Quechua, and Aymara are official languages. Have students find out what languages family members from South and Central America speak. Do they speak an indigenous language as well as Spanish?

Cultura INTERACTIVA *See these pages come alive!*
ClassZone.com

Ecuador

Indígenas ecuatorianas A dance group from the Paktarinmi cultural organization forms a "sacred circle" with grains of corn, a pre-Incan rite. In Ecuador, which lies on the equator, this date is considered the summer solstice, rather than the winter.

Vocabulario para celebrar

el aymara	language of indigenous group from Bolivia and Peru
los incas	Incas, an ancient South American people
el quechua	language common to many South American indigenous groups and adopted and spread by Incas
el sol	sun

Bolivia

Los aymaras In the pre-Columbian ruins of Tihuanaku, an Aymara priest blows on a shell to celebrate the winter solstice, which marks the new year. The Aymara are one of two dominant indigenous groups in Bolivia, comprising 25 percent of the population. The other group, Quechua, makes up 30 percent.

Comparación cultural

1. In North America, June 21 is the summer solstice, or the longest day of the year, and December 21 is the winter solstice, or the shortest day of the year. What important holidays or events occur during this time of year?
2. In ancient civilizations, the appearance of the sun and moon were important events that helped mark the passing of time and the seasons. If you were to celebrate the winter or summer solstice, what would you include in your celebration?

Celebraciones **C23**

Inti Raymi

Connections

Science

The different seasons of the year exist due to the tilt of the earth. In the Southern Hemisphere, the winter solstice is in June and the summer solstice is in December. When it is the winter solstice in the Southern Hemisphere, it is the summer solstice in the Northern Hemisphere. Have students note Ecuador's position in relationship to the equator. Discuss why Ecuadorians consider the June solstice their summer solstice.

Culture

About the Photos

Peru, Ecuador, and Bolivia were all part of the Inca empire.
Perú The fortress of Sacsayhuaman was largely destroyed by the Spanish. Its ruins with stones expertly fit closely together illustrate the building skills of the Incas.
Ecuador The equator runs through the capital city of Quito, Ecuador. The name of the country is the Spanish word for equator.
Bolivia Once ruled by the Aymara people, Bolivia became part of the Inca empire in the 1400s.

Comparación cultural

Possible Answers

1. Many communities enjoy winter festivals in December. Many holidays take place in late December, such as the African American celebration of Kwanzaa.
2. Students may identify seasonal outdoor objects, such as flowers, lightning bugs, snow, and ice, with the solstices. They should name the items and explain how they would use them.

Enrichment

Science

Seasonal Changes Have students use drawings or models to demonstrate the solstices and equinoxes in the Southern Hemisphere. Have them provide an explanation of what happens on those days including facts such as the number of hours of sunlight.

Foods

Quinoa Have students make a quinoa salad. Quinoa is an ancient Peruvian grain. If quinoa is not available in an ethnic food store, substitute rice or another grain. To make the salad, seed and chop a jalapeño pepper, peel and chop a cucumber, and dice a tomato. Add these to four cups of the cooked grain. Add fresh mint as well. Make a salad dressing of olive oil, lime juice, and salt and pepper.

C23

Objectives

- Provide biographical data on Simón Bolívar.
- Familiarize students with Día de Simón Bolívar.

Presentation Strategies
20-minute lesson

- Read pages C24–C25.
- Identify the present-day nations of South America that made up Gran Colombia.
- Locate Venezuela, Panama, Colombia, Ecuador, Bolivia, and Peru on a map.
- Conduct a class discussion of the Comparación cultural questions.

50-minute lesson

- Complete 20-minute lesson.
- Review the vocabulary in the Vocabulario para celebrar.
- Identify the meaning of **el libertador** and explain why Simón Bolívar was called el Libertador.
- Discuss the text, photographs, and captions.

STANDARDS

2.1 Practices and perspectives
2.2 Products and perspectives
3.1 Knowledge of other disciplines
4.2 Compare cultures

Long-term Retention
Critical Thinking

Have students identify the historical leaders who are on the American one dollar (George Washington), five dollar (Abraham Lincoln), ten dollar (Alexander Hamilton), and twenty dollar (Andrew Jackson) bills. Then remind students who is depicted on the Venezuelan currency. Why are these people depicted on the money? What does it show about their contribution to the nation? Which leaders do you think are most like Simón Bolívar? Why?

Día de Simón Bolívar

Simón Bolívar, known as *El Libertador,* envisioned a united South America, a union for which he fought, but never attained. Despite this, he was instrumental in bringing about much of South America's independence from Spain and became one of its most revered leaders. His birthday is a national holiday in Venezuela, Ecuador, and Bolivia, and many cities and towns have plazas or monuments in his honor.

Born on July 24, 1783, in Caracas, Venezuela, Simón Bolívar strongly believed in freedom from Spanish rule and worked toward that goal as a political leader, writer, and military commander. With his troops, he liberated present-day Venezuela, then Colombia. He was then named president of Gran Colombia, a federation comprised of what is now Venezuela, Colombia, Panama, and Ecuador. He went on to lead his troops into Peru, aiding in the final defeat of Spain. For two more years, Bolívar maintained his leadership, writing the constitution of Bolivia, a country named in his honor. By 1827, his dream of unification dissolved amidst growing rivalries between the South American military leaders. Three years later Bolívar died, on December 17, 1830.

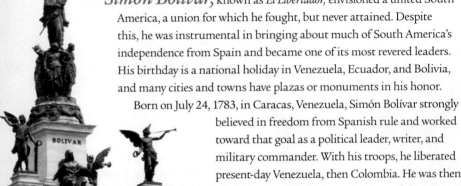

Colombia

Bolívares Venezuela's currency carries both Bolívar's name and image.

Venezuela

Monumento a Simón Bolívar This monument marks the location of the Battle of Boyacá, where Bolívar's forces defeated the Spanish resulting in the liberation of Gran Colombia. To celebrate the anniversary of the battle, students form the colors of the Colombian flag.

C24   Celebraciones

Bridging Cultures

Heritage Language Learners

Support What They Know Students with South American roots might ask family members whether they celebrated Simón Bolívar Day as children. Encourage them to identify ways the day was celebrated.

English Learners

Increase Interaction Have students proficient in English read the pages with English learners. Encourage students to summarize each paragraph and caption in simple terms. Students should consult a dictionary when necessary to understand the meaning of terms such as *instrumental, amidst, crucial,* and *commemorates.*

Cultura INTERACTIVA *See these pages come alive!*
ClassZone.com

Ecuador

Líder de la Batalla de Pichincha Each year, the city of Quito commemorates the Battle of Pichincha, where Simón Bolívar sent troops under the command of Antonio José de Sucre to defeat the Spanish in one of the crucial battles in the fight for independence.

Simón Bolívar (1830), José Gil de Castro
José Gil de Castro, renowned painter of Chilean society and of the independence leaders, painted this portrait of Bolívar in the early 1800s.

Venezuela

Vocabulario para celebrar

la batalla   battle
la independencia
                          independence
El Libertador
                          the liberator

Plaza de Bolívar This statue of Bolívar is located in the Plaza Bolívar, the historic, political, and commercial center of Caracas.

Comparación cultural

1. What famous leader in U.S. history would you compare with Simón Bolívar? Why? What do both leaders have in common?
2. What U.S. holidays are in honor of famous leaders? How are they celebrated? What other ways do we honor our important leaders?

Celebraciones   **C25**

Culture

About the Photos

Colombia The Battle of Boyacá took place on August 7, 1819. It was a great victory for the independence movement.

Ecuador Antonio José de Sucre defeated the Spanish near Quito on May 24, 1822. He later served as Bolivia's first president.

Simón Bolívar (1830) José Gil de Castro also painted two other great South American liberators—Bernardo O'Higgins of Chile and José de San Martín of Argentina.

Venezuela In addition to the statue of Simón Bolívar in the center of the plaza, the Bolívar Plaza has statues in each of its four corners that represent the nations once part of Gran Colombia.

Comparación cultural

Possible Answers

1. Answers may vary, but students are likely to compare Simón Bolívar with George Washington. Both leaders commanded armed forces to help their countries gain freedom, and both served as presidents of new American nations.
2. Students might mention such holidays as Presidents' Day and Martin Luther King, Jr., Day. Celebrations include memorial services, speeches, and parades. Other ways of honoring leaders include writing and reading books about them and making movies about them.

Enrichment

Arts and Crafts

Simón Bolívar Have students use clay or papier-mâché to make a miniature statue of Simón Bolívar. Alternatively, they might use markers or paints to do a portrait of the leader.

Timeline

Independence Many Central and South American nations gained their independence in the 1800s. Have students make a list of all the Central and South American nations and record their dates of independence. Students should then arrange the nations on a timeline to show the sequence of independence.

Culture at a Glance ❖

Topic & Activity	Essential Question
¡Hola! p. C26	How do Spanish-speaking people living in New York City celebrate their culture?
A mural at the metro, p. 9	How can artists give back to their neighborhood through their work?

Practice at a Glance ❖

	Objective	Activity & Skill
Vocabulary	Greetings	1: Reading; 2: Writing; 3: Speaking; 4: Reading; 5: Reading/Writing; 6: Speaking; 7: Speaking; Repaso 1: Listening; Repaso 4: Writing
	Alphabet	8: Listening/Writing; 9: Speaking; 10: Speaking
	Countries	11: Writing/Speaking; 12: Speaking; 13: Speaking; Repaso 3: Writing
	Numbers from 0 to 10	14: Speaking/Writing; 15: Speaking; 16: Speaking; Repaso 3: Writing
	Days of the week	17: Speaking/Writing; 18: Listening; 19: Speaking
	Weather expressions	20: Listening; 21: Speaking; 22: Speaking; Repaso 2: Writing
	Classroom commands	23: Reading; 24: Writing/Speaking; Repaso 1: Listening
Communication	Greet people and say goodbye	1: Reading; 2: Writing; 3: Speaking; Repaso 1: Listening; Repaso 2: Writing
	Introduce yourself and others	4: Reading; 5: Reading/Writing; 6: Speaking; 7: Speaking; Repaso 2: Writing
	Ask and say how to spell names	8: Listening/Writing; 9: Speaking; 10: Speaking; 25: Speaking
	Say where you are from	11: Writing/Speaking; 12: Speaking; 13: Speaking; 22: Speaking; Repaso 3: Writing
	Exchange phone numbers	15: Speaking; 16: Speaking; Repaso 3: Writing; Repaso 4: Writing
	Say what day of the week it is	17: Speaking/Writing; 18: Listening; 19: Speaking
	Describe the weather	20: Listening; 21: Speaking; 22: Speaking; Repaso 2: Writing
	Respond to classroom instructions	23: Reading; 24: Writing/Speaking
	Pronunciation: The letter **h**	**Pronunciación: La letra h,** p. 5: Listening/Speaking
	Pronunciation: The vowels	**Pronunciación: Las vocales,** p. 11: Listening/Speaking

The following activities are recorded in the Audio Program for *¡Avancemos!*

- **¡A responder!** *pages 3, 7, 10, 13, 16, 18, 20, 23*
- **8: Lista** *page 11*
- **18: ¿Lógico o ilógico?** *page 19*
- **20: El tiempo** *page 21*
- **Repaso de la lección** *page 26*
- **1 Listen and Understand** *page 26*

¡A responder!

TXT CD 1 track 2 Page 3

1. Buenos días.
2. Hasta mañana.
3. Adiós.
4. ¿Qué tal?
5. Buenas tardes.
6. ¡Hasta luego!

TXT CD 1 track 5 Page 7

1. Te presento a Sonia.
2. Hola. Me llamo Ricardo.
3. Me llamo Carolina. ¿Y tú?
4. Le presento a la señora Vargas.

TXT CD 1 track 7 Page 10

1. ele
2. e
3. jota
4. eñe
5. pe
6. i
7. hache
8. be grande

TXT CD 1 track 11 Page 13

1. Es de Costa Rica.
2. Es de Puerto Rico.
3. Es de Argentina.
4. Es de España.
5. Es de Ecuador.
6. Es de la República Dominicana.

TXT CD 1 track 13 Page 16

a. ocho
b. cinco
c. nueve
d. seis
e. cuatro
f. uno
g. diez
h. siete

TXT CD 1 track 15 Page 18

1. martes
2. domingo
3. lunes
4. miércoles
5. sábado
6. jueves

TXT CD 1 track 18 Page 20

1. Hace viento.
2. Nieva.
3. Hace sol.
4. Llueve.
5. Hace frío.
6. Hace calor.

TXT CD 1 track 21 Page 23

1. Abran los libros en la página 10.
2. Levanten la mano.
3. Cierren los libros.
4. Repitan: "buenos días".
5. Saquen una hoja de papel.

8 | Lista TXT CD 1 track 8

1. equis, i, eme, e, ene, a
2. ge, u, i, ele, ele, e, ere, eme, o
3. a, ele, e, jota, a, ene, de, ere, o
4. i griega, o, ele, a, ene, de, a
5. be grande, e, a, te, ere, i, zeta
6. jota, o, ese, e, efe, i, ene, a
7. hache, u, ge, o
8. te, o, eñe, o

18 | ¿Lógico o ilógico? TXT CD 1 track 16

1. Hoy es martes. Mañana es miércoles.
2. Hoy es jueves. Mañana es sábado.
3. Hoy es lunes. Mañana es viernes.
4. Hoy es sábado. Mañana es domingo.
5. Hoy es miércoles. Mañana es jueves.
6. Hoy es viernes. Mañana es martes.

20 | El tiempo TXT CD 1 track 19

1. Hace sol.
2. Llueve.
3. Hace viento.
4. Nieva.

Repaso de la lección TXT CD 1 track 22

1 Listen and understand

1. Te presento a Victoria. Es de España.
2. ¿Cómo se llama usted?
   Me llamo Rodrigo León.
   ¿Cuál es su número de teléfono?
   Cinco - dos - tres - siete - uno - nueve - cero.
3. Abran los libros en la página ocho.
4. Buenos días, señor. ¿Cómo está usted?

On your desktop

Everything you need to ...

Plan	Present	Assess
 **easyPlanner** DVD-ROM	**POWER PRESENTATIONS**	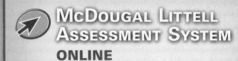 **McDOUGAL LITTELL ASSESSMENT SYSTEM** ONLINE
All resources including audio and video	Ready-made PowerPoint™ presentations with  **Animated Grammar**	✓ Assess, score, prescribe, and remediate online ✓ Create customized tests with the Test Generator CD-ROM ✓ Individualized Assessment for on-level, modified, pre-AP, and heritage language learners

 ## Print

Plan	Practice
URB 1: • Video Scripts p. 97 **Lesson Plans** **Best Practices Toolkit**	• *SuperBruno y Nati* **URB 1** • Back to School Resources pp. 1–24 • Audio Scripts pp. 101–103

 ## Unit Transparency Book 1

Culture	Classroom Management
• Atlas Maps UTB 1 1–6	• Warm up Transparencies 22–25 **MSRB** • Student Book Answer Transparencies 24–27

Audio and Video

Audio	Video
• Student Book Audio CD 1 Tracks 1–22 • Assessment Audio CD 1 Tracks 1–2 • *Música del mundo hispano* • Sing-along Audio CD	• *Telehistoria Prólogo* DVD 1

Online and CD-ROM Resources

Student	Teacher
Available online and on CD-ROM: • eEdition • @HomeTutor • Animated Grammar **Available online:** • *Cultura Interactiva* • Culture Links • WebQuests • Flashcards • Conjuguemos.com • Review Games • Self-check Quiz	**Available online and on CD-ROM:** **EasyPlanner only resources:** • Learning Scenarios • Conversation Cards • Family Letters in Spanish • Family Letters in Creole **Available online:** • McDougal Littell Assessment System **Available on CD-ROM:** • Test Generator • Power Presentation

Differentiated Assessment

On-level	Modified	Pre-AP	Heritage Learners
• On-level Preliminary Lesson Test pp. 1–6	• Preliminary Modified Lesson Test pp. 1–6	• Preliminary Pre-AP Lesson Test pp. 1–6	• Heritage Learners Diagnostic Test pp. 1–6 • Heritage Learners Preliminary Lesson Test pp. 7–12

	Objectives/Focus	Teach	Practice	Assess/HW Options
DAY 1	**Culture:** learn about the culture of Spanish-speaking people in New York City • Learn about greetings **5 min**	Lesson Opener pp. 0–1 **Hola, ¿qué tal?** pp. 2–5 • Read A–H • Play audio TXT CD 1 track 1 • *¡A responder!* TXT CD 1 track 2 • *Nota: ¿Cómo estás?* • *Pronunciación* TXT CD 1 track 3 **20 min**	**Hola, ¿qué tal?** pp. 2–5 • Acts. 1, 2, 3 **20 min**	**Assess:** *Para y piensa* p. 5 **5 min**
DAY 2	Learn about introductions • Warm Up OHT 22 **5 min**	**¡Mucho gusto!** pp. 6–9 • Read A–G • Play audio TXT CD 1 track 4 • *¡A responder!* TXT CD 1 track 5 • *Nota: ¿Cómo te llamas?* **20 min**	**¡Mucho gusto!** pp. 6–9 • Acts. 4, 5, 6, 7 **20 min**	**Assess:** *Para y piensa* p. 9 **5 min**
DAY 3	Learn how to spell using the Spanish alphabet • Warm Up OHT 22, 23 Learn how to say where people are from **5 min**	**El abecedario** pp. 10–11 • Read the alphabet • Play audio TXT CD 1 track 6 • *¡A responder!* TXT CD 1 track 7 • *Pronunciación:* TXT CD 1 track 9 **¿De dónde eres?** pp. 12–15 • Play audio TXT CD 1 track 10 • *¡A responder!* TXT CD 1 track 11 • *Nota:* Asking questions **20 min**	**El abecedario** pp. 10–11 • Act. 8 TXT CD 1 track 8 • Acts. 9, 10 **¿De dónde eres?** pp. 12–15 • Acts. 11, 12, 13 **20 min**	**Assess:** *Para y piensa* pp. 11, 15 **5 min**
DAY 4	Learn the numbers 0–10 and exchange phone numbers • Warm Up OHT 23 **5 min**	**Mi número de teléfono** pp. 16–17 • Read p. 16 • Play audio TXT CD 1 track 12 • *¡A responder!* TXT CD 1 track 13 **20 min**	**Mi número de teléfono** pp. 16–17 • Acts. 14, 15, 16 **20 min**	**Assess:** *Para y piensa* p. 17 **5 min**
DAY 5	Learn the days of the week • Warm Up OHT 24 **5 min**	**Los días de la semana** pp. 18–19 • Read A–B • Play audio TXT CD 1 track 14 • *¡A responder!* TXT CD 1 track 15 **15 min**	**Los días de la semana** pp. 18–19 • Acts. 17, 19 • Act. 18 TXT CD 1 track 16 **25 min**	**Assess:** *Para y piensa* p. 19 **5 min**
DAY 6	Learn to describe the weather • Warm Up OHT 24 **5 min**	**¿Qué tiempo hace?** pp. 20–21 • Read A–F • Play audio TXT CD 1 track 17 • *¡A responder!* TXT CD 1 track 18 **15 min**	**¿Qué tiempo hace?** pp. 20–21 • Act. 20 TXT CD 1 track 19 • Acts. 21, 22 **25 min**	**Assess:** *Para y piensa* p. 21 **5 min**
DAY 7	Learn classroom phrases • Warm Up OHT 25 **5 min**	**En la clase** pp. 22–24 • Read pp. 22–23 • Play audio TXT CD 1 track 20 • *¡A responder!* TXT CD 1 track 21 **15 min**	**En la clase** pp. 22–24 • Acts. 23, 24, 25 **25 min**	**Assess:** *Para y piensa* p. 24 **5 min**
DAY 8	**Review:** Lesson review • Warm Up OHT 25 **5 min**	**Repaso de la lección** pp. 26–27 **20 min**	**Repaso de la lección** pp. 26–27 • Act. 1 TXT CD 1 track 22 • Acts. 2, 3, 4 **20 min**	**Assess:** pp. 26–27 **5 min** **Homework:** *En resumen* p. 25
DAY 9	Assessment			**Assess:** Preliminary lesson test **50 min**

	Objectives/Focus	Teach	Practice	Assess/HW Options
DAY 1	**Culture:** learn about the culture of Spanish-speaking people in New York City • Learn about greetings **5 min**	Lesson Opener pp. 0–1 **Hola, ¿qué tal?** pp. 2–5 • Read A–H • Play audio TXT CD 1 track 1 • *¡A responder!* TXT CD 1 track 2 • *Nota: ¿Cómo estás?* • *Pronunciación* TXT CD 1 track 3 **20 min**	**Hola, ¿qué tal?** pp. 2–5 • Acts. 1, 2, 3 **15 min**	**Assess:** *Para y piensa* p. 5 @HomeTutor **5 min**
	Learn about introductions • Warm Up OHT 22 **5 min**	**¡Mucho gusto!** pp. 6–9 • Read A–G • Play audio TXT CD 1 track 4 • *¡A responder!* TXT CD 1 track 5 • *Nota: ¿Cómo te llamas?* **15 min**	**¡Mucho gusto!** pp. 6–9 • Acts. 4, 5, 6, 7 **20 min**	**Assess:** *Para y piensa* p. 9 **5 min**
DAY 2	Learn how to spell using the Spanish alphabet • Warm Up OHT 22 **5 min**	**El abecedario** pp. 10–11 • Read the alphabet • Play audio TXT CD 1 track 6 • *¡A responder!* TXT CD 1 track 7 • *Pronunciación* TXT CD 1 track 9 **20 min**	**El abecedario** pp. 10–11 • Act. 8 TXT CD 1 track 8 • Acts. 9, 10 **15 min**	**Assess:** *Para y piensa* p. 11 **5 min**
	Learn how to say where people are from **5 min**	**¿De dónde eres?** pp. 12–15 • Play audio TXT CD 1 track 10 • *¡A responder!* TXT CD 1 track 11 **20 min**	**¿De dónde eres?** pp. 12–15 • Acts. 11, 12, 13 **20 min**	**Assess:** *Para y piensa* p. 15 **5 min**
DAY 3	Learn the numbers 0–10 and exchange phone numbers • Warm Up OHT 23 **5 min**	**Mi número de teléfono** pp. 16–17 • Read p. 16 • Play audio TXT CD 1 track 12 • *¡A responder!* TXT CD 1 track 13 **15 min**	**Mi número de teléfono** pp. 16–17 • Acts. 14, 15, 16 **20 min**	**Assess:** *Para y piensa* p. 17 **5 min**
	Learn the days of the week **5 min**	**Los días de la semana** pp. 18–19 • Read A–B • Play audio TXT CD 1 track 14 • *¡A responder!* TXT CD 1 track 15 **15 min**	**Los días de la semana** pp. 18–19 • Acts. 17, 19 • Act. 18 TXT CD 1 track 16 **20 min**	**Assess:** *Para y piensa* p. 19 **5 min**
DAY 4	Learn to describe the weather • Warm Up OHT 24 **5 min**	**¿Qué tiempo hace?** pp. 20–21 • Read A–F • Play audio TXT CD 1 track 17 • *¡A responder!* TXT CD 1 track 18 **15 min**	**¿Qué tiempo hace?** pp. 20–21 • Act. 20 TXT CD 1 track 19 • Acts. 21, 22 **25 min**	**Assess:** *Para y piensa* p. 21 **5 min**
	Learn classroom phrases **5 min**	**En la clase** pp. 22–24 • Read pp. 22–23 • Play audio TXT CD 1 track 20 • *¡A responder!* TXT CD 1 track 21 **5 min**	**En la clase** pp. 22–24 • Acts. 23, 24, 25 **25 min**	**Assess:** *Para y piensa* p. 24 **5 min**
DAY 5	**Review:** Lesson review **5 min**	**Repaso de la lección** pp. 26–27 **10 min**	**Repaso de la lección** pp. 26–27 • Act. 1 TXT CD 1 track 22 • Acts. 2, 3, 4 **20 min**	**Assess:** pp. 26–27 **5 min** **Homework:** *En resumen* p. 25
	Assessment **50 min**			**Assess:** Preliminary lesson test

Objectives

- Introduce lesson theme: **¡Hola!**
- **Culture:** Learn about New York City's Hispanic population and its cultural celebrations.

Presentation Strategies

- Ask students to study the photos on this spread, identify the city, and tell what they know about it.
- Ask students to talk about their initial impression of the city. Have them make a list of four important aspects of New York City.
- Have students talk about cultural celebrations in their own area and compare them to those in New York City.

STANDARDS

2.1 Practices and perspectives
4.2 Compare cultures

Comparación cultural

Exploring the Theme

Ask the following:

1. Is the architecture of the buildings seen here similar to buildings in your area?
2. Have you ever visited any area with this type of architecture? Do you like these buildings? Why or why not?
3. Think of the parades in the area where you live. What is the occasion for these celebrations? What do the people that participate in the parade wear? What do they do?

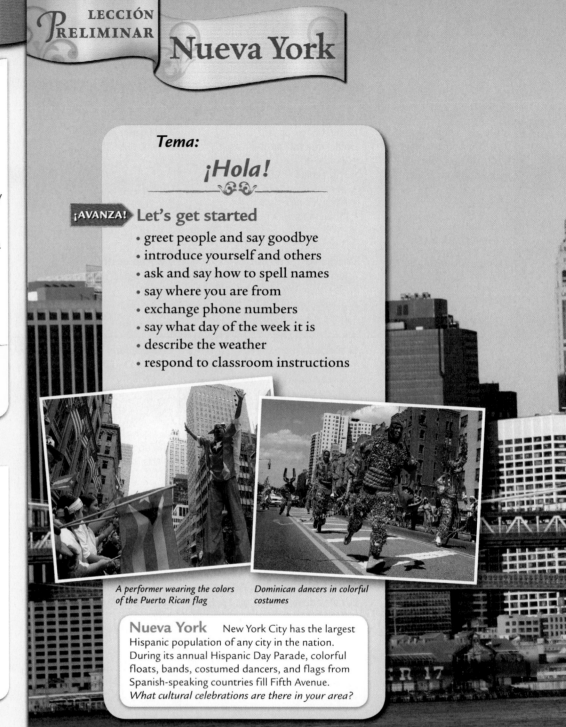

LECCIÓN
PRELIMINAR
Nueva York

Tema:

¡Hola!

¡AVANZA! **Let's get started**

- greet people and say goodbye
- introduce yourself and others
- ask and say how to spell names
- say where you are from
- exchange phone numbers
- say what day of the week it is
- describe the weather
- respond to classroom instructions

A performer wearing the colors of the Puerto Rican flag

Dominican dancers in colorful costumes

Nueva York   New York City has the largest Hispanic population of any city in the nation. During its annual Hispanic Day Parade, colorful floats, bands, costumed dancers, and flags from Spanish-speaking countries fill Fifth Avenue. *What cultural celebrations are there in your area?*

Lección preliminar

Differentiating Instruction

Multiple Intelligences

Visual Learners Students who are visual learners learn better when provided with visual input: photos, drawings, shapes, colors, etc. Encourage these students to create vocabulary flashcards with drawings, magazine cutouts, or color coding to help them remember the meanings of words.

Heritage Language Learners

Support What They Know Ask Spanish-speaking students to talk about their experiences attending a parade in their country of origin. What was the occasion for the parade? Where and when did it take place? Who participated in the parade? What did the participants wear? What were they doing? Were there floats? Who attended the parade?

A view of Lower Manhattan from the East River
New York, New York

Nueva York
uno 1

Using the Photo

Location Information

New York City lies about 100 miles south of Boston at the mouth of the Hudson River with more than eight million residents. It is divided into five boroughs. Most Americans are familiar with their names: the Bronx, Brooklyn, Queens, Staten Island, and Manhattan.

Expanded Information

Spanish-speaking Population Approximately one in eight people in the U.S. is of Latin American origin. New York City has the highest Spanish-speaking population of any U.S. city. Puerto Ricans make up almost 40 percent of the Latin American population in New York City. While Spanish-speaking people in the southwestern part of the U.S. primarily come from Mexico, New York City draws people from Puerto Rico, the Dominican Republic, and other areas of the Caribbean.

Differentiating Instruction

English Learners

Build Background Students whose first language is not English may need extra support with the information on these pages. Inform them that New York is very diverse, meaning that people of many different backgrounds live there. Ask students what their images and impressions of this city are.

Slower-paced Learners

Personalize It Have students express their opinions about the photos.

Objectives
- Present vocabulary: greetings and saying goodbye.
- Check for recognition.

Core Resource
- Audio Program TXT CD 1 tracks 1, 2

Presentation Strategies
- Tell students that the ¡Avanza! sets the goals for this segment and that the Para y piensa is a self-check to see if they have accomplished those goals.
- Ask students how they greet the following people: a friend, a teacher, a parent of a classmate.
- Have students look at the photos on pp. 2–3 and ask them to point out any similarities and differences they notice between greeting styles in Spanish-speaking cultures and those in English-speaking cultures.
- Point to each photo on the spread, and ask students to guess in English what the people are saying. Are the greetings casual? Are they formal? Do they take place in the morning? In the afternoon? In the evening?
- Play the audio as students read A–H.

STANDARDS
1.2 Understand language

Communication
Pair Work

Students should go around the room and practice the mini-conversations on this spread with their classmates. They should shake hands or wave goodbye as they engage in conversation. After the mini-conversation, each one should raise his/her hand and switch partners with someone else who has a hand raised. Time this activity for five minutes to give students time to greet several classmates.

Students may be fearful of speaking a foreign language, so initially they should not be expected to produce the language in front of the entire class. Give them multiple opportunities for partner and group practice to help them feel more comfortable. When you do hear something that needs to be corrected, do so as gently as possible.

Hola, ¿qué tal?

¡AVANZA! **Goal:** Learn how various Spanish speakers greet each other. Then practice what you have learned to greet and say goodbye to others. *Actividades 1–3*

A
Hola.
¿Cómo estás?

Bien.
¿Y tú?

Mal.

B **Juan:** ¡Hola, Miguel! ¿Qué tal?
Miguel: Hola, ¿qué pasa?

C **Juan:** ¡Hasta luego, Ana!
Ana: Hasta luego.

D **Srta. Daza:** Adiós.
Sr. Ortega: Adiós, señorita.

Differentiating Instruction

English Learners

Build Background Explain to students whose native language is not English the different gestures English-speaking people use to say hello and goodbye. They wave, shake hands, hug, or give a kiss on the cheek. Ask students to share the common gestures associated with greetings in their culture. Are they the same or different from those shown on pp. 2 and 3?

Multiple Intelligences

Interpersonal Interpersonal learners enjoy interacting with people and are sensitive to other people's feelings. Have these students work with a partner to develop a short role-play. Partners should greet each other, ask each other how they are, and then say goodbye. Remind students to use appropriate gestures and facial expressions to support the meaning of their words.

E **Sr. Martínez:** Buenos días, señora Ramos. ¿Cómo está usted?
Sra. Ramos: Regular. ¿Y usted?
Sr. Martínez: Más o menos.

F **Juan:** Buenas tardes. ¿Cómo estás?
Esteban: Muy bien.

G **Sra. Acevedo:** Hola, **buenas noches.**
Diana: Buenas noches, señora.

H **Sr. García:** Buenas noches, Diana.
Diana: **Hasta mañana, señor** García.

¡A responder! Escuchar

Listen to these people greeting and saying goodbye. Wave toward the front of the room if you hear a greeting or toward the back of the room if you hear a goodbye.

Comparisons
English Language Connection

Buenos días literally translates as *good days* but is primarily used for saying *good morning*. **Buenas tardes** is used for *good afternoon* and **buenas noches** for *good night, good evening*. After going over the expressions, have students give the appropriate greeting for the following times of day: **1.** 11:00 a.m.; **2.** 8 p.m.; **3.** 7 a.m.; **4.** 3 p.m. ; **5.** 11 p.m.; **6.** 1:30 p.m.

Answers: 1. Buenos días. 2. Buenas noches. 3. Buenos días. 4. Buenas tardes. 5. Buenas noches. 6. Buenas tardes.

Communication
 ## Regionalisms

Young people in Spanish-speaking countries have informal ways of greeting each other. For example, in Mexico they say **¿Qué hubo?** and **¿Qué onda?** to express *What's up?* or *What's going on?* In Argentina, they use **Chau** to say *goodbye*.

Differentiating Instruction

Inclusion

Clear Structure Create the following headings on the board: **Hola, ¿Cómo estás?** and **Adiós.** Review the meanings of these words and phrases. Then have students organize the vocabulary presented on pp. 2–3 into these three categories. Which words and phrases can be used to say hello, ask or tell how someone is, or say goodbye?

Heritage Language Learners

Support What They Know Ask students to share other greetings that they have heard or used. Are there words and phrases popular among teenagers to say *hi* and *bye*? Ask students to model these words and phrases for the group. Then have the whole group repeat. Encourage all students to practice these terms when they arrive at or leave Spanish class.

Answers MSRB Transparency 24

¡A responder! Audio Script, TE p. C25b
1. Students wave toward the front.
2. Students wave toward the back.
3. Students wave toward the back.
4. Students wave toward the front.
5. Students wave toward the front.
6. Students wave toward the back.

3

Objectives

· Practice greetings and saying goodbye.
· Practice familiar and formal greetings.
· Learn to say names in Spanish.
· Pronunciation: Learn about the letter **h** in Spanish.

Core Resource

· Audio Program: TXT CD 1 track 3

Practice Sequence

· **Activity 1:** Controlled practice: greetings and farewells
· **Activity 2:** Transitional practice: greetings and farewells
· **Activity 3:** Transitional practice: familiar and formal greetings
· **Pronunciation:** Oral comprehension and production of the letter **h**.

STANDARDS

1.1 Engage in conversation, Acts. 2–3
1.3 Present information, Acts. 2–3, PYP

Communication

Interpersonal Mode

Read aloud the list of Spanish names and have students repeat each name. Have each student select a Spanish name and create a name tag. Then have students go around the room and greet each other using their new names. Be sure to point out the correct pronunciation of **Me llamo**. It may be helpful to write a phonetic spelling on the board: /*may*//*yahmo*/.

Communication

Role-Playing and Skits

Divide students into groups of three or four. Have them prepare mini-dialogues to be presented to the rest of the class. Ask them to write on the board the time of day that the conversation occurs so that you, and classmates, can check to see if they are using the proper greetings. You may wish to assign the time of day to be sure that all greetings besides simply **hola** are used.

See Activity Answers on page 5.

---

1 | Muy bien

Leer   Complete each expression.

1. ¿Cómo está…   a. tal?
2. Buenas…   b. mañana.
3. ¿Qué…   c. usted?
4. Muy bien…   d. tardes.
5. Hasta…   e. ¿Y usted?

2 | ¿Cómo estás?

Escribir   Create a conversation to complete the speech bubbles of this cartoon strip.

NOMBRES DE CHICOS		NOMBRES DE CHICAS	
Alejandro	Juan	Alejandra	Juana
Andrés	Luis	Alicia	Luisa
Carlos	Manuel	Ana	María
Cristóbal	Mateo	Bárbara	Marta
Daniel	Miguel	Carmen	Natalia
David	Nicolás	Carolina	Patricia
Eduardo	Pablo	Cristina	Raquel
Esteban	Pedro	Diana	Rosa
Felipe	Ramón	Elena	Sofía
Guillermo	Ricardo	Emilia	Susana
Jaime	Roberto	Florencia	Teresa
Jorge	Tomás	Gabriela	Verónica
José	Vicente	Isabel	Yolanda

Manuel

Isabel

Lección preliminar
4   cuatro

Differentiating Instruction

Multiple Intelligences

Visual Learners Have students create a **¿Cómo estás?** poster. The poster should include possible answers to the question, such as **bien, muy bien, más o menos, regular,** and **mal**, as well as a drawing expressing the meaning of each. For example, students might draw a face with a big smile for **muy bien**, and a face with a big frown for **mal**. Display the posters in the classroom for reference.

Inclusion

Alphabetic/Phonetic Awareness Model for students the pronunciation of Spanish names. Point out that even though some names are spelled the same in English and Spanish, they are pronounced differently. Some examples would include **Daniel, David, Diana**, and **Verónica**. Invite students to choose names to use in class. They could be similar to or different from their English names.

Nota

¿**Cómo estás?** and ¿**Cómo está usted?** both mean *How are you?*

¿**Cómo estás?** and ¿**Y tú?** are familiar phrases used with:
- a person your own age
- a relative
- a person you call by his or her first name

Other familiar greetings:
¿**Qué tal?** and ¿**Qué pasa?**

¿**Cómo está usted?** and ¿**Y usted?** are formal phrases used with:
- a person you don't know
- someone older
- a person with whom you want to show respect

3 | Buenos días

 Hablar

According to the time of day, greet your partner as if he or she were the following people. Use a formal greeting or a familiar greeting depending on whom you address.

modelo: Sr. (Sra.) Vargas / 7 a.m.

A Buenos días, señor (señora) Vargas. ¿Cómo está usted?

B Muy bien.

1. your best friend / 10 p.m.
2. the school principal / 2 p.m.
3. Sr. (Srta.) López / 7 p.m.
4. your mother/father / 9 a.m.
5. Sr. (Sra.) Santos / 4 p.m.
6. your brother/sister / 9 p.m.
7. your coach / 11 a.m.
8. your Spanish teacher / 10 a.m.

Pronunciación   La letra h

 AUDIO

In Spanish, the letter **h** is always silent.

Listen and repeat.

ha	he	hi	ho	hu
hace	helado	hispano	hola	humano

¡Hola, Hugo!

Hasta mañana, Héctor.

PARA Y PIENSA

Did you get it?
1. Tell a friend good morning.
2. Ask a friend how he or she is.
3. Say goodbye to your teacher.

Get Help Online
ClassZone.com

Lección preliminar
cinco   **5**

Differentiating Instruction

Slower-paced Learners

Peer-study Support Have students work with their partners to create a script for each exchange in Activity 3. Instruct pairs to look at the person and time presented in the prompt, and then discuss the best greeting and response to use. Advise them to write each of their lines down before saying them aloud.

Inclusion

Alphabetic/Phonetic Awareness To teach students the sound of the Spanish letter **h,** write the following words on the board: **hola, helado, hilo, hombre, humano,** and **hispano.** Say each aloud, and have students repeat. Then ask students to describe what they notice about the *h* at the beginning of each word. Reinforce that the letter *h* is always silent in Spanish.

Nota

In some Spanish-speaking countries, people follow the custom of using formal speech to show respect to parents and grandparents. They are taught to use **usted** when addressing an older family member.

✓ Ongoing Assessment

Dictation After practicing the sounds under the pronunciation heading, dictate the following sentences and have students write them in their notebooks.
Hola, Hugo. Hasta luego. Hasta mañana. Hola, Héctor.

✓ Ongoing Assessment

@HomeTutor
More Practice
ClassZone.com

 PARA Y PIENSA

Quick Check The Para y piensa is a quick self-assessment tool that allows students to evaluate their understanding of the lesson's topic. If students have difficulty with the sentences in Para y piensa, ask them to review pp. 2–4.

Answers MSRB Transparency 24

Answers for Activities on pp. 4, 5.

Activity 1 1. c; 2. d; 3. a; 4. e; 5. b

Activity 2 Answers will vary.
Sample answers include:
A. Buenos días, Juan, **B.** Hola, Pablo. ¿Cómo estás?
B. Bien. ¿Y tú? **B.** Mal.
A. Hasta luego. **B.** Hasta mañana.

Activity 3 Answers to each question may include: Muy bien, regular, más o menos. ¿Y tú?
1. Buenas noches. ¿Cómo estás?
2. Buenas tardes, señor/señora _____. ¿Cómo está usted?
3. Buenas noches, señor/señorita López. ¿Cómo está usted?
4. Buenos días. ¿Cómo estás?
5. Buenas tardes, señor/señora Santos. ¿Cómo está usted?
6. Buenas noches. ¿Cómo estás?
7. Buenos días. ¿Cómo está usted?
8. Buenos días, señor/señorita _____. ¿Cómo está usted?

Para y piensa
1. Buenos días.
2. ¿Cómo estás?
3. Adiós/Hasta mañana/Hasta luego, señor/señora _____.

¡Mucho gusto!

 Goal: Notice how certain speakers introduce themselves and others. Then practice what you have learned to make introductions. *Actividades 4–7*

AUDIO

A **Esteban:** Hola. **Me llamo** Esteban. ¿Y tú? **¿Cómo te llamas?**
Diana: Me llamo Diana.
Esteban: Encantado, Diana.
Diana: Igualmente.

B **Diana:** **Te presento a** Esteban.
Ana: Encantada.
Esteban: Igualmente.

C **Srta. Machado:** Perdón. ¿Cómo se llama?
Srta. Daza: Me llamo Raquel Daza.

D **Srta. Machado:** Le presento a Ana Vega.
Sr. Ortega: Mucho gusto.
Ana: El gusto es mío.

6 Lección preliminar
seis

Differentiating Instruction

Heritage Language Learners

Writing Skills Heritage language learners may need practice with punctuation, spelling, and grammar. Have students choose one of the photos on pp. 6, 7. Then invite them to write down an expansion of the conversation based on what they see in the photo. What else might these two or three people say to each other? Remind students to focus on using correct punctuation, spelling, and grammar.

Slower-paced Learners

Sentence Completion Copy one of the dialogues on the board replacing some of the words with blanks. For example:

Hola. Me llamo _____.
Me _____ Diana.
Encantado, Diana.
_____.

Then have volunteers fill in each blank with an appropriate word.

E ¿Quién es? ¿Es Raúl?

No. Es Juan.

F ¿Cómo se llama?

Se llama Diana.

G **Rosa:** ¿Se llama Miguel?

Esteban: Sí. Se llama Miguel Luque.

¡A responder! Escuchar

Listen to four people make introductions. Point to yourself if you hear someone introducing themselves. Point to the person next to you if you hear someone introducing someone else.

Lección preliminar
siete **7**

Differentiating Instruction

English Learners

Build Background Discuss with students the different phrases used in different languages to tell someone your name. Point out that in English, you say *My name is...,* while in Spanish you say **Me llamo...,** or *I call myself...* Ask students to share how to tell someone your name in their first language. Have students practice saying **Me llamo...** in several different languages.

Slower-paced Learners

Yes/No Questions Use yes/no questions to help students practice saying their names, and the names of their classmates. Point to a student as you ask: **¿Se llama Isabel?** Students should answer **sí** or **no**. If it is the wrong name, they should follow up with an explanation. **No, se llama Natalia.**

Communication
Common Error Alert

Students may be confused with the **se llama** structures. Explain that **Me llamo** does not literally mean *My name is.* Instead, it is literally translated as *I call myself.* **Se llama** can mean *You (formal) call yourself* or *He/she calls himself/herself.* English speakers, of course, would be more likely to say *Your name is* or *His/her name is.* To avoid confusion with **se llama,** include the appropriate pronoun in the question. For example: **¿Cómo se llama usted?** *How do you call yourself? (What is your name?)*

Communication
Grammar Activity

Read the following sentences and have students write **tú** if the statement or question is familiar; have them write **usted** if the speaker is addressing someone formally.
  1. Buenos días, señor. ¿Cómo está usted?
  2. Hola. ¿Cómo te llamas?
  3. Te presento a Felipe.
  4. Le presento a María.
  5. Me llamo Juan Carlos. ¿Cómo te llamas?
  6. Muy bien. ¿Y usted?
  7. ¿Cómo se llama, señora?

Answers: 1. usted; 2. tú; 3. tú; 4. usted; 5. tú; 6. usted; 7. usted

Communication
Role-Playing and Skits

Divide students into groups of three. Ask them to create a conversation between a teacher and two students (three students for a group of four). They should greet each other, ask names, perform introductions, and say goodbye.

Answers MSRB Transparency 24

¡A responder! Audio Script, TE p. C25b
  1. Student points to person next to him or her.
  2. Student points to himself or herself.
  3. Student points to himself or herself.
  4. Student points to person next to him or her.

Objectives
· Practice greetings, make introductions.
· **Culture:** Discuss the murals of Manuel Vega.
· Ask someone's name.

Practice Sequence
· **Activity 4:** Controlled practice: introductions
· **Activity 5:** Controlled practice: greetings, introductions
· **Activity 6:** Transitional practice: introductions
· **Activity 7:** Transitional practice: introductions

STANDARDS
1.1 Engage in conversation, Acts. 6–7
1.3 Present information, Acts. 4–7, PYP
2.2 Products and perspectives, CC
4.2 Compare cultures, CC

Communication
Interpersonal Mode

Write a series of statements or questions on the board and ask student pairs to read them and provide a logical answer. For example, student reads and says: **¿Quién es?** (Student points to another student in the class). Partner answers: **Es Margarita.** Continue with the following examples:
1. Te presento a Miguel.
2. ¿Cómo te llamas?
3. Buenas tardes. ¿Cómo estás?
4. Encantada.
Check for use of correct rejoinder and pronunciation.

Communication

Role-Playing and Skits

Ask students to complete Activity 5 using their own names. Then have them repeat their lines until they have memorized them. Ask them to act out the scene in front of the class using appropriate gestures to accompany their lines.

See Activity answers on p. 9.

8

---

4 | ¿Cómo te llamas?

Leer | Choose the correct response to each question or statement.

1. ¿Quién es?
  a. Es Hugo.
  b. Encantado.
  c. Me llamo Carlos.

2. Encantada.
  a. Le presento a Sergio.
  b. ¿Y tú?
  c. Igualmente.

3. Te presento a Joaquín.
  a. ¿Cómo se llama?
  b. Mucho gusto.
  c. Igualmente.

4. ¿Cómo te llamas?
  a. Perdón.
  b. Me llamo Isabel.
  c. Bien.

5. Me llamo Gabriel.
  a. Igualmente.
  b. Encantado.
  c. El gusto es mío.

6. Mucho gusto.
  a. Buenas tardes.
  b. ¿Quién es?
  c. El gusto es mío.

5 | Conversación

Leer
Escribir
 | Complete the conversation with the correct words.

  Carlos: Hola. Me **1.** Carlos. ¿ **2.** te llamas?
  Beatriz: Me **3.** Beatriz.
  Carlos: **4.** , Beatriz.
  Beatriz: **5.** .

6 | Mucho gusto

Hablar | Work in a group of four. Introduce yourself to each member of the group.

Hola, me llamo...

Encantado. Me llamo...

Differentiating Instruction

Inclusion
Metacognitive Support Help students to think how language is structured before they do Activity 4. Ask them to explain why some answers make sense, and why the others do not. The question in number 4 is **¿Cómo te llamas? Perdón** is a polite way of saying excuse me, but it doesn't answer the question. **Bien** answers the question **¿Cómo estás?** The correct answer is **Me llamo Isabel.**

Heritage Language Learners
Support What They Know Invite students to expand on the possibilities for their conversations in Activity 6. As part of the introduction, they might also talk about where they live, where they go to school, and some of their hobbies or interests.

Nota

¿Cómo te llamas? and ¿Cómo se llama? both are used to ask *What is your name?*
Te presento a... and Le presento a... both mean *I'd like you to meet . . .*

¿Cómo te llamas? and
Te presento a... are familiar
phrases used with:

- a person your own age
- a relative
- a person you call by
  his or her first name

¿Cómo se llama? and
Le presento a... are formal
phrases used with:

- a person with whom
  you want to show respect
- a person you don't know
- someone older

7 | Te presento a...

Hablar Work in a group of three. Take turns introducing each other.

A Te presento a Tomás.

B Encantado(a), Tomás.

C Igualmente.

Comparación cultural

Un mural del metro

How can artists give back to their neighborhood through their work? Artist Manuel Vega moved with his family from Puerto Rico to **New York** at a young age. He created a series of mosaic murals called *Sábado en la Ciento Diez* that decorate the walls of the 110th Street subway station, located in East Harlem where he grew up. These works depict neighborhood scenes inspired by Vega's childhood. This mosaic shows a woman and child in front of a local store.

Compara con tu mundo *What childhood memory would you paint if you were creating a neighborhood mural? Compare it with the scene in Vega's mural.*

Sábado en la Ciento Diez
(1996), Manuel Vega

PARA Y PIENSA

Did you get it? Complete each statement.

1. Me llamo...   a. a Maricela.
2. Te presento...   b. gusto, señor.
3. Mucho...   c. Walter.

Get Help Online
ClassZone.com

Lección preliminar
nueve   **9**

Comparación cultural

Essential Question

Suggested Answer Artists can give back to their neighborhood by depicting its landscape, people, and activities in their work. This can give residents a sense of pride in their community and themselves.

Background Information

Manuel Vega, or Manny as he is called, grew up in the Bronx. His work is not limited to painting. He also designs mosaics and prints and has been active in creating and restoring murals in New York City. He often involves the youth of the city in the mural restoration projects. African, Latino and Caribbean influences can be seen in his art. He has been named the Artist in Residence at New York's Guggenheim Museum.

✓ Ongoing Assessment

@HomeTutor
More Practice
ClassZone.com

PARA Y PIENSA **Peer Assessment** Have pairs of students read aloud the sentences in Para y piensa and correct each other.

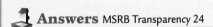
Answers MSRB Transparency 24

Answers for Activities on pp. 8, 9.

Activity 4
1. a; 2. c; 3. b; 4. b; 5. b; 6. c

Activity 5
1. llamo; 2. Cómo; 3. llamo;
4. Mucho gusto/Encantado; 5. El gusto es mío/Igualmente

Activity 6 Answers will vary. Suggested answers include:
A. Hola, me llamo Debbie.
B. Encantado. Me llamo Luis.

Activity 7 Answers will vary. Sample answers include:
A. Te presento a Margarita. **B.** Mucho gusto, Margarita. **C.** El gusto es mío.

Para y piensa 1. c; 2. a; 3. b

Differentiating Instruction

Inclusion

Clear Structure Create two columns on the board. At the top of one, write **¿Cómo te llamas?** and **Te presento a...** At the top of the other, write **¿Cómo se llama?** and **Le presento a...** Then ask for volunteers to come add names to one column or the other. With whom would students use these phrases?

Multiple Intelligences

Visual Learners Give students the opportunity to paint or draw a scene depicting people in their own neighborhood. Then have them use their artwork to practice naming and introducing people. Have them point out and introduce characters in their paintings. **Te presento a ... Se llama...**

Objectives

- Learn and say the Spanish alphabet.
- Practice spelling words in Spanish.
- Practice pronouncing the Spanish vowels **a, e, i, o, u.**

Core Resource

- Audio Program: TXT CD 1 tracks 6, 7, 8, 9

Presentation Strategies

- Say the Spanish alphabet and have students repeat after you.
- Point out the letter **ñ** and reinforce the difference between the pronunciation of **n** and **ñ.**
- Say a Spanish alphabet letter and the word that starts with it. **Jota: jabón.** Have students repeat after you. Continue with the rest of the alphabet.
- Play the audio as students follow the script in their text.

Practice Sequence

- **Activity 8:** Vocabulary recognition: spelling words
- **Activity 9:** Vocabulary production: spelling words
- **Activity 10:** Vocabulary production: spelling words
- **Pronunciation:** Oral comprehension and production of the vowels.

STANDARDS

- **1.1** Engage in conversation, Acts. 9-10
- **1.2** Understand language, Act. 8
- **1.3** Present information, Acts. 8-10, PYP
- **4.1** Compare languages, Pronunciación

Warm Up UTB 1 Transparency 22

Familiar vs. Formal Have students read the following sentences and write **Familiar** or **Formal** depending on whom they address.
1. ¿Cómo está usted?
2. Señor Ortega, le presento a Ana Vega.
3. ¿Qué tal? ¿Cómo estás?
4. Te presento a Carolina.
5. Perdón. ¿Cómo se llama?

Answers: 1. Formal; 2. Formal; 3. Familiar; 4. Familiar; 5. Formal

Answers MSRB Transparency 24

¡A responder! Audio Script, TE p. C25b
Students should write and hold up the following letters.
1. L; **2.** E; **3.** J; **4.** Ñ; **5.** P; **6.** I; **7.** H; **8.** B

El abecedario

 ¡AVANZA! **Goal:** Learn to say the Spanish alphabet. Then practice how to say the letters to spell different things. *Actividades 8–10*

AUDIO

A (a) **a**lfombra	**B** (be, be grande) **b**ate	**C** (ce) **c**ine	**D** (de) **d**inero	**E** (e) **e**ntrada
F (efe) **f**ruta	**G** (ge) **g**ato	**H** (hache) **h**elado	**I** (i) **i**glú	**J** (jota) **j**abón
K (ka) **k**arate	**L** (ele) **l**ápiz	**M** (eme) **m**ochila	**N** (ene) **n**ariz	**Ñ** (eñe) **ñ**u
O (o) **o**reja	**P** (pe) **p**atines	**Q** (cu) **q**ueso	**R** (ere) **r**egalo	**RR** (erre) guita**rr**a
S (ese) **s**ofá	**T** (te) **t**iza	**U** (u) **u**vas	**V** (uve, ve chica) **v**entana	
W (doble uve, doble ve) **w**afle	**X** (equis) **x**ilófono	**Y** (i griega) **y**ogur	**Z** (zeta) **z**apato	

¡A responder! Escuchar

Listen to letters of the Spanish alphabet. Write each letter that you hear on a piece of paper and hold it up.

Differentiating Instruction

Multiple Intelligences

Musical/Rhythmic Musical learners are sensitive to music and rhythm. To appeal to these students, lead them in a version of the traditional ABC song, using the Spanish alphabet. Point out that there are two additional letters in Spanish that will need to be incorporated into the song.

Inclusion

Multisensory Input/Output Whenever possible, present topics both orally and visually. Help students remember the letters of the Spanish alphabet through this activity.
1. Say a letter aloud. Have students repeat.
2. Have students point to the letter on p. 10.
3. Have students write the letter on a separate piece of paper.

8 | Lista

Escuchar
Escribir

Listen to someone dictate an invitation list for a party. Write down each name as it is spelled.

🎧 Audio Program
TXT CD 1 Track 8
Audio Script, TE p.
C25b

> **modelo:** You hear: de, a, ene, i, e, ele
> You write: Daniel

9 | Me llamo...

Hablar

Work in a group of three. Ask each person his or her name and write down the name as he or she spells it.

A ¿Cómo te llamas?

B Me llamo Shawna, S - H - A - W - N - A. (ese, hache, a, doble uve, ene, a)

10 | ABC

Hablar

Spell aloud the following things for a partner. He or she will write the word. Then verify that your partner spelled the word correctly.

your middle name	your favorite singer	the name of your town
the name of your school	your favorite sports team	¿?

AUDIO

Pronunciación — **Las vocales**

In Spanish, the vowels are **a, e, i, o,** and **u.** Each vowel is always pronounced the same way. Spanish vowels are always short and crisp.

Listen to and repeat these words.

a → as in *father*	**encantada**	**mal**	**mañana**
e → as in *hey*	**menos**	**señor**	**presento**
i → sounds like *meet*	**igualmente**	**adiós**	**bien**
o → as in *woke*	**hola**	**noches**	**cómo**
u → sounds like *boot*	**usted**	**mucho**	**tú**

PARA Y PIENSA

Did you get it? Recite the Spanish alphabet.

📝 **Get Help Online**
ClassZone.com

Differentiating Instruction

Multiple Intelligences

Visual Learners Invite students to create a name poster of their original or Spanish name. The poster should include each letter of the name written as a character and as a word. For example, **J-jota, U-u, A-a, N-ene.** It should also include a picture of something that starts with each letter. Refer students back to the chart on page 10 for ideas.

Inclusion

Alphabetic/Phonetic Awareness Ask students to write the vowels, **a, e, i, o,** and **u** on small pieces of paper. Review with students the sound represented by each of these letters. Then say a one-syllable word aloud, such as **tú** or **mal.** Have students hold up the letter whose sound they hear. Continue the activity with two-syllable words, and have students hold up the two vowels they hear.

LECCIÓN PRELIMINAR

⚠ Common Error Alert

Explain to students that there is generally only one sound for each Spanish vowel. Have students write down phonetic spellings for the vowels: /ah/; /ay/; /ee/; /oh/; /oo/. Model their pronunciation and have students repeat.

Long-term Retention

Personalize It

Give students the opportunity to make what they've learned their own. Ask them to illustrate their own examples of alphabet letters and display them in the classroom. They can use vocabulary from the glossary if they run out of word ideas.

✓ Ongoing Assessment

@HomeTutor
More Practice
ClassZone.com

PARA Y PIENSA

Alternative Strategy Prepare in advance a randomized alphabet list and ask students to take turns saying the letters.

📠 Answers MSRB Transparency 25

Activity 8
1. Ximena
2. Guillermo
3. Alejandro
4. Yolanda
5. Beatriz
6. Josefina
7. Hugo
8. Toño

Activity 9 Answers will vary. Sample answers:
A. ¿Cómo te llamas? **B.** Me llamo Thomas, T-H-O-M-A-S. (te, hache, o, eme, a, ese)

Activity 10 Answers will vary. Sample answers:
Middle name: be grande, e, ene, jota, a, eme, i, ene

Name of school: de, a, ye; hache, i, ge, hache; ese, ce, hache, o, o, ele

Favorite singer: eme, a, ere, i, a; ce, a, ere, e, i griega

Favorite sports team: jota, e, te, ese

Name of your town: te, a, eme, pe, a

Para y piensa Students should recite the Spanish alphabet.

Objectives
- Learn the names of countries in the Spanish-speaking world
- Learn to say where someone is from.

Core Resource
- Audio Program: TXT CD 1 tracks 10, 11

Presentation Strategies
- Read aloud the text on p. 12 and have students repeat after you.
- Ask students yes/no questions about the people in the text. For example: ¿**Es Pablo de Costa Rica?** (No.) ¿**Es Marisol de Puerto Rico?** (Sí).
- Point to **Los países hispanohablantes** on p. 13, say the countries, and have students repeat them. Correct pronunciation as needed.
- Point to a country on the map on p. 12, and ask individual students to identify it, using the list on p. 13.
- Play the audio as students follow in their texts.

STANDARDS
1.2 Understand language

 Warm Up UTB 1 Transparency 23

Spelling Spell the following words in Spanish.
1. zapato
2. encantado
3. helado
4. bate
5. usted

Answers: 1. zeta, a, pe, a, te, o; 2. e, ene, ce, a, ene, te, a, de, o; 3. hache, e, ele, a, de, o; 4. be grande, a, te, e; 5. u, ese, te, e, de

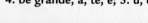

Communication

Pair Work

Have students practice asking each other ¿**De dónde eres?** and answering with **Soy de _____**.

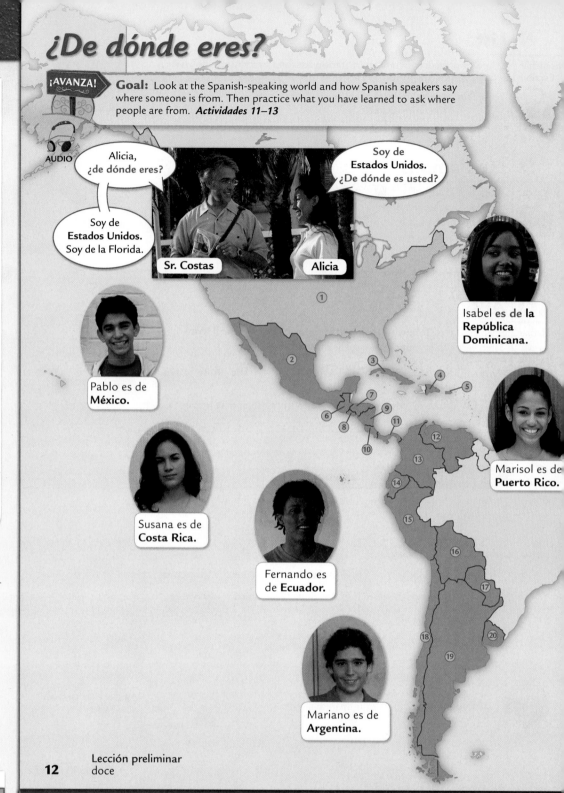

¿De dónde eres?

¡AVANZA! **Goal:** Look at the Spanish-speaking world and how Spanish speakers say where someone is from. Then practice what you have learned to ask where people are from. *Actividades 11–13*

Alicia, ¿de dónde eres?

Soy de **Estados Unidos**. ¿De dónde es usted?

Soy de **Estados Unidos**. Soy de la Florida.

Sr. Costas — **Alicia**

Isabel **es de la República Dominicana.**

Pablo es de **México.**

Susana es de **Costa Rica.**

Fernando es de **Ecuador.**

Marisol es de **Puerto Rico.**

Mariano es de **Argentina.**

12 Lección preliminar doce

Differentiating Instruction

Slower-paced Learners

Yes/No Questions Ask students yes or no questions about the people and countries presented on pages 12 and 13. Here are a few possibilities:
¿**Es Fernando de Ecuador?** (Sí)
¿**Es Marisol de Costa Rica?** (No)

Heritage Language Learners

Support What They Know Invite students with a personal or family connection to one of the countries listed to share something about that country with the group. Encourage students to give a general description of the place, its culture and people. Also, encourage them to share memories or impressions of the place.

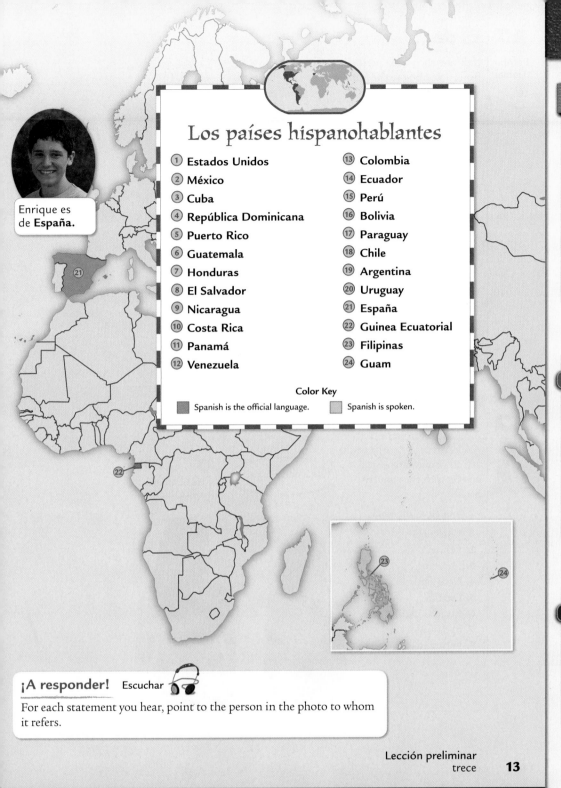

Los países hispanohablantes

1. Estados Unidos
2. México
3. Cuba
4. República Dominicana
5. Puerto Rico
6. Guatemala
7. Honduras
8. El Salvador
9. Nicaragua
10. Costa Rica
11. Panamá
12. Venezuela
13. Colombia
14. Ecuador
15. Perú
16. Bolivia
17. Paraguay
18. Chile
19. Argentina
20. Uruguay
21. España
22. Guinea Ecuatorial
23. Filipinas
24. Guam

Color Key

■ Spanish is the official language. ■ Spanish is spoken.

Enrique es de **España**.

¡A responder! Escuchar

For each statement you hear, point to the person in the photo to whom it refers.

Culture

Teaching with Maps

Have the students draw or trace the map on p. 12. Have them label and color each Spanish-speaking country in bright colors. The countries that are not Spanish-speaking should be colored a neutral color such as gray. Students should not use the same color for two countries that border each other. Have the students glue their colored maps on construction paper. You may wish to laminate them to preserve the surface.

Communication
Group Work

As students enter the classroom, give them a sheet with a Spanish name and a country. For example, one card may be **Diego/Venezuela**. Have them locate that country on a map. They will introduce themselves to each other and show each classmate the country on the map. For example: **Me llamo Diego. Soy de Venezuela. Y tú, ¿cómo te llamas? ¿De dónde eres?**

Long-term Retention
Critical Thinking

Ask students to look at the map on p. 12 and the list on p. 13 and count in English the number of countries where Spanish is spoken. Based on this information, have them discuss why it is important to learn Spanish.

Differentiating Instruction

Inclusion

Alphabetic/Phonetic Awareness Model for students the pronunciation of country names in Spanish. Point out that even though some names are spelled the same in English and Spanish, they are pronounced differently. Some examples would include **Panamá, Chile, México**, and **Cuba**.

Pre-AP*

Expand and Elaborate Ask students to choose one of the countries presented on p. 13, say the name, and share with the class what they know about that country. Allow them time to do some research, and then report to the class something about the country.

* Pre-AP is a registered trademark of the College Entrance Examination Board, which was not involved in the production of and does not endorse this product.

Answers MSRB Transparency 25

¡A responder! Audio Script, TE p. C25b
Students should point to the following people.
1. Susana
2. Marisol
3. Mariano
4. Enrique
5. Fernando
6. Isabel

13

Objectives

· Practice saying where someone is from and asking others where they are from.
· Identify the countries in a map of Latin America.

Practice Sequence

· **Activity 11:** Controlled practice: identifying countries on a map, telling where a person is from
· **Activity 12:** Controlled practice: asking and telling where someone is from
· **Activity 13:** Transitional practice: asking and telling where someone is from

 STANDARDS

1.1 Engage in conversation, Acts. 12–13
1.3 Present information, Acts. 11–13, PYP

Culture

Teaching with Maps

Have students write the name of the northernmost country from each pair.

1. Chile/Ecuador
2. Panamá/Paraguay
3. Argentina/Venezuela
4. Perú/Cuba
5. Puerto Rico/Honduras
6. Bolivia/Guatemala
7. El Salvador/Estados Unidos

Answers: 1. Ecuador 2. Panamá 3. Venezuela 4. Cuba 5. Puerto Rico 6. Guatemala 7. Estados Unidos

Long-term Retention

Study Tips

When memorizing the location of countries on a map, it may be helpful for some students to create a mnemonic device. For example, when trying to remember the placement of the islands in the Caribbean, students may create a sentence such as *Charlie Really Digs Purple Rice.* Have students come up with their own sentences.

See Activity answers on p. 15.

14

---

11 | Es de...

Escribir Hablar

Indicate where each person is from, according to the number on the map.

modelo: Guillermo / ⑦

Guillermo es de Uruguay.

1. Andrea / ⑤
2. Tomás / ⑧
3. Nicolás / ④
4. Sofía / ②
5. Verónica / ③
6. Mateo / ⑨
7. Consuelo / ①
8. Pablo / ⑥

12 | ¿De dónde eres?

Hablar

Ask a partner where he or she is from. Your partner will answer with the country listed.

modelo: Colombia

1. Venezuela
2. Panamá
3. México
4. Uruguay
5. España
6. Estados Unidos
7. El Salvador
8. Nicaragua

 A ¿De dónde eres? **B** Soy de Colombia.

Lección preliminar
14 catorce

Differentiating Instruction

Inclusion

Cumulative Instruction Ask students to work in pairs. Then instruct partners to read their answers to Activity 11 aloud to each other. Tell students to spell out the names of the people and countries for their partner.
Guillermo: ge-u-i-ele-ele-e-ere-eme-o.

Multiple Intelligences

Interpersonal Have students work with a partner to develop a short role-play. Partners should greet each other, ask each other their names and where they are from, and then say goodbye. Remind students to use appropriate gestures and facial expressions to support the meaning of their words. Give each pair the chance to present their exchange to the class.

Nota

When you are speaking, one way to change a statement into a question is to simply raise the intonation of your voice.

Beto es de Paraguay.   ¿Beto es de Paraguay?

Answer simple yes/no questions with **sí** (*yes*) or **no** (*no*).

¿Eres de California?   No. Soy de Nueva York.

In written Spanish, all questions begin with an upside-down question mark (¿) and end with a question mark (?).

13 | ¿Eres de Honduras?

Hablar Ask a partner if he or she is from the country indicated. He or she will answer according to the number.

modelo: ① / ⑩

A ¿Eres de **México**?

B No. Soy de **Panamá**.

Estudiante A		Estudiante B	
1. ⑨	4. ⑩	1. ③	4. ⑩
2. ④	5. ⑤	2. ④	5. ⑤
3. ⑥	6. ⑧	3. ②	6. ⑦

PARA Y PIENSA

Did you get it? Match each question with the correct response.
1. ¿De dónde eres?
2. ¿De dónde es Hugo?
3. ¿Eres de México?

a. Es de Puerto Rico.
b. Soy de Colombia.
c. Sí, soy de México.

Get Help Online
ClassZone.com

Differentiating Instruction

Heritage Language Learners

Writing Skills Review with students the different punctuation marks used to indicate a question versus a sentence. Have students write down five sentences. Then have them convert each sentence into a question by changing the punctuation and/or word order.

Slower-paced Learners

Personalize It Have students answer the question ¿De dónde eres? supplying information about themselves. They might respond with the name of their neighborhood, city, state, or country.

Long-term Retention
 Recycle

Have students work in small groups to create chain stories. The first student says hello; the next introduces himself or herself and a Spanish-speaking friend. The next student says where he or she is from.

Communication
 TPR Activity

Using a large wall map, play a game by dividing students into two groups. They will line up, relay style, behind a marked line. Give a fly swatter to the first student in each line. Call out a country name. The first student to hit that country with the fly swatter scores a point for his or her team. He or she then goes to the back of the line and it is the next student's turn.

✓ Ongoing Assessment

@HomeTutor
More Practice
ClassZone.com

PARA Y PIENSA **Alternative Assessment** Cover the questions 1–3 in Para y piensa and have students say the questions that go with each response.

Answers MSRB Transparency 25

Activity 11
1. Andrea es de Bolivia.
2. Tomás es de Chile.
3. Nicolás es de Perú.
4. Sofía es de Colombia.
5. Verónica es de Ecuador.
6. Mateo es de Argentina.
7. Consuelo es de Venezuela.
8. Pablo es de Paraguay.

Activity 12
A. ¿De dónde eres?
B. Soy de + *country*.

Activity 13
1. A. ¿Eres de Costa Rica? B. No, soy de la República Dominicana.
2. A. ¿Eres de Puerto Rico? B. Sí, soy de Puerto Rico.
3. A. ¿Eres de Honduras? B. No, soy de Cuba.
4. A. ¿Eres de Panamá? B. Sí, soy de Panamá.
5. A. ¿Eres de Guatemala? B. Sí, soy de Guatemala.
6. A. ¿Eres de Nicaragua? B. No, soy de El Salvador.

Para y piensa 1. b; 2. a; 3. c

Objectives
- Say the numbers from zero to ten.
- Exchange phone numbers.

Core Resource
- Audio Program: TXT CD 1 tracks 12, 13

Presentation Strategies
- Say the numbers from zero to ten and have students repeat after you.
- Call on students at random and ask them to say their phone number. **¿Cuál es tu número de teléfono? Es 2-2-3-5-4-9-2.**
- Point out the formal and familiar ways of asking for someone's phone number.
- Play the audio.

Practice Sequence
- **Activity 14:** Controlled practice: numbers and math
- **Activity 15:** Transitional practice: phone numbers
- **Activity 16:** Transitional practice: phone numbers

STANDARDS
1.1 Engage in conversation, Acts. 15–16

 Warm Up UTB 1 Transparency 23

Names of countries Complete the names of the following countries.
1. _ O _ O M _ I _
2. B _ _ I _ I _
3. _ H _ L E
4. _ I C _ R _ _ U A
5. _ _ N _ U R _ S

Answers: 1. Colombia; 2. Bolivia; 3. Chile;
4. Nicaragua; 5. Honduras

 Answers MSRB Transparency 25

¡A responder! Audio Script, TE p. C25b
a. Student should raise their right hand.
b. Student should raise their left hand.
c. Student should raise their left hand.
d. Student should raise their right hand.
e. Student should raise their right hand.
f. Student should raise their left hand.
g. Student should raise their right hand.
h. Student should raise their left hand.

16

Mi número de teléfono

 ¡AVANZA! **Goal:** Learn how to say the numbers from zero to ten and how to exchange phone numbers. Then use what you have learned to say your home (or cellular) phone number. *Actividades 14–16*

 AUDIO

¿Cuál es tu número de teléfono?

Es 7-6-4-9-0-8-1.

Perdón. ¿Cuál es su número de teléfono?

Mi número de teléfono es 2-5-3-7-1-0-9.

¡A responder! Escuchar

Listen to these numbers. If you hear an even number, raise your right hand. If you hear an odd number, raise your left hand.

Differentiating Instruction

Inclusion

Metacognitive Support Point out to students that when asking for someone's phone number in Spanish, the question word **cuál** is used. The direct translation of the question would be *Which is your phone number?* as opposed to the English phrasing *What is your phone number?*

Multiple Intelligences

Visual Learners Invite students to create a number poster of the numbers **uno** through **diez**. The poster should include each number written as a numeral and as a word. It should also include a picture to represent each number, such as an octopus next to the word **ocho**.

14 | Matemáticas

Give the answers to the following math problems using words.

modelo: 2 + 4
seis

1. 8 − 3   **3.** 3 + 6   **5.** 1 + 9   **7.** 6 − 5   **9.** 10 − 8
2. 4 + 4   **4.** 7 − 7   **6.** 5 − 2   **8.** 7 + 0   **10.** 1 + 3

15 | Teléfono

Hablar

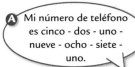

Work in a group of five. Whisper a phone number to the person at your right. He or she will repeat it to the person at his or her right, and so on. Verify that the phone number you gave was repeated accurately.

A Mi número de teléfono es cinco - dos - uno - nueve - ocho - siete - uno.

B Cinco - dos - uno - nueve - ocho - siete - uno.

C Cinco - dos - uno...

16 | ¿Quién es?

Hablar

Work with a partner. Look at this Buenos Aires phone directory and read a phone number at random. Your partner will say whose phone number it is.

A Cuatro - tres - cero - tres - ocho - siete - cuatro - cero.

B Gianmarco Santander.

> **Santander Gemma**
> Lauerbach 3472 Pb 11- Capital Federal
> Ciudad de Buenos Aires 4301-9203
>
> **Santander Genoveva**
> Löschner 244- Capital Federal
> Ciudad de Buenos Aires 4921-4808
>
> **Santander Geraldo**
> López de Padilla 12 Pb 4- Capital Federal
> Ciudad de Buenos Aires 4704-5960
>
> **Santander Giancarlo**
> Filippozzi 9903 Pb Casa- Capital Federal
> Ciudad de Buenos Aires 4638-3123
>
> **Santander Gianmarco**
> Filippozzi 1099- Capital Federal
> Ciudad de Buenos Aires 4303-8740
>
> **Santander Gregorio**
> Sta Marta 374 Pb 7- Capital Federal
> Ciudad de Buenos Aires 4941-7819

PARA Y PIENSA

Did you get it? Say these phone numbers.
1. 6251-4209   2. 3708-9263   3. 4185-2760

Get Help Online
ClassZone.com

Communication
TPR Activity

Have students create flashcards with the numerals 1–10 on each—the numbers should be large enough for you to see. They may use both sides of the paper, such as having 1 on one side and 2 on the other. Call out numbers at random in Spanish and have students hold up the correct numeral.

Communication
Group Work

Pronounce the numbers for the students and have them repeat. Then have them write the numeral as you say them in random order. For example: 7, 9, 4, 2, 10, 1, 8, 6, 5, 3. Have them check each other's papers as you call out the correct answers.

✓ Ongoing Assessment

@HomeTutor
More Practice
ClassZone.com

PARA Y PIENSA **Peer Assessment** Have pairs of students say the phone numbers in Para y piensa aloud and correct each other.

Answers MSRB Transparencies 25–26

Activity 14 1. cinco; **2.** ocho; **3.** nueve; **4.** cero; **5.** diez; **6.** tres; **7.** uno; **8.** siete; **9.** dos; **10.** cuatro

Activity 15 Answers will vary. Sample answers:
A. Mi número de teléfono es cinco-cinco-cinco-dos-nueve-tres-siete. **B.** Cinco-cinco-cinco-dos... **C.** Cinco-cinco...

Activity 16 Answers will vary. Sample answers:
A. cuatro-tres-cero-uno-nueve-dos-cero-tres
B. Gemma Santander
A. cuatro-nueve-dos-uno-cuatro-ocho-cero-ocho
B. Genoveva Santander
Para y piensa
1. seis-dos-cinco-uno-cuatro-dos-cero-nueve
2. tres-siete-cero-ocho-nueve-dos-seis-tres
3. cuatro-uno-ocho-cinco-dos-siete-seis-cero

Differentiating Instruction

Pre-AP

Expand and Elaborate Invite students to brainstorm other numbers they use and can say in Spanish. These may include numbers in addresses, classroom numbers, or their school's phone number. Ask for volunteers to write a number on the board, and then read it aloud.

Multiple Intelligences

Logical/Mathematical Point out to students that the symbol + is read as **más** in Spanish, while the symbol − is read as **menos**. Then invite students to create their own simple math problems on the front of an index card. Have students exchange cards with a partner, read the problems aloud, and find the answers.

Objective

· Learn and practice the days of the week.

Core Resource

· Audio Program: TXT CD 1 tracks 14, 15, 16

Presentation Strategies

· Show students the agenda from p. 18. Explain that in most Spanish-speaking countries, the week starts with Monday.
· Prompt students to ask you **¿Qué día es hoy?** Respond and point to the day at the top of the agenda. Then ask students **¿Qué día es mañana?**
· Play the audio.

Practice Sequence

· **Activity 17:** Controlled practice: days of the week
· **Activity 18:** Controlled practice: days of the week
· **Activity 19:** Transitional practice: days of the week

 STANDARDS

1.1 Engage in conversation, Act. 19
1.2 Understand language, Act. 18
1.3 Present information, Acts. 17–19, PYP

 Warm Up UTB 1 Transparency 24

Numbers Write the missing number(s) in each sequence.
1. uno, _____, _____, cuatro
2. dos, _____, seis, _____, diez
3. tres, _____, nueve
4. _____, cinco, _____, nueve

Answers 1. dos, tres; **2.** cuatro, ocho; **3.** seis; **4.** tres, siete

 Answers MSRB Transparency 26

¡A responder! Audio Script, TE p. C25b
Answers will vary. Possible answers:
1. Students stand up.
2. Students remain seated.
3. Students stand up.
4. Students stand up.
5. Students remain seated.
6. Students stand up.

18

Los días de la semana

 ¡AVANZA! **Goal:** Learn to talk about the days of the week. Then practice what you have learned to say what day of the week it is. *Actividades 17–19*

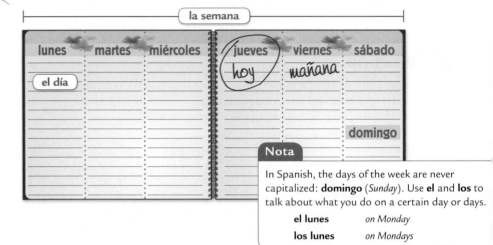

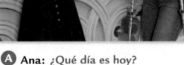 **A** **Ana:** ¿Qué día es hoy?
Rosa: Hoy es jueves.

B **Juan:** ¿Hoy es viernes?
Esteban: No. Mañana es viernes.

¡A responder! Escuchar

Listen to the days of the week. If you hear a day that you have Spanish class, stand up. If you hear a day that you don't have Spanish class, remain seated.

Differentiating Instruction

Slower-paced Learners

Memory Aids Have students create a chart to help remember the names of the days of the week in Spanish. Encourage students to start each class by talking about the name of the day, and which day will follow. **Hoy es lunes. Mañana es martes.**

Slower-paced Learners

Yes/No Questions Write the names of the days of the week on the board. Circle the current day, and write the word **hoy** below it. Then ask students yes or no questions about the days of the week. **¿Hoy es jueves? ¿Mañana es domingo? ¿Mañana es lunes?** Continue the questions by changing the day that is today.

17 | Los días

**Hablar
Escribir**

Complete each list with the missing day of the week.

1. lunes, _____, miércoles, jueves
2. viernes, _____, domingo, lunes
3. _____, martes, miércoles, jueves
4. lunes, martes, miércoles, _____
5. _____, jueves, viernes, sábado
6. domingo, _____, martes, miércoles
7. sábado, _____, lunes, martes
8. martes, miércoles, jueves, _____

18 | ¿Lógico o ilógico?

Escuchar

Listen to these statements about the days of the week. Write **L** if the statement you hear is **lógico** (*logical*) or **I** if it is **ilógico** (*not logical*).

modelo: You hear: Hoy es viernes. Mañana es domingo.
You write: I

Audio Program
TXT CD 1 Track 16
Audio Script, TE p. C25b

19 | ¿Qué día es?

Hablar

Ask a partner what day of the week it is. He or she will tell you what day of the week today is and what tomorrow is.

modelo: 6

A ¿Qué día es hoy?

B Hoy es **martes**. Mañana es **miércoles**.

1. 2
2. 12
3. 28
4. 15
5. 18
6. 3
7. 20
8. 16

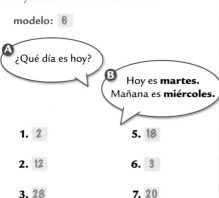

SEPTIEMBRE

L	M	M	J	V	S	D
			1	2	3	4
5	6	7	8	9	10	11
12	13	14	15	16	17	18
19	20	21	22	23	24	25
26	27	28	29	30		

PARA Y PIENSA

Did you get it?
1. Tell someone that today is Monday. Hoy es _____.
2. Ask what day tomorrow is. ¿Qué día es _____?

Get Help Online
ClassZone.com

Differentiating Instruction

Inclusion

Alphabetic/Phonetic Awareness Remind students of phonetic points related to talking about the days of the week. Here are a few examples:
· The **h** at the beginning of **hoy** is silent.
· The **ñ** in **mañana** sounds like *ny* in *canyon*.
· The **es** at the end of each day's name sounds similar to the English *ace*.

Multiple Intelligences

Intrapersonal Have students create a diary of a typical week. Instruct them to write the name of each day of the week, and draw pictures of activities they do on each day. As students learn new vocabulary for everyday activities, have them return to these diaries to add the words and phrases they have learned.

LECCIÓN PRELIMINAR

Communication

Group Work

Have students repeat the days of the week after you. Tell them you will say a day of the week. They are to say what the next day of the week would be. **martes → miércoles.** Continue with the other days of the week.

Communication

Class Work

Game Using numerals 0–10, the days of the week, and the words **semana, hoy, mañana, día, qué**, have students create a Bingo grid with sixteen squares. They are to write one word or numeral in each square. They will not use all of the words as there are 23 in the list. Call out the English word or the Spanish number. The first student to get four in a row wins.

✓ **Ongoing Assessment**

@HomeTutor
More Practice
ClassZone.com

PARA Y PIENSA
Peer Assessment Have student pairs say their sentences and correct each other.

Answers MSRB Transparency 26

Activity 17 **1.** martes; **2.** sábado; **3.** lunes; **4.** jueves; **5.** miércoles; **6.** lunes; **7.** domingo; **8.** viernes

Activity 18 **1.** L; **2.** I; **3.** I; **4.** L; **5.** L; **6.** I

Activity 19
1. ¿Qué día es hoy? Hoy es viernes. Mañana es sábado.
2. ¿Qué...? Hoy es lunes. Mañana es martes.
3. ¿...? Hoy es miércoles. Mañana es jueves.
4. ¿...? Hoy es jueves. Mañana es viernes.
5. ¿...? Hoy es domingo. Mañana es lunes.
6. ¿...? Hoy es sábado. Mañana es domingo.
7. ¿...? Hoy es martes. Mañana es miércoles.
8. ¿...? Hoy es viernes. Mañana es sábado.

Para y piensa
1. lunes; 2. mañana

Objective
· Learn and practice weather expressions.

Core Resource
· Audio Program: TXT CD 1 tracks 17, 18, 19

Presentation Strategies
· Point to the map on p. 20 and ask **¿Qué tiempo hace?** Read each of the weather descriptions and have students repeat.
· Assign students the roles of the teens in A–F and ask them **¿Qué tiempo hace?** Students respond according to their role.
· Play the audio.

Practice Sequence
· **Activity 20:** Vocabulary recognition: weather expressions
· **Activity 21:** Vocabulary production: weather expressions
· **Activity 22:** Vocabulary production: weather expressions, tell where someone is from

STANDARDS
1.1 Engage in conversation, Acts. 21–22
1.2 Understand language, Act. 20
1.3 Present information, Acts. 20–22, PYP

Warm Up UTB 1 Transparency 24

Days of the Week Unscramble the days of the week.
1. absodá
2. senul
3. seléimroc
4. tmraes
5. ogniodm

Answers: 1. sábado; 2. lunes; 3. miércoles; 4. martes; 5. domingo

Answers MSRB Transparency 26

¡A responder! Audio Script, TE p. C25b
Students should point to the following students.
1. Diego
2. Mariana
3. Natalia
4. Jorge
5. Andrea
6. Luis

20

¡AVANZA! **Goal:** Learn how to describe the weather. Then practice what you have learned to describe a sunny day, a rainy day, and a windy day. *Actividades 20–22*

¿Qué tiempo hace?

AUDIO

A Luis: Hace calor.

B Natalia: Hace sol.

C Jorge: Llueve.

D Andrea: Hace frío.

E Diego: Hace viento.

F Mariana: Nieva.

¡A responder! Escuchar

Listen to weather descriptions. Point to the photo of the person that corresponds to the description you hear.

Lección preliminar
20 veinte

Differentiating Instruction

Slower-paced Learners

Yes/No Questions Use yes/no questions to help students practice talking about the weather. Point to one of the people on p. 20 as you ask: **¿Hace viento?** or **¿Hace calor?** Students should answer **sí** or **no**. If the answer is **no**, they should follow up with an explanation. **No, no hace calor. Hace frío.**

Inclusion

Cumulative Instruction Use the pictures on p. 20 to help students review skills they have learned so far in the lesson. Here are a few possibilities:
· Ask someone their name.
· Ask someone where they are from.
· Spell out the name of a person or place.

20 | El tiempo

Escuchar

Listen to four meteorologists describe the weather in their region. Write the letter of the photo that corresponds to the weather description you hear.

a. **b.**  **c.**  **d.**

🎧 **Audio Program**
TXT CD 1 Track 19
Audio Script, TE p. C25b

21 | ¿Hace calor o hace frío?

Hablar

Work with a partner. Say whether it is cold or hot, according to the temperature given.

modelo: 32°F / 0°C
Hace frío.

1. 15°F / –9°C   **3.** 20°F / –6°C   **5.** 88°F / 32°C
2. 94°F / 35°C   **4.** 4°F / –16°C   **6.** 104°F / 40°C

22 | ¿Qué tiempo hace?

Hablar

Tell what city you are from, and ask a partner what the weather is like. He or she will give you the weather conditions for that city.

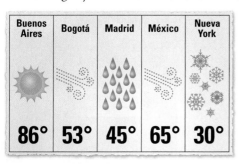

Buenos Aires	Bogotá	Madrid	México	Nueva York
86°	53°	45°	65°	30°

A Soy de la Ciudad de México. ¿Qué tiempo hace?

B Hace viento.

PARA Y PIENSA

Did you get it? Match each question with the correct response.

1. ¿Qué tiempo hace?   **a.** No. Hace frío.
2. ¿Hace calor?   **b.** Hace viento.
3. ¿Llueve?   **c.** No. Hace sol.

🖱 **Get Help Online**
ClassZone.com

Differentiating Instruction

Multiple Intelligences

Naturalist Have students work in small groups to create a weather chart. Their charts should include words to describe different types of weather, as well as a picture to represent each phrase. Start each class by having students update their charts and talk about the day's weather.

Slower-paced Learners

Personalize It Ask students to write a few sentences about the weather in their own city or a place they have visted. When they finish writing, ask them to read their sentences aloud.

LECCIÓN PRELIMINAR

Communication
⚠ Common Error Alert

Because **hace** is used with so many weather expressions, students tend to use it with **nieva** and **llueve**. Explain to students that **hace** is a verb and is only needed with nouns such as **calor, frío, viento. Nieva** and **llueve** are verbs that express complete thoughts and do not require the use of **hace**.

Communication
👥 TPR Activity

Instruct students to draw a picture that reflects the weather condition as you say it in Spanish.
1. Hace sol. 2. Nieva. 3. Hace viento.
4. Hace calor. 5. Llueve. 6. Hace frío.
Send volunteers to the board to draw pictures. Have them write the weather expression underneath each.

✓ Ongoing Assessment

@HomeTutor
More Practice
ClassZone.com

PARA Y PIENSA **Quick Check** If students have problems matching the questions and responses from Para y piensa, refer them to p. 20.

Answers MSRB Transparencies 26–27

Activity 20
  1. b; **2.** a; **3.** d; **4.** c

Activity 21
  1. Hace frío; **2.** Hace calor; **3.** Hace frío;
  4. Hace frío; **5.** Hace calor; **6.** Hace calor.

Activity 22
  A. Soy de Buenos Aires. ¿Qué tiempo hace?
    B. Hace sol. Hace calor.
  A. Soy de Bogotá. ¿Qué...? **B.** Hace viento.
  A. Soy de Madrid. ¿...? **B.** Llueve. Hace frío.
  A. Soy de Nueva York. ¿...? **B.** Nieva. Hace frío.

Para y piensa
  1. b; **2.** a; **3.** c

Objective
· Learn useful classroom phrases.

Objective
· Learn useful classroom phrases.

Core Resource
· Audio Program: TXT CD 1 tracks 20, 21

Presentation Strategies
· Remind students that this material is to help them understand recurring Spanish phrases used in class.
· Read aloud the phrases for En la clase and Otras instrucciones on pp. 22–23 and use gestures whenever possible to clarify meaning.
· Review these phrases often and post them in the classroom until students are comfortable using them.
· Play the audio. Practice the phrases with sample situations.

STANDARDS
1.2 Understand language

 Warm Up UTB 1 Transparency 25

Vocabulary Unscramble the weather.
1. ¿Qué tiempo hace? Hace r c l a o
2. ¿Qué tiempo hace? Hace e n o v t i
3. ¿Qué tiempo hace? Hace l o s
4. ¿Qué tiempo hace? L u v e l e
5. ¿Qué tiempo hace? N a v e i

Answers: 1. calor; 2. viento; 3. sol; 4. Llueve; 5. Nieva

Communication
TPR Activity

Go over the expressions on p. 22 and add the expression **Levántense** *Stand up,* on the board. Model two of the commands and have students imitate what you do. Then say the commands and have students obey them. Gradually add more commands as they master two at a time. Sample script:
Levántense. Levanten la mano. Siéntense. Levanten la mano. Levántense. Siéntense. Abran los libros. Levanten la mano. Cierren los libros. Levántense. Siéntense. Abran los libros. Saquen una hoja de papel. Cierren los libros.

En la clase

 Goal: Learn some useful phrases used by teachers and students. Then practice what you have learned to use classroom phrases with others.
Actividades 23–25

 AUDIO

Maestro, ¿cómo se dice Wednesday?

Se dice miércoles.

la clase

En la clase

Abran los libros (en la página...)	*Open your books (to page . . .)*
Cierren los libros.	*Close your books.*
¿Cómo se dice...?	*How do you say . . .?*
Se dice...	*You say . . .*
¿Cómo se escribe (tu nombre)?	*How do you spell (your name)?*
Se escribe...	*It is spelled . . .*
¿Comprendes?	*Do you understand?*
Levanten la mano.	*Raise your hand.*
Más despacio, por favor.	*More slowly, please.*
No sé.	*I don't know.*
¿Qué quiere decir...?	*What does . . . mean?*
Quiere decir...	*It means . . .*
Repitan, por favor.	*Please repeat.*
Saquen una hoja de papel.	*Take out a piece of paper.*
Siéntense.	*Sit down.*
¿Tienen preguntas?	*Do you have questions?*
¿Verdad?	*Right?*

Muchas gracias.

De nada.

el maestro de español

22 Lección preliminar
veintidós

Differentiating Instruction

Inclusion

Multisensory Input/Output Model for students how to follow important commands from the list on p. 22. For example, say **abran los libros** as you open a book. Say **levanten la mano** as you raise your hand. Have students find and point to each phrase on p. 22, and then practice following the command.

Multiple Intelligences

Interpersonal Have students work in groups of three to develop a short role-play. One student will play the part of the teacher, and the others will be students. The scene should involve a classroom situation. The teacher might ask the students questions, such as **¿Cómo te llamas?** or give the students instructions, such as **Siéntense**.

Otras instrucciones

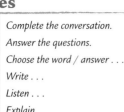

Completa la conversación.	*Complete the conversation.*
Contesta las preguntas.	*Answer the questions.*
Escoge la palabra / la respuesta...	*Choose the word / answer . . .*
Escribe...	*Write . . .*
Escucha...	*Listen . . .*
Explica...	*Explain . . .*
Indica si es cierto o falso.	*Indicate whether it is true or false.*
Lee...	*Read . . .*
Pregúntale a otro(a) estudiante.	*Ask another student.*
Trabaja con otro(a) estudiante.	*Work with another student.*
Trabaja en un grupo de...	*Work in a group of . . .*

Perdón, ¿qué quiere decir *número*?

Quiere decir *number*.

la maestra de español

¡A responder!   Escuchar

Listen to each classroom instruction and respond appropriately.

Lección preliminar
veintitrés   **23**

Communication
Group Activity

Divide students into two groups to act out the expressions on pp. 22–23. The other students will try to guess which classroom command they are demonstrating.

Communication
Pair Work

Before students arrive to class, write isolated words and phrases from the classroom commands on index cards. For example, write **Pregúntale** on one card and **a otro(a) estudiante** on another. They should find their match to create the correct phrase. They will then take turns reading and demonstrating the expressions to the class.

Communication
Pair Work

Have students work with a partner to give the commands on pp. 22–23. Each should give five commands for the other to follow before switching roles.

Long-term Retention
Study Tips

Ask student pairs to go through the list and note the items that each of them has difficulty remembering. Partners then devise a way to help each other remember (flashcards, drawings, graphic organizers) according to their preferred learning style.

Differentiating Instruction

English Learners

Build Background Ask students to share information about teachers, students, and classrooms in their country of origin. What are some phrases that might be heard in a typical classroom? Are they similar to or different from the phrases listed on pp. 22 and 23?

Slower-paced Learners

Memory Aids Have students create a set of flashcards to help practice vocabulary related to common classroom phrases. Using index cards, have them write the vocabulary word or phrase on one side, and draw a simple picture on the other. Encourage students to use their cards individually or with a partner.

Answers MSRB Transparency 27

¡A responder! Audio Script, TE p. C25b
Answers will vary. Possible answers:
1. Students open their books to page 10.
2. Students raise their hand.
3. Students close their books.
4. Students repeat: "Buenos días."
5. Students take out a sheet of paper.

Objective
· Practice classroom phrases.

Practice Sequence
· **Activity 23:** Vocabulary recognition: classroom phrases
· **Activity 24:** Vocabulary production: classroom phrases.
· **Activity 25:** Vocabulary production: classroom phrases, greetings, days of the week, weather

STANDARDS
1.1 Engage in conversation, Act. 25
1.3 Present information, Acts. 24–25, PYP

✓ **Ongoing Assessment**
@HomeTutor
More Practice
ClassZone.com

PARA Y PIENSA **Peer Assessment** Before writing the correct answers on the board, have students exchange papers and correct each other's statements.

Answers MSRB Transparency 27

Activity 23 **1.** d; **2.** c; **3.** b; **4.** a

Activity 24
1. Muchas gracias.
2. Más despacio, por favor.
3. ¿Cómo se dice *book*?
4. ¿Qué quiere decir **página**?
5. No sé.
6. ¿Comprendes?

Activity 25
1. A. ¿Cómo se dice *Spanish*? B. Se dice español. A. ¿Cómo se escribe español? B. Se escribe: e, ese, pe, a, eñe, o, ele.
2. A. ¿Cómo se dice *week*? B. Se dice semana. A. ¿Cómo se escribe semana? B. Se escribe: ese, e, eme, a, ene, a.
3. A. ¿Cómo se dice *Thank you very much*? B. Se dice Muchas gracias. A. ¿Cómo se escribe Muchas gracias? B. Se escribe: eme, u, ce, hache, a, ese, ge, ere, a, ce, i, a, ese.
4. A. ¿Cómo se dice *male teacher*? B. Se dice maestro. A: ¿Cómo se escribe maestro? B: Se escribe: eme, a, e, ese, te, ere, o.
5. A. ¿Cómo se dice *See you later*? B. Se dice Hasta luego. A. ¿Cómo se escribe Hasta luego? B. Se escribe hache, a, ese, te, a, ele, u, e, ge, o.
6. A. ¿Cómo se dice *Friday*? B. Se dice viernes. A. ¿Cómo se escribe viernes? B. Se escribe uve, i, e, ere, ene, e, ese.
7. A. ¿Cómo se dice *It's raining*? B. Se dice Llueve. A. ¿Cómo se escribe Llueve? Se escribe ele, ele, u, e, uve, e.

Para y piensa
1. ¿Cómo se dice *please*?   2. ¿Comprendes?

24

---

23 | Instrucciones

Leer   Match each picture with the correct instruction.

a. Abran los libros en la página 7.
b. Levanten la mano.
c. Repitan, por favor.
d. Siéntense.

24 | ¿Qué dices?

Escribir Hablar

Indicate what you would say in each situation. Refer to the expressions on pages 22–23.

1. You want to thank your Spanish teacher.
2. Your teacher is speaking too fast.
3. You want to know how to say *book* in Spanish.
4. You want to know what **página** means.
5. You must admit that you don't have the answer to a question.
6. You wonder if your friend understands the lesson.

25 | ¿Cómo se dice?

Hablar

Ask a partner to say the following words in Spanish and how to spell them.

modelo: Tuesday
1. Spanish
2. week
3. Thank you very much.
4. male teacher
5. See you later.
6. Friday
7. It's raining.

A ¿Cómo se dice *Tuesday*?
B Se dice *martes*.
¿Cómo se escribe *martes*?
Se escribe eme, a, ere, te, e, ese.

PARA Y PIENSA **Did you get it?** 1. Ask how to say the word *please.*
2. Ask a friend if he or she understands.

⚡ **Get Help Online** ClassZone.com

Differentiating Instruction

Multiple Intelligences

Kinesthetic Help students review common classroom instructions by playing a modified Simon Says game. Give students a command, such as **Levanten la mano.** Direct all students to follow the command as quickly as possible. Continue with other commands, such as **Abran los libros.** After a few rounds, give volunteers the chance to act as the leader.

Heritage Language Learners

Support What They Know Partner students with a non-heritage language learner for Activity 25. Have the other students use their partner as a resource to ask about additional words and phrases they are interested in.

A: **¿Cómo se dice** *play the piano*? B: **Se dice** *tocar el piano.* A: **¿Cómo se escribe** *piano*? B: **Se escribe** *pe-i-a-ene-o.*

LECCIÓN PRELIMINAR

En resumen
Vocabulario

Vocabulario

Greet People and Say Goodbye

Greetings

Buenos días.	Good morning.
Buenas tardes.	Good afternoon.
Buenas noches.	Good evening.
Hola.	Hello./Hi.

Say Goodbye

Adiós.	Goodbye.
Buenas noches.	Good night.
Hasta luego.	See you later.
Hasta mañana.	See you tomorrow.

Say How You Are

¿Cómo estás?	How are you? (familiar)
¿Cómo está usted?	How are you? (formal)
¿Qué tal?	How is it going?
Bien.	Fine.
Mal.	Bad.
Más o menos.	So-so.
Muy bien.	Very well.
Regular.	Okay.
¿Y tú?	And you? (familiar)
¿Y usted?	And you? (formal)
¿Qué pasa?	What's up?

Make Introductions

¿Cómo se llama?	What's his/her/ your (formal) name?
Se llama...	His/Her name is . . .
¿Cómo te llamas?	What's your (familiar) name?
Me llamo...	My name is . . .
Te/Le presento a...	Let me introduce you (familiar/ formal) to . . .
El gusto es mío.	The pleasure is mine.
Encantado(a).	Delighted./Pleased to meet you.
Igualmente.	Same here./ Likewise.
Mucho gusto.	Nice to meet you.
¿Quién es?	Who is he/she/it?
Es...	He/She/It is . . .

Say Which Day It Is

¿Qué día es hoy?	What day is today?
Hoy es...	Today is . . .
Mañana es...	Tomorrow is . . .
el día	day
hoy	today
mañana	tomorrow
la semana	week

Days of the week p. 18

Exchange Phone Numbers

¿Cuál es tu/su número de teléfono?	What's your (familiar/ formal) phone number?
Mi número de teléfono es...	My phone number is . . .

Numbers from zero to ten p. 16

Other Words and Phrases

la clase	class
el (la) maestro(a) de español	Spanish teacher (male/female)
el país	country
Perdón.	Excuse me.
por favor	please
(Muchas) Gracias.	Thank you (very much).
De nada.	You're welcome.
el señor (Sr.)	Mr.
la señora (Sra.)	Mrs.
la señorita (Srta.)	Miss
sí	yes
no	no

Describe the Weather

¿Qué tiempo hace?	What is the weather like?
Hace calor.	It is hot.
Hace frío.	It is cold.
Hace sol.	It is sunny.
Hace viento.	It is windy.
Llueve.	It is raining.
Nieva.	It is snowing.

Say Where You Are From

¿De dónde eres?	Where are you (familiar) from?
¿De dónde es?	Where is he/she from?
¿De dónde es usted?	Where are you (formal) from?
Soy de...	I am from . . .
Es de...	He/She is from . . .

Spanish-speaking countries p. 13

Objective
· Review lesson vocabulary.

Online SPANISH CLASSZONE.COM

Interactive Flashcards Students can hear every target vocabulary word pronounced in authentic Spanish. Flashcards have Spanish on one side, and a picture or a translation on the other.

Self-Quiz Students can check their understanding and get instant results with our online multiple-choice quizzes. These quizzes provide immediate feedback, making them a great way to prepare for a quiz or test.

Review Games Matching, concentration, hangman, and word search are just a sampling of the fun, interactive games students can play to review for the test.

Featuring...

- Cultura INTERACTIVA
- Animated Grammar
- @HomeTutor

And more...
- Get Help Online
- Interactive Flashcards
- Review Games
- WebQuest
- Self-Check Quiz

Communication
Role-Playing and Skits

Divide students into groups of three or four. They should create a skit in which they greet each other, make introductions, ask how each other is doing, ask where each other is from, and say goodbye. Have them present in front of the class.

Long-term Retention
Critical Thinking

Categorize Have students group vocabulary from En resumen into questions and answers for easy recall. Students should write a question on one side of an index card and the corresponding answer(s) on the other side using different color markers.

Differentiating Instruction

Inclusion

Cumulative Instruction Write the headings **Preguntas** and **Respuestas** on the board. Review the meaning of these terms with students. Then ask students to list as many questions as they can that they learned in the lesson. After each question, have students brainstorm as many possible responses as possible.

Multiple Intelligences

Visual Learners Have students create a comic strip involving two or three characters. The characters should greet each other, ask each other two or three questions, and then say goodbye. Advise students to use word bubbles to show the characters' dialogue. Give students the opportunity to share their comic strips with the whole group.

LECCIÓN PRELIMINAR

Objective
· Review lesson vocabulary.

Core Resource
· Audio Program: TXT CD 1 track 22

Review Options
· Draw students' attention to the ¡Llegada!
· Before starting the audio for Activity 1, ask students to listen carefully to each conversation and pay special attention to expressions that tie in with the drawings.
· Before doing Activity 2, ask students to look at the word bank and identify those words that refer to greetings, those that refer to introductions, and those that refer to the weather.
· Review numbers by saying one number and asking students to say the next number. For example, say **ocho**. Students say **nueve**.
· Before doing Activity 4, review the meaning of question words by saying a statement and asking students to choose the correct question from the ones in the activity. For example: **Me llamo Luis Aguirre.** Students respond: **¿Cómo te llamas?**

STANDARDS
1.2 Understand language, Act. 1
1.3 Present information, Acts. 1–4

 Warm Up UTB 1 Transparency 25

Vocabulary Complete the sentences with the correct word.

presento   mañana   gusto   dónde   día

1. ¿Qué _____ es hoy?
2. Te _____ a Matilde.
3. ¿De _____ eres?
4. Hasta _____.
5. Mucho _____.

Answers: 1. día; 2. presento; 3. dónde; 4. mañana; 5. gusto

Answers MSRB Transparency 27

Activity 1 1. d; 2. a; 3. c; 4. b
Activity 2 1. Hola; 2. Cómo; 3. llamo; 4. Soy; 5. Hoy; 6. calor; 7. tiempo; 8. Hace; 9. Adiós

26

 LECCIÓN PRELIMINAR ***Repaso de la lección***

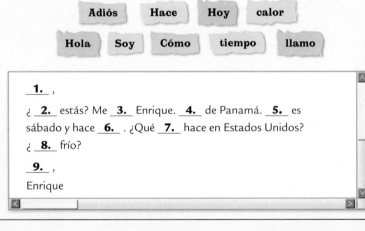

¡LLEGADA!

@HomeTutor
ClassZone.com

Now you can
· greet people and say goodbye
· introduce yourself and others
· ask and say how to spell names
· say where you are from
· exchange phone numbers
· say what day of the week it is
· describe the weather
· respond to classroom instructions

Audio Progra
TXT CD 1 Track 2
Audio Script, TE
C25b

To review
· introductions pp. 6–7
· classroom instructions pp. 22–23

1 Listen and understand

You will hear four separate conversations. Put the drawings in order according to what you hear.

a.    b.   c.   d.

To review
· greet people pp. 2–3
· introductions pp. 6–7
· weather p. 20

2 Introduce yourself and others

Complete Enrique's e-mail message to his new e-pal.

Adiós   Hace   Hoy   calor

Hola   Soy   Cómo   tiempo   llamo

___**1.**___ ,

¿ ___**2.**___ estás? Me ___**3.**___ Enrique. ___**4.**___ de Panamá. ___**5.**___ es sábado y hace ___**6.**___ . ¿Qué ___**7.**___ hace en Estados Unidos? ¿ ___**8.**___ frío?

___**9.**___ ,

Enrique

26 Lección preliminar
veintiséis

Differentiating Instruction

Slower-paced Learners
Read Before Listening Before students listen to the conversations in Activity 1, have them preview the pictures. Direct them to brainstorm possible words and phrases related to each picture. For example, in picture **a.**, what might the two characters be saying to each other? Have students write their ideas on a separate piece of paper, and refer to their notes as they listen.

Heritage Language Learners
Writing Skills Ask students to imagine they are writing to a new e-pal. Have them draft a message in which they introduce themselves, ask questions about the e-pal's home, and talk about their own home and interests. Remind students to use proper punctuation to differentiate questions from statements.

o review
origin pp. 12–13
numbers p. 16

3 Say where you are from

Look at these students' ID cards from the International Club.
Then complete the sentences that follow.

Club Internacional NOMBRE: **Cristina Villaveces** PAÍS DE ORIGEN: **Venezuela** DOMICILIO: **332 Avenida de las Américas** TELÉFONO: **241-0976**	**Club Internacional** NOMBRE: **Yolanda Hoyos** PAÍS DE ORIGEN: **Chile** DOMICILIO: **1902 Rúa Mayor** TELÉFONO: **397-2261**
Club Internacional NOMBRE: **Alejandro Cruz** PAÍS DE ORIGEN: **México** DOMICILIO: **214 Paseo Suárez** TELÉFONO: **898-1035**	**Club Internacional** NOMBRE: **Guillermo Morales** PAÍS DE ORIGEN: **España** DOMICILIO: **38 Calle Toro, 3°D** TELÉFONO: **460-1853**

1. _____ es de España.
2. El número de teléfono es ocho - nueve - ocho - uno - cero - tres - cinco. Se llama _____ .
3. Se llama Cristina. El número de teléfono es _____ .
4. La señorita de Chile se llama _____ .
5. Se llama Guillermo. El número de teléfono es _____ .
6. _____ es de México.

o review
alphabet p. 10
numbers p. 16
days of the week
p. 18

4 Answer personal questions

Answer these questions using complete sentences.

1. ¿Cómo te llamas?
2. ¿Cómo se escribe tu nombre?
3. ¿De dónde eres?
4. ¿Cuál es tu número de teléfono?
5. ¿Quién es el (la) maestro(a) de español? ¿De dónde es?
6. ¿Cómo se llama el libro de español?
7. ¿Qué día es mañana?
8. ¿Qué tiempo hace hoy?
9. ¿Cómo se dice *country* en español?

 Get Help Online
ClassZone.com

Differentiating Instruction

Multiple Intelligences

Linguistic/Verbal Model introducing yourself in Spanish, then have students follow your model: **Hola, buenos días, me llamo... Yo soy de...** Then ask volunteers to introduce themselves and expand the introduction. For example, **Hola, me llamo Carlos, soy de Puerto Rico. En Puerto Rico hace sol.**

Slower-paced Learners

Peer-study Support Organize students into pairs to check their answers for Activity 4. Have partners take turns reading the questions aloud. Both partners should then read or say their responses aloud. Encourage partners to give each other constructive feedback when appropriate.

LECCIÓN PRELIMINAR

✓ **Ongoing Assessment**   @HomeTutor
More Practice
ClassZone.com

Intervention and Remediation If students achieve less than 80% accuracy with the activities, direct them to pp. 2-3, 6-7,10, 12-13, 16, 18, 20, 22-23 and to get help online at ClassZone.com.

✓ **Ongoing Assessment**

Alternative Strategy After doing Activity 2 in class, have students write a letter to a classmate. You may wish to assign partners or have them draw names. They will tell their names, where they're from, what day of the week it is, and what the weather is like. They may add additional information. They should include at least two questions to be answered by the receiver.

✓ **Ongoing Assessment**

Peer Assessment Have student pairs exchange answers for Activity 4, and correct each other's work.

Answers MSRB Transparency 27

Activity 3
1. Guillermo Morales
2. Alejandro Cruz
3. dos-cuatro-uno-cero-nueve-siete-seis
4. Yolanda Hoyos
5. cuatro-seis-cero-uno-ocho-cinco-tres
6. Alejandro Cruz

Activity 4 Answers will vary. Sample answers include:
1. Me llamo George.
2. Se escribe ge-e-o-ere-ge-e.
3. Soy de Nueva York.
4. Mi número de teléfono es cinco-siete-siete-tres-dos-nueve-cero.
5. El(la) maestro(a) de español es el señor (la señora) Ramos. Es de Miami.
6. El libro de español se llama ¡*Avancemos!*
7. Mañana es jueves.
8. Hace calor.
9. Se dice país.

Proyectos adicionales

❋ Art Project

Create a mosaic. Have students look at the maps found on pages xxx–xxxv of their text. Work with students to generate a list of Spanish-speaking countries and write them on the board. Ask students to select six countries. Bring students to the library where they can research various flags and make notes about color, and so forth.

1. Hand out pieces of cardboard and have students fold it into a cube.

2. On each side, have students create mosaic images of six of the flags they choose. They can tear colored construction paper into very small pieces and paste it onto the outer surface of the box. Each side should have a different flag representing one of the various countries.

3. Ask for volunteers to talk about their mosaic. Students should say which countries their mosaic represents, where the countries are located, and what the weather is like there.

4. Make a small hole in one corner of each box and tie string or fishing line on them in order to hang the mosaics from the ceiling.

PACING SUGGESTION: One 50-minute class period.

❋ Bulletin Board

¿Qué me gusta hacer? Ask students to look through magazines and newspapers, to draw, or to go online to find three things that they like to do in their free time and/or during a particular season of the year. Be sure they identify who they are, and what they like to do. After you've created the bulletin board, go around the classroom and ask each student to tell the class what they like to do and why.

PACING SUGGESTION: One 50-minute class period.

❋ Web Research

Cities online. Find out about different Spanish-speaking cultures in the U.S. Pair students up and assign them one of the following cities: Miami, San Antonio, Los Angeles.

Encourage students to provide the following information:
- tell where the majority of the population comes from (e.g., Miami–Cuba etc.)
- describe any cultural practices and/or typical foods that can be found in the community
- have students imagine they live in one of the cities and describe three things they would do there in their free time.

Students report what they have learned. Encourage them to print out interesting things they found online or to provide a drawing of things they would like to do in the particular city.

Search Key Words: "Little Havana," "the Greater Miami Chamber of Commerce," "San Antonio," "the Los Angeles Visitors Bureau." Also visit **ClassZone.com** for more information.

PACING SUGGESTION: Two-day project for one 50-minute class. One-day project for one 90-minute class.

Get Help Online
ClassZone.com

❊ Games

Diez

Have students stand up at their desks. Begin in one corner of the room. The first student starts with number **"Uno"** and has the option to name up to three numbers in sequence. (For example, the student who begins has the option to say **"Uno,"** **"Uno, Dos,"** or **"Uno, Dos, Tres."**) The next student continues, and again may name up to three sequential numbers, following from where the first student left off. The student who arrives at the point where he or she must say **"Diez"** is automatically out and has to sit down. The game then starts again at **"Uno"** and continues as long as there are players left standing.

PACING SUGGESTION: Twenty minutes of classtime.

Espalda con espalda

Select a student to be "it." Have him/her sit on a chair at the front of the class blindfolded. Have another student also sit on a chair at the front of the class. One-by-one, the rest of the class provides clues describing the second student to the blindfolded student. The blindfolded student gets one guess after each clue. When correct, the student who provided the last clue is the next one to be "it." Play continues until a predetermined time limit is reached. To keep hesitations to a minimum, keep a reference vocabulary list available for students.

PACING SUGGESTION: Twenty minutes of classtime.

¿Quién es?

Alternatively, hand out 3x5 index cards. Ask students to provide the following information:

- where they are from
- a short description of what they look like
- two adjectives to describe themselves
- what they like to do in their free time

Collect the cards. Then either read the descriptions and have students guess who is who or distribute the cards to various students to read aloud (make sure they don't read their own). Students guess who is who.

PACING SUGGESTION: Thirty minutes of classtime.

❊ Recipe

Guacamole is the second most popular dip in the southwestern U.S. (after salsa). It is generally served with fried corn chips, tostadas, but can also be served with flour tortillas cut into strips. With your students, try this quick-and-easy recipe for Olé Guacamole.

Olé Guacamole

Ingredientes

6 aguacates bien maduros

1 tomate: pelado, sin semillas y en trozos pequeños

1/4 taza de cebolla bien picada

1/4 taza de hojas de cilantro picadas

8 cdas. de jugo fresco de limón verde

sal al gusto

Instrucciones

Cortar los aguacates por la mitad, quitar la semilla y sacar la pulpa. Pisar la pulpa con un tenedor; añadir el tomate, la cebolla, el cilantro, el jugo de limón verde y la sal al gusto. Refrigerar cubierto con papel de plástico por 1/2 hora. Servir con tortillas.

(Sirve a 6-8.)

Tiempo de preparación 40 minutos
Tiempo total 90 minutos

❊ Music

Pop music. Both Spanish and English speakers in the U.S. enjoy Spanish language music. Some popular singers are Gloria Estefan, Jennifer Lopez, and Marc Anthony. Have student go to a music store or to an online music store and find out the names of other Spanish-speaking singers and groups. Play some of the music they research. Discuss what music they like and why. Samples can be heard on music sites.

UNIT THEME
Time with friends

UNIT STANDARDS
COMMUNICATION
· Talk about activities
· Say what you like and don't like to do
· Tell where you are from
· Describe yourself and others
· Identify people and things

CULTURES
· *Los Premios Juventud*
· Art of Xavier Cortada
· Favorite activities of Florida teenagers
· Mexican and Tex-Mex food
· Art of Carmen Lomas Garza

CONNECTIONS
· Geography: Cities—old and new
· Mathematics: Calculate distances
· Language: Places in the U.S. with Spanish names
· Music: Tex-Mex

COMPARISONS
· Florida beaches, places students go in their free time.
· Famous performers and athletes
· The Spanish **p, t,** and **ñ,** the English *p, t,* and /*ny*/ sound
· Representing communities in art
· Paseo del Río, places of interest
· Restaurants with foods from other countries
· Family traditions
· Places of interest in San Antonio and Miami
· Traditional dishes of Mexico and Cuba
· Personal descriptions

COMMUNITIES
· Restaurants with food from Spanish-speaking countries

Estados Unidos
Un rato con los amigos

Lección 1
Tema: **¿Qué te gusta hacer?**

Lección 2
Tema: **Mis amigos y yo**

Chicago · Filadelfia · Nueva York
· San José
Denver
Estados Unidos
Los Ángeles
· Phoenix · Albuquerque
San Diego · Tucson
· Dallas
· El Paso · Houston
Océano Atlántico
San Antonio
Miami ·
Golfo de México
México
Cuba
Océano Pacífico
Mar Caribe
Honduras
Nicaragua
Costa Rica
Guatemala
El Salvador
Panamá

Alaska

Islas Hawai

«¡Hola!
Nosotras somos Alicia y Sandra.
Somos de Estados Unidos.»

Población: 293.655.404

Población de ascendencia hispana: 41.322.070

Ciudad con más latinos: Nueva York (más de 2.000.000)

Ciudad con mayor porcentaje de latinos: El Paso, Texas (77%)

Comida latina: el sándwich cubano, burritos, fajitas

El sándwich cubano

Gente famosa: Sandra Cisneros (escritora), Gloria Estefan (cantante), Eva Mendes (actriz), Eloy Rodríguez (bioquímico)

28 veintiocho

Cultural Geography

Setting the Scene
· Where are we? South America or North America? (North America)
· What are the girls' names? (Alicia and Sandra)
· Which city has a larger Latino population, Boston or New York? (New York)

Teaching with Maps
· Which countries have borders with the United States? (Mexico and Canada)
· The United States has coasts along which bodies of water? (Pacific Ocean, Atlantic Ocean, Gulf of Mexico)

◄ **La ascendencia hispana** The over 40 million Hispanics living in the United States trace their roots to more than 20 nations. From September 15 to October 15, Hispanic Heritage Month celebrates the diverse backgrounds and cultures of these Americans. *Do you know anyone from a Spanish-speaking country?*

Hispanic teens gather for a celebration in Miami, Florida

La comunidad cubana de Miami The Cuban American community thrives in Miami's Little Havana. **Calle Ocho** is known for its Cuban restaurants, cafés, and shops, and the nearby Freedom Tower houses the Cuban American Museum. *How have people from other countries shaped your community?* ►

Miami's Freedom Tower, home to the Cuban American Museum

Dancers in traditional dress during the Fiesta San Antonio

◄ **Las celebraciones** San Antonio is proud of its unique multicultural history. The **Fiesta San Antonio,** a ten-day celebration with food, music, and parades, honors the heroes of the Alamo and the Battle of San Jacinto. La Villita, the city's oldest neighborhood, hosts many of the festival events. *How do people celebrate history and culture where you live?*

Estados Unidos
veintinueve **29**

Cultura INTERACTIVA
ClassZone.com

Send your students to www.ClassZone.com to explore authentic Latin culture in the United States. Tell them to click on Cultura interactiva to see these pages come alive!

Culture

About the Photos
· The photo of the teens shows a very diverse group of people. According to the 2000 U.S. Census, the term *Hispanic* refers to Spanish-speaking people in the U.S. of any race.
· The Freedom Tower's octagonal shape was inspired by the Cathedral Tower at Sevilla Cathedral in Seville, Spain.
· The Fiesta San Antonio grew out of the Battle of the Flowers (1891). A group of women adorned horse-drawn carriages, paraded in front of the Alamo, and bombarded each other with flower blossoms—as homage to the heroes of the Alamo and San Jacinto.

Expanded Information
· Hispanic Heritage Month begins on the anniversary of independence of five Latin American countries—Costa Rica, El Salvador, Guatemala, Honduras, and Nicaragua.
· La Villita is home to a thriving arts and crafts community.

Video Character Guide
Alicia and Sandra are friends from the U.S. Alicia lives in Miami. She likes to ride her bike, play soccer, and skateboard.

Bridging Cultures

Heritage Language Learners

Support What They Know If there are students from Spanish-speaking countries in class, ask them to talk about where their families are from. Encourage them to share some traditions they celebrate in their countries, typical foods, famous people, and so forth.

English Learners

Build Background Encourage students to think about other cities with large Latino communities (New York, El Paso) and list them on the board. Organize students into groups and have them select a city that interests them. Ask them to create an almanac similar to the one on p. 28, based on the information they find about their communities.

Lesson Overview

Culture at a Glance ✣

Topic & Activity	Essential Question
Beaches in Florida pp. 30–31	Where do teenagers go during their free time in Florida?
Youth awards show p. 43	How have Latino performers and athletes affected popular culture in the United States?
Art in Miami p. 45	How would being Cuban American influence an artist's work?
What teens like to do pp. 52–53	What are the favorite activities of teens in a dual-language school in Florida?
Culture review p. 57	What Latino cultural elements exist in San Antonio and Miami?

COMPARISON COUNTRIES  Estados Unidos Colombia México

Practice at a Glance ✣

	Objective	Activity & Skill
Vocabulary	Activities	1: Reading/Writing; 3: Listening/Reading; 4: Speaking; 5: Writing/Speaking 15: Writing; 16: Speaking; 17: Speaking/Writing; 18: Listening/Writing; 20: Listening/Reading; 21: Listening/Reading; 22: Speaking; 23: Reading/Listening/Speaking; 24: Writing; Repaso 1: Listening; Repaso 2: Writing; Repaso 4: Writing
	Foods and beverages	2: Speaking/Writing; 23: Reading/Listening/Speaking; Repaso 1: Listening; Repaso 2: Writing
Grammar	Subject pronouns and **ser**	6: Writing; 7: Reading/Writing; 8: Speaking/Writing; 9: Writing; 10: Speaking; 11: Writing; 12: Listening/Reading; 13: Reading/Speaking; 14: Speaking; 20: Listening/Reading; 22: Speaking; 24: Writing; Repaso 1: Listening; Repaso 3: Writing
	de to describe where you are from	7: Reading/Writing; 8: Speaking/Writing; 9: Writing; 10: Speaking; 11: Writing; 12: Listening/Reading; 13: Reading/Speaking; 14: Speaking; 20: Listening/Reading; 22: Speaking; 24: Writing; Repaso 1: Listening; Repaso 3: Writing
	gustar with an infinitive	2: Speaking/Writing; 3: Listening/Reading; 4: Speaking; 5: Writing/Speaking; 15: Writing; 16: Speaking; 17: Speaking/Writing; 18: Listening/Writing; 19: Speaking; 20: Listening/Reading; 21: Listening/Reading; 22: Speaking; 23: Reading/Listening/Speaking; 24: Writing; Repaso 1: Listening; Repaso 2: Writing; Repaso 4: Writing
Communication	Talk about activities	4: Speaking; 5: Writing/Speaking; 16: Speaking; 17: Speaking/Writing; 19: Speaking; 22: Speaking; 23: Reading/Listening/Speaking; 24: Writing; Repaso 2: Writing; Repaso 4: Writing
	Tell where you are from	10: Speaking; 13: Reading/Speaking; 14: Speaking; 22: Speaking; 23: Reading/Listening/Speaking; 24: Writing; Repaso 3: Writing
	Say what you like and don't like to do	2: Speaking/Writing; 4: Speaking; 5: Writing/Speaking; 16: Speaking; 19: Speaking; 22: Speaking; 23: Reading/Listening/Speaking; 24: Writing; Repaso 2: Writing
	Pronunciation: The letters **p** and **t**	*Pronunciación: Las letras **p** y **t**,* p. 47: Listening/Speaking
Recycle	Weather expressions	4: Speaking

The following activities are recorded in the Audio Program for *¡Avancemos!*

- **¡A responder!** *page 34*
- **18: Las actividades** *page 47*
- **23: Integración** *page 50*
- **Repaso de la lección** *page 56*
  - **1: Listen and understand**

¡A responder! TXT CD 1 track 24

1. beber
2. descansar
3. hablar por teléfono
4. comer
5. tocar la guitarra
6. leer un libro
7. jugar al fútbol
8. dibujar

18 | Las actividades TXT CD 1 track 28

Hola. Me llamo Mariana. Hoy es sábado. A mis amigos Jorge y Federico y a mí nos gusta descansar. A Federico le gusta pasear pero a Jorge no. Me gusta pasear pero hoy no hace sol. Me gusta más tocar la guitarra. A ellos les gusta escuchar música pero no les gusta tocar la guitarra. A los dos les gusta mirar la televisión. A mí no me gusta mirar la televisión.

23 | Integración TXT CD 1 tracks 30, 31

¡Hola, Vanessa! Me llamo Carmen. Soy de Carolina, Puerto Rico. Después de las clases, me gusta practicar deportes, hacer la tarea o estudiar. No me gusta escuchar música. Y no me gusta mirar la televisión. Los sábados y domingos me gusta pasar un rato con los amigos. Me gusta comer pizza o papas fritas y descansar.

Repaso de la lección TXT CD 1 track 33

1 Listen and understand

Pablo: Me llamo Pablo. Soy de Miami. Después de las clases me gusta andar en patineta y escuchar música. Sara es de Puerto Rico. Sara, ¿qué te gusta hacer después de las clases? ¿Te gusta andar en patineta y escuchar música?

Sara: ¿Andar en patineta? No, no me gusta andar en patineta. Pero me gusta escuchar música. También me gusta comer frutas.

Pablo: ¡Uy! ¡No me gusta comer frutas! Me gusta comer helado.

Sara: A mí también. A nosotros nos gusta comer helado. Mmmmmm...

Complete Resource List

On your desktop

Everything you need to ...

Plan

easyPlanner
DVD-ROM

All resources including audio and video

Present

POWER PRESENTATIONS

Ready-made PowerPoint™ presentations with

Animated Grammar

Assess

 McDOUGAL LITTELL ASSESSMENT SYSTEM
ONLINE

✓ Assess, score, prescribe, and remediate online

✓ Create customized tests with the Test Generator CD-ROM

✓ Individualized Assessment for on-level, modified, pre-AP, and heritage language learners

Print

Plan	Present	Practice	Assess
URB 1 • Video Scripts pp. 97–98 • Family Letter p. 123 • Absent Student Copymasters pp. 125–132 **Lesson Plans** p. 21 **Best Practices Toolkit**	**URB 1** • Video Activities pp. 79–86 **TPRS** pp. 1–7	• *Cuaderno* pp. 1–23 • *Cuaderno para hispanohablantes* pp. 1–23 • *Lecturas para todos* pp. 2–6 • *Lecturas para hispanohablantes* • *¡AvanzaCómics! SuperBruno y Nati*, Episodio 1 **URB 1** • Practice Games pp. 57–64 • Audio Scripts pp. 104–107 • Map/Culture Activities pp. 113–114 • Fine Art Activities pp. 117–118	**URB 1** • Did you get it? Reteaching and Practice Copymasters pp. 29–38

Unit Transparency Book 1

Culture	Presentation and Practice	Classroom Management
• Atlas Maps 1–6 • U.S. Map 7 • Fine Art Transparencies 8, 9	• Vocabulary Transparencies 12, 13 • Grammar Presentation Transparencies 16, 17	• Warm Up Transparencies 26–29 **MSRB** • Student Book Answer Transparencies 28–31

Audio and Video

Audio	Video

• Student Book Audio CD 1 Tracks 23–33
• Workbook Audio CD 1 Tracks 1–10
• Heritage Learners Audio CD 1 Tracks 1–4, CD 3 Tracks 3–4
• Assessment Audio CD 1 Tracks 3–4
• *Lecturas para todos* Audio CD 1 Track 1, CD 2 Tracks 1–6
• *Música del mundo hispano*
• Sing-along Audio CD
	• Vocabulary Video DVD 1
	• *Telehistoria* DVD 1
	    Escena 1
	    Escena 2
	    Escena 3
	    Completa

Online and CD-ROM Resources

Student	Teacher
Available online and on CD-ROM: • eEdition • @HomeTutor • Animated Grammar **Available online:** • *Cultura Interactiva* • Culture Links • WebQuests • Flashcards • Conjuguemos.com • Review Games • Self-check Quiz	**Available online and on CD-ROM:** **EasyPlanner CD-ROM resources:** • Learning Scenarios • Conversation Cards • Family Letters in Spanish • Family Letters in Creole **Available online:** • McDougal Littell Assessment System **Available on CD-ROM:** • Test Generator • Power Presentation

Differentiated Assessment

On-level	Modified	Pre-AP	Heritage Learners
• Vocabulary Recognition Quiz p. 11 • Vocabulary Production Quiz p. 12 • Grammar Quizzes pp. 13–14 • Culture Quiz p. 15 • On-level Lesson Test pp.16–22	• Modified Lesson Test pp. 11–17	• Pre-AP Lesson Test pp. 11–17	• Heritage Learners Lesson Test pp. 17–23

Core Pacing Guide

50 Minute (9 Day)

	Objectives/Focus	Teach	Practice	Assess/HW Options
DAY 1	**Culture:** Learn about Hispanic culture in the U.S. **Vocabulary:** activities, what you like to do • Warm Up OHT 26 5 min	Unit Opener pp. 28–29 Lesson Opener pp. 30–31 **Presentación de vocabulario** pp. 32–34 • Read A–F • View video DVD 1 • Play audio TXT CD 1 track 23 • *¡A responder!* TXT CD 1 track 24 25 min	Lesson opener pp. 30–31 **Práctica de vocabulario** p. 35 • Acts. 1, 2 15 min	**Assess:** *Para y piensa* p. 35 5 min **Homework:** *Cuaderno* pp. 1–3 @HomeTutor
DAY 2	**Communication:** talking about activities, saying what you like to do • Warm Up OHT 26 • Check Homework 5 min	**Vocabulario en contexto** pp. 36–37 • *Telehistoria escena I* DVD 1 20 min	**Vocabulario en contexto** pp. 36–37 • Act. 3 TXT CD 1 track 25 • Acts. 4, 5 20 min	**Assess:** *Para y piensa* p. 37 5 min **Homework:** *Cuaderno* pp. 1–3 @HomeTutor
DAY 3	**Grammar:** subject pronouns, **ser**, **ser de** • Warm Up OHT 27 • Check Homework 5 min	**Presentación de gramática** p. 38 • Subject pronouns and **ser** **Práctica de gramática** pp. 39–41 • *Nota gramatical:* **ser de** 20 min	**Práctica de gramática** pp. 39–41 • Acts. 6, 7, 8, 9, 10, 11 20 min	**Assess:** *Para y piensa* p. 41 5 min **Homework:** *Cuaderno* pp. 4–6 @HomeTutor
DAY 4	**Communication:** using **ser de** to talk about where people are from • Warm Up OHT 27 • Check Homework 5 min	**Gramática en contexto** pp. 42–43 • *Telehistoria escena 2* DVD 1 15 min	**Gramática en contexto** pp. 42–43 • Act. 12 TXT CD 1 track 26 • Acts. 13, 14 25 min	**Assess:** *Para y piensa* p. 43 5 min **Homework:** *Cuaderno* pp. 4–6 @HomeTutor
DAY 5	**Grammar:** using **gustar** to talk about what people like to do • Warm Up OHT 28 • Check Homework 5 min	**Presentación de gramática** p. 44 • **Gustar** with an infinitive **Práctica de gramática** pp. 45–47 • *Pronunciación* TXT CD 1 track 27 **Culture:** *El arte de Miami* 15 min	**Práctica de gramática** pp. 45–47 • Acts. 15, 16, 17, 19 • Act 18 TXT CD 1 track 28 25 min	**Assess:** *Para y piensa* p. 47 5 min **Homework:** *Cuaderno* pp. 7–9 @HomeTutor
DAY 6	**Communication:** Culmination: what you like to do, **ser**, **ser de**, **gustar** • Warm Up OHT 28 • Check Homework 5 min	**Todo junto** pp. 48–50 • *Escenas 1, 2: Resumen* • *Telehistoria completa* DVD 1 15 min	**Todo junto** pp. 48–50 • Acts. 20, 21 TXT CD 1 tracks 25, 26, 29 • Act. 23 TXT CD 1 tracks 30, 31 • Acts. 22, 24 25 min	**Assess:** *Para y piensa* p. 50 5 min **Homework:** *Cuaderno* pp. 10–11 @HomeTutor
DAY 7	**Reading:** What do you like to do? **Connections:** Geography • Warm Up OHT 29 • Check Homework 5 min	**Lectura** pp. 52–53 • *¿Qué te gusta hacer?* TXT CD 1 track 32 **Conexiones** p. 54 • *La geografía* 20 min	**Lectura** pp. 52–53 • *¿Qué te gusta hacer?* **Conexiones** p. 54 • *Proyectos* 1, 2, 3 20 min	**Assess:** *Para y piensa* p. 53 5 min **Homework:** *Cuaderno* pp. 15–17 @HomeTutor
DAY 8	**Review:** Lesson review • Warm Up OHT 29 • Check Homework 5 min	**Repaso de la lección** pp. 56–57 15 min	**Repaso de la lección** pp. 56–57 • Act. 1 TXT CD 1 track 33 • Acts. 2, 3, 4, 5 20 min	**Assess:** *Repaso de la lección* pp. 56–57 10 min **Homework:** *En resumen* p. 55; *Cuaderno* pp. 12–14, 18–23 (optional) Review Games Online @HomeTutor
DAY 9	**Assessment**			**Assess:** Lesson 1 test 50 min

	Objectives/Focus	Teach	Practice	Assess/HW Options
DAY 1	**Culture:** learn about Hispanic culture in the U.S. **Vocabulary:** activities, what you like to do • Warm Up OHT 26 **5 min**	Unit Opener pp. 28–29 Lesson Opener pp. 30–31 **Presentación de vocabulario pp. 32–34** • Read A–F • View video DVD 1 • Play Audio TXT CD 1 track 23 • *¡A responder!* TXT CD 1 track 24 **20 min**	Lesson Opener pp. 30–31 **Práctica de vocabulario p. 35** • Acts. 1, 2 **20 min**	**Assess:** *Para y piensa* p. 35 **5 min** @HomeTutor
	Communication: talking about activities, saying what you like to do **5 min**	**Vocabulario en contexto** pp. 36–37 • *Telehistoria escena I* DVD 1 **15 min**	**Vocabulario en contexto** pp. 36–37 • Act. 3 TXT CD 1 track 25 • Acts. 4, 5 **15 min**	Assess: *Para y piensa* p. 37 **5 min** **Homework:** *Cuaderno* pp. 1–3 @HomeTutor
DAY 2	**Grammar:** subject pronouns **ser, ser de** • Warm Up OHT 27 • Check Homework **5 min**	**Presentación de gramática p. 38** • Subject pronouns and **ser** **Práctica de gramática pp. 39–41** • *Nota gramatical:* **ser de** **20 min**	**Práctica de gramática pp. 39–41** • Acts. 6, 7, 8, 9, 10, 11 **15 min**	Assess: *Para y piensa* p. 41 **5 min**
	Communication: using **ser de** to talk about where people are from **5 min**	**Gramática en contexto** pp. 42–43 • *Telehistoria escena 2* DVD 1 **20 min**	**Gramática en contexto** pp. 42–43 • Act. 12 TXT CD 1 track 26 • Acts. 13, 14 **15 min**	**Assess:** *Para y piensa* p. 43 **5 min** **Homework:** *Cuaderno* pp. 4–6 @HomeTutor
DAY 3	**Grammar:** using **gustar** to talk about what people like to do • Warm Up OHT 28 • Check Homework **5 min**	**Presentación de gramática p. 44** • **Gustar** with an infinitive **Práctica de gramática pp. 45–47** • *Pronunciación* TXT CD 1 track 27 **Culture:** *El arte de Miami* **15 min**	**Práctica de gramática pp. 45–47** • Acts. 15, 16, 17, 19 • Act. 18 TXT CD 1 track 28 **20 min**	**Assess:** *Para y piensa* p. 47 **5 min**
	Communication: Culmination: what you like to do, **ser, ser de, gustar** **5 min**	**Todo junto** pp. 48–50 • *Escenas 1, 2: Resumen* • *Telehistoria completa* DVD 1 **10 min**	**Todo junto** pp. 48–50 • Acts. 20, 21 TXT CD 1 tracks 25, 26, 29 • Act. 23 TXT CD 1 tracks 30, 31 • Acts. 22, 24 **25 min**	Assess: *Para y piensa* p. 50 **5 min** **Homework:** *Cuaderno* pp. 7–11 @HomeTutor
DAY 4	**Reading:** What do you like to do? • Warm Up OHT 29 • Check Homework **5 min**	**Lectura** pp. 52–53 • *¿Qué te gusta hacer?* TXT CD 1 track 32 **15 min**	**Lectura** pp. 52–53 • *¿Qué te gusta hacer?* **15 min**	**Assess:** *Para y piensa* p. 53 **5 min**
	Review: Lesson review **5 min**	**Repaso de la lección** pp. 56–57 **15 min**	**Repaso de la lección** pp. 56–57 • Act. 1 TXT CD 1 track 33 • Acts. 2, 3, 4, 5 **25 min**	**Assess:** *Repaso de la lección* pp. 56–57 **5 min** **Homework:** *En resumen* p. 55; *Cuaderno* p. 12–23 (optional) Review Games Online @HomeTutor
DAY 5	**Assessment**			**Assess:** Lesson 1 test **45 min**
	Connections: Geography **5 min**	**Conexiones** p. 54 • *La geografía* **10 min**	**Conexiones** p. 54 • *Proyectos* 1, 2, 3 **30 min**	

¡AVANZA! Objectives

· Introduce lesson theme: **¿Qué te gusta hacer?**
· **Culture:** Compare everyday activities.

Presentation Strategies

· Introduce characters' names: Alicia, Teresa, Miguel, Sandra.
· Ask students to make a list of their favorite activities and foods.
· Ask students to talk about beaches they know.

STANDARDS

2.1 Practices and perspectives
4.2 Compare cultures

Warm Up   UTB 1 Transparency 26

Numbers Write the names of the following numbers:

0. _____		6. _____
1. _____		7. _____
2. _____		8. _____
3. _____		9. _____
4. _____		10. _____
5. _____		

Answers: 0. cero; 1. uno; 2. dos; 3. tres; 4. cuatro; 5. cinco; 6. seis; 7. siete; 8. ocho; 9. nueve; 10 diez

Comparación cultural

Exploring the Theme

Ask the following:
1. How might the activities the students enjoy in the photo differ from activities you enjoy?
2. Which activities do you think they prefer?
3. Which climate do you think they prefer? Why?
4. What are some kinds of activities that are more easily done in their preferred climate?

¿Qué ves? Possible answers include:
· It is sunny and warm.
· They are friends.
· The boy likes to play soccer and the girl likes to draw.

30

UNIDAD 1
Estados Unidos

Lección 1

Tema:
¿Qué te gusta hacer?

¡AVANZA! **In this lesson you will learn to**
· talk about activities
· tell where you are from
· say what you like and don't like to do

using
· subject pronouns and **ser**
· **de** to describe where you are from
· **gustar** with an infinitive

♻ *¿Recuerdas?*
· weather expressions

Comparación cultural

In this lesson you will learn about
· *Los Premios Juventud,* an awards show in Miami
· Cuban-American artist Xavier Cortada
· free-time activities of students at a Florida school

Compara con tu mundo

This group of teenagers is spending the day at a beach. In southern Florida, beaches are open year-round and are popular places to do many different activities. *Where do you like to go with your friends in your free time? What do you like to do?*

¿Qué ves?

Mira la foto

What is the weather like?

Do you think that these teenagers are friends?

What activities do they like to do?

Differentiating Instruction

Multiple Intelligences

Visual Learners After viewing and discussing the opening photo, ask students to illustrate their ideal vacation spot—real or imaginary. Students can create a drawing or a collage by cutting pictures from magazines. Be sure their drawing illustrates people engaged in some of their favorite activities. Have them share their work with the class.

Pre-AP

Draw Conclusions Using a map, point out the city of Miami. Ask students to think about why Miami is so greatly influenced by Latin culture. Why does its location and neighbors make this a logical conclusion? Point out the Spanish-speaking countries that are close to Miami, such as Cuba, the Dominican Republic, and so on.

Online SPANISH CLASSZONE.COM

Featuring...	And more...
Cultura INTERACTIVA	• Get Help Online
	• Interactive Flashcards
Animated Grammar	• Review Games
	• WebQuest
@HomeTutor	• Self-Check Quiz

Una playa de Miami Beach
Miami Beach, Florida

Estados Unidos
treinta y uno **31**

Online SPANISH CLASSZONE.COM

WebQuest Provides step-by-step guidance for your students to help them explore this unit's theme and location online. Students are given a task and a set or pre-approved links to conduct research, answer questions, and submit their findings to the class.

Featuring...	And more...
Cultura INTERACTIVA	• Get Help Online
	• Interactive Flashcards
Animated Grammar	• Review Games
	• WebQuest
@HomeTutor	• Self-Check Quiz

Using the Photo

Location Information

Miami Beach The photo shows Miami Beach, Florida; downtown Miami can be seen in the background. Miami's 35-mile stretch of sand and sea offers ample space for activities such as jogging, surfing, kite flying, volleyball and, of course, swimming.

Expanded Information

South Beach, located at the southern end of Miami Beach, has a mix of first-class hotels, youth hostels, cafés, and trendy Latin and Caribbean restaurants.

Population Since the 2000 U.S. Census figures for Miami-Dade County, non–Cuban Hispanics have outnumbered the more than 650,000 people of Cuban descent in Miami-Dade. The Mexican population was up by 65 percent and the Colombian population grew 31 percent.

Long-term Retention
Interest Inventory

If you need more information on what students like to do after school, ask them now and list their responses on the board. Read the list aloud and have students raise their hands to indicate their favorite things. Record their responses so that students with similar interests can work together.

Differentiating Instruction

Heritage Language Learners

Expand and Elaborate Ask students to share what they know about the city of Miami. Students might mention:
· Miami is the most populous city in the state of Florida.
· Nearly 60 percent of Miami residents are of Latin origin.
· Miami is the only city in the United States founded by a woman, Julia Tuttle.

Multiple Intelligences

Naturalist Have students study the photo and write down the elements that indicate what kind of physical environment is shown (clothing, sand, ocean, etc.). Students can then compare and contrast the area pictured with their local area.

¡AVANZA! Objective

- Present vocabulary about daily activities, snack foods, and likes and dislikes.

Core Resources

- Video Program: DVD 1
- Audio Program: TXT CD 1, track 23

Presentation Strategies

- Draw students' attention to the ¡Avanza! which shows objectives that begin each section, and the Para y piensa, which ends each section and shows what students will be able to do at the end of each section.
- Play the audio as students read A–D.
- Show the video.

STANDARD

1.2 Understand language

Communication

Interpersonal Mode

Have student pairs identify who likes to do the activities depicted on p. 32. One student says **Me gusta hablar por teléfono.** The other students responds: **Miguel.** Then have students exchange roles.

Comparisons

English Language Connection

Cognates are words in Spanish that resemble English. **Teléfono,** for example, is a cognate of the English word *telephone*. Scan the three pages for other cognates. Possible answers include: **guitarra** = *guitar;* **música** = *music.*

Presentación de VOCABULARIO

¡AVANZA! **Goal:** Learn about what Alicia and her friends like to do. Then use what you have learned to talk about activities. *Actividades 1–2*

VIDEO DVD

AUDIO

A ¡Hola! Me llamo Teresa. Después de las clases, me gusta pasar un rato con los amigos. Me gusta escuchar música o tocar la guitarra.

hablar por teléfono

escuchar música

leer un libro

Miguel   **Teresa**   **Alicia**

dibujar

tocar la guitarra

32 Unidad 1 Estados Unidos
treinta y dos

Differentiating Instruction

Inclusion

Multisensory Input/Output Write the activities from pp. 32–34 on the board, modeling pronunciation, and ask students to repeat. Ask students to indicate, by a show of hands, which is their favorite. Record preferences, and ask students to draw pictures of their two or three favorite activities.

Slower-paced Learners

Yes/No Questions Ask students yes/no questions to help reinforce new vocabulary. Use gestures to support the meaning of each question. **¿Te gusta dibujar? ¿Te gusta escuchar música?** Instruct students to point to the picture of the activity in each question and then answer **sí** or **no.**

B ¡Hola! Me llamo Miguel. A mí me gusta **hablar por teléfono, dibujar** y **estudiar.** Me gusta **pasear,** pero me gusta **más correr.** A ti, ¿qué te gusta hacer?

estudiar

pasear

correr

C ¡Hola! Me llamo Alicia. A mí me gusta **montar en bicicleta** y **jugar al fútbol.** También me gusta **andar en patineta.**

montar en bicicleta

jugar al fútbol

andar en patineta

D Hoy hace calor en Miami. **Antes de practicar deportes** me gusta **comprar agua.**

comprar

las papas fritas

la fruta

el agua

la pizza

el refresco

el helado

las galletas

Continuará...

TEACHER to TEACHER
Matt Cavanaugh
Rye, New York

Tips for Presenting Vocabulary

I choose five to eight words from the vocabulary list that are most easily illustrated by dramatic gestures. I display the target words on the board and point to each one. The class repeats them several times as they imitate my gestures. I repeat the drill, mixing up the order of the words and gradually erasing the words as students master them. The presentation is complete when students can produce the words upon seeing the gestures as easily as they can act out their meanings when they hear or read them.

Communication
Common Error Alert

· In Spanish, there is more than one verb that means *to play*. **Jugar** means *to play a game,* and **tocar** means *to play an instrument.*
· Point out that although the noun **agua** is feminine, it's always preceded by the masculine article **el**.

Communication
Regionalisms

Explain to students that there are regional variations for some of the words and phrases on these pages, for example: **patineta** (Argentina), **monopatín** (México); **el refresco** (México), **la gaseosa** (España); **el jugo** (Latinoamérica), **el zumo** (España).

Communication

TPR Activity

After modeling the terms below, select students to act out the following activities as you say them aloud:
· hablar por teléfono   · dibujar
· leer un libro   · andar en patineta
· tocar la guitarra   · jugar al fútbol

Differentiating Instruction

Heritage Language Learners

Support What They Know Ask students to expand on each of the activities, according to their cultural background. For example: **Me gusta escuchar merengue. Me gusta tocar la marimba. Me gusta comprar empanadas.**

Inclusion

Alphabetic/Phonetic Awareness Have students divide a piece of paper into two columns, **Acciones** and **Objetos.** Students should list the new vocabulary words on pp. 32–34 in the appropriate column. Point out phonetic differences between Spanish and English, such as the silent **h** at the beginning of **helado** and **hablar,** or the pronunciation of the **ll** in **galletas.**

Objectives
· Present vocabulary about daily activities.
· Check for recognition.

Core Resources
· Video Program: DVD 1
· Audio Program: TXT CD 1, tracks 23, 24

Presentation Strategies
· Play the audio as students read E–F.
· Show the video.

 STANDARD
1.2 Understand language

 Communication
Group Work

Have students work in groups to brainstorm "active" and "passive" activities and write them under the headings **actividades activas** and **actividades pasivas.** Have them present their lists to the class.

Communication
Interpersonal Mode

Ask students to create a short dialogue based on the photo showing the family eating and drinking. Ask them to talk about the foods they like to eat and beverages they like to drink. For example: **¿Te gusta preparar la comida? Sí, me gusta preparar la comida. ¿Qué te gusta comer? Me gusta comer fruta. También me gusta comer pizza. ¿Qué te gusta beber? Me gusta beber jugo pero no me gusta beber agua.**

 Answers MRSB Transparency 28

¡A responder! Audio Script, TE p. 29b
Students should act out the following:

1. to drink
2. to rest
3. to talk on the phone
4. to eat
5. to play the guitar
6. to read a book
7. to play soccer
8. to draw

34

E Me gusta **beber** agua o **jugo** pero no me gusta beber **refrescos.**

preparar la comida
comer
beber
el jugo

Más vocabulario
la actividad *activity*
alquilar un DVD *to rent a DVD*
aprender el español
  to learn Spanish
la escuela *school*
hacer la tarea *to do homework*
Expansión de vocabulario p. R2

F No me gusta **trabajar** los sábados y domingos. Me gusta **escribir correos electrónicos** y **descansar.** También me gusta **mirar la televisión.** ¿Te gusta pasar un rato con los amigos?

escribir correos electrónicos

descansar
mirar la televisión

¡A responder! Escuchar
Listen to the list of activities. As you listen, act out the activities.

@HomeTutor VideoPlus
Interactive Flashcards
ClassZone.com

Differentiating Instruction

Multiple Intelligences
Logical/Mathematical Create a Venn diagram on the board. Label one circle "Indoors" and the other "Outdoors." Have students brainstorm a list based on the activities on pp. 32–34. Volunteers come to the board and place each activity in the appropriate circle. There might be overlapping activities.

Inclusion
Frequent Review/Repetition Provide frequent practice of new vocabulary by writing on the board the following:
¿Qué te gusta hacer? Me gusta... ¿Qué no te gusta hacer? No me gusta... Have student pairs take turns asking and answering each other's questions. Encourage them to expand their answers. For example: **¿Qué no te gusta hacer? No me gusta trabajar los domingos.**

Práctica de VOCABULARIO

1 | El sábado

Leer
Escribir

Miguel, Teresa, and Alicia are talking about the activities they like to do. Complete the conversation with the appropriate words.

un libro

la tarea

deportes

bicicleta

un DVD

música

la comida

Alicia: Miguel, ¿te gusta escuchar __1.__ los sábados?

Miguel: Sí, pero me gusta más practicar __2.__ .
Teresa, ¿te gusta montar en __3.__ ?

Teresa: No, no me gusta. Me gusta más leer __4.__ .

Alicia: Teresa, ¿te gusta hacer __5.__ los sábados?

Teresa: ¿Los sábados? No, sólo me gusta preparar __6.__ , alquilar __7.__ y descansar.

> **Expansión:**
> Teacher Edition Only
> Ask students to write a dialogue based on the conversation in Activity 1.

2 | ¿Te gusta?

Hablar
Escribir

Tell whether you like or don't like to eat or drink these foods and beverages.

modelo: beber
(No) Me gusta beber refrescos.

1. comer

2. beber

3. comer

4. comer

5. beber

6. comer

> **Expansión:**
> Teacher Edition Only
> Ask students to add two more items and tell whether they like or don't like to eat or drink them.

Más práctica   Cuaderno *pp. 1–3*   Cuaderno para hispanohablantes *pp. 1–4*

PARA Y PIENSA

Did you get it?
1. Tell someone that you like to listen to music.   Me gusta _____.
2. Ask a friend if he or she likes to do homework.   ¿Te gusta _____?

Get Help Online
ClassZone.com

Lección 1
treinta y cinco   **35**

Differentiating Instruction

Slower-paced Learners

Sentence Completion Before doing Activity 1, read aloud the dialogue. Invite volunteers to play the parts of Alicia, Miguel, and Teresa. As students read each sentence aloud, model gestures to support key vocabulary (e.g., pantomime putting on headphones for the word **escuchar**). Instruct students to point to the word in the list that they believe goes in each blank.

Heritage Language Learners

Support What They Know Have students share any additional information describing the foods presented in Activity 2. For example, someone from the Dominican Republic might call French fries something different than someone from Spain would. Generate a list on the board to compare similarities and differences.

Objectives
· Practice vocabulary: daily activities, snack foods, likes and dislikes.
· State preferences about favorite activities.

Core Resource
· *Cuaderno*, pp. 1–3

Practice Sequence
· **Activity 1:** Vocabulary recognition: everyday activities, stating preferences
· **Activity 2:** Vocabulary production: stating preferences

 STANDARDS
1.2 Understand language, Act. 1
1.3 Present information, Acts. 1–2, PYP

Long-term Retention

Personalize It

Use Expansión de vocabulario on p. R2. Encourage students to list words and phrases used for after-school activities. Have them use their list to answer questions about the activities they like and dislike. Ask students: **¿Qué te gusta?** Encourage them to give complete answers: **Me gusta escuchar música.**

✓ **Ongoing Assessment**

@HomeTutor
More Practice
ClassZone.com

PARA Y PIENSA   **Quick Check** These activities are self-checks. If students have trouble completing them, they can practice online. For additional practice, use Reteaching & Practice Copymasters URB 1 pp. 29, 30.

 Answers   MSRB Transparency 28

Activity 1
1. música   **4.** un libro   **6.** la comida
2. deportes   **5.** la tarea   **7.** un DVD
3. bicicleta

Activity 2   Answers will vary. Sample answers include:
1. (No) Me gusta comer galletas.
2. (No) Me gusta beber jugo.
3. (No) Me gusta comer helado.
4. (No) Me gusta comer papas fritas.
5. (No) Me gusta beber agua.
6. (No) Me gusta comer fruta.

Para y piensa
1. escuchar música
2. hacer la tarea

35

¡AVANZA! Objectives

- Understand activity vocabulary in context.
- Practice using vocabulary in context.
- Recycle: weather expressions.
- Practice using **gustar** + infinitive.

Core Resources

- Video Program: DVD 1
- Audio Program: TXT CD 1, track 25

Practice Sequence

- **Activity 3:** Telehistoria comprehension
- **Activity 4:** Vocabulary production: **gustar**; Recycle: weather expressions
- **Activity 5:** Vocabulary production: **gustar**

Presentation Strategies

- Draw students' attention to the ¡Avanza!
- Ask students to predict Alicia and Sandra's conversation.
- Show the video and/or play the audio.

STANDARDS

1.1 Engage in conversation, Acts. 4–5
1.2 Understand language, Act. 3
1.3 Present information, Acts. 3–5; PYP

Warm Up UTB 1 Transparency 26

Vocabulary Choose a verb to complete each sentence: **mirar, escribir, escuchar, pasar, montar.**

1. Me gusta _____ música.
2. A mí me gusta _____ en bicicleta.
3. Los sábados me gusta _____ la televisión.
4. Después de las clases me gusta _____ un rato con los amigos.
5. No me gusta _____ correos electrónicos.

Answers: 1. escuchar; 2. montar; 3. mirar; 4. pasar; 5. escribir

Video Summary

@HomeTutor VideoPlus ClassZone.com

Alicia and Sandra, friends who met through playing soccer, talk about what they like to do in their free time. Alicia's father listens to her side of the conversation, and is very surprised to hear her say that she doesn't like to talk on the phone.

36

VOCABULARIO *en contexto*

Goal: Listen to the words Alicia and Sandra use to talk about activities. Then practice what you have heard to talk about the activities you and others like to do. *Actividades 3–5*

♻ *¿Recuerdas?* Weather expressions p. 20

Telehistoria escena 1

@HomeTutor VideoPlus
ClassZone.com

STRATEGIES

Cuando lees

Search for clues Look for clues in the picture before starting to read. Who's in the photos? What are they doing?

Cuando escuchas

Listen for intonation The way people speak, not just what they say, often reflects how they feel. Listen for Alicia's intonation. How does she feel about the activities mentioned?

VIDEO
DVD

AUDIO

Sandra

Alicia

Papá

Alicia: *(on phone, to Sandra, a friend in San Antonio, Texas)* En Miami, hace calor. ¿Te gusta andar en patineta?

Sandra: No, me gusta más pasear o montar en bicicleta. Los sábados me gusta hacer la tarea.

Alicia: ¿Sí? Los sábados me gusta pasar un rato con amigos... ¡y dibujar! Y los domingos, ¡jugar al fútbol! Los viernes me gusta alquilar un DVD y comer pizza.

Sandra: Sí, sí. Mmm. Me gusta comer pizza y hablar por teléfono.

Alicia: ¿Hablar por teléfono? No me gusta hablar por teléfono. *(Father gives a look of disbelief.)*

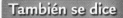

También se dice

Miami To talk about riding bicycles, Sandra uses the phrase **montar en bicicleta**. In other Spanish-speaking countries you might hear:
- **muchos países** **andar en bicicleta**

Continuará... p. 42

Unidad 1 Estados Unidos
36 treinta y seis

Differentiating Instruction

Inclusion

Clear Structure Write phrases from the Telehistoria on individual sentence strips (e.g., **Me gusta montar en bicicleta.**). Label one half of the board Alicia, and the other Sandra. Have students read each sentence aloud and post it under the name of the character who said it. If both girls enjoy an activity, they should post the sentence in the center.

Heritage Language Learners

Increase Accuracy Have student pairs create their own short dialogue, describing what they like to do in their free time. They should use the Telehistoria as a model. Invite volunteers to act out their conversations in front of the class after they have had a chance to practice.

3 | A Alicia y a Sandra les gusta... *Comprensión del episodio*

Escuchar Leer

Tell if what Alicia and Sandra say is true or false. Correct the false statements.

modelo: Alicia: Los viernes no me gusta comer pizza.
Falso. Los viernes me gusta comer pizza.

1. **Alicia:** Llueve en Miami.
2. **Sandra:** Me gusta correr los sábados.
3. **Alicia:** Me gusta pasar un rato con los amigos.
4. **Sandra:** Me gusta hacer la tarea los domingos.
5. **Alicia:** Los sábados me gusta alquilar un DVD.
6. **Sandra:** Me gusta hablar por teléfono.

Expansión: Teacher Edition Only

Have students write an activity they like to do for each day of the week.

---

4 | ¡Hace frío! ♻ *¿Recuerdas?* Weather expressions p. 20

Hablar

Tell a partner what you like to do in each situation.

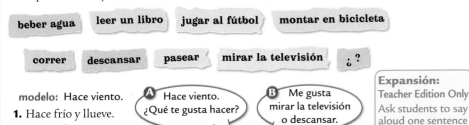

beber agua   leer un libro   jugar al fútbol   montar en bicicleta

correr   descansar   pasear   mirar la televisión   ¿ ?

modelo: Hace viento.

Ⓐ Hace viento. ¿Qué te gusta hacer?

Ⓑ Me gusta mirar la televisión o descansar.

1. Hace frío y llueve.
2. Hace sol.
3. Hace viento y hace frío.
4. Hace calor.
5. Nieva y hace sol.
6. Llueve y hace calor.

Expansión: Teacher Edition Only

Ask students to say aloud one sentence describing what they like to do.

---

5 | ¡Me gusta!

Escribir Hablar

Write a list of your after-school activities and then compare them with other students' activities.

– escribir correos electrónicos
– practicar deportes
– dibujar
– andar en patineta

Ⓐ ¿Te gusta pasear después de las clases?

Ⓑ Sí, me gusta pasear.

Ⓒ No, me gusta pasear antes de las clases.

Expansión: Teacher Edition Only

Have students write their list of activities in order of preference.

PARA Y PIENSA

Did you get it? Fill in Alicia's sentences with the appropriate vocabulary word.

1. Me gusta _____ al fútbol.
2. ¿Te gusta escuchar _____ ?
3. También me gusta _____ pizza.

Get Help Online ClassZone.com

Differentiating Instruction

Slower-paced Learners

Memory Aids Divide the class into groups to create posters illustrating each of the weather phrases listed in Activity 4. Instruct each group to write the weather phrase in large letters and draw a picture illustrating that specific weather condition. Keep the posters displayed to assist in daily discussions of the weather.

Pre-AP

Expand and Elaborate Have students ask and answer questions regarding their activity preferences. For example, Student A may ask **¿Te gusta más practicar deportes o mirar la televisión?** and Student B may answer **Me gusta más practicar deportes.**

Long-term Retention

Personalize It

Have students write a list of the activities they like to do during the day. Then have them exchange their list with another student and compare them.

Communication

Group Work

Write on the board a list of eight after-school activities. Ask students to copy the list and rate the activities in order of preference. Have them share their preferences with the rest of the class.

✓ Ongoing Assessment

@HomeTutor More Practice ClassZone.com

PARA Y PIENSA **Dictation** Have students read aloud the sentences in the Para y piensa. Then have them write the sentences as you dictate them. For additional practice, use Reteaching & Practice Copymasters URB 1, pp. 29, 31, 38.

Answers   MSRB Transparency 28

Activity 3
1. Falso. Hace calor en Miami.
2. Falso. Me gusta pasear o montar en bicicleta.
3. Cierto.
4. Falso. Me gusta hacer la tarea los sábados.
5. Falso. Los viernes me gusta alquilar un DVD.
6. Cierto.

Activity 4 Answers will vary. Sample answers should follow this pattern:
1. **A:** Hace frío y llueve. ¿Qué te gusta hacer?
   B: Me gusta leer un libro.
2. ... Me gusta jugar al fútbol.
3. ... Me gusta descansar.
4. ... Me gusta beber agua.
5. ... Me gusta pasear.
6. ... Me gusta correr.

Activity 5 Answers will vary. Sample answers include:
A. ¿Te gusta escuchar música? **B.** Sí, me gusta escuchar música. **C.** No, me gusta más andar en patineta.

A. ¿Te gusta mirar la televisión? **B.** Sí, me gusta mirar la televisión. **C.** No, me gusta más alquilar un DVD.

Para y piensa 1. jugar; 2. música; 3. comer

¡AVANZA! **Objective**
· Present subject pronouns and **ser**.

Core Resource
· *Cuaderno,* pp. 4-6

Presentation Strategies
· Present forms and uses of subject pronouns and **ser**. Check understanding: one student gives a pronoun and another student gives the corresponding verb form.
· Discuss uses of formal and familiar forms.

STANDARDS
3.1 Knowledge of other disciplines
4.1 Compare languages

Warm Up UTB 1 Transparency 27

Vocabulary Copy the sentences onto a separate piece of paper and number them according to the sequence in which they appear in the Telehistoria. The first one is done for you.

  1. En Miami hace calor.
_____ No, me gusta más pasear o montar en bicicleta.
_____ No me gusta hablar por teléfono.
_____ ¿Te gusta andar en patineta?
_____ Me gusta comer pizza y hablar por teléfono.
_____ Los sábados me gusta hacer la tarea.
Answers: 3; 6; 2; 5; 4

Comparisons
English Grammar Connection

Unlike English, subject pronouns can often be omitted in Spanish because the verb form indicates the subject: **Soy de Venezuela.**

Presentación de GRAMÁTICA

¡AVANZA! **Goal:** Learn how to use subject pronouns and the verb **ser**. Then practice the verb forms of **ser** with **de** to talk about where you and others are from. *Actividades 6–11*

English Grammar Connection: Pronouns are words that take the place of nouns. **Subject pronouns** indicate who is being described or who does the action in a sentence.

| We are friends. | Nosotros somos amigos. |

Subject Pronouns and *ser*

Animated Grammar
ClassZone.com

Ser means *to be.* Use **ser** to identify a person or say where he or she is from. How do you use this verb with **subject pronouns**?

Here's how:

	Singular			Plural		
	yo	soy	*I am*	nosotros(as)	somos	*we are*
familiar →	tú	eres	*you are*	vosotros(as)	sois	*you are* ← *familiar*
formal →	usted	es	*you are*	ustedes	son	*you are*
	él, ella	es	*he, she is*	ellos(as)	son	*they are*

| Yo soy de Buenos Aires. | Ellas son de Venezuela. |
| *I am from Buenos Aires.* | *They are from Venezuela.* |

Singular

Use **tú** with
• a friend
• a family member
• someone younger

Use **usted** with
• a person you don't know
• someone older
• someone for whom you want to show respect

Plural

• Use **vosotros(as)** with friends, family, and younger people only in Spain.

• Use **ustedes** with people you don't know, older people, and people for whom you want to show respect in Spain; use it in Latin America with any group of people.

• Use **nosotras, vosotras,** and **ellas** when all the people you are talking about are female.

Más práctica
  Cuaderno *pp. 4–6*
  Cuaderno para hispanohablantes *pp. 5–7*

@HomeTutor
Leveled Grammar Practice
ClassZone.com

Differentiating Instruction

Slower-paced Learners

Personalize It Have students fold a piece of paper in half lengthwise. Instruct them to label one column **tú,** and the other column **usted.** Then tell students to list the names of people in their own lives whom they would address using these pronouns. Possible names in the **tú** column: friends and family members. Names in the **usted** column: teachers, principals, and other adults.

Heritage Language Learners

Regional Variations Encourage students to share a sentence describing their family's country or region of origin. **Yo soy de Venezuela. Yo soy de Madrid.** Then ask students to discuss whether they are more familiar with the pronoun **vosotros** or **ustedes.** How does this relate to their country or region of origin?

Práctica de GRAMÁTICA

6 ¿Quién?

Escribir

Write the corresponding pronoun.

 modelo: ella

 1.  2.  3.

 4.  5.  6.

Expansión:
Teacher Edition Only
Have student groups use TPR to demonstrate subject pronouns. One student says a subject pronoun, the other points to the appropriate person(s).

Nota gramatical

Use **de** with the verb **ser** to talk about where someone is from.

Daniela y Sonia **son de** Miami.   Martín **es de** Honduras.
*Daniela and Sonia **are from** Miami.*   *Martín **is from** Honduras.*

7 ¿De dónde son?

Leer
Escribir

Lucía's friends and teachers are from different places. Write the correct form of **ser** to learn where they are from.

Hola, me llamo Lucía. Mi amigo Andrés y yo **1.** de la República Dominicana. Yo **2.** de Santo Domingo y él **3.** de San Pedro de Macorís. La señora Muñoz y el señor Vázquez **4.** de Puerto Rico. Son mis maestros favoritos. Mis amigas Laura y Ana **5.** de Colombia. Laura **6.** de Bogotá y Ana **7.** de Cartagena. Y tú, ¿de dónde **8.** ?

Expansión:
Teacher Edition Only
Have students write an e-mail message telling where at least five of their teachers and friends are from.

Lección 1
treinta y nueve   **39**

Objectives
· Practice using subject pronouns.
· Use **ser de** + location to tell where someone is from.

Practice Sequence
· **Activity 6:** Controlled practice: subject pronouns
· **Activity 7:** Controlled practice: **ser de**

 STANDARD
1.3 Present information, Acts. 6-7

 Communication
Common Error Alert

Give students names, as well as combinations of names and subject pronouns. Have them provide the appropriate pronoun. For example: **Marcos y yo = nosotros**.

Comparisons
English Language Connection

Unlike English, plural subject pronouns in Spanish corresponding to *we, you* (familiar), and *they* have feminine and masculine forms: **nosotros/nosotras, vosotros/vosotras, ellos/ellas.**

Differentiating Instruction

Inclusion

Frequent Review/Repetition Before doing Activity 6, have students go through the activity orally. Instruct them to point to each picture as they say aloud the corresponding pronoun. Then reverse the activity. Say a pronoun aloud, and have students point to the corresponding picture. After students have written their answers, ask them to share their responses aloud once again.

Heritage Language Learners

Writing Skills Have students use the text in Activity 7 as a model to draft an e-mail message to a friend. Remind students to capitalize proper nouns. If students have questions regarding the spelling of place names, refer them to a dictionary or atlas. Once students have drafted their e-mails, have them exchange papers to peer-edit each other's work.

 Answers MSRB Transparency 28

Activity 6
1. ellos	**3.** yo	**5.** nosotras
2. tú	**4.** usted	**6.** ellas

Activity 7
1. somos	**4.** son	**7.** es
2. soy	**5.** son	**8.** eres
3. es	**6.** es	

Objectives
· Practice using subject pronouns.
· Use **ser + de** to tell where someone is from.

Core Resource
· *Cuaderno*, pp. 4–6

Practice Sequence
· **Activity 8:** Controlled practice: **ser de**
· **Activity 9:** Controlled practice: **ser de**
· **Activity 10:** Transitional practice: subject pronouns and **ser de**
· **Activity 11:** Open-ended practice: **ser de**

STANDARDS
1.1 Engage in conversation, Act. 10
1.3 Present information, Acts. 8–11, PYP

Long-term Retention
Recycle

Give students ten minutes to study the spelling of the names of the places mentioned on p. 40 (Uruguay, Bolivia, Chile, Paraguay, El Salvador, Nicaragua, Cuba, Venezuela, Panamá, España, México, Puerto Rico, Miami, Ecuador, and la República Dominica). Then hold a spelling bee.

Communication
Group Work

Assign seven students roles to play as students mentioned in Activity 9: Maribel, Enrique, Claudia, Pablo, Marisol, Fernando, and Mario. Ask each of these students to write the name of the character and the place of origin on a piece of paper. Ask them to stand and hold the paper in front of them so that the rest of the class can see. Going in order, ask other students to make sentences using the character's name and stating where the character is from.

Answers MSRB Transparency 28

Activity 8
1. c; **2.** d; **3.** b; **4.** e; **5.** b; **6.** a; **7.** c; **8.** d

Answers continue on p. 41.

40

---

8 | Ella es de...

Hablar
Escribir

Choose the correct form of **ser** to say where each person is from. Some forms may be used more than once.

modelo: Ella _____ de Uruguay.
Ella **es** de Uruguay.

1. Nosotros _____ de Bolivia.
2. Ellos _____ de Chile.
3. Usted _____ de Paraguay.
4. Yo _____ de El Salvador.
5. Él _____ de Nicaragua.
6. Tú _____ de Cuba.
7. Nosotras _____ de Venezuela.
8. Ustedes _____ de Panamá.

a. eres
b. es
c. somos
d. son
e. soy

Expansión:
Teacher Edition Only
Have students make a map with captions, illustrating where the people in the activity are from.

9 | Los amigos de Alicia

Escribir

Alicia has a lot of friends that you are going to meet in the following chapters. Write where they are from.

modelo: Maribel y Enrique / España
Maribel y Enrique son de España.

1. yo / Miami

2. Claudia y Pablo / México

3. Marisol / Puerto Rico

4. papá y yo / Miami

5. Fernando / Ecuador

6. Mario / la República Dominicana

Expansión:
Teacher Edition Only
Ask students to name three famous people and tell where they are from.

Differentiating Instruction

Inclusion

Multisensory Input/Output Distribute index cards to students, and assign a different country or place to each student. Then, in pairs, have students interview their partner to learn where he or she is from, and write it down on the index card. Students will glue their index cards to a piece of poster board, creating a poster telling where each member of the class is from.

Multiple Intelligences

Visual Learners Direct students to find the countries and cities mentioned on p. 40 on a map or in an atlas. For the city mentioned, have students identify the state. For each country mentioned, have students name some of its major cities. Invite students to add this information as they talk about **Los amigos de Alicia**.

10 | De muchos países

Hablar

Ask another student where Miguel's friends are from. Your partner should use pronouns to answer.

modelo: Luis

A ¿De dónde es Luis?

B Él es de Colombia.

1. Leticia
2. Álvaro y Linda
3. Isabel y Ángela
4. Andrés y Jorge
5. Ana Sofía y Elena
6. Y tú, ¿ ?

Expansión:
Teacher Edition Only

Have students replace the name in each question with its corresponding subject pronoun. For example: ¿De dónde es Luis? = ¿De dónde es él?

Océano Atlántico

Océano Pacífico

Expansión:
Teacher Edition Only

Have students organize their sentences in order of distance, from farthest to closest to students' current location.

11 | Mis amigos

Escribir

Write five sentences telling where your friends are from.

modelo: Amy es de Minnesota. Mike es de Indiana...

Más práctica Cuaderno *pp. 4–6* Cuaderno para hispanohablantes *pp. 5–7*

PARA Y PIENSA

Did you get it? Match the phrases to make a complete sentence.

1. Cristóbal y yo
2. Tomás
3. Yo

a. soy de México.
b. somos de Honduras.
c. es de la República Dominicana.

Get Help Online
ClassZone.com

Differentiating Instruction

Pre-AP

Expand and Elaborate Give students the opportunity to create a simple scrapbook showing where their friends are from. Have students choose five or six of their friends to write about. Direct them to model their sentences after those in Activitiy 11. Students might use a photo of each friend or draw a picture to illustrate each page. **Isabella es de California. Jorge es de Denver.**

Slower-paced Learners

Metacognitive Support Before doing Activity 10, review name/subject pronoun replacements. For example: **Leticia = ella, Álvaro y Linda = ellos.** Have students provide the subject pronouns for the remaining questions.

Connections
Geography

Activities 8–10 Have students use a map to locate the places mentioned in the activities. Then have them create a table with the headings **América del Norte, América del Sur, América Central, El Caribe,** and **Europa.** Have them list the places mentioned under the appropriate heading.

Communication
⚠ Common Error Alert

Be sure that students understand that questions asked with one pronoun may require a different pronoun in the answer. For example: **¿Tú eres/Usted es...? Sí, yo soy...**

✓ Ongoing Assessment

@HomeTutor
More Practice
ClassZone.com

PARA Y PIENSA

Intervention Have student pairs practice asking each other where they are from. For additional practice, use Reteaching & Practice Copymasters URB 1, pp. 32, 33.

Answers MSRB Transparencies 28–29

Answers continued from p. 40.

Activity 9

1. Yo soy de Miami.
2. Claudia y Pablo son de México.
3. Marisol es de Puerto Rico.
4. Papá y yo somos de Miami.
5. Fernando es de Ecuador.
6. Mario es de la República Dominicana.

Activity 10

1. ¿De dónde es Leticia? Leticia es de Perú.
2. ¿De dónde son Álvaro y Linda? Ellos son de Costa Rica.
3. ¿De dónde son Isabel y Ángela? Ellas son de la Florida.
4. ¿De dónde son Andrés y Jorge? Ellos son de Bolivia.
5. ¿De dónde son Ana Sofía y Elena? Ellas son de Panamá.
6. ¿De dónde eres tú? Yo soy de (answers will vary.)

Activity 11 Answers will vary. Sample answers include:

Martha es de Washington. James es de Idaho. Julian es de Massachusetts. Greta es de South Carolina. Tom es de Texas.

Para y piensa 1. b; **2.** c; **3.** a

41

Objectives
- Practice **ser** in context.
- **Culture:** Learn about Los Premios Juventud, a Latino award show in Miami.
- Practice names of Latin American countries.

Core Resources
- Video Program: DVD 1
- Audio Program: TXT CD 1, track 26

Presentation Strategies
- Ask students to scan the Telehistoria script before watching the video.
- Show the video. Point out gestures/intonations and uses of **ser de.**
- Play audio.

Practice Sequence
- **Activity 12:** Telehistoria comprehension
- **Activity 13:** Transitional practice: **ser de**
- **Activity 14:** Open-ended practice: **ser de**

STANDARDS
1.1 Engage in conversation, Acts. 13–14
1.2 Understand language, Act. 12
2.2 Products and perspectives, Act. 12
4.2 Compare cultures, Act. 13

Warm Up · UTB 1 Transparency 27

Pronouns Match the letter of the pronoun to its corresponding subject.

1. el Sr. Ruiz _____
2. Mi amigo Miguel y yo _____
3. tú y Marta _____
4. Sandra _____
5. Alicia y Teresa _____

a. ella
b. ustedes
c. ellas
d. él
e. nosotros

Answers: 1. d; 2. e; 3. b; 4. a; 5. c

42

GRAMÁTICA *en contexto*

¡AVANZA! **Goal:** Notice how Alicia and her friends say where they are from. Then use **ser** with **de** to tell where people are from. *Actividades 12–14*

Telehistoria escena 2

@HomeTutor VideoPlus ClassZone.com

STRATEGIES

Cuando lees
Scan for details Quickly look ahead for certain details before you read the scene. Scan for names and people. What do you think this scene is about?

Cuando escuchas
Listen for guesses Listen as Mr. Costas guesses where Teresa and Miguel are from. What does he guess? What does Miguel guess about where Mr. Costas is from?

VIDEO DVD

AUDIO

Alicia: ¡Hola! Señor Costas, le presento a dos amigos... Teresa y Miguel. Ellos son de...

Mr. Costas stops her because he wants to guess.

Sr. Costas: Tú eres de... ¿Puerto Rico? ¿Panamá? ¿Costa Rica?

Teresa: No, yo soy de...

Mr. Costas interrupts and gestures toward Miguel.

Sr. Costas: ¿Él es de México? ¿El Salvador? ¿Colombia?

Miguel: No, nosotros somos de *(pointing to himself)* Cuba y *(pointing to Teresa)* de Honduras. Y usted, ¿de dónde es?

Sr. Costas: Soy de...

Miguel: ¿Argentina? ¿Chile? ¿Cuba?

Sr. Costas: Soy de la Florida.

Continuará... p. 48

Differentiating Instruction

Slower-paced Learners

Read Before Listening Have students read aloud the Telehistoria before listening to it. Instruct them to raise their hands when they come across the name of a state or country. Assign one student to write it on the board. Model for students how to pronounce each place name, and have them repeat after you.

Heritage Language Learners

Writing Skills Invite students to write their own script for an original scene based on the Telehistoria. Tell them that their scenes will have a similar theme, but can use different characters and place names. Point out the punctuation used in the Telehistoria script. Remind students to use question marks correctly to make their script easy to read.

12 | Los orígenes *Comprensión del episodio*

Escuchar
Leer

Answer the questions about the episode.

1. Teresa y Miguel son los amigos de
   a. Alicia.
   b. el señor Costas.
   c. el señor Díaz.
2. ¿De dónde es Miguel?
   a. Es de Puerto Rico.
   b. Es de Cuba.
   c. Es de la República Dominicana.

3. ¿De dónde es Teresa?
   a. Es de Puerto Rico.
   b. Es de Costa Rica.
   c. Es de Honduras.
4. ¿Quién es de la Florida?
   a. Miguel
   b. el señor Costas
   c. Teresa

Expansión:
Teacher Edition Only
Ask students to write one additional question about the Telehistoria followed by three answer options.

13 | Los famosos en Miami

Leer
Hablar

Comparación cultural

Los Premios Juventud

How have Latino performers and athletes affected popular culture in the United States? Los Premios Juventud is an awards show held in **Miami** *and broadcast on Spanish-language television. Teens vote for their favorite stars in music, film, and sports. Past nominees include Shakira and Juanes (Colombia), Paulina Rubio and Gael García Bernal (Mexico), Miguel Cabrera (Venezuela), and Jennifer Lopez (New York).*

Compara con tu mundo *Who are your favorite figures in music, film, and sports, and why?*

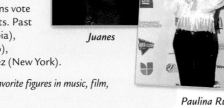
Juanes

Paulina Rubio

Talk with a partner about where the nominees are from.

 A ¿De dónde es Juanes?

 B Juanes es de Colombia.

14 | ¿De dónde somos?

Hablar

Ask other students where they are from.

A Nora, ¿de dónde eres?
B Soy de Miami. ¿Y tú?
También soy de Miami.

Expansión:
Teacher Edition Only
As a class, have students compile the results into a chart to show where everyone is from.

PARA Y PIENSA

Did you get it? Create sentences to tell where the people are from.

1. el Sr. Costas / la Florida
2. Alicia / Miami
3. Teresa y Miguel / Honduras y Cuba

Get Help Online
ClassZone.com

Differentiating Instruction

Inclusion

Alphabetic/Phonetic Awareness In groups, have students compile a list of the place names they find on pp. 42–43. Have the groups organize their lists in alphabetical order. Then invite volunteers to read the names from their lists. Model the Spanish pronunciation of names that may be spelled the same, but pronounced differently in English. Examples include **México, Miami,** and **Puerto Rico.**

Slower-paced Learners

Personalize It Write the following headings on the chalkboard or chart paper: **Música** (music), **Cine** (movies), **Deportes** (sports). Explain to students the meanings of these words. Then ask for volunteers to add names of their own favorite stars under each heading and say where they are from. Point out stars who are from Spanish-speaking countries or of Hispanic origin.

Comparación cultural

Essential Question

Suggested Answer Since Latinos became the largest ethnic minority in the United States, there has been a massive growth in Spanish media, music, art, and literature, which in turn is having an increasingly dramatic effect on U.S. culture.

Background Information

Premios Juventud gives awards in 22 unconventional subcategories such as **¡Qué actorazo!** (Can He Act or What?); **Actriz que se roba la pantalla** (She Steals the Show); **Voz del momento** (All Over the Dial); **Novato del año** (Rookie that Rocks). Shakira, Juanes, and Paulina Rubio are all musicians (pop/rock). Gael García Bernal is an actor, and Miguel Cabrera is a professional baseball player. Jennifer Lopez is a singer/actress.

✓ Ongoing Assessment

@HomeTutor
More Practice
ClassZone.com

PARA Y PIENSA **Peer Assessment** Have pairs of students read aloud the sentences and correct each other. For additional practice, use Reteaching & Practice Copymasters URB 1, pp. 32, 34.

Answers MSRB Transparency 29

Activity 12
1. a; 2. b; 3. c; 4. b

Activity 13 Answers will vary.
¿De dónde es Shakira? Shakira es de Colombia.
¿De dónde es Paulina Rubio? Paulina Rubio es de México.

Activity 14 Answers will vary but should follow the format: (Name), ¿de dónde eres? Soy de (name of city, state, or country).

Para y piensa
1. El Sr. Costas es de la Florida.
2. Alicia es de Miami.
3. Teresa y Miguel son de Honduras y Cuba.

43

Objectives
· Present **gustar** + infinitives.
· Present **a** + noun/pronoun.

Core Resource
· *Cuaderno,* pp. 7–9

Presentation Strategies
· Ask students what an infinitive is.
· Point out the verb form **gusta** and the pronouns used with it.

 STANDARDS
3.1 Knowledge of other disciplines
4.1 Compare languages

 Warm Up UTB 1 Transparency 28

Ser de Complete the following sentences with the correct form of **ser + de.**
1. Julio _____ Colombia.
2. Marta y Teresa _____ Ecuador.
3. Yo _____ Miami.
4. Tú _____ Puerto Rico.
5. Estela y yo _____ California.
Answers: 1. es de; 2. son de; 3. soy de;
4. eres de; 5. somos de

Comparisons
English Grammar Connection

Gustar does not literally mean *to like,* but rather *to be pleasing.* **Me gusta** = *It is pleasing to me.* Use indirect object pronouns **me, te, le, nos, os, les** to indicate to whom an activity is pleasing. Place the indirect object pronoun immediately before the conjugated form of **gustar.** To say that someone does not like something, **no** is used directly before the indirect object pronoun.

Verbs Students Know

Keep in mind that students have studied the meanings of the following infinitives:

alquilar	dibujar	montar
andar	escribir	(en bicicleta)
(en patineta)	escuchar	pasar (un rato)
aprender	hablar	pasear
beber	hacer	practicar
comer	(la tarea)	preparar
comprar	jugar	tocar (un
correr	leer	instrumento)
descansar	mirar	trabajar

44

Presentación de GRAMÁTICA

 **Goal:** Learn how to express what people like to do using the verb **gustar.** Then use **gustar** to say what you and others like to do. *Actividades 15–19*

English Grammar Connection: An **infinitive** is the basic form of a **verb,** a word that expresses action or a state of being. In English, most infinitives include the word *to.* In Spanish, infinitives are always one word that ends in **-ar, -er,** or **-ir.**

I like **to run.**   Me gusta **correr.**
↑   ↑
infinitive   infinitive

Gustar with an Infinitive

Animated Grammar
ClassZone.com

Use **gustar** to talk about what people like to do.

Here's how: Use phrases like **me gusta** + **infinitive.**

Me gusta **dibujar.**	*I like to draw.*
Te gusta **dibujar.**	*You (familiar singular) like to draw.*
Le gusta **dibujar.**	*You (formal singular) like to draw. He/She likes to draw.*
Nos gusta **dibujar.**	*We like to draw.*
Os gusta **dibujar.**	*You (familiar plural) like to draw.*
Les gusta **dibujar.**	*You (plural) like to draw. They like to draw.*

When you want to really emphasize or identify the person that you are talking about, add **a** + noun/pronoun.

A Sonia le gusta **leer.**   A ella le gusta **leer.**
Sonia likes to read.   *She likes to read.*

These are the **pronouns** that follow **a.**

A mí me gusta dibujar.   A nosotros(as) nos gusta dibujar.
A ti te gusta dibujar.   A vosotros(as) os gusta dibujar.
A usted le gusta dibujar.   A ustedes les gusta dibujar.
A él, ella le gusta dibujar.   A ellos(as) les gusta dibujar.

Más práctica
Cuaderno *pp. 7–9*
Cuaderno para hispanohablantes *pp. 8–11*

@HomeTutor
Leveled Grammar Practice
ClassZone.com

Differentiating Instruction

Inclusion

Clear Structure Create the following four-column chart on the chalkboard or chart paper and write an example under each column head.

A + name(s)/pronoun + **le/les gusta** + activity
A Ana y a Adela les gusta comer helado.
Have students complete the chart with examples of their own. Help students organize their sentences in the correct order.

Heritage Language Learners

Support What They Know Invite students to share a short paragraph explaining what they, their family members, and their friends like to do. Encourage students to use gestures or picture clues to clarify vocabulary that may not be familiar to all.

Práctica de GRAMÁTICA

15 | ¿Les gusta o no?

Escribir

Write what these people like and don't like to do.

modelo: a Luisa / preparar la comida 😞
No le gusta preparar la comida.

1. a nosotras / 🙂
comer pizza

2. a ustedes / estudiar 😞

3. a ti / montar en bicicleta 😐

4. a mí / escuchar música 🙂

5. a Alicia y a Miguel / 🙂
aprender el español

6. a usted / trabajar 😞

7. a Teresa / tocar la guitarra 🙂

8. a ellos / hacer la tarea 😞

Expansión:
Teacher Edition Only
Have students tell you that someone else has the opposite opinion of the activity indicated. For example: A nosotras nos gusta comer pizza. A ti no te gusta comer pizza.

Comparación cultural

El arte de Miami

How would being Cuban American influence an artist's work? Growing up in **Miami**, artist Xavier Cortada learned about his Cuban heritage through his family and community around him. Many of his paintings reflect his identity as a Cuban American. His colorful painting *Music* presents a variety of instruments found in traditional Cuban music *(son, rumba, mambo, Afro-Latin jazz)* as well as American music. How many instruments can you identify?

Music (2005), Xavier Cortada

Compara con tu mundo *What would you paint to represent your community? Where would you display your painting?*

Objectives

· State likes and dislikes with **gustar** + infinitives.
· **Culture:** Miami's artwork.

Practice Sequence

· **Activity 15:** Controlled practice: **gustar** + infinitive

STANDARDS

1.3 Present information, Act. 15
2.2 Products and perspectives
4.1 Compare cultures, CC

Comparación cultural

Essential Question

Suggested Answer A Cuban-American artist might create art depicting themes that mix elements of both American and Cuban cultures.

About the Artist

Xavier Cortada is active in his community and has created a variety of public artwork in Miami. This piece, *Music*, was created for Festival Miami 2005, a music festival at the University of Miami (Cortada's alma mater).

Comparisons

English Language Connection

Infinitives In English, an infinitive consists of *to* + verb (to sing); in Spanish, an infinitive is one word, a verb ending in **-r** (**dibujar**).

Differentiating Instruction

Multiple Intelligences

Visual Learners Have students create their own paintings or murals to express the things they like to do. Provide materials such as poster boards, colored pencils, or markers. Have students title their paintings. They may wish to present or exhibit their artwork to the rest of the class.

Pre-AP

Expand and Elaborate Invite students to keep their own personal Spanish-language journals. Encourage them to make entries about themselves and their own lives. At this point, they might include information about where they and their friends are from, and some of their favorite activities.

Answers MSRB Transparency 29

Activity 15
1. A nosotras nos gusta comer pizza.
2. A ustedes no les gusta estudiar.
3. A ti no te gusta montar en bicicleta.
4. A mí me gusta escuchar música.
5. A Alicia y a Miguel les gusta aprender el español.
6. A usted no le gusta trabajar.
7. A Teresa le gusta tocar la guitarra.
8. A ellos no les gusta hacer la tarea.

Objectives
- Practice **gustar** + infinitives.
- Pronunciation: Compare pronunciation of the letters **p** and **t** in Spanish and English.

Core Resources
- *Cuaderno*, pp. 7–9
- Audio Program: TXT CD 1, tracks 27, 28

Practice Sequence
- **Activity 16:** Transitional practice: **gustar** + infinitive
- **Activity 17:** Transitional practice: **gustar** + infinitive
- **Activity 18:** Transitional practice: **gustar** + infinitive
- **Activity 19:** Open-ended practice: **gustar** + infinitive

STANDARDS
- **1.1** Engage in conversation, Act. 16, Act. 19
- **1.2** Understand language, Act. 18, Pronunciación
- **1.3** Present information, Acts. 16–19, PYP
- **4.1** Compare languages, Pronunciación

Communication
TPR Activity

Before Activity 16, ask students to act out each of the pastimes illustrated in the photos. Then ask them to perform the actions again, this time saying the name of the activity as they are doing it.

Answers MSRB Transparencies 29–30

Activity 16
1. A: ¿Qué le gusta hacer a Alicia? B: Le gusta escribir correos electrónicos.
2. A: ¿Qué le gusta hacer a ella? B: Le gusta andar en patineta.
3. A: ¿Qué le gusta hacer a él? B: Le gusta comprar agua.
4. A: ¿Qué les gusta hacer a Alicia y a Miguel? B: Les gusta pasear.
5. A: ¿Qué le gusta hacer a Teresa? B: Le gusta tocar la guitarra.
6. A: ¿Qué les gusta hacer a ustedes? B: Nos gusta pasar un rato con los amigos.

Activity 17
1. Les gusta pasear.
2. Le gusta descansar.
3. Le gusta leer un libro.
4. Le gusta tocar la guitarra.
5. No le gusta escuchar música.
6. No le gusta andar en patineta.
7. Le gusta hablar por teléfono.
8. No le gusta jugar al fútbol.

46

---

16 | ¿Qué les gusta hacer?

Hablar With a partner, use the photos to say what Alicia and others like to do.

Teresa

 A ¿Qué le gusta hacer a Teresa?

 B Le gusta leer un libro.

1. Alicia
2. ella
3. él
4. Alicia y Miguel
5. Teresa
6. ustedes

> **Expansión:**
> Teacher Edition Only
> Have students write a sentence stating what each person pictured doesn't like to do.

17 | En el parque

Hablar Escribir

Look at the drawing and say whether the people like or don't like what they are doing.

modelo: Le gusta jugar al fútbol.

> **Expansión:**
> Teacher Edition Only
> Have students draw their own scene with people doing activities they like or don't like to do.

Differentiating Instruction

Slower-paced Learners

Sentence Completion Before students discuss their responses to Activity 16, provide them with the following template on the board:

Estudiante A: ¿Qué _____ gusta hacer a _____?
Estudiante B: _____ gusta _____.

Have students draft their responses by filling in the blanks with the appropriate pronoun, name, and activity.

Multiple Intelligences

Visual Learners Ask students to draw maps of the park in Activity 17. Then ask them to place the people on the map, using symbols such as circles or squares. As the class completes Activity 17, ask students to point to the appropriate place on their maps as they reply.

18 | Las actividades

Escuchar
Escribir

Copy this chart on a piece of paper. Listen to Mariana's description of what she and her friends like to do on Saturdays, and complete your chart with **sí** or **no**. Then answer the questions.

¿Le gusta...?	descansar	pasear	mirar la televisión	tocar la guitarra
A Mariana	sí			
A Jorge		no		
A Federico				

1. ¿Qué le gusta hacer a Jorge?
2. ¿Qué le gusta hacer a Mariana?
3. ¿Qué le gusta hacer a Federico?
4. ¿Qué no le gusta hacer a Mariana?
5. ¿Qué no les gusta hacer a Jorge y a Federico?
6. ¿Qué les gusta hacer a los tres amigos?

Audio Program
TXT CD 1 Track 28
Audio Script, TE
p. 29b

19 | A mi amigo(a) le gusta

Hablar

Ask a classmate what he or she likes to do on Saturdays and Sundays. Then tell the class.

Expansión:
Teacher Edition Only
Have students write a paragraph telling what they like or don't like to do on Sundays.

¿Te gusta montar en bicicleta?

Pronunciación — Las letras p y t

AUDIO

When you pronounce the **p** and **t** in English, a puff of air comes out of your mouth. In Spanish, there is no puff of air. Listen and repeat.

pasar	**p**or favor	**P**uerto Rico
pizza	**p**ero	**p**apas

Pepe **pre**para las **p**apas fritas.

fru**t**a	**t**elevisión	prac**t**icar
tocar	es**t**udiar	**t**area

Más práctica   Cuaderno *pp. 7–9*   Cuaderno para hispanohablantes *pp. 8–11*

PARA Y PIENSA

Did you get it? Complete each sentence with the correct **gustar** phrase.

1. _____ correr. (a ella)
2. ¿_____ andar en patineta? (a ti)
3. _____ tocar la guitarra. (a nosotros)

Get Help Online
ClassZone.com

Lección 1
cuarenta y siete **47**

Unidad 1 Lección 1
GRAMÁTICA

Communication
Pair Work

Ask students to work in pairs to talk about activities they like to do on weekends. Their partner will agree or disagree. Example: **A: Me gusta montar en bicicleta los sábados. B: A mí también me gusta montar en bicicleta.** or: **A mí no me gusta montar en bicicleta.**

✓ Ongoing Assessment

Dictation Have students write the following dictation with the letters **p** and **t**:
Por favor, prepara la pizza y las papas fritas.
Teresa toca la guitarra y practica todos los martes.

✓ Ongoing Assessment

@HomeTutor
More Practice
ClassZone.com

Remediation If students have problems saying the sentences in Para y piensa, have them review p. 44 and repeat Activities 15 on p. 45 and 16 on p. 46. For additional practice, use Reteaching & Practice Copymasters URB 1, pp. 35, 36.

Answers MSRB Transparency 30

Activity 18
1. ...le gusta descansar, mirar la televisión y escuchar música.
2. ...le gusta descansar, pasear y tocar la guitarra.
3. ...le gusta descansar, pasear, mirar la televisión y escuchar música.
4. ...no le gusta mirar la televisión.
5. ...no les gusta tocar la guitarra. A Jorge no le gusta pasear.
6. ...les gusta descansar.

Activity 19 Answers will vary. Sample answers include:
A: ¿Qué te gusta hacer los sábados y domingos?
B: Me gusta pasear y tocar la guitarra.

Para y piensa
1. le gusta; 2. te gusta; 3. nos gusta

47

Differentiating Instruction

Inclusion

Alphabetic/Phonetic Awareness Have students make lists of all the Spanish words they know that contain the letters **p** and **t.**

Slower-paced Learners

Memory Aids Ask students to draw cartoons of five activities on index cards. Ask them to name the activity, spell it, and state if they like to do it. Then have them write that information on the back of the card.

Objective

· Integrate lesson content.

Core Resources

· Video Program: DVD 1
· Audio Program: TXT CD 1, tracks 25, 26, 29

Presentation Strategies

· Ask students what they remember about the Telehistoria so far.
· Show the video and/or play the audio.

Practice Sequence

· **Activity 20:** Telehistoria comprehension
· **Activity 21:** Telehistoria comprehension
· **Activity 22:** Open-ended practice: speaking

 STANDARDS

1.1 Engage in conversation, Act. 22
1.2 Understand language, Act. 20
1.3 Present information, Acts. 21–22

 Warm Up UTB 1 Transparency 28

Gustar + infinitive Unscramble the following sentences.
1. le gusta / a Mariana / beber jugos
2. mirar la televisión / nos gusta / a nosotros
3. no / a mí / preparar la comida / me gusta
4. les gusta / a Federico y a Jorge / descansar

**Answers: 1. A Mariana le gusta beber jugos.
2. A nosotros nos gusta mirar la televisión.
3. A mí no me gusta preparar la comida.
4. A Federico y a Jorge les gusta descansar.**

Video Summary
@HomeTutor VideoPlus ClassZone.com

Alicia, Teresa, and Miguel are trying to decide what to do. They all agree that they like to eat, but then disagree on what to eat or drink. Teresa points to a story in the newspaper about Trini Salgado. Alicia calls her friend Sandra in San Antonio.

▶ ❙❙

Todo junto

 ¡AVANZA! **Goal: *Show what you know*** Pay attention to Alicia and her friends as they describe the activities they like to do. Then use **ser** and **gustar** to say where you are from and what you like to do. *Actividades 20–24*

Telehistoria completa

@HomeTutor VideoPlus
ClassZone.com

STRATEGIES

Cuando lees
Unlock the main idea Find repeated phrases that can unlock the overall meaning. Find all the phrases that contain the verb **gustar**. What is this scene about?

Cuando escuchas
Listen for cognates A cognate is a Spanish word that sounds like an English word and means the same thing. For example, *telephone* and **teléfono**. In the video, listen for at least three cognates.

Escena 1 *Resumen*
A Alicia y a Sandra les gusta hacer muchas actividades. Les gusta dibujar, comer pizza y más.

Escena 2 *Resumen*
Miguel es de Cuba y Teresa es de Honduras. El señor Costas es de la Florida.

VIDEO DVD

AUDIO

Escena 3

Alicia: ¿Qué les gusta hacer?
Miguel: Me gusta mirar la televisión.
Teresa: No me gusta mirar la televisión. Me gusta más tocar la guitarra o escuchar música.
Miguel: Me gusta comer.
Teresa: Sí, me gusta comer.
Alicia: ¡Nos gusta comer!

They stand to go eat.
Alicia: ¿Qué les gusta comer? ¿Pizza? ¿Les gusta comer helado? ¿Fruta? ¿Beber jugos?
Both say no, and they all sit. Teresa shows them the paper.
Alicia: ¿Trini Salgado? ¿En San Antonio? (*She quickly takes out her cell phone.*) ¡Sandra!

48 Unidad 1 Estados Unidos
cuarenta y ocho

Differentiating Instruction

Slower-paced Learners

Yes/No Questions Ask students yes/no questions to reinforce their understanding of Escena 3 of the Telehistoria. **¿A Miguel le gusta mirar la televisión? (Sí) ¿A Teresa le gusta mirar la televisión? (No)** Encourage students to point to the place in the text where they found their information.

English Learners

Provide Comprehensive Input Explain to students that cognates are words that are similar in spelling and have the same meaning in two languages. For example: **música** and *music*. Ask students to share words in their own language that are English cognates. Ask students to find Spanish/English cognates in the Telehistoria.

20 | ¿Quiénes son? *Comprensión de los episodios*

Escuchar
Leer

Write the name(s) of the character(s) according to the descriptions.

1. No le gusta andar en patineta.
2. Es de Honduras.
3. Les gusta comer.
4. Es de la Florida.
5. Le gusta tocar la guitarra.
6. Es de San Antonio, Texas.
7. Le gusta hablar por teléfono.
8. Le gusta escuchar música.

Expansión:
Teacher Edition Only
Ask students to write clues for another Telehistoria character and have a partner guess who it is.

21 | Los amigos *Comprensión de los episodios*

Escuchar
Leer

Answer the questions according to the episodes.

1.
a. ¿Cómo se llama?
b. ¿Qué le gusta hacer?
c. ¿Qué no le gusta hacer?

2.
a. ¿Cómo se llama?
b. ¿De dónde es?
c. ¿Qué le gusta hacer?

Expansión:
Teacher Edition Only
Have students write one additional detail about Alicia and Miguel.

22 | Nuevos amigos

Hablar

STRATEGY Hablar

Boost your "speaking self-confidence" with positive statements
To increase your speaking self-confidence, say something positive to yourself like: *I learn from my mistakes. I can say things now that I couldn't say last week.* Create your own positive statement. Say it to yourself before the speaking activity below.

You are a new student at school. Talk with other students about where you are from and what you like and don't like to do. Make a list of the things you have in common.

A Hola, me llamo Víctor. Soy de Chicago. Me gusta escuchar música y correr.

B Hola, me llamo Carolina y soy de Chicago también. No me gusta escuchar música pero me gusta practicar deportes.

C Hola. Me llamo Alex...

Expansión:
Teacher Edition Only
Have students write a list of the things they don't have in common.

Differentiating Instruction

Slower-paced Learners

Read Before Listening Have students read aloud the questions in Activity 21 before listening to the episodes. Discuss what kind of information they should listen for to answer each question. For example, to answer the question **¿Cómo se llama?,** students should listen for the name of a person.

Multiple Intelligences

Interpersonal After students introduce themselves in Activity 22, have them choose a partner and repeat their introductions to each other. Next have students introduce their partner to the group. Review how to change the sentences they have heard. For example, **Me llamo Carolina** becomes **Se llama Carolina.**

✓ Ongoing Assessment

Rubric Activity 22

Speaking Criteria	Maximum Credit	Partial Credit	Minimum Credit
Content	Conversation includes all the information.	Conversation includes some information.	Conversation includes little information.
Communication	Conversation is well-organized.	Conversation is fairly well-organized.	Conversation is disorganized.
Accuracy	Few mistakes in grammar and vocabulary.	Some mistakes in grammar and vocabulary.	Many mistakes in grammar and vocabulary.

Answers MSRB Transparency 30

Activity 20
1. Sandra
2. Teresa
3. Alicia, Miguel y Teresa
4. el Sr. Costas
5. Teresa
6. Sandra
7. Sandra
8. Teresa

Activity 21
1. a. Alicia. b. A Alicia le gusta dibujar, jugar al fútbol y pasar un rato con los amigos. c. A Alicia no le gusta hablar por teléfono.
2. a. Miguel. b. Miguel es de Cuba. c. Le gusta mirar la televisión y comer.

Activity 22 Answers will vary. Sample answers include: Hola, me llamo María. Soy de Costa Rica. Me gusta montar en bicicleta y dibujar.

49

Objective
· Practice using and integrating lesson vocabulary and grammar.

Core Resources
· *Cuaderno*, pp. 10–11
· Audio Program: TXT CD 1, tracks 30, 31

Practice Sequence
· **Activities 23:** Open-ended practice: reading, listening, speaking
· **Activities 24:** Open-ended practice: writing

 STANDARDS

1.2 Understand language, Act. 23
1.3 Present information, Acts. 23–24, PYP

Long-term Retention
 Pre-AP Integration

Activity 23 Help students take notes for this activity. They should create a two-column, two-row chart. They can label the columns with the girls' names, and each row as **Le gusta** or **No le gusta.** They can make notes in the corresponding columns as they read the e-mail and listen to the audio, and then compare the girls' likes and dislikes.

✓ Ongoing Assessment

Rubric Activity 23

Speaking/Listening

Proficient	Not There Yet
Student takes detailed notes and names most or all the activities that both girls like and dislike.	Student takes few notes and only names some of the activities that both girls like and dislike.

✓ Ongoing Assessment
@HomeTutor More Practice ClassZone.com

PARA Y PIENSA **Intervention** If students have difficulty completing the Para y piensa, refer them to the Telehistorias on pp. 36, 42, and 48. For additional practice, use Reteaching & Practice Copymasters URB 1 pp. 36, 37.

See Activity answers on p. 51.

50

---

23 | Integración

Leer
Escuchar
Hablar

Read the e-mail from Vanessa, then listen to Carmen and take notes. Say what both of them like and don't like.

Fuente 1 Correo electrónico

¡Hola, Carmen! Soy Vanessa. Soy de Morelos, México. Me gusta mucho practicar deportes. También me gusta andar en patineta. No me gusta escuchar música. Después de las clases me gusta pasar un rato con los amigos y comer pizza. Los sábados y domingos no me gusta hacer la tarea. Me gusta más alquilar un DVD o descansar. ¿Y a ti? ¿Qué te gusta hacer?

Fuente 2 Escucha a Carmen

Listen and take notes
· ¿Qué le gusta hacer a Carmen?
· ¿Qué no le gusta hacer?

modelo: A las chicas les gusta...

🎧 **Audio Program**
TXT CD 1 Tracks 30, 31
Audio Script, TE p. 29b

24 | Un correo electrónico

Escribir

Write to your new e-pal in Puebla, Mexico. Introduce yourself and tell him or her where you are from and what you like and don't like to do. Also write three questions for him or her to answer.

modelo: Hola, Eva. Me llamo Ana, y soy de la Florida. Me gusta leer un libro, pero no me gusta mirar la televisión. ¿Te gusta hablar por teléfono?

Writing Criteria	Excellent	Good	Needs Work
Content	Your e-mail includes a lot of information and questions.	Your e-mail includes some information and questions.	Your e-mail includes little information and not enough questions.
Communication	Most of your e-mail is organized and easy to follow.	Parts of your e-mail are organized and easy to follow.	Your e-mail is disorganized and hard to follow.
Accuracy	Your e-mail has few mistakes in grammar and vocabulary.	Your e-mail has some mistakes in grammar and vocabulary.	Your e-mail has many mistakes in grammar and vocabulary.

Expansión:
Teacher Edition Only
Have students exchange what they wrote and answer the questions as if they were each other's e-pal.

Más práctica Cuaderno *pp. 10–11* Cuaderno para hispanohablantes *pp. 12–13*

PARA Y PIENSA

Did you get it? Tell where these people are from and what they like to do, based on the Telehistoria.

1. Teresa / Honduras / tocar la guitarra
2. Alicia / Miami / comer
3. Miguel / Cuba / mirar la televisión

💬 **Get Help Online** ClassZone.com

Differentiating Instruction

Heritage Language Learners

Writing Skills Have students expand on the e-mail they write for Activity 24 by including information about their heritage countries. For example, students may want to describe in detail a city or region of their country, write about foods and dishes, or discuss in more detail the types of activities one can do.

Slower-paced Learners

Peer Study Support Review with students the writing rubric that accompanies Activity 24. After students have completed their e-mail messages, have them exchange papers with a partner. Each student reads his or her partner's work and applies the rubric. Model for students how to give constructive criticism to help their partners improve their writing.

Juegos y diversiones

Review the verb **ser** by playing a game.

The Setup

Your teacher will hand you a card with the name of a country on it. This will be your country of origin for use in the game. Do not show your card to anyone. The object of the game is to find another person in your class with the same country card.

Materials

index cards with names of Spanish-speaking countries (two cards for each country)

Colombia   Perú   Honduras

Playing the Game

You will go around asking your classmates where they are from in order to find the person who has the same country card as you. You must use the correct Spanish phrasing and answer in complete sentences.

¿Eres de Honduras?

No, soy de Perú.

The Winners!

The first two students to match country cards and say the word **¡Ganamos!** (we win) are the winners.

Objective
Review the verb **ser** by playing a game.

STANDARD
5.2 Life-long learners

Long-term Retention

♻ Recycle

Ask students to create a song using the names of Spanish-speaking countries. They should choose a tune they know, and fit the names of the countries into the rhythm of the song.

Communication

Group Work

Ask students to make the cards for the game, using the shapes as well as the names of the countries in Latin America. There will be two maps of each country, each held by a different student. The object of the game is to find other students with different maps and to construct a map of Latin America from the cards. The winner of this game is the first group of students to complete a map of Latin America.

Communication

⚠ Common Error Alert

Monitor students' correct intonation and pronunciation.

Answers MSRB Transparency 30

Answers for Activities on p. 50.

Activity 23 Answers will vary. Sample answers include: A las chicas les gusta comer pizza y pasar un rato con los amigos.

Activity 24 Answers will vary. Sample answers include: Hola, Juan. Me llamo Pedro y soy de Puerto Rico. Me gusta comer pizza, pero no me gusta preparar la comida. ¿Te gusta mirar la televisión? Hasta luego.

Para y piensa
1. Teresa es de Honduras y le gusta tocar la guitarra.
2. Alicia es de Miami y le gusta comer.
3. Miguel es de Cuba y le gusta mirar la televisión.

Differentiating Instruction

Multiple Intelligences

Intrapersonal Ask students to write a short journal entry about their experience finding a partner while playing **Sí, es mi país.** Was it easier for them to speak Spanish with their classmates when they were trying to find the answers to specific questions? Did they feel comfortable answering questions?

Inclusion

Alphabetic/Phonetic Awareness Ask students to repeat the names of the countries in **Sí, es mi país** several times. Then write the names on the board, and ask students to write the names on paper. Draw their attention to important pronunciation points such as the silent **h** in **Honduras** and the **ú** indicating stress on the second syllable of **Perú.**

¡AVANZA! Objectives

- Use surveys to talk about favorite activities.
- **Culture:** learn what students in a dual-language school in Florida like to do in their free time.
- Interpret information recorded in a bar graph about favorite activities.
- Compare favorite activities of teens.

Core Resource

- Audio Program: TXT CD 1 track 32

Presentation Strategies

- Ask students: What are the activities listed on the survey and graph? Which activity is your favorite? Create a conversation about those activities.
- Explain how to interpret the information in the bar graph.
- Ask students what activities they would list in their own survey or graph.

STANDARDS

1.2 Understand language
2.1 Practices and perspectives
4.2 Compare cultures

Warm Up UTB 1 Transparency 29

Ser de and gustar Write an appropriate question for each statement.

1. Nos gusta dibujar.
2. Soy de Costa Rica.
3. A Trini le gusta escuchar música.
4. A Jorge y a Federico no les gusta pasear.
5. Ana y yo somos de San Antonio.

**Answers: 1. ¿Qué les gusta hacer a ustedes?
2. ¿De dónde eres? 3. ¿Qué le gusta hacer a Trini? 4. ¿Qué no les gusta hacer a Jorge y a Federico? 5. ¿De dónde son ustedes?**

Culture

Background Information
Explain that dual-language programs allow students to develop proficiency in two languages by learning academic subjects in both languages.

Lectura

¡AVANZA! **Goal:** Read about what students in a dual-language school in Florida like to do in their free time. Then compare the activities they like to do with what you like to do.

AUDIO

¿Qué te gusta hacer?

This is a survey about what students like to do in their free time. It was conducted among students at a dual-language school in Florida.

> **STRATEGY Leer**
> **Use a judgment line** Draw a line like this one with *least popular* on the left and *most popular* on the right. On the line, list all the activities in the survey according to their popularity.
>
> leer estudiar   dibujar
> _____
> least popular   most popular

Una encuesta en la escuela

52 Unidad 1 Estados Unidos
cincuenta y dos

¿Qué te gusta hacer?

Me gusta...
- **mirar la televisión** ☐
- **pasar un rato con los amigos** ☑
- **jugar videojuegos** [1] ☐
- **trabajar** ☑
- **jugar con los amigos** ☐
- **dibujar** ☑
- **practicar deportes** ☐
- **escribir** ☐
- **leer** ☑
- **estudiar** ☐
- **otras** [2] **actividades** _tocar la guitarra_

[1] videogames   [2] other

Differentiating Instruction

Heritage Language Learners

Support What They Know Ask students to share any knowledge or experience they have with dual-language schools or programs. Have they, their friends, or family members ever participated in such a program? Encourage students to discuss the advantages of attending a dual-language school. Do they see any disadvantages? Have students express and support their opinions on this topic.

Multiple Intelligences

Interpersonal Have students brainstorm activities they like to do in their free time. For example, **Me gusta dibujar.** Ask a volunteer to write his/her responses on the board in a survey chart similar to the one on p. 52. Have another volunteer tally the results. Call on students to report which are the most popular and least popular activities.

Resultados de la encuesta[3]

25 estudiantes respondieron[4] a las 11
categorías o actividades.

Actividades

- mirar la tele
- pasar un rato
- videojuegos
- trabajar
- jugar
- dibujar
- deportes
- escribir
- leer
- estudiar
- otras

5   10   15   20   25
Número de estudiantes

---
[3] survey   [4] replied

¡Interpreta!

Based on the chart and survey, answer the following questions.

1. How many students took the survey?
2. What are the three most popular activities and the three least popular activities?
3. Would you get the same results if you used the survey with your classmates? Give specific reasons why or why not.

¿Y tú?

Record your answers to the survey on the previous page and compare them to the results of these students.

Lección 1
cincuenta y tres   **53**

Connections
Mathematics

Before working on Para y piensa, remind students that a bar graph shows the relationship between different things. Also remind them that percentages show the proportion of something or the number of parts in every hundred.

Communication
Pair Work

Oral Presentation Have student pairs ask each other whether they like or dislike each activity on the bar graph. Have pairs share conclusions in a presentation to the class.

Communication
Pair Work

Have students ask each other which activities from the survey they like more. For example:
A: ¿Qué te gusta más, jugar o dibujar? B: Me gusta más jugar. After three exchanges, have them switch roles.

Differentiating Instruction

Slower-paced Learners

Personalize It Direct students' attention to the bar graph. Ask for volunteers to read aloud the different activities listed along the y-axis. Then ask students to point to their favorite activity on the graph. Ask how many students in the survey chose that same activity. Repeat the discussion having students point to their second and third favorite activities.

Inclusion

Cumulative Instruction In order to interpret the results of the bar graph in Spanish, review with students the names for numbers one through twenty. Then ask a series of questions that students must use numbers to answer. If necessary, give two possible choices for students to choose from. **¿A cuántos estudiantes les gusta leer? ¿A dos estudiantes o a veinte estudiantes?**

Objectives

· Read about Hernando de Soto's exploration of the southeastern U.S.
· Calculate geographical distances.
· Find places in the U.S. with Spanish names.
· Describe Tex-Mex music.

Presentation Strategies

· Ask students if they know any places that have Spanish names. Do they know why the names are in Spanish?
· Point out on a map the area Hernando de Soto explored. Ask students to name the states that currently form that area.
· Tell students that the areas explored by the Spaniards were often populated by Native Americans. Ask students how they think the two cultures might have interacted.

STANDARDS

2.2 Products and perspectives
3.1 Knowledge of other disciplines

Connections

La historia

Ask students to write a brief historical biography in English of an explorer of their choice. Their bio should include the explorer's birthplace and the regions he explored. Suggest names of explorers, such as Hernando de Soto, Francisco Pizarro and Hernán Cortés.

Answers

Conexiones

Ucita: Tampa, FL; Casqui: Parkin, AR; Mabila: Mobile, AL; Anhayca: Tallahassee, FL

Proyecto 1

Ucita to Anhayca: 58 leguas; Anhayca to Mobila: 64 leguas; Mabila to Casqui: 99 leguas

Proyecto 2

Students should be able to come up with some just by looking at a map of the U.S. Other Spanish place names may be found by using online search engines. Possible answers:
Nevada—snowy
Colorado—colored red
Montana—from montaña (mountain)
Puerto Rico—rich port

Proyecto 3

Answers will vary. Common instruments in Tex/Mex include the accordion, guitar, drums, bass, and saxophone.

54

Conexiones *La geografía*

La expedición de Hernando de Soto

Hernando de Soto

The map below shows one account of the expedition of Hernando de Soto, a sixteenth-century Spanish explorer. It is believed that de Soto's team traveled through ten present-day U.S. states, and through many Native American villages. The following table gives the latitude and longitude of four U.S. cities, as well as the villages that were close to these locations. Use the coordinates to find the city that corresponds to each Native American village.

NATIVE AMERICAN VILLAGE	LOCATION OF CITY	NAME OF CITY
Ucita	27° 56' N 82° 27' O	
Casqui	35° 15' N 90° 34' O	
Mabila	30° 41' N 88° 02' O	
Anhayca	30° 26' N 84° 16' O	

La expedición (1539–1543)

Proyecto 1 *Las matemáticas*

A common form of measurement during the time of de Soto was the league (**legua**). A league was based on the distance an average person could walk in an hour: 3.5 miles. Calculate what these distances would be in leagues.

Ucita to Anhayca:	204 miles
Anhayca to Mabila:	224 miles
Mabila to Casqui:	347 miles

Proyecto 2 *El lenguaje*

Many places in the United States have Spanish names. **Florida,** for instance, means *full of flowers*. Use an atlas or the Internet to find three places in the United States with Spanish names. Then write the meaning of each place.

Proyecto 3 *La música*

The term "Tex–Mex" also describes music that blends elements of Mexico and the southwestern U.S. Most Tex–Mex music features the accordion, brought to Texas in the 1890s by German immigrants. Find an example of Tex–Mex music—such as Selena or Los Tigres del Norte—and listen to it. Then write a paragraph describing the instruments and the music and list the Spanish names of the instruments.

Los Tigres del Norte

Differentiating Instruction

Multiple Intelligences

Logical/Mathematical Most Spanish-speaking countries around the world use the metric system of measurement. Have small groups of students research the Spanish names of both the standard and metric units (**millas**, **leguas**) for measuring distance, and then ask them to create tables showing the conversions between these units.

English Learners

Check Comprehension Read **La expedición de Hernando de Soto** aloud with students. Stop after each sentence to ask follow-up questions and gauge their comprehension. During each pause, ask *who, what, where,* and *when* questions to help students identify the key ideas in each sentence. For example, after the second sentence you might ask, *Who* is this sentence about? *What* did they do?

LECCIÓN 1

En resumen
Vocabulario y gramática

Animated Grammar
Interactive Flashcards
ClassZone.com

Vocabulario

Talk About Activities

alquilar un DVD	to rent a DVD	hacer la tarea	to do homework
andar en patineta	to skateboard	jugar al fútbol	to play soccer
aprender el español	to learn Spanish	leer un libro	to read a book
beber	to drink	mirar la televisión	to watch television
comer	to eat	montar en bicicleta	to ride a bike
comprar	to buy		
correr	to run	pasar un rato con los amigos	to spend time with friends
descansar	to rest	pasear	to go for a walk
dibujar	to draw	practicar deportes	to practice / play sports
escribir correos electrónicos	to write e-mails	preparar la comida	to prepare food / a meal
escuchar música	to listen to music	tocar la guitarra	to play the guitar
estudiar	to study	trabajar	to work
hablar por teléfono	to talk on the phone		

Say What You Like and Don't Like to Do

¿Qué te gusta hacer?	What do you like to do?	Me gusta...	I like . . .
¿Te gusta...?	Do you like . . . ?	No me gusta...	I don't like . . .

Snack Foods and Beverages

el agua (fem.)	water
la fruta	fruit
la galleta	cookie
el helado	ice cream
el jugo	juice
las papas fritas	French fries
la pizza	pizza
el refresco	soft drink

Other Words and Phrases

la actividad	activity
antes de	before
después (de)	afterward, after
la escuela	school
más	more
o	or
pero	but
también	also

Gramática

Nota gramatical: **de** to describe where you are from *p. 39*

Pronouns and *ser*

Ser means *to be*. Use **ser** to identify a person or say where he or she is from.

Singular		Plural	
yo	soy	nosotros(as)	somos
tú	eres	vosotros(as)	sois
usted	es	ustedes	son
él, ella	es	ellos(as)	son

Gustar with an Infinitive

Use **gustar** to talk about what people like to do.

A mí me gusta dibujar.
A ti te gusta dibujar.
A usted le gusta dibujar.
A él, ella le gusta dibujar.
A nosotros(as) nos gusta dibujar.
A vosotros(as) os gusta dibujar.
A ustedes les gusta dibujar.
A ellos(as) les gusta dibujar.

Lección 1
cincuenta y cinco **55**

Objective
· Review lesson vocabulary and grammar.

Online SPANISH CLASSZONE.COM

Interactive Flashcards Students can hear every target vocabulary word pronounced in authentic Spanish. Flashcards have Spanish on one side, and a picture or a translation on the other.

Review Games Matching, concentration, hangman, and word search are just sampling of the fun, interactive games students can play to review for the test.

Featuring...
Cultura INTERACTIVA
Animated Grammar
@HomeTutor

And more...
· **Get Help Online**
· **Interactive Flashcards**
· **Review Games**
· **WebQuest**
· **Self-Check Quiz**

Communication
Group Work

Game Bring a small ball to class. Write on the board the following vocabulary categories in Spanish: **Comidas** (Foods), **Bebidas** (Beverages), **Acciones** (Actions.) Call out a category and toss a ball to a student. The student says a word that belongs to that category and tosses the ball to another student who names another word in that category. When a student cannot come up with a word, he or she is out of the game.

Long-term Retention
Study Tips

Help students think of categories for the different activities listed in the Vocabulario. For example: Activities to do at home and Activities to do outside, Activities I do alone and Activities I do with friends. Have them write the activities under the categories they have chosen.

Differentiating Instruction

Slower-paced Learners

Memory Aids Give students the opportunity to create their own flashcards to review the words and phrases in the "Talk About Activities" and "Snack Foods and Beverages" lists. Instruct students to write the word or phrase on one side of the card, and draw or paste a picture from a magazine on the other side. Have students work in pairs to use their flashcards.

Inclusion

Frequent Review/Repetition With a partner, have students study each group of vocabulary words. One partner goes down the list and tries to give the meaning of each word while covering the English definition. The other partner checks his or her partner's work. If students cannot recall a word's meaning, or offer the wrong meaning, have the partners study the word together, and try again.

Objective

· Review lesson grammar and vocabulary.

Core Resources

· *Cuaderno*, pp. 12–23
· Audio Program: TXT CD 1 track 33

Presentation Strategies

· Direct students' attention to the ¡Llegada!
· As students listen to Activity 1, instruct them to pay special attention to the uses of **gustar** + infinitive.
· Before doing Activity 4, ask students to identify the activities in the photos.
· Review forms of **ser** by saying a subject pronoun and asking students to provide the correct form of **ser.**
· Ask students to generate three questions to ask their classmates based on the Comparación cultural.

 STANDARDS

1.2 Understand language, Acts. 1,3
1.3 Present information, Acts. 2, 4
4.2 Compare cultures, Act. 5

Warm Up UTB 1 Transparency 29

Vocabulary Complete the sentences with the correct word from the group below.
beber más helado pero hablar

1. Me gusta dibujar, _____ no me gusta leer.
2. ¿Qué te gusta _____, escuchar música o mirar la televisión?
3. A Marta le gusta _____ por teléfono.
4. Hoy hace calor. Me gusta _____ agua.
5. Mmm. Me gusta comer _____.

Answers: 1. pero; 2. más; 3. hablar; 4. beber; 5. helado

✓ Ongoing Assessment @HomeTutor More Practice ClassZone.com

Intervention/Remediation If students achieve less than 80% accuracy on each activity, direct them to review pages 29, 38–39, 43–45 and to get help online at ClassZone.com.

See Activity answers on p. 57.

56

Lección 1
Repaso de la lección

 ¡LLEGADA!

@HomeTutor ClassZone.com

Now you can
· talk about activities
· tell where you are from
· say what you like and don't like to do

Using
· subject pronouns and **ser**
· **de** to describe where you are from
· **gustar** with an infinitive

To review
· **gustar** with an infinitive p. 44
· **de** to describe where you are from p. 39

 AUDIO

1 Listen and understand

Listen to Pablo and Sara talk about their activities. Then match the descriptions with the name or names.

1. Es de Puerto Rico.
2. Es de Miami.
3. Le gusta escuchar música.
4. No le gusta andar en patineta.
5. No le gusta comer frutas.
6. Le gusta comer helado.

a. Pablo
b. Sara
c. Pablo y Sara

🎧 **Audio Program**
TXT CD 1 Track 33
Audio Script, TE
p. 29b

To review
· **gustar** with an infinitive p. 44

2 Say what you like and don't like to do

Write sentences describing the activities you like and don't like to do.
modelo: alquilar un DVD
(No) Me gusta alquilar un DVD.

1. beber refrescos
2. preparar la comida
3. hacer la tarea
4. descansar
5. escribir correos electrónicos
6. pasar un rato con los amigos
7. practicar deportes
8. trabajar
9. comprar libros
10. comer pizza

Differentiating Instruction

Slower-paced Learners

Read Before Listening Before students listen to the script in Activity 1, have them read aloud the sentences in the left-hand column. Discuss which key words they should be listening for and ask them if that is a good key word. For example, for sentence 6, you might ask if **le** is a good key word to listen for. What about **gusta**? What about **helado**?

Inclusion

Metacognitive Support Read aloud the **modelo** in Activity 4. Point out the order in which the parts of the sentence are put together. Have them write these components on three separate index cards: Card 1: **A Sonia** Card 2: **le gusta** Card 3: **hablar por teléfono.** Then have them put their cards together to form the complete sentence. Repeat this for every item.

To review
- subject pronouns and **ser** p. 38
- **de** to describe where you are from p. 39

3 | Tell where you are from

Complete the e-mail with the appropriate form of **ser**.

Hola, me llamo Eduardo. Yo **1.** de Miami. Y tú, ¿de dónde **2.** ? Mis amigos y yo **3.** de diferentes países. Roberto **4.** de Chile y Yolanda **5.** de Perú. Nosotros **6.** estudiantes. El señor Santana y la señora Zabala **7.** maestros. Ellos **8.** de Cuba.

To review
- **gustar** with an infinitive p. 44

4 | Talk about activities

Tell what activities these people like to do, according to the photos.

modelo: a José
A José le gusta tocar la guitarra.

1. a Sonia

2. a ellos

3. a usted

4. a nosotras

5. a ustedes

6. a ti

To review
- Miami's Freedom Tower p. 29
- Fiesta San Antonio p. 29
- Comparación cultural pp. 43, 45

5 | United States

Comparación cultural

Answer these culture questions.

1. What is inside Miami's Freedom Tower?
2. What occurs during Fiesta San Antonio?
3. Who votes for the winners of **Los Premios Juventud**?
4. What is Xavier Cortada's heritage?

Más práctica   Cuaderno *pp. 12–23*   Cuaderno para hispanohablantes *pp. 14–23*

Get Help Online
ClassZone.com

Lección 1
cincuenta y siete   **57**

Differentiating Instruction

Heritage Language Learners

Writing Skills Have students draft their own e-mail messages based on the model in Activity 3. Instruct them to explain where they, their friends, family, and teachers are from. Encourage them to give a short description of each of the places they are familiar with. If possible, have students send their e-mail messages to other classmates or pen pals.

Multiple Intelligences

Musical/Rhythmic Have students create a short poem or song describing who they are and the things they like to do. Since many of the action verbs have similar sounds (**comer/correr, descansar/trabajar**), students may find it easy to create verses that rhyme. Invite students to read their poems to the class.

✓ Ongoing Assessment

Peer Assessment   Activity 3 Have student pairs exchange the completed e-mail messages and check each other's work.

✓ Ongoing Assessment

Alternative Strategy   Activity 4 Have students combine sentences by using such words as **más, pero,** and **también.** For example, a student may combine the first two sentences and write **A ella le gusta hablar por teléfono y también le gusta escuchar música.**

Answers MSRB Transparency 31

Answers for Activities on pp. 56, 57.

Activity 1
1. b	**3.** c	**5.** a
2. a	**4.** b	**6.** c

Activity 2
1. (No) Me gusta beber refrescos.
2. (No) Me gusta preparar la comida.
3. (No) Me gusta hacer la tarea.
4. (No) Me gusta descansar.
5. (No) Me gusta escribir correos electrónicos.
6. (No) Me gusta pasar un rato con los amigos.
7. (No) Me gusta practicar deportes.
8. (No) Me gusta trabajar.
9. (No) Me gusta comprar libros.
10. (No) Me gusta comer pizza.

Activity 3
1. soy
2. eres
3. somos
4. es
5. es
6. somos
7. son
8. son

Activity 4
1. A Sonia le gusta hablar por teléfono.
2. A ellos les gusta jugar al fútbol.
3. A usted le gusta leer un libro.
4. A nosotras nos gusta correr.
5. A ustedes les gusta pasar un rato con los amigos.
6. A ti te gusta montar en bicicleta.

Activity 5
1. The Cuban-American Museum is inside Miami's Freedom Tower.
2. During Fiesta San Antonio, there is a ten-day celebration with food, music, and parades to honor the heroes of the Álamo, and Battle of San Jacinto.
3. Teens vote for the winners of Los Premios Juventud.
4. Xavier Cortada is of Cuban heritage.

Culture at a Glance ❖

Topic & Activity	Essential Question
The Paseo del Río pp. 58–59	What do teenagers do at the Paseo del Río and where you live?
Mexican and Tex-Mex food p. 65	How does local environment affect the food that people eat?
Art in Texas p. 75	How do cultural traditions influence an artist's work?
Free time activities pp. 80–81	What kinds of things are there to do in San Antonio, Miami, and where you live?
Traditional dishes of Mexico and Cuba p. 82	Why do traditional dishes change when they are brought from one country to another?
Culture review p. 85	What are some leisure activities and traditional foods in San Antonio and Miami?

COMPARISON COUNTRIES  Estados Unidos  Colombia México

Practice at a Glance ❖

	Objective	Activity & Skill
Vocabulary	Adjectives	1: Reading; 2: Speaking/Writing; 3: Listening/Reading; 4: Reading/Speaking; 5: Reading; 8: Speaking/Writing; 15: Writing; 16: Speaking/Writing; 17: Writing; 18: Writing/Speaking; 19: Speaking; 21: Listening/Reading; 22: Writing/Speaking; 23: Reading/Listening/Speaking; 24: Writing; Repaso 1: Listening; Repaso 2–4: Writing
Vocabulary	Nouns for identifying people	5: Reading; 8: Speaking/Writing; 13: Speaking; 18: Writing/Speaking; 19: Speaking; 20: Listening/Reading; 22: Writing/Speaking; 24: Writing; Repaso 1: Listening; Repaso 2, 3: Writing
Grammar	**ser** to describe what someone is like	2: Speaking/Writing; 5: Reading; 8: Speaking/Writing; 14: Reading; 15: Writing; 16: Speaking/Writing; 17: Writing; 18: Writing/Speaking; 19: Speaking; 20: Listening/Reading; 21: Listening/Reading; 22: Writing/Speaking; 23: Reading/Listening/Speaking; 24: Writing; Repaso 1: Listening; Repaso 2–4: Writing
Grammar	Definite and indefinite articles	5: Reading; 6: Listening/Writing; 7: Speaking/Writing; 8: Speaking/Writing; 9: Writing; 10: Speaking; 11: Speaking; 13: Speaking; 19: Speaking; Repaso 2: Writing
Grammar	Noun-adjective agreement	14: Reading; 15: Writing; 16: Speaking/Writing; 17: Writing; 18: Writing/Speaking; 19: Speaking; 20: Listening/Reading; 22: Writing/Speaking; 23: Reading/Listening/Speaking; 24: Writing; Repaso 1: Listening; Repaso 2–4: Writing
Communication	Describe yourself and others	2: Speaking/Writing; 4: Reading/Speaking; 8: Speaking/Writing; 15: Writing; 17: Writing; 18: Writing/Speaking; 19: Speaking; 21: Listening/Speaking; 22: Writing/Speaking; 23: Reading/Listening/Speaking; 24 Writing; Repaso 3, 4: Writing
Communication	Identify people and things	6: Listening/Writing; 7: Speaking/Writing; 8: Speaking/Writing; 9: Writing; 10: Speaking; 11: Speaking; 13: Speaking; 18: Writing/Speaking; 22: Writing/Speaking; Repaso 2: Writing
Communication	Pronunciation: The letter **ñ**	*Pronunciación: La letra **ñ**, p. 71: Listening/Speaking*
Recycle	**gustar** with an infinitive	10: Speaking
Recycle	Snack foods	7: Speaking/Writing
Recycle	After-school activities	13: Speaking

The following activities are recorded in the Audio Program for *¡Avancemos!*

- **¡A responder!** *page 62*
- **6: La lista de Sandra** *page 67*
- **23: Integración** *page 78*
- **Repaso de la lección** *page 84*
  - **1: Listen and understand**
- **Repaso inclusivo** *page 88*
  - **1: Listen, understand, and compare**

¡A responder! TXT CD 1 track 35

1. pelirroja
2. atlético
3. organizada
4. cómico
5. grande
6. perezoso
7. joven
8. trabajador

6 La lista de Sandra TXT CD 1 track 37

Me gusta comprar libros, DVDs, frutas, helados, papas fritas, jugo, galletas y pizza.

23 Integración TXT CD 1 tracks 41, 42

¡Hola! Soy Alejandro. Tengo pelo rubio. No soy muy alto pero no soy bajo. Soy simpático y tengo muchos amigos. Me gusta escribir correos electrónicos. ¿Y tú? ¿Cómo eres? ¿Qué te gusta hacer?

¡Hola! Me llamo Édgar. ¿Y tú? ¿Cómo te llamas? ¿De dónde eres? A mí me gusta escuchar música. También me gusta escribir correos electrónicos y hablar por teléfono. ¡Hasta luego!

Repaso de la lección TXT CD 1 track 44

1 Listen and understand

Hola. Me llamo Carlos. Soy estudiante de español. Soy alto, pero no soy muy grande. Tengo pelo rubio. Soy un chico cómico, pero soy estudioso. Me gusta aprender el español. La maestra de español es la señora Pérez. Ella es muy buena. También es organizada y trabajadora. Es una mujer pequeña. Es baja y tiene pelo castaño. Le gusta dibujar porque es muy artística.

Repaso inclusivo TXT CD 1 track 46

1 Listen, understand, and compare

Buenos días. Yo soy Magdalena Canseco. Después de las clases, a los estudiantes de Miami les gusta pasar un rato con los amigos. Son muy estudiosos pero les gusta más practicar deportes. Les gusta montar en bicicleta y jugar al fútbol. Los estudiantes de Miami son muy atléticos.

Yo soy Magdalena Canseco, Radio Sol, Miami. David...

Gracias, Magdalena. Soy David Guzmán. En San Antonio, los estudiantes también son atléticos. Les gusta correr y jugar al fútbol. Pero hoy hace calor. Les gusta más leer o descansar. Pero no son perezosos. Los estudiantes de San Antonio son muy trabajadores.

Yo soy David Guzmán, Radio Sol, San Antonio.

On your desktop

Everything you need to ...

Plan	Present	Assess
easyPlanner DVD-ROM	**POWER PRESENTATIONS**	**McDougal Littell Assessment System** ONLINE
All resources including audio and video	Ready-made PowerPoint™ presentations with  **Animated Grammar**	✓ Assess, score, prescribe, and remediate online ✓ Create customized tests with the Test Generator CD-ROM ✓ Individualized Assessment for on-level, modified, pre-AP, and heritage language learners

Print

Plan	Present	Practice	Assess
URB 1 • Video Scripts pp. 99–100 • Family Involvement Activity p. 124 • Absent Student Copymasters pp. 133–143 **Lesson Plans** p. 29 **Best Practices Toolkit**	**URB 1** • Video Activities pp. 87–94 **TPRS** pp. 8–14	• *Cuaderno* pp. 24–49 • *Cuaderno para hispanohablantes* pp. 24–49 • *Lecturas para todos* pp. 7–11 • *Lecturas para hispanohablantes* • *¡AvanzaCómics! SúperBruno y Nati,* Episodio 1 **URB 1** • Practice Games pp. 65–72 • Audio Scripts pp. 108–112 • Fine Art Activities pp. 119–120	**URB 1** • Did you get it? Reteaching and Practice Copymasters pp. 39–50

Unit Transparency Book 1

Culture	Presentation and Practice	Classroom Management
• Atlas Maps 1–6 • U.S. Map 7 • Fine Art Transparencies 10, 11	• Vocabulary Transparencies 14, 15 • Grammar Presentation Transparencies 18, 19 • Situational Transparencies and label overlay 20, 21 • Situational Student Copymasters pp. 1, 2	• Warm Up Transparencies pp. 30–33 **MSRB** • Student Book Answer Transparencies 32–35

Audio and Video

Audio	Video

• Student Book Audio CD 1 Tracks 34–46
• Workbook Audio CD 1 Tracks 11–20
• Heritage Learners Audio CD 1 Tracks 5–8, CD 3 Tracks 5–8
• Assessment Audio CD 1 Tracks 5–8
• *Lecturas para todos* Audio CD 1 Track 2, CD 2 Tracks 1–6
• *Música del mundo hispano*
• Sing-along Audio CD
	• Vocabulary Video DVD 1
	• *Telehistoria* DVD 1
	   Escena 1
	   Escena 2
	   Escena 3
	   Completa
	• Culture Video DVD 1

Online and CD-ROM Resources

Student	Teacher
Available online and on CD-ROM: • eEdition • @HomeTutor • Animated Grammar **Available online:** • *Cultura Interactiva* • Culture Links • WebQuests • Flashcards • Conjuguemos.com • Review Games • Self-check Quiz	**Available online and on CD-ROM:** **EasyPlanner CD-ROM resources:** • Learning Scenarios • Conversation Cards • Family Letters in Spanish • Family Letters in Creole **Available online:** • McDougal Littell Assessment System **Available on CD-ROM:** • Test Generator • Power Presentations

Differentiated Assessment

On-level	Modified	Pre-AP	Heritage Learners
• Vocabulary Recognition Quiz p. 28 • Vocabulary Production Quiz p.29 • Grammar Quizzes pp. 30–31 • Culture Quiz p. 32 • On-level Lesson Test pp. 33–39 • On-level Unit Test pp. 45–51	• Modified Lesson Test pp. 23–29 • Modified Unit Test pp. 35–41	• Pre-AP Lesson Test pp. 23–29 • Pre-AP Unit Test pp. 35–41	• Heritage Learners Lesson Test pp. 29–35 • Heritage Learners Unit Test pp. 41–47

| **Core Pacing Guide** | **50 Minute (9 Day)**

	Objectives/Focus	Teach	Practice	Assess/HW Options
DAY 1	**Culture:** learn about Hispanic culture in the United States **Vocabulary:** describe yourself and others, identify people and things • Warm Up OHT 30 **5 min**	Lesson Opener pp. 58–59 **Presentación de vocabulario** pp. 60–62 • Read A–F • View video DVD 1 • Play audio TXT CD 1 track 34 • *¡A responder!* TXT CD 1 track 35 **Práctica de vocabulario** p. 63 • *Nota gramatical:* **ser**　　**25 min**	Lesson opener pp. 58–59 **Práctica de vocabulario** p. 63 • Acts. 1, 2 **15 min**	**Assess:** *Para y piensa* p. 63　**5 min** **Homework:** *Cuaderno* pp. 24–26 @HomeTutor
DAY 2	**Communication:** describing yourself and others • Warm Up OHT 30 • Check Homework　**5 min**	**Vocabulario en contexto** pp. 64–65 • *Telehistoria escena 1* DVD 1 **Culture:** *Comida mexicana y Tex-Mex* **20 min**	**Vocabulario en contexto** pp. 64–65 • Act. 3 TXT CD 1 track 36 • Act. 4 **20 min**	**Assess:** *Para y piensa* p. 65　**5 min** **Homework:** *Cuaderno* pp. 24–26 @HomeTutor
DAY 3	**Grammar:** definite and indefinite articles • Warm Up OHT 31 • Check Homework　**5 min**	**Presentación de gramática** p. 66 • Definite and indefinite articles **20 min**	**Práctica de gramática** pp. 67–69 • Acts. 5, 7, 8, 9, 10, 11 • Acts. 6 TXT CD 1 track 37 **20 min**	**Assess:** *Para y piensa* p. 69　**5 min** **Homework:** *Cuaderno* pp. 27–29 @HomeTutor
DAY 4	**Communication:** using definite and indefinite articles to talk about people • Warm Up OHT 31 • Check Homework　**5 min**	**Gramática en contexto** pp. 70–71 • *Telehistoria escena 2* DVD 1 • *Pronunciación* TXT CD 1 track 39 **15 min**	**Gramática en contexto** pp. 70–71 • Act. 12 TXT CD 1 track 38 • Act. 13 **25 min**	**Assess:** *Para y piensa* p. 71　**5 min** **Homework:** *Cuaderno* pp. 27–29 @HomeTutor
DAY 5	**Grammar:** noun-adjective agreement, using adjectives to describe people • Warm Up OHT 32 • Check Homework　**5 min**	**Presentación de gramática** p. 72 • Noun-adjective agreement **15 min**	**Práctica de gramática** pp. 73–75 • Acts. 14, 15, 16, 17, 18, 19 **25 min**	**Assess:** *Para y piensa* p. 75　**5 min** **Homework:** *Cuaderno* pp. 30–32 @HomeTutor
DAY 6	**Communication:** Culmination: describing people, definite and indefinite articles, descriptive adjectives • Warm Up OHT 32 • Check Homework　**5 min**	**Todo junto** pp. 76–78 • *Escenas 1, 2: Resumen* • *Telehistoria completa* DVD 1 **20 min**	**Todo junto** pp. 76–78 • Acts. 20, 21 TXT CD 1 tracks 36, 38, 40 • Act. 23 TXT CD 1 tracks 41, 42 • Acts. 22, 24 **20 min**	**Assess:** *Para y piensa* p. 78　**5 min** **Homework:** *Cuaderno* pp. 33–34 @HomeTutor
DAY 7	**Reading:** Greetings from San Antonio and Miami **Review:** Lesson review • Warm Up OHT 33 • Check Homework　**5 min**	**Lectura cultural** pp. 80–81 • *Saludos desde San Antonio y Miami* TXT CD 1 track 43 **Repaso de la lección** pp. 84–85 **15 min**	**Lectura cultural** pp. 80–81 • *Saludos desde San Antonio y Miami* **Repaso de la lección** pp. 84–85 • Act. 1 TXT CD 1 track 44 • Acts. 2, 3, 4, 5　**20 min**	**Assess:** *Para y piensa* p. 81; *Repaso de la lección* pp. 84–85 **10 min** **Homework:** *En resumen* p. 83; *Cuaderno* pp. 35–46 (optional) Review Games Online @HomeTutor
DAY 8	**Assessment**			**Assess:** Lesson 2 test or Unit 1 test **50 min**
DAY 9	**Unit Culmination** **5 min**	**Comparación cultural** pp. 86–87 TXT CD 1 track 45 **Repaso inclusivo** pp. 88–89 **15 min**	**Comparación cultural** pp. 86–87 **Repaso inclusivo** pp. 88–89 • Act. 1 TXT CD 1 track 46 • Acts. 2, 3, 4, 5, 6 **25 min**	**Homework:** *Cuaderno* pp. 47–49 **5 min**

	Objectives/Focus	Teach	Practice	Assess/HW Options
DAY 1	**Culture:** learn about Hispanic culture in the United States **Vocabulary:** describe yourself and others, identify people and things • Warm Up OHT 30 **5 min**	Lesson Opener pp. 58–59 **Presentación de vocabulario** pp. 60–62 • Read A–F • View video DVD 1 • Play audio TXT CD1 track 34 • *¡A responder!* TXT CD 1 track 35 **Práctica de vocabulario** p. 63 • *Nota gramatical:* ser **20 min**	Lesson Opener pp. 58–59 **Práctica de vocabulario** p. 63 • Acts. 1, 2 **20 min**	**Assess:** *Para y piensa* p. 63 **5 min**
	Communication: describing yourself and others **5 min**	**Vocabulario en contexto** pp. 64–65 • *Telehistoria escena 1* DVD 1 **Culture:** *Comida mexicana y Tex-Mex* **15 min**	**Vocabulario en contexto** pp. 64–65 • Act. 3 TXT CD 1 track 36 • Act. 4 **15 min**	Assess: *Para y piensa* p. 65 **5 min** **Homework:** *Cuaderno* pp. 24–26 @HomeTutor
DAY 2	**Grammar:** definite and indefinite articles • Warm Up OHT 31 • Check Homework **5 min**	**Presentación de gramática** p. 66 • Definite and indefinite articles **20 min**	**Práctica de gramática** pp. 67–69 • Acts. 5, 7, 8, 9, 10, 11 • Act. 6 TXT CD 1 track 37 **15 min**	Assess: *Para y piensa* p. 69 **5 min**
	Communication: using definite and indefinite articles to talk about people **5 min**	**Gramática en contexto** pp. 70–71 • *Telehistoria escena 2* DVD 1 • *Pronunciación* TXT CD 1 track 39 **20 min**	**Gramática en contexto** pp. 70–71 • Act. 12 TXT CD 1 track 38 • Act. 13 **15 min**	**Assess:** *Para y piensa* p. 71 **5 min** **Homework:** *Cuaderno* pp. 27–29 @HomeTutor
DAY 3	**Grammar:** noun adjective agreement, using adjectives to describe people • Warm Up OHT 32 • Check Homework **5 min**	**Presentación de gramática** p. 72 • Noun-adjective agreement **15 min**	**Práctica de gramática** pp. 73–75 • Acts. 14, 15, 16, 17, 18, 19 **20 min**	**Assess:** *Para y piensa* p. 75 **5 min**
	Communication: Culmination: describing people, definite and indefinite articles, descriptive adjectives **5 min**	**Todo junto** pp. 76–78 • *Escenas 1, 2: Resumen* • *Telehistoria completa* DVD 1 **15 min**	**Todo junto** pp. 76–78 • Acts. 20, 21 TXT CD 1 tracks, 36, 38, 40 • Act 23 TXT CD 1 tracks 41, 42 • Acts. 22, 24 **20 min**	Assess: *Para y piensa* p. 78 **5 min** **Homework:** *Cuaderno* pp. 30–34 @HomeTutor
DAY 4	**Reading:** Greetings from San Antonio and Miami • Warm Up OHT 33 • Check Homework **5 min**	**Lectura cultural** pp. 80–81 • *Saludos desde San Antonio y Miami* TXT CD 1 track 43 **15 min**	**Lectura cultural** pp. 80–81 • *Saludos desde San Antonio y Miami* **15 min**	**Assess:** *Para y piensa* p. 81 **10 min**
	Review: Lesson review **5 min**	**Repaso de la lección** pp. 84–85 **15 min**	**Repaso de la lección** pp. 84–85 • Act. 1 TXT CD 1 track 44 • Acts. 2, 3, 4, 5 **20 min**	**Assess:** *Repaso de la lección* pp. 84–85 **5 min** **Homework:** *En resumen* p. 83; *Cuaderno* pp. 35–46 (optional) @HomeTutor
DAY 5	**Assessment**			Assess: Lesson 2 test or Unit 1 test **50 min**
	Unit Culmination **5 min**	**Comparación cultural** pp. 86–87 TXT CD 1 track 45 **Repaso inclusivo** pp. 88–89 **10 min**	**Comparación cultural** pp. 86–87 **Repaso inclusivo** pp. 88–89 • Act. 1 TXT CD 1 track 46 • Acts. 2, 3, 4, 5, 6 **20 min**	Homework: *Cuaderno* pp. 47–49 **5 min**

¡AVANZA! Objectives

- Introduce lesson theme: **Mis amigos y yo.**
- **Culture:** Learn about activities teens enjoy in the U.S. and in Spanish-speaking countries.

Presentation Strategies

- Introduce the characters' names: Sandra, Ricardo and Alberto.
- Ask students to look at the photo on pp. 58–59.
- Ask students to identify the city, tell what they know about it, and identify what they see in the photo.
- Have students make a list of what they would like to do if they were to visit that city.

STANDARDS

1.3 Present information
2.1 Practices and perspectives
4.2 Compare cultures

Warm Up UTB 1 Transparency 30

Ser Complete the sentences with the correct form of **ser.**
1. Juan, ¿de dónde _____ tú?
2. Yo _____ de Costa Rica.
3. Y Ana y María, ¿de dónde _____ ellas?
4. Ana _____ de Panamá y María de Honduras.
5. Pablo y yo _____ de Uruguay.

Answers: 1. eres; 2. soy; 3. son; 4. es; 5. somos

Comparación cultural

Exploring the Theme

Ask the following:
1. Are there places in your neighborhood that sell Mexican and/or Tex-Mex food?
2. Have you tried any Mexican and/or Tex-Mex food? Can you name some examples?

¿Qué ves? Possible answers include:
- Sí, son amigos.
- Hace sol.
- Les gusta pasar un rato con los amigos, hablar, pasear.

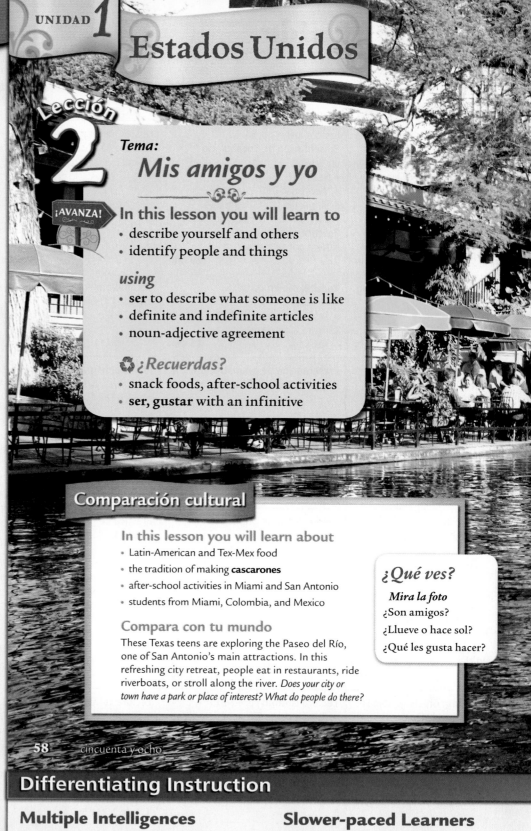

UNIDAD **1**
Estados Unidos

Lección

2

Tema:
Mis amigos y yo

¡AVANZA!

In this lesson you will learn to
- describe yourself and others
- identify people and things

using
- **ser** to describe what someone is like
- definite and indefinite articles
- noun-adjective agreement

¿Recuerdas?
- snack foods, after-school activities
- **ser, gustar** with an infinitive

Comparación cultural

In this lesson you will learn about
- Latin-American and Tex-Mex food
- the tradition of making **cascarones**
- after-school activities in Miami and San Antonio
- students from Miami, Colombia, and Mexico

Compara con tu mundo

These Texas teens are exploring the Paseo del Río, one of San Antonio's main attractions. In this refreshing city retreat, people eat in restaurants, ride riverboats, or stroll along the river. *Does your city or town have a park or place of interest? What do people do there?*

58 cincuenta y ocho

¿Qué ves?
Mira la foto
¿Son amigos?
¿Llueve o hace sol?
¿Qué les gusta hacer?

Differentiating Instruction

Multiple Intelligences

Naturalist Brainstorm with students to create a list of natural resources in your region or state. Then have students draft a design for an outdoor space that would allow the public access to, and enjoyment of, one of these natural resources. Encourage students to use San Antonio's **Paseo del Río** as one possible model.

Slower-paced Learners

Yes/No Questions Ask students yes or no questions about what they see in the photo on pp. 58–59. Point to the different items and ask questions about them. **¿Hace frío? ¿Les gusta pasar un rato con los amigos? ¿Les gusta practicar deportes?**

Online SPANISH CLASSZONE.COM

Featuring...
Cultura INTERACTIVA
Animated Grammar
@HomeTutor

And more...
• Get Help Online
• Interactive Flashcards
• Review Games
• WebQuest
• Self-Check Quiz

Online SPANISH CLASSZONE.COM

Get Help Online If students need a little extra help with vocabulary, grammar, or a recycled topic, they can download the exact copymaster they need. The Did you get it? Reteaching and Practice Copymasters provide extensive reteaching and additional practice for every vocabulary and grammar presentation in *¡Avancemos!*, and they are all available online.

Featuring...
Cultura INTERACTIVA
Animated Grammar
@HomeTutor

And more...
• Get Help Online
• Interactive Flashcards
• Review Games
• WebQuest
• Self-Check Quiz

Using the Photo

Location Information

Paseo del Río The **Paseo del Río** shown in the photo is in San Antonio, a city located in south-central Texas. It is a walkway that borders the San Antonio River. Around 1986, it became a popular tourist attraction. It has a large mall, shops, restaurants, open-air cafés, and an amphitheater.

Expanded Information

San Antonio Native Americans first called the place that is now San Antonio *Yanaguana,* which means "refreshing waters." San Antonio is approximately 150 miles from Mexico.

The Alamo San Antonio is home to the famous Alamo, the first Spanish mission established in the area.

Paseo del Río
San Antonio, Texas

Estados Unidos
cincuenta y nueve   59

Differentiating Instruction

Heritage Language Learners

Support What They Know Display photos of historical places in Texas and a map of San Antonio. Invite students who have visited or have relatives in Texas to share what they know about the state. Based on the information they have given, ask students what places they would like to visit and why. What type of food would they eat there?

Pre-AP

Expand and Elaborate San Antonio is a city rich in history and culture. Have students use the library or Internet to research one aspect of the city's history. Some key words for their search could include **historia**/history of San Antonio. Then give students the opportunity to share what they have learned with the rest of the group.

Long-term Retention

Connect to Previous Learning

Review weather vocabulary from Lección preliminar and **ser** and **gustar** from Unidad 1, Lección 1, by having students generate questions and answers about the photo: **¿Qué tiempo hace? Hace sol; ¿De dónde son los amigos? Son de San Antonio.**

¡AVANZA! **Goal:** Learn how Sandra describes herself and her friends. Then practice what you have learned to describe yourself and others. *Actividades 1–2*

♻ *¿Recuerdas?* The verb **ser** p. 38

¡AVANZA! Objective

- Present vocabulary: adjectives to describe yourself and friends.

Core Resources

- Video Program: DVD 1
- Audio Program: TXT CD 1, track 34

Presentation Strategies

- Have students look at pp. 60–61 and repeat each vocabulary word after you.
- Ask **sí/no** questions to verify comprehension. For example: **¿Laura es alta? (no) ¿Rosita es joven? (sí)**
- Play the audio as students read A–D.
- Show the video.

✦ STANDARD

1.2 Understand language

Comparisons

English Language Connection

Point out that the verb **tener,** *to have,* is also used to talk about the features a person has: **tiene pelo castaño.**

Long-term Retention

Study Tips

Introduce students to the practice of learning new adjectives and their opposites. Have them write an adjective on index cards and its opposite from the vocabulary, for example: **trabajador/perezoso; bueno/malo; organizada/desorganizada.**

Communication

🌐 Regionalisms

Explain to students that in Cuba and Puerto Rico, **guapo(a)** also means bold, daring, or defiant.

VIDEO
DVD

AUDIO

A ¡Hola! Soy Sandra. Soy **artística** y **tengo pelo castaño.** A mi **amigo** Ricardo le gusta practicar deportes **porque** es **atlético.**

artística

atlético

B Alberto es **trabajador** y **estudioso.** Le gusta estudiar. David es **un poco perezoso.** No es **un estudiante muy bueno.** No le gusta trabajar.

trabajador

perezoso

60 Unidad 1 Estados Unidos
sesenta

Differentiating Instruction

Inclusion

Multisensory Input/Output Say one of the featured vocabulary words aloud as you write it on the board. Then have students copy the word onto a small slip of paper as they repeat it aloud. After students have written all of the words, say each aloud again. This time, have students place their slips of paper on top of the appropriate photo in the text.

Multiple Intelligences

Intrapersonal Invite students to reflect on their own traits and personalities by creating a personality page. On their pages students might include a photo, a self-portrait, or other drawing of things they like. They should also include adjectives that describe themselves. **Soy organizada. No soy muy alta.**

C Soy **una persona** muy **organizada.** Mi **amiga** Ana es **inteligente** pero un poco **desorganizada.**

organizada

desorganizada

D Rafael es muy **alto,** pero Laura es **baja.** Manuel es **grande,** pero Francisco es **pequeño.** La señora Santa Cruz es un poco **vieja,** pero Rosita es **joven.**

alto

baja

grande

pequeño

vieja

joven

Más vocabulario

bonito(a) *pretty*
guapo(a) *good-looking*
malo(a) *bad*

Expansión de vocabulario p. R2

Continuará...

Lección 2
sesenta y uno **61**

Communication
Common Error Alert

Often, students forget to use the definite article before the titles **señor (Sr.), señora (Sra.),** and **señorita (Srta.).** Remind students to use **el** or **la** before these titles except when addressing a person directly. For example: **Hola, Sr. Sánchez. Le presento a la Sra. García.**

Communication
Regionalisms

Explain to students that in Argentina and Mexico, the word **grande** means *big* but is also used when referring to an older person. For example, **Él es un señor grande.** This means that he is an old man. Instead of using the word **viejo** (old), they use **grande.**

Differentiating Instruction

Multiple Intelligences

Visual Learners Ask students to make a Venn diagram in which they compare and contrast themselves and a friend, using the adjectives they've learned in this lesson.

Slower-paced Learners

Personalize It Have students compare themselves with the people in the photos on pp. 60–61. Ask: **¿Eres organizado(a)? Sí, soy organizado(a). ¿Eres alto(a)? No, soy bajo(a). ¿Eres joven? Sí, soy joven.** Continue with the rest of the photos. Then have students ask their classmates similar questions: **¿Eres perezosa? No, no soy perezosa. Soy trabajadora.**

62

Objective

- Present vocabulary, adjectives to describe yourself and friends.

Core Resources

- Video Program: DVD 1
- Audio Program: TXT CD 1 tracks 34, 35

Presentation Strategies

- Have students look at the photos on p. 62, and have them repeat each vocabulary word after you.
- Ask simple comprehension questions: ¿Quién es la mujer pelirroja? ¿Quién tiene pelo rubio?
- Play the audio as students read E and F.

 STANDARD

1.2 Understand language

 Communication
Group Work

Place students in groups of four or five. Ask each group to review the adjectives on pp. 60–62 and then close their books. Ask them to work together to write down as many adjectives as they can in 60 seconds.

Long-term Retention
Personalize It

Ask students to draw a chart with three columns. They should head one column with their own names. The second column they should head with the name of a family member. The third column they should head with the name of a friend. They should write the adjectives they've learned under the names of the people to whom those adjectives apply.

Communication
Interpersonal Mode

Memory Game Ask a student to start the game by saying **"Yo tengo un amigo alto."** The next student must add an adjective and say **"Yo tengo un amigo alto y pelirrojo."** The game continues from student to student until all of the adjectives from the lesson have been used.

See answers on p. 63.

62

Presentación de VOCABULARIO
(continuación)

E La señora Guardado es **pelirroja** y el señor Guardado **tiene** pelo castaño. Marco y Laura son **chicos** muy buenos. Marco tiene **pelo rubio** y Laura tiene pelo castaño.

pelirroja
la mujer

pelo castaño
el hombre

pelo rubio
el chico   la chica

F Yo soy un poco **seria,** pero mi amigo Alberto es muy **cómico. Todos** mis amigos son muy **simpáticos.** ¿Y tú? ¿**Cómo eres?**

cómico   seria

¡A responder! Escuchar

Listen to these descriptions of Sandra and her friends. Point to the person in the photo who matches each description you hear.

@HomeTutor VideoPlus
Interactive Flashcards
ClassZone.com

Unidad 1 Estados Unidos
62 sesenta y dos

Differentiating Instruction

Pre-AP

Expand and Elaborate Have students choose three people from the photos. Ask them to describe those people using as many details as possible. For example: **La mujer pelirroja se llama Sra. Guardado. Ella es bonita y simpática. Le gusta tocar la guitarra y dibujar.**

Heritage Language Learners

Regional Variations Ask students to discuss other words they know and use that mean the same as the words presented on pp. 60–62. For example, other words that mean the same thing as **chico(a)** are **muchacho(a)** and **niño(a)** in many Latin American countries; **chaval(a)** in Spain; **chavo(a)** in Mexico, and **pibe(a)** in Argentina.

Práctica de VOCABULARIO

1 | Los opuestos

Leer | Sandra describes her friends but Ricardo says the opposite. Match Sandra's description with Ricardo's response.

Sandra

1. Marco es pequeño.
2. Luisa es trabajadora.
3. Pablo es organizado.
4. Joaquín es malo.
5. Anabel es joven.
6. Francisco es cómico.

Ricardo

a. No, es bueno.
b. No, es grande.
c. No, es desorganizado.
d. No, es perezosa.
e. No, es serio.
f. No, es vieja.

Expansión:
Teacher Edition Only
Ask students to write other examples of a description and its opposite.

Nota gramatical **¿Recuerdas?** The verb **ser** p. 38

Use **ser** to describe what people are like.

La mujer **es** alta.
The woman **is** tall.

Los chicos **son** organizados.
The boys **are** organized.

---

2 | Porque...

Hablar
Escribir

Explain why Ricardo and Alberto like or don't like the following activities.

serio   atlético   artístico

estudioso   desorganizado   trabajador

modelo: A Ricardo le gusta practicar deportes porque es atlético.

1. A Ricardo le gusta hacer la tarea.
2. A Ricardo le gusta dibujar.
3. A Alberto no le gusta ser cómico.
4. A Alberto le gusta correr.
5. A Alberto no le gusta ser perezoso.
6. A Alberto no le gusta ser organizado.

Expansión:
Teacher Edition Only
Have students draw, cut out, or use clip art to illustrate all of the adjectives in the list.

Más práctica   Cuaderno pp. 24–26   Cuaderno para hispanohablantes pp. 24–27

PARA Y PIENSA **Did you get it?**
1. Say that Juan is short.
2. Say that David is artistic.
3. Say that Carlos is serious.

Get Help Online
ClassZone.com

Lección 2
sesenta y tres   **63**

Objectives
· Practice vocabulary: adjectives, likes and dislikes.
· Recycle: **ser** to describe people.

Core Resource
· *Cuaderno,* pp. 24–26

Practice Sequence
· **Activity 1:** Vocabulary recognition: descriptive adjectives, opposites
· **Activity 2:** Vocabulary production: associating preferences with characteristics

STANDARDS
1.2 Understand language, Act. 1
1.3 Present information, Act. 2

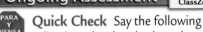

✓ Ongoing Assessment   @HomeTutor More Practice ClassZone.com

PARA Y PIENSA **Quick Check** Say the following adjectives aloud and ask students to say the opposite: **bueno, pequeño, viejo, cómico, organizado. Answers:** malo; grande; joven; serio; desorganizado
For additional practice, use Reteaching & Practice Copymasters URB 1 pp. 39, 40.

Answers MSRB Transparency 32

Answers for Activities on pp. 62, 63.

¡A responder! Audio Script, TE p. 57b
Students should point to:

1. la señora Guardado   5. Manuel
2. Ricardo   6. David
3. Sandra   7. Rosita
4. Alberto   8. Alberto

Activity 1
1. b   3. c   5. f
2. d   4. a   6. e

Activity 2
1. A Ricardo le gusta hacer la tarea porque es estudioso.
2. ... le gusta dibujar porque es artístico.
3. A Alberto no le gusta ser cómico porque es serio.
4. ... le gusta correr porque es atlético.
5. ... no le gusta ser perezoso porque es trabajador.
6. ... no le gusta ser organizado porque es desorganizado.

Para y piensa
1. Juan es bajo.
2. David es artístico.
3. Carlos es serio.

Differentiating Instruction

Slower-paced Learners

Yes/No Questions Have students bring in photos of sports teams, family members, or friends. Create yes/no questions about physical and personal traits of the people represented in each photo and have the class respond **sí** or **no.** For example: **¿John es atlético?** (sí) **¿La maestra es vieja?** (no)

Pre-AP

Expand and Elaborate Have students write a paragraph about their favorite celebrity. They may include information about where this person is from, what he or she likes to do and why, and a description. Have students read their paragraph to the class and have the class guess the identity of the celebrity.

- Understand vocabulary in context: descriptive words.
- Practice using vocabulary in context.
- **Culture:** Compare Mexican and Tex-Mex food.

Core Resources

- Video Program: DVD 1
- Audio Program: TXT CD 1, track 36

Presentation Strategies

- Ask students to predict what Sandra, Alberto, and Ricardo are talking about.
- Show the video. Encourage students to find examples of humor in the scene.
- Play audio while students follow the script in the text.

Practice Sequence

- **Activity 3:** Telehistoria comprehension
- **Activity 4:** Vocabulary production: descriptive adjectives; **gustar** + infinitive

STANDARDS

1.1 Engage in conversation, Act. 4
1.2 Understand language, Acts. 3–4
1.3 Present information, Acts. 3–4
2.2 Products and perspectives, CC

 Warm Up UTB 1 Transparency 30

Vocabulary Match each adjective with its appropriate like or dislike.

1. perezoso
2. estudiosa
3. artística
4. atlético

a. le gusta dibujar
b. le gusta correr
c. le gusta leer y estudiar
d. no le gusta trabajar

Answers: 1. d; 2. c; 3. a; 4. b

Video Summary

At River Walk Café, Sandra sets up her laptop and Webcam. She contacts her friend Alicia, who has sent her a T-shirt to get Trini Salgado's autograph. Sandra is joined by her friends Alberto and Ricardo, who introduce themselves to Alicia via the Webcam. Each boy describes himself favorably in a humorous way. Sandra rolls her eyes.

VOCABULARIO *en contexto*

 Goal: Notice how Sandra and her friends describe themselves and each other. Then practice these words to describe others. *Actividades 3–4*

Telehistoria escena 1

STRATEGIES

Cuando lees

Skim Find the main idea by skimming (rapidly glancing over) the text before reading it carefully. What is the main idea of the scene below?

Cuando escuchas

Find the humor Humor makes a scene fun and memorable. Listen for exaggeration, teasing, and jokes. What are some examples of humor in the following scene?

VIDEO
DVD

AUDIO

Sandra, speaking to Alicia via webcam, holds up Alicia's T-shirt.

Sandra: Es bonita. Pero te gusta más con el autógrafo de Trini Salgado, ¿no?

Alberto and Ricardo join Sandra.

Sandra: Alicia, te presento a mis amigos: Alberto y Ricardo.

Alberto: Hola, Alicia. Me llamo Alberto. Soy alto... no soy muy alto. Tengo pelo castaño, y soy muy trabajador. Pero me gusta mirar la televisión y escuchar música. *(He pulls CDs from his backpack.)*

Sandra: No, él no es perezoso pero es un poco desorganizado.

Ricardo: Hola, Alicia. ¿Qué tal? Me llamo Ricardo. Soy inteligente, simpático y estudioso. Me gusta practicar deportes porque soy atlético. Y me gusta dibujar porque soy muy artístico.

Sandra shows one of Ricardo's drawings that is not very good.

Sandra: Sí. Él es muy artístico.

Ricardo: Ella es cómica, ¿no?

Alberto: Ella no es muy seria.

Sandra: OK, OK. Adiós, Alicia. Hasta luego.

Continuará... p. 70

Differentiating Instruction

Inclusion

Frequent Review/Repetition Organize students into groups of three. Give them the opportunity to read through the Telehistoria four times. The first time, instruct students to read the script silently. The second time, have each group member read the part of one character. Then have students change roles, and read through the script twice more. Each student should get a chance to play each role.

Pre-AP

Identify Main Idea Write the following words on individual index cards: **trabajador, desorganizado, inteligente, simpático, estudioso, atlético.** Then create two concept webs on the board, one for **Ricardo,** and the other for **Alberto.** Invite volunteers to post each word around the appropriate name. Have students point to the place in the text where they found their information and read the text.

3 | Las características *Comprensión del episodio*

Escuchar Leer

Copy the Venn diagram on a piece of paper and use it to compare Ricardo and Alberto. Write their differences below their names. In the center, write what they have in common.

Ricardo   Alberto

Le gusta dibujar.

Expansión:
Teacher Edition Only
Ask students to compare two people they know using a Venn diagram.

4 | Una entrevista

Leer Hablar

Read the interview with Raúl López, a famous young soccer player. Then talk to another student about the article. Use at least three adjectives to ask him or her questions.

A ¿Es Raúl perezoso?

B No, es trabajador porque le gusta estudiar.

ENTREVISTA

¡ESTRELLA DEL FUTURO!

Revista Estrella: Raúl, ¿cómo eres?

Raúl: Soy muy atlético. Me gusta mucho jugar al fútbol y practicar deportes. Pero también me gusta descansar.

Revista Estrella: Y eres un estudiante serio, ¿no?

Raúl: Sí, me gusta leer libros y estudiar.

Revista Estrella: ¿Te gusta escuchar música?

Raúl: Sí, me gusta escuchar música, pero me gusta más tocar la guitarra. También me gusta dibujar.

Expansión:
Teacher Edition Only
Ask students to generate three more questions for Raúl.

Comparación cultural

Comida mexicana y Tex-Mex

How does local environment affect the food that people eat? Tex-Mex is a regional cuisine that combines styles of cooking from **Mexico** and **Texas.** Did you know that *nachos,* crispy tacos, tortilla chips with salsa, *fajitas,* and *chili con carne* are all Tex-Mex dishes? Common Tex-Mex ingredients include flour tortillas, yellow cheese, refried beans, and beef. In the interior of Mexico, traditional ingredients are corn tortillas, white cheese, black beans, chicken, seafood, and pork.

Unas fajitas

Compara con tu mundo *What are some restaurants in your community that serve foods from other countries? Have you eaten at any of them?*

PARA Y PIENSA

Did you get it? Fill in the appropriate adjective.
1. Alberto es trabajador. No es _____ .
2. A Ricardo le gusta practicar deportes. Es _____ .
3. A Ricardo le gusta hacer la tarea. Es _____ .

Get Help Online
ClassZone.com

Differentiating Instruction

Slower-paced Learners

Personalize It Ask students to talk about experiences they have had with Tex-Mex cuisine. Perhaps it was at a restaurant, a friend's house, or at home. Perhaps it was a recipe they prepared themselves. Encourage students to talk about their personal preferences in Spanish. **Me gusta comer chili con carne. Me gusta más comer fajitas.**

Pre-AP

Support Ideas with Details Write the following adjectives describing Raúl López on the board: **atlético, estudioso, artístico.** Then ask students to find details in the interview to support each of these ideas. For example, under **atlético** you might add **le gusta jugar al fútbol** and **le gusta practicar deportes.**

Comparación cultural

Essential Question

Suggested Answer Local agriculture often dictates the foods people eat. For example, many Mexican foods contain corn and chile peppers because those crops grow abundantly in Mexico's climate.

✓ Ongoing Assessment

@HomeTutor
More Practice
ClassZone.com

PARA Y PIENSA **Quick Check** Play a word association game before students do the Para y piensa. You say an activity and students supply an appropriate adjective. For example: **Le gusta correr. Es atlético.** For additional practice, use Reteaching & Practice Copymasters URB 1 pp. 39, 41.

Answers MSRB Transparency 32

Activity 3 Answers will vary. Possible answers include:

Ricardo   Alberto

es inteligente
es simpático

son amigos de Sandra

es trabajador

Activity 4 Answers will vary. Sample answers include:

¿Es Raúl atlético? Sí. Le gusta mucho jugar al fútbol.

¿Es Raúl un estudiante serio? Sí. Le gusta leer libros.

¿Es Raúl viejo? No. Es joven.

Para y piensa
1. perezoso; 2. atlético; 3. estudioso

Presentación de GRAMÁTICA

Goal: Learn about definite and indefinite articles. Then practice using these articles to identify people and things. *Actividades 5–11*

♻ *¿Recuerdas?* Snack foods p. 33, **gustar** with an infinitive p. 44

Objective

· Present definite and indefinite articles.

Core Resource

· *Cuaderno,* pp. 27–29

Presentation Strategies

· Check students' understanding of definite and indefinite articles by saying a noun and asking them to provide the correct article. For example: **el chico**.

· Say a singular noun and ask students to provide the corresponding indefinite article: **un niño.** Repeat with plural nouns: **unos niños.**

· Check formation of plural nouns by saying a singular noun and asking students to provide the plural noun: **mujer/mujeres.**

✿ STANDARD

4.1 Compare languages

Warm Up   UTB 1 Transparency 31

Vocabulary Complete the sentences using the correct word.

> mujer   chicos   hombre   chica   pelo

1. Marco y Lauro son _____ muy buenos.
2. Marco tiene el _____ rubio.
3. La señora Díaz es una _____ joven.
4. El señor Roldán es un _____ alto.
5. Sara es una _____ muy simpática.

Answers: 1. chicos; 2. pelo; 3. mujer; 4. hombre; 5. chica

English Grammar Connection: **Definite articles** (in English, *the*) are used with nouns to indicate *specific* persons, places, or things. **Indefinite articles** (*a, an*) are used with nouns to indicate *nonspecific* persons, places, or things.

The boy is **a** friend.   **El** chico es **un** amigo.

| definite article | indefinite article | | definite article | indefinite article |

Definite and Indefinite Articles

Animated Grammar
ClassZone.com

In Spanish, articles match nouns in gender and number.

Here's how: All Spanish nouns, even if they refer to objects, are either **masculine** or **feminine**.

· Nouns ending in **-o** are usually **masculine**.
· Nouns ending in **-a** are usually **feminine**.

		Definite Article	Noun	Indefinite Article	Noun
Masculine	Singular	el *the*	chico *boy*	un *a*	chico *boy*
	Plural	los *the*	chicos *boys*	unos *some*	chicos *boys*
Feminine	Singular	la *the*	chica *girl*	una *a*	chica *girl*
	Plural	las *the*	chicas *girls*	unas *some*	chicas *girls*

matches   *matches*
Los libros son para **la maestra.**   **The** books are for **the** teacher.

To form the **plural** of a noun, add **-s** if the noun ends in a vowel. Add **-es** if the noun ends in a consonant.

vowel ↴   *consonant* ↴
estudiante → estudiant**es**   mujer → muje**res**

Más práctica
Cuaderno *pp. 27–29*
Cuaderno para hispanohablantes *pp. 28–30*

@HomeTutor
Leveled Grammar Practice
ClassZone.com

Differentiating Instruction

English Learners

Provide Comprehensible Input Have students fold a piece of paper in half lengthwise. Tell them to label the left column **Singular** and the right column **Plural**. Then invite students to create a list of ten things that they see in the classroom. Tell them to write the singular form of each word on the left, and the plural form on the right. Allow students to read their lists aloud for the group.

Inclusion

Metacognitive Support Direct students to the chart within the grammar box that explains *Definite and Indefinite Articles.* Ask students to describe the patterns they notice within the information presented. For example, they might point out that all plural articles end in **s,** or that there are four ways to say *the* in Spanish.

Answers   MSRB Transparency 32

Activity 5

| 1. Las | 3. Los | 5. Las | 7. Las | 9. Los |
| 2. La | 4. El | 6. El | 8. Las | 10. La |

Activity 6
los libros; los DVDs; las frutas; los helados; las papas fritas; el jugo; las galletas; la pizza

Activity answers continue on page 67.

Práctica de GRAMÁTICA

5 | ¿Cómo son las personas en la oficina?

Leer Miguel is describing various people in the school office. Complete his sentences with **el, la, los, las.**

1. ____ chicas son atléticas.
2. ____ maestra es inteligente.
3. ____ amigos son simpáticos.
4. ____ chico es pelirrojo.
5. ____ mujeres son artísticas.
6. ____ hombre es guapo.
7. ____ personas son organizadas.
8. ____ amigas son jóvenes.
9. ____ estudiantes son bajos.
10. ____ mujer es cómica.

> **Expansión:**
> Teacher Edition Only
> Have students choose three of the sentences and illustrate them.

6 | La lista de Sandra

Escuchar
Escribir Sandra likes to buy many things. Listen and write a list of what she likes to buy, using **el, la, los, las.**

> 🎧 **Audio Program**
> TXT CD 1 Track 37
> Audio Script, TE p. 57b

7 | ¿Qué es? ♻ ¿Recuerdas? Snack foods p. 33

Hablar
Escribir Identify these foods, using **un, una, unos, unas.**

modelo: Son unas galletas.

> **Expansión:**
> Teacher Edition Only
> Ask students to write another sentence for each picture. They can say if they like each food or not, or add an adjective to describe the food.

1.
2.
3.
4.

5.
6.
7.
8.

Lección 2
sesenta y siete **67**

Differentiating Instruction

Inclusion

Alphabetic/Phonetic Awareness Before students complete Activity 5, have them copy it on a separate sheet of paper. Have them circle the letters in each noun that will help them determine whether it is masculine or feminine, singular or plural. For example, in item 1, students circle the **-as** in **chicas.** This indicates the noun is feminine and plural and requires the article **las.**

Multiple Intelligences

Visual Learners Divide the class into two teams to play a "Draw and Guess" game. In advance, copy a number of familiar nouns onto index cards. Have one player choose a card and draw a picture of the noun for his or her team. The teammates need to guess the item using an indefinite article. **¡Es un teléfono! ¡Son unas chicas!**

Objectives
· Practice using definite and indefinite articles.
· Recycle: snack foods.

Core Resource
· Audio Program: TXT CD 1 track 37

Practice Sequence
· **Activity 5:** Controlled practice: definite articles
· **Activity 6:** Transitional practice: definite and indefinite articles
· **Activity 7:** Transitional practice: indefinite articles; **Recycle:** snack foods

✿ STANDARD
1.3 Present information, Acts. 5–7

Communication
Grammar Activity

Before doing Activity 5, divide students into four groups and give each group an index card. One group writes **el** on an index card. Another group writes **la** on another index card. The third group writes **los**, and the last group writes **las.** Read aloud the nouns from the activity at random, and have groups take turns raising the corresponding card. For example, you say **chico**, group one raises the card with **el.**

✓ Ongoing Assessment

Alternative Strategy Have students practice when to ask **¿Qué es?** and when to ask **¿Qué son?** using the illustrations from Activity 7. For additional practice, use Reteaching & Practice Copymasters URB 1, p. 48.

 Answers MSRB Transparency 32

Answers continued from p. 66.

Activity 7
1. Son unas papas fritas.
2. Es un refresco.
3. Es una galleta.
4. Es un helado.
5. Es una pizza.
6. Son unos helados.
7. Son unas frutas.
8. Es un jugo.

67

Objectives

- Practice using definite and indefinite articles, adjectives
- **Recycle: gustar** + infinitive.

Core Resource

- *Cuaderno*, pp. 27–29

Practice Sequence

- **Activity 8:** Transitional practice: **ser** + indefinite articles
- **Activity 9:** Transitional practice: **gustar** + infinitive, definite and indefinite articles
- **Activity 10:** Open-ended practice: **gustar** + infinitive, definite and indefinite articles
- **Activity 11:** Open-ended practice: indefinite articles

 STANDARDS

1.1 Engage in conversation, Acts. 10–11
1.3 Present information, Acts 8–11, PYP

Long-term Retention

 Recycle

Activity 8 Remind students that to make a sentence negative, they must place the word **no** before the verb. **Las chicas no son estudiosas.** Expand Activity 8 by having students make all the sentences negative.

✓ **Ongoing Assessment**

Alternative Strategy After completing Activity 9, each student should report to the class some of his or her sentences using: **A Marta le gusta...**

 Answers MSRB Transparency 33

Activity 8
1. Sara y Laura son unas chicas estudiosas.
2. Óscar y Justino son unos chicos serios.
3. Sara y Laura son unas amigas trabajadoras.
4. Daniel es un chico desorganizado.
5. Diana es una chica alta.
6. Óscar es un chico alto.
7. Sara es una estudiante pelirroja.
8. Justino es un chico grande.

Activity answers continue on p. 69.

68

---

8 | ¿Son estudiosos?

Hablar Escribir

Describe these people, using **ser** and **un, una, unos, unas.**

modelo: chico cómico
Daniel es un chico cómico.

1. chicas estudiosas
2. chicos serios
3. amigas trabajadoras
4. chico desorganizado
5. chica alta
6. chico alto
7. estudiante pelirroja
8. chico grande

Expansión:
Teacher Edition Only
Have students choose one of the students from the picture and invent a complete description of him or her.

9 | Después de las clases

Escribir

Describe what Marta likes to do after school. Combine elements from the three columns to create six different sentences. You may use each article more than once.

modelo: tocar / la / guitarra
Le gusta tocar la guitarra.

tocar		guitarra
aprender		DVD
preparar	la	libro
alquilar	los	amigos
leer	un	televisión
mirar	el	español
pasar un rato con		comida

Expansión:
Teacher Edition Only
Ask students to use the three columns to write six sentences describing what other people like to do.

68 Unidad 1 Estados Unidos
sesenta y ocho

Differentiating Instruction

Slower-paced Learners

Personalize It Have students replace the names in Activity 8 with names of their own classmates. Who among their friends could be described as **chicas estudiosas,** or **un chico alto?**

Multiple Intelligences

Kinesthetic Have students dramatize gestures associated with the following people from Activity 8: chicas estudiosas, chico(a) alto(a), chico desorganizado, chicos serios, chico grande.

10 | ¿Qué te gusta más? ♻ *¿Recuerdas?* **gustar** with an infinitive p. 44

Hablar

Ask a partner what he or she likes more.

modelo: comprar

A ¿Te gusta más comprar una fruta o unas papas fritas?

B Me gusta más comprar una fruta.

1. leer

2. hablar con

3. pasar un rato con

Expansión:
Teacher Edition Only
Ask students to write and illustrate three more items like those in the activity.

4. comer

5. beber

6. comprar

11 | En una isla desierta

Hablar

Work in a group of five. Take turns naming some of the items you would wish for if you were stranded on a desert island. Repeat the items other group members wished for, and then add one of your own. Include the definite or indefinite article with each item.

A Una pizza.

B Una pizza, unos libros.

C Una pizza, unos libros, un refresco.

Expansión:
Teacher Edition Only
Have groups of students compete to see who can come up with the longest list of items.

Más práctica   Cuaderno pp. 27–29   Cuaderno para hispanohablantes pp. 28–30

PARA Y PIENSA

Did you get it?
Match the article to its corresponding noun.

1. la
2. unas
3. el
4. unos

a. libro
b. hombres
c. televisión
d. frutas

Get Help Online
ClassZone.com

Differentiating Instruction

Inclusion

Sequential Organization Have students write a subject (male or female), the verb form **es,** the articles **un** and **una** + noun, and adjectives they know on separate index cards. Use the cards to practice forming sentences using the correct word order. Use color coding to reinforce sentence pattern. For example: blue = subject, yellow = verb, and so on.

Pre-AP

Expand and Elaborate Have students explain why they chose the items they did for Activity 11. For example: Una pizza, porque me gusta comer pizza. Unos libros, porque me gusta leer. Un refresco, porque me gusta beber refrescos.

♻ Recycle   **Long-term Retention**

Ask students to work with a partner to ask and answer a minimum of 5 questions about what they like to do most. Ask them to prepare in advance a list of activities to include in their questions. They should not be the same as the ones in Activity 10. When they have completed the activity, have students reverse roles.

✓ Ongoing Assessment   @HomeTutor More Practice ClassZone.com

PARA Y PIENSA
Peer Assessment Have pairs of students explain to each other when to use **un/una** or **unos/unas** and when to use **el/la** or **los/las**. Monitor to be sure they are on the right track. For additional practice, use Reteaching & Practice Copymasters URB 1 pp. 42, 43, 49.

Answers   MSRB Transparency 33

Answers continued from p. 68.

Activity 9 Answers will vary. Sample answers include:
Le gusta aprender el español.
Le gusta preparar la comida.
Le gusta alquilar un DVD.
Le gusta leer un libro.
Le gusta mirar la televisión.
Le gusta pasar un rato con los amigos.

Activity 10 Answers will vary. Answers may include:
1. A: ¿Te gusta más leer un libro o un correo electrónico? B: Me gusta más leer un libro.
2. A: ¿Te gusta más hablar con unas chicas o con unos chicos? B: Me gusta más hablar con unos chicos.
3. A: ¿Te gusta más pasar un rato con unos chicos o un maestro? B: Me gusta más pasar un rato con unos chicos.
4. A: ¿Te gusta más comer unas galletas o una pizza?
B: Me gusta más comer una pizza.
5. A: ¿Te gusta más beber un jugo o un refresco? B: Me gusta más beber un refresco.
6. A: ¿Te gusta más comprar unos libros o unos DVDs? B: Me gusta más comprar unos libros.

Activity 11 Answers will vary. Answers must include correct definite or indefinite article with each item:
Una bicicleta, una patineta, una guitarra, unas galletas, unos helados.

Para y piensa 1. c; **2.** d; **3.** a; **4.** b

69

¡AVANZA! **Objectives**

- Practice definite and indefinite articles in context.
- **Culture:** Compare regional variations: foods.
- Recycle: after-school activities.
- Pronunciation: the letter **ñ** and its /ny/ sound.

Core Resources

- Video Program: DVD 1
- Audio Program: TXT CD 1, tracks 38, 39

Presentation Strategies

- Have students read the script.
- Show the video and/or play the audio.
- Ask who the people in the picture are.
- Ask what interests Ricardo and Alberto.

Practice Sequence

- **Activity 12:** Telehistoria comprehension
- **Activity 13:** Transitional practice: definite and indefinite articles; Recycle: after-school activities

STANDARDS

1.1 Engage in conversation, Act. 13
1.2 Understand language, Act. 12, Pronunciación
1.3 Present information, Act. 13
4.1 Compare languages, Pronunciación

 Warm Up UTB 1 Transparency 31

Indefinite Articles Write the appropriate indefinite article for the following.

1. _____ chico   4. _____ amigas
2. _____ mujeres   5. _____ refresco
3. _____ galleta   6. _____ hombres

Answers: 1. un; 2. unas; 3. una; 4. unas; 5. un; 6. unos

Video Summary

@HomeTutor VideoPlus ClassZone.com

Ricardo, Alberto, and Sandra are at the café. The boys inquire about a girl, Ana, who is sitting with a group of girls from Mrs. García's class. Sandra tells them what she knows about Ana, and the boys become more interested. Sandra signals that it is time to leave and the boys follow. Alberto almost bumps into Ana. Sandra, once again, rolls her eyes.

▶ ‖

70

GRAMÁTICA *en contexto*

¡AVANZA! **Goal:** Listen to the conversation between Sandra and her friends. Then use definite and indefinite articles to talk about people. *Actividades 12–13*

♻ *¿Recuerdas?* After-school activities p. 32

Telehistoria escena 2

@HomeTutor VideoPlus ClassZone.com

STRATEGIES

Cuando lees
Answer questions related to context Knowing the context helps you understand the meaning. Ask yourself: Where is the action taking place?

Cuando escuchas
Listen for unstated wishes People often reveal their wishes without saying them out loud. How do Alberto and Ricardo make it obvious that they want to meet Ana?

 VIDEO DVD / AUDIO

Ricardo: Un helado.
Alberto: Unas papas fritas y un refresco.
Sandra: Un jugo y una pizza. *(Alberto looks over at another table.)*
Alberto: ¿Son las chicas de la clase de la señora García?
Ricardo: Sí, son Marta, Carla y...
Sandra: Ana.
Both boys look interested.
Alberto: ¿Quién es ella?
Sandra: Ella es la amiga de Carla. Es muy inteligente. Le gusta leer y tocar la guitarra.
Alberto: Me gusta escuchar música. Ana, ¿no?
Sandra: Sí. Y le gusta practicar deportes.
Ricardo: Yo soy atlético. Soy muy bueno.
Sandra: ¡Ay, los chicos! *(Leaving, Alberto trips and lands in the seat next to Ana and her friends.)*
Alberto: Uh... hola. Perdón.   **Continuará...** p. 76

También se dice

San Antonio Alberto says **unas papas fritas** to talk about French fries. In other Spanish-speaking countries you might hear:
- **España** las patatas fritas
- **Colombia, México** las papitas

To talk about juice, Sandra says **un jugo**. In other Spanish-speaking countries you might hear:
- **España** el zumo

Differentiating Instruction

Multiple Intelligences

Interpersonal Invite three volunteers to play the parts of Ricardo, Alberto, and Sandra. As these students read through the script, encourage them to emphasize the facial expressions appropriate to each character's emotions. When Sandra says, **¡Ay, los chicos!** what might her expression be?

Slower-paced Learners

Memory Aids Have students create their own "Snack Bar Menus" to help them remember active vocabulary. Menus should include the name of each item preceded by the appropriate definite article and an illustration or photo from a magazine. Display the menus for future reference.

12 | A corregir *Comprensión del episodio*

Escuchar
Leer

All of these sentences are false. Correct the errors.

1. Las chicas se llaman Marta, Beatriz y Ana.
2. Ana es la amiga de Sandra.
3. A Ricardo le gusta escuchar música.
4. Ana no es inteligente.
5. A Alberto le gusta tocar la guitarra.
6. Ricardo no es atlético.

Expansión:
Teacher Edition Only
Have students write three false statements about the Telehistoria and ask a partner to correct them.

13 | En el parque ♻ *¿Recuerdas?* After-school activities p. 32

Hablar

Choose a person or a group of people from the drawings. Follow the model to give clues to another student, who will guess the people you describe. Change roles and describe everyone.

A Es una chica. Le gusta tocar la guitarra.

B Es la chica de San Antonio.

San Antonio

Bogotá

Expansión:
Teacher Edition Only
Have students work in pairs. One student gives clues about a person who both students know, following the **modelo.** The other student guesses who that person is.

Pronunciación La letra ñ

AUDIO

The **ñ** sounds like the /ny/ of the word *canyon.* The letter **ñ** does not exist in English, but the sound does. Listen and repeat.

señor   España   mañana   pequeño   castaño

La señora es española.   El señor es de España y tiene pelo castaño.

PARA Y PIENSA

Did you get it? Change the article to make the noun more or less specific.

1. Ricardo es el amigo de Alberto.
2. Marta y Carla son las chicas de la clase de Juan.
3. Ana es la chica muy inteligente.

Get Help Online
ClassZone.com

Lección 2
setenta y uno **71**

Differentiating Instruction

Multiple Intelligences

Visual Learners Give students the opportunity to create their own illustrations similar to those in Activity 13. Encourage them to include two different people engaged in two different activities and a place name. Suggest that students review the vocabulary they have learned so far when making their choice of whom and what to draw. Have students describe their illustrations.

Inclusion

Alphabetic/Phonetic Awareness Say each of the following words: **señora, España, Antonio, uno, mañana, organizado, pequeño, castaño.** Have students raise a hand when they hear a word with the /ny/ sound and ask them to pronounce it.

Unidad 1 Lección 2
GRAMÁTICA

Communication
Role-Playing and Skits

Turn the class into a café in Madrid. Bring in a tablecloth and ask one student to be the waiter. Place a napkin on his or her arm. Have students practice the first six lines of the Telehistoria. Remind them that they are now in a café in Madrid and must use the terms **zumo** and **patatas fritas** when they order their food.

✓ Ongoing Assessment

Dictation Read aloud the sentences below as students copy what you say. Have students make the necessary corrections in spelling.
1. **Soy de España, no de San Antonio.**
2. **Me gusta la clase de español porque es pequeña.**
3. **Hasta mañana, señor Salgado.**
4. **¿Tiene el señor Costas pelo castaño?**

✓ Ongoing Assessment

@HomeTutor
More Practice
ClassZone.com

PARA Y PIENSA

Peer Assessment Have students exchange the Para y piensa answers and correct each other's work. For additional practice, use Reteaching & Practice Copymasters URB 1 pp. 42, 44, 50.

Answers MSRB Transparency 33

Activity 12
1. Las chicas se llaman Marta, Carla y Ana.
2. Ana es la amiga de Carla.
3. A Alberto le gusta escuchar música.
4. Ana es inteligente.
5. A Ana le gusta tocar la guitarra.
6. Ricardo es atlético.

Activity 13 Answers will vary. Students must follow this structure: **Es/Son** + indefinite article + noun. **Le/Les gusta** + infinitive + noun. **Es/Son** + definitive article + noun + **de** + name of place. For example: **Es un chico. Le gusta escuchar música. Es el chico de Bogotá.**

Para y piensa
1. Ricardo es un amigo de Alberto.
2. Marta y Carla son unas chicas de una clase de Juan.
3. Ana es una chica muy inteligente.

71

¡AVANZA! Objective
· Present noun-adjective agreement.

Core Resource
· *Cuaderno,* pp. 30–32

Presentation Strategy
· Say or write expressions with noun-adjective agreement **La chica bonita. El chico alto.** Ask students to note the changes according to the gender and number of the nouns in the expressions.

☘ STANDARDS
3.1 Knowledge of other disciplines
4.1 Compare languages

 Warm Up UTB 1 Transparency 32

Definite articles Write the appropriate definite article for the following words:
1. _____ pelo
2. _____ guitarra
3. _____ hombre
4. _____ chicos
5. _____ mujeres
Answers: 1. el; 2. la; 3. el; 4. los; 5. las

Communication
⚠ Common Error Alert

In Spanish, when an adjective describes a group that contains both masculine and feminine forms, the masculine plural form of the adjective is used: **Mi amigo y mi amiga son muy serios.**

Adjectives Students Know

Students have learned the following adjectives whose masculine singular forms end in **-o** and whose feminine singular forms end in **-a**:

alto(a)	cómico(a)	pequeño(a)
artístico(a)	desorganizado(a)	perezoso(a)
atlético(a)	estudioso(a)	rubio(a)
bajo(a)	guapo(a)	serio(a)
bonito(a)	malo(a)	simpático(a)
bueno(a)	organizado(a)	viejo(a)
castaño(a)	pelirrojo(a)	

72

Presentación de GRAMÁTICA

 ¡AVANZA! **Goal:** Learn how to use adjectives with nouns. Then practice using adjectives to describe people. *Actividades 14–19*

English Grammar Connection: Adjectives are words that describe **nouns.** In English, the adjective almost always comes before the noun. In Spanish, the adjective usually comes after the noun.

┌─ *before the noun*   *after the noun* ─┐
the **serious** students   los estudiantes **serios**

Noun-Adjective Agreement

Animated Grammar ClassZone.com

In Spanish, adjectives match the gender and number of the nouns they describe.

Here's how:

	Singular	Plural
Masculine	el chic**o** alt**o** *the tall boy*	los chic**os** alt**os** *the tall boys*
Feminine	la chic**a** alt**a** *the tall girl*	las chic**as** alt**as** *the tall girls*

· Adjectives that end in **-e** match both genders.
     el maestro inteligent**e**
     la maestra inteligent**e**

· Many adjectives that end in a **consonant** match both genders.
     el amigo jove**n**
     la amiga jove**n**

· Some adjectives that end in a **consonant** add **-a** to form the feminine singular. These exceptions have to be memorized.
     el chico trabajado**r**
     la chica trabajado**ra**

· To make an adjective plural, add **-s** if it ends in a **vowel;** add **-es** if it ends in a **consonant.**
     las chicas trabajado**ras**
     los chicos trabajado**res**

Más práctica
     Cuaderno pp. 30–32
     Cuaderno para hispanohablantes *pp. 31–34*

@HomeTutor
Leveled Grammar Practice
ClassZone.com

Differentiating Instruction

English Learners
Build Background Review with English learners the terms *noun* and *adjective.* Remind students that a *noun* is a person, place, or thing, and that an *adjective* describes a noun. Model a few sample phrases in English, such as *the tall girl* or *the serious boy.* Write the phrases on the board, and ask for volunteers to underline the adjective and circle the noun in each.

Inclusion
Metacognitive Support Create a Venn diagram. Label one side **English,** and the other **Español.** Ask students to think about the similarities and differences between nouns and adjectives in the two languages. Similarity: Nouns and adjectives often appear next to each other; Difference: In English the adjective almost always precedes the noun, while in Spanish the adjective usually follows the noun.

Práctica de GRAMÁTICA

14 | Un correo electrónico

Leer Help Sandra solve the puzzle in Alicia's e-mail by choosing the correct words in parentheses.

A: Sandra

Asunto: ¡Una persona famosa en Miami!

Hola, amiga. Te gusta jugar al fútbol y eres **1.** (inteligente / inteligentes), ¿no? ¿Quién es la persona famosa en Miami? No es un chico **2.** (grande / grandes). No es una chica **3.** (pequeño / pequeña). Tiene pelo **4.** (castaño / castaña) y es una persona **5.** (simpático / simpática). Es una mujer **6.** (serio / seria) pero le gusta pasar un rato con los amigos. Los amigos de ella son **7.** (atléticos / atlético) también y les gusta practicar deportes. Ella se llama Trini...

Alicia

Expansión:
Teacher Edition Only
Have students write an e-mail describing themselves to a new friend.

15 | Descripciones

Escribir Write descriptions of the people in the drawing.

alto(a)   guapo(a)   cómico(a)   atlético(a)

estudioso(a)   desorganizado(a)   serio(a)   ¿?

la Sra. De Silva

Rafael

Mónica

Mario

Expansión:
Teacher Edition Only
Have students use additional adjectives to describe the people in the drawing.

Lección 2
setenta y tres **73**

Differentiating Instruction

Slower-paced Learners

Sentence Completion Organize students into pairs to complete Activity 14. Instruct partners to take turns reading sentences aloud. If necessary, tell them to try out both choices in the parentheses, and listen for which one "sounds right." Point out that **chica pequeña** sounds like it goes together, while **chica pequeño** is a mismatch.

Heritage Language Learners

Writing Skills Encourage students to elaborate on their descriptions in Activity 15. Ask them to add other appropriate adjectives that may not have been included in the lesson. Tell students to consult a dictionary for the accurate spelling of words they are unsure of. Remind students to pay attention to the agreement of articles, nouns, and adjectives.

Objectives
- Practice noun-adjective agreement.
- Practice using adjectives that describe people.

Practice Sequence
- **Activity 14:** Controlled practice: noun-adjective agreement
- **Activity 15:** Transitional practice: noun-adjective agreement

 STANDARD
1.3 Present information, Acts. 14–15

Communication
Grammar Activity

Explain to students that in Spanish some adjectives do not have different masculine/feminine forms. Those adjectives are known as invariable in gender, meaning they describe both masculine or feminine nouns. For example, **la chica es inteligente, el chico es inteligente** or **la maestra es joven, el maestro es joven.**

Activity 14
 1. inteligente
 2. grande
 3. pequeña
 4. castaño
 5. simpática
 6. seria
 7. atléticos

Activity 15 Answers will vary. Sample answers include:
 Mario es alto. Él es estudioso. Es serio.
 La señora De Silva es desorganizada. Ella es baja.
 Mónica es atlética. Ella es guapa.
 Rafael es cómico. Él es joven.

Objectives

- Practice noun-adjective agreement.
- **Culture:** Learn about the art of Carmen Lomas Garza.
- Practice **ser** with adjectives.

Core Resource

- *Cuaderno*, pp. 30–32

Practice Sequence

- **Activity 16:** Transitional practice: descriptive adjectives, noun-adjective agreement
- **Activity 17:** Open-ended practice: descriptive adjectives, **gustar** + infinitive, noun-adjective agreement
- **Activity 18:** Open-ended practice: noun-adjective agreement
- **Activity 19:** Open-ended practice: descriptive adjectives

STANDARDS

1.1 Engage in conversation, Acts. 18–19
1.2 Understand language, Act. 18
1.3 Present information, Acts. 16–19
2.1 Practices and perspectives, Act. 19
4.2 Compare cultures, Act. 19

Long-term Retention

Study Tips

Ask students to find the cognates in the adjectives they've learned in this lesson. Have them write the cognates in one column, and the adjectives that are not cognates in another. Then ask them to develop mnemonics to help them remember the meanings of the adjectives that are not cognates, and make notes about the mnemonics next to the adjectives.

Answers MSRB Transparency 33

Activity 16
1. Luis es bajo.
2. Laura es organizada.
3. Luis es pelirrojo.
4. Laura es cómica.
5. Luis es joven.
6. Laura es artística.
7. Luis es estudioso.
8. Laura es guapa.

Activity answers continue on p. 75.

74

---

16 | ¡No son iguales!

Hablar Escribir

Laura and her brother Luis are almost total opposites. Change each statement about one to say what the other is like. Use an adjective in each answer. Be careful! Laura and Luis do have a few things in common.

modelo: A Luis no le gusta practicar deportes.
Laura es atlética.

1. Laura es alta.
2. Luis es desorganizado.
3. Laura es pelirroja.
4. Luis es serio.
5. Laura es joven.
6. A Luis no le gusta dibujar.
7. A Laura no le gusta estudiar.
8. Luis es guapo.

Expansión:
Teacher Edition Only
Ask students to draw their own two scenes and tell how the people in them are the same or different.

17 | Un amigo

Escribir

Write a short description of a friend. Be sure to describe what your friend looks like, his or her personality, and what he or she likes to do.

modelo: Cristina tiene pelo rubio. Es baja. Le gusta leer libros. Ella es inteligente...

Expansión:
Teacher Edition Only
Ask students to write a short description of themselves.

Differentiating Instruction

Slower-paced Learners

Memory Aids If students have difficulties completing Activity 16, have them draw a Venn diagram on a piece of paper. Ask them to label Luis's oval "masculine (-o)," Laura's oval "feminine (-a)," and the overlapping portions "invariable." Then have them list the adjectives from Activity 16 in the correct oval.

Pre-AP

Support Ideas with Details Ask students to choose three or four words to describe themselves. For each of the words, have them write a sentence telling what they like or do not like to do. For example: **Soy simpático. Me gusta pasar un rato con los amigos y hablar por teléfono.**

18 | ¿Cómo son los amigos de clase?

Escribir
Hablar

Write descriptions of three people in the class. Read the descriptions to a partner, who will guess the people being described.

A Es un chico. Es alto, inteligente y atlético. Es un poco serio también. Tiene pelo castaño.

B Es Felipe.

Expansión:
Teacher Edition Only
Have students describe someone they know to a partner, who will try to draw that person.

19 | La Fiesta San Antonio

Hablar

Comparación cultural

Los cascarones

How do cultural traditions influence an artist's work? Cascarones are painted eggs filled with confetti. They are popular at Easter and events such as parties or graduations. They are also a common sight during Fiesta San Antonio, an annual citywide celebration that honors the history and culture of San Antonio, **Texas.** But *cascarones* are not meant for decoration. Children sneak up on their friends and try to crack the eggs over their heads. If a *cascarón* is broken over your head, it is supposed to bring you good luck. Artists are often influenced by traditions like these. Carmen Lomas Garza is a Mexican-American artist who depicts scenes of traditional celebration. In her 1989 painting *Cascarones,* Lomas Garza presents a family making the colorful eggs.

Fiesta San Antonio

Compara con tu mundo *What are some traditions in your family and why are they important to you? Which is your favorite tradition?*

Point to a person in the photo and ask a partner what he or she is like. Your partner will answer. Change roles. Describe all of the people.

 A ¿Cómo es la chica?

 B La chica es bonita.

Expansión:
Teacher Edition Only
Have students write their descriptions of the people in the picture.

Más práctica   Cuaderno *pp. 30–32*   Cuaderno para hispanohablantes *pp. 31–34*

PARA Y PIENSA

Did you get it? Give the correct ending for each adjective.
1. una estudiante desorganizad____
2. unos chicos simpátic____
3. unas mujeres trabajador____
4. un hombre grand____

Get Help Online
ClassZone.com

Differentiating Instruction

Multiple Intelligences

Visual Learners Ask students to paint or draw a depiction of one of their own family traditions. Tell students they might model their style on that of Carmen Lomas Garza, or utilize their own personal aesthetic. Once paintings or drawings are complete, have them describe the people they have depicted. **Es Gabriela. Es una chica pequeña.**

Heritage Language Learners

Support What They Know Ask students to discuss the traditions their families and communities practice during the holidays, at parties, or at graduations. Also, ask all students to talk about traditions in their cultures that are supposed to bring good luck. What kinds of things do people do, or not do, to bring good luck?

Comparación cultural

Essential Question

Suggested Answer Many artists include in their work aspects of their culture such as family ritual activities including games, crafts, and foods. For the artist Carmen Lomas Garza, family is an important component in Mexican-American culture.

About the Artist

Carmen Lomas Garza was born in Kingsville, Texas in 1948. Most of Garza's paintings are recollections of her childhood in South Texas. Much of Lomas Garza's work focuses on the traditions and daily activities in Mexican-American culture. The painting *Cascarones* represents the artist as a child with her mother and siblings. Lomas Garza is located in the center, wearing a red dress.

✓ Ongoing Assessment

@HomeTutor
More Practice
ClassZone.com

PARA Y PIENSA
Remediation If students have problems supplying the correct adjective endings in Para y piensa, have them review p. 72 and repeat Activities 14 and 15 on p. 73. For additional practice, use Reteaching & Practice Copymasters URB 1 pp. 45, 46.

 Answers MSRB Transparency 34

Answers continued from p. 74.

Activity 17 Answers will vary. Sample answers include:
Jorge tiene pelo castaño. Es alto. Le gusta tocar la guitarra y pasar un rato con los amigos. Él es inteligente y estudioso.

Activity 18 Answers will vary. Students must use the structure: verb + adjective in their response. For example: Es una chica. Es alta y simpática.

Activity 19 Answers will vary.
Sample answers:
A: ¿Cómo es la señora? B: La señora es grande.

Para y piensa 1. desorganizada;
2. simpáticos; 3. trabajadoras; 4. grande

Objective
· Integrate lesson content

Core Resources
· Video Program: DVD 1
· Audio Program: CD 1, tracks 36, 38, 40

Presentation Strategies
· Ask students what they remember about the Telehistoria so far.
· Before showing the video or playing the audio, tell students to watch for the surprise ending and to be ready to talk about it.

Practice Sequence
· **Activities 20 and 21:** Telehistoria comprehension
· **Activity 22:** Open-ended practice: writing, speaking

STANDARDS
1.1 Engage in conversation, Act. 20
1.2 Understand language, Acts. 20–22
1.3 Present information, Acts. 21–22

Warm Up UTB 1 Transparency 32

Noun-Adjective Agreement Match the following nouns with their corresponding adjectives.

1. unos estudiantes   a. trabajadoras
2. unas señoras   b. alto
3. una amiga   c. serios
4. un chico   d. atlética

Answers: 1. c; 2. a; 3. d; 4. b

Video Summary @HomeTutor VideoPlus ClassZone.com

The trio walks into a store where Trini Salgado will be signing autographs. Ricardo finds a sign that says that Trini signed autographs yesterday. The next stop on her tour is Puebla, Mexico. Sandra says she knows a friend of Alicia's in Puebla.

▶❚ ❚❚

Todo junto

 ¡AVANZA! **Goal:** *Show what you know* Pay attention to how Sandra and her friends describe specific people. Then use definite and indefinite articles and adjectives to tell what someone is like. *Actividades 20–24*

Telehistoria completa
@HomeTutor VideoPlus ClassZone.com

STRATEGIES

Cuando lees
Discover a problem Scenes often reveal problems that the characters must solve. While reading the text below, search for a problem. What is it? Can it be solved?

Cuando escuchas
Listen for the parts Even a short scene can have parts, each with a somewhat different topic or action. These can be keys to meaning. How would you divide this scene?

 **Escena 1** *Resumen*
Alberto y Ricardo son amigos de Sandra. Alberto es un poco desorganizado. Ricardo es artístico.

 **Escena 2** *Resumen*
Ana es la amiga de Carla. A Ricardo y a Ana les gusta practicar deportes, y a Alberto y a Ana les gusta escuchar música.

Escena 3

 VIDEO DVD

 AUDIO

Ricardo: ¿Es Trini Salgado?

Alberto: ¿Quién?

Ricardo: La mujer seria. Tiene pelo castaño.

Sandra: No es ella. Es un poco baja. Trini es alta y más joven.

Ricardo finds the sign announcing Trini Salgado and points to the date.

The group enters a store where Trini Salgado will be signing autographs.
Alberto: Ana es bonita, inteligente, simpática... y nosotros somos inteligentes y simpáticos, ¿no?
Sandra: Sí, sí, ustedes son inteligentes, atléticos, cómicos. Ricardo, tú eres estudioso y Alberto, tú eres trabajador.
Ricardo notices a woman in the store.

Sandra: Pero... es el sábado. Hoy es domingo.
Ricardo: Sí, el sábado en San Antonio y el lunes en México.
Sandra: ¿México? ¿Puebla, México? Pablo, un amigo muy simpático de Alicia, es de México.
Sandra thinks of a plan to send the T-shirt to Pablo.

Differentiating Instruction

Slower-paced Learners

Read Before Listening Have students read the script before listening to the audio or viewing the video. Ask them to make a list of adjectives for each character, for example:
Ricardo: estudioso. Have them refer to this list as they listen to the audio or view the video.

Inclusion

Sequential Information Write sentences from the Telehistoria on individual sentence strips. Scramble the sentences. Have students arrange them in order, based on what they read or hear.

20 | ¿Cómo son? *Comprensión de los episodios*

Escuchar
Leer

Combine phrases from the two columns to make sentences about the people in the Telehistoria.

1. Alberto y Ricardo son
2. Sandra es
3. Ana es
4. Ricardo es
5. Alberto es
6. Todos los chicos son
7. La mujer seria es
8. Pablo es

a. un poco baja.
b. una amiga de Ricardo y Alberto.
c. un amigo de Alicia.
d. jóvenes.
e. alto y trabajador.
f. cómicos.
g. inteligente y le gusta leer.
h. artístico y atlético.

Expansión:
Teacher Edition Only
Ask students to think of other characteristics of each person in the Telehistoria.

21 | Los amigos *Comprensión de los episodios*

Escuchar
Leer

Write descriptions of the Telehistoria characters, based on the three episodes.

Expansión:
Teacher Edition Only
Have students choose a photo of people from a magazine and describe the people in the photo.

22 | Las personas famosas

Escribir
Hablar

STRATEGY Hablar

Practice pronunciation To speak more fluently and accurately, practice the sounds of words you need to use in your descriptions. Paying attention to pronunciation will help you with cognates.

Write descriptions of three famous people. Include what they like and don't like to do. Read your descriptions to a partner, who will guess the people being described.

A Es un hombre. Tiene pelo rubio. Es muy atlético. Le gusta montar en bicicleta. No es muy joven y no es muy viejo. Es de Estados Unidos. ¿Quién es?

B Es Lance Armstrong.

Expansión:
Teacher Edition Only
Ask students to pick another celebrity and have a partner ask five yes/no questions to find out who it is.

Long-term Retention
Study Tips

Write a T table on the board. Using colored chalk, write **una chica** on one side of the table and using a different color, write **un chico** on the other side. Ask for volunteers to write adjectives under each, being sure to make the adjective agree in gender with the column heading. If the adjective applies to both, have them write it in both columns.

✓ Ongoing Assessment

Rubric Activity 22

Speaking Criteria	Maximum Credit	Partial Credit	Minimum Credit
Content	The description is complete.	The description is partially complete.	The description is incomplete.
Communication	Description and pronunciation are easy to follow and clear.	Parts of the description and pronunciation are organized and clear.	Description and pronunciation are disorganized and unclear.
Accuracy	There are few mistakes in grammar and vocabulary.	There are some mistakes in grammar and vocabulary.	There are many mistakes in grammar and vocabulary.

Differentiating Instruction

Multiple Intelligences

Interpersonal Invite students to expand on Activity 20 by describing their own friends and family. Direct students to substitute names of people they know in the first column, and then combine those names with appropriate phrases from the second column. Remind students to modify articles and adjective endings when necessary.

Heritage Language Learners

Support What They Know Ask students to name a famous person from their country of origin and describe that person using the vocabulary they have learned. For example: **Antonio Banderas es un actor de España. No es muy joven y no es muy viejo. Es alto y tiene pelo castaño. Es muy inteligente y le gusta leer.**

Answers MSRB Transparency 34

Activity 20
1. f; **2.** b; **3.** g; **4.** h; **5.** e; **6.** d; **7.** a; **8.** c

Activity 21 Answers will vary. Students must follow this structure: Name + es + adjective.

Activity 22 Answers will vary. Sample descriptions will follow this outline:

Es un(a)... Tiene pelo... Es... Le gusta... Es (joven/viejo). Es de... ¿Quién es?

77

Objective

· Practice and integrate lesson vocabulary and grammar.

Core Resources

· *Cuaderno*, pp. 33–34
· Audio Program: TXT CD 1 tracks 41, 42

Practice Sequence

· **Activity 23:** Open-ended practice: reading, listening, speaking
· **Activity 24:** Open-ended practice: writing

✿ STANDARDS

1.2 Understand language, Act. 23
1.3 Present information, Acts. 23–24, PYP

Long-term Retention

 Pre-AP Integration

Activity 23 Have students work in pairs. Have one student write an e-mail describing himself/herself following the activity model. As that student reads the e-mail, his or her partner takes notes.

✓ Ongoing Assessment

Rubric Activity 23

Writing/Speaking	
Proficient	**Not There Yet**
Student takes detailed notes and provides a complete oral description.	Student takes few notes and provides an incomplete oral description.

✓ Ongoing Assessment

@HomeTutor More Practice ClassZone.com

 Intervention If students have difficulty creating sentences for Para y piensa ask them to review p. 72. For additional practice, use Reteaching & Practice Copymasters URB 1 pp. 45, 47.

See Activity answers on p. 79.

78

---

23 | Integración

Leer
Escuchar
Hablar

Read the Web page and listen to the boys' messages. Describe the two boys.

Fuente 1 Página Web

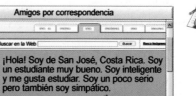

Amigos por correspondencia

Buscar en la Web

Alejandro ¡Hola! Soy de San José, Costa Rica. Soy un estudiante muy bueno. Soy inteligente y me gusta estudiar. Soy un poco serio pero también soy simpático.
¡Escucha!

Édgar Soy de Colombia. Soy alto y tengo pelo castaño. Soy cómico y simpático. Soy inteligente pero no soy muy trabajador. No me gusta estudiar. ;-)
¡Escucha!

Fuente 2 Audio en Internet

 Listen and take notes
· ¿Cómo es Alejandro? ¿Qué le gusta hacer?
· ¿Cómo es Édgar? ¿Qué le gusta hacer?

modelo: Alejandro es un poco serio, pero Édgar es cómico...

🎧 **Audio Program**
TXT CD 1 Tracks 41, 42
Audio Script, TE p. 57b

24 | Un(a) amigo(a) perfecto(a)

Escribir

Describe the perfect friend for a special page in the yearbook. What is this person like? What does he or she like to do? Why?

modelo: Ella se llama Megan. Es bonita, inteligente y artística. Es una chica muy simpática. Le gusta escuchar música y...

Writing Criteria	Excellent	Good	Needs Work
Content	Your description includes a lot of information.	Your description includes some information.	Your description includes little information.
Communication	Most of your description is organized and easy to follow.	Parts of your description are organized and easy to follow.	Your description is disorganized and hard to follow.
Accuracy	Your description has few mistakes in grammar and vocabulary.	Your description has some mistakes in grammar and vocabulary.	Your description has many mistakes in grammar and vocabulary.

Expansión:
Teacher Edition Only

Have students describe another person that they like.

Más práctica Cuaderno *pp. 33–34* Cuaderno para hispanohablantes *pp. 35–36*

PARA Y PIENSA **Did you get it?** Create sentences with the following information.
1. Alberto / chico(a) / simpático(a)
2. Ricardo / estudiante / trabajador(a)
3. Sandra / persona / organizado(a)

🔎 **Get Help Online** ClassZone.com

Differentiating Instruction

Inclusion

Clear Structure Remind students to follow the steps of the writing process in order to create their descriptions in Activity 24. Have them brainstorm important vocabulary, draft complete sentences, revise, and then proofread before turning in their final drafts.

Pre-AP

Self-correct After students have completed their descriptions in Activity 24, encourage them to read their writing aloud. Remind them to listen for agreement between articles, nouns, and adjectives. If something does not sound right, tell students to take a closer look and confirm they have used the correct endings.

Juegos y diversiones

Review descriptive adjectives, noun-adjective agreement, and indefinite articles by playing a game.

20 preguntas

The Setup

Get a good look at your classmates, as you will need to identify them based on descriptions used in the game. Form two teams.

Palabras útiles

equipo *team*
puntos *points*

Playing the Game

First: One person from each team will go to the board and face the class, with his or her back to the board.

Then: Your teacher will write on the board the name of someone in the class. Each player at the board will alternate asking a yes/no question to his or her teammates about the mystery person. The player at the board who correctly identifies the mystery person first gets a point for his or her team.

Two new players go to the board, and the game continues.

The Winner!

The team with the most points at the end wins.

¿Es una chica alta?

¿Es un chico bajo?

Lección 2
setenta y nueve **79**

Communication

Group Work

Game Have students play a game of "Jeopardy." Divide the class into teams. One student says the name of a class, student, or person all students know. The team that can generate the most questions about that person wins. For example: One student says "George." Teams ask: **¿Tiene pelo castaño? ¿Es bajo? ¿Le gusta jugar al fúbol?**

Communication

Group Work

Game During the game **20 preguntas,** monitor students' questions to avoid judgmental adjectives such as **perezoso, malo** and so on.

Differentiating Instruction

Multiple Intelligences

Visual Learners Ask students to write a description of a friend or family member doing an activity. Make sure they include physical characteristics. Ask one student to read his or her description while the other students draw the person being described. The student who read the description, looks at the pictures and decides which one comes closest to the description.

Heritage Language Learners

Support What They Know Ask students what kind of word games they play in their country of origin. What are their names? Are the players grouped in pairs or teams? What are the game rules? Who is the winner?

Answers MSRB Transparency 34

Answers for Activities on p. 78.

Activity 23 Sample answers include:

Alejandro es inteligente y un poco serio, pero también es simpático.

Activity 24 Answers will vary. Sample descriptions will follow this outline:

Él/Ella se llama... Es..., ... y... Es un(a) chico/chica muy... Le gusta... y...

Para y piensa

1. Alberto es un chico simpático.
2. Ricardo es un estudiante trabajador.
3. Sandra es una persona organizada.

LECTURA CULTURAL

¡AVANZA! **Objectives**

- Learn about after-school activities in Miami and San Antonio.
- Build vocabulary with new terms for activities, food, and interesting places.

Core Resource

- Audio Program: TXT CD 1 track 43

Presentation Strategies

- Ask students to look at the photos on pp. 80 and 81. Ask quick comprehension questions: **¿Qué tiempo hace? ¿Qué le gusta hacer al chico en Miami?**
- Have students listen to the audio paying special attention to all activities mentioned.

STANDARDS

1.2 Understand language
2.1 Practices and perspectives
4.2 Compare cultures

 Warm Up UTB 1 Transparency 33

Noun-Adjective Agreement Fill in the blanks with the appropriate **–o/–a** ending.
1. Alejandro es un estudiante muy buen _____.
2. Él es un poco seri _____.
3. Megan es artístic _____.
4. Ella es una chica muy simpátic _____.

Answers: 1. bueno; 2. serio; 3. artística 4. simpática

Comparación cultural

Background Information

El Álamo The Álamo was named for the grove of cottonwood trees in which it stands. It was the chapel of the Mission San Antonio de Valero, founded in 1716. In December 1835, Texans were at war with Mexico, seeking independence. Members of the volunteer army captured the city of San Antonio, and occupied the Álamo. The leader of the Texas independence movement, Sam Houston, advised the volunteers to abandon the Álamo, but they refused. In February 1836, Mexican troops under the command of General Antonio López de Santa Anna began a seige of the Álamo.

 Goal: Read about things to do in San Antonio and Miami. Then compare what teens do in those cities with what you like to do where you live.

Comparación cultural

AUDIO

Saludos desde [1]
San Antonio y Miami

STRATEGY Leer

Make a comparison chart
Create a chart like the one below to compare San Antonio and Miami.

	San Antonio	Miami
sitios de interés		
actividades		
comida		

En San Antonio, Texas, hay [2] parques de diversiones [3], museos [4], el Paseo del Río y el Álamo. Después de las clases, a los chicos y a las chicas les gusta pasar un rato con los amigos en El Mercado, donde es posible escuchar música de los mariachis y comer comida típica mexicana.

[1] **Saludos...** Greetings from   [2] there are
[3] amusement parks   [4] museums

San Antonio

El Álamo en San Antonio, Texas

Differentiating Instruction

Multiple Intelligences

Interpersonal Have students form groups of three or four. Ask each group to discuss favorite after-school activities in their hometown. Are any the same as or similar to those of students in San Antonio or Miami? Ask each group to give an informal oral report to the class.

Heritage Language Learners

Writing Skills Have students do research about some of San Antonio's famous sites such as the Álamo, Paseo del Río, and La Villita. Have them use the information to write a short report to present to the class. Monitor correct spelling, pronunciation, and word usage.

En Miami, Florida, si[5] hace buen tiempo, a los chicos y a las chicas les gusta andar en patineta o montar en bicicleta. Después de las clases, a muchos chicos les gusta pasear con los amigos por la Calle Ocho, en la Pequeña Habana de Miami. ¡Es una pequeña Cuba en la Florida! Allí[6] es posible comer sándwiches cubanos y beber jugo de mango.

[5] if   [6] There

Miami

Andar en patineta en Miami, Florida

PARA Y PIENSA

¿Comprendiste?
1. ¿Qué hay en San Antonio?
2. ¿Qué les gusta hacer a muchos chicos en Miami?
3. ¿Qué hay en la Pequeña Habana de Miami?

¿Y tú?
¿De dónde eres? ¿Qué te gusta hacer después de las clases?

Differentiating Instruction

Slower-paced Learners

Sentence Completion If students have trouble responding to the ¿Comprendiste? questions, ask them to complete sentences that begin with:
En San Antonio les gusta...
A muchos chicos les gusta pasear...
En la Pequeña Habana de Miami...

Pre-AP

Communicate Preferences After students have read the selection, ask them to discuss what they have read about San Antonio and Miami. For example: **¿Dónde te gusta pasear en Miami? ¿Qué te gusta hacer en San Antonio?** Have them share their preferences about places, activities, foods, and explain why.

Communication
Group Work

Organize students in groups of four to talk about activities they do on weekends with their families or friends. Have them discuss if their activities are similar to or different from the activities young people do in San Antonio and Miami. Allow them to work by themselves and record their findings using a Venn diagram.

Comparisons
English Language Connection

Cognates Have students look for cognates in the reading. Ask them to write the words down, give their meanings in English, and then share the words with the class.

Long-term Retention
Personalize It

Ask students what activities they would like to do if they were in Miami or in San Antonio and explain why. For example, **En San Antonio me gusta pasar un rato en El Mercado porque me gusta escuchar música de los mariachis. En Miami me gusta pasear por la Calle Ocho porque me gusta comer sándwiches cubanos.**

Answers

Para y piensa
¿Comprendiste?
1. En San Antonio, hay parques de diversiones, museos, el Paseo del Río, el Álamo y El Mercado.
2. A muchos chicos les gusta pasear por la Calle Ocho.
3. La Calle Ocho está en la Pequeña Habana. Allí es posible comer sándwiches cubanos y beber jugo de mango.

¿Y tú?
Answers will vary. Sample answers will follow this format: **Soy de... Después de las clases me gusta...**

Objectives

- Read about traditional dishes from Mexico and Cuba.
- **Culture:** Discuss how traditional dishes change from one country to another.
- **Community:** Investigate sources of Latin American food in your community.

Presentation Strategies

- Ask students to describe Latin dishes they have tasted. Have they eaten **salsa fresca** or **sándwiches cubanos?**
- Have students read the two recipes. Assign two students to look up these words in an English-Spanish dictionary and come up with a list of ingredients in Spanish.
- Conduct a class survey to find out which dish the class prefers, and why.

STANDARDS

3.1 Knowledge of other disciplines
5.1 Spanish in the community

Comparación cultural

Essential Question

Suggested Answer Traditional dishes change because certain ingredients might not be available in other countries. For example, the abundance of wheat in the U.S. caused flour to become the basis for many Tex-Mex dishes instead of the corn meal used in Mexico.

Expanded Information

Mexican restaurants in the U.S. have followed the form and style of "Tex-Mex" food, a combination of Northern Mexican food with Texas farm and cowboy fare. Chili, which some consider Texas' state dish, was unknown in Mexico and derived from an ample supply of beef in Texas.

Communities
Spanish in the Marketplace

Have students visit a grocery store that sells traditional Latin American foods. Ask students to write down the names of Mexican and/or Cuban foods that are sold and report back to the class.

82

Comparación cultural

Proyectos culturales

Platos tradicionales de México y Cuba

Why do traditional dishes change when they are brought from one country to another? In the U.S. we enjoy foods from many different Spanish-speaking countries. In many parts of the U.S. you can easily find dishes from Mexico, the Caribbean, Central America, and South America. Yet you might be surprised that those dishes aren't exactly the same as they are in their countries of origin. Here are two traditional recipes. The original list of ingredients for both has been modified to include foods more readily available in the U.S. They also reflect the widespread cooking practices and tastes that were already in place when the recipes were brought to this country.

Proyecto 1 Salsa fresca

México This is a common sauce in Mexico and all Central America. It is made from scratch and can be eaten as a dip with tortilla chips.

Ingredients for salsa fresca
4–5 fresh tomatoes, diced
1 onion, diced
1 green chile, diced
1 clove of garlic, crushed
Juice of 1 fresh lime

Instructions
Combine the ingredients in a bowl. Cover and let stand for an hour in the refrigerator so that the flavors mix. Serve with tortilla chips.

Proyecto 2 Sándwich cubano

Cuba This is a traditional Cuban lunch dish found throughout Florida. The sandwich is pressed in a special grill or on a skillet.

Ingredients for sándwich cubano
1 long sandwich roll
Slices of roast pork, ham, turkey, or bacon
Slice of Swiss or monterey jack cheese
Mustard or mayonnaise
Olive oil

Instructions
First brush the outside of the roll with olive oil. Then split it open and lay meat, cheese, and mustard or mayonnaise as desired. Put the sandwich in a hot skillet, placing a small, heavy skillet on top and pressing lightly. Cook three minutes or until cheese melts and bread is toasted.

En tu comunidad

Check your phone book for restaurants that serve foods from Mexico, Cuba, or other Spanish-speaking countries. Do any of the restaurants in your area serve **salsa fresca** or **sándwiches cubanos?**

Differentiating Instruction

Heritage Language Learners

Support What They Know Ask student pairs to cut from magazines or download from the Internet recipes from their country of origin. Have them present their recipe as if they were doing it in front of a TV audience. Have props available as needed. As one student reads the recipe, the other student pantomimes its preparation.

Multiple Intelligences

Logical/Mathematical Ask students to name multiple-ingredient sandwiches that are popular in their hometowns. They might be hoagies, submarines, po'boys, or grinders. Ask them to create tables that show how similar ingredients are used in Cuban sandwiches and other locally popular sandwiches.

Lección 2

En resumen
Vocabulario y gramática

Animated Grammar
Interactive Flashcards
ClassZone.com

Vocabulario

Describe Yourself and Others

¿Cómo eres?	What are you like?

Personality

artístico(a)	artistic
atlético(a)	athletic
bueno(a)	good
cómico(a)	funny
desorganizado(a)	disorganized
estudioso(a)	studious
inteligente	intelligent
malo(a)	bad
organizado(a)	organized
perezoso(a)	lazy
serio(a)	serious
simpático(a)	nice
trabajador(a)	hard-working

Appearance

alto(a)	tall
bajo(a)	short (height)
bonito(a)	pretty
grande	big, large; great
guapo(a)	good-looking
joven (pl. jóvenes)	young
pelirrojo(a)	red-haired
pequeño(a)	small
viejo(a)	old
Tengo...	I have . . .
Tiene...	He / She has . . .
pelo rubio	blond hair
pelo castaño	brown hair

People

el (la) amigo(a)	friend
la chica	girl
el chico	boy
el (la) estudiante	student
el hombre	man
la mujer	woman
la persona	person

Other Words and Phrases

muy	very
un poco	a little
porque	because
todos(as)	all

Gramática

Nota gramatical: **ser** to describe what someone is like *p. 63*

Definite and Indefinite Articles

In Spanish, articles match nouns in gender and number.

		Definite Article	Noun	Indefinite Article	Noun
Masculine	Singular	el	chico	un	chico
	Plural	los	chicos	unos	chicos
Feminine	Singular	la	chica	una	chica
	Plural	las	chicas	unas	chicas

Noun-Adjective Agreement

In Spanish, adjectives match the gender and number of the nouns they describe.

	Singular	Plural
Masculine	el chico alto	los chicos altos
Feminine	la chica alta	las chicas altas

Lección 2
ochenta y tres   **83**

Online SPAN- CLASSZONE.

Interactive Flashcards Students can hear every target vocabulary word pronounced in authentic Spanish. Flashcards have Spanish on one side, and a picture or a translation on the other.

Review Games Matching, concentration, hangman, and word search are just a sampling of the fun, interactive games students can play to review for the test.

Featuring...
Cultura INTERACTIVA
Animated Grammar
@HomeTutor

And more...
· Get Help Online
· Interactive Flashcards
· Review Games
· WebQuest
· Self-Check Quiz

Long-term Retention
Personalize It

Help students create personal Spanish-English dictionaries using two-column tables. They may illustrate the words as well as define them.

Long-term Retention
Study Tips

Ask students to list vocabulary terms that have English cognates, and create a mnemonic device that helps them remember the cognate pair.

Communication
Interpersonal Mode

Have students quiz each other on the vocabulary. One pantomimes an adjective and the other classmate guesses which word his/her partner is acting out.

Differentiating Instruction

Multiple Intelligences

Interpersonal Using the Vocabulario, ask students to create poems that describe themselves. They may arrange the phrases creatively on colored paper and draw illustrations, borders, and other decorations.

English Learners

Build Background Ask students to draw pictures of their immediate families. Under the image of each family member, students should write the person's name and the appropriate term from the vocabulary for *People*.

Objective

¡AVANZA!
- Review lesson content: vocabulary, definite and indefinite articles, noun-adjective agreement, the verb **ser**.

Core Resources
- *Cuaderno*, pp. 35–46
- Audio Program: TXT CD 1 track 44

Presentation Strategies
- Direct students' attention to the ¡Llegada!
- As students listen to the audio, instruct them to pay special attention to the endings of nouns and adjectives.
- Monitor correct use of **ser** and noun-adjective agreement as students do the activities.
- Go over the Comparación cultural with students and clarify any questions that arise.
- Review may be done in class or given as homework.
- You may want students to access the review online.

STANDARDS
1.2 Understand language, Acts. 1, 3
1.3 Present information, Acts. 2, 4
4.2 Compare cultures, Act. 5

Warm Up   UTB 1 Transparency 33

Noun-Adjective Agreement Complete each phrase with the correct adjective form.
1. una chica _____ (alto)
2. un chico _____ (guapo)
3. las mujeres _____ (bajo)
4. los hombres _____ (viejo)
5. una maestra _____ (simpático)

Answers: 1. alta; 2. guapo; 3. bajas;
4. viejos; 5. simpática

✓ Ongoing Assessment

@HomeTutor
More Practice
ClassZone.com

Remediation If students achieve less than 80% accuracy with the activities, direct them to review pages 58, 63, 65–66, 72, 75, 80–81 and to get help online at ClassZone.com.

See Activity answers on p. 85.

84

Repaso de la lección

¡LLEGADA!

@HomeTutor
ClassZone.com

Now you can
- describe yourself and others
- identify people and things

Using
- **ser** to describe what someone is like
- definite and indefinite articles
- noun-adjective agreement

To review
- definite and indefinite articles p. 66
- **ser** to describe what someone is like p. 63
- noun-adjective agreement p. 72

1 Listen and understand
AUDIO

Listen to Carlos talk about himself and his teacher. Then write a description of Carlos and Mrs. Pérez, according to what Carlos says.

Audio Progr
TXT CD 1 Track
Audio Script, TB
p. 57b

To review
- definite and indefinite articles p. 66

2 Identify people and things

Identify the people in the drawing.

modelo: señor viejo / hombre
El señor viejo es un hombre de Honduras.

México   Honduras   Uruguay   Panamá   Bolivia   Argentina   Estados Unidos

1. chica pelirroja / estudiante
2. hombre grande / maestro
3. chicos pelirrojos / amigos
4. mujer joven / maestra

5. señora alta / mujer
6. chico atlético / estudiante
7. chico desorganizado / persona
8. hombres simpáticos / amigos

Differentiating Instruction

Multiple Intelligences

Musical/Rhythmic After students have completed Activity 2, divide them into groups of four or five. In turn, ask groups to chant each of the sentences, tapping out a strong rhythm to keep time.

Inclusion

Multisensory Input/Output Ask students to draw a T-table in their notebooks. Ask them to write **Carlos** on one column, and **Sra. Pérez** on the other. As students listen to the audio, ask them to write the descriptions for Carlos and for Sra. Pérez under the appropriate headings.

3 | Describe yourself and others

To review
• noun-adjective agreement p. 72

Read this entry in Alejandra's diary. Complete the entry with the correct form of the word in parentheses.

> **lunes**
>
> Todos mis amigos son muy **1.** (simpático). Miguel es un chico **2.** (inteligente) y muy **3.** (guapo). Beatriz es **4.** (bonito) y **5.** (estudioso). A Miguel y a Beatriz les gusta practicar deportes porque son **6.** (atlético). Carmen y yo no somos **7.** (atlético). Nosotras somos **8.** (artístico). Todos nosotros somos unos estudiantes **9.** (serio) y muy **10.** (bueno).

4 | Describe yourself and others

To review
• **ser** to describe what someone is like p. 63
• noun-adjective agreement p. 72

Ramón and Ramona are complete opposites. Write sentences describing them, based on the descriptions.

modelo: Ramón es malo.
Ramona es buena.

1. Ramón es viejo.
2. Ramona es seria.
3. Ramón es organizado.
4. Ramona es pequeña.
5. Ramón es perezoso.
6. Ramona es baja.

5 | United States

To review
• Comparación cultural pp. 58, 65, 75
• Lectura cultural pp. 80–81

Comparación cultural

Answer these culture questions.

1. What can people do at San Antonio's Paseo del Río?
2. Give an example of a Tex-Mex dish and a Mexican dish.
3. When do people generally use **cascarones** and what do they do with them?
4. What can people do in San Antonio's El Mercado and Miami's Calle Ocho?

Más práctica   Cuaderno *pp. 35–46*   Cuaderno para hispanohablantes *pp. 37–46*

 **Get Help Online**
ClassZone.com

Lección 2
ochenta y cinco   **85**

Differentiating Instruction

Slower-paced Learners

Read Before Listening Give students the script for Activity 1. First, ask them to read the script silently. Second, ask them to use their index fingers to track the text as you read it to them slowly. Then have them listen to the audio.

Multiple Intelligences

Visual Learners Ask students to choose three of the characteristics that describe Ramón and/or Ramona in Activity 4. Have students draw a picture of the fictional Ramón/Ramona illustrating these qualities and write three sentences describing the person. Example: **Ramona es seria. Ramona es desorganizada. Ramona es baja.**

✓ Ongoing Assessment

Alternative Strategy Activity 2
Have students make all sentences plural. For example: **Los señores viejos son unos hombres de Honduras.**

✓ Ongoing Assessment

Peer Assessment Activity 3
Have students exchange the complete paragraph and check each other's work.

Answers MSRB Transparencies 34–35

Answers for Activities on pp. 84, 85.

Activity 1

Carlos es estudiante de español. Él es alto y tiene pelo rubio. Es cómico pero es estudioso. La señora Pérez es buena, organizada y trabajadora. Ella es baja y tiene pelo castaño. Ella es muy artística.

Activity 2

1. La chica pelirroja es una estudiante de Panamá.
2. El hombre grande es un maestro de Argentina.
3. Los chicos pelirrojos son unos amigos de Uruguay y Panamá.
4. La mujer joven es una maestra de Bolivia.
5. La señora alta es una mujer de México.
6. El chico atlético es un estudiante de Uruguay.
7. El chico desorganizado es una persona de Estados Unidos.
8. Los hombres simpáticos son unos amigos de Honduras y Argentina.

Activity 3

1. simpáticos; 2. inteligente; 3. guapo; 4. bonita; 5. estudiosa; 6. atléticos; 7. atléticas; 8. artísticas; 9. serios; 10. buenos

Activity 4

1. Ramona es joven.
2. Ramón es cómico.
3. Ramona es desorganizada.
4. Ramón es grande.
5. Ramona es trabajadora.
6. Ramón es alto.

Activity 5

1. People can eat in restaurants, ride riverboats, or stroll along the river.
2. Chili con carne, fajitas, and nachos.
3. People use cascarones at Easter time; children crack them over their friends' heads.
4. In Calle Ocho people eat Cuban sandwiches and drink mango juice. In El Mercado people eat typical Mexican food and listen to mariachi music.

85

Objectives
- Read three personal accounts about personal descriptions and favorite activities.
- Compare favorite activities of teens with your favorite activities.
- Write a self-description.

Core Resources
- *Cuaderno,* pp. 47–49
- Audio Program: TXT CD 1 track 45
- Video Program: DVD 1

Presentation Strategies
- Ask students to read the headings on p. 86 and look at the photos on p. 87 and predict what they will read in the text. List their responses on the board.
- Have students listen to audio as they follow it in their text.
- Assign students to read each of the three accounts. Encourage them to say if they also like to do activities described by these young people.

STANDARDS
1.2 Understand language
1.3 Present information
2.1 Practices and perspectives
4.2 Compare cultures

Communication
Role-Playing and Skits

Ask students to work in pairs to write and perform skits based on conversations between the following people: José Manuel and one of his teammates, Martina and María, and Mónica and Maite.

Comparación cultural

Estados Unidos
México
Colombia

 AUDIO
Me gusta...

Lectura y escritura

 WebQuest
ClassZone.com

1 Leer Read how José Manuel, Martina, and Mónica describe themselves and state their favorite activities.

2 Escribir Using the three descriptions as models, write a short paragraph about yourself.

STRATEGY Escribir
Use a personal chart
Make a chart showing information about yourself. This will help you write your description.

Categoría	Detalles
país de origen	
descripción física	
personalidad	
actividades favoritas	
comidas favoritas	

Step 1 Complete the chart by adding details about where you are from, a physical description, personality, and favorite activities and foods.

Step 2 Write your paragraph, including all the information from your chart. Check your writing by yourself or with help from a friend. Make final corrections.

Compara con tu mundo
Use the paragraph you wrote to compare your personal description to a description by *one* of the three students. What similarities do you find? What differences?

Cuaderno *pp. 47–49*   Cuaderno para hispanohablantes *pp. 47–49*

Differentiating Instruction

Inclusion
Clear Structure Lead a discussion about each of the categories described in Escribir. Use a discussion to help guide students in creating brainstorming webs as part of their prewriting strategy.

Multiple Intelligences
Naturalist Ask students to use an online weather information source to research weather conditions for the day in Bogotá, Mexico City, Miami, and their hometowns. Then ask them which activities mentioned in the Comparación cultural would be appropriate or inappropriate for the day's weather in each city.

Cultura INTERACTIVA *See these pages come alive!*
ClassZone.com

Colombia — José Manuel

Me llamo José Manuel. Soy de Bogotá. Soy cómico y un poco desorganizado pero también soy estudioso. Después de hacer la tarea me gusta jugar al fútbol con mis amigos en el parque El Tunal. También me gusta mirar el fútbol en la televisión.

Estados Unidos — Martina

¡Hola! Me llamo Martina y soy de Miami. Soy inteligente, alta y atlética. Los domingos, me gusta montar en bicicleta. También me gusta preparar jugo de mango o de melón con mi amiga, María. Nos gusta beber mucho jugo porque en Miami hace calor.

México — Mónica

¿Qué tal? Me llamo Mónica y soy de México, D.F. Tengo pelo castaño y soy seria. Mis amigas Maite y Alejandra también tienen pelo castaño y son muy simpáticas. Maite y yo somos artísticas. Nos gusta tocar la guitarra. También nos gusta dibujar.

Estados Unidos
ochenta y siete **87**

Comparación cultural

Exploring the Theme

Soccer, or **fútbol**, has long been popular in Europe and Latin America, and has gained in popularity in the United States in the past 20 years. The sport originated with the Olmecs, who flourished in Mexico about 1200 BC. It was a ritual ball game played by all the peoples of Mexico and Central America. The ruins of almost every ancient city include a walled court for this sacred game. The ball used was small but extremely heavy because it was made of solid rubber. The Aztecs thought its movements during the ball game symbolized the sun's east-west journey across the sky. The players were not allowed to hit the ball with their hands and feet. They could use only their knees, hips, and elbows.

✓ Ongoing Assessment

Quick Check Ask students quick comprehension questions about each of the three descriptions and write their responses on the board. For example: **¿Cómo se llama la chica de Estados Unidos?**

✓ Ongoing Assessment

Rubric Lectura y escritura

Writing Criteria	Very Good	Proficient	Not There Yet
Content	Paragraph contains a lot of information.	Paragraph contains some information.	Paragraph lacks information.
Communication	Paragraph is organized and easy to follow.	Paragraph is fairly well organized and easy to follow.	Paragraph is disorganized and hard to follow.
Accuracy	Paragraph has few mistakes in vocabulary and grammar.	Paragraph has some mistakes in vocabulary and grammar.	Paragraph has many mistakes in vocabulary and grammar.

Differentiating Instruction

Pre-AP

Expand and Elaborate Have students respond to three young people from Bogotá, Miami, and Mexico City by writing an e-mail to each one. In their e-mails they should take into account the information given by José Manuel, Martina, and Mónica and then write about their own likes and dislikes.

Slower-paced Learners

Yes/No Questions Check students' comprehension of the readings by asking yes/no questions. For example: **José Manuel es muy organizado, ¿verdad? (No.) ¿Mónica tiene pelo castaño? (Sí.) ¿A Martina le gusta montar en bicicleta? (Sí.)**

UNIDAD
1

Repaso inclusivo
♻ Options for Review

Objective
· Cumulative review.

Core Resource
· Audio Program: TXT CD 1 track 46

Review Options
· **Activity 1:** Listening
· **Activity 2:** Speaking
· **Activity 3:** Speaking
· **Activity 4:** Writing
· **Activity 5:** Speaking
· **Activity 6:** Reading, Writing

STANDARDS

1.1 Engage in conversation, Act. 3
1.2 Understand language, Acts. 1, 3
1.3 Present information, Acts. 2–6
2.1 Practices and perspectives, Act. 1
4.2 Compare cultures, Act. 1

Long-term Retention

Study Tips
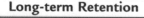

Ask students to make flashcards with Spanish words on one side and English translations on the other. An alternate design for flashcards would be pictures drawn by students or clipped from magazines and pasted on the cards.

---

1 | Listen, understand, and compare

Escuchar

Listen to two teen radio reporters talk about typical after-school activities in Miami and San Antonio. Then answer the questions.

1. ¿Cómo son los estudiantes de Miami?
2. ¿Qué les gusta hacer a los estudiantes de Miami?
3. ¿Cómo son los estudiantes de San Antonio?
4. ¿Qué tiempo hace en San Antonio?
5. ¿Qué les gusta hacer a los estudiantes de San Antonio?

> 🎧 **Audio Program**
> TXT CD 1 Track 46
> Audio Script, TE
> p. 57b

Are you and your friends like the students in Miami and/or San Antonio? Do you like to do the same kinds of activities?

2 | Oral presentation

Hablar

Your principal is making a video about your school and you are going to be a featured student. In a segment that lasts at least 30 seconds, introduce yourself, say where you are from, describe yourself, and talk about what you like to do after school.

3 | Role-play conversation

Hablar

Role-play a conversation with a new student at your school. The new student, played by your partner, will introduce himself or herself and ask you what you are like and what you and your friends like to do. Answer the new student's questions and ask questions of your own to get to know him or her. Your conversation should be at least two minutes long.

¿Cómo eres?

Soy inteligente y atlética.

Differentiating Instruction

Inclusion

Metacognitive Support Ask students to read all six options for review. Hold a short discussion on the various options, and then ask students to think about which of the options would best help them, as individuals, review the material. Ask students to share their thoughts with the class. Finally, have the class vote on three or four different ways they will review the lesson.

Multiple Intelligences

Linguistic/Verbal After listening to the audio in "Listen, understand, and compare," ask students to write a short newspaper story based on the audio. In addition to the audio, students should interview a partner and include that information in their article.

Answers

Activity 1
1. Son muy estudiosos y atléticos.
2. Les gusta pasar un rato con los amigos, estudiar, practicar deportes, montar en bicicleta y jugar al fútbol.
3. Son atléticos y trabajadores.
4. Hace calor.
5. Les gusta correr, jugar al fútbol, leer, y descansar.

4 | Create a yearbook entry

Escribir

Bring in a photo of yourself and create a caption that could be used in a yearbook. Give your name, where you are from, what you are like, who you like to spend time with, and what activities you like to do. Copy this chart on a piece of paper and use it to organize your information.

¿Cómo te llamas?	
¿De dónde eres?	
¿Cómo eres?	
¿Qué te gusta hacer?	

5 | Create a collage

Hablar

Work with a partner to create individual collages. Use magazine clippings, photos, or your own drawings. Use the collage to introduce yourself to your partner, say where you are from, and show some of the things you like to do. When you finish, exchange your collages and use them to introduce each other to the class.

6 | Write a profile

Leer
Escribir

You are collecting information for this school's Web site. Read the questionnaire and write a profile of this student. Include his name, where he is from, and what he likes and doesn't like to do.

Escuela Secundaria Cuauhtémoc
Cuestionario estudiantil

Nombre: Esteban Leñeros

País de origen: México

ACTIVIDADES

¿Qué te gusta hacer? practicar deportes, estudiar, comer enchiladas, escuchar música

¿Qué no te gusta hacer? andar en patineta, comer helado, dibujar

Communication
Group Work

Ask students to think of an activity they like to do using the vocabulary from this unit. Select one student to go first, asking him or her to say the activity. That student should then ask another student who will describe his or her favorite activity. Continue until each student in the class has had a turn. Repeat the activity, asking students to share an activity they don't like.

✓ Ongoing Assessment

Integrated Performance Assessment Rubric Oral Activities 2, 3, 5
    Written Activities 4, 6

Very Good	Proficient	Not There Yet
The student thoroughly develops all requirements of the task.	The student develops most requirements of the task.	The student does not develop the requirements of the task.
The student demonstrates excellent control of verb forms.	The student demonstrates good to fair control of verb forms.	The student demonstrates poor control of verb forms.
Good variety of appropriate vocabulary.	Adequate variety of appropriate vocabulary.	The vocabulary is not appropriate.
The pronunciation is excellent to very good.	The pronunciation is good to fair.	The pronunciation is poor.

Differentiating Instruction

Multiple Intelligences

Naturalist Ask students to identify latitude and longitude for San Antonio, Miami, Bogotá, México, D.F., and their hometowns. Ask students to discuss how latitude could affect after-school activities. Ask them to use longitude to determine the time zone for each city. When their school day is over, what time is it in each of the other cities?

Slower-paced Learners

Memory Aids To adapt Activity 3, ask students to form pairs and discuss the questions they plan to ask each other, and the answers they want to give. Each pair should work together to create cue cards by writing the answers in enlarged print on 8″ x 10″ sheets of paper. They can read from the cue cards during the conversation.

Proyectos adicionales

❋ Planning Ahead

Projects **Create a mural.** Have students work collaboratively to create a "public art" mural that represents their individuality and interests. Using large pieces of butcher paper, have each student create a nearly life-sized drawing of him- or herself doing one of his or her favorite activities. Students can use magic markers, or paint if time allows. Also, ask each student to create one or two items for the mural's background. These might include school items, a clock, or a window. Once the drawings are complete and the paint is dry, have students cut out their figures. Then have them work together to arrange and display their characters and objects on a classroom or hallway wall.

After the mural is complete, distribute two index cards to each student. On one card, instruct students to write as much as they can about their own figure in the mural. On another card, have them choose a friend's figure and write as much as they can about that. Post these cards next to or underneath their corresponding figures in the mural.

> **PACING SUGGESTION:** Upon completion of **Lección 2** to review vocabulary related to school, activities, emotions, and personal traits.

❋ Bulletin Board

Create a bulletin board with the following title: **¿A qué hora?** Using a large cardboard circle and two cardboard "hands," create a large clock on the bulletin board. Attach the hands with a brass brad or paper fastener so that they can be moved into different positions. You can use the clock to help students talk about time, as well as to play different games. Here's one. Write a number of different school activities on separate index cards. Place these in an envelope and attach it to the bulletin board. Have volunteers come choose a card and then set the clock at the right time for that activity. **La clase de ciencias es a la una y veinte.**

> **PACING SUGGESTION:** Before **Lección 1** to preview telling time, and throughout the lesson for reinforcement as time allows.

❋ Web Research

Go online to connect with a pen pal in Mexico. There are many Web sites that can help students connect with a pen pal. A simple search of the words "Mexico" and "pen pal" will lead you to many potential sites.

Begin by having students work together to brainstorm ideas for their first message. Advise them to include some kind of greeting, an introduction, a description of their family, a description of their school, and an explanation of their daily schedule of activities. Once students have finished brainstorming ideas, have them draft their own e-mail messages on a separate piece of paper. Once students have identified potential recipients, have each student send his or her message. Alternatively, you could draft one message for the whole class, and send it as a group.

Hopefully, students will receive a response. Give students the opportunity to share the messages they receive, and to discuss what they will write about next.

> **PACING SUGGESTION:** Upon completion of **Lección 1,** and throughout **Lección 2** as messages arrive.

Get Help Online
ClassZone.com

❋ Games

¿Tienes?

This game is similar to Go Fish. Begin by having students create the cards for the game. Have students draw on index cards the classroom items presented on p. 122. There should be four index cards for each item.

To play, organize students into groups of three or four. Each group needs one deck of cards. One student deals each player five cards, then places the remaining cards face down. The goal is to get matching pairs. The dealer begins by asking whether another player has a card: **¿Tienes un lápiz?** If the player has the card, he or she responds affirmatively and gives the card to the dealer. The dealer than sets the pair aside and takes another turn. If the player doesn't have the card, the dealer must draw one from the pile and the next player takes a turn. The game ends when one player puts down or gives away the last card. The player with the most pairs wins.

> **PACING SUGGESTION:** After vocabulary is presented in **Lección 2** to reinforce classroom items. Can be replayed using different sets of cards.

Tengo... Estoy...

Before playing, collect a number of classroom items, such as those listed on p. 122. Have a group of five or six students sit in a circle. The first player chooses one of the items, and tells the player to his or her right, **Tengo una pluma.** That player responds with a question: **¿Tienes una pluma?** The first player repeats his or her assertion: **Sí, tengo una pluma.** The second player then takes the item, stating, **No,** *yo* **tengo la pluma.** The conversation then begins again between this player and the player to his or her right. Allow the item to travel all the way around the circle. Then repeat with a new item. For a variation, the game can also be played using emotion words. Have the first player begin: **Estoy cansado(a).** Encourage students to act out an appropriate facial expression. The next player responds with the question: **¿Estás cansado(a)?** The first player repeats his or her assertion: **Sí, estoy cansado(a).** The second player then imitates the face, stating, **Yo estoy cansado(a) también.**

For an added challenge, don't wait for the item or emotion to travel all the way around the circle before introducing the next one.

> **PACING SUGGESTION:** Upon completion of **Lección 2.**

❋ Recipe

Natilla is an easy-to-make Mexican dessert. It is very similar to a basic **flan,** another traditional custard dessert served across the Spanish-speaking world.

Natilla

Ingredientes

4 huevos separados
1 taza de leche
1/8 cucharadita de sal
1/4 taza de harina
3/4 taza de azúcar
1 cucharadita de nuez
   moscada

Instrucciones

En una fuente, hacer una pasta con las yemas de los huevos, la harina y 1/2 taza de leche. En una cacerola mediana, añadir el azúcar y la sal a la leche sobrante y calentar hasta que casi hierva a temperatura mediana. Añadir la mezcla de yemas a la leche y continuar cociendo a temperatura mediana hasta que cobre una consistencia cremosa. Retirar la cacerola del fuego y enfriar. Cuando esté fría, ponerle la nuez moscada por encima.

❋ Music

Mexican music is diverse and ever-changing. Some traditional styles include **mariachi, ranchera, norteña,** and **banda.** Some contemporary styles combine these traditions with rock and hip-hop. Have students go to a music store or to an online music store to find examples of traditional and modern Mexican music. Play some of the music they research. Discuss what music they like and why. Samples can be heard on music sites online.

UNIT THEME
Let's go to school

✿ UNIT STANDARDS

COMMUNICATION
- Talk about daily schedules
- Ask and tell time
- Say what you have and have to do
- Say what you do and how often you do it
- Describe classes and classroom objects
- Say where things are located
- Say where you are going
- Talk about how you feel

CULTURES
- School uniforms
- Diego Rivera and Frida Kahlo
- Bilingual school in Mexico
- The National Museum of Anthropology

CONNECTIONS
- History: Reading historical maps
- Art: Creating maps and symbols
- Social Studies: Technology in education
- Health: Health benefits of cacti

COMPARISONS
- Meeting places in Spanish-speaking countries and in the U.S.
- School uniforms in Mexico, the Dominican Republic, and the U.S.
- Public artwork in Mexico and the U.S.
- The Spanish **ch** and **d** and the English *ch* and *d*
- School years in Mexico and the U.S.
- Ancient artifacts and future artifacts
- Self-portraits
- Favorite classes of Mexican and Dominican students
- A culture's view of the natural world reflected in art
- School schedules in Mexico, the Dominican Republic, and Paraguay
- Huichol yarn painting, Taino rock art

COMMUNITIES
- Arts and crafts influenced by Spanish-speaking cultures in a local store

UNIDAD 2

México
¡Vamos a la escuela!

Lección 1
Tema: **Somos estudiantes**

Lección 2
Tema: **En la escuela**

Estados Unidos

Ciudad Juárez

Chihuahua

BAJA CALIFORNIA

Golfo de California

Monterrey

Golfo de México

México

Bahía de Campeche

Chichén Itzá

Océano Pacífico

Zempoala

San Miguel de Allende

PENÍNSULA DE YUCATÁN

Guadalajara

México, D.F.

Puebla

Oaxaca

Guatemala

El Salvador

«¡Hola!
Somos Pablo y Claudia.
Somos de México.»

Población: 104.959.594

Área: 761.606 millas cuadradas

Capital: México, D.F. (Ciudad de México)

Moneda: el peso mexicano

Idiomas: español, maya y otras lenguas indígenas; el país con más hispanohablantes del mundo

Comida típica: tortillas, tacos, enchiladas

Gente famosa: Carlos Fuentes (escritor), Salma Hayek (actriz), Mario Molina (químico), Thalía (cantante)

Chocolate

90 noventa

Cultural Geography

Setting the Scene
- What is the currency of Mexico? (peso)
- What are the colors of Mexico's flag? (red, white, green)
- What is the boy's name? (Pablo) What is the girl's name? (Claudia)

Teaching with Maps
- Mexico shares a border with which country to the north? (United States)
- Chichén Itzá is located in which peninsula? (Yucatán)

Jóvenes en el Jardín Principal de San Miguel de Allende

◄ **Un rato con familia y amigos** In San Miguel de Allende, people of all ages go to the **Jardín Principal,** a tree-lined park in the center of town, to stroll, listen to live music, and spend time with family and friends. *When you want to spend time outside, where do you go?*

Las ruinas de Chichén Itzá The ruins of the ancient Mayan city of Chichén Itzá include structures built for worship, sports, and studying astronomy. The pyramid of **Kukulcán** was used as a temple. *What are some important buildings in your area used for?* ►

La estatua de Chac-Mool y la pirámide de Kukulcán

◄ **Una universidad con mucha historia y arte** **La Universidad Nacional Autónoma de México (UNAM)** is one of the oldest universities in the Americas, and the largest public university in Mexico, with over 270,000 students. The library's mosaic mural depicts moments in the cultural history of Mexico. *What are some well-known universities in your area?*

La biblioteca de la UNAM con el mural mosaico

Bridging Cultures

Heritage Language Learners

Support What They Know Invite students, with a personal or family connection to Mexico, to add to the information presented on pp. 90 and 91. What are their memories and/or impressions of this country? How would they compare schools and students in Mexico with those in the United States?

English Learners

Build Background Direct students to read p. 91 in order to identify the main idea of each paragraph. Remind them that the title and topic sentence can be good clues toward finding the main idea. After students have defined the main idea, ask them to draw connections between these elements of Mexican life and those in their own home country. Are there any similarities?

Send your students to www.ClassZone.com to explore authentic Mexican culture. Tell them to click on Cultura interactiva to see these pages come alive!

Culture

About the Photos

· Music is an ever-present feature of the Jardín Principal. Saturday afternoons and evenings are the liveliest times, when both mariachis and amateur musicians meander around the central square.

· **Kukulcán** is the Mayan name for the Plumed Serpent, a deity frequently shown in Central American art. The Spanish name for the pyramid is **El Castillo de la Serpiente Emplumada,** or The Castle of the Plumed Serpent.

· The Mexico City campus of the university boasts a number of architecturally impressive buildings. One of them bears the university's coat of arms, with the motto **Por mi raza hablará el espíritu** (For my race the spirit will speak).

Expanded Information

· San Miguel de Allende is a charming tourist town that draws many artists, artisans, and musicians every year. In its network of narrow streets are brightly painted red, orange, and yellow buildings that house tiny shops, eateries, and art galleries.

· Chichén Itzá was once a great Mayan city, complete with a plaza, marketplace, athletic fields, and numerous temples. Between A.D. 700 and A.D. 1200, it was the Yucatán's seat of power for government, religion, and the military.

· The university, founded over 500 years ago, has been attended by dozens of Mexico's presidents, statesmen, scientists, writers, and artists.

Video Character Guide

Pablo and Claudia are classmates. They are both good students.

▶l ll

Lesson Overview

Culture at a Glance ❖

Topic & Activity	Essential Question
Town squares or plazas pp. 92–93	Does your city or town have a main square?
School uniforms p. 102	How does the way students dress reflect a culture?
Mexican murals p. 109	How does society affect public artwork?
A bilingual school in Mexico pp. 114–115	What are some of the requirements to graduate from a bilingual school in Mexico?
Culture review p. 119	What are some cultural elements in Mexico and the Dominican Republic?

COMPARISON COUNTRIES México República Dominicana Paraguay

Practice at a Glance ❖

	Objective	Activity & Skill
Vocabulary	Numbers from 11 to 100	1: Speaking/Writing; 2: Speaking; 13: Writing; 23: Reading/Listening/Speaking
	School subjects, classroom activities	1: Speaking/Writing; 2: Speaking; 3: Listening/Reading; 4: Writing; 6: Writing; 8: Listening/Writing; 12: Speaking/Writing; 14: Speaking/Writing; 17: Speaking/Writing; 18: Speaking; 21: Listening/Reading; 22: Speaking; 23: Reading/Listening/Writing; 24: Writing; Repaso 1: Listening
	Expressions of frequency	9: Speaking; 14: Speaking/Writing; 16: Speaking; 19: Writing/Speaking; 24: Writing; Repaso 1: Listening; Repaso 4: Writing
Grammar	The verb **tener**	5: Reading/Writing; 6: Writing; 7: Speaking; 8: Listening/Writing; 9: Speaking; 11: Writing; 12: Speaking/Writing; 20: Listening/Reading; 21: Listening/Reading; 22: Speaking; 24: Writing; Repaso 2: Writing
	Present tense of **-ar** verbs	13: Writing; 14: Speaking/Writing; 15: Reading/Writing; 16: Speaking; 17: Speaking/Writing; 18: Speaking; 19: Writing/Speaking; 20: Listening/Reading; 21: Listening/Reading; 22: Speaking; Repaso 3, 4: Writing
Communication	Talk about daily schedules	1: Speaking/Writing; 3: Listening/Reading; 4: Writing; 12: Speaking/Writing; 18: Speaking; 23: Reading/Listening/Writing; 24: Writing; Repaso 3: Writing
	Ask and tell time	1: Speaking/Writing; 12: Speaking/Writing; 13: Writing; 23: Reading/Listening/Writing; Repaso 2: Writing
	Say what you have and have to do	7: Speaking; 8: Listening/Writing; 9: Speaking; 10: Listening/Reading; 11: Writing; 12: Speaking/Writing; 22: Speaking; 24: Writing; Repaso 2: Writing
	Say what you do and how often you do things	9: Speaking; 12: Speaking/Writing; 14: Speaking/Writing; 15: Reading/Writing; 16: Speaking; 19: Writing/Speaking; 22: Speaking; 24: Writing; Repaso 4: Writing
	Pronunciation: The **ch** sound	*Pronunciáción: El sonido ch* p. 101: Listening
Recycle	After-school activities	9: Speaking
	Days of the week	11: Writing

The following activities are recorded in the Audio Program for *¡Avancemos!*

- **¡A responder!** *page 96*
- **8: ¿Qué tienen que hacer?** *page 102*
- **23: Integración** *page 112*
- **Repaso de la lección** *page 118*
  1: Listen and Understand

¡A responder! TXT CD 2 track 2

1. La clase de matemáticas es a las siete.
2. La clase de español es a la una y media.
3. La clase de arte es a las doce menos diez.
4. La clase de inglés es a las diez y cuarto.
5. La clase de historia es a las doce y media.
6. La clase de ciencias es a las ocho y diez.

8 | ¿Qué tienen que hacer?

TXT CD 2 track 4

Hola, me llamo Pablo. Mis amigos y yo tenemos mucho que hacer.
Claudia tiene un examen mañana. Son las ocho y tiene que estudiar.
Me gusta escribir correos electrónicos. Son las diez menos cuarto y tengo que usar la computadora.
Pepe tiene que hacer la tarea porque son las cuatro y diez.
Es la una y media. Laura y Diana tienen que tocar la guitarra.
Hoy es lunes. Son las seis y cuarto y Carlos tiene que trabajar.
Son las once menos veinte. Manuel y yo tenemos que leer un libro para la clase de historia.

23 | Integración TXT CD 2 tracks 8, 9

Atención, estudiantes. Mañana los maestros tienen una reunión y el horario de clases es diferente. Todos los estudiantes tienen que llegar 45 minutos después de la hora normal a las clases de la mañana y 15 minutos después de la hora normal a las clases de la tarde. Repito. Mañana el horario de clases es diferente. Todos los estudiantes tienen que llegar 45 minutos después de la hora normal a las clases de la mañana y 15 minutos después de la hora normal a las clases de la tarde. Gracias.

Repaso de la lección TXT CD 2 track 11

1 Listen and understand

Martín: Hola, Lupe.

Lupe: ¡Martín! ¿Cómo estás?

Martín: Regular. ¿Qué hora es?

Lupe: Son las diez y cuarto.

Martín: Tengo la clase de historia a las diez y media. Me gusta llegar temprano porque necesito sacar una buena nota.

Lupe: ¿Ustedes tienen que tomar muchos apuntes?

Martín: Sí. Tomamos apuntes todos los días. También tomamos muchos apuntes en la clase de inglés, y contestamos preguntas. ¡Hay muchas preguntas!

Lupe: Yo tengo la clase de ciencias a las diez y media. La maestra es joven y es muy buena. De vez en cuando usamos la computadora. También tenemos que contestar muchas preguntas.

Martín: ¡Uy! Es la hora de clase, ¿no?

Lupe: Sí. Casi son las diez y media. Hasta luego.

Martín: Adiós.

On your desktop

Everything you need to ...

Plan	Present	Assess
easyPlanner DVD-ROM	**POWER PRESENTATIONS**	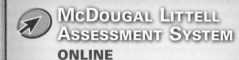 **McDougal Littell Assessment System** ONLINE
All resources including audio and video	Ready-made PowerPoint™ presentations with  **Animated Grammar**	✓ Assess, score, prescribe, and remediate online ✓ Create customized tests with the Test Generator CD-ROM ✓ Individualized Assessment for on-level, modified, pre-AP, and heritage language learners

 ## Print

Plan	Present	Practice	Assess
URB 2 • Video Scripts pp. 67–68 • Family Letter p. 90 • Absent Student Copymasters pp. 92–99 **Lesson Plans** p. 39 **Best Practices Toolkit**	**URB 2** • Video Activities pp. 51–56 **TPRS** pp. 15–21	• *Cuaderno* pp. 51–73 • *Cuaderno para hispanohablantes* pp. 51–73 • *Lecturas para todos* pp. 12–16 • *Lecturas para hispanohablantes* • *¡AvanzaCómics! SuperBruno y Nati*, Episodio 1 **URB 2** • Practice Games pp. 29–36 • Audio Scripts pp. 71–74 • Map/Culture Activities pp. 81–83 • Fine Art Activities pp. 85–86	**URB 2** • Did you get it? Reteaching and Practice Copymasters pp. 1–10

 ## Unit Transparency Book 2

Culture	Presentation and Practice	Classroom Management
• Atlas Maps UTB 1 1–6 • Map of Mexico 1 • Fine Art Transparencies 2, 3	• Vocabulary Transparencies 6, 7 • Grammar Presentation Transparencies 10, 11	• Warm Up Transparencies 16–19 **MSRB** • Student Book Answer Transparencies 36–39

Audio and Video

Audio	Video

• Student Book Audio CD 2 Tracks 1–11
• Workbook Audio CD 1 Tracks 21–30
• Heritage Learners Audio CD 1 Tracks 9–12, CD 3 Tracks 9, 10
• Assessment Audio CD 1 Tracks 9, 10
• *Lecturas para todos* Audio CD 1 Track 3, CD 2 Tracks 1–6
• *Música del mundo hispano*
• Sing-along Audio CD
	• Vocabulary Video DVD 1
	• *Telehistoria* DVD 1
	   Escena 1
	   Escena 2
	   Escena 3
	   Completa

 # Online and CD-ROM Resources

Student	Teacher
Available online and on CD-ROM: • eEdition • @HomeTutor • Animated Grammar **Available online:** • *Cultura Interactiva* • Culture Links • WebQuests • Flashcards • Conjuguemos.com • Review Games • Self-check Quiz	**Available online and on CD-ROM:** **EasyPlanner CD-ROM resources:** • Learning Scenarios • Conversation Cards • Family Letters in Spanish • Family Letters in Creole **Available online:** • McDougal Littell Assessment System **Available on CD-ROM:** • Test Generator • Power Presentations

✓ Differentiated Assessment

On-level	Modified	Pre-AP	Heritage Learners
• Vocabulary Recognition Quiz p. 57 • Vocabulary Production Quiz p. 58 • Grammar Quizzes pp. 59–60 • Culture Quiz p. 61 • On-level Lesson Test pp. 62–68	• Modified Lesson Test pp. 47–53	• Pre-AP Lesson Test pp. 47–53	• Heritage Learners Lesson Test pp. 53–59

	Objectives/Focus	Teach	Practice	Assess/HW Options
DAY 1	**Culture:** learn about Mexican culture **Vocabulary:** daily schedules • Warm up OHT 16 5 min	**Unit Opener** pp. 90–91 **Lesson Opener** pp. 92–93 **Presentación de vocabulario** pp. 94–96 • Read A–D • View video DVD 1 • Play audio TXT CD 2 track 1 • *¡A responder!* TXT CD 2 track 2 20 min	**Lesson Opener** pp. 92–93 **Práctica de vocabulario** p. 97 • Acts. 1, 2 • *Nota gramatical* 20 min	**Assess:** *Para y piensa* p. 97 5 min **Homework:** *Cuaderno* pp. 51–53 @HomeTutor
DAY 2	**Communication:** talking about daily schedules • Warm up OHT 16 • Check Homework 5 min	**Vocabulario en contexto** pp. 98–99 • *Telehistoria escena 1* DVD 1 • *Nota gramatical* 20 min	**Vocabulario en contexto** pp. 98–99 • Act. 3 TXT CD 2 track 3 • Act. 4 20 min	**Assess:** *Para y piensa* p. 99 5 min **Homework:** *Cuaderno* pp. 51–53 @HomeTutor
DAY 3	**Grammar:** verb **tener** • Warm up OHT 17 • Check Homework 5 min	**Presentación de gramática** p. 100 • The verb **tener** • Pronunciación TXT CD 2 track 6 **Culture:** School uniforms 20 min	**Práctica de gramática** pp. 101–103 • Acts. 5, 6, 7, 9 • *Nota gramatical* • Act. 8 TXT CD 2 track 4 20 min	**Assess:** *Para y piensa* p. 103 5 min **Homework:** *Cuaderno* pp. 54–56 @HomeTutor
DAY 4	**Communication:** using **tener** to talk about daily schedules • Warm up OHT 17 • Check Homework 5 min	**Gramática en contexto** pp. 104–105 • *Telehistoria escena 2* DVD 1 20 min	**Gramática en contexto** pp. 104–105 • Act. 10 TXT CD 2 track 5 • Acts. 11–12 20 min	**Assess:** *Para y piensa* p. 105 5 min **Homework:** *Cuaderno* pp. 54–56 @HomeTutor
DAY 5	**Grammar:** present tense of **-ar** verbs • Warm up OHT 18 • Check Homework 5 min	**Presentación de gramática** p. 106 • Present tense of **-ar** verbs 15 min	**Práctica de gramática** pp. 107–109 • Acts. 13–19 25 min	**Assess:** *Para y piensa* p. 109 5 min **Homework:** *Cuaderno* pp. 57–59 @HomeTutor
DAY 6	**Communication:** Culmination: use **tener** and **-ar** verbs to talk about daily activities • Warm up OHT 18 • Check Homework 5 min	**Todo junto** pp. 110–112 • *Escenas 1, 2: Resumen* • *Telehistoria completa* DVD 1 15 min	**Todo junto** pp. 110–112 • Acts. 20, 21 TXT CD 2 track 7 • Act. 23 TXT CD 2 tracks 8, 9 • Acts. 22, 24 25 min	**Assess:** *Para y piensa* p. 112 5 min **Homework:** *Cuaderno* pp. 60–61 @HomeTutor
DAY 7	**Reading:** A Bilingual School in Mexico • Warm up OHT 19 • Check Homework 5 min	**Lectura** pp. 114–115 • *Una escuela bilingüe en México* TXT CD 2 track 10 15 min	**Lectura** pp. 114–115 • *Una escuela bilingüe en México* 25 min	**Assess:** *Para y piensa* p. 115 5 min **Homework:** *Cuaderno* pp. 65–67 @HomeTutor
DAY 8	**Review:** Lesson review • Warm up OHT 19 5 min	**Repaso de la lección** pp. 118–119 15 min	**Repaso de la lección** pp. 118–119 • Activity 1 CD 2 track 11 • Activities 2, 3, 4, 5 25 min	**Assess:** *Repaso de la lección* 5 min pp. 118–119 **Homework:** *En resumen* p. 117 *Cuaderno* pp. 62–64, 68–73 (optional) Review Games Online @HomeTutor
DAY 9	**Assesssment**			**Lesson 1 test** 50 min

	Objectives/Focus	Teach	Practice	Assess/HW Options
DAY 1	**Culture:** learn about Mexican culture **Vocabulary:** daily schedule • Warm Up OHT 16 **5 min**	**Unit Opener** pp. 90–91 **Lesson Opener** pp. 92–93 **Presentación de vocabulario** pp. 94–96 • Read A–D • View video DVD 1 • Play audio TXT CD 2 track 1 • ¡A responder! TXT CD 2 track 2 **20 min**	**Lesson Opener** pp. 92–93 **Práctica de vocabulario** p. 97 • Acts. 1, 2 • Nota gramatical **20 min**	**Assess:** Para y piensa p. 97 **5 min** @HomeTutor
	Communication: talking about daily schedules **5 min**	**Vocabulario en contexto** pp. 98–99 • Telehistoria escena 1 DVD 1 • Nota gramatical **15 min**	**Vocabulario en contexto** pp. 98–99 • Act. 3 TXT CD 2 track 3 • Activity 4 **15 min**	**Assess:** Para y piensa p. 99 **5 min** **Homework:** Cuaderno pp. 51–53 @HomeTutor
DAY 2	**Grammar:** verb **tener** • Warm Up OHT 17 • Check Homework **5 min**	**Presentación de gramática** p. 100 • The verb **tener** **Práctica de gramática** pp. 101–103 • Nota gramatical • Pronunciación TXT CD 2 track 6 **Culture:** School uniforms **20 min**	**Práctica de gramática** pp. 101–103 • Acts. 5, 6, 7, 9 • Act. 8 TXT CD 2 track 4 **15 min**	**Assess:** Para y piensa p. 103 **5 min**
	Communication: using **tener** and **tener que** to talk about what you have to do **5 min**	**Gramática en contexto** pp. 104–105 • Telehistoria escena 2 DVD 1 **20 min**	**Gramática en contexto** pp. 104–105 • Act. 10 TXT CD 2 track 5 • Activities 11, 12 **15 min**	**Assess:** Para y piensa p. 105 **5 min** **Homework:** Cuaderno pp. 54–56 @HomeTutor
DAY 3	**Grammar:** present tense of **-ar** verbs • Warm Up OHT 18 • Check Homework **5 min**	**Presentación de gramática** p. 106 • Present tense of **-ar** verbs **15 min**	**Práctica de gramática** pp. 107–109 • Acts. 13, 14, 15, 16, 17, 18, 19 **20 min**	**Assess:** Para y piensa p. 109 **5 min**
	Communication: Culmination: use **tener** and **-ar** verbs to talk about daily activities **5 min**	**Todo junto** pp. 110–112 • Escenas 1 & 2: Resumen • Telehistoria completa DVD 1 **15 min**	**Todo junto** pp. 110–112 • Acts. 20, 21 TXT CD 2 track 7 • Activity 23 TXT CD 2 tracks 8,9 • Acts. 22, 24 **20 min**	**Assess:** Para y piensa p. 112 **5 min** **Homework:** Cuaderno pp. 57–59 @HomeTutor
DAY 4	**Reading:** A Bilingual School in Mexico • Warm Up OHT 19 • Check Homework **5 min**	**Lectura** pp. 114–115 • Una escuela bilingüe en México TXT CD 2 track 10 **15 min**	**Lectura** pp. 114–115 • Una escuela bilingüe en México **15 min**	**Assess:** Para y piensa p. 115 **5 min**
	Review: lesson review **5 min**	**Repaso de la lección** pp. 118–119 **15 min**	**Repaso de la lección** pp. 118–119 • Activity 1 CD 2 track 11 • Activities 2 ,3, 4, 5 **25 min**	**Assess:** Repaso de la lección pp. 118–119 **5 min** **Homework:** En resumen p. 117 Cuaderno pp. 62–73 (optional) Review Games Online @HomeTutor
DAY 5	**Assessment**			**Assessment:** Lesson Test **50 min**
	Connections: History	**Conexiones** p. 116 • El pueblo de Zempoala **10 min**	**Conexiones** p. 116 • Proyecto 1,2,3 **30 min**	

México

Objectives
- Introduce lesson theme: **Somos estudiantes.**
- Culture: **zócalos** and **plazas**

Presentation Strategies
- Introduce the characters' names: Claudia and Pablo.
- Have students make a list of their daily schedule.
- Have students talk about places to visit in their city.

STANDARDS
2.1 Practices and perspectives
4.2 Compare cultures

Warm Up · UTB 2 Transparency 16

Vocabulary Write *Carlos* if the sentence describes a boy. Write *Carla* if the sentence describes a girl.
1. Es inteligente y estudioso.
2. Es cómico y un poco artístico.
3. Es alta y seria.
4. Es bonita y tiene pelo castaño.
5. Es joven y atlética.

Answers: 1. Carlos; 2. Carlos; 3. Carla; 4. Carla; 5. Carla

Comparación cultural

Exploring the Theme
Ask the following:
1. Does your town have a central or town square?
2. How is it different from the one in this photo? How is it similar?
3. What historical buildings do you know of in your town?

¿Qué ves? Possible answers include:
- Hace sol.
- Es lunes.
- El chico es guapo, simpático, alto y joven. La chica es bonita, baja y simpática.

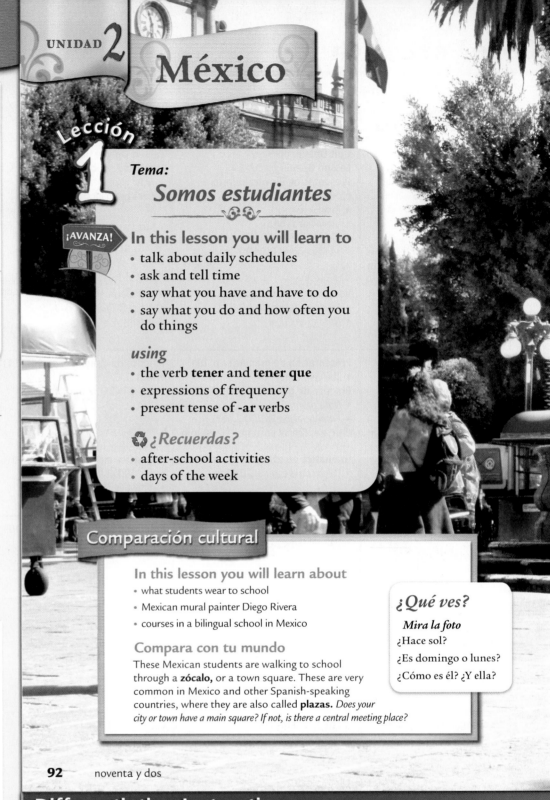

Lección 1

Tema:
Somos estudiantes

¡AVANZA! **In this lesson you will learn to**
- talk about daily schedules
- ask and tell time
- say what you have and have to do
- say what you do and how often you do things

using
- the verb **tener** and **tener que**
- expressions of frequency
- present tense of **-ar** verbs

♻ **¿Recuerdas?**
- after-school activities
- days of the week

Comparación cultural

In this lesson you will learn about
- what students wear to school
- Mexican mural painter Diego Rivera
- courses in a bilingual school in Mexico

Compara con tu mundo
These Mexican students are walking to school through a **zócalo,** or a town square. These are very common in Mexico and other Spanish-speaking countries, where they are also called **plazas.** *Does your city or town have a main square? If not, is there a central meeting place?*

¿Qué ves?
Mira la foto
¿Hace sol?
¿Es domingo o lunes?
¿Cómo es él? ¿Y ella?

92 noventa y dos

Differentiating Instruction

English Learners
Build Background Ask students to share experiences they have had attending schools in other countries. What are the similarities and differences? For example, do they have to wear school uniforms? What is their school year calendar?

Slower-paced Learners
Personalize It Explain to students that a **zócalo** is similar to a town square. Ask students to name locations in their own town or city that might be referred to as a **zócalo.** What features do these areas have? Why do people congregate there?

La fuente de San Miguel en el Zócalo
Puebla, México

México
noventa y tres   **93**

Using the Photo

Location Information

Puebla, Mexico Puebla, established in 1531, is the most European of Mexico's colonial cities. The town square, **El Zócalo**, is in the heart of the historic district that includes architecture dating to the 17th century.

Expanded Information

History El **Cinco de Mayo** is a celebration of the Mexican victory over French invaders at Puebla on May 5, 1862. It is not to be confused with Mexico's Independence Day from Spain celebrated September 16. In the early hours of this day in 1810, Father Hidalgo, followed by other Mexican patriots, rang the bell of his church calling all Mexicans to fight for their independence from Spain. The war lasted 10 years. Today, just like the 4th of July in the United States, Mexicans celebrate September 16th with a big **fiesta** with fireworks and the Mexican flag is displayed in every house and building.

Differentiating Instruction

Heritage Language Learners

Support What They Know Divide a piece of chart paper into two columns. First, invite students to share what they know about the country of Mexico. Record their responses in the left-hand column. Then ask students to share questions that they have about Mexico. Record these questions in the right-hand column. Invite students to choose one question to research and report back on.

Multiple Intelligences

Kinesthetic Assign two students to play the roles of the students in the photo. Have them create a dialogue about the weather, what they like to do, and what their friends are like. Then have them perform the dialogue, acting out the meanings of the expressions they use.

Long-term Retention
Connect to Previous Learning

Remind students that they have learned words and phrases to describe primarily after-school and extracurricular activities. Explain that in this lesson they will be able to describe their time spent at school. Ask them to share Spanish words and phrases already learned about what would take place during a typical school day. Write them on the board.

Objective
- Present vocabulary: time, school and class schedules, numbers, school subjects, classroom activities.

Core Resources
- Video Program: DVD 1
- Audio Program: TXT CD 2, track 1

Presentation Strategies
- Say the vocabulary words on pp. 94–96 and have students repeat after you.
- Play the audio as students read A–B.
- Show the video.

STANDARDS
1.2 Understand language

Comparisons
English Language Connection

Cognates Remind students that there are many Spanish words that look similar to their English meanings and that these are called cognates. Discuss some of the cognates seen on pp. 94–96.

Communication
Class Work

Have students practice numbers from 11 to 100. Go row by row, asking students to count by 2s, 3s, 5s, and 10s. For example, the first student in the 1st row says **dos**, the second says **cuatro**, the third says **seis**. Continue until all students have spoken.

Long-term Retention
Connect to Previous Learning

Mention that neither school subjects nor languages are capitalized in Spanish. Ask students what other words they have learned are capitalized in English but not in Spanish. Answers include the days of the week and the subject pronoun **yo.**

Presentación de VOCABULARIO

 Goal: Learn about Pablo's school and class schedule. Then practice what you have learned to talk about daily schedules. *Actividades 1–2*

VIDEO
DVD

AUDIO

A ¡Hola! Me llamo Pablo. Mi amiga es Claudia. Somos estudiantes en Puebla, México. Me gusta **llegar** a clase **temprano.** Claudia, ¿qué hora es?

7:00 matemáticas
8:10 ciencias
9:15 usar la computadora
10:15 inglés
11:50 arte
12:30 historia
1:30 español
3:30 jugar al fútbol

el horario

Numbers from 11 to 100

11 once	20 veinte	30 treinta
12 doce	21 veintiuno	31 treinta y uno
13 trece	22 veintidós	
14 catorce	23 veintitrés	40 cuarenta
15 quince	24 veinticuatro	50 cincuenta
16 dieciséis	25 veinticinco	60 sesenta
17 diecisiete	26 veintiséis	70 setenta
18 dieciocho	27 veintisiete	80 ochenta
19 diecinueve	28 veintiocho	90 noventa
	29 veintinueve	100 cien

Más vocabulario

de vez en cuando *once in a while*
muchas veces *often, many times*
nunca *never*
todos los días *every day*
casi *almost*
difícil *difficult*
fácil *easy*
hay... *there is, there are . . .*
la hora *hour; time*
el minuto *minute*
¿Cuántos(as)...? *How many . . . ?*
Expansión de vocabulario p. R3

94 Unidad 2 México
noventa y cuatro

Differentiating Instruction

Inclusion

Cumulative Instruction Before introducing the vocabulary on pp. 94–96, review with students the numbers 1 through 10. Write a number on the board, and have students call out its name in Spanish. Then invite volunteers to the board to write down a number whose name you say aloud. Preview the list of numbers 11 to 100 on p. 94 by reading each aloud and having students repeat.

Multiple Intelligences

Intrapersonal Invite students to create a sample page from a daily planner that represents their own daily schedule. The page should include the time and name of each class, and a symbol or picture representing each class. Have students describe their schedules and classes using the vocabulary on pp. 94–96. For example, **La clase de ciencias es difícil. Me gusta llegar temprano a la clase de arte.**

B ¿A qué hora son mis clases? Tengo **muchas** clases.

las matemáticas

La clase de **matemáticas** es **a las siete** de la mañana.

las ciencias

La clase de **ciencias** es **a las ocho y diez** de la mañana.

el inglés

La clase de **inglés** es **a las diez y cuarto** de la mañana.

el arte

La clase de **arte** es **a las doce menos diez** de la mañana.

la historia

La clase de **historia** es a las **doce y media** de la tarde.

el español

La clase de **español** es a la **una y media** de la tarde.

Continuará...

Lección 1
noventa y cinco **95**

TEACHER to TEACHER

Rosa Jacks
Mountain Lakes, New Jersey

Tips for Presenting Vocabulary

Whenever I teach time, I bring a large plastic clock or one made from a paper plate and movable hands. I say a time on the hour, half hour, and quarter hour and call on one student to come and move the hands to that time and then hold up the clock to the class and say that time. I repeat the process with several more students.

Communication
Interpretive Mode

Have students keep the following questions in mind:
1. Where are Pablo and Claudia students?
2. What time is **las diez y cuarto de la mañana**?
3. What time is **las siete de la mañana**?
4. What time is **la una y media de la tarde**?
Answers: 1. Puebla, México; 2. 10:15 A.M.; 3. 7:00 A.M.; 4. 1:30 P.M.

Communication
Pair Work

Ask students to write the order in which they have these classes: **el inglés, el español, la historia, las ciencias, las matemáticas.** Next to each course, have them write the time at which they have each class. When they finish, have pairs compare their schedule.

Long-term Retention
Study Tips

Use Photos Explain to students that photos provide clues to help them understand what the main idea is without understanding every word in the passage. When learning a new word, they should think about the theme of the lesson—and look for clues in the photos.

Differentiating Instruction

Slower-paced Learners

Memory Aids Ask students to write the new vocabulary words in their notebooks. Encourage them to accompany each word with a picture that will help them remember it. For **arte**, for example, they could draw an easel or paints and brushes. For **historia**, they could draw a map.

Heritage Language Learners

Support What They Know Ask students who have attended school in a Spanish-speaking country to describe the differences in scheduling between school there and school in the United States. Ask them to describe when school starts and ends, how many classes students take, and if there are other breaks besides lunch.

Objectives
- Present vocabulary: school and class schedules, school activities.
- Check for recognition.

Core Resources
- Video Program: DVD 1
- Audio Program: TXT CD 2, tracks 1, 2

Presentation Strategies
- Read a sentence from the text and ask whether it refers to Claudia or Pablo. For example: **Ella es muy inteligente. (Claudia) Tengo que sacar una buena nota en la clase de inglés. (Pablo)**
- Play the audio as students read C–D.
- Play the video.

STANDARDS
1.2 Understand language

Comparisons
English Language Connection

False Cognates Point out that **nota** as used on p. 96 is a false cognate. It does not mean *note*; in this case, it means *grade*.

Long-term Retention
Connect to Previous Learning

Remind students of the verbs ending in **-ar** that they learned in Unidad 1, Lección 1. Ask them to read p. 96 and find new verbs ending in **-ar**. (**contestar, tomar, sacar, necesitar, usar, enseñar**) Ask them to write these verbs in their notebooks along with their English equivalents for future reference.

Answers MSRB Transparency 36

¡A responder!
1. la mañana 3. la mañana 5. la tarde
2. la tarde 4. la mañana 6. la mañana

Activity 1
1. A las once menos cuarto Claudia tiene la clase de inglés.
2. A las siete y media Claudia tiene la clase de ciencias.
3. A las doce Claudia tiene la clase de historia.
4. A las nueve menos veinte Claudia tiene la clase de arte.
5. A las nueve y cuarto Claudia tiene la clase de matemáticas.
6. A las dos y media Claudia tiene la clase de música.

Answers continue on p. 97.

96

Presentación de VOCABULARIO
(continuación)

C Son **las** ocho y diez y tengo la clase de ciencias. A Claudia **siempre** le gusta **contestar** las preguntas del maestro. Ella es muy inteligente. Yo **tengo que** estudiar **mucho** y **tomar apuntes** en clase.

D Tengo que **sacar una buena nota** en la clase de inglés. A Claudia y a mí nos gusta estudiar a las ocho **de la noche.** Es un poco **tarde** pero **necesito** estudiar. ¡No me gusta **sacar una mala nota**!

¡A responder! Escuchar

On separate pieces of paper, write the words **la mañana** and **la tarde**. Listen to Pablo describe his schedule. Hold up the piece of paper that indicates when he has each class.

@HomeTutor VideoPlus
Interactive Flashcards
ClassZone.com

Differentiating Instruction

Pre-AP

Communicate Preferences Ask students to talk about what they do and do not like to do and explain why. **¿Te gusta contestar preguntas? Sí, me gusta contestar preguntas porque soy inteligente. ¿Te gusta tomar apuntes? Sí, me gusta tomar apuntes porque tengo que estudiar mucho.**

Multiple Intelligences

Visual Learners Give students a piece of drawing paper. Then instruct them to choose one of the vocabulary words from pp. 94–96 to draw. For example, they might draw **la computadora** or a scene from **la clase de inglés.** Have students share their completed drawings with a group. The rest of the group must name the vocabulary word or phrase represented.

Práctica de VOCABULARIO

1 | Las clases de Claudia

**Hablar
Escribir**

Identify Claudia's classes according to the time.

modelo: a la una y diez
A la una y diez Claudia tiene la clase de español.

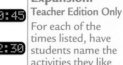

1. a las once menos cuarto
2. a las siete y media
3. a las doce
4. a las nueve menos veinte
5. a las nueve y cuarto
6. a las dos y media

Expansión:
Teacher Edition Only
For each of the times listed, have students name the activities they like to do during the weekend at that time.

Nota gramatical

For the numbers **21, 31,** and so on, use **veintiún, treinta y un,** and so on before a masculine noun and **veintiuna, treinta y una,** and so on before a feminine noun.

Hay **veintiún** maestros en la escuela.   Hay **treinta y una** personas en mi clase.
*There are **twenty-one** teachers in the school.*   *There are **thirty-one** people in my class.*

2 | ¿Cuántas personas?

Hablar

Ask a partner how many people there are in these classes.

modelo: chicos / historia
y arte (29)

 A ¿Cuántos chicos hay en las clases de historia y arte?

B Hay veintinueve chicos en las clases de historia y arte.

1. chicas / matemáticas (16)
2. estudiantes / inglés y arte (58)
3. chicos / historia y ciencias (27)
4. estudiantes / historia y arte (62)
5. chicas / música y español (33)
6. estudiantes / arte (40)
7. chicas / todas las clases (71)
8. chicos / todas las clases (74)

Expansión:
Teacher Edition Only
Have students tell how many people are in their other classes.

Más práctica   Cuaderno *pp. 51–53*   Cuaderno para hispanohablantes *pp. 51–54*

PARA Y PIENSA

Did you get it?
1. Tell someone you like to draw in art class.
2. Say that there are 23 boys in math class.

Get Help Online
ClassZone.com

Differentiating Instruction

Inclusion

Synthetic/Analytic Support Help students break down, and then put together, the names of numbers greater than 20. Write a two-digit number on the board, such as 43. Then break the number down by writing 40 + 3. Have students repeat the name of each component. Point to the 40 as you say **cuarenta**; point to the + as you say **y**; and point to the 3 as you say **tres**. Repeat with other examples.

Pre-AP

Expand and Elaborate Write the words **hay, hoy,** and **hora** on the board. Read them aloud, and have students repeat. Then circle the **h** at the beginning of each word. Ask students to describe what they notice about this letter. Elicit that the **h** in each word is silent. Ask students to brainstorm other words they know that begin with **h**. Examples might include **hola, historia,** and **horario.**

Objectives

- Practice vocabulary: time and class schedules.
- Practice numbers, school subjects.

Core Resource

- *Cuaderno,* pp. 51–53

Practice Sequence

- **Activity 1:** Vocabulary recognition: time, school subjects
- **Activity 2:** Vocabulary production: practice numbers, school subjects

STANDARDS

1.1 Engage in conversation, Act. 2
1.3 Present information, Act. 1

Nota gramatical

Expanded Information Numbers always replace the articles when they come before the noun. **Veintiuno** adds an accent mark when the **o** is dropped: **veintiún.** However, when it is written as three separate words—**veinte y un**—no accent mark is needed, just as it is never needed when writing **treinta y un, cuarenta y un,** and so on.

✓ Ongoing Assessment

@HomeTutor
More Practice
ClassZone.com

PARA Y PIENSA   **Peer Assessment** Before you write the correct answers on the board, have students exchange papers and read their partners' sentences, making corrections as needed. For additional practice, use Reteaching & Practice Copymasters URB 2, pp. 1, 2.

 Answers MSRB Transparency 36

Answers continued from p. 96.

Activity 2 Answers should follow this format: ¿Cuántos/Cuántas + people + **hay en la/las clase/clases de** + class? **Hay** + number + people + **en la/las clase/clases de** + class.

Para y piensa
1. Me gusta dibujar en la clase de arte.
2. Hay veintitrés chicos en la clase de matemáticas.

Objectives

- Understand vocabulary in context.
- Practice using vocabulary in context.
- Practice telling time.

Core Resources

- Video Program: DVD 1
- Audio Program: TXT CD 2, track 3

Presentation Strategies

- Have students look at the photo, and ask quick comprehension questions such as, **¿Cuántos chicos hay en la foto?**
- Show the video with books open; then with books closed.
- Play audio while students follow the script in the text.

Practice Sequence

- **Activity 3:** Telehistoria comprehension
- **Activity 4:** Vocabulary production: time, class schedules, school subjects

STANDARDS

1.2 Understand language, Act. 3, PYP
1.3 Present information, Act. 4

 Warm Up UTB 2 Transparency 16

Numbers Write the correct number in Spanish.

1. 11 cuadernos
2. 21 maestros
3. 31 mochilas
4. 71 chicos
5. 57 clases

Answers: 1. once; 2. veintiún; 3. treinta y una; 4. setenta y un; 5. cincuenta y siete

---

 Video Summary
@HomeTutor VideoPlus ClassZone.com

Claudia and Pablo are classmates discussing a science test they have tomorrow. Pablo likes getting good grades, but today he wants to play soccer instead of studying for the test. They make plans to meet at school tomorrow at 7AM to study, although Pablo would prefer to arrive at 8:00.

 ▶ ❚❚

98

VOCABULARIO en contexto

 ¡AVANZA! **Goal:** Listen to how Pablo and Claudia talk about at what time they will study. Then practice these words to ask and tell time. *Actividades 3–4*

Telehistoria escena 1

@HomeTutor VideoPlus ClassZone.com

STRATEGIES

Cuando lees
Focus on time Read for expressions of time like **hoy** or **a las ocho.** How many can you find in this scene? What do they mean?

Cuando escuchas
Listen for questions Listen to find all the questions in this scene. Who asks most of the questions? What does that person ask about?

Claudia / Pablo

Claudia: Pablo, hay examen de ciencias mañana, ¿no?

Pablo: Sí... Me gusta la clase de ciencias, pero... sacar una buena nota, un 90 o un 100, ¡es difícil!

Claudia: Necesitas estudiar una o dos horas... ¿Te gusta estudiar con amigos?

Pablo: Sí... pero hoy no. ¡Hay fútbol! ¿Mañana?

Claudia: Sí. ¿En la escuela?

Pablo: Sí. ¿A las ocho de la mañana? ¿O más temprano?

Claudia: A las siete de la mañana. ¿Está bien?

Pablo: ¡Sí!

The bell rings, and they part ways for class.

Pablo: Hmmm... Hay chicas muy inteligentes en la escuela...

Continuará... p. 104

VIDEO DVD

AUDIO

Differentiating Instruction

Multiple Intelligences

Logical/Mathematical Before listening to the Telehistoria, have students preview the text silently. Tell them to look specifically for numbers or number words. Then have two volunteers read the roles of Claudia and Pablo aloud. Instruct students to raise their hands when they hear a number. Discuss what each number refers to: a grade, an amount, or a time of day.

Slower-paced Learners

Sentence Completion Provide students with sentence starters related to the Telehistoria. Instruct students to find the place in the script that gives them the information, and then have them complete each sentence. Here are a few examples:

- **Claudia y Pablo tienen un examen de _____.**
- **Sacar una buena nota es _____.**
- **A Pablo le gusta estudiar con _____.**

3 | Planes para estudiar *Comprensión del episodio*

Escuchar
Leer

True or false? If the statement is false, say what is true.

1. Hay un examen en la clase de español mañana.
2. A Pablo le gusta estudiar con amigos, pero hoy no.
3. A Pablo le gusta la clase de ciencias.
4. Hay fútbol hoy.
5. La clase de ciencias es fácil.

> **Expansión:**
> Teacher Edition Only
> Ask students to make two more true statements based on the dialogue.

Nota gramatical

- Use **Es la una** to say that it is one o'clock; use **Son las...** for any other time.
  Son las cinco.   *It is 5:00.*

- Use **y** + **minutes** for the number of minutes after the hour (up to 30).
  Son las dos **y diez**.   *It is 2:10.*

- Use **menos** + **minutes** for the number of minutes before the hour.
  Es la una **menos veinte**.   *It is 12:40.*

- Use **y** or **menos cuarto** for a quarter of an hour and **y media** for half an hour.

- To say at what time something happens, use **a la(s)...**
  La clase de arte es **a la** una y la clase de inglés es **a las** dos.

4 | El horario de clases

Escribir

Write the times of Marisol's classes.

modelo: La clase de historia es a las siete de la mañana.

MARISOL AGUILAR

HORA	LUNES
7:00	HISTORIA
8:15	MATEMÁTICAS
9:30	INGLÉS
10:45	ARTE
1:05	CIENCIAS
2:10	ESPAÑOL

> **Expansión:**
> Teacher Edition Only
> Ask students to draw five clocks showing different times. Have them ask a partner what time it is.

PARA Y PIENSA

Did you get it? Complete each sentence with the appropriate time.
1. El jueves Claudia tiene que llegar a la escuela _____ . (10:15)
2. Son _____ . (8:20)
3. A Pablo le gusta hacer la tarea _____ de la noche. (7:00)

Get Help Online
ClassZone.com

Differentiating Instruction

English Learners

Build Background Use a model clock to review the terms *before* and *after* with English language learners. Also, remind them of other English terms that can be used with time, such as *past, until,* or *to.* Set a time on the model clock, and ask students to read it aloud in English and Spanish. *It's twenty past two.* **Son las dos y veinte.**

Inclusion

Metacognitive Support Read with students the information presented in **Nota gramatical.** Then ask them to reflect on the aspects of telling time in Spanish that differ from English. For example, in Spanish you use an article, **la** or **las,** before the number. And whereas you might say *three-fifty* in English, in Spanish you would say **las cuatro menos diez.**

Pair Work

Ask students to take turns asking and answering questions about Marisol's schedule from Activity 4. For example: A: **¿A qué hora es la clase de matemáticas?** B: **La clase de matemáticas es a las ocho y cuarto.**

✓ Ongoing Assessment

@HomeTutor
More Practice
ClassZone.com

PARA Y PIENSA **Alternative Strategy** Have students practice saying at what time and day of the week they like to do their favorite activity. For example, **Me gusta patinar los sábados a las tres y media de la tarde.** For additional practice, use Reteaching & Practice Copymasters URB 2, pp. 1, 3.

Answers MSRB Transparency 36

Activity 3
1. Falso. Hay un examen en la clase de ciencias.
2. Cierto
3. Cierto
4. Cierto
5. Falso. La clase de ciencias es difícil.

Activity 4
La clase de matemáticas es a las ocho y cuarto de la mañana.
La clase de inglés es a las nueve y media de la mañana.
La clase de arte es a las once menos cuarto de la mañana.
La clase de ciencias es a la una y cinco de la tarde.
La clase de español es a las dos y diez de la tarde.

Para y piensa
1. a las diez y cuarto
2. las ocho y veinte
3. a las siete

Objective

· Present the verb **tener.**

Core Resource

· *Cuaderno,* pp. 54–56

Presentation Strategies

· Present forms of the verb **tener.**

· Tell students that they can use the verb **tener** to denote possession, and also as an equivalent of the expression *to have to* + verb.

⚙ STANDARDS

4.1 Compare languages

🖥 Warm Up UTB 2 Transparency 17

Telling Time Fill in the times.
1. Tengo que estudiar _____. (11:00)
2. Tenemos la clase de ciencias _____. (12:30)
3. Tienes la clase de matemáticas _____. (2:15)
4. Tengo la clase de inglés _____. (8:00)
5. Tienen que llegar a la escuela _____. (6:40)

Answers: 1. a las once; 2. a las doce y media; 3. a las dos y cuarto; 4. a las ocho; 5. a las siete menos veinte

Nota gramatical

The word **que** has several meanings but is not translated into English when used with **tener.** However, it is essential in Spanish when telling what someone has to do. **Tienes que llegar temprano.** (You have to arrive early.)

Comparisons
English Language Connection

Tell students that in some countries in Central America, people might use **a la(s)** to say the time. For example, **un cuarto a las cinco** or **veinte a las cuatro,** which in English would be a *quarter to five* or *twenty to five.*

 Goal: Learn how to form the verb **tener.** Then use this verb to say what people have and have to do and how often. *Actividades 5–9*

♻ *¿Recuerdas?* After-school activities p. 32

English Grammar Connection: Conjugating is changing the forms of a verb to indicate who is doing the action. For example, the English verb *to have* is conjugated as *I have, you have, he/she/it has, we have, they have.*

Claudia **has** a computer.   Claudia **tiene** una computadora.

[**conjugated verb**]   [**conjugated verb**]

The Verb tener

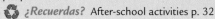 *Animated* **Grammar** ClassZone.com

Use the verb **tener** to talk about what you have. How do you conjugate this verb?

Here's how:

tener *to have*			
yo	**tengo**	nosotros(as)	**tenemos**
tú	**tienes**	vosotros(as)	**tenéis**
usted, él, ella	**tiene**	ustedes, ellos(as)	**tienen**

Tenemos clase el lunes.   ¿**Tienes** una bicicleta?
We have class on Monday.   *Do you have* a bike?

Tener + **que** + **infinitive** is used to talk about what someone has to do.

Tengo que estudiar.   Miguel **tiene que leer** un libro.
I have to study.   Miguel *has to* read a book.

Más práctica
Cuaderno *pp. 54–56*
Cuaderno para hispanohablantes *pp. 55–57*

@HomeTutor
Leveled Grammar Practice
ClassZone.com

Differentiating Instruction

Inclusion

Multisensory Input/Output Say a form of the verb **tener** aloud as you write it on the board. For example, **Yo tengo.** Have students copy the phrase as they repeat it aloud. After you have gone through all of the forms, repeat the exercise. This time, only provide students with the pronoun. They must provide the correct form of the verb.

Pre-AP

Timed Answer Create two sets of cards. The first set will have pronouns: **yo, tú, él,** etc. The second set will have familiar nouns: **una computadora, una bicicleta,** etc. Invite a volunteer to choose five cards from each set. Have the student speak for at least one minute using a variety of sentences with the verb **tener** and the chosen pronouns and nouns.

Práctica de GRAMÁTICA

5 | Los amigos de Raquel

Leer
Escribir

Use the appropriate forms of the verb **tener** to complete Raquel's description of her closest friends.

Yo __1.__ muchos amigos diferentes. Mi mejor amigo, Rafael, es un estudiante muy serio. Él __2.__ seis clases muy difíciles, y __3.__ que estudiar muchas horas todos los días. Mis amigas Clara y Linda son altas y __4.__ pelo castaño. ¡Son muy atléticas! Los lunes, martes y miércoles ellas __5.__ que practicar fútbol. Los viernes, mis amigos y yo __6.__ que trabajar. ¿Qué tipo de amigos __7.__ tú?

Expansión:
Teacher Edition Only
Have students change the subject of each sentence and then give to a partner to fill in the correct form of **tener**.

6 | Las clases

Escribir

Write what classes these people have, using forms of **tener**.

1. yo

2. nosotros

3. Claudia y Pablo

4. tú

5. Claudia

6. ustedes

Expansión:
Teacher Edition Only
Have students make up sentences using **tener** and their schedule of classes.

AUDIO

Pronunciación   El sonido ch

In Spanish, the **ch** sounds like the *ch* of the English word *chip*.

Listen and repeat.

cha	mucha
che	noche
chi	chico
cho	dieciocho
chu	churro

Muchas chicas escuchan música de Pancho Sánchez.

Differentiating Instruction

Multiple Intelligences

Intrapersonal Ask students to write down all the classes they are taking and then write what they have to do for those classes this week using the expression **tengo que...** Have them exchange their papers with partners and check them for correct spelling and verb forms. Have students report to the class what their partners have written.

Slower-paced Learners

Yes/No Questions Preview Activity 6 by asking students yes/no questions about the photos. Point to photo # 1 and ask: **¿Es la clase de arte? (No.) ¿Es la clase de matemáticas? (Sí.)** Continue until you've identified all the photos. Have students write the class names before doing the activity.

Objectives
· Practice **tener** and school subjects.
· **Pronunciation:** the **ch** sound in Spanish.

Core Resource
· Audio: TXT CD 2, track 6

Practice Sequence
· **Activity 5:** Controlled practice: **tener**
· **Activity 6:** Controlled practice: **tener**

 STANDARDS
1.3 Present information, Acts. 5–6
4.1 Compare languages, Pronunciación

✓ Ongoing Assessment

Dictation Dictate to students words containing **ch** and check their answers. **El chico estudia mucho. Son las ocho de la noche.**

Communication
Grammar Activity

Ask students to make a list of five things they have to do at school using the expression **tener que**. For example: **Tengo que tomar muchos apuntes. Tengo que estudiar. Tengo que usar la computadora.** Have them compare their lists with their classmates.

Answers MSRB Transparencies 36–37
Actividad 5

1. tengo; **2.** tiene; **3.** tiene; **4.** tienen; **5.** tienen; **6.** tenemos; **7.** tienes

Activity 6

1. Yo tengo la clase de matemáticas.
2. Nosotros tenemos la clase de inglés.
3. Claudia y Pablo tienen la clase de ciencias.
4. Tú tienes la clase de arte.
5. Claudia tiene la clase de historia.
6. Ustedes tienen la clase de español.

Objectives

- Practice **tener**, lesson vocabulary, expressions of frequency.
- **Culture:** compare school uniforms.
- Recycle: after-school activities.

Core Resources

- *Cuaderno*, pp. 54–56
- Audio Program: TXT CD 2, track 4

Practice Sequence

- **Activity 7:** Transitional practice: **tener**
- **Activity 8:** Transitional practice: **tener que**, telling time
- **Activity 9:** Open-ended practice: **tener que**, expressions of frequency; Recycle: after-school activities

STANDARDS

1.1 Engage in conversation, Acts. 7, 9
1.2 Understand language, Act. 8
1.3 Present information, Acts. 7–9
2.1 Practices and perspectives, CC
4.2 Compare cultures, CC

Comparación cultural

Essential Question

Suggested Answer Most schools in Spanish-speaking countries require students to wear uniforms. Oftentimes, students are even required to wear a certain kind of shoes. Wearing uniforms prevents students from feeling pressure to dress a certain way, or to be influenced by advertising and trends.

Expanded Information

In many Latin American high schools, students do not change classrooms as they do in the United States. Except for physical education and art, students remain in the same classroom, while the teachers come to them. In many schools, it is common to have as much as fifteen minutes between each class. During their break, students often play **fútbol** or have a snack.

See Activity answers on p. 103.

---

7 | ¿Qué tienes?

Hablar Find out what items your partner has in his or her room by forming questions with the verb **tener.** Take turns asking and answering.

modelo: una computadora

A ¿Tienes **una computadora**?

B Sí, tengo **una computadora.** (No, no tengo **computadora.**)

1. un DVD
2. una patineta
3. un refresco
4. una bicicleta

5. un teléfono
6. una guitarra
7. un libro de matemáticas
8. una galleta

Expansión:
Teacher Edition Only
Have students write three questions asking a partner what he or she has to do, using **tener que.**

8 | ¿Qué tienen que hacer?

Escuchar
Escribir

Listen to Pablo's description of what he and his friends have to do. Then write sentences indicating what time it is and who has to do these activities.

1. estudiar
2. usar la computadora
3. hacer la tarea

4. tocar la guitarra
5. trabajar
6. leer un libro

🎧 **Audio Program**
TXT CD 2 Track 4
Audio Script, TE p. 91b

Comparación cultural

Uniformes escolares

How does the way students dress reflect a culture? In **Mexico,** it is common for students to wear uniforms in both public and private schools. The type and color of the uniforms can vary depending on the individual school. Most students in the **Dominican Republic** also wear uniforms. Public schools have the same uniforms, while private school uniforms may vary.

Compara con tu mundo *Why do some schools require uniforms? Are they common in your community? If you were a principal, would you have uniforms at your school?*

Estudiantes en México y la República Dominicana

Differentiating Instruction

Slower-paced Learners

Read Before Listening Have students copy the words and phrases from Activity 8 onto a separate piece of paper. Then tell them to draw a simple picture next to each word or phrase to help recall its meaning. As students listen to Pablo's description, have them take notes on their own page, recording each person's name next to the proper picture.

Multiple Intelligences

Interpersonal Prepare in advance a list of things to do, using vocabulary students have learned. For example: **preparar la comida, hacer la tarea, estudiar, trabajar, usar la computadora, tomar apuntes.** Conduct a class survey to find how many students have to do these activities today. Ask, **¿Quién tiene que preparar la comida hoy? ¿Quién tiene que hacer la tarea hoy?**

Nota gramatical

The expressions of frequency **siempre** and **nunca** are usually placed before the verb.

Antonio **siempre** toma apuntes.　　*Antonio **always** takes notes.*

Rafael **nunca** llega a clase tarde.　*Rafael **never** arrives late to class.*

Mucho is usually placed after the verb.

Raquel estudia **mucho**.　　*Raquel studies **a lot**.*

De vez en cuando, muchas veces, and **todos los días** are usually placed at the beginning or the end of the sentence.

Todos los días Jaime trabaja.　　*Jaime works **every day**.*

Jaime trabaja **todos los días**.

9 Las obligaciones ♻ ¿*Recuerdas?* After-school activities p. 32

Hablar

Ask other students whether they have to do these activities. They will respond using an expression of frequency.

A ¿Tienen que tomar apuntes ustedes?

B Sí, tengo que tomar apuntes muchas veces.

C Sí, tengo que tomar apuntes de vez en cuando.

1.
2.
3.
4.
5.
6.

Expansión:
Teacher Edition Only
Have students write three or four sentences about the activities they and their friends never have to do.

Más práctica　Cuaderno *pp. 54–56*　Cuaderno para hispanohablantes *pp. 55–57*

PARA Y PIENSA

Did you get it? Answer each question with the word(s) in parentheses.
1. ¿Tiene que preparar la comida Juan? (nunca)
2. ¿Cuándo tenemos la clase de inglés? (todos los días)
3. ¿Tienes que usar la computadora? (siempre)

Get Help Online
ClassZone.com

Communication
Grammar Activity

Activity 9 Give a blank sheet of paper to the first person in each row. The first student will write a subject pronoun; the student after him or her will write the correct form of **tener que** next to it. The third person will supply a different subject pronoun and pass the paper to the fourth person for that form of **tener que.** Continue to the end of the row.

✓ Ongoing Assessment

@HomeTutor
More Practice
ClassZone.com

PARA Y PIENSA
Quick Check Ask students if any of the expressions of frequency can be placed both at the beginning or at the end of the sentence. For additional practice, use Reteaching & Practice Copymasters URB 2, pp. 4, 5, 10.

Answers MSRB Transparency 37

Answers for Activities on pp. 102, 103.
Activity 7
1. A: ¿Tienes un DVD? B: Sí, tengo un DVD. (No, no tengo DVD.)
2. A: ¿Tienes una patineta? B: Sí, tengo una patineta. (No, no tengo patineta.)
3. A: ¿Tienes un refresco? B: Sí, tengo un refresco. (No, no tengo refresco.)
4. A: ¿Tienes una bicicleta? B: Sí, tengo una bicicleta. (No, no tengo bicicleta.)
5. A: ¿Tienes un teléfono? B: Sí, tengo un teléfono. (No, no tengo teléfono.)
6. A: ¿Tienes una guitarra? B: Sí, tengo una guitarra. (No, no tengo guitarra.)
7. A: ¿Tienes un libro de matemáticas? B: Sí, tengo un libro de matemáticas. (No, no tengo libro de matemáticas.)
8. A: ¿Tienes una galleta? B: Sí, tengo una galleta. (No, no tengo galleta.)

Activity 8
1. Son las ocho y Claudia tiene que estudiar.
2. Son las diez menos cuarto y Pablo tiene que usar la computadora.
3. Son las cuatro y diez y Pepe tiene que hacer la tarea.
4. Es la una y media, y Laura y Diana tienen que tocar la guitarra.
5. Son las seis y cuarto y Carlos tiene que trabajar.
6. Son las once menos veinte, y Manuel y Pablo tienen que leer un libro.

Activity 9 Answers should follow this format:
　¿Tienen que + activity?
　Sí/No, tengo que + activity + expression of frequency.

Para y piensa
1. Juan nunca tiene que preparar la comida.
2. Tenemos la clase de inglés todos los días.
3. Siempre tengo que usar la computadora.

103

Differentiating Instruction

Multiple Intelligences

Interpersonal Write the expressions of frequency outlined on p. 103 on the board. Then ask students questions about their own classmates using vocabulary phrases from the lesson. **¿Llega Diana a la clase tarde? ¿Usa Javier la computadora?**

Inclusion

Frequent Review/Repetition As students answer each other's questions in Activity 9, advise them to refer to the Nota gramatical after each response. Have students confirm that they used the expression of frequency in the correct place in the sentence. If they did not, have them rearrange the sentence and repeat their answers as many times as necessary.

¡AVANZA! Objectives
- Practice **tener** in context.
- Recycle: days of the week.

Core Resources
- Video Program: DVD 1
- Audio Program: TXT CD 2, track 5

Presentation Strategies
- Have students read the script and talk about what they say when they answer the phone.
- Show the video or play the audio.

Practice Sequence
- **Activity 10:** Telehistoria comprehension
- **Activity 11:** Transitional practice: **tener que**; Recycle: days of the week
- **Activity 12:** Open-ended practice: **tener**, telling time, **tener que**

STANDARDS
1.2 Understand language, Act. 10
1.3 Present information, Acts. 11–12, PYP

Warm Up   UTB 2 Transparency 17

Tener Write the correct form of the verb **tener** for each pronoun.
1. yo _____
2. tú _____
3. ella _____
4. nosotros _____
5. ustedes _____
6. ellos _____

Answers: 1. tengo; 2. tienes; 3. tiene; 4. tenemos; 5. tienen; 6. tienen

Communication
Regionalisms

Point out to students that in Colombia the word for *grades* is **calificaciones**.

@HomeTutor
VideoPlus
ClassZone.com

Video Summary

Claudia calls Pablo to remind him of their plans to meet at school at 7:00 to study for a science test. As they walk to class the next morning, Claudia gently reminds Pablo that he likes to get good grades and should study more.

▶l ll

GRAMÁTICA en contexto

 ¡AVANZA!

Goal: Notice how Pablo and Claudia use the verb phrase **tener que** to talk about what they do at school. Then use **tener** and **tener que** to say what you and others have and have to do. *Actividades 10–12*

♻ *¿Recuerdas?* Days of the week p. 18

Telehistoria escena 2

@HomeTutor VideoPlus
ClassZone.com

STRATEGIES

Cuando lees
Find the "tag questions" This scene contains the "tag question" **¿no?** Where are the tag questions in a sentence? How do they differ from questions like **¿Quién es?**

Cuando escuchas
Weigh the motive Listen for Pablo's reasons for not studying for the test. What are his reasons? Do they sound credible to you? Have you ever used them?

VIDEO
DVD

AUDIO

Pablo's cell phone rings.
Pablo: Hola... ¿Quién es? ¡Claudia! ¿Qué tal?... Sí, sí, a las siete. ¡Tenemos que estudiar mucho!
The next morning, Claudia and Pablo walk to class.
Claudia: Pablo, tienes que estudiar más, ¿no?
Pablo: Sí. Tenemos mucha tarea y los exámenes son muy difíciles.
Claudia: Pero te gusta sacar buenas notas, ¿no?
Pablo: Sí. Tenemos que estudiar más.

También se dice

México Pablo uses the word **tarea** to talk about homework. In other Spanish-speaking countries you might hear:
- **muchos países** los **deberes**

Continuará... p. 110

Unidad 2 México
104 ciento cuatro

Differentiating Instruction

Pre-AP

Draw Conclusions Have students reread Pablo's side of the cell phone conversation in the Telehistoria. Based on what Pablo says, have students draft the lines for Claudia to say in between. For example, after Pablo asks **¿Quién es?** Claudia might say, **Claudia.** What might Claudia be asking before Pablo says, **Sí, sí, a las siete?**

Heritage Language Learners

Writing Skills Have students copy the following story starter on a piece of paper: **Tengo que estudiar más, pero...** Then have students create an imaginary excuse explaining why they can't study more. Encourage students to be as creative as possible. Give students the opportunity to read their work to the rest of the group.

10 | Un examen importante *Comprensión del episodio*

Escuchar
Leer

Choose the correct answers to the questions.

1. ¿Qué tienen que hacer Pablo y Claudia?
   a. Tienen que descansar mucho.
   b. Tienen que estudiar.
   c. Tienen que enseñar.

2. ¿A qué hora tienen que estudiar?
   a. a las siete
   b. a las siete y media
   c. a las ocho

3. ¿Qué tienen Pablo y Claudia?
   a. muchos libros
   b. un poco de tarea
   c. mucha tarea

4. ¿Qué le gusta hacer a Pablo?
   a. Le gusta estudiar.
   b. Le gusta llegar tarde.
   c. Le gusta sacar buenas notas.

Expansión:
Teacher Edition Only
Have students write a fourth answer to each question.

11 | Las responsabilidades ♻ *¿Recuerdas?* Days of the week p. 18

Escribir

You have a lot to do this week. Write an e-mail explaining five things that you have to do this week.

modelo:

> Hola, Jeff.
> Tengo mucho que hacer. El lunes tengo que practicar la guitarra. El martes tengo que hacer la tarea...

Expansión:
Teacher Edition Only
Have students talk with classmates to find out how many people have to do the same activity.

12 | ¿Y tú?

Hablar
Escribir

Answer the questions in complete sentences.

1. ¿Qué clases tienes? ¿Son fáciles o difíciles?
2. ¿A qué hora tienes la clase de español?
3. ¿Tienes que tomar apuntes? ¿En qué clases?
4. ¿Qué tienes que hacer todos los días?
5. ¿Qué tienes que hacer todos los sábados y domingos?
6. ¿Qué nunca tienes que hacer?
7. ¿Tienes que trabajar? ¿A qué hora?
8. ¿A qué hora necesitas llegar a la escuela?

Expansión:
Teacher Edition Only
Have students add two more questions, with their answers, about things they have to do.

PARA Y PIENSA

Did you get it? ¿**Tener** or **tener que**? Complete each sentence based on the Telehistoria with the correct form of the verb or expression.
1. Pablo y Claudia _____ mucha tarea.
2. Pablo _____ estudiar mucho.
3. Ellos _____ un examen en la clase de ciencias.

🔵 **Get Help Online** ClassZone.com

Lección 1
ciento cinco **105**

Differentiating Instruction

Slower-paced Learners

Read Before Listening Provide scripts to students before listening to the audio and doing Activity 10. Then go over each of the choices given to make sure students understand their meaning.

Inclusion

Clear Structure Remind students of the elements of a sentence to draft their answers for Activity 12.
1. Record ideas for the answer in words or phrases.
2. Underline the words in the question that you'll need in the answer.
3. Conjugate the verb in the correct form.
4. Put the pieces of the sentence together.

Unidad 2 Lección 1
GRAMÁTICA

Communication
Common Error Alert

Remind students not to use **en** when saying on Monday, on Tuesday, etc. They should use **el: el lunes, el martes**. When saying on Mondays, on Tuesdays, the **el** changes to **los**.

✓ **Ongoing Assessment**
@HomeTutor
More Practice
ClassZone.com

PARA Y PIENSA **Peer Assessment** After students have completed the sentences, each student should compare answers with two other students and correct each other's work. For additional practice, use Reteaching & Practice Copymasters URB 2, pp. 4, 6.

Answers MSRB Transparency 37

Activity 10
1. b   2. a   3. c   4. c

Activity 11 Answers will vary. Sample answers include:

Hola, Carla:
Tengo mucho que hacer. El lunes tengo que trabajar. El martes tengo que llegar temprano a la escuela. El miércoles tengo que usar la computadora. El jueves tengo que estudiar inglés. El viernes tengo que preparar la comida.

Activity 12 Answers will vary. Sample answers include:
1. Tengo las clases de matemáticas, español, historia y ciencias. Son fáciles.
2. Tengo la clase de español a las once de la mañana.
3. Sí, tengo que tomar apuntes todos los días. Tengo que tomar apuntes en las clases de historia y ciencias.
4. Tengo que usar la computadora todos los días.
5. Tengo que trabajar todos los sábados y domingos.
6. Nunca tengo que preparar la comida.
7. Sí, tengo que trabajar todos los días. Tengo que trabajar a las tres de la tarde.
8. Necesito llegar a la escuela a las ocho de la mañana.

Para y piensa
1. tienen   2. tiene que   3. tienen

¡AVANZA! Objective

- Present the present tense of regular **-ar** verbs.

Core Resource

- *Cuaderno,* pp. 57–59

Presentation Strategy

- Reassure students that the pattern of **-ar** verb conjugations in Spanish is very predictable for regular verbs.

✿ STANDARDS

4.1 Compare languages

Warm Up   UTB 2 Transparency 18

Tener que Create sentences using the following phrases and the correct form of **tener que** + pronoun in parenthesis.

1. escuchar música (yo)
2. montar en bicicleta (ellos)
3. dibujar (nosotras)
4. hablar por teléfono (tú)
5. tocar la guitarra (ustedes)

Answers: 1. Tengo que escuchar música.
2. Tienen que...; **3.** Tenemos que...;
4. Tienes que...; **5.** Tienen que...

Verbs Students Know

Students have learned the following **-ar** verbs, which are all regular in the present tense:

alquilar	estudiar	practicar
andar	hablar	preparar
comprar	llegar	sacar
contestar	mirar	tocar
descansar	montar	tomar
dibujar	necesitar	trabajar
enseñar	pasar	usar
escuchar	pasear	

Note that the verb **jugar** is not regular; its conjugation will be taught in 1b, Unit 6.

Answers   MSRB Transparency 37

Activity 13

1. Nosotros llegamos a las cinco y media. Llegamos temprano.
2. Marta llega a las siete y cuarto. Llega tarde.
3. Yo llego a las siete menos cuarto. Llego temprano.
4. Marcos y Benito llegan a las seis. Llegan temprano.
5. La señora Jiménez llega a las ocho menos veinte. Llega tarde.

Answers continue on p. 107.

Presentación de GRAMÁTICA

¡AVANZA!   **Goal:** Learn the forms of **-ar** verbs. Then practice using the verbs to say what people do. *Actividades 13–19*

English Grammar Connection: A **verb tense** is the form of the verb that shows *when* an action is happening. The **present tense** shows that an action is happening *now*. The Spanish present-tense verb form **estudiamos** can be expressed in English in three different ways: *we study, we are studying,* or *we do study.*

We **study** Spanish.   **Estudiamos** español.

↑ present-tense verb   ↑ present-tense verb

Present Tense of **-ar** Verbs

Animated Grammar
ClassZone.com

Many infinitives in Spanish end in **-ar.** How do you form the present tense of these verbs?

Here's how: In Spanish, the present tense is formed by changing the ending of the verb.

To form the present tense of a regular verb that ends in **-ar,** drop the **-ar** and add the appropriate **ending.**

hablar ◄ [**o, as, a, amos, áis,** or **an**]

hablar *to talk, to speak*		
yo	**habl**o	nosotros(as)	**habl**amos
tú	**habl**as	vosotros(as)	**habl**áis
usted, él, ella	**habl**a	ustedes, ellos(as)	**habl**an

Hablo inglés.   ¿**Habl**an español?

I speak English.   *Do they speak Spanish?*
I am speaking English.   *Are they speaking Spanish?*
I do speak English.

Más práctica
   Cuaderno pp. 57–59
   Cuaderno para hispanohablantes *pp. 58–61*

@HomeTutor
Leveled Grammar Practice
ClassZone.com

Differentiating Instruction

Slower-paced Learners

Memory Aids Have students create their own set of verb reference cards. On an index card, have students copy the forms of the verb **hablar** as presented on p. 106. Then have them recall the forms of the verb **tener** and create a card for this verb. Each time students encounter a new verb, have them take the time to create a new verb card.

Inclusion

Metacognitive Support Ask students to think about why subject pronouns are not always necessary in Spanish. Why, for example, does **hablo inglés** suffice in Spanish, while the pronoun would be necessary to express the same phrase in English? Point out that verb endings help to indicate the subject pronoun.

Práctica de GRAMÁTICA

13 | ¿Tarde o temprano?

Escribir

Claudia is throwing a surprise party for Pablo and wants all the guests to arrive at seven o'clock sharp. Use the cues to state at what time people arrive at the party. Then tell whether they arrive early or late.

> **modelo:** Luis y Carmen / 8:00
> Luis y Carmen llegan a las ocho. Llegan tarde.

1. nosotros / 5:30
2. Marta / 7:15
3. yo / 6:45
4. Marcos y Benito / 6:00
5. la señora Jiménez / 7:40
6. ellas / 9:25
7. tú / 6:05
8. María y Enrique / 8:10
9. Sara y yo / 6:50
10. Pablo / 7:20

> **Expansión:**
> Teacher Edition Only
> Have students talk with classmates to find out at what time people arrive at school.

14 | Somos buenos estudiantes

Hablar
Escribir

Pablo, Claudia, and their friends are good students. Explain whether they always or never do the following.

> **modelo:** Claudia / llegar a clase temprano
> Claudia **siempre** llega a clase temprano.

1. yo / escuchar en clase
2. Pablo / tomar apuntes
3. nosotros / sacar malas notas
4. Claudia y Pablo / estudiar
5. tú / contestar preguntas
6. Diego y yo / llegar a clase tarde
7. Lorena / mirar la televisión
8. ustedes / sacar buenas notas

> **Expansión:**
> Teacher Edition Only
> Ask students to add other -ar verbs to their lists and create sentences with them.

15 | El fin de semana

Leer
Escribir

Sandra likes to spend time with her friends. Complete the paragraph with the correct form of the appropriate verb.

> escuchar   tocar   alquilar   estudiar
>
> pasar   montar   dibujar   practicar

Nosotros __1.__ en bicicleta después de las clases. Amy y Rosa __2.__ deportes y yo __3.__ la guitarra. A mi amigo Eduardo no le gusta descansar. Él __4.__ inglés o __5.__ para la clase de arte. Es muy artístico. Si llueve, nosotros __6.__ música en un café o __7.__ un DVD. ¿Dónde __8.__ tú un rato con los amigos?

> **Expansión:**
> Teacher Edition Only
> Have students rewrite the paragraph using different subjects so they can practice different present tense forms.

Lección 1
ciento siete **107**

Differentiating Instruction

Multiple Intelligences

Kinesthetic Toss a soft ball to a student as you say an **-ar** infinitive and a subject pronoun **(contestar: nosotros).** The student gives the correct verb form, then tosses the ball back to you. Continue with other students.

Inclusion

Clear Structure Have students copy the paragraph in Activity 15 onto a separate sheet of paper. Instruct them to break Activity 15 into smaller steps, like these for item 1.
1. Note a key word. **bicicleta**
2. Choose the correct verb. **montar**
3. Underline the subject. **nosotros**
4. Write the correct form of the verb in the blank. **montamos**

Objectives
· Practice the present tense of regular **-ar** verbs.
· Practice lesson vocabulary.

Practice Sequence
· **Activity 13:** Controlled practice: Present tense of **-ar** verbs, telling time
· **Activity 14:** Controlled practice: Present tense of **-ar** verbs, expressions of frequency
· **Activity 15:** Controlled practice: Present tense of **-ar** verbs

STANDARDS
1.3 Present information, Acts. 13–15

Long-term Retention

Personalize It

Ask students to write a paragraph about how they spend their time with friends. Encourage them to include the verbs in Activity 15, as well as the expression **tener que.**

Answers MSRB Transparencies 37–38

Answers continued from p. 106.

6. Ellas llegan a las nueve y veinticinco. Llegan tarde.
7. Tú llegas a las seis y cinco. Llegas temprano.
8. María y Enrique llegan a las ocho y diez. Llegan tarde.
9. Sara y yo llegamos a las siete menos diez. Llegamos temprano.
10. Pablo llega a las siete y veinte. Llega tarde.

Activity 14
1. Yo siempre escucho en clase.
2. Pablo siempre toma apuntes.
3. Nosotros nunca sacamos malas notas.
4. Claudia y Pablo siempre estudian.
5. Tú siempre contestas preguntas.
6. Diego y yo nunca llegamos a clase tarde.
7. Lorena nunca mira la televisión.
8. Ustedes siempre sacan buenas notas.

Activity 15
1. montamos
2. practican
3. toco
4. estudia
5. dibuja
6. escuchamos
7. alquilamos
8. pasas

107

Objectives

- Practice the present tense of regular **-ar** verbs.
- **Culture:** Learn about the murals of Diego Rivera.
- Practice lesson vocabulary, expressions of frequency.

Core Resource

- *Cuaderno*, pp. 57–59

Practice Sequence

- **Activity 16:** Transitional practice: present tense of **-ar** verbs, expressions of frequency
- **Activity 17:** Transitional practice: present tense of **-ar** verbs
- **Activity 18:** Open-ended practice: present tense of **-ar** verbs, **tener**
- **Activity 19:** Open-ended practice: present tense of **-ar** verbs, expressions of frequency

 STANDARDS

1.1 Engage in conversation, Acts. 16, 18
1.3 Present information, Acts. 16–19, PYP
2.2 Products and perspectives, Act. 18
4.2 Compare cultures, Act. 18

 Answers MSRB Transparency 38

Activity 16 Answers will vary. Sample answers include:

1. A. ¿Estudias en la escuela? B. Sí, siempre estudio en la escuela.
2. A. ¿Escuchas música...? B. No, nunca escucho música...
3. A. ¿Compras refrescos...? B. Sí, compro refrescos... de vez en cuando.
4. A. ¿Practicas deportes...? B. Sí, siempre practico deportes...
5. A. ¿Tocas la guitarra...? B. No, nunca toco la guitarra...
6. A. ¿Pasas un rato con los amigos...? B. Sí, paso un rato con los amigos todos los días.

Activity 17

En septiembre, Marcos descansa. En mayo, él usa la computadora.

En septiembre, Álvaro saca una mala nota. En mayo, él saca una buena nota.

En septiembre, Paula y Federico hablan mucho en clase. En mayo, ellos contestan las preguntas.

En septiembre, la señorita Solar llega tarde. En mayo, ella enseña bien.

108

---

16 | ¿En la escuela?

Hablar

Ask another student whether he or she does these activities at school. Use expressions of frequency.

modelo: dibujar

A ¿Dibujas en la escuela?

B No, nunca dibujo en la escuela.

1. estudiar
2. escuchar música
3. comprar refrescos
4. practicar deportes
5. tocar la guitarra
6. pasar un rato con los amigos

Expansión: Teacher Edition Only
Have students say how often they do these activities at home.

17 | De septiembre a mayo

Hablar
Escribir

Señorita Solar and her students have changed a great deal over the course of the school year. Look at the two drawings below and note the differences between the beginning and the end of the school year.

modelo: En septiembre, Susana escucha música. En mayo, ella toma apuntes.

Septiembre — la Srta. Solar, Paula y Federico, Marcos, Álvaro, Susana

Mayo — la Srta. Solar, Álvaro, Paula y Federico, Susana, Marcos

Expansión: Teacher Edition Only
Have students write sentences describing three of the people in the drawings.

Differentiating Instruction

Multiple Intelligences

Visual Learners Have student pairs create a Venn diagram. Give them a list of verbs that end in **-ar.** One student writes five activities he or she does a lot, using the **yo** form of the verb in the left oval. That student interviews a partner about activities and lists them in the right oval, using the **él/ella** form of the verb. Ask them to list the activities they have in common in the center, using the **nosotros(as)** form.

Slow-paced Learners

Memory Aids For Activity 17, ask students to divide a sheet of paper in two columns. Ask them to label one column **septiembre** and the other column **mayo.** Have them label each row with the names of the people in the picture. Students then write the activities that these people are doing under the appropriate column. Have them exchange papers with a classmate and check for correct verb forms.

18 | ¿Qué estudias?

Hablar

Comparación cultural

Los murales en México

How does society affect public artwork? The Mexican government commissioned Diego Rivera to paint murals about **Mexico's** history. *Alfabetización* reflects the idea of free public education. Between 1920 and 1924, more than 1,000 schools were established in rural areas to teach children to read and study subjects such as history and math.

Compara con tu mundo *What would you paint in a mural representing your community? What objects or people would you include? What would your mural's message be?*

Talk with a partner about your schedule and what you study.

Detalle de Alfabetización (1926), Diego Rivera

A ¿Estudias ciencias?

B Sí, tengo la clase de ciencias a las once.

Expansión: Teacher Edition Only
Have students write a summary of their partner's schedule.

19 | Un sábado típico

Escribir Hablar

Describe what you do on Saturdays and how often you do it. Use verbs from the list. Then compare your activities with other students'.

> alquilar   estudiar   descansar   comprar
>
> escuchar   usar   trabajar   ¿ ?

modelo: Siempre hablo por teléfono los sábados. Muchas veces paso un rato con las amigas. Nosotras alquilamos un DVD...

Expansión: Teacher Edition Only
Have students use two additional verbs in their descriptions.

Más práctica Cuaderno *pp. 57–59*   Cuaderno para hispanohablantes *pp. 58–61*

 PARA Y PIENSA

Did you get it? Complete each sentence with the correct form of the verb in parentheses.

Get Help Online ClassZone.com

1. Nosotros _____ la computadora mucho. (usar)
2. Yo _____ la comida de vez en cuando. (preparar)
3. Los chicos _____ en la clase de arte. (dibujar)
4. ¿ _____ tú sacar una buena nota? (necesitar)

Differentiating Instruction

Pre-AP

Expand and Elaborate After students complete Activity 19, have them reread their descriptions. Encourage them to add a sentence after each existing sentence. This new sentence should elaborate upon the one preceding it. **Siempre hablo por teléfono los sábados. Me gusta hablar mucho con mi amiga Melissa.**

Heritage Language Learners

Literacy Skills Encourage students to use the library or Internet to research other murals by Diego Rivera. Then ask students to explain how the name of the work and the content are related. Give students the opportunity to present their findings to the whole group.

✓ Ongoing Assessment

@HomeTutor More Practice ClassZone.com

Intervention If students miss more than one or two of the Para y piensa items, suggest that they review p. 106 and repeat Activities 13–15 on p. 107. For additional practice, use Reteaching and Practice Copymasters, URB 2, pp. 7, 8.

Comparación cultural

Essential Question

Suggested Answer There are situations in society that inspire artists to reproduce them in artwork. Those situations could be related to education, industrialization, or historical events happening at a certain time.

Background Information

Alfabetización is a mural painted by Diego Rivera. It took him four years to finish it, sometimes painting 18 hours per day. It is painted in vivid colors and simplified lines and it illustrates the importance education has in the lives of Mexicans.

♦ Answers   MSRB Transparency 38

Activity 18 Answers will vary. Sample answers include:

A. ¿Estudias matemáticas? **B.** Sí, tengo la clase de matemáticas a las ocho.

A. ¿Estudias historia? **B.** Sí, tengo la clase de historia a la una.

Activity 19 Answers will vary. Sample answers include:

Siempre estudio. Muchas veces descanso. Nunca trabajo.

Para y piensa
1. usamos; 2. preparo; 3. dibujan; 4. Necesitas

109

¡AVANZA! Objective

- Integrate lesson content.

Core Resources

- Video Program: DVD 1
- Audio Program: TXT CD 2, tracks 3, 5, 7

Presentation Strategies

- Ask students what they remember about the Telehistoria so far.
- Show the video or play the audio.

Practice Sequence

- **Activity 20:** Telehistoria comprehension
- **Activity 21:** Telehistoria comprehension
- **Activity 22:** Open-ended practice: speaking

STANDARDS

1.1 Engage in conversation, Act. 22
1.2 Understand language, Act. 20
1.3 Present information, Acts. 20–22

Warm Up   UTB 2 Transparency 18

-ar verbs Write on a separate piece of paper all forms of the verb **pasar. yo..., tú...,
usted/él/ella..., nosotros..., vosotros...,
ustedes/ellos/ellas...**

Answers: paso; pasas; pasa; pasamos; pasáis; pasan

Video Summary   @HomeTutor VideoPlus ClassZone.com

Pablo is not happy because Claudia got a higher grade on her science test than he did. She tells him that he has to take better notes. Claudia asks Pablo what time he has soccer practice tomorrow and he asks her what she's doing tomorrow. She tells him that she is going to study and do her science homework. Pablo is going to soccer practice early. As he walks away, he puts on Alicia's T-shirt and Roberto teases him about the T-shirt.

▶❙ ❙❙

Todo junto

¡AVANZA!

Goal: *Show what you know* Pay attention to how Pablo and Claudia use **tener** and **-ar** verbs to talk about their test and what they do after school. Then use these verbs to say what you and others do during and after school. *Actividades 20–24*

Telehistoria completa

@HomeTutor VideoPlus
ClassZone.com

STRATEGIES

Cuando lees
Look for the unexpected As you read, look for two surprises involving Pablo. What are they? Why are they unexpected? What did you expect to happen?

Cuando escuchas
Listen for cognates Listen for cognates like **examen** (exam, test). What cognates do you hear? What English word(s) do they sound like? What do they mean?

Escena 1 *Resumen*
Pablo y Claudia necesitan estudiar porque tienen un examen de ciencias.

Escena 2 *Resumen*
Pablo y Claudia hablan por teléfono. Tienen que estudiar más.

VIDEO
DVD

AUDIO

Escena 3

Roberto

Pablo: ¡Claudia! En el examen de ciencias, tengo... ¡un 90!

Claudia: ¡Y yo, un 100!

Pablo: ¿Estudiamos, tú y yo, todos los días?

Claudia: Sí... pero tú necesitas tomar buenos apuntes, ¿no? *(Pablo grins.)* ¿A qué hora practican fútbol?

Pablo: Muchas veces practicamos a las cinco. Mañana practicamos temprano, a las tres y media. ¿Y tú? ¿Qué necesitas hacer mañana?

Claudia: ¿Mañana? Estudiar y hacer la tarea de ciencias.

Claudia says goodbye and leaves. As his friend Roberto walks up, Pablo distractedly pulls Alicia's T-shirt out of his bag and puts it on.

Roberto: ¡Ay, Pablo, qué interesante!

Pablo, embarrassed, takes the shirt off quickly.

Pre-AP

Summarize Direct students to review Escena 1 on p. 98 and Escena 2 on p. 104. Then ask them to summarize each of these scenes in their own words. They might begin by brainstorming important words or phrases, and then drafting a summarizing sentence. After students have given their own summaries, have them read those presented on p. 110. How do they compare?

Multiple Intelligences

Interpersonal Invite three volunteers to play the parts of Pablo, Claudia, and Roberto. As these students read the script, encourage them to emphasize the facial expressions appropriate to each character's emotions. When Pablo says **tengo... ¡un 90!,** what emotion might he be feeling? When Roberto says **¡Ay, Pablo, qué interesante!,** what might Pablo's expression be?

20 ¿Quién es? *Comprensión de los episodios*

Escuchar
Leer

Do these sentences refer to Claudia, Pablo, or Claudia and Pablo? Write the name or names and the correct form of the verb in parentheses.

Pablo

Claudia y Pablo

Claudia

1. _____ (tener) que practicar fútbol.
2. _____ (llegar) a la escuela a las siete de la mañana.
3. _____ (hablar) por teléfono.
4. _____ (necesitar) estudiar una o dos horas.
5. _____ (tener) un examen de ciencias.
6. _____ (sacar) una buena nota.
7. _____ (estudiar) para la clase de ciencias mañana.
8. _____ (practicar) a las tres y media mañana.

Expansión:
Teacher Edition Only
Have students make up other sentences about Claudia and Pablo from the Telehistoria.

21 ¿Qué hacen? *Comprensión de los episodios*

Escuchar
Leer

Complete the sentences with information from the episodes.

1. Pablo y Claudia tienen que...
2. A las siete Pablo y Claudia...
3. Mañana Claudia...
4. Pablo necesita tomar...
5. Claudia y Pablo sacan...

Expansión:
Teacher Edition Only
Ask students to write a summary of the Telehistoria.

22 ¿Qué tienes que hacer?

Hablar

STRATEGY Hablar

Create a dialogue of your own Use the model question and substitute different school subjects. Use the model answer, but change verbs, or use multiple verbs in a single sentence. Bring in humor if you can.

Talk with a partner about what you do and what you have to do in your classes.

A ¿Qué tienes que hacer en la clase de matemáticas?

B Tengo que tomar apuntes. Siempre escucho en clase...

Expansión:
Teacher Edition Only
Ask students to talk about things they have to do outside school.

Lección 1
ciento once **111**

Differentiating Instruction

Pre-AP

Expand and Elaborate After they complete Activity 20, pair students and have them change each sentence into a question to ask their partner. For example:
1. ¿Y tú? ¿Tienes que practicar fútbol?
If the partner answers no, he or she must provide an explanation. **No, tengo que hacer la tarea.**

Slower-paced Learners

Sentence Completion Help students complete the sentences in Activity 21 by providing two choices. For example, **Pablo y Claudia tienen que estudiar. Pablo y Claudia tienen que montar en bicicleta.** Have students repeat and then write the correct choice. Also, help them locate the place in the text where the information for the correct answer is presented.

Communication
Group Work

Telehistoria Ask students to work in groups and write a summary of the dialogue in Spanish, using Pablo and Claudia as the subjects of the sentences instead of **yo, tú,** or **nosotros.**

✓ Ongoing Assessment

Rubric Activity 22

Speaking Criteria	Maximum Credit	Partial Credit	Minimum Credit
Content	Dialogue includes all the information.	Dialogue includes some of the information.	Dialogue includes little information.
Communication	Most of the information is well organized.	Part of the information is well organized.	The information is disorganized.
Accuracy	There are few mistakes in grammar and vocabulary.	There are some mistakes in grammar and vocabulary.	There are many mistakes in grammar and vocabulary.

Answers MSRB Transparency 38

Activity 20
1. Pablo tiene que practicar fútbol.
2. Claudia y Pablo llegan a la escuela a las siete de la mañana.
3. Claudia y Pablo hablan por teléfono.
4. Pablo necesita estudiar una o dos horas.
5. Claudia y Pablo tienen un examen de ciencias.
6. Pablo y Claudia sacan una buena nota.
7. Claudia estudia para la clase de ciencias mañana.
8. Pablo practica a las tres y media mañana.

Activity 21 Answers will vary. Sample answers include:
1. estudiar mucho.
2. estudian para el examen de ciencias.
3. tiene que estudiar y hacer la tarea de ciencias.
4. buenos apuntes.
5. buenas notas.

Activity 22 Answers will vary. Sample answers include: A. ¿Qué tienes que hacer en la clase de historia? B. Tengo que estudiar. Siempre tomo apuntes.

Objective
· Practice and integrate lesson vocabulary and grammar.

Core Resources
· *Cuaderno*, pp. 60–61
· Audio Program: TXT CD 2, tracks 8, 9

Practice Sequence
· **Activity 23:** Open-ended practice: reading, listening, speaking
· **Activity 24:** Open-ended practice: writing

 STANDARDS

1.1 Understand language, Act. 23
1.3 Present information, Acts. 23–24, PYP

 **Ongoing Assessment**

Rubric Activity 23

Listening/Speaking	
Proficient	**Not There Yet**
Student correctly says the times in complete sentences.	Student does not say the correct time and does not complete sentences.

 Ongoing Assessment

@HomeTutor
More Practice
ClassZone.com

PARA Y PIENSA **Peer Assessment** Have students correct each other's papers. For additional practice, use Reteaching & Practice Copymasters URB 2, pp. 7, 9.

 Answers MSRB Transparencies 38–39

Activity 23

Manuel necesita llegar a la clase de ciencias a las 7:55... a la clase de arte a las 9:15... a la clase de inglés a las 10:35... a la clase de historia a las 11:55... a la clase de español a la 1:35... a la clase de matemáticas a las 2:55.

Activity 24 Answers will vary. Sample answers include:

Tengo la clase de inglés los lunes. Tengo que tomar apuntes. A las diez tengo la clase de matemáticas.

Para y piensa
1. toma; **2.** practicar; **3.** estudian

112

---

23 | Integración

Leer
Escuchar
Hablar

Tomorrow is a teachers' meeting, so the class schedule is different. Read Manuel's schedule and listen to the principal's message. Tell at what time Manuel needs to arrive at each of his classes.

Fuente 1 Horario de clases

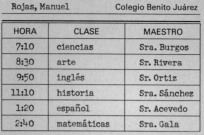

Rojas, Manuel		Colegio Benito Juárez
HORA	**CLASE**	**MAESTRO**
7:10	ciencias	Sra. Burgos
8:30	arte	Sr. Rivera
9:50	inglés	Sr. Ortiz
11:10	historia	Sra. Sánchez
1:20	español	Sr. Acevedo
2:40	matemáticas	Sra. Gala

Fuente 2 Mensaje del director

Listen and take notes
· ¿Cuántos minutos después de la hora normal son las clases de la mañana? ¿Las clases de la tarde?

modelo: Manuel necesita llegar a la clase de... a las...

Audio Program
TXT CD 2 Tracks 8, 9
Audio Script, TE p. 91b

24 Tu horario

Escribir

Describe your school schedule. What classes do you have? At what times? What do you have to do every day? What do you do once in a while? What activities do you never do in class?

modelo: Tengo muchas clases en mi horario. Tengo la clase de español todos los días a las nueve menos cuarto. Llego a clase temprano...

Writing Criteria	Excellent	Good	Needs Work
Content	Your description includes a lot of information.	Your description includes some information.	Your description includes little information.
Communication	Most of your description is organized and easy to follow.	Parts of your description are organized and easy to follow.	Your description is disorganized and hard to follow.
Accuracy	Your description has few mistakes in grammar and vocabulary.	Your description has some mistakes in grammar and vocabulary.	Your description has many mistakes in grammar and vocabulary.

Expansión:
Teacher Edition Only
Ask students to write about what their teachers do and have to do at school.

Más práctica Cuaderno *pp. 60–61* Cuaderno para hispanohablantes *pp. 62–63*

Did you get it? Write the correct form of **tomar, estudiar,** or **practicar.**
1. Claudia siempre ___ buenos apuntes.
2. Pablo tiene que ___ fútbol a las cinco.
3. Pablo y Claudia ___ todos los días.

Get Help Online ClassZone.com

Differentiating Instruction

Multiple Intelligences

Visual Learners Once students have completed Activity 23, give them the opportunity to create a new schedule for Manuel, based on their answers. Provide them with chart paper and colored pencils or pens. Students may want to present their schedules to the rest of the class.

Pre-AP

Expand and Elaborate Have students use Activity 24 as a model to write about their ideal school schedule with as many details as possible. For example: **Llego a la escuela a las diez y media de la mañana. A las once tengo la clase de matemáticas. La clase es muy fácil. Nunca tenemos que tomar apuntes y ¡nunca tenemos exámenes!**

Juegos y diversiones

Review numbers by playing a game.

Silencio

The Setup

The object of this game is to demonstrate understanding without speaking. For each round of play, your teacher will give each player an index card with a number written out in Spanish.

Your teacher will divide the class into several teams with one or two members of each team competing at a given time.

Playing the Game

Each round will have a different number line for highest and lowest. You will be asked to silently line up in order according to what is on your index card and where your card fits in the number line. Your teacher will use a timer, so you need to line up quickly or you will be disqualified and not have a chance to gain points.

The Winner!

Each student who lines up correctly will gain a point. The team with the most points at the end wins.

Materials
- index cards with Spanish words for various numbers
- timer
- cards for number line

Objective
· To review numbers by playing a game.

 STANDARDS
5.2 Life-long learners

Communication
Group Work

After starting out with numbers written out, you may progress to addition and subtraction problems and then to multiplication and division problems. Add more times for rounds with math problems. Give students index cards with the following terms: **Más** = plus; **menos** = minus; **por** = times; **dividido por** = divided by; **son** = equals. Ask students to line up to form a problem: **trece por tres es treinta y nueve.**

Long-term Retention
Recycle

Use this game to review telling times. Write different times of the day on separate index cards. **Es la una de la mañana. Son las cinco de la tarde. Son las diez de la noche.** Distribute the index cards to the class. Keep a list of the times on the index cards on a separate sheet of paper. Using the list to call times at random, have students line up from the earliest time in the morning to the latest time at night.

Differentiating Instruction

Inclusion

Frequent Review/Repetition Have student pairs alternate counting aloud from one to one hundred. Student A: **uno;** Student B: **dos,** Student A: **tres,** and so on. Then have one student dictate ten numbers to his partner. Monitor correct spelling and have them switch roles.

Multiple Intelligences

Musical/Rhythmic Ask students to develop a chant to help recall **los números,** counting by ten. Then challenge them to develop chants adding numbers. Give them the words **y** for *plus* and **son** for *equals.* For example: **dos y dos son cuatro, cuatro y dos son seis, seis y dos son ocho y ocho dieciséis.**

113

¡AVANZA! Objectives

- Learn about a bilingual school in Mexico.
- Learn about graduation requirements from a bilingual school in Mexico.
- Compare these requirements with graduation requirements in U.S. schools.

Core Resources

- Audio Program: TXT CD 2 track 10

Presentation Strategies

- Explain that the goal of bilingual schools is to educate students in content areas in two languages.
- Ask students what they think might be the advantages of bilingual schooling.
- Ask students if they would like to attend a bilingual school and why or why not.
- Play the audio while students read the handbook and course requirements.

STANDARDS

1.2 Understand language
2.1 Practices and perspectives
4.2 Compare cultures

Warm Up UTB 2 Transparency 19

-ar Verbs Write the correct form of **sacar, llegar, dibujar,** or **necesitar.**

1. Nosotros _____ buenas notas en las clases.
2. Yo _____ a la escuela a las siete de la mañana.
3. Ustedes _____ en la clase de arte.
4. ¿ _____ tú tomar muchos apuntes?

Answers: 1. sacamos; 2. llego; 3. dibujan; 4. Necesitas

Culture

Background Information

The **bachillerato** is a three-year high-school program and students are usually between 15 and 18 years old. The objective of these schools is to prepare students for further study in a university. Although the course of study varies, all high schools (called **Preparatorias** in Mexico) have a curriculum of social studies, language, culture, science, and technology. These schools are managed privately, by the nation, or occasionally housed within a university.

Lectura

¡AVANZA! **Goal:** Read about the requirements for graduating from a bilingual school in Mexico. As you read these documents, compare them with the course requirements needed to graduate from your school.

AUDIO

Una escuela bilingüe en México

The following pages are from the student handbook for Colegio Americano, a bilingual school in Guadalajara, Mexico.

STRATEGY Leer
Use what you know As you read the graduation requirements of Colegio Americano, use what you know. Find words that sound and look somewhat similar to those in English — cognates like **ciencias** or **matemáticas.** Then use the context and what you already know to guess what **desarrollo humano** and **optativas** mean.

MANUAL DEL ESTUDIANTE

Estudiantes en el Colegio Americano

«A mí me gusta mucho el Colegio Americano. Las clases son muy buenas. Los maestros son trabajadores y muy inteligentes. Y los estudiantes son súper simpáticos. Siempre tenemos que trabajar mucho, pero... ¡¿dónde no?! Y también en la escuela hay muchas actividades después de las clases. ¡Es una escuela excelente!»
–Marta Ramos, estudiante

COLEGIO AMERICANO
Colomos 2100 Colonia Providencia
Guadalajara, Jalisco 44640 México
http://www.asfg.mx

Unidad 2 México
114 ciento catorce

Differentiating Instruction

Multiple Intelligences

Interpersonal Ask student pairs to visit the website of a bilingual school in Mexico. They can search using these key words: Bilingual Schools Mexico. Have them click on the home page of one of these schools to find additional information about school subjects offered, extracurricular activities, and graduation requirements. Ask them to write a brief report in English and use it for class discussion.

Slower-paced Learners

Personalize It Ask students to look closely at the photo on the cover of the **Manual del Estudiante.** Ask them: What are the different groups of students doing? Do the students in the photo look as if they enjoy their school? Does this look like a school you'd like to attend?

Requisitos para graduarse de bachillerato

A continuación [1], los requisitos para graduarse con los dos certificados: el certificado mexicano y el certificado estadounidense.

Clase	Número de unidades
Inglés	4 unidades
Español	4 unidades
Matemáticas	4 unidades
Ciencias	4 unidades
Ciencias Sociales de México	1 unidad
Historia de México II	1 unidad
Geografía de México	1 unidad
Derecho [2]	1 unidad
Ciencias Sociales	3 unidades
Computación	0,5 unidades
Educación Física	0,5 unidades
Desarrollo Humano [3]	1 unidad
Optativas [4]	2 unidades
Total	**27 unidades**

COLEGIO AMERICANO

[1] A... following are   [2] Law
[3] Human Development   [4] Electives

PARA Y PIENSA

¿Comprendiste?
1. ¿Cuántas clases necesitas para los dos programas?
2. ¿Cuántas unidades de matemáticas tienes que tomar?

¿Y tú?
¿Qué clases del Colegio Americano hay en tu escuela? ¿Cómo son?

Lección 1
ciento quince **115**

Communication
Presentational Mode

Ask students to write their own statement for the cover of a **Manual del Estudiante** for their own school. Give them the following questions as a guide: **¿Cómo se llama tu escuela? ¿Cómo son las clases? ¿Cómo son los maestros? ¿Qué tienes que hacer en la escuela? ¿Qué actividades tienes después de las clases? ¿Cómo es la escuela?** Encourage them to add a photo or poster of their school to accompany their class presentation.

Communication
Pair Work

Assign students the roles of school admissions counselor in a Mexican school and prospective student. The student asks questions about the school, required subjects, and graduation requirements. Encourage them to use the vocabulary from the **Manual del Estudiante** and the **Requisitos para graduarse de bachillerato**. Example: **A: ¿Cómo son los maestros de la escuela? B: Son muy simpáticos. A: ¿Cuántas unidades de ciencias sociales tengo que tomar? B: Tienes que tomar tres unidades.**

Long-term Retention
Critical Thinking

Evaluate Play the audio once without pausing and then play it once again, stopping along the way to check comprehension. Make a list of difficult words on the board for review. Add a list of topics to help students evaluate the school: **las clases, los maestros, los requisitos, los números de unidades.** Possible answers: **Es una escuela muy difícil porque tienes que tomar muchas clases.**

Differentiating Instruction

Heritage Language Learners

Writing Skills Ask students if anyone they know ever attended a bilingual school. If so, ask them to compare a bilingual school and their school. Write their opinions in two lists on the board. Have students use the lists to write their comparisons in paragraph form.

Pre-AP

Expand and Elaborate Ask students to work in groups to design a four-year curriculum for a bilingual school based on the **Requisitos para graduarse de bachillerato**. How long would the day be? How long would each period be? What courses would they offer, and in what years?

Answers

Para y piensa ¿Comprendiste?
1. Necesitas trece clases para los dos programas.
2. Tienes que tomar cuatro unidades de matemáticas.

¿Y tú? Answers will vary, but should follow the pattern: En mi escuela hay inglés, español, matemáticas, ciencias, ciencias sociales, computación, educación física y las optativas.

Objectives

- Analyze an antique map over 400 years old to learn about an ancient Mexican city.
- Deduce the meaning of symbols in the map's key.

Presentation Strategies

- Ask students to think about as many different kinds of maps as they can, and list the responses on the board (weather maps, road maps, etc.).
- Ask them which maps they have used, and if they think it is helpful to have illustrations on maps.
- Ask them to think about the different purposes for maps.
- Tell them that in 1577, Spain asked for information about its territories in the New World, and received maps like the one on this page. Ask how they think the information on the map was used.

STANDARDS

1.3 Present information
3.1 Knowledge of other disciplines
3.2 Acquire information

El pueblo de Zempoala

In 1577, the Spanish crown sent a questionnaire to Mexico to get information about its territories in the New World. The responses that were sent back included local maps drawn by indigenous mapmakers.

The map below depicts the town (**pueblo**) of Zempoala, located in the modern Mexican state of Hidalgo. Research Zempoala to learn more about the town and this map. Then choose three specific map symbols not listed in the legend (**leyenda**) and explain what you think they mean.

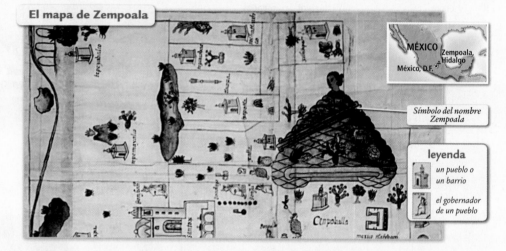

El mapa de Zempoala

Símbolo del nombre Zempoala

leyenda
- un pueblo o un barrio
- el gobernador de un pueblo

Proyecto 1 *El arte*

Draw a map of your town or city similar to the one of Zempoala. Give information about people, buildings, roads, and vegetation. Use symbols like the ones in the map above and label them in Spanish.

Proyecto 2 *Las ciencias sociales*

In 1968, Mexico established a televised system of secondary schools called **Telesecundaria.** Today, educational video programs are broadcast via satellite to more than 15,000 schools. Write two paragraphs about the use of technology in education. How is it used in your school? Can you think of other ways it can be used in education?

Proyecto 3 *La salud*

The map of Zempoala shows a number of cacti. The cactus has been an important source of food and medicine for people in Mexico for many years. Make a list of different types of cacti found in Mexico and create a chart showing how people have used them for health and beauty purposes.

Un nopal con flores

Connections

La historia

The name *Zempoala* means *place of the 20 waters,* for the several rivers that converge near the site. At the time of the Conquest, Zempoala was the largest city on the Gulf of Mexico, with a population of about 30,000. The map on this page is part of a collection of maps called the **Relaciones Gráficas** Collection. Many of them are held at the Universty of Texas at Austin in the Benson Latin American Collection, and can be viewed online. The map is labeled in Nahuatl, the language of the Aztec empire, which is still spoken widely in Mexico.

Answers

Conexiones Historians are still trying to decipher the meanings of the symbols on this map. Students should write their opinion of what the symbols mean.

Answers continue on page 117.

Answers continue on page 117.

Differentiating Instruction

Pre-AP

Draw Conclusions Point out that the **Telesecundaria** system of instruction is capable of transmitting 24 hours a day. Nowadays programs are more interactive and have corresponding textbooks. Lessons can be watched live on TV or can be recorded. Based on this information, ask students: **¿Es una buena idea tener clases 24 horas al día? ¿Por qué?**

English Learners

Increase Interaction Pair English learners with native English-speaking students to discuss the information on p. 116. Have them work together on the planning and creation of maps for Proyecto 1.

Lección 1

En resumen
Vocabulario y gramática

Animated Grammar
Interactive Flashcards
ClassZone.com

Vocabulario

Tell Time and Discuss Daily Schedules

¿A qué hora es...?	At what time is...?	la hora	hour; time
¿Qué hora es?	What time is it?	el horario	schedule
A la(s)...	At . . . o'clock.	menos	to, before (telling time)
Es la... / Son las...	It is . . . o'clock.		
de la mañana	in the morning (with a time)	el minuto	minute
		...y cuarto	quarter past
de la tarde	in the afternoon (with a time)	...y (diez)	(ten) past
		...y media	half past
de la noche	at night (with a time)		

Describe Classes

School Subjects		Classroom Activities	
el arte	art	contestar	to answer
las ciencias	science	enseñar	to teach
el español	Spanish	llegar	to arrive
la historia	history	necesitar	to need
el inglés	English	sacar una buena / mala nota	to get a good / bad grade
las matemáticas	math	tomar apuntes	to take notes
		usar la computadora	to use the computer

Describe Frequency

de vez en cuando	once in a while
muchas veces	often, many times
mucho	a lot
nunca	never
siempre	always
todos los días	every day

Other Words and Phrases

casi	almost
¿Cuántos(as)...?	How many . . . ?
difícil	difficult
en	in
el examen (pl. los exámenes)	exam, test
fácil	easy
hay...	there is, there are . . .
muchos(as)	many
tarde	late
temprano	early
tener que	to have to

Numbers from 11 to 100 *p. 94*

Gramática

Notas gramaticales: Numbers *p. 97*, Telling time *p. 99*, Expressions of frequency *p. 103*

The Verb tener

Use the verb **tener** to talk about what you have.

tener *to have*			
yo	tengo	nosotros(as)	tenemos
tú	tienes	vosotros(as)	tenéis
usted, él, ella	tiene	ustedes, ellos(as)	tienen

Tener + **que** + **infinitive** is used to talk about what someone has to do.

Present Tense of -ar Verbs

To form the present tense of a regular verb that ends in **-ar**, drop the **-ar** and add the appropriate **ending**.

hablar *to talk, to speak*			
yo	**habl**o	nosotros(as)	**habl**amos
tú	**habl**as	vosotros(as)	**habl**áis
usted, él, ella	**habl**a	ustedes, ellos(as)	**habl**an

Lección 1
ciento diecisiete **117**

Objective
· Review lesson vocabulary and grammar.

Online SPANISH CLASSZONE.COM

Self-Quiz Students can check their understanding and get instant results with our online multiple-choice quizzes. These quizzes provide immediate feedback, making them a great way to pepare for a quiz or test.

Featuring...
Cultura INTERACTIVA
Animated Grammar
@HomeTutor

And more...
· Get Help Online
· Interactive Flashcards
· Review Games
· WebQuest
· Self-Check Quiz

Long-term Retention
Study Tips

Have students study the first category of words in En resumen for 1 minute. Then tell them to close their books and write down as many words as they can remember in 2 minutes. They should then open their book and check their work. Continue with the other categories.

Answers

Answers continued from page 116.

(This is a continuation of the answer for main project) Possible answers include: The plant life may represent fields used for farming. The places where earth is shown could be hills or mountains. The buildings may represent the center of town.

Proyecto 1 Students should draw maps that incorporate similar images and orientations as the map of Zempoala.

Proyecto 2 Answers will vary. Sample answers include computers, the Internet, overhead projectors, TVs, VHS, DVDs.

Proyecto 3 Examples of cacti include maguey and nopal. Several parts of the nopal are eaten–the actual cactus leaves as well as the fruit that comes off it, called the prickly pear or **tuna** in Spanish. The fruit is also used to make juice. The maguey is used to produce soap, food, medicine, rope, fibers, furniture, and paper.

Differentiating Instruction

Multiple Intelligences

Musical/Rhythmic Lead students in chanting **yo hablo, tú hablas, usted habla, él habla, ella habla, nosotros hablamos, vosotras habláis, ustedes hablan, ellos hablan, ellas hablan.** As they progress through the sequence, have them gesture to indicate about whom they are talking. Conduct this exercise first as a large group and then in pairs.

Inclusion

Synthetic/Analytic Support Ask students to make flashcards with the subject pronoun on one side and the correct form of **tener** on the other side. Ask students to work in pairs, taking turns as one student shows the pronoun and the other says the verb form, then one student shows the verb form and the other says the pronoun.

Objectives
· Review lesson grammar and vocabulary.

Core Resources
· *Cuaderno*, pp. 62–73
· Audio Program: TXT CD 2 track 11

Review Options
· Before listening to the audio for Activity 1, ask students to listen to it and pay special attention to the subjects and times mentioned.
· Before doing Activity 2, review forms of **tener** and telling time with students.
· Review present tense forms of **-ar** verbs by saying a subject and an infinitive and asking students to supply the correct verb form. For example: **él/practicar: él practica.**
· Review expressions of frequency before doing Activity 4.
· Ask students to generate two questions to ask their classmates, based on the Comparación cultural.

STANDARDS
1.2 Understand language, Act. 1
1.3 Present information, Acts. 2–5
4.2 Compare cultures, Act. 5

Warm Up UTB 2 Transparency 19

Vocabulary Complete the sentences with the correct word.

difícil   notas   hora   tarde   apuntes

1. No me gusta sacar malas _____.
2. De vez en cuando, llego _____ a clase.
3. En la clase de historia tenemos que tomar muchos _____.
4. La clase de matemáticas no es _____.
5. ¿A qué _____ es la clase de arte?

Answers: 1. notas; 2. tarde; 3. apuntes; 4. difícil; 5. hora

See Activity answers on p. 119.

118

¡LLEGADA!

@HomeTutor
ClassZone.com

Now you can
· talk about daily schedules
· ask and tell time
· say what you have and have to do
· say what you do and how often you do things

Using
· the verb **tener** and **tener que**
· expressions of frequency
· present tense of **-ar** verbs

To review
· the verb **tener** and **tener que** p. 100
· expressions of frequency p. 103
· present tense of **-ar** verbs p. 106

1 Listen and understand

Listen to Martín and Lupe talk about their classes. Then match the questions and anwers.

1. ¿Qué hora es?
2. ¿A qué hora es la clase de historia?
3. ¿En qué clase tiene que sacar una buena nota Martín?
4. ¿En qué clases contestan muchas preguntas?
5. ¿Cómo es la maestra de ciencias?
6. ¿En qué clase usan la computadora?

a. joven
b. en la clase de ciencias
c. Son las diez y cuarto.
d. Es a las diez y media.
e. en las clases de historia y ciencias
f. en la clase de historia

Audio Program
TXT CD 2 Track 1
Audio Script, TE
p. 91b

To review
· the verb **tener** and **tener que** p. 100

2 Say what you have and have to do

Tell what classes Beto and his friends have at these times and what they have to do.

8:00   **modelo:** Adela: arte / dibujar
Adela tiene la clase de arte a las ocho.
Tiene que dibujar.

1. **9:15** yo: historia / tomar muchos apuntes
2. **10:30** ustedes: matemáticas / trabajar con problemas
3. **11:45** tú: español / hablar español
4. **1:20** David y yo: inglés / contestar muchas preguntas
5. **2:15** Lilia: ciencias / usar la computadora
6. **3:30** Eva y Víctor: música / tocar la guitarra

Differentiating Instruction

Pre-AP

Draw Conclusions For Activity 1, ask students to discuss why Martín needs to take a lot of notes in history and why he has to answer many questions. Why does the history class differ from Martín's other classes?

Multiple Intelligences

Visual Learners To help visual learners with Activity 3, ask students to create a chart that shows Pati León's schedule. Direct them to use symbols or pictures as well as words to indicate what Pati will be doing on each day.

3 | Talk about daily schedules

To review
• present tense of -ar verbs p. 106

Read the information about Pati León. Then complete the information with the correct form of the verbs in parentheses.

Mi horario es muy bueno. Yo __1.__ (trabajar) mucho los lunes, martes y miércoles. Los jueves Gustavo y yo __2.__ (andar) en patineta. Los viernes Gustavo __3.__ (descansar), pero yo __4.__ (montar) en bicicleta con Eloísa y Héctor. Ellos __5.__ (practicar) deportes casi todos los días. Los viernes nosotros __6.__ (comprar) una pizza y __7.__ (mirar) la televisión. ¿Y los sábados y domingos? Muchas veces mis amigos y yo __8.__ (pasear). ¿Y tú? ¿También __9.__ (pasar) un rato con los amigos los sábados y domingos?

4 | Say what you do and how often you do things

To review
• expressions of frequency p. 103
• present tense of -ar verbs p. 106

Write sentences telling how often these people do the following activities.

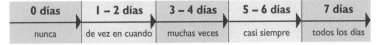

0 días	1 – 2 días	3 – 4 días	5 – 6 días	7 días
nunca	de vez en cuando	muchas veces	casi siempre	todos los días

modelo: nosotros / mirar un DVD (2 días)
Miramos un DVD de vez en cuando.

1. Roberta / contestar preguntas (0 días)
2. tú / hablar español (5 días)
3. Nicolás / practicar deportes (6 días)
4. yo / escuchar música (3 días)
5. Carlos y Pilar / estudiar historia (2 días)
6. nosotros / tocar la guitarra (4 días)
7. los maestros / usar la computadora (7 días)

5 | Mexico and the Dominican Republic

To review
• Chichén Itzá p. 91
• Comparación cultural pp. 92, 102, 109

Comparación cultural

Answer these culture questions.

1. What is Chichén Itzá and what can you find there?
2. What are **zócalos**?
3. What do many students in Mexico and the Dominican Republic wear to school?
4. What does the mural *Alfabetización* represent?

Más práctica | Cuaderno *pp. 62–73* Cuaderno para hispanohablantes *pp. 64–73*

Get Help Online
ClassZone.com

Differentiating Instruction

Inclusion

Clear Structure Ask students to write a description of their school schedule. Encourage them to brainstorm ideas in these categories: class subjects and times, class activities, frequency of activities, lunch time, and after-school activities. Ask them to use a concept web to organize their ideas before they start writing. Make sure they write their schedule in chronological order.

Slower-paced Learners

Yes/No Questions Ask students yes/no questions about their school activities. Use frequency words, such as **de vez en cuando, muchas veces, siempre,** and **todos los días** in your questions. **¿Usas la computadora muchas veces?** Encourage students to add to their responses after answering **sí** or **no.**

✓ Ongoing Assessment

Peer Assessment Have students complete Activity 3 individually. Then ask pairs of students to read answers aloud and check each other's written work.

✓ Ongoing Assessment

Quick Check Ask students how often they do the activities listed in Activity 4. For example: **Carlos, ¿con qué frecuencia escuchas música? Peter y Alice, ¿con qué frecuencia usan la computadora?**

Answers MSRB Transparency 39

Answers for Activities on pp. 118, 119.

Actividad 1 1. c; 2. d; 3. f; 4. e; 5. a; 6. b

Actividad 2
1. Yo tengo la clase de historia a las nueve y cuarto. Tengo que tomar muchos apuntes.
2. Ustedes tienen la clase de matemáticas a las diez y media. Tienen que trabajar con problemas.
3. Tú tienes la clase de español a las doce menos cuarto. Tienes que hablar español.
4. David y yo tenemos la clase de inglés a la una y veinte. Tenemos que contestar muchas preguntas.
5. Lilia tiene la clase de ciencias a las dos y cuarto. Tiene que usar la computadora.
6. Eva y Víctor tienen la clase de música a las tres y media. Tienen que tocar la guitarra.

Actividad 3 1. trabajo; 2. andamos; 3. descansa; 4. monto; 5. practican; 6. compramos; 7. miramos; 8. paseamos; 9. pasas

Actividad 4
1. Roberta nunca contesta preguntas.
2. Tú hablas español casi siempre.
3. Nicolás practica deportes casi siempre.
4. Yo escucho música muchas veces.
5. Carlos y Pilar estudian historia de vez en cuando.
6. Nosotros tocamos la guitarra muchas veces.
7. Los maestros usan la computadora todos los días.

Actividad 5
1. Chichén Itzá is an ancient Mayan city. You can find there the statue of Chac-Mool and the pyramid of Kukulcán.
2. A zócalo is a town square or plaza.
3. Many students in Mexico and the Dominican Republic wear uniforms to school.
4. The mural *Alfabetización* represents the idea of free public education.

Culture at a Glance ❖

Topic & Activity	Essential Question
School in Mexico pp. 120–121	How is Mexico's school year different or similar to your school year?
The National Museum of Anthropology p. 130	What do ancient artifacts teach us about a culture?
A self-portrait of Frida Kahlo p. 137	What does a self-portrait reveal about an artist?
Favorite classes of Mexican and Dominican students pp. 142–143	How would you talk about your favorite class?
Huichol yarn painting and Taino rock art p. 144	How does art reflect a culture's view of the natural world?
Culture review p. 147	What are some cultural elements of Mexico and the Dominican Republic?

COMPARISON COUNTRIES **República Dominicana** 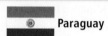 **Paraguay** **México**

Practice at a Glance ❖

	Objective	Activity & Skill
Vocabulary	Classroom objects	1: Speaking/Writing; 3: Speaking; 12: Speaking; 26: Writing; Repaso 4: Writing
	Feelings	8: Speaking; 11: Speaking/Writing; 14: Speaking; 23: Listening/Reading; Repaso 2: Writing
	Places in school	2: Reading/Writing; 6: Speaking/Writing; 7: Speaking/Writing; 9: Speaking; 15: Speaking; 17: Writing; 18: Listening/Writing; 19: Speaking/Writing; 20: Speaking; 23: Listening/Reading; 24: Speaking; Repaso 1: Listening
Grammar	The verb **estar**	6: Speaking/Writing; 7: Speaking/Writing; 8: Speaking; 9: Speaking; 10: Writing; 11: Speaking/Writing; 12: Speaking; 13: Listening/Reading; 14: Speaking; 15: Speaking; 23: Listening/Reading; Repaso 2, 4: Writing
	The conjugated verb before the subject to ask a question	8: Speaking; Repaso 2: Writing
	The verb **ir**	16: Reading/Writing; 17: Writing; 18: Listening/Writing; 19: Speaking/Writing; 20: Speaking; 21: Speaking/Writing; 24: Speaking; 25: Reading/Listening/Speaking; 26: Writing; Repaso 3: Reading/Writing
Communication	Describe classes and classroom objects	1: Speaking/Writing; 3: Speaking; 5: Speaking; 26: Writing
	Say where things are located	6: Speaking/Writing; 7: Speaking/Writing; 9: Speaking; 10: Writing; 12: Speaking; Repaso 4: Writing
	Say where you are going	16: Reading/Writing; 17: Writing; 18: Listening/Writing; 19: Speaking/Writing; 20: Speaking; 21: Speaking/Writing; 24: Speaking; 26: Writing; Repaso 3: Reading/Writing
	Talk about how you feel	8: Speaking; 11: Speaking/Writing; 14: Speaking; 23: Listening/Reading; Repaso 2: Writing
	Pronunciation: The letter **d**	*Pronunciación: La letra **d**, p. 135:* Listening
Recycle	Class subjects	5: Speaking
	Telling time	24: Speaking

The following activities are recorded in the Audio Program for *¡Avancemos!*

- **¡A responder!** *page 124*
- **18: ¿Adónde van?** *page 136*
- **25: Integración** *page 140*
- **Repaso de la lección** *page 146*
   1: Listen and understand
- **Repaso inclusivo** *page 150*
   1: Listen, understand, and compare

¡A responder! TXT CD 2 track 13

1. enojado
2. nervioso
3. cansado
4. contento
5. deprimido
6. emocionado
7. tranquilo

18 ¿Adónde van? TXT CD 2 track 16

Pablo: Hola, me llamo Pablo. ¡Me gusta practicar deportes! A las ocho de la mañana yo voy al gimnasio.

Hola, Claudia. ¿Adónde vas?

Claudia: ¡Hola, Pablo! Voy a la clase de inglés.

Pablo: Martín y Sara, ¿adónde van ustedes?

Sara: Son las doce y Martín y yo tenemos que comer. Vamos a la cafetería.

Pablo: Pero, ¿adónde va la maestra de inglés? La clase de inglés es a la una.

Claudia: ¡Ay, Pablo! Ella va a la biblioteca. Necesita un libro para la clase.

Pablo: María y Claudia, ¿qué tal? Ustedes van al gimnasio, ¿no?

Claudia: María y yo vamos a la clase de matemáticas.

Pablo: Sr. Treviño, ¿adónde va usted después de clase?

Sr. Treviño: Después de clase voy a la oficina de la directora. Necesito hablar con ella.

25 Integración TXT CD 2 tracks 19, 20

Hola, Raquel. Soy yo, Mario. Tenemos el examen de historia mañana, a las tres menos cuarto. ¡Necesitamos estudiar!

Vamos a la biblioteca mañana, ¿no? Voy a la clase de ciencias a las siete y media de la mañana. No tengo clase a las nueve menos veinte pero a las diez menos diez tengo la clase de matemáticas. A las doce necesito comer con Andrés. A las doce y media descanso. A la una y media estoy en la clase de inglés. ¡Estoy muy nervioso! ¿Cuándo estudiamos?

Repaso de la lección TXT CD 2 track 22

1 Listen and understand

Hola. ¿Dónde estás? Son las ocho de la mañana. Estoy delante de la clase de arte. Voy a la clase de español. Hasta luego.

Hola. Mmmm. No contestas. Son las diez y cuarto. Estoy en el pasillo. Del pasillo, voy a la clase de inglés. Adiós.

¿Qué pasa? ¿Dónde estás? Son las doce y media. Estoy en la cafetería. De la cafetería, voy a la clase de matemáticas. Hasta luego.

Hola. Soy yo... Ana. Son las tres menos cuarto de la tarde. Estoy en la oficina. De la oficina, voy a la clase de historia. Adiós.

¡Hola! ¡Hola! ¡Contesta, por favor! Son las cuatro y diez. Estoy en la biblioteca. De la biblioteca, voy al gimnasio. ¿Y tú? ¿Dónde estás? ¿Estás en el gimnasio?

Repaso inclusivo TXT CD 2 track 24

1 Listen, understand, and compare

Javier: Los maestros enseñan pero a ellos también les gusta hacer otras cosas. El señor Minondo enseña la clase de historia y después de las clases practica deportes con amigos.

Sr. Minondo: Soy estudioso y atlético también. Después de enseñar, voy al gimnasio con los amigos para jugar al fútbol... y estoy más tranquilo.

Javier: La señora Cruz es la directora de la escuela.

Sra. Cruz: Tengo que ser organizada y seria pero también soy artística. Después de un día difícil, voy a mi oficina y toco la guitarra.

Javier: Cuando estás en el pasillo después de las cuatro de la tarde y escuchas música, es la directora y ella está contenta. Los maestros y directores son muy interesantes.

On your desktop

Everything you need to ...

Plan

DVD-ROM

All resources including audio and video

Present

POWER PRESENTATIONS

Ready-made PowerPoint™ presentations with

Grammar

Assess

ONLINE

✓ Assess, score, prescribe, and remediate online
✓ Create customized tests with the Test Generator CD-ROM
✓ Individualized Assessment for on-level, modified, pre-AP, and heritage language learners

 Print

Plan	Present	Practice	Assess
URB 2 • Video Scripts pp. 69, 70 • Family Letter p. 90 • Family Involvement Activity p. 91 • Absent Student Copymasters pp. 100–110 **Lesson Plans** pp. 47–55 **Best Practices Toolkit**	**URB 2** • Video Activities pp. 57–64 TPRS pp. 22–28	• *Cuaderno* pp. 73–95 • *Cuaderno para hispanohablantes* pp. 73–95 • *Lecturas para todos* pp. 17–21 • *Lecturas para hispanohablantes* • *¡AvanzaCómics! SuperBruno y Nati*, Episodio 1 **URB 2** • Practice Games pp. 37–44 • Audio Scripts pp. 75–80 • Map/Culture Activities pp. 81–82 • Fine Art Activities pp. 87–88	**URB 2** • Did you get it? • Reteaching and Practice Copymasters pp. 11–22

 Unit Transparency Book 2

Culture	Presentation and Practice	Classroom Management
• Atlas Maps UTB 1 1–6 • Map of Mexico 1 • Fine Art Transparencies 4, 5	• Vocabulary Transparencies 8, 9 • Grammar Presentation Transparencies 12, 13 • Situational Transparencies and label overlay 14, 15 • Situational Student Copymasters 1, 2	• Warm Up Transparencies 20–23 **MSRB** • Student Book Answer Transparencies 40–43

Audio and Video

Audio	Video

• Student Book Audio CD 2 Tracks 12–24
• Workbook Audio CD 1 Tracks 31–40
• Heritage Learners Audio CD 1 Tracks 13–16, CD 3 Tracks 11–14
• Assessment Audio CD 1 Tracks 11–14
• *Lecturas para todos* Audio CD 1 Track 4, CD 2 Tracks 1–6
• *Música del mundo hispano*
• Sing-along Audio CD
	• Vocabulary Video DVD 1
	• *Telehistoria* DVD 1
	   Escena 1
	   Escena 2
	   Escena 3
	   Completa
	• Culture Video DVD 1

 Online and CD-ROM Resources

Student	Teacher
Available online and on CD-ROM: • eEdition • @HomeTutor • Animated Grammar **Available online:** • *Cultura Interactiva* • Culture Links • WebQuests • Flashcards • Conjuguemos.com • Review Games • Self-check Quiz	**Available online and on CD-ROM:** **EasyPlanner CD-ROM resources:** • Learning Scenarios • Conversation Cards • Family Letters in Spanish • Family Letters in Creole **Available online:** • McDougal Littell Assessment System **Available on CD-ROM:** • Test Generator • Power Presentations

✓ Differentiated Assessment

On-level	Modified	Pre-AP	Heritage Learners
• Vocabulary Recognition Quiz p.74 • Vocabulary Production Quiz p.75 • Grammar Quizzes pp. 76–77 • Culture Quiz p.78 • On-level Lesson Test pp. 79–85 • On-level Unit 2 Unit Test pp. 91–97	• Modified Lesson Test pp. 59–65 • Modified Unit 2 Unit Test pp. 71–77	• Pre-AP Lesson Test pp. 59–65 • Pre-AP Unit 2 Unit Test pp. 71–77	• Heritage Learners Lesson Test pp. 65–71 • Heritage Learners Unit 2 Unit Test pp. 77–83

Core Pacing Guide

	Objectives/Focus	Teach	Practice	Assess/HW Options
DAY 1	**Vocabulary:** typical school day • Warm Up OHT 20 **5 min**	**Lesson Opener pp.** 120–121 **Presentación de vocabulario pp.** 122–124 • Read A–D • View video DVD 1 • Play Audio TXT CD 2 track 12 • *¡A responder!* TXT CD 2 track 13 **25 min**	**Lesson Opener pp.** 120–121 **Práctica de vocabulario p.** 125 • Acts. 1, 2, 3 **15 min**	**Assess:** *Para y piensa* p. 125 **5 min** **Homework:** *Cuaderno* pp. 74–76 @HomeTutor
DAY 2	**Communication:** describing classes and classroom objects • Warm Up OHT 20 • Check Homework **5 min**	**Vocabulario en contexto pp.** 126–127 • *Telehistoria escena 1* DVD 1 **20 min**	**Vocabulario en contexto** pp. 126–127 • Act 4, TXT CD 2 track 14 • Act. 5 **20 min**	**Assess:** *Para y piensa* p. 127 **5 min** **Homework:** *Cuaderno* pp. 74–76 @HomeTutor
DAY 3	**Grammar:** the verb **estar** • Warm Up OHT 21 • Check Homework **5 min**	**Presentación de gramática p.** 128 • the verb **estar** **Práctica de gramática pp.** 129–131 • *Nota gramatical* **20 min**	**Práctica de gramática pp.** 129–131 • Acts. 6, 7, 8, 9, 10, 11, 12 **20 min**	**Assess:** *Para y piensa* p. 131 **5 min** **Homework:** *Cuaderno* pp. 77–79 @HomeTutor
DAY 4	**Communication: estar** to talk about emotions and locations • Warm Up OHT 21 • Check Homework **5 min**	**Gramática en contexto pp.** 132–133 • *Telehistoria escena 2* DVD 1 **15 min**	**Gramática en contexto** pp. 132–133 • Activity 13 TXT CD 2 track 15 • Acts. 14, 15 **25 min**	**Assess:** *Para y piensa* p. 133 **5 min** **Homework:** *Cuaderno* pp. 77–79 @HomeTutor
DAY 5	**Grammar:** using the verb **ir** to say where you go during and after school • Warm Up OHT 22 • Check Homework **5 min**	**Presentación de gramática p.** 134 • the verb **ir** **Práctica de gramática pp.** 135–137 • *Pronunciación* TXT CD 2 track 17 **Culture:** Self-portraits **15 min**	**Práctica de gramática pp.** 135–137 • Act. 18 TXT CD 2 track 16 • Acts. 16, 17, 19, 20, 21 **25 min**	**Assess:** *Para y piensa* p. 137 **5 min** **Homework:** *Cuaderno* pp. 80–82 @HomeTutor
DAY 6	**Communication:** Culmination: use **ir** and **estar** • Warm Up OHT 22 • Check Homework **5 min**	**Todo junto pp.** 138–140 • *Escenas 1, 2: Resumen* •*Telehistoria completa* DVD 1 **15 min**	**Todo junto pp.** 138–140 • Acts. 22, 23 TXT CD 2 tracks 14, 15, 18 • Act. 25 TXT CD 2 tracks 19, 20 • Acts. 24, 26 **25 min**	**Assess:** *Para y piensa* p. 140 **5 min** **Homework:** *Cuaderno* pp. 83–84 @HomeTutor
DAY 7	**Reading:** My favorite class • Warm Up OHT 23 • Check Homework **Review:** Lesson Review **5 min**	**Lectura cultural pp.** 142–143 • *Mi clase favorita* TXT CD 2 track 21 **Repaso de la lección pp.** 146–147 **20 min**	**Lectura cultural pp.** 142–143 • *Mi clase favorita* **Repaso de la lección pp.** 146–147 • Act. 1 TXT CD 2 track 22 • Acts. 2, 3, 4, 5 **20 min**	**Assess:** *Para y piensa* **5 min** p. 143; *Repaso de la lección* pp. 146–147 **Homework:** *En resumen* p. 145 *Cuaderno* pp. 85–87, 91–96 (optional) Review Games Online @HomeTutor
DAY 8	**Assessment**			**Assess:** Lesson 2 Test or Unit 2 Test **50 min**
DAY 9	**Unit Culmination** **5 min**	**Comparación cultural pp.** 148–149 TXT CD 2 track 23 **Repaso inclusivo pp.** 150–151 **20 min**	**Comparación cultural pp.** 148–149 **Repaso inclusivo pp.** 150–151 • Act. 1 TXT CD 2 track 24 • Acts. 2, 3, 4, 5, 6 **25 min**	

	Objectives/Focus	Teach	Practice	Assess/HW Options
DAY 1	**Vocabulary:** typical school day • Warm Up OHT 20 5 min	Lesson Opener pp. 120–121 **Presentación de vocabulario** pp. 122–124 • Read A–D • View video DVD 1 • Play Audio TXT CD 2 track 12 • *¡A responder!* TXT CD 2 track 13 20 min	Lesson Opener pp. 120–121 **Práctica de vocabulario** p. 125 • Acts. 1, 2, 3 20 min	**Assess:** *Para y piensa* p. 125 5 min
	Communication: describing classes and classroom objects 5 min	**Vocabulario en contexto** pp. 126–127 • *Telehistoria escena 1* DVD 1 15 min	**Vocabulario en contexto** pp. 126–127 • Act 4, TXT CD 2 track 14 • Act. 5 15 min	**Assess:** *Para y piensa* p. 127 5 min **Homework:** *Cuaderno* pp. 74–76 @HomeTutor
DAY 2	**Grammar:** the verb **estar** • Warm Up OHT 21 • Check Homework 5 min	**Presentación de gramática** p. 128 • the verb **estar** **Práctica de gramática** pp. 129–131 • *Nota gramatical* 20 min	**Práctica de gramática** pp. 129–131 • Acts. 6, 7, 8, 9, 10, 11, 12 15 min	**Assess:** *Para y piensa* p. 131 5 min
	Communication: estar to talk about emotions and locations 5 min	**Gramática en contexto** pp. 132–133 • *Telehistoria escena 2* DVD 1 20 min	**Gramática en contexto** pp. 132–133 • Act. 13 TXT CD 2 track 15 • Acts. 14, 15 15 min	**Assess:** *Para y piensa* p. 133 5 min **Homework:** *Cuaderno* pp. 77–79 @HomeTutor
DAY 3	**Grammar:** using the verb **ir** to say where you go during and after school • Warm Up OHT 22 • Check Homework 5 min	**Presentación de gramática** p. 134 • the verb **ir** **Práctica de gramática** pp. 135–137 • *Pronunciación* TXT CD 2 track 17 **Culture:** Self-portraits 15 min	**Práctica de gramática** pp. 135–137 • Act. 18 TXT CD 2 track 16 • Acts. 16, 17, 19, 20, 21 20 min	**Assess:** *Para y piensa* p. 137 5 min
	Communication: Culmination: use **ir** and **estar** 5 min	**Todo junto** pp. 138–140 • *Escenas 1 & 2: Resumen Telehistoria completa* DVD 1 10 min	**Todo junto** pp. 138–140 • Acts. 22, 23 TXT CD 2 tracks 14, 15, 18 • Act. 25 TXT CD 2 tracks 19, 20 • Acts. 24, 26 25 min	**Assess:** *Para y piensa* p. 140 5 min **Homework:** *Cuaderno* pp. 80–84 @HomeTutor
DAY 4	**Reading:** My favorite class • Warm Up OHT 23 • Check Homework 5 min	**Lectura cultural** pp. 142–143 • *Mi clase favorita* TXT CD 2 track 21 15 min	**Lectura cultural** pp. 142–143 • *Mi clase favorita* 15 min	**Assess:** *Para y piensa* p. 143 5 min
	Review: Lesson Review 5 min	**Repaso de la lección** pp. 146–147 15 min	**Repaso de la lección** pp. 146–147 • Act. 1 TXT CD 2 track 22 • Acts. 2, 3, 4, 5 25 min	**Assess:** *Repaso de la lección* pp. 146–147 5 min **Homework:** *En resumen* p. 145, *Cuaderno* pp. 85–96 Review Games Online @HomeTutor
DAY 5	**Assessment**			**Assess:** Lesson 2 Test or Unit 2 Test 45 min
	Unit Culmination 5 min	**Comparación cultural** pp. 148–149 TXT CD 2 track 23 **Repaso inclusivo** pp. 150–151 10 min	**Comparación cultural** pp. 148–149 **Repaso inclusivo** pp. 150–151 • Act. 1 TXT CD 2 track 24 • Acts. 2, 3, 4, 5, 6 30 min	

Objectives

- Introduce lesson theme: **En la escuela.**
- **Culture:** Discuss different school systems in the Spanish-speaking world.

Presentation Strategies

- Introduce characters' names: Pablo and Claudia.
- Ask students to look at the photo on pp. 120–121.
- Have students talk about their school and their classes.
- Have students make a list of things in their classroom.

 STANDARDS

1.3 Present information
4.2 Compare cultures

Warm Up UTB 2 Transparency 20

-ar Verbs Write the form of **mirar** for each subject.

1. nosotros	5. Juan y Nicolás
2. Carla	6. tú
3. yo	7. María y yo
4. ustedes	8. usted

Answers: 1. miramos; 2. mira; 3. miro; 4. miran; 5. miran; 6. miras; 7. miramos; 8. mira

---

Comparación cultural

Exploring the Theme

Ask students the following:

1. Are all schools in the United States on the same yearly schedule?
2. School breaks are often set around important holidays. Why do you think schools in Mexico do not have a break at the end of November as we do?
3. Schools south of the equator, such as those in Chile and Argentina, are in session June through August while U.S. students are enjoying summer vacation. Why do you think this is so?

¿Qué ves? Possible answers include:
- Sí, hay una escuela en la foto.
- Pablo dibuja.
- Las chicas practican fútbol.

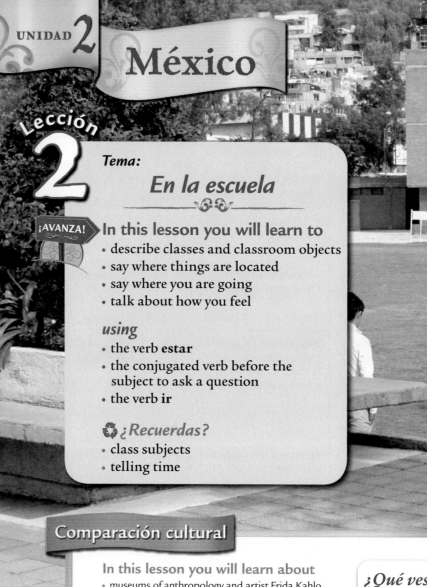

UNIDAD 2
México

Lección 2

Tema:
En la escuela

¡AVANZA! **In this lesson you will learn to**
- describe classes and classroom objects
- say where things are located
- say where you are going
- talk about how you feel

using
- the verb **estar**
- the conjugated verb before the subject to ask a question
- the verb **ir**

♻ *¿Recuerdas?*
- class subjects
- telling time

Comparación cultural

In this lesson you will learn about
- museums of anthropology and artist Frida Kahlo
- schools in Mexico, the Dominican Republic, and Paraguay
- Huichol yarn painting and Taino rock art

Compara con tu mundo

School years vary from country to country. Mexican students go to school from the end of August until June, with short breaks in December and April. *How is this different or similar to your school year?*

¿Qué ves?

Mira la foto

¿Hay una escuela en la foto?

¿Pablo dibuja o escucha música?

¿Qué practican las chicas?

120 ciento veinte

Differentiating Instruction

Multiple Intelligences

Visual Learners Have students work in small groups to create a floor plan of their ideal school. What would the school have both outside and inside? As students learn vocabulary related to school items and places, have them label the objects and rooms in their floor plan. Encourage students to use vocabulary from previous lessons where applicable.

Pre-AP

Communicate Preferences Discuss with students the information presented in the Comparación cultural. Ask them to discuss some of the advantages and disadvantages of different school year models.

Online SPANISH CLASSZONE.COM

Featuring...
Cultura INTERACTIVA
Animated Grammar
@HomeTutor

And more...
• Get Help Online
• Interactive Flashcards
• Review Games
• WebQuest
• Self-Check Quiz

El patio de una escuela secundaria
México

México
ciento veintiuno **121**

Online SPANISH CLASSZONE.COM

Animated Grammar This entertaining animated tutor helps students learn Spanish grammar in a fun and lively way. Verbs are conjugated before students' eyes, and direct and indirect object pronouns pop into place! Animated characters walk students through every explanation, adding a special zing to Spanish grammar that students won't forget!

Featuring...
Cultura INTERACTIVA
Animated Grammar
@HomeTutor

And more...
• Get Help Online
• Interactive Flashcards
• Review Games
• WebQuest
• Self-Check Quiz

Using the Photo

Location Information

The School Yard Recess areas are usually very big in schools not only in Mexico, but in all of Latin America.

Expanded Information

Recess In Mexico, recess lasts approximately thirty minutes. During this time students are permitted to buy refreshments, play a quick game of soccer, eat lunch together, or just sit around and relax.

Long-term Retention
Connect to Previous Learning

Read the following list of activities, and have students write **sí** if the activity is taking place in the photo, and **no** if it is not: **tocar la guitarra (no), hablar por teléfono (no), jugar al fútbol (sí), andar en patineta (no), hablar (sí), preparar la comida (no).**

Communication
TPR Activity

To ensure that students recognize and respond to words they've learned, play Simon Says by saying **abran el libro, cierren el libro, levanten la mano,** etc. If one or more students cannot respond to one command, repeat it and model the action.

Differentiating Instruction

Inclusion

Frequent Review/Repetition Have students create a list of words and phrases they already know that could be applied to the photo on pp. 120 and 121. Some examples might include **estudiantes atléticos, amigos,** or **fútbol.** After students finish, have them compare their lists with a partner and add any new words or phrases.

Heritage Language Learners

Support what they know Have students talk about the school year in their country of origin. What months are students in school? When are the breaks?

¡AVANZA! Objective
- Present vocabulary: classroom objects, places in school, and adjectives.

Core Resources
- Video Program: DVD 1
- Audio Program: TXT CD 2, track 12

Presentation Strategies
- Point to items in the classroom, say the word, and have students repeat after you.
- Play the audio as students read A–C.
- Show the video.

 STANDARDS
1.2 Understand language

Communication
Common Error Alert

If you have told your students that most nouns that end in **-a** are feminine, they may question the word **el mapa.** Explain to them that many Spanish words that are masculine and that end in **-a** are of Latin/Greek origin. Students should learn nouns with the correct article in order to learn the gender of the nouns.

Long-term Retention
 ### Recycle

Review adjectives by having students write the adjective that means the opposite of each adjective below.

1. cómico	6. desorganizada
2. mala	7. viejo
3. trabajadora	8. seria
4. pequeño	9. alta
5. bajo	

Answers: 1. serio; 2. buena; 3. perezosa; 4. grande; 5. alto; 6. organizada; 7. joven; 8. cómica; 9. baja

---

Presentación de VOCABULARIO

 ¡AVANZA! **Goal:** Learn about Pablo and Claudia's school and how they spend their day. Then practice what you have learned to talk about your school day. *Actividades 1–3*

 VIDEO DVD

 AUDIO

A La clase de historia no es **aburrida** porque la maestra es **interesante**. La clase es **divertida** pero es difícil. **Cuando** una clase no es fácil, tengo que trabajar mucho. Necesito sacar buenas notas.

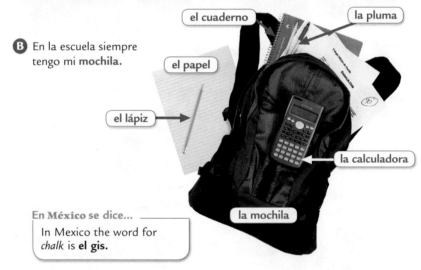

B En la escuela siempre tengo mi **mochila**.

En México se dice...
In Mexico the word for *chalk* is **el gis**.

122 Unidad 2 México
ciento veintidós

Differentiating Instruction

Heritage Language Learners

Regional Variations Ask students if they use any words different than those that appear on this page, but mean the same thing. For instance, in Argentina a pen is **la lapicera** and in Venezuela and Peru is **el lapicero**. A student's desk in Venezuela and Argentina is referred to as **el pupitre**. Remind students that many words are said differently in some countries, but they all have the same meaning.

Slower-paced Learners

Yes/No Questions Assess students' understanding of new vocabulary by walking around the room pointing at classroom items and asking **Sí/No** questions. For example: **¿Es un escritorio? Sí, es un escritorio. ¿Es el pizarrón? No, no es el pizarrón.** Put labels on classroom items to increase retention.

C Mi escuela es grande. Hay **una cafetería**, **un gimnasio** y **una biblioteca**.

la cafetería

el gimnasio

la biblioteca

los baños

el pasillo

la oficina del director

Más vocabulario

¿(A)dónde?	*(To) Where?*	ocupado(a)	*busy*
¿Cuándo?	*When?*	el problema	*problem*
deprimido(a)	*depressed*	la puerta	*door*
emocionado(a)	*excited*		

Expansión de vocabulario p. R3

Continuará...

Differentiating Instruction

Inclusion

Multisensory Input/Output Collect examples of the school supplies shown on p. 122. Pass the items out to students, and then ask questions regarding who has what. Instruct students to hold their item up as they answer. **¿Quién tiene la pluma? Yo tengo la pluma.** After a few rounds, have students switch items. Then allow students to ask, as well as answer, the questions.

Multiple Intelligences

Visual Learners Have students draw a plan of the layout of the school showing the rooms on p. 123. Provide them with vocabulary for the following: **el laboratorio** (lab), **el auditorio** (auditorium), **el estudio** (art studio). Ask them to create icons to identify each room and to include labels for each room. Students will present their plans to the class.

TEACHER to TEACHER
Jorge Dominguez
Valley Stream, New York

Tips for Presenting Vocabulary

To present classroom vocabulary, I prepare in advance a transparency of two classrooms (labeled A and B) that are similar except for five or six details. I call on students to identify the objects that are similar and different in both pictures. For example: En el dibujo A y en el dibujo B hay un mapa. En el dibujo A hay dos ventanas, pero en el dibujo B hay una ventana. *These pictures can also be used later to practice prepositions of location. For example:* En el dibujo A el mapa está al lado de la ventana, pero en el dibujo B el mapa está debajo del reloj.

Communication
TPR Activity

Write the names of different areas of your school (in English) on construction paper and place them around your classroom. Include places such as the hallway, the principal's office, the library, the cafeteria, the restrooms, and the gymnasium. Go to each sign and say the name of each area in Spanish. Select six students and have them go to each place as you give the command in Spanish. For example: **Cindy, ve al gimnasio. Jason, ve a la cafetería,** etc. Choose a different group and make the sentences more difficult. For example: **Rolanda, ve a la biblioteca para leer un libro. Matt, ve al gimnasio para la clase de educación física.**

Long-term Retention
Study Tips

Have students prepare index cards with a picture of a school item on one side and the corresponding vocabulary word on the reverse side. Students can use the flashcards to test one another.

123

Objective

· Present vocabulary: adjectives.

Core Resources

· Video Program: DVD 1
· Audio Program: TXT CD 2 tracks 12, 13

Presentation Strategies

· Say the adjectives on page 124 and have students repeat them after you. Encourage them to use appropriate gestures and facial expressions.
· Play the audio and show the video.

 STANDARDS

1.2 Understand language

 Communication
TPR Activity

Call students to the front and give them a situation where they have to act out the words **cansado(a), emocionado(a), nervioso(a), contento(a), ocupado(a), enojado(a), triste, tranquilo(a).** For example, **Hay un examen muy difícil de ciencias mañana.** Students act out the word **nervioso(a).** The class guesses the word.

D Me gusta pasar un rato con Claudia en la biblioteca. Claudia usa la computadora pero yo tengo que estudiar.

 cansado(a)

 nervioso(a)

 contento(a)

  enojado(a)

 triste

 tranquilo(a)

¡A responder! Escuchar *Text CD 2, track 13*

Listen to the list of adjectives and draw a face representing each one.

@HomeTutor VideoPlus
Interactive Flashcards ClassZone.com

Differentiating Instruction

Multiple Intelligences

Kinesthetic Copy the names of rooms and emotion words onto index cards. Then invite a volunteer to choose one card to act out for the group. If it is a room in the school, the student might show the actions that people do there. If it is an emotion, the student can use facial expressions and gestures. The rest of the group must guess the word being portrayed.

Pre-AP

Relate Opinions Have students interview their classmates about how they feel in each class. Suggest that they use the words **cansado(a), emocionado(a), nervioso(a), contento(a), ocupado(a), enojado(a), triste, tranquilo(a)** as categories in their poll. Have them present the results in chart form, with the adjectives on the left and the names of classes on top.

 Answers MSRB Transparency 40

¡A responder! Students will draw faces representing the following adjectives:
1. angry
2. nervous
3. tired
4. happy
5. depressed
6. excited
7. calm

124

Práctica de VOCABULARIO

1 | Para la escuela

Hablar
Escribir

What do they have at Tienda Martínez? Name the items.

PARA LA ESCUELA...

250 pesos
3 pesos
5 por 30 pesos
2 por 80 pesos
300 pesos
5 por 10 pesos

Tenemos todo para tus clases en
TIENDA MARTÍNEZ
Avenida Hermanos Soriano 80, Puebla, México

Expansión:
Teacher Edition Only
Have students list other items with their prices that could be sold in Tienda Martínez.

2 | ¿Qué lugar es?

Leer
Escribir

Claudia is talking about various places in the school. Complete the sentences with the appropriate place words.

biblioteca   gimnasio   oficina del director

cafetería   baños   clase

En el gimnasio hay dos __1.__, uno para chicas y uno para chicos. Tenemos que correr y practicar deportes en el __2.__. Hay muchos libros en la __3.__. Nos gusta comer pizza y pasar un rato con los amigos en la __4.__. Hablamos con el director en la __5.__. Hay escritorios y pizarrones en la __6.__.

Expansión:
Teacher Edition Only
Have students pick a place word and write an additional sentence for it.

3 | ¿Cuántos hay en la clase?

Hablar

Talk with another student about objects in the classroom.

puerta   ventana   mapa   pizarrón

tiza   escritorio   reloj   ¿?

modelo: mapa

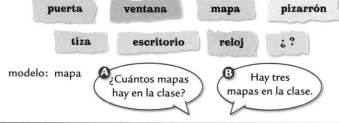

A ¿Cuántos mapas hay en la clase?

B Hay tres mapas en la clase.

Expansión:
Teacher Edition Only
Have students tell what objects aren't in your classroom.

Más práctica   Cuaderno *pp. 74–76*   Cuaderno para hispanohablantes *pp. 74–77*

PARA Y PIENSA

Did you get it?
1. Name three rooms in your school.
2. Name three objects you could find in your classroom.

Get Help Online
ClassZone.com

Differentiating Instruction

Multiple Intelligences

Logical/Mathematical For Activity 1, assign students the roles of client and salesclerk at Tienda Martínez. The client asks for several of each item and the salesclerk tells how much the total cost is. Provide students with the following sample dialogue: **Necesito seis lápices./18 pesos, por favor.**

Heritage Language Learners

Writing Skills Have students write a paragraph about a particular class and classroom in as much detail as possible. They should include the time the class takes place, the subject, the items found in the classroom, the number of students, what the class is like, what the teacher is like, and why they like or don't like that class. Make sure they use correct spelling, grammar, and punctuation.

Objective
· Practice vocabulary: classroom objects and places in school.

Core Resource
· *Cuaderno,* pp. 74-76

Practice Sequence
· **Activity 1:** Vocabulary recognition: classroom objects
· **Activity 2:** Vocabulary recognition: places in school
· **Activity 3:** Vocabulary production: classroom objects

STANDARDS

1.1 Engage in conversation, Act. 3
1.3 Present information, Acts. 1–3, PYP

Communication
Common Error Alert

Before doing Activity 1, remind students that the plural of **lápiz** is **lápices.** Explain that the word **por** is used here to express how much for something: **5 plumas por 30 pesos.**

✓ Ongoing Assessment

@HomeTutor
More Practice
ClassZone.com

PARA Y PIENSA **Peer Assessment** Have students share their answers with a partner without looking at the textbook. Partners will listen to see if they can understand. They will then reverse roles. For additional practice, use Reteaching & Practice Copymasters URB 2, pp. 11, 12.

Answers   MSRB Transparency 40

Activity 1
los lápices; la calculadora; los cuadernos; los borradores; la mochila; las plumas

Activity 2
1. baños   4. cafetería
2. gimnasio   5. oficina del director
3. biblioteca   6. clase

Activity 3 Answers will vary. Answers should follow format:
A ¿Cuántos/Cuántas... hay en la clase? B Hay... en la clase.

Para y piensa Answers will vary. Sample answers include:
1. la cafetería, la oficina del director, la clase
2. el escritorio, el lápiz, el cuaderno

¡AVANZA! Objective

- Understand vocabulary in context: classroom objects and places in school.

Core Resources

- Video Program: DVD 1
- Audio Program: TXT CD 2, track 14

Presentation Strategies

- Have students skim the Telehistoria and identify uses of exclamation points in Spanish.
- Show the video with books open, then with books closed.
- Play audio while students follow the script in the text.

Practice Sequence

- **Activity 4:** Telehistoria comprehension
- **Activity 5:** Vocabulary production: descriptive adjectives; Recycle: class subjects

STANDARDS

1.1 Engage in conversation, Act. 5
1.2 Understand language, Act. 4
1.3 Present information, Act. 5, PYP

Warm Up UTB 2 Transparency 20

Vocabulary Complete the sentences with a correct word from the list below.

biblioteca tiza mochila aburrida cafetería

1. Necesito una ＿＿＿ para escribir en el pizarrón.
2. No me gusta comer en la ＿＿＿.
3. Hay muchos libros en la ＿＿＿.
4. La clase de historia no es divertida, es ＿＿＿.
5. Tengo tres cuadernos en mi ＿＿＿.

Answers: 1. tiza; 2. cafetería; 3. biblioteca; 4. aburrida; 5. mochila

Video Summary

@HomeTutor VideoPlus ClassZone.com

Pablo and Claudia plan to go to the school's gym to see Trini Salgado. In science class, the teacher sends Pablo to the board to solve a problem, but he gets it wrong. After class, Claudia suggests that they go to the library to study and do homework. Pablo agrees. He notices that she doesn't have her backpack.

▶ ‖

126

VOCABULARIO *en contexto*

Goal: Identify the words Pablo and Claudia use to talk about what they do after school. Then use the words you have learned to describe classes and classroom objects. *Actividades 4–5*

♻ *¿Recuerdas?* Class subjects p. 95

Telehistoria escena 1

@HomeTutor VideoPlus ClassZone.com

STRATEGIES

Cuando lees

Look for exclamations Many sentences below are exclamations. Exclamations reveal emphasis, warning, or emotions. How many exclamation-type sentences can you find? Why is each one used?

Cuando escuchas

Listen for emotions What different emotions do Claudia and Pablo show? How do they express them? How would you feel in their place?

 VIDEO DVD

 AUDIO

A poster announces Trini Salgado's guest appearance in the school gym.

Maestro: Trini Salgado, ¿eh? ¿Y vas tú al gimnasio?

Pablo: ¡Sí!

Maestro: ¡Muy divertido! *(later on in science class...)* ¿Quién contesta la pregunta? ¿Pablo? Bueno, ¡al pizarrón!

Pablo tries, but gets the problem wrong. Claudia goes to the board and corrects it. The bell rings and they leave class together.

Claudia: Pablo, ¿vamos a la biblioteca? Estudiamos, hacemos la tarea y llegamos bien al gimnasio... ¡Trini Salgado, Pablo!

Pablo: ¡Sí! Necesito estudiar, ¡y tú enseñas muy bien! ¿Y tu mochila? *(He points to her backpack, which she has left in the classroom.)*

Claudia: ¡Gracias, Pablo!   Continuará... p. 132

También se dice

México The teacher uses the word **pizarrón** to call Pablo to the board. In other Spanish-speaking countries you might hear:
- **muchos países** la pizarra

Differentiating Instruction

Slower-paced Learners

Read Before Listening Before listening to the Telehistoria, have students preview the text silently. Instruct them to copy any unfamiliar words onto a separate piece of paper. Then have them refer to pp. 122–124 to review the meanings of the words on their list.

Heritage Language Learners

Writing Skills Have students draft their own versions of a short conversation between a teacher and two friends at school. Point out to students the punctuation that is used in the Telehistoria to indicate exclamations and questions. Advise students to proofread their own scripts for correct punctuation.

4 En clase *Comprensión del episodio*

Escuchar
Leer

Describe what happens in the episode by matching phrases from each column.

1. Pablo no contesta la pregunta
2. Después de Pablo, Claudia contesta
3. Pablo y Claudia necesitan ir
4. Pablo necesita
5. Claudia no tiene
6. Claudia enseña

a. la pregunta en el pizarrón.
b. la mochila.
c. estudiar con Claudia.
d. a la biblioteca y al gimnasio.
e. porque el problema es difícil.
f. muy bien.

Expansión:
Teacher Edition Only
Have students take turns reading aloud the complete sentences they formed.

5 ¿Cómo son las clases?

¿Recuerdas? Class subjects p. 95

Hablar Describe your classes to another student.

A ¿Cómo es la clase de español?

B Es divertida y fácil.

1.
2.
3.
4.
5.
6.

Expansión:
Teacher Edition Only
Have students give reasons for two of their descriptions.

Did you get it? Tell where Pablo and Claudia are going by writing **la biblioteca** or **el gimnasio**.
1. Pablo y Claudia tienen que estudiar.
2. Pablo necesita practicar fútbol.
3. Ellos necesitan un libro.

Get Help Online ClassZone.com

Lección 2
ciento veintisiete **127**

Differentiating Instruction

Slower-paced Learners

Sentence Completion Before students attempt Activity 5, write the following sentence on the board. **La clase de _____ es _____.** Ask students to list as many possibilities as they can for each of the blanks. Record these words underneath each blank. Then have students use this information as they converse during Activity 5.

Pre-AP

Expand and Elaborate As students talk about their classes in Activity 5, encourage them to follow up each statement with an explanation to support their statement. **La clase de ciencias es difícil. Tenemos muchos exámenes. Muchos estudiantes sacan malas notas.**

Personalize It

Ask students to write sentences describing the classroom, using numbers or prepositions of location. For example, their sentences may be: **Hay un mapa al lado de la puerta. Hay un pizarrón cerca de la ventana. Hay veinticinco escritorios.**

Communication
Pair Work

Have pairs of students take turns making statements and answering with the name of the person from the Telehistoria to which the statement applies.

✓ **Ongoing Assessment**
@HomeTutor
More Practice ClassZone.com

PARA Y PIENSA **Quick Check** Ask students to write other activities that can be done in the library and the gym. For additional practice, use Reteaching & Practice Copymasters URB 2, pp. 11, 13, 20.

Answers MSRB Transparency 40

Activity 4
1. e; 2. a; 3. d; 4. c; 5. b; 6. f
Activity 5 Answers should follow this format:
A. ¿Cómo es la clase de + class?
B. Es + descriptive adjectives.
Para y piensa
1. la biblioteca; 2. el gimnasio; 3. la biblioteca

128

 Objective

· Present the uses of the verb **estar**.

Core Resource

· *Cuaderno,* pp. 77–79

Presentation Strategies

· Explain the different uses of the verb **estar**.
· Remind students that in Spanish adjectives need to agree in gender and number with the nouns they describe.

 STANDARDS

4.1 Compare languages

 Warm Up UTB 2 Transparency 21

Vocabulary Write the location where each activity would take place:

1. practicar deportes
2. comer pizza y hablar con amigos
3. hablar con el director de la escuela
4. hacer la tarea o leer un libro

Answers: 1. el gimnasio; 2. la cafetería; 3. la oficina del director; 4. la biblioteca

Communication

Common Error Alert

The inclusion of the accent mark over the **a** in **estás, está,** and **están** is very important. The accent marks change the pronunciation of the words but in the case of **estás** and **está**, they also change the meaning. **Estas** means *these* and **esta** means *this*.

Comparisons

English Grammar Connection

Remind students that there are words that combine to form contractions in English; for example, *is + not → isn't*. English contractions use apostrophes.

Communication

Common Error Alert

Point out that **estar** is conjugated like other **-ar** verbs except for the **yo** form (**estoy**) and the accents on most of the other forms.

Presentación de GRAMÁTICA

 ¡AVANZA! **Goal:** Learn to use the verb **estar** to talk about location and condition. Then practice using **estar** to say and ask where things are located and how people feel. *Actividades 6–12*

English Grammar Connection: There are two ways to say the English verb *to be* in Spanish: **ser** and **estar**. You already learned **ser** (see p. 38).

The Verb estar

Animated Grammar
ClassZone.com

Use **estar** to indicate location and say how people feel.

Here's how:

estar *to be*			
yo	estoy	nosotros(as)	estamos
tú	estás	vosotros(as)	estáis
usted, él, ella	está	ustedes, ellos(as)	están

Pedro **está** en la cafetería.   *Pedro is in the cafeteria.*

Use **estar** with the following words of location.

al lado (de)	debajo (de)	dentro (de)	encima (de)
cerca (de)	delante (de)	detrás (de)	lejos (de)

Use the word **de** after the location word when a specific location is mentioned. When **de** is followed by the word **el**, they combine to form the contraction **del**.

La biblioteca **está al lado** de la cafetería.   La tiza **está encima del** borrador.
The library is next to the cafeteria.   *The chalk is on top of the eraser.*

Estar is also used with **adjectives** to say how someone feels at a given moment.

El maestro **está tranquilo.**   Las chicas **están cansadas.**
The teacher is calm.   *The girls are tired.*

♻ **¿Recuerdas?** Adjectives agree in gender and number with the nouns they describe (see p. 72).

Más práctica
Cuaderno *pp. 77–79*
Cuaderno para hispanohablantes *pp. 78–80*

@HomeTutor
Leveled Grammar Practice
ClassZone.com

Differentiating Instruction

Inclusion

Metacognitive Support Write the following sentences on the board. You can add additional examples as well. **Claudia _____ de Argentina. Pablo _____ nervioso. La clase _____ fácil. Mi pluma _____ en mi mochila.** Then ask students to identify whether each sentence calls for the verb **ser** or the verb **estar,** and to explain why.

Multiple Intelligences

Kinesthetic Help students practice words of location by playing this game. Each student will need a pen. Place a pen on top of a desk, and ask: **¿Dónde está la pluma?** Have students copy your action as they respond: **La pluma está encima del escritorio.** Change the relationship of the pen to the desk each time you ask the question.

Práctica de GRAMÁTICA

6 ¿Dónde están?

Hablar
Escribir

Tell where the people are, according to Pablo.

modelo: el señor Díaz
El señor Díaz está en la oficina.

1. ustedes

2. yo

3. Miguel y Alejo

4. Sergio

5. Claudia y yo

6. Cristina y Sarita

Expansión:
Teacher Edition Only
Ask students to choose two places and name something they would find in each.

7 El horario

Hablar
Escribir

Indicate the most logical place at school for each person to be.

modelo: Víctor llega a la escuela.
Está en el pasillo.

1. Carlos y Juan dibujan.

2. Maya habla español.

3. Yo toco la guitarra.

4. Nosotros compramos la comida.

5. Luz practica deportes.

6. Tú necesitas muchos libros.

7. Ustedes usan la calculadora.

8. El maestro habla con el director.

Expansión:
Teacher Edition Only
Have students write other clues for four of the places.

Lección 2
ciento veintinueve **129**

Differentiating Instruction

Pre-AP

Expand and Elaborate Encourage students to elaborate on their sentences in Activity 6. After expressing where each person is, have students describe that person's personality, activity, or emotion. **El señor Díaz está en la oficina. Es trabajador.**

Slower-paced Learners

Yes/No Questions Help students with Activity 7 by asking them yes/no questions about logical places for each activity. As you read each statement, use gestures to help students figure out the meaning. For example, pretend you are strumming a guitar as you say **Yo toco la guitarra.** Then ask, **¿Estoy en la clase de música?**

Objectives

- Practice using **estar**.
- Practice using vocabulary for places in school.
- Practice using prepositions of place and vocabulary.

Practice Sequence

- **Activity 6:** Controlled practice: **estar**
- **Activity 7:** Controlled practice: **estar**

STANDARDS

1.3 Present information, Acts. 6–7

Long-term Retention
Recycle

Write a list of times during the school day on the board. Ask students to say the time in Spanish and then say where they are on a typical day at that time. For example: **12:00 A las doce estoy en la cafetería. 3:00 A las tres estoy en el gimnasio.**

Communication
Pair Work

Ask students to create a list of activities. Exchange lists with a partner and have each person tell how he or she feels doing each activity.

Answers MSRB Transparency 40

Activity 6
1. Ustedes están en el gimnasio.
2. Yo estoy en la clase de ciencias.
3. Miguel y Alejo están en el pasillo.
4. Sergio está en el baño.
5. Claudia y yo estamos en la biblioteca.
6. Cristina y Sarita están en la cafetería.

Activity 7
1. Están en la clase de arte.
2. Está en la clase de español.
3. Estoy en la clase de música.
4. Estamos en la cafetería.
5. Está en el gimnasio.
6. Estás en la biblioteca.
7. Están en la clase de matemáticas.
8. Está en la oficina del director.

129

Objectives
· Practice using adjectives to describe feelings.
· **Culture:** artifacts and their impact.
· Practice using prepositions of place.

Core Resource
· *Cuaderno,* pp. 77–79

Practice Sequence
· **Activity 8:** Transitional practice: feelings, **estar**
· **Activities 9, 10:** Transitional practice: **estar** and prepositions of location
· **Activity 11:** Transitional practice: **estar,** feelings
· **Activity 12:** Open-ended practice: **estar** and prepositions of location

STANDARDS
1.1 Engage in conversation, Acts. 8, 9, 12
1.3 Present information, Acts. 8–12, PYP
3.1 Knowledge of other disciplines, Act. 9
4.2 Compare cultures, Act. 9

Nota gramatical

Expanded Presentation When inverting the subject and verb to form a question, the subject may come immediately after the verb or at the end of the question. This is especially true when the subject contains more than one word. For example: **¿Tiene una mochila la chica pelirroja?**

Comparison
English Language Connection

English speakers add words like *do* and *does* when asking questions. Spanish speakers do not. For example: *Does Juana have a pencil?* **¿Tiene Juana un lápiz?**

Comparación cultural

Essential Question
Suggested Answer Often artifacts show whether a society was agrarian based or depended on hunting for survival. Artifacts can also show how people constructed their homes and measured time.

See Activity answers on p. 131.

130

Nota gramatical
You already know that you can use rising intonation to ask a yes/no question. You can also switch the position of the **verb** and the **subject** to form a question.

María tiene una patineta.   **¿Tiene María** una patineta?
María has a skateboard.   *Does María have a skateboard?*

8 | Las emociones

Hablar
Talk with another student about how these people are feeling.

modelo: el maestro / nervioso(a)
el maestro 🙂

A ¿Está nervioso el maestro?
B No, está tranquilo.

Estudiante A
1. Pablo / tranquilo(a)
2. Claudia / triste
3. los maestros / cansado(a)
4. los amigos / enojado(a)
5. las amigas / emocionado(a)
6. tú / ocupado(a)

Pablo 😳
Claudia 🙁
los maestros 😔
los amigos 😠
las amigas 🙁
yo ¿ ?

Expansión:
Teacher Edition Only
Have students come up with two additional questions and answers about people they know.

9 | Las salas del museo

Hablar
Comparación cultural

El museo de antropología
What do ancient artifacts teach us about a culture? The National Museum of Anthropology in Mexico City contains artifacts from **Mexico's** many indigenous cultures. A main attraction is the *Piedra del Sol,* or Sun Stone, an Aztec calendar that weighs almost 25 tons. In **Paraguay,** the Andrés Barbero Museum of Ethnography in Asunción contains tools, musical instruments, and artwork from its indigenous cultures.

Compara con tu mundo
What items might people find 1,000 years from now that give clues about life in the 21st century? What would you put in a time capsule?

Use the map to tell a partner where the rooms are located in the museum.

A ¿Dónde está la Sala Tolteca?
B La Sala Tolteca está al lado de la Sala Teotihuacán.

Piedra del Sol
El Museo Nacional de Antropología

1. Sala Mexica (Azteca)
2. el patio central
3. la oficina
4. Sala Norte de México
5. Sala Maya
6. Sala Oaxaca
7. Sala Tolteca
8. Sala Teotihuacán
9. Sala Preclásico
10. Sala de Introducción a la Antropología
11. el auditorio

Un plano de El Museo Nacional de Antropología en la Ciudad

Expansión:
Teacher Edition Only
Have students writ[...] sentences using a subject, a form of **estar**, and a room in the museum.

Unidad 2 México
130 ciento treinta

Differentiating Instruction

Inclusion
Synthetic/Analytic Support Write the following words on index cards: **Pablo, está,** and **contento.** Discuss with students which of these words is a noun, verb, and adjective. Then color-code the cards by shading each with a different colored highlighter. Display the cards in the order to form a question. **¿Está contento Pablo?** Then ask for a volunteer to come change the order to create an answer. Repeat with other examples.

Heritage Language Learners
Literacy Skills Brainstorm with students a list of things they would be interested in learning about an ancient culture. Some topics might include food, clothing, tools, and music. Then have students choose one ancient culture to research, such as the Aztec or Maya. Give them the opportunity to report to the group what they learned about each topic.

10 | ¿Lejos de la escuela?

Escribir

Rewrite the statements below to say that the opposite is true.

1. Nosotros estamos lejos de la escuela.
2. El cuaderno está detrás de la silla.
3. El libro está debajo del escritorio.
4. Los lápices están delante de la mochila.
5. Yo estoy cerca de la biblioteca.
6. La pluma está encima del papel.

Expansión:
Teacher Edition Only
Ask students to give a sentence about the position of an object and have a partner say that the opposite is true.

11 | ¿Cómo estás?

Hablar
Escribir

Describe how you feel in the following situations.

modelo: hablar español
Estoy nerviosa cuando hablo español.

1. pasar un rato con los amigos
2. tener que hacer la tarea
3. sacar una mala nota
4. llegar tarde a clase
5. sacar una buena nota
6. escuchar música
7. mirar la televisión
8. tener un examen
9. practicar deportes
10. estudiar mucho

Expansión:
Teacher Edition Only
Have students write three sentences about when they feel nervous, happy, and angry.

12 | ¿Qué es?

Hablar

Give clues about an object in the drawing to another student. He or she has to guess the object.

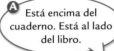
A — Está encima del cuaderno. Está al lado del libro.

B — Es la calculadora.

Expansión:
Teacher Edition Only
Have students give clues to a partner about objects in the classroom.

Más práctica   Cuaderno *pp. 77–79*   Cuaderno para hispanohablantes *pp. 78–80*

PARA Y PIENSA

Did you get it? 1. Tell someone that you are near the windows.
2. Ask Pablo if he is nervous.

Get Help Online ClassZone.com

✓ **Ongoing Assessment**   @HomeTutor More Practice ClassZone.com

PARA Y PIENSA   **Peer Assessment** Ask students to write the answers to Para y piensa, exchange them with a partner, and check each other's work. For additional practice, use Reteaching & Practice Copymasters URB 2, pp. 14, 15.

Answers MSRB Transparency 41

Answers for Activities on pp. 130, 131.

Activity 8
1. ¿Está tranquilo Pablo? No, está nervioso.
2. ¿Está triste Claudia? Sí, está triste.
3. ¿Están cansados los maestros? Sí, están cansados.
4. ¿Están enojados los amigos? Sí, están enojados.
5. ¿Están emocionadas las amigas? No, están tristes.
6. ¿Estás ocupado(a) tú? Sí, yo estoy ocupado(a) or No, yo estoy (will vary).

Activity 9 Answers should follow this format:
¿Dónde está + room?
La/El + room + está + location + room.

Activity 10
1. Nosotros estamos cerca de la escuela.
2. El cuaderno está delante de la silla.
3. El libro está encima del escritorio.
4. Los lápices están detrás de la mochila.
5. Yo estoy lejos de la biblioteca.
6. La pluma está debajo del papel.

Activity 11 Answers will vary. Answers may include:
1. Estoy contento(a) cuando paso un rato con los amigos.
2. Estoy deprimido(a) cuando tengo que hacer la tarea.
3. Estoy triste cuando saco una mala nota.
4. Estoy nervioso(a) cuando llego tarde a clase.
5. Estoy emocionado(a) cuando saco una buena nota.
6. Estoy contento(a) cuando escucho música.
7. Estoy tranquilo(a) cuando miro la televisión.
8. Estoy nervioso(a) cuando tengo un examen.
9. Estoy contento(a) cuando practico deportes.
10. Estoy cansado(a) cuando estudio mucho.

Activity 12 Answers will vary. Sample answers include:
Está detrás del escritorio. Está detrás de la silla.
Es el pizarrón.

Para y piensa
1. Estoy cerca de las ventanas.
2. ¿Estás nervioso, Pablo?

Differentiating Instruction

Slower-paced Learners

Memory Aids To help students with Activity 11, create on the board a concept web around the word **estoy.** Then brainstorm adjectives that can be applied to describe how they are feeling in a particular situation. They might think of **contento, deprimido, triste, ocupado, nervioso, cansado,** and so on. Remind them of the feminine forms of these adjectives.

Multiple Intelligences

Intrapersonal Provide students with the following situations:

· **Cuando saco una mala nota...**
· **Cuando tengo un examen...**
· **Cuando paso un rato con los amigos...**

You can add additional examples as well. Ask students to reflect on how they feel in each of the situations presented. Students might record their responses in their journals.

¡AVANZA! **Goal:** Listen to how Pablo and Claudia use **estar** to talk about how Pablo feels. Then practice using **estar** to talk about emotions and locations. *Actividades 13–15*

¡AVANZA! Objective

· Practice **estar** in context.

Core Resources

· Video Program: DVD 1
· Audio Program: TXT CD 2, track 15

Presentation Strategies

· Ask students to describe the photo by asking quick comprehension questions.
· Have students read the script.
· Show the video and/or play the audio.

Practice Sequence

· **Activity 13:** Telehistoria comprehension
· **Activity 14:** Transitional practice: **estar** and emotions
· **Activity 15:** Open-ended practice: **estar** and places in school

✿ STANDARDS

1.1 Engage in conversation, Acts. 14–15
1.2 Understand language, Act. 13
1.3 Present information, Acts. 14–15, PYP

Telehistoria escena 2

@HomeTutor VideoPlus
ClassZone.com

STRATEGIES

Cuando lees 📖
Read for motives behind actions
This scene contains a physical action related to Pablo's complaints. What is the action, and what are his complaints? Are his complaints justified?

Cuando escuchas 🎧
Listen for feelings What feelings are mentioned in this scene? How does Pablo explain how he feels? Have you ever felt this way?

VIDEO DVD

AUDIO

Claudia: Eh, Pablo, ¿qué pasa? ¿Estás deprimido? ¿Estás enojado?

Pablo: No, no estoy enojado... Estoy nervioso... Tengo que estar en el gimnasio a las cinco pero tengo que hacer la tarea.

Pablo leaves the library. Later Claudia joins him outside.

Pablo: Ay, Claudia, nunca descanso... Me gusta pasar un rato con los amigos... Y ¡esta mochila!

Claudia: ¿Qué pasa?

Pablo starts swinging his backpack back and forth.

Pablo: Aquí tengo libros, cuadernos, plumas, calculadoras... ¡estoy cansado!

Suddenly Pablo lets go of his backpack.

Pablo: ¡Ay! ¿Dónde está mi mochila?

Claudia: ¡Pablo, tu mochila!

She points to his backpack, which is caught in a basketball hoop.

Continuará... p. 138

También se dice

México To say he has pens in his backpack, Pablo uses the word **plumas.** In other Spanish-speaking countries you might hear:
· **muchos países** el bolígrafo, el boli

✿ Warm Up UTB 2 Transparency 21

Estar and Words of Location Use the given pronoun and the location to write sentences with the correct form of the verb **estar:**

1. yo/biblioteca
2. tú/cafetería
3. nosotros/pasillo
4. él/cerca de la ventana

Answers: 1. Estoy en la biblioteca; 2. Estás en la cafetería; 3. Estamos en el pasillo; 4. Él está cerca de la ventana.

Video Summary

@HomeTutor VideoPlus ClassZone.com

Claudia asks Pablo if he is depressed or angry. He tells her he is nervous because he has to be at the gym at 5:00, but he also has to do homework. Later, Pablo complains that he never rests. He points out that his backpack is full of school supplies and begins to swing it back and forth. Pablo loses his grip on the backpack and it gets caught in a basketball net.

▶ ❚❚

Differentiating Instruction

Multiple Intelligences

Interpersonal Divide students into two groups. Assign one group the role of Claudia, and the other the role of Pablo. Have the groups read their assigned parts chorally. As they do, instruct students to exaggerate the emotions and facial expressions of their character. Then have groups switch roles.

Slower-paced Learners

Read Before Listening Direct students to preview the Telehistoria silently. Tell them their goal is to locate all of the emotion words used in the conversation. Have students copy these words onto a separate piece of paper. Then ask them to draw a face to represent the emotion of each word in their list.

13 | El problema de Pablo *Comprensión del episodio*

Escuchar
Leer

Read the sentences and decide whether they are true or false. Correct the false statements.

1. Claudia y Pablo están en la oficina.
2. Pablo está nervioso porque tiene que jugar al fútbol.
3. Claudia tiene que estar en el gimnasio a las cinco.
4. Pablo está enojado.
5. A Claudia y a Pablo les gusta pasar un rato con los amigos.
6. Pablo está deprimido porque tiene libros, cuadernos, plumas y calculadoras en la mochila.

Expansión:
Teacher Edition Only
Have students expand the activity by asking each other about other emotions.

14 | ¿Cuándo?

Hablar

Ask another student when he or she feels these emotions.

A ¿Cuándo estás triste?

B Estoy triste cuando saco una mala nota.

Estudiante A
1. 2.
3. 4.
5. 6.

Estudiante B
sacar una buena / mala nota
escuchar música
practicar deportes
trabajar
estudiar
¿ ?

Expansión:
Teacher Edition Only
Have students talk about their family's emotions when they get good grades and when they don't.

15 | ¡A jugar! ¿Dónde estoy?

Hablar

Give clues for other students to guess where you are in the school.

A Compro papas fritas y jugo. Paso un rato con los amigos. Estoy tranquilo.

B ¿Estás en la cafetería?

Expansión:
Teacher Edition Only
Have students describe where these places are located.

PARA Y PIENSA

Did you get it? Give three sentences about Pablo and Claudia using the verb **estar.** Use one of the following words in each sentence: **la biblioteca, nervioso(a), el gimnasio.**

Get Help Online
ClassZone.com

Lección 2
ciento treinta y tres **133**

Differentiating Instruction

Multiple Intelligences

Visual Learners Have students come up with additional emoticons. They can illustrate them and use a dictionary to help them translate the emotion into Spanish.

Heritage Language Learners

Support What They Know After students complete Activity 14, ask them to think about a specific time when they felt one of the emotions listed. Encourage students to share an anecdote about a time they felt sad, nervous, or angry. What was the situation, and why did it make them feel that way?

Communication

Interpersonal Mode

Play a simple memory game with each row of students by conjugating the verb **estar** + adjective of emotion. The first student in the row begins by saying, for example, **Estoy emocionado.** The second student says, **Él/Ella está emocionado(a).** The third student could say **Ustedes están emocionados,** the next one would say **Nosotros estamos emocionados,** and they continue until the present tense of the verb has been conjugated.

✓ Ongoing Assessment

@HomeTutor
More Practice
ClassZone.com

PARA Y PIENSA

Peer Assessment Allow students to work in pairs to correct each statement. For additional practice, use Reteaching & Practice Copymasters URB 2, pp. 14, 16.

Answers MSRB Transparency 41

Activity 13
1. Falsa: Pablo y Claudia están en la biblioteca.
2. Falsa: Pablo está nervioso porque tiene que estar en el gimnasio a las cinco pero tiene que hacer la tarea.
3. Falsa: Pablo tiene que estar en el gimnasio a las cinco.
4. Falsa: Pablo está nervioso.
5. Falsa: A Pablo le gusta pasar un rato con los amigos.
6. Falsa: Pablo está cansado porque tiene libros, cuadernos, plumas y calculadoras en la mochila.

Activity 14 Answers should follow this format:
A. ¿Cuándo estás + emotion?
B. Estoy + emotion + cuando + reason.

Activity 15 Answers will vary. Sample answers include:
A. Hay muchos libros. Estoy ocupado.
B. ¿Estás en la biblioteca?

Para y piensa Answers will vary. Sample answers include:
Claudia está en la biblioteca.
Pablo está nervioso.
Pablo tiene que estar en el gimnasio a las cinco.

¡AVANZA! **Objective**

· Present the verb **ir.**

Core Resource

· *Cuaderno,* pp. 80–82

Presentation Strategies

· Practice using **ir** by conjugating the verb as a class.
· Explain to students the use of the words **a** and **adónde** to say or ask where someone is going.

 STANDARDS

4.1 Compare languages

 Warm Up UTB 2 Transparency 22

Adjectives Look at the following emoticons below. Then write the corresponding emotion for each.

1. ☹
2. 😠
3. ☺
4. 😔

Answers: 1. triste; 2. enojado; 3. contento; 4. cansado

Comparisons
English Grammar Connection

Forms of **ir** can be translated as *go* or *am/is/are going,* depending upon the context of the conversation. Although **ir** looks nothing like **–ar** verbs, its forms are very similar. A helpful memorization technique is to learn the **yo** form—**voy**—and, for the rest of the forms, use the letter **v** + the regular **–ar** endings, except for the **vosotros** form, which has no accent.

Communication
Common Error Alert

In English, it is common to hear prepositions used at the end of questions and answers. *Where are you going to?* is very frequently heard. Spanish avoids this by combining the preposition **a** with **dónde** to create the word **adónde. Dónde** is used to ask where someone or something is; **adónde** is used to ask to where someone is going.

134

Presentación de GRAMÁTICA

 ¡AVANZA! **Goal:** Learn how to form the verb **ir** in order to say where you and others are going. Then practice using **ir** to say where you go during and after school. *Actividades 16–21*

English Grammar Connection: Remember that **conjugating** is changing the forms of a verb to indicate who is doing the action (see p. 100). In English, *to go* is conjugated as *I go, you go, he/she/it goes, we go, they go.*

Pablo **goes** to the cafeteria at twelve.

Pablo **va** a la cafetería a las doce.

conjugated verb	conjugated verb

The Verb ir

Animated Grammar
ClassZone.com

Use **ir** to talk about where someone is going. How do you form the present tense of this verb?

Here's how:

ir *to go*			
yo	voy	nosotros(as)	vamos
tú	vas	vosotros(as)	vais
usted, él, ella	va	ustedes, ellos(as)	van

Use **ir** with the word **a** to say that someone is going to a specific place. When **a** is followed by the word **el,** they combine to form the contraction **al.**

Voy a la biblioteca.
I'm going to the library.

Los estudiantes **van al** gimnasio.
The students are going to the gym.

To ask where someone is going, use ¿**adónde**...?

¿**Adónde** vas?
Where are you going?

Más práctica
Cuaderno *pp. 80–82*
Cuaderno para hispanohablantes *pp. 81–84*

@HomeTutor
Leveled Grammar Practice
ClassZone.com

Differentiating Instruction

Slower-paced Learners

Memory Aids Have students copy the forms of the verb **ir** onto an index card. Instruct them to write a capital *I* in the upper right hand corner of the card to indicate that **ir** is an *irregular* verb. Then have students add this card to their collection of verb cards. Have them add an *I* for irregular or *R* for regular to each verb card they have already created.

Pre-AP

Timed Answer Have pairs of students take turns reciting the conjugated verb forms as the partners call out the different subject pronouns. Partners can time themselves to see who can recite the conjugated forms the fastest.

Práctica de GRAMÁTICA

16 | ¿Un estudiante serio?

Leer
Escribir

Claudia and Pablo are talking at school. Complete their conversation with forms of **ir**.

Claudia: ¡Tengo mucha tarea en la clase de inglés! Yo __1.__ a la biblioteca... ¿ __2.__ tú y yo?

Pablo: No, yo no __3.__ a la biblioteca hoy.

Claudia: ¿No __4.__ tú a la biblioteca? ¡Tienes que hacer la tarea!

Pablo: Sí, pero necesito comprar pizza y un refresco. Mis amigos y yo __5.__ a la cafetería. Después yo __6.__ al gimnasio y ellos __7.__ a la clase de matemáticas.

Claudia: ¿ __8.__ Carlos al gimnasio?

Pablo: No, él __9.__ a la biblioteca.

Claudia: ¡Ay, Pablo! Tú también necesitas ir. ¿ __10.__ tú y Carlos mañana?

Pablo: Sí, todos nosotros __11.__ mañana.

> **Expansión:**
> Teacher Edition Only
> Have students write their own dialogue with forms of **ir**.

17 | ¿Por qué vas allí?

Escribir

Match the statements with the places the people would go. Then write a sentence saying that they are going to these places.

1. Claudia tiene una calculadora.
2. Yo necesito libros.
3. A ti te gusta practicar deportes.
4. Nosotros tenemos lápices para dibujar.
5. A Pablo le gusta comer pizza.
6. Los amigos llegan tarde a la escuela.

   a. la clase de arte
   b. la oficina del director
   c. la clase de matemáticas
   d. el gimnasio
   e. la biblioteca
   f. la cafetería

> **Expansión:**
> Teacher Edition Only
> Have pairs of students ask each other where they are going.

AUDIO

Pronunciación   La letra d

In Spanish, the letter **d** has two sounds. At the beginning of a sentence, after a pause, or after the letters **l** or **n,** the **d** sounds like the English *d* in *door.* In all other cases, the **d** sounds like the *th* of the word *the.*

Listen and repeat, paying close attention to the two sounds of **d.**

comida	divertido	¿Dónde está David?
adiós	falda	Daniel está al lado de la puerta.
lado	grande	¿Adónde vas con mi cuaderno?

Soy Diego. Dibujo en mi cuaderno.

Differentiating Instruction

Multiple Intelligences

Linguistic/Verbal Organize students into a circle. The first student asks the student on his or her right: **¿Adónde vas?** That student gives an answer: **Voy a la oficina.** The first student then reports the answer to the group. **Él/Ella va a la oficina.** The second student then asks the question of the next in line: **¿Adónde vas?**

Inclusion

Clear Structure Instruct students to break Activity 16 into smaller steps. First, have them circle the noun or pronoun near the blank. Second, have them choose the correct verb form. Third, ask them to read the sentence aloud. Remind students that two pronouns together have a different meaning than each separately. For example, **tú y yo** means **nosotros.**

· Practice using **ir.**
· Practice naming places in school.
· **Pronunciation:** Practice pronouncing the different sounds of the letter **d.**

Core Resource

· Audio Program: TXT CD 2, track 17

Practice Sequence

Activity 16: Controlled practice: **ir**
Activity 17: Controlled practice: **ir** and places in school

✿ STANDARDS

1.3 Present information, Acts. 16–17
4.1 Compare languages, Pronunciación

Communication
Reluctant Speakers

Have students repeat the forms of **ir** as a group. Then ask them, as a group, to supply the missing verb form after you say a subject, or hold up a flashcard with a subject written on it.

Answers   MSRB Transparencies 41–42

Activity 16

1. voy	**7.** van
2. Vamos	**8.** Va
3. voy	**9.** va
4. vas	**10.** van
5. vamos	**11.** vamos
6. voy	

Activity 17

1. c Claudia va a la clase de matemáticas.
2. e Yo voy a la biblioteca.
3. d Tú vas al gimnasio.
4. a Nosotros vamos a la clase de arte.
5. f Pablo va a la cafetería.
6. b Los amigos van a la oficina del director.

Objectives

· Practice using **ir** and lesson vocabulary.
· **Culture:** discuss the work of Mexican artist Frida Kahlo.

Core Resource

· *Cuaderno,* pp. 80–82
· Audio Program: TXT CD 2, track 16

Practice Sequence

· **Activity 18:** Controlled practice: **ir** and places in school
· **Activity 19:** Transitional practice: **ir** and places in school
· **Activity 20:** Open-ended practice: **ir** and lesson vocabulary
· **Activity 21:** Open-ended practice: **ir**

STANDARDS

1.1 Engage in conversation, Act. 20
1.2 Understand language, Act. 18
1.3 Present information, Acts. 19–21, PYP
2.2 Products and perspectives, CC
4.2 Compare cultures, CC

Communication

TPR Activity

Write destinations, such as going to the library or going to the gym, on slips of paper. Have students in turn draw a slip and act it out, using appropriate gestures and props. The other students must guess where that student is going.

Answers   MSRB Transparency 42

Activity 18
1. Pablo va al gimnasio.
2. Claudia va a la clase de inglés.
3. Sara y Martín van a la cafetería.
4. La maestra de inglés va a la biblioteca.
5. María y Claudia van a la clase de matemáticas.
6. El señor Treviño va a la oficina de la directora.

Activity 19
Yo voy a la clase de matemáticas.
Frida va a la clase de arte.
El Sr. Molina va a la clase de ciencias.
Victoria va a la biblioteca.
Esteban va a la oficina del director.
Diego y Pepe van al gimnasio.

136

---

18 | ¿Adónde van?

Escuchar
Escribir

Where are Pablo and other people going? Listen to the description and write sentences saying where these people are going.

| la oficina de la directora | el gimnasio | la biblioteca |

| la clase de inglés | la clase de matemáticas | la cafetería |

1. Pablo
2. Claudia
3. Martín y Sara
4. la maestra de inglés
5. María y Claudia
6. el señor Treviño

🎧 **Audio Program**
TXT CD 2 Track 16
Audio Script, TE
p. 119b

19 | En el pasillo

Hablar
Escribir

The bell has just rung to change classes. Tell where the students and the teachers are going, based on the clues in the drawing.

modelo: Las amigas van a la cafetería.

Expansión:
Teacher Edition Only
Have students write sentences describing four of the people in the drawing.

Differentiating Instruction

Slower-paced Learners

Read before Listening Provide scripts for Activity 18 before listening to the audio. Have students prepare a chart with the headings **Persona(s)** and **Lugar.** Have them fill the first column with the names of the people in the activity. As they listen to the audio, have them write the name of the place where the people are going. For example: **Pablo / el gimnasio.**

Heritage Language Learners

Writing Skills Challenge students to provide additional details about each of the people pictured in Activity 19. For example: **Diego y Pepe van al gimnasio porque son muy atléticos y les gusta mucho jugar al básquetbol. Frida va a la clase de arte porque es artística y le gusta dibujar.** Have them check their sentences for correct spelling, punctuation, and grammar.

20 ¿Cuándo vas a...?

Hablar

Ask a partner when he or she goes to these places.

modelo: la oficina

A ¿Cuándo vas a la oficina?

B Voy a la oficina cuando tengo problemas.

Estudiante A

1. el gimnasio
2. la oficina
3. la escuela
4. la biblioteca
5. la cafetería
6. la clase de...

Estudiante B

tengo (que)
necesito
hay
¿ ?

Expansión:
Teacher Edition Only
Have students tell the class when their partner goes to the places in the activity.

21 ¿Y tú?

Hablar
Escribir

Answer the questions in complete sentences.

1. ¿A qué hora vas a la escuela?
2. ¿Cuándo van tú y tus amigos(as) a la cafetería?
3. ¿Adónde vas después de la clase de español?
4. ¿Vas mucho a la oficina del (de la) director(a)?
5. ¿Adónde vas cuando tienes que estudiar?
6. ¿Qué hay dentro de tu mochila?

Expansión:
Teacher Edition Only
Have students use question 6 to conduct a brief survey about the contents of their backpacks.

Comparación cultural

El autorretrato

What does a self-portrait reveal about an artist?
Mexican artist Frida Kahlo painted many self-portraits, including *Autorretrato con collar*. She was influenced by the indigenous cultures of **Mexico** in both her style of painting and style of clothing. She often wore traditional native clothing, as depicted in the photograph. What similarities and differences do you see between the two images?

Compara con tu mundo *What would you include in a portrait of yourself and why? What would your clothing be like?*

Autorretrato con collar (1933), Frida Kahlo

Una fotografía de Frida Kahlo (1941), Nickolas Muray

Más práctica   Cuaderno *pp. 80–82*   Cuaderno para hispanohablantes *pp. 81–84*

PARA Y PIENSA

Did you get it? Tell where the following people are going.

1. Teresa / la cafetería
2. los estudiantes / la oficina del director
3. nosotros / el gimnasio
4. yo / la clase de matemáticas

Get Help Online
ClassZone.com

Lección 2
ciento treinta y siete   **137**

Differentiating Instruction

Pre-AP

Self-correct After students complete Activity 21, have them read their answers aloud to a partner. Remind students to listen for the correct form of the verb **ir,** as well as appropriate word order. If an answer does not sound correct, have the partners analyze the problem.

Multiple Intelligences

Visual Learners Give students the opportunity to create a sketch of a self-portrait. They might depict themselves engaged in a favorite activity, or just show their face as in Frida Kahlo's example. Have students create five sentences describing themselves, based on their sketches. Sentences might describe fixed traits. **No soy muy alta.** Or they might describe current emotions. **Estoy tranquilo.**

Comparación cultural

Essential Question

Suggested Answer In addition to capturing what the artist looks like, self-portraits reveal something about the artist's personality, feelings, and lifestyle.

About the Artist

Frida Kahlo, a native of Mexico City, was stricken with polio as a child and suffered throughout her life, both emotionally and physically. She was married to the Mexican muralist Diego Rivera, but her art was very different from that of her husband. She died in 1954 at the age of 47.

✓ Ongoing Assessment

@HomeTutor
More Practice
ClassZone.com

PARA Y PIENSA

Peer Assessment Have students exchange papers with a partner and check each other's answers. Ask for a show of hands as to how many made no mistakes. For additional practice, use Reteaching & Practice Copymasters URB 2, pp. 17, 18.

Answers   MSRB Transparency 42

Activity 20 Answers should follow this format:
¿Cuándo vas al/a la + place?
Voy al/a la + place + cuando + reason.

Activity 21 Answers will vary but will include these elements:

1. Voy a la escuela a las _____.
2. Vamos a la cafetería a las _____.
3. Voy a la (al) _____ después de la clase de español.
4. No, no voy (Sí, voy) mucho a la oficina del (de la) director(a).
5. Voy a la (al) _____ cuando tengo que estudiar.
6. En mi mochila hay _____.

Para y piensa

1. Teresa va a la cafetería.
2. Los estudiantes van a la oficina del director.
3. Nosotros vamos al gimnasio.

137

Objective

- Integrate lesson content.

Core Resources

- Video Program: DVD 1
- Audio Program: TXT CD 2 tracks 14, 15, 18

Presentation Strategies

- Ask students what they remember about the Telehistoria so far.
- Before showing the video or playing the audio, tell students to watch for the surprise ending and to be ready to talk about it.

Practice Sequence

- **Activities 22, 23:** Telehistoria comprehension
- **Activity 24:** Open-ended practice: speaking

STANDARDS

1.1 Engage in conversation, Act. 24
1.2 Understand language, Acts. 22–23
1.3 Present information, Act. 24

 Warm Up UTB 2 Transparency 22

Ir Write the corresponding form of the verb for each pronoun.

1. yo
2. tú
3. él
4. nosotros
5. vosotros
6. ustedes

Answers: 1. voy; 2. vas; 3. va; 4. vamos; 5. vais; 6. van

Video Summary
@HomeTutor VideoPlus ClassZone.com

Pablo and Claudia meet a friend, Roberto, who has a poster. Pablo is in a hurry as it is 4:45 and he has to be at the gym at 5:00. Claudia says he needs the backpack because Alicia's shirt is inside of it. Roberto tells Pablo that Trini Salgado was at the gym at 4:00 instead of 5:00 and points it out on the poster that has been autographed by Trini Salgado.

▶ ❚❚

138

Todo junto

 ¡AVANZA! **Goal:** *Show what you know* Notice how Pablo and Claudia use **ir** to talk about where they are going, and **estar** to say where things are. Then use **ir** and **estar** to talk about your own schedule. *Actividades 22–26*

♻ *¿Recuerdas?* Telling time p. 99

Telehistoria completa

@HomeTutor VideoPlus ClassZone.com

STRATEGIES

Cuando lees
Read for locations This scene mentions specific places people are going. What are those places? Alicia's T-shirt is now located in a specific place. Where is it?

Cuando escuchas
Notice the problems In this scene, Pablo's problems go from bad to worse. What are the problems? How does he react?

Escena 1 *Resumen*
Pablo no contesta la pregunta en la clase de ciencias porque el problema es difícil. Claudia contesta la pregunta.

Escena 2 *Resumen*
Pablo no está contento porque tiene mucho que hacer y no tiene la mochila con la camiseta de Alicia.

Escena 3

 VIDEO DVD

 AUDIO

Roberto   Pablo   Claudia

Roberto approaches, holding a poster.
Roberto: ¿Qué pasa?
Claudia: Vamos al gimnasio. Bueno, Pablo va al gimnasio, yo voy a la cafetería...
Pablo: ¡Necesito ir al gimnasio a las cinco, y son las cinco menos cuarto!
Claudia: ¡Y necesita la mochila! Dentro está la camiseta de Alicia.

Pablo: A las cinco Trini Salgado va al gimnasio, y yo...
Roberto: No, no. ¡A las cuatro!
Pablo: No... ¡A las cinco!
Roberto: Mira... a las cuatro.
He shows his autographed poster to Pablo. It says four o'clock.
Pablo: *(dejectedly)* No...

138   Unidad 2 México
ciento treinta y ocho

Differentiating Instruction

Inclusion

Frequent Review/Repetition Organize students into pairs. Ask each pair to use **ir** in a sentence to say somewhere they go at school, for example, **Yo voy a...,** or **Vamos a...,** using as many vocabulary words as possible. Have other pairs correct pronunciation or add other words to the sentences.

Slower-paced Learners

Peer-study Support Have students work in pairs to draft a question about the Telehistoria. Have them write the question on an index card. Then have each pair switch cards with another group. Tell students to read the question they received, and discuss the answer with their partner. Repeat the activity with each pair getting a new question each time.

22 | ¡A organizar! *Comprensión de los episodios*

Escuchar
Leer

Put the sentences in order to describe the episodes.

1. La camiseta está en la mochila y Pablo no tiene la mochila.
2. Pablo y Claudia hablan con Roberto.
3. Claudia y Pablo van a la biblioteca y estudian.
4. Pablo está nervioso; tiene que ir al gimnasio a las cinco.
5. Pablo va a la clase de ciencias y no contesta la pregunta.

> **Expansión:**
> Teacher Edition Only
> Have students add dialogue to the descriptions.

23 | ¡A describir! *Comprensión de los episodios*

Escuchar
Leer

Describe what is happening in the photos. Include where the people in the photos are and how they feel.

modelo: Pablo está en la clase de ciencias. Va al pizarrón porque tiene que contestar una pregunta. Está nervioso.

1.  **2.**  **3.**

> **Expansión:**
> Teacher Edition Only
> Ask students to look through all the photos in their books and discuss the emotions of the characters.

24 | ¿Adónde vamos? ♻ *¿Recuerdas?* Telling time p. 99

Hablar

STRATEGY Hablar
Make it lively Keep the discussion interesting! Add as many details about your classes as possible. Don't just talk about your classes; include other places in your school.

> **Expansión:**
> Teacher Edition Only
> Have students write a summary of the classes they have in common with other members of their group.

Talk with other students about schedules: where they go and at what times.

A ¿A qué hora van ustedes a la cafetería?

B Voy a la cafetería a las doce y media.

C Voy a la cafetería a la una.

✓ Ongoing Assessment

Rubric Activity 24

Speaking Criteria	Maximum Credit	Partial Credit	Minimum Credit
Content	Numerous words from previous lessons as well as words from this unit.	Few words from previous lessons and unit.	Words are limited to this lesson and unit.
Communication	Easy to understand. Good pronunciation.	Can be understood. Some errors in pronunciation.	Hard to understand. Many errors in pronunciation.
Accuracy	Few mistakes in grammar and vocabulary.	Some mistakes in grammar and vocabulary.	Many mistakes in grammar and vocabulary.

 Answers MSRB Transparency 42

Activity 22 The correct order for the sequence of events is as follows: 5; 3; 4; 1; 2

Activity 23 Answers will vary. Sample answers:
1. Claudia está en la clase de ciencias. Contesta la pregunta. Está contenta.
2. Pablo y Claudia están delante de la escuela. Hablan. Pablo está nervioso porque tiene que estar en el gimnasio a las cinco y tiene que hacer la tarea.
3. Pablo y Roberto están delante de la escuela. Hablan de Trini Salgado. Pablo está deprimido.

Activity 24 Answers will vary. Sample answer:
A. ¿Qué van a hacer a la una? **B.** Yo voy a estudiar ciencias. **C.** Yo voy a la clase de español.

139

Differentiating Instruction

Pre-AP

Expand and Elaborate Have volunteers share their descriptions of the photos in Activity 23. Then challenge the group to add more information to each description. For example, the following might be added to the model. **Pablo está nervioso. La clase de ciencias es muy difícil.**

Inclusion

Clear Structure Before students discuss Activity 24, have them create a two-column chart. Tell them to write the heading **¿adónde?** at the top of the left-hand column, and **¿a qué hora?** at the top of the right. Then have students brainstorm places in school on the left, and record the appropriate time for each on the right. Encourage students to use their charts as they ask and answer questions.

Objective
· Practice using and integrating lesson vocabulary and grammar.

Core Resources
· *Cuaderno*, pp. 83–84.
· Audio Program: TXT CD 2 tracks 19, 20

Practice Sequence
· **Activity 25:** Open-ended practice: reading, listening, speaking
· **Activity 26:** Open-ended practice: writing

 STANDARDS

1.2 Understand language, Act. 25
1.4 Present information, Acts. 25–26, PYP

Long-term Retention
Pre-AP Integration

Ask student pairs to write a short script about what they do during the day and at what time. Ask them to follow the schedule in Act. 25, and use **estar, ir, al,** and **del.**

✓ Ongoing Assessment

Rubric Activity 25

Listening/Speaking

Proficient	Not There Yet
Student correctly uses **ir + a.**	Student incorrectly uses **ir + a.**

✓ Ongoing Assessment
@HomeTutor
More Practice
ClassZone.com

PARA Y PIENSA **Peer Assessment** Ask students to read aloud the completed sentences, and ask the class to correct their pronunciation. For additional practice, use Reteaching & Practice Copymasters URB 2, pp. 17, 19, 22.

See Activity answers on p. 141.

140

---

25 | Integración

Leer
Escuchar
Hablar

Raquel and Mario need to study in the library. Read Raquel's daily planner and listen to Mario's message. Then tell when Raquel and Mario will go to the library to study. Explain why they won't go at the other times mentioned.

Fuente 1 Agenda personal

28 de octubre

7:30 clase de matemáticas
8:40 estudiar
9:50 clase de ciencias
11:00 inglés: presentación oral
12:30 descansar
1:40 cafetería con Amanda
2:45 examen de historia
4:00 estudiar en la biblioteca

Fuente 2 Un mensaje por teléfono

 Listen and take notes
· Escribe qué hace Mario y a qué hora.

modelo: Ellos van a la biblioteca a las... No estudian a las siete y media porque...

🎧 **Audio Program**
TXT CD 2 Tracks 19, 20
Audio Script, TE p. 119b

26 | El periódico escolar

Escribir

You have to write an article for the school newspaper about your typical school day. Explain what classes you go to, what they are like, and what you use in each class.

modelo: Yo siempre estoy muy ocupado. A las siete y media voy a la clase de matemáticas. La clase es muy divertida. Usamos calculadoras, pero no es fácil. A las ocho y cuarto...

Writing Criteria	Excellent	Good	Needs Work
Content	Your article includes a lot of information.	Your article includes some information.	Your article includes little information.
Communication	Most of your article is organized and easy to follow.	Parts of your article are organized and easy to follow.	Your article is disorganized and hard to follow.
Accuracy	Your article has few mistakes in grammar and vocabulary.	Your article has some mistakes in grammar and vocabulary.	Your article has many mistakes in grammar and vocabulary.

Expansión:
Teacher Edition Only
Have students interview you and write about your typical day.

Más práctica Cuaderno *pp. 83–84* Cuaderno para hispanohablantes *pp. 85–86*

PARA Y PIENSA

Did you get it? Complete each sentence with the correct forms of **estar** and **ir + a.**

Get Help Online
ClassZone.com

1. A la una Pablo _____ en la clase de arte, pero a las dos _____ la cafetería.
2. ¿Dónde _____ Roberto y Claudia? Ellos _____ la cafetería.
3. Claudia _____ nerviosa porque _____ la oficina de la directora.

Differentiating Instruction

Multiple Intelligences

Musical/Rhythmic Have students create a poem or song based on the schedule shown in Activity 25. For example: **A las nueve menos veinte, Raquel tiene que estudiar. A las diez menos diez tiene la clase de ciencias, y a las once tiene una presentación oral.** Students may want to read their poems or sing their songs for the rest of the class.

Heritage Language Learners

Writing Skills After students have completed their articles for Activity 26, organize them into groups of three. Provide each student with copies of the three articles. Tell students that they will each play the part of the writer, editor, and editor-in-chief. The writer reads his or her article aloud. The editor reads along, suggesting revisions and proofreading. The editor-in-chief checks the editor's work.

Juegos y diversiones

Review **estar,** classroom objects, and location words by playing a game.

¿Cierto o falso?

The Setup

Your teacher will divide the class into two teams. Each student will make up a sentence using classroom objects and location words.

Playing the Game

Players from each team go up to the front of the class with their sentences in hand.

The player from Team A reads the sentence to the player from Team B. The player from Team B has to say whether the sentence is true (**cierto**) or false (**falso**). Then they change roles.

Scoring

Players receive one point for correct answers. Points are taken away for incorrectly formed sentences.

A player can earn an extra point by correcting a false sentence to say something true about the location of the object. A player can also earn an extra point by adding more information to a true sentence.

The Winner!

The team with the most points at the end is the winner.

El libro está debajo del escritorio.

Falso. El libro está encima del escritorio.

Lección 2
ciento cuarenta y uno **141**

Objective

· Review **estar,** classroom objects, and location words.

STANDARDS

5.2 Life-long learners

Long-term Retention

Recycle

You may want to use this game to review other grammar and vocabulary students have learned. Suggestions: telling time, after-school activities, weather expressions, numbers, days of the week. Example: Student A points to the clock and says: **Son las diez y media.** Student B says: **Falso, son las diez y cuarto.**

Communication

Group Work

Challenge students to add more information to a true sentence to earn an extra point. For example: A: **El libro de español está encima del escritorio.** B: **Cierto. El libro de español está al lado del cuaderno también.**

Answers MSRB Transparencies 42–43

Answers for Activities on p. 140.

Activity 25 Ellos van a la biblioteca a las nueve menos viente. No estudian a las siete y media porque Mario tiene la clase de ciencias. No estudian a las diez menos diez porque Mario tiene la clase de matemáticas. ... a las doce porque Mario necesita comer con Andrés. ...a las doce y media porque Mario descansa. ...a la una y media porque Mario tiene la clase de inglés.

Activity 26 Answers will vary. Sample answer: Yo voy a la escuela a las ocho de la mañana. Tengo examen de ciencias. Tengo que estudiar...

Para y piensa **1.** está, va a; **2.** están, van a; **3.** está, va a

---

Differentiating Instruction

Multiple Intelligences

Interpersonal Ask students to write the location of five different people in the classroom. For example: **Está lejos del maestro. Está detrás de Paco y Celia.** After each student reads his or her statement, the class must guess who that person is. The student with the correct answer gets a point.

Pre-AP

Expand and Elaborate Make sure there's a map available for this activity. Ask students to select five countries from Latin America and describe where they are located in relation to one another. You may want to teach the word **entre** (between) for this activity. For example: Student points to Bolivia and says: **Está al lado de Brasil, de Chile y de Perú.** Or, **está entre Brasil y Perú.**

- Read two compositions about **Mi clase favorita.**
- Compare ways of explaining and talking about favorite classes.
- **Culture:** Learn how students in Mexico and the Dominican Republic plan to prepare for their careers.

Core Resource

- Audio Program: TXT CD 2 track 21

Presentation Strategies

- Ask students to name their favorite classes.
- Review the classes listed in both compositions.
- Lead a discussion on how students will prepare for the careers they want. Point out how their favorite classes may help them in their career planning.

 STANDARDS

1.2 Understand language
4.2 Compare cultures

Warm Up UTB 2 Transparency 23

Ir Complete the sentences with the correct form of **ir.**

1. Yo _____ a la biblioteca.
2. Pablo _____ a la cafetería.
3. ¿Adónde _____ ustedes?
4. Nosotros _____ al gimnasio.
5. Y tú, ¿adónde _____?

Answers: 1. voy; 2. va; 3. van; 4. vamos; 5. vas

Comparación cultural

Background Information

Graduation Requirements in Dominican Schools A minimum of 25 credits must be earned in Grades 9–12. Eight semesters of successful full-time attendance in high school is required. Students must maintain an academic GPA of 2.0 (70%). Required courses include a modern language, social studies, mathematics, science, Spanish, physical and health education, fine arts and computer technology.

Lectura cultural

¡AVANZA! **Goal:** Read the excerpts from the essays of two students from Mexico and the Dominican Republic. Then compare the descriptions of their favorite classes and talk about your favorite class.

Comparación cultural

 # Mi clase favorita

AUDIO

STRATEGY Leer

Use the title The title *Mi clase favorita* helps you anticipate the contents of the reading. Write down the things that you would expect to find, then search for them.

Expected contents	Actual contents
El (La) maestro(a)...	
La clase...	
Más información:	

México

Below are compositions by two finalists who entered the essay contest called "Mi clase favorita."

Tomás Gutiérrez Moreno
Colegio de la Providencia
Guadalajara, México

Mi nombre es Tomás Gutiérrez Moreno. Soy de Guadalajara, México. Estudio en el Colegio de la Providencia.

La historia es muy interesante; es mi clase favorita. Me gusta mucho estudiar el pasado[1] de México. Soy estudioso y siempre saco buenas notas en la clase.

En la universidad deseo[2] estudiar historia. Deseo ser maestro y enseñar historia mexicana en Guadalajara.

_____
[1] past   [2] I wish to

Mural en la Biblioteca Central de la Universidad Nacional Autónoma de México en la Ciudad de México

Unidad 2 México
142 ciento cuarenta y dos

Differentiating Instruction

Heritage Language Learners

Writing Skills Ask students to write a composition about their favorite class. Instruct them to use pp. 142–143 as a model. Provide them with the following questions as a guide: **¿Cómo te llamas? ¿De dónde eres? ¿Dónde estudias? ¿Cuál es tu clase favorita? ¿Por qué te gusta? ¿Qué deseas hacer después de terminar la escuela?** Check for correct spelling, punctuation, and grammar.

Multiple Intelligences

Linguistic/Verbal Explain that people reveal a great deal about themselves through their writing. Ask half the class to reread Tomás's essay and the other half to reread María's. Ask students to write short reflections in Spanish in which they explain how much they can tell about the personalities of María and Tomás; then ask students to share their reflections with the rest of the class.

María González
Colegio San Esteban
San Pedro de Macorís, República Dominicana

Me llamo María González. Soy de la República Dominicana. Estudio en el Colegio San Esteban.

Tengo dos clases favoritas: el inglés y el español. Deseo estudiar idiomas[3] en Santo Domingo, la capital, y después, trabajar en mi país.

El turismo es muy importante para[4] la economía de la República Dominicana. Deseo trabajar en un hotel, en las famosas playas[5] de Punta Cana o de Puerto Plata.

---

[3] languages   [4] for   [5] beaches

Mural en la Universidad Nacional en Santo Domingo, República Dominicana

República Dominicana

PARA Y PIENSA

¿Comprendiste?
1. ¿Dónde estudia Tomás?
2. ¿Cómo es Tomás?
3. ¿De dónde es María?
4. ¿Qué le gusta estudiar más a María?

¿Y tú?
¿Cuál es tu clase favorita? ¿Cómo es?

Differentiating Instruction

Slower-paced Learners

Personalize It Organize students into pairs. Then have partners ask each other questions based on the content of both compositions. Instruct students to answer from their own perspective.

Estudiante A: ¿Cuál es tu clase favorita?
Estudiante B: Mi clase favorita es inglés.
Estudiante A: ¿Sacas buenas notas en inglés?
Estudiante B: Sí, saco buenas notas.

Inclusion

Metacognitive Support Teach students how to use context clues to find the meanings of words they don't know. Have them skim the two compositions on pp. 142-143. Then ask them to look at the glossed words without looking at the English translation and guess their meaning. For example, students read that Tomás's favorite class is history, which provides them with the context clue to the word **el pasado** (the past).

Answers

Para y piensa

¿Comprendiste?
1. Tomás estudia en el Colegio de la Providencia.
2. Tomás es estudioso.
3. María es de la República Dominicana.
4. A María le gusta más estudiar el inglés y el español.

¿Y tu? Answers will vary but should follow the model: **Mi clase favorita es...**

143

Proyectos culturales

Comparación cultural

Objectives

- Read about yarn painting in Mexico and rock drawing in the Dominican Republic.
- **Culture:** Compare the art of two indigenous cultures: the Huichol of Mexico and the Taino of the Greater Antilles.
- **Community:** Investigate sources of arts and crafts influenced by Spanish-speaking cultures in the community.

Presentation Strategies

- Ask students to look at the illustrations on this page and identify similarities and differences between the two kinds of folk art.
- Have students tell about folk art traditions they have seen (beaded moccasins, hand-woven blankets, etc.) or may own.
- Bring in samples of indigenous art for students to see.
- Ask students to read the **proyectos** and choose the one they want to create.

STANDARDS

1.3 Present information
2.2 Products and perspectives
4.2 Compare cultures
5.1 Spanish in the community

Comparación cultural

Essential Question

Suggested Answer The natural world can be portrayed in various ways through art; realistic, idealistic, even fantastic. The type of portrayal can show how a culture thinks or feels about the natural world.

Expanded Information

The yarn paintings of the Huichol are still being made. Originally intended as religious offerings, these paintings describe the way the Huichol people saw the world they lived in and the way they saw the world they hoped for.

Experiences
Spanish in the Marketplace

Ask students to visit local craft stores to search for supplies that are imported from Latin America. Ask them to keep records of what they find and where it comes from. In the classroom, have students combine their findings in a list of words and countries.

144

Comparación cultural

Arte de México y la República Dominicana

How does art reflect a culture's view of the natural world? Many cultures use art to capture the beauty and wonder of their natural surroundings. Two indigenous groups whose art can still be appreciated are the Huichol of **Mexico** and the Taino of the Greater Antilles (including what is now known as the **Dominican Republic**).

Proyecto 1 Yarn Painting

México Some Huichol still live in the isolated mountains of western Mexico. They make yarn paintings of birds, flowers, and other natural shapes. Make your own Huichol-style yarn painting.

Materials for yarn painting
Cardboard
2–3 colors yarn
Glue

Instructions
1. On a piece of cardboard, draw a pencil outline of the design you'd like to make.
2. Place one strand of yarn along the outline's length. Glue the yarn to the cardboard.
3. Fill in the design by laying yarn just inside the outline you made, coiling the yarn around until the figure is filled.
4. Section off the background and fill it in the same way.

Proyecto 2 Rock Drawing

República Dominicana The Taino lived in the islands of the Caribbean until the 16th century. Their rock art can still be seen in the caverns of the Dominican Republic. Try making your own rock art.

Materials for rock drawing
Rock
Pencil
Optional: Markers, pens, or chalk

Instructions
1. Begin by finding a smooth, oval rock about the size of your hand with an adequate surface for drawing.
2. Use a pencil to sketch the animal or design you'd like to make.
3. Then use a black felt tip pen to make it permanent. Add color by using colored felt tip pens or colored chalk.

En tu comunidad

Visit an arts and crafts store or a museum in your community. Look for any items that have been influenced by Spanish-speaking cultures.

144 Unidad 2 México
ciento cuarenta y cuatro

Differentiating Instruction

Heritage Language Learners

Support What They Know Encourage students to bring in samples of folk art from their country of origin. Have students describe who makes them, where are they made, what they are made of, and if they are used for decoration or other purposes.

English Learners

Provide Comprehensible Input Provide English learners with extra illustrations of Huichol yarn paintings and Taino rock drawings. If possible, show them examples of other students' completed work. Model the processes for completing these **proyectos** then encourage the student to make his or her own. Also be sure the student has a dual-language dictionary available for clarification.

LECCIÓN 2

En resumen
Vocabulario y gramática

Animated Grammar
Interactive Flashcards
ClassZone.com

Vocabulario

Describe Classroom Objects

el borrador	eraser	el pizarrón (pl.	board, chalkboard
la calculadora	calculator	los pizarrones)	
el cuaderno	notebook	la pluma	pen
el escritorio	desk	la puerta	door
el lápiz	pencil	el reloj	clock; watch
(pl. los lápices)		la silla	chair
el mapa	map	la tiza	chalk
la mochila	backpack	la ventana	window
el papel	paper		

Say Where Things Are Located

al lado (de)	next to	dentro (de)	inside (of)
cerca (de)	near (to)	detrás (de)	behind
debajo (de)	underneath, under	encima (de)	on top (of)
delante (de)	in front (of)	lejos (de)	far (from)

Talk About How You Feel

cansado(a)	tired	nervioso(a)	nervous
contento(a)	content, happy	ocupado(a)	busy
deprimido(a)	depressed	tranquilo(a)	calm
emocionado(a)	excited	triste	sad
enojado(a)	angry		

Describe Classes

aburrido(a)	boring
divertido(a)	fun
interesante	interesting

Places in School

el baño	bathroom
la biblioteca	library
la cafetería	cafeteria
el gimnasio	gymnasium
la oficina	principal's
del (de la)	office
director(a)	
el pasillo	hall

Other Words and Phrases

¿(A)dónde?	(To) Where?
¿Cuándo?	When?
cuando	when
el problema	problem

Gramática

Nota gramatical: Conjugated verb before the subject to ask a question *p. 130*

The Verb estar

Use **estar** to indicate location and say how people feel.

estar *to be*			
yo	estoy	nosotros(as)	estamos
tú	estás	vosotros(as)	estáis
usted, él, ella	está	ustedes, ellos(as)	están

The Verb ir

Use **ir** to talk about where someone is going.

ir *to go*			
yo	voy	nosotros(as)	vamos
tú	vas	vosotros(as)	vais
usted, él, ella	va	ustedes, ellos(as)	van

Lección 2
ciento cuarenta y cinco **145**

Communication
Humor and Creativity

Ask students to write vocabulary words from En resumen on small slips of paper and place them, by category, in containers. One at a time, have students pull a word from each of three or four containers and put them together in a sentence. Possible combinations: **(Yo estoy) (debajo de) (la pluma).**

Long-term Retention
Study Tips

Ask students to sort the vocabulary into smaller categories of their choice. For example: **en la mochila, en la clase.** Have them use graphic organizers such as charts or word webs to do so. Ask them to share their work and discuss the reasons for assigning an item to a particular category.

Differentiating Instruction

Inclusion

Multisensory Input/Output First lead the class in creating facial expressions that match the Talk About How You Feel vocabulary. Then divide the class into pairs and ask each pair to quiz each other on the vocabulary words. One student will give the Spanish word, and the other will make the appropriate facial expression.

Multiple Intelligences

Visual Learners Give students two options: mapping their school or mapping their classroom. Ask them to draw detailed maps and label each space or item in Spanish.

Objective
· Review lesson grammar and vocabulary.

Core Resources
· *Cuaderno*, pp. 85–96
· Audio Program: TXT CD 2 track 22

Presentation Strategies
· Before playing the audio for Activity 1, ask students to listen to it carefully, especially to the times and the forms of **estar** and **ir**.
· Monitor correct use of **ser, estar,** and prepositions of location.
· Read the Comparación cultural with students and clarify any questions that arise.
· Review may be done in class or given as homework.
· Students can also access the review activities on line at ClassZone.com.

STANDARDS
1.2 Understand language, Act. 1
1.3 Present information, Acts. 1–5
4.2 Compare cultures, Act. 5

 Warm Up UTB 2 Transparency 23

Vocabulary Complete the sentences with the correct word.

cafetería   al lado   divertida   biblioteca   tiza
1. En la _____ hay muchos libros.
2. No me gusta comer la pizza en la _____.
3. Necesito _____ para escribir en el pizarrón.
4. La clase de español es interesante y _____.
5. El reloj está _____ del mapa.

Answers: 1. biblioteca; 2. cafetería; 3. tiza; 4. divertida; 5. al lado

Intervention and Remediation If students achieve less than 80% accuracy with the activities, direct them to review pp. 120, 128, 130, 134, 137, 142–143 and to get help online at ClassZone.com.

See Activity answers on p. 147.

146

Repaso de la lección

¡LLEGADA!

@HomeTutor
ClassZone.com

Now you can
· describe classes and classroom objects
· say where things are located
· say where you are going
· talk about how you feel

Using
· the verb **estar**
· the conjugated verb before the subject to ask a question
· the verb **ir**

To review
· the verb **estar** p. 128
· the conjugated verb before the subject to ask a question p. 130
· the verb **ir** p. 134

AUDIO

1 Listen and understand

Copy this chart on a piece of paper. Listen to the phone messages and complete the chart. Write sentences using the information.

La hora	¿Dónde está Ana?	¿Adónde va Ana?
modelo: 8:00	delante de la clase de arte	clase de español
10:15		
12:30		
2:45		
4:10		

modelo: A las ocho Ana está delante de la clase de arte. Ella va de la clase de arte a la clase de español.

🎧 **Audio Program**
TXT CD 2 Track 22
Audio Script, TE p. 119b

To review
· the verb **estar** p. 128
· the conjugated verb before the subject to ask a question p. 130

2 Talk about how you feel

Write questions to verify how these people are feeling.

 modelo: Bárbara
¿Está emocionada Bárbara?

1.  Jorge y Pilar   **4.** usted

2. 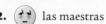 las maestras   **5.** tú

3. la directora   **6.** ustedes

Differentiating Instruction

Multiple Intelligences

Intrapersonal Ask students to create a table like the one in Activity 1. The headings for columns in this table, though, should be **La hora, ¿Dónde estoy?** and **¿Adónde voy?** Have them fill out the table according to their own schedule.

Pre-AP

Expand and Elaborate Ask students to explain their class schedules to a partner, identifying the subjects they take, what time they meet, and how often they have them. For example: **Tengo inglés a las ocho de la mañana. Tengo inglés todos los días. A las nueve estoy en la clase de historia.** Then ask them to exchange schedules and explain the sequence of each other's classes.

To review
• the verb **ir** p. 134

3 Say where you are going

Read Mario's e-mail message and complete it with the correct form of **ir**.

> Hola, Luis. Yo **1.** a la clase de ciencias en quince minutos. Es una clase interesante, pero es difícil. A las doce y media mis amigos y yo **2.** a la cafetería. Después Inés **3.** al gimnasio y Jerónimo **4.** a la oficina del director. A las cinco ellos **5.** a la biblioteca para estudiar. ¿Adónde **6.** tú después de las clases?

To review
• the verb **estar** p. 128

4 Say where things are located

Write sentences telling where Señora Romero's students have put the erasers.

modelo: el pizarrón (cerca / lejos)
Un borrador está cerca del pizarrón.

1. reloj (al lado / debajo)
2. silla (debajo / encima)
3. mochila (dentro / debajo)
4. ventana (delante / detrás)
5. escritorio (encima / delante)
6. maestra (lejos / detrás)

To review
• Comparación cultural pp. 120, 130, 137
• Lectura cultural pp. 142–143

5 Mexico and the Dominican Republic

Comparación cultural

Answer these culture questions.

1. When do Mexican students attend school?
2. How did indigenous cultures influence Frida Kahlo?
3. What can you find in Mexico City's National Museum of Anthropology?
4. Why is tourism important in the Dominican Republic?

Más práctica Cuaderno *pp. 85–96* Cuaderno para hispanohablantes *pp. 87–96*

Get Help Online
ClassZone.com

Differentiating Instruction

Slower-paced Learners

Yes/No Questions As an alternative to Activity 4, ask students questions following the model: **¿Está un borrador cerca del pizarrón?** Have them answer in complete sentences. **Sí, un borrador está cerca del pizarrón.** Continue asking about the other items in the picture.

Heritage Language Learners

Increase Accuracy Ask students to reply to Mario's e-mail in Activity 3. They should use forms of **ir** and **ser** to describe their school schedule. For example: **Hola, Mario. Yo voy a la clase de matemáticas en diez minutos. Es una clase difícil pero el maestro es muy bueno. A las doce, mis amigo y yo vamos a...** Correct common spelling mistakes such as **boy** and **siensas.**

✓ Ongoing Assessment

Alternative Assessment Activity 2 Ask students to draw their own emoticon faces and label them **cansado(a), contento(a), deprimido(a), emocionado(a), enojado(a), nervioso(a), ocupado(a), tranquilo(a),** and **triste.**

✓ Ongoing Assessment

Peer Assessment Activity 4 Ask students to take turns quizzing each other by taking an eraser and moving it around the room to the places indicated in Activity 4. Example: One student moves the eraser and the other says where it is. They should keep score of right and wrong answers.

Answers MSRB Transparency 43

Answers for Activities on pp. 146, 147.

Activity 1 A las diez y cuarto Ana está en el pasillo. Ella va del pasillo a la clase de inglés.

A las doce y media Ana está en la cafetería. Ella va de la cafetería a la clase de matemáticas.

A las tres menos cuarto Ana está en la oficina. Ella va de la oficina a la clase de historia.

A las cuatro y diez Ana está en la biblioteca. De la biblioteca, ella va al gimnasio.

Activity 2
1. ¿Están enojados Jorge y Pilar?
2. ¿Están cansadas las maestras?
3. ¿Está contenta la directora?
4. ¿Está usted nervioso?
5. ¿Estás tú triste?
6. ¿Están ustedes cansados?

Activity 3
1. voy
2. vamos
3. va
4. va
5. van
6. vas

Activity 4
1. Un borrador está debajo del reloj.
2. Un borrador está debajo de la silla.
3. Un borrador está dentro de la mochila.
4. Un borrador está delante de la ventana.
5. Un borrador está encima del escritorio.
6. Un borrador está detrás de la maestra.

Activity 5
1. Mexican students attend school from the end of August until June.
2. Indigenous cultures influenced Frida Kahlo's style of painting and style of clothing. She often wore traditional native clothing.
3. In Mexico City's National Museum of Anthropology I can find the *Piedra del Sol*, which is an Aztec calendar, as well as other artifacts from Mexico's indigenous cultures.
4. Tourism is very important to the economy of the Dominican Republic, particularly for the travel and hotel industries.

Objectives

- Read personal narratives about school and classes in three different countries.
- Have students compare the favorite classes of the authors with their own favorite classes.
- Ask students to write about their school schedule.

Core Resources

- *Cuaderno*, pp. 97–99
- Audio Program: TXT CD 2, track 23
- Video Program: DVD 1

Presentation Strategies

- Ask students to look at the photos on pp. 148 and 149 and describe what they see.
- Instruct students to follow the text in the book as they listen to the audio.
- Tell students to think about their own class schedules while they are reading the three personal accounts.

STANDARDS

1.2 Understand language
1.3 Present information
2.1 Practices and perspectives
4.2 Compare cultures

Communication
Group Work

Ask students to work in groups of three to write e-mail messages from Juan Carlos to Rafael, from Rafael to Andrea, and from Andrea to Juan Carlos. The subject of the e-mails should be school schedules.

Long-term Retention
Recycle

Review telling time by asking individual students to generate a list of activities. For example: **llegar a la escuela, ir a la cafetería, mirar la televisión, descansar.** Have them use the list to ask their partners when they do these activities. **A: ¿A qué hora llegas a la escuela? B: Llego a la escuela a las siete y cuarto.**

148

Comparación cultural

Horarios y clases
AUDIO

Lectura y escritura

WebQuest
ClassZone.com

1 **Leer** School subjects and daily schedules vary around the world. Read how Rafael, Andrea, and Juan Carlos spend a typical day at school.

2 **Escribir** Using the three descriptions as models, write a short paragraph about your daily schedule.

> **STRATEGY** **Escribir**
> **Create a schedule** Draw two large clocks, one for a.m. and the other for p.m. Write your school schedule on these clocks.
>
>
> actividad
> clase   a.m.   p.m.

Step 1 Complete the two clocks by listing your classes and after-school activities. Use arrows to point to the correct times.

Step 2 Write your paragraph. Make sure to include all the classes, activities, and times. Check your writing by yourself or with help from a friend. Make final corrections.

Compara con tu mundo

Use the paragraph you wrote to compare your school schedule to the schedule of *one* of the three students. What are the similarities in the schedules? What are the differences?

Cuaderno *pp. 97–99*   Cuaderno para hispanohablantes *pp. 97–99*

Differentiating Instruction

Multiple Intelligences

Naturalist Ask students to determine the time zone differences between Santo Domingo, Asunción, México, D.F., and their hometown. Have students write down what time it is where they live and in the other cities when Rafael leaves school. Then ask them to determine what they, Andrea, and Juan Carlos are doing at those times.

Inclusion

Read Before Listening Ask students to read the descriptions silently. Then read them aloud to the class, asking students to track your voice by tracing their index fingers along the printed words as you pronounce them.

Cultura INTERACTIVA *See these pages come alive!*
ClassZone.com

República Dominicana
Rafael

¡Hola a todos! Me llamo Rafael y estudio en una escuela en Santo Domingo. Tengo clases todos los días de las ocho de la mañana a la una de la tarde. A las diez tenemos un descanso de quince minutos. Luego, voy a la clase de historia. Es interesante y yo tomo muchos apuntes. En la tarde muchas veces paso un rato con los amigos.

Paraguay
Andrea

¿Qué tal? Me llamo Andrea y estudio en Asunción, Paraguay. Mis clases son en la tarde, de la una a las cinco. En la escuela los estudiantes tienen muchas clases. Todos los días, tengo clases de español, ciencias, historia y matemáticas. También tengo clase de guaraní[1]. Después de las clases, voy al gimnasio y practico deportes. De vez en cuando uso la computadora en la biblioteca.

[1] an indigenous language spoken in Paraguay

México
Juan Carlos

¡Hola! Soy Juan Carlos. Soy estudiante en México, D.F. En la escuela necesito trabajar mucho porque tengo nueve clases. Las clases son de las siete de la mañana a las dos de la tarde. ¡Tengo que llegar muy temprano! Mi clase favorita es la clase de matemáticas. Es interesante y divertida. Después de las clases mis amigos y yo estudiamos en la biblioteca.

México
ciento cuarenta y nueve **149**

Comparación cultural

Exploring the Theme
The Guarani language, which was being used in South America at the time the Spaniards explored the area, is one of the official languages of Paraguay. It is spoken by 94% of the population, and by many Paraguayans who have emigrated to other countries. The constitution of Paraguay is written in both Spanish and Guarani, and state-produced textbooks are printed with half the text in Spanish and half in Guarani. It is the second official language in the province of Corrientes in Argentina. The English words *tapioca, toucan,* and *jaguar* can be traced to Guarani roots.

✓ Ongoing Assessment

Quick Check Ask students yes or no questions to assess comprehension. For example: **¿Es Rafael de México?** (no)

✓ Ongoing Assessment

Rubric Lectura y escritura

Writing Criteria	Excellent	Good	Needs Work
Content	Paragraph contains a lot of information about daily schedule.	Paragraph contains some information about daily schedule.	Paragraph lacks information about daily schedule.
Communication	Paragraph is organized and easy to follow.	Paragraph is fairly well organized and easy to follow.	Paragraph is disorganized and hard to follow.
Accuracy	Paragraph has few mistakes in vocabulary and grammar.	Paragraph has some mistakes in vocabulary and grammar.	Paragraph has many mistakes in vocabulary and grammar.

Differentiating Instruction

Pre-AP

Expand and Elaborate Have students scan the three descriptions on p. 149 and explain the different lengths of the students' school days and number of classes. Then ask students to express their opinion on the reasons for such differences.

Slower-paced Learners

Yes/No Questions Ask students yes or no questions to assess their comprehension of the descriptions presented on pp. 148–149. If the answer to a question is no, ask students to supply the correct information. For example:
¿Tiene Andrea clases en la mañana?
No, Andrea tiene clases en la tarde.

Long-term Retention

Study Tips

Ask students to think of new ways to organize vocabulary and grammar notes. This may include color-coding, alphabetizing, or sorting according to another set of categories the student proposes. Remind students that sorting is not the goal, but that organizing material should make it easier to remember.

Answers MSRB Transparency 43

Activity 1
1. El señor Minondo enseña la clase de historia.
2. El señor Minondo practica fútbol.
3. La señora Cruz es la directora de la escuela.
4. A la señora Cruz le gusta tocar la guitarra.
5. Los maestros son muy interesantes.

150

---

1 | Listen, understand, and compare

Escuchar

Javier interviewed teachers and administrators at his school for Teacher Appreciation Day. Listen to his report and answer the questions.

1. ¿Qué enseña el señor Minondo?
2. ¿Qué deporte practica el señor Minondo?
3. ¿Quién es la señora Cruz?
4. ¿Qué le gusta hacer a la señora Cruz?
5. ¿Cómo son los maestros?

> 🎧 **Audio Program**
> TXT CD 2 Track 24
> Audio Script, TE p. 119b

Are your teachers and administrators like those at Javier's school? What kind of activities do your teachers like to do after classes?

2 | Give a school orientation

Hablar

You are giving a talk at an orientation meeting for students who are new to your school. Greet the new students, introduce yourself, and give them some background information about yourself: what classes you have, what you like to do after school, etc. Then tell them where the gym, cafeteria, and other locations around the school are. Finish by describing some of the classes that are available and what they have to do in each class. Your talk should be at least two minutes long.

3 | Talk with a school counselor

Hablar

Role-play a conversation with a school counselor. The counselor wants to know what your classes are like and what you like to do after classes. Answer your partner's questions, tell him or her what you do in each class, and ask a few questions of your own about the school. Your conversation should be at least two minutes long.

> ¿Cómo son tus clases?

> Son difíciles. Estudio mucho.

Differentiating Instruction

Pre-AP

Self-correct Have students audiotape their performances in Activities 2, 3 and 5. Ask them to listen closely to themselves and identify errors or hesitations. Encourage students to write down and correct their errors. Then give them the opportunity to present the activity again, being mindful of correcting themselves as they speak.

Inclusion

Clear Structure Before students begin their interviews in Activity 3, have each pair of students draw a large concept web. First, have them write their topic in the center (**Entrevista**). Then have them record useful vocabulary around the web (**clases, ¿Cómo son?; actividades**). Advise students to refer to their webs as they talk.

4 | Write a brochure

Escribir

Create a brochure about your school that would be helpful to a new student from a Spanish-speaking country. Include some of the following: places in the school, classes offered, school supplies needed, teachers, and extracurricular activities. Copy this chart on a piece of paper and use it to organize your information. Your brochure should have illustrations and at least six sentences.

Lugares	Clases	Materiales	Maestros	Actividades

5 | Hold a press conference

Hablar Escribir

Hold a mock press conference. You and your classmates are reporters and have to ask your teacher questions about his or her school schedule and favorite activities. Use the answers to write a short profile of your teacher that could appear in a Spanish edition of the school newspaper. The profile should have at least five sentences.

6 | Write a postcard

Leer Escribir

You received the following postcard from your new pen pal in Mexico. Write back, answering all of your pen pal's questions and asking a few of your own. Your letter should have at least eight sentences.

> PUEBLA
>
> Hola. Me llamo Manuel Salazar. Soy de Puebla, México. Soy estudioso y atlético. Soy un estudiante organizado. Siempre saco buenas notas. ¿Cómo eres tú? ¿Cómo son tus clases? Tengo clases difíciles pero los maestros son muy simpáticos. Estudio mucho y también paso un rato con los amigos. Me gusta jugar al fútbol y andar en patineta. ¿Qué te gusta hacer con los amigos?
>
> Tu amigo,
>
> Manuel

REPASO INCLUSIVO

Communication
Group Work

Assign students to work in groups in which there are a variety of learning styles/multiple intelligences. Ask each group to select a favorite part of the lesson. Within each group, ask each person to describe the favorite part according to his or her strength: to draw it, sing it, chart it, etc.

✓ Ongoing Assessment

Rubric Integrated Performance Assessment
Oral Activities 2, 3, 5
Written Activities 4, 6

Very Good	Proficient	Not There Yet
The student thoroughly develops all requirements of the task.	The student develops most requirements of the task.	The student does not develop the requirements of the task.
The student demonstrates excellent control of grammar.	The student demonstrates good to fair control of grammar.	The student demonstrates poor control of grammar.
Good variety of appropriate vocabulary.	Adequate variety of appropriate vocabulary.	The vocabulary is not appropriate.
The pronunciation is excellent to very good.	The pronunciation is good to fair.	The pronunciation is poor.

Differentiating Instruction

Multiple Intelligences

Musical/Rhythmic Ask students to take information about their school, their schedules, and their classes, and use it as lyrics to create a song or a chant. Ask for volunteers to bring in musical instruments to play accompaniments.

Slower-paced Learners

Sentence Completion Write a list of classes on the board. For example: **la historia, la música, el arte, las ciencias.** Below the list, write the following sentence frame: **La clase favorita de** _____ **es** _____ . Ask students to copy the sentence frame several times. Then ask them to fill in a person's name (a classmate) and a class for each sentence frame.

Proyectos adicionales

❊ Planning Ahead

Projects **Create a calendar.** Have students create their own calendars for the next few months, or the entire year. Encourage them to be creative and original in their designs, and to use a theme related to Puerto Rico, such as Old San Juan, **la comida criolla,** or famous Puerto Ricans. Once their calendars are complete, have students label specific dates with special events, such as the birthdays of family members. Also, have students review vocabulary related to school activities to record upcoming events, such as specific classes, sports practices, or exams.

PACING SUGGESTION: Upon completion of **Lección 2** to review vocabulary related to dates, family members, school, and activities.

❊ Bulletin Board

Create a bulletin board with the title **¡A comer!** Provide students with paper plates and a selection of cooking magazines. Instruct students to find favorite food items in the magazines, cut them out, and glue them onto their plates to create a favorite meal. Staple the completed plates to a bulletin board. Use these "dishes" to ask questions about what students see, as well as foods they like and don't like.

PACING SUGGESTION: After **Lección 1** to reinforce food vocabulary and questions and answers using the verb **gustar.**

Create a bulletin board with the title **Nuestras familias.** Invite students to bring in photographs of one or more family members. Then have them create and decorate frames for their photos using construction paper, stickers, glitter, or other craft supplies. After displaying the photos on a bulletin board, use this "family album" to spark discussions about names, ages, birthdays, favorite foods, and favorite activities.

PACING SUGGESTION: After **Lección 2** to reinforce vocabulary related to ages, birthdays, food, and favorite activities.

Projects **Play house.** Using large shoe boxes or boxes of similar size, have students create a miniature family dining room. They can create furniture out of clay or cardboard, and cut plates and food out of construction paper. They might bring in small dolls or action figures to serve as the family in their scenes, or use clay or paper to create their people. Encourage students to add a calendar to the wall in their scenes, as well as other objects for which they know the vocabulary. On different days, give students the opportunity to rearrange their scenes, and say something new about the people and objects in their "dining room." **Es el siete de diciembre. Es el cumpleaños de la hermana. La familia come pastel.**

PACING SUGGESTION: Throughout the unit as time allows.

Get Help Online
ClassZone.com

Games

Dominós

Domino games are a common sight in the parks and plazas throughout Puerto Rico. Obtain several sets of dominos and have students learn how to play. Throughout the unit, hold an ongoing tournament. Keep track of the results on a grid so play can continue as time allows on different days.

Alternately, have students create their own domino sets using pieces of cardboard or index cards. Instead of dots, have students draw simple pictures of food items and family members. As students add to the "train" of tiles, have them name the item they are connecting with. **Tengo una hermana. Tengo un café.**

> **PACING SUGGESTION:** For regular dominos, at any time during the unit. For vocabulary dominos, after vocabulary is presented in **Lección 1** and **2** to reinforce food items and family names. Can be replayed using different sets of tiles.

Music

Create a lyrics poster of the words to **La Borinqueña,** the Puerto Rican national anthem. You can find the lyrics on the Internet. To teach students the melody, locate a recording or download one from the Internet.

Also, invite interested students to research an aspect of Puerto Rican music, such as the musical styles **bomba** or **plena;** or international music stars from Puerto Rico, such as Danny Rivera, Ricky Martin, Chayanne, or the group Menudo.

Recipe

Piraguas are sold by **piragüeros** in the parks and on the streets of Puerto Rico. These refreshing treats are like snow cones with tropical fruit flavors. You can make them in your classroom using a blender.

Piraguas

Ingredientes

1 bolsa de hielo

3 o más latas de jugo concentrado de sabores tropicales (piña, mango, papaya, etc.)

Instrucciones

En un jarrón, diluir cada lata de jugo concentrado a 1/3 de lo que indican las instrucciones (usualmente una lata de agua en vez de tres). Triturar hielo en la licuadora y ponerlo en pequeños vasos de cartón. Verter el almíbar sobre el hielo y servir con una cucharita.

La comida criolla. Plan a Puerto Rican tasting day! Have students research recipes for traditional Puerto Rican dishes, such as **empanadillas, asopao, tostones,** or **arroz con pollo.** Organize volunteers to bring in their culinary creations, as well as paper plates, napkins, and plastic silverware. Invite each "chef" to speak about his or her dish, and then **¡Buen provecho!**

UNIT THEME
Eating with the family

🏵 UNIT STANDARDS
COMMUNICATION
- Talk about foods and beverages
- Ask questions
- Say which foods you like and don't like
- Talk about family
- Ask and tell ages
- Express possession
- Give dates
- Make comparisons

CULTURES
- Traditional cooking of Puerto Rico, El Salvador
- Manuel Hernández Acevedo and La Plaza de Colón in Old San Juan
- Grocery shopping
- Government elections in Puerto Rico
- Rafael Tufiño and Fernando Sayán Polo
- Instruments from Puerto Rico and Peru

CONNECTIONS
- Science: Researching severe weather
- Math: Calculating the speed of a storm
- History: Researching Caribbean hurricanes
- Geography: Tracking Hurricane Georges

COMPARISONS
- Hot weather foods and drinks
- Traditional Puerto Rican and Salvadoran dishes
- The Spanish letters **r** and **rr**; the letter **j** in Spanish and in English
- The **quinceañera** celebration in Peru and Puerto Rico
- Landmarks in Puerto Rico and the U.S.
- The **sobremesa,** and other mealtime traditions
- Elections in Puerto Rico and the U.S.
- Portraits by Rafael Tufiño (Puerto Rico) and Fernando Sayán Polo (Peru)
- Instruments from Puerto Rico and Peru
- Sunday meals in El Salvador, Peru, Puerto Rico, the U.S.

COMMUNITIES
- Andean music and music of other countries in a local store

UNIDAD **3**
Puerto Rico
Comer en familia

Océano Atlántico

Lección 1
Tema: **Mi comida favorita**

Lección 2
Tema: **En mi familia**

«¡Hola!
Somos Marisol y Rodrigo. Somos de Puerto Rico.»

Población: 3.897.960

Área: 3.515 millas cuadradas

Capital: San Juan

Moneda: el dólar estadounidense

Idiomas: español, inglés (los dos son oficiales)

Comida típica: pasteles, arroz con gandules, pernil

Pasteles

Gente famosa: Julia de Burgos (poetisa), Roberto Clemente (beisbolista), Rosario Ferré (escritora), Luis Muñoz Marín (político)

152 ciento cincuenta y dos

Cultural Geography

Setting the Scene
- How many stars does the Puerto Rican flag have? (one)
- What are the two official languages of Puerto Rico? (Spanish, English)
- What is the currency of Puerto Rico? (U.S. dollar) Why? (Puerto Rico is a U.S. commonwealth.)

Teaching with Maps
- Which country is Puerto Rico's closest Spanish-speaking neighbor? (Dominican Republic)
- Where on the island is San Juan located? (the Northern coast)
- What are the names of two smaller islands that belong to Puerto Rico? (Culebra, Vieques)

Una familia come en la playa

◄ **Comidas al aire libre** Many Puerto Ricans enjoy informal gatherings at a beach or park, where families can spend the day together, barbecue, and listen to music. **Pinchos** (skewers of chicken or pork) are popular at barbecues and snack stands. *Where do people like to eat outdoors where you live?*

Casas de colores vivos San Juan is famous for its well-preserved colonial quarter, called **Viejo San Juan.** Its narrow streets are lined with brightly-colored houses with balconies. *What are some historic areas close to where you live?* ►

Casas coloniales en Viejo San Juan

La Cascada de la Coca en El Yunque

◄ **Un parque nacional** El Yunque is the only tropical rain forest in the care of the U.S. Forest Service. The park has many waterfalls, such as the Cascada de la Coca, and is home to the **coquí,** a tiny tree frog named for its distinctive song. *What are some features of other parks in the United States?*

Puerto Rico
ciento cincuenta y tres   **153**

Bridging Cultures

Heritage Language Learners

Support What They Know Invite those students who have a personal or family connection to Puerto Rico to enrich the information presented on pp. 152 and 153. What are their memories and/or impressions of this island? How would they compare family life and food in Puerto Rico with that of the United States? What are some of their favorite traditional Puerto Rican dishes?

English Learners

Build Background Encourage students to make connections with the information on p. 153. After reading each paragraph, ask the follow-up question in reference to their home country. Substitute the name of the country for the phrase *where you live*. For example: *Where do people like to eat outdoors in Korea? What are some historic areas in Haiti?*

Send your students to www.ClassZone.com to explore authentic Puerto Rican culture. Tell them to click on Cultura interactiva to see these pages come alive!

Culture

About the Photos

· The photo of the picnickers shows Puerto Ricans participating in a typical pastime. The are enjoying **pinchos de carne** on the beach.
· The architecture of **Viejo San Juan** dates from the 16th century and mimics the majestic, yet charming, architecture of many southern Spanish cities. These well-preserved, pastel-colored buildings are the pride of the Old City.
· The young explorers pictured here are enjoying the beauty of an ancient rain forest, just a short distance from San Juan. The forest offers a variety of trees, flowers, and wildlife.

Expanded Information

· Puerto Rican food, or **comida criolla,** has a distinctive taste, which comes from the herbs and spices that enhance it. A combination of local ingredients produces **sofrito,** the seasoning used in popular dishes such as **arroz con pollo.**
· Old San Juan has other centuries-old, historically important structures: El Morro Fortress, San Juan Cathedral, and the Dominican Convent.
· **El Yunque,** which lies in the Luquillo Mountain Range, was once considered a sacred place by Puerto Rico's native Taino people. The name **El Yunque** means *White Lands* and refers to the cloud-covered mountaintops in this part of the island.

Video Character Guide

Marisol and Rodrigo are friends who live in Puerto Rico. They both enjoy food, but disagree about what the best choices are when grocery shopping or eating.

Lesson Overview

Culture at a Glance ❖

Topic & Activity	Essential Question
Hot weather foods and beverages pp. 154–155	What do you like to eat or drink during hot weather?
Traditional cooking p. 164	How do historical influences affect the food that people eat?
La Plaza de Colón, artist Manuel Hernández Acevedo p. 170	How does an artist's work represent historic landmarks of a country?
Let's go grocery shopping! pp. 176–177	What are some of the food items that people from Puerto Rico buy on a regular basis?
Culture review p. 181	What are some aspects of Puerto Rican and Salvadoran culture?

COMPARISON COUNTRIES 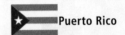 Puerto Rico  El Salvador Perú

Practice at a Glance ❖

	Objective	Activity & Skill
Vocabulary	Food and beverages	1: Writing; 2: Speaking; 4: Speaking; 6: Reading/Writing; 8: Speaking; 9: Reading/Speaking; 10: Speaking/Writing; 11: Writing; 12: Listening/Reading; 13: Writing; 14: Speaking/Writing; 15: Speaking/Writing; 19: Speaking/Writing; 23: Speaking; 24: Reading/Listening/Speaking; Repaso 1: Listening; Repaso 2: Writing
	Interrogative words	3: Listening/Reading; 18: Speaking; 22: Listening/Reading; Repaso 3: Writing
Grammar	Interrogative words	3: Listening/Reading; 22: Listening/Reading; Repaso 3: Writing
	Gustar with nouns	5: Speaking/Writing; 6: Reading/Writing; 7: Speaking; 8: Speaking; 9: Reading/Speaking; 10: Speaking/Writing; 11: Writing; 12: Listening/Reading; 13: Writing; 14: Speaking/Writing; 24: Reading/Listening/Speaking; 25: Writing; Repaso 4: Writing
	Present tense of **-er** and **-ir** verbs	15: Speaking/Writing; 16: Speaking/Writing; 17: Listening/Writing; 18: Speaking; 19: Speaking/Writing; 20: Speaking; 23: Speaking; 24: Reading/Listening/Speaking; Repaso 2: Writing
	The verb **hacer**	18: Speaking; 23: Speaking; Repaso 2: Writing
Communication	Talk about foods and beverages	1: Writing; 2: Speaking; 4: Speaking; 5: Speaking/Writing; 6: Reading/Writing; 7: Speaking; 8: Speaking; 9: Reading/Speaking; 10: Speaking/Writing; 11: Writing; 12: Listening/Reading; 13: Writing; 14: Speaking/Writing; 15: Speaking/Writing; 25: Writing; Repaso 4: Writing
	Ask questions	2: Speaking; 3: Listening/Reading; 7: Speaking; 9: Reading/Speaking; 14: Speaking/Writing; 18: Speaking; 20: Speaking; 25: Writing; Repaso 3: Writing;
	Say which foods you like and don't like	2: Speaking; 6: Reading/Writing; 7: Speaking; 8: Speaking; 9: Reading/Speaking; 10: Speaking/Writing; 11: Writing; 12: Listening/Reading; 13: Writing; 14: Speaking/Writing; 24: Reading/Listening/Speaking; 25: Writing; Repaso 4: Writing
	Pronunciation: The letters **r** and **rr**	Las letras *r* y *rr*, p. 163: Listening/Speaking
Recycle	**Gustar** with an infinitive	2: Speaking
	Snack foods	4: Speaking
	The verb **estar**	16: Speaking/Writing
	Telling time	23: Speaking

The following presentations are recorded in the Audio Program for *¡Avancemos!*

- **¡A responder!** *page 158*
- **17: Actividades en el almuerzo** *page 169*
- **24: Integración** *page 174*
- **Repaso de la lección** *page 180*
  1: Listen and understand

¡A responder! TXT CD 3 track 2

1. la hamburguesa
2. la leche
3. el pan
4. el sándwich de jamón y queso
5. el cereal
6. la sopa
7. el huevo
8. el café

17 | Actividades en el almuerzo

TXT CD 3 track 6

Marisol: ¡Hola! Soy Marisol. Antes del almuerzo, tengo la clase de inglés. Escribo en el cuaderno, pero es difícil porque tengo mucha hambre.

Rodrigo: Soy Rodrigo. Es la hora del almuerzo. Hmmm... la cafetería vende sopa, uvas y bananas.

Mateo: Me llamo Mateo. ¡Me gusta la comida nutritiva! Hoy Rodrigo y yo comemos uvas.

Carmen: Hola, me llamo Carmen. Ahora estoy en la cafetería. Bebo jugo de naranja porque tengo sed. ¡Es rico!

Raúl y David, ¿qué hacen ustedes? ¿Por qué no comen?

Raúl: Leemos un libro. Nos gustan los libros.

Laura: Hola, soy Laura. Hoy la cafetería no vende sándwiches. ¡Qué horrible! Pero mi amiga Diana tiene un sándwich y nosotras compartimos. Es una buena amiga.

24 | Integración TXT CD 3 tracks 8, 9

¿Tienes hambre? En Supermercado Econo vendemos todo para el desayuno: cereal, huevos y muchas frutas. También hay almuerzo todos los días en la cafetería dentro del supermercado. Vendemos hamburguesas muy ricas, sándwiches de jamón, sopas nutritivas y ¡más!

Repaso de la lección TXT CD 3 track 11

1 Listen and understand

Roque: Gracias por estar con nosotros, Lola.

Lola: El gusto es mío, Roque. Me gusta hablar de la comida.

Roque: Ah, ¿sí? ¿Qué te gusta comer más?

Lola: Las hamburguesas son muy ricas. En el desayuno como dos hamburguesas casi todos los días.

Roque: ¿Te gustan las hamburguesas en el desayuno? Interesante... ¿Y bebes café también?

Lola: No, el café es para la cena. Bebo café todas las noches.

Roque: ¿Qué te gusta comer en la cena?

Lola: Siempre como huevos y pan.

Roque: ¿Qué comes y bebes en el almuerzo?

Lola: Como cereal y una banana.

Roque: ¿Bebes leche?

Lola: Sí, bebo leche en el almuerzo porque es muy buena.

Roque: También bebes leche en el desayuno, ¿no?

Lola: No, me gusta más beber un refresco en el desayuno.

Roque: Gracias, Lola. Eres una persona muy interesante.

On your desktop

Everything you need to ...

Plan	Present	Assess
 **easyPlanner** DVD-ROM	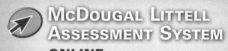 **POWER PRESENTATIONS**	**McDougal Littell Assessment System** ONLINE
All resources including audio and video	Ready-made PowerPoint™ presentations with  **Animated** Grammar	✓ Assess, score, prescribe, and remediate online ✓ Create customized tests with the Test Generator CD-ROM ✓ Individualized Assessment for on-level, modified, pre-AP, and heritage language learners

 ## Print

Plan	Present	Practice	Assess
URB 3 • Video Scripts pp. 69–70 • Family Letter p. 91 • Absent Student Copymasters pp. 93–100 **Lesson Plans** p. 57 **Best Practices Toolkit**	**URB 3** • Video Activities pp. 51–58 **TPRS** pp. 29–35	• *Cuaderno* pp. 101–123 • *Cuaderno para hispanohablantes* pp. 101–123 • *Lecturas para todos* pp. 22–26 • *Lecturas para hispanohablantes* • *¡AvanzaCómics! SúperBruno y Nati, Episodio 2* **URB 3** • Practice Games pp. 31–38 • Audio Scripts pp. 73–77 • Map/Culture Activities pp. 83–84 • Fine Art Activities pp. 86–87	**URB 3** • Did you get it? Reteaching and Practice Copymasters pp. 1–12

 ## Unit Transparency Book 3

Culture	Presentation and Practice	Classroom Management
• Atlas Maps UTB 1 1–6 • Map of Puerto Rico 1 • Fine Art Transparencies 2, 3	• Vocabulary Transparencies 6, 7 • Grammar Presentation Transparencies 10, 11	• Warm Up Transparencies 16–19 **MSRB** • Student Book Answer Transparencies 44–47

Audio and Video

Audio	Video

• Student Book Audio CD 3 Tracks 1–11
• Workbook Audio CD 2 Tracks 1–10
• Heritage Learners Audio CD 1 Tracks 17–20, CD 3 Tracks 15,16
• Assessment Audio CD 1 Tracks 15,16
• *Lecturas para todos* Audio CD 1 Track 5, CD 2 Tracks 1–6
• *Música del mundo hispano*
• Sing-along Audio CD
	• Vocabulary Video DVD 1
	• *Telehistoria* DVD 1
	   Escena 1
	   Escena 2
	   Escena 3
	   Completa

Online and CD-ROM Resources

Student	Teacher
Available online and on CD-ROM: • eEdition • @HomeTutor • Animated Grammar **Available online:** • *Cultura interactiva* • Culture Links • WebQuests • Flashcards • Conjuguemos.com • Review Games • Self-check Quiz	**Available online and on CD-ROM:** **EasyPlanner CD-ROM resources:** • Learning Scenarios • Conversation Cards • Family Letters in Spanish • Family Letters in Creole **Available online:** • McDougal Littell Assessment System **Available on CD-ROM:** • Test Generator • Power Presentations

✓ Differentiated Assessment

On-level	Modified	Pre-AP	Heritage Learners
• Vocabulary Recognition Quiz p. 103 • Vocabulary Production Quiz p. 104 • Grammar Quizzes pp. 105–106 • Culture Quiz p. 107 • On-level Lesson Test pp. 108–114	• Modified Lesson Test pp. 83–89	• Pre-AP Lesson Test pp. 83–89	• Heritage Learners Lesson Test pp. 89–95

Core Pacing Guide

	Objectives/Focus	Teach	Practice	Assess/HW Options
DAY 1	**Culture:** learn about Puerto Rican culture **Vocabulary:** breakfast, lunch, and dinner foods and beverages • Warm Up OHT 16 **5 min**	Unit Opener pp. 152–153 Lesson Opener pp. 154–155 **Presentación de vocabulario** pp. 156–158 • Read A–D • View video DVD 1 • Play audio TXT CD 3 track 1 • *¡A responder!* TXT CD 3 track 2 **25 min**	Lesson opener pp. 154–155 **Práctica de vocabulario** p. 159 • Acts. 1, 2 **15 min**	**Assess:** *Para y piensa* p. 159 **5 min** **Homework:** *Cuaderno* pp. 101–103 @HomeTutor
DAY 2	**Communication:** identify question words, practice using them to ask questions and give answers • Warm Up OHT 16 • Check Homework **5 min**	Vocabulario en contexto pp. 160–161 • *Telehistoria escena 1* DVD 1 • *Nota gramatical:* interrogative words **20 min**	Vocabulario en contexto pp. 160–161 • Act. 3 TXT CD 3 track 3 • Act. 4 **20 min**	**Assess:** *Para y piensa* p. 161 **5 min** **Homework:** *Cuaderno* pp. 101–103 @HomeTutor
DAY 3	**Grammar: gustar** with nouns • Warm Up OHT 17 • Check Homework **5 min**	**Presentación de gramática** p. 162 • **gustar** with nouns **Práctica de gramática** pp. 163–165 • *Pronunciación:* TXT CD 3 track 4 **20 min**	**Práctica de gramática** pp. 163–165 • Acts. 5, 6, 7, 8, 9, 10, 11 **20 min**	**Assess:** *Para y piensa* p. 165 **5 min** **Homework:** *Cuaderno* pp. 104–106 @HomeTutor
DAY 4	**Communication:** talk about likes and dislikes using **gustar** • Warm Up OHT 17 • Check Homework **5 min**	Gramática en contexto pp. 166–167 • *Telehistoria escena 2* DVD 1 **15 min**	Gramática en contexto pp. 166–167 • Act. 12 TXT CD 3 track 5 • Acts. 13, 14 **25 min**	**Assess:** *Para y piensa* p. 167 **5 min** **Homework:** *Cuaderno* pp. 104–106 @HomeTutor
DAY 5	**Grammar:** present tense of **-er** and **-ir** verbs • Warm Up OHT 18 • Check Homework **5 min**	**Presentación de gramática** p. 168 • Present tense of **-er** and **-ir** verbs **Práctica de gramática** pp. 169–171 • *Nota gramatical:* the verb **hacer** **Culture:** *La Plaza de Colón* **15 min**	**Práctica de gramática** pp. 169–171 • Acts. 15, 16, 18, 19, 20 • Act. 17 TXT CD 3 track 6 **25 min**	**Assess:** *Para y piensa* p. 171 **5 min** **Homework:** *Cuaderno* pp. 107–109 @HomeTutor
DAY 6	**Communication:** Culmination: talk about eating healthy foods; using **-er** and **-ir** verbs • Warm Up OHT 18 • Check Homework **5 min**	Todo junto pp. 172–174 • *Escenas 1, 2: Resumen* • *Telehistoria completa* DVD 1 **20 min**	Todo junto pp. 172–174 • Acts. 21, 22 TXT CD 3 tracks 3, 5, 7 • Act. 24 TXT CD 3 tracks 8, 9 • Acts. 23, 25 **20 min**	**Assess:** *Para y piensa* p. 174 **5 min** **Homework:** *Cuaderno* pp. 110–111 @HomeTutor
DAY 7	**Reading:** Let's shop and eat! **Connections:** Science • Warm Up OHT 19 • Check Homework **5 min**	Lectura pp. 176–177 • *¡A comprar y a comer!* TXT CD 3 track 10 Conexiones p. 178 • *Las ciencias* **15 min**	Lectura pp. 176–177 • *¡A comprar y a comer!* Conexiones p. 178 • *Proyectos 1, 2, 3* **25 min**	**Assess:** *Para y piensa* p. 177 **5 min** **Homework:** *Cuaderno* pp. 115–117 @HomeTutor
DAY 8	**Review:** Lesson review • Warm Up OHT 19 • Check Homework **5 min**	Repaso de la lección pp. 180–181 **15 min**	Repaso de la lección pp. 180–181 • Act. 1 TXT CD 3 track 11 • Acts. 2, 3, 4, 5 **25 min**	**Assess: Repaso de la lección** pp. 180–181 **5 min** **Homework:** *En resumen* p. 179; *Cuaderno* pp. 112–114, 118–123 (optional) Review Games Online @HomeTutor
DAY 9	Assessment			**Assess:** Lesson 1 test **50 min**

	Objectives/Focus	Teach	Practice	Assess/HW Options
DAY 1	**Culture:** learn about Puerto Rican culture **Vocabulary:** breakfast, lunch, and dinner foods and beverages • Warm Up OHT 16 **5 min**	Unit Opener pp. 152–153 Lesson Opener pp. 154–155 **Presentación de vocabulario** pp. 156–158 • Read A–D • View video DVD 1 • Play audio TXT CD 3 track 1 • *¡A responder!* TXT CD 3 track 2 **25 min**	Lesson Opener pp. 154–155 **Práctica de vocabulario** p. 159 • Acts. 1, 2 **15 min**	**Assess:** *Para y piensa* p. 159 **5 min**
	Communication: identify question words, practice using them to ask questions and give answers **5 min**	**Vocabulario en contexto** pp. 160–161 • *Telehistoria escena 1* DVD 1 • *Nota gramatical:* interrogative words **15 min**	**Vocabulario en contexto** pp. 160–161 • Act. 3 TXT CD 3 track 3 • Act. 4 **15 min**	**Assess:** *Para y piensa* p. 161 **5 min** **Homework:** *Cuaderno* pp. 101–103 @HomeTutor
DAY 2	**Grammar: gustar** with nouns • Warm Up OHT 17 • Check Homework **5 min**	**Presentación de gramática** p. 162 • **gustar** with nouns **Práctica de gramática** pp. 163–165 • *Pronunciación:* TXT CD 3 track 4 **15 min**	**Práctica de gramática** pp. 163–165 • Acts. 5, 6, 7, 8, 9, 10, 11 **20 min**	**Assess:** *Para y piensa* p. 165 **5 min**
	Communication: talk about likes and dislikes using **gustar** **5 min**	**Gramática en contexto** pp. 166–167 • *Telehistoria escena 2* DVD 1 **15 min**	**Gramática en contexto** pp. 166–167 • Act. 12 TXT CD 3 track 5 • Acts. 13, 14 **20 min**	**Assess:** *Para y piensa* p. 167 **5 min** **Homework:** *Cuaderno* pp. 104–106 @HomeTutor
DAY 3	**Grammar:** present tense of **-er** and **-ir** verbs • Warm Up OHT 18 • Check Homework **5 min**	**Presentación de gramática** p. 168 • Present tense of **-er** and **-ir** verbs **Práctica de gramática** pp. 169–171 • *Nota gramatical:* the verb **hacer** **Culture:** *La Plaza de Colón* **15 min**	**Práctica de gramática** pp. 169–171 • Acts. 15, 16, 18, 19, 20 • Act. 17 TXT CD 3 track 6 **20 min**	**Assess:** *Para y piensa* p. 171 **5 min**
	Communication: Culmination: talk about eating healthy foods; using **-er** and **-ir** verbs **5 min**	**Todo junto** pp. 172–174 • *Escenas 1, 2: Resumen* • *Telehistoria completa* DVD 1 **15 min**	**Todo junto** pp. 172–174 • Acts. 21, 22 TXT CD 3 tracks 3, 5, 7 • Act. 24 TXT CD 3 tracks 8, 9 • Acts. 23, 25 **20 min**	**Assess:** *Para y piensa* p. 174 **5 min** **Homework:** *Cuaderno* pp. 107–111 @HomeTutor
DAY 4	**Reading:** Let's shop and eat! • Warm Up OHT 19 • Check Homework **5 min**	**Lectura** pp. 176–177 • *¡A comprar y a comer!* TXT CD 3 track 10 **15 min**	**Lectura** pp. 176–177 • *¡A comprar y a comer!* **20 min**	**Assess:** *Para y piensa* p. 177 **5 min**
	Review: Lesson review **5 min**	**Repaso de la lección** pp. 180–181 **15 min**	**Repaso de la lección** pp. 180–181 • Act. 1 TXT CD 3 track 11 • Acts. 2, 3, 4, 5 **20 min**	**Assess: Repaso de la lección** pp. 180–181 **5 min** **Homework:** *En resumen* p. 179; *Cuaderno* pp. 112–123 (optional); Review Games Online @HomeTutor
DAY 5	**Assessment**			**Assess:** Lesson 1 test **45 min**
	Connections: Science **5 min**	**Conexiones** p. 178 • *Las ciencias* **10 min**	**Conexiones** p. 178 • *Proyectos 1, 2, 3* **30 min**	

Objectives
- Introduce lesson theme: **Mi comida favorita.**
- **Culture:** Learn about and compare foods from different countries.

Presentation Strategies
- Introduce the characters' names: Rodrigo and Marisol.
- Ask students to make a list of their favorite foods and beverages.
- Have students from other countries talk about foods and beverages typical of their countries.

STANDARDS
2.2 Products and perspectives
4.2 Compare cultures

 Warm Up   UTB 3 Transparency 16

Ir Fill in the blanks with the appropriate form of **ir.**
1. Anita y Juan _____ a la cafetería a las doce.
2. Selena y yo _____ al gimnasio después de las clases.
3. ¿_____ ustedes a la biblioteca? Tengo que ir también.
4. ¿_____ tú al baño?
5. Yo _____ a la oficina.
Answers: 1. van; 2. vamos; 3. Van; 4. Vas; 5. voy

Comparación cultural

Exploring the Theme
Ask the following:
1. Do you buy food from street vendors?
2. Do you like to try new types of foods when you travel?
3. Are there any grocery shops where you live that sell foods from other countries?

¿Qué ves? Sample answers include:
- Sí, los chicos están contentos.
- Están delante del señor.
- A los chicos les gusta comer helado.

154

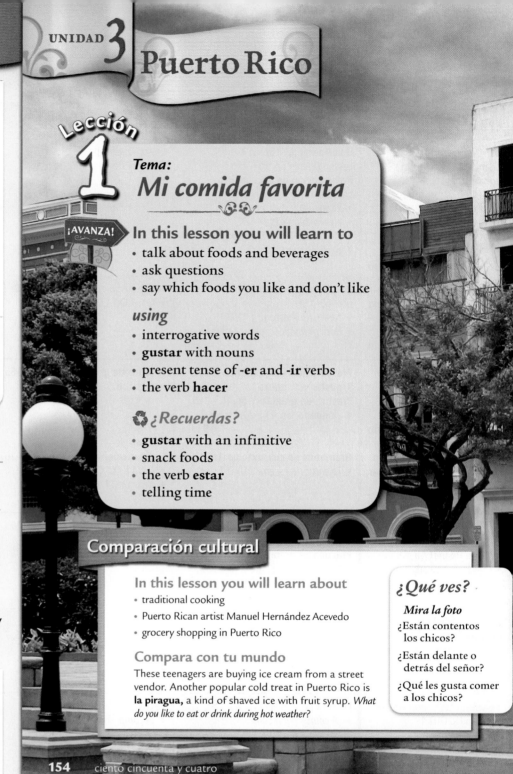

UNIDAD 3 Puerto Rico

Lección 1

Tema:
Mi comida favorita

¡AVANZA! **In this lesson you will learn to**
- talk about foods and beverages
- ask questions
- say which foods you like and don't like

using
- interrogative words
- **gustar** with nouns
- present tense of **-er** and **-ir** verbs
- the verb **hacer**

¿Recuerdas?
- **gustar** with an infinitive
- snack foods
- the verb **estar**
- telling time

Comparación cultural

In this lesson you will learn about
- traditional cooking
- Puerto Rican artist Manuel Hernández Acevedo
- grocery shopping in Puerto Rico

Compara con tu mundo
These teenagers are buying ice cream from a street vendor. Another popular cold treat in Puerto Rico is **la piragua,** a kind of shaved ice with fruit syrup. *What do you like to eat or drink during hot weather?*

¿Qué ves?

Mira la foto
¿Están contentos los chicos?

¿Están delante o detrás del señor?

¿Qué les gusta comer a los chicos?

154 ciento cincuenta y cuatro

Differentiating Instruction

Heritage Language Learners

Support What They Know Ask students what are some popular or typical dishes from their country of origin. What are the main ingredients, and how are they prepared? If you have students of Puerto Rican descent, ask them to share what they know about typical Puerto Rican cuisine. You can also have students research the topic at the library or via the Internet.

Inclusion

Cumulative Instruction Remind students that they already learned some vocabulary related to food in Unidad 1, Lección 1. Ask students to review this vocabulary by writing each familiar word and then drawing a corresponding picture. Then ask students to draw pictures of new food items for which they would like to learn the Spanish word.

La Plaza de Colón
en el Viejo San Juan
San Juan, Puerto Rico

Puerto Rico
ciento cincuenta y cinco   155

Using the Photo

Location Information

Plaza de Colón, shown in the photo, is in the heart of San Juan's Old Town. Originally called **Plaza Santiago,** it was renamed in 1893 to honor the 400th anniversary of Columbus's arrival to that island. The plaza hosts several quaint cafés and ice cream stands.

Expanded Information

Puerto Rico The island of Puerto Rico is 100 miles long, and only 35 miles wide. Both Spanish and English are official languages of Puerto Rico. Puerto Rico is not a state. It is a self-governing commonwealth in association with the United States. Its official name is **Estado Libre Asociado de Puerto Rico.**

Long-term Retention

Recycle

Have students write a list of snack foods or beverages that they enjoy eating or drinking. Then have them practice these words by using them in the following sentence: **Me gusta comer/beber _____.**

Differentiating Instruction

Pre-AP

Expand and Elaborate Have students write three to five things they know about Puerto Rico. Topics can include history, geography, daily life, climate, language, etc. Have them post this information around a map of Puerto Rico, and call on volunteers to give a short description of the island.

Slower-paced Learners

Yes/No Questions Ask students yes/no questions about what they see in the photo on pp. 154–155. Point to the appropriate item in the photo when the answer is yes. **¿Hay dos chicos en la foto?** Use familiar vocabulary on other topics when the answer is no. **¿Hay una chica enojada? ¿Hay un gimnasio?**

¡AVANZA! Objective

- Present vocabulary: food, meals.

Core Resources

- Video Program: DVD 1
- Audio Program: TXT CD 3 track 1

Presentation Strategies

- Have students look at pp. 156–157, and present vocabulary.
- Make **cierto/falso** statements to verify comprehension. For example: **La leche es una comida. (Falso, es una bebida.)**
- Play the audio as students read A–C.
- Show the video.

STANDARDS

1.2 Understand language

Comparisons
English Language Connection

Spanish often requires the use of **tener** rather than an English equivalent of the verb *to be* to express a condition. Note: **tener hambre** and **tener sed.** To say that one is very thirsty or very hungry, use **tener mucha sed** and **tener mucha hambre. Tener ganas de** + an infinitive means *to feel like.*

Long-term Retention
Personalize It

Read the names of the food items on pp. 156–157 and ask students to vote with a show of hands whether they are **rico(a)(os)(as)** or **horrible(s).** Tally the votes on the board.

Presentación de VOCABULARIO

¡AVANZA! **Goal:** Learn about what Rodrigo and Marisol eat for breakfast, lunch, and dinner. Then practice what you have learned to talk about foods and beverages. ***Actividades 1–2***

♻ *¿Recuerdas?* **gustar** with an infinitive p. 44

VIDEO
DVD

AUDIO

A ¡Hola! Me llamo Rodrigo y ella es Ana. Son las ocho de la mañana. **Es importante** comer **un desayuno nutritivo** todos los días.

el desayuno

los huevos

el pan

B Cuando **tengo hambre**, me gusta comer **huevos** y **pan.** Cuando **tengo sed**, bebo **jugo de naranja.** Me gusta mucho porque es **rico.** Nunca bebo **café** porque es **horrible.**

el cereal

el yogur

En Puerto Rico se dice...
In Puerto Rico the word for *orange juice* is **el jugo de china.**

las bebidas

el jugo de naranja

el café

la leche

Differentiating Instruction

English Learners

Build Background Before introducing the Spanish vocabulary on p. 156, give English learners the opportunity to familiarize themselves with the photos. Discuss the food items presented and whether similar items exist in their countries of origin. If items do not exist, is there something similar that people eat or drink?

Multiple Intelligences

Logical/Mathematical Say aloud the name of one of the breakfast foods presented on p. 156. Tell students to raise their hands if they had that item for breakfast that morning. Record the findings of your survey on the board. Then have students present the information in the form of a bar graph that represents which breakfast foods are most popular among their classmates.

C Es la una y **ahora** Marisol y yo comemos **el almuerzo.** En la cafetería **venden** muchas **comidas: sándwiches, hamburguesas** y **sopa.** También venden **bebidas: leche,** jugos y refrescos.

el almuerzo

el sándwich de jamón y queso

la hamburguesa

la sopa

Más vocabulario

¿Cómo? *How?*	¿Quién(es)? *Who?*
¿Cuál(es)? *Which?*	compartir *to share*
¿Por qué? *Why?*	otro(a) *other*
¿Qué? *What?*	*Expansión de vocabulario* p. R4

Continuará...

Comparisons
English Language Connection

Point out that in English a noun is often used to describe another noun: *orange juice, ham sandwich.* The describing noun comes first and the noun that's being described comes second. In Spanish, the noun that's being described comes first and is followed by **de** + the describing noun: **jugo de naranja, sándwich de jamón.**

Communication
Humor/Creativity

Hold a contest in which students write and read aloud horrible combinations of foods and/or beverages. For example: **jugo de huevo, yogur de jamón,** and so on. The class can vote for the most horrible combination.

Communication
Regionalisms

In Spain and Mexico many people use **la comida** instead of **el almuerzo.** In Spain **un sándwich** is called **un bocadillo** and in Mexico it is called **una torta.**

Differentiating Instruction

Pre-AP

Expand and Elaborate Have students bring empty food packages to class such as soup, milk, juice, and yogurt containers. Have them create short TV food ads for a fictitious food item brand and present them to the class. For example: **Cuando tengo hambre, siempre como el cereal Nutrirrico porque es rico y nutritivo.**

Heritage Language Learners

Support What They Know In small groups, have students create a skit based on the vocabulary presented on pp. 156 and 157. Have students pick one of the following: **en el desayuno,** or **en el almuerzo.** Then instruct them to write a short script wherein they each play a part. Give students the opportunity to perform their plays for the group.

157

Objectives
- Present vocabulary: foods, meals
- Check for recognition.

Core Resources
- Video Program: DVD 1
- Audio Program: TXT CD 3 tracks 1, 2

Presentation Strategies
- Have students look at p. 158 and make a list of all the fruits mentioned in it.
- Play the audio as students read D.
- Show the video.

STANDARDS
1.2 Understand language

Long-term Retention
Personalize It

Ask students what they feel like eating for breakfast and lunch. Say: **¿Qué tienes ganas de comer para el almuerzo? ¿Qué tienes ganas de comer para el desayuno?**

Communication
Pair Work

Ask student pairs to make a list of breakfast foods and lunch foods, including beverages. Then ask them to use the list to ask each other questions about which foods or beverages they like best. For example: **A: ¿Te gusta más beber jugo de naranja o jugo de manzana? B: Me gusta más beber jugo de naranja. A: ¿Te gusta más comer una hamburguesa o un sándwich de queso? B: Me gusta más comer una hamburguesa.**

Communication
Group Work

Place students in groups of four. Ask them to work together to create a table with three columns and two rows. They should head the columns **el desayuno, el almuerzo,** and **los dos.** The rows should be labeled **para beber, para comer.** Ask them to complete the chart with food vocabulary from this lesson as well as from Unidad 1, Lección 1.

See ¡A responder! answers on p. 159.
158

Presentación de VOCABULARIO
(continuación)

D Marisol y yo compramos fruta **para** mi papá: **manzanas, bananas** y **uvas. La cena** es a las siete y **tengo ganas de** comer. Siempre como mucho cuando mi mamá prepara la comida.

la manzana

las uvas

la banana

En Puerto Rico se dice...
The word for *banana* is **el guineo.**

la cena

¡A responder! Escuchar

Write **desayuno** and **almuerzo** on separate pieces of paper. Listen to the list of foods. Hold up the correct piece or pieces of paper to indicate when you eat each food.

@HomeTutor VideoPlus
Interactive Flashcards
ClassZone.com

Differentiating Instruction

Multiple Intelligences
Kinesthetic Have pictures or drawings of the food items on pp. 156–158 arranged on a table, at the front of the classroom. Call students individually to come up and take the item you name. Have them hold the item up and repeat the name.

Pre-AP
Communicate Preferences Ask students to read pp. 156–158 again and make a list of all the food items mentioned. Then ask them to read each word aloud, state whether they like to eat or drink that item and express why or why not. For example: **El café: no me gusta beber café porque no es nutritivo y porque es horrible.**

Práctica de VOCABULARIO

1 | ¡A jugar! Busca, busca

Escribir   Find and write the names of the eight foods hidden in the cafeteria scene.

> **Expansión:**
> **Teacher Edition Only**
> Have students create three sentences about the people in the picture and the food they like to eat.

2 | ¿Qué te gusta más? ♻ *¿Recuerdas?* **gustar** with an infinitive p. 44

Hablar   Talk with a partner about which foods and drinks you like more.

A ¿Te gusta más comer papas fritas o pizza?

B Me gusta más comer pizza.

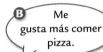

 **1.** **2.** **3.**

4. **5.** **6.**

> **Expansión:**
> **Teacher Edition Only**
> Ask students to talk with a partner about which foods and drinks they do not like.

Más práctica   Cuaderno *pp. 101–103*   Cuaderno para hispanohablantes *pp. 101–104*

PARA Y PIENSA

Did you get it?
1. Name three breakfast foods.   2. Name three lunch foods.

Get Help Online ClassZone.com

Differentiating Instruction

Inclusion

Multisensory Input/Output In pairs, have students create a deck of food cards. Have them draw a sketch of each of the foods shown on p. 159 on index cards. Then have each partner choose two cards. Students must use yes/no questions to figure out which foods their partner is holding. **¿Tienes la manzana? No, no tengo la manzana. ¿Tienes la sopa? No, no tengo la sopa.**

Heritage Language Learners

Regional Variations Ask students to share the expressions that people in their country or region of origin use when food is really delicious. What do people say when a meal is not so good? Also, ask students to share the expressions people use before starting a meal or making a toast. What are some common phrases heard around the table?

Objectives
· Practice vocabulary: food, meals.
· Recycle: **gustar** with an infinitive.

Core Resource
· *Cuaderno,* pp. 101–103

Practice Sequence
· **Activity 1:** Vocabulary recognition: foods
· **Activity 2:** Vocabulary production: stating preferences; Recycle: **gustar** with an infinitive

✿ STANDARDS
1.1 Engage in conversation, Act. 2
1.3 Present information, Acts. 1–2, PYP

✓ Ongoing Assessment

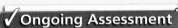
@HomeTutor More Practice ClassZone.com

PARA Y PIENSA **Alternative Strategy** Have students use whiteboards to complete the Para y piensa. On the count of three, direct students to display their answers. For additional practice, use Reteaching & Practice Copymasters URB 3, pp. 1, 2, 10.

Answers MSRB Transparency 44

¡A responder! Audio Script, TE p. 153b
Students will hold up the following pieces of paper:
1. almuerzo (la hamburguesa)
2. desayuno (la leche)
3. desayuno (el pan)
4. almuerzo (el sándwich de jamón y queso)
5. desayuno (el cereal)
6. almuerzo (la sopa)
7. desayuno (el huevo)
8. desayuno (el café)

Activity 1
la sopa; el pan; el huevo; el yogur; el sándwich; las uvas; la manzana; la hamburguesa

Activity 2
1. A. ¿Te gusta más comer cereal o huevos? B. Me gusta más comer...
2. A. ¿Te gusta más beber leche o jugo de naranja? B. Me gusta más beber...
3. A. ¿Te gusta más comer sopa o un sándwich de jamón y queso? B. Me gusta más comer...
4. A. ¿Te gusta más comer una hamburguesa o pizza? B. Me gusta más comer...
5. A. ¿Te gusta más comer una manzana o una banana? B. Me gusta más comer...
6. A. ¿Te gusta más beber un refresco o un café? B. Me gusta más beber...

Para y piensa Answers will vary. Sample answers: **1.** huevos, cereal, yogur; **2.** hamburguesa, sopa, sándwich de jamón y queso

159

Objective

· Understand vocabulary in context: interrogative words.

Core Resources

· Video Program: DVD 1
· Audio Program: TXT CD 3 track 3

Presentation Strategies

· Ask students to make a list of the question words they hear.
· Show the video with the books closed. Then show it again with the books open.
· Play the audio while students follow the script in the text.

Practice Sequence

· **Activity 3:** Telehistoria comprehension
· **Activity 4:** Vocabulary production; Recycle: snack foods

STANDARDS

1.1 Engage in conversation, Act. 4
1.2 Understand language, Act. 3
1.3 Present information, Act. 4, PYP

Warm Up UTB 3 Transparency 16

Asking Questions Match each question with its appropriate answer.

a. Es una bebida. **b.** Es una amiga.
c. Es nutritivo. **d.** Porque no tengo ganas.

1. ¿Cómo es el desayuno?
2. ¿Qué es el café?
3. ¿Quién es Ana?
4. ¿Por qué no comes?

Answers: 1. c; 2. a; 3. b; 4. d

Video Summary

@HomeTutor
VideoPlus
ClassZone.com

As Rodrigo counts his money on his way to the store, Marisol distracts him with several annoying questions. He tells Marisol that he is going to school to get Trini Salgado's autograph.

▶︎ ‖

VOCABULARIO en contexto

Goal: Identify the words Rodrigo and Marisol use to ask questions. Then practice these words to ask questions and give answers. **Actividades 3–4**
♻ *¿Recuerdas?* Snack foods p. 33

Telehistoria escena 1

@HomeTutor VideoPlus
ClassZone.com

STRATEGIES

Cuando lees

List the question words As you read, list the words that indicate questions, such as **Qué** in **¿Qué amiga?** Save the list so that you can add more question words as you encounter them.

Cuando escuchas

Think about motives In this scene, Marisol asks questions repeatedly. Think of possible reasons why she does this. Which reason seems the most probable to you?

VIDEO
DVD

AUDIO

Marisol

Rodrigo

Rodrigo and Marisol walk to the grocery store. Rodrigo is counting his money.

Marisol: ¿A la escuela? ¿Por qué vas a la escuela hoy? Es sábado.

Rodrigo: Trini Salgado llega hoy y necesito un autógrafo en una camiseta. Es importante.

Marisol: ¿En una camiseta? ¿Qué camiseta?

Rodrigo: Tengo una amiga...

Marisol: *(teasing him)* ¿Una amiga? ¿Qué amiga? ¿Cómo se llama?

Rodrigo: Se llama Alicia.

Marisol: ¿De dónde es?

Rodrigo: Es de Miami. *(He loses count and starts over, sighing.)*

Marisol: ¿Cuándo tienes que estar en la escuela?

Rodrigo: A las cuatro de la tarde. *(Rodrigo loses count.)* ¡Y por favor! ¡No más preguntas! *(He starts to count again.)*

Marisol: Quince, veinte, cuarenta...   Continuará... p. 166

También se dice

Puerto Rico Rodrigo uses the word **la camiseta** when he mentions Alicia's T-shirt. In other Spanish-speaking countries you might hear:
· **Argentina** la remera
· **Perú** el polo
· **Venezuela** la franela
· **México** la playera

Differentiating Instruction

English Learners

Provide Comprehensible Input Before listening to the Telehistoria, have students preview the text for question words. Help them remember their meanings by providing an accompanying gesture for each. Say **¿dónde?** and look around the room pointing to different places. Say **¿cuándo?** and look at your watch or the clock. Say **¿qué?** as you hold your hands out and shrug your shoulders slightly.

Inclusion

Frequent Review/Repetition Provide student pairs with sentence starters related to the Telehistoria. Direct each pair to find the place in the text that gives them the information, and then complete each sentence. Here are a few examples:
    Rodrigo va a _____.
    Rodrigo necesita un autógrafo en _____.

Nota gramatical

You learned interrogative words on p. 157. Use an **interrogative word** followed by a **conjugated verb** to ask a question. Notice that each interrogative has an accent.

¿Cómo está usted?   **¿Por qué estás** triste?

How are you?   *Why are you sad?*

3 Muchas preguntas *Comprensión del episodio*

Escuchar
Leer

Complete each question with the appropriate interrogative word and choose the correct answer according to the episode.

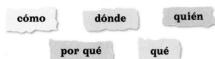

cómo   dónde   quién

por qué   qué

1. ¿ _____ necesita Rodrigo?
2. ¿ _____ se llama la amiga de Rodrigo?
3. ¿De _____ es Alicia?
4. ¿ _____ va a la escuela Rodrigo?
5. ¿ _____ es Trini Salgado?

a. Es de Miami.
b. porque Trini Salgado está allí
c. un autógrafo
d. Alicia
e. una atleta famosa

Expansión:
Teacher Edition Only
Have students write all the questions that appear in the Telehistoria. Ask them to write the answers to each of them.

4 ¿Cómo es? ♲ *¿Recuerdas?* Snack foods p. 33

Hablar

Work with a partner to describe the following foods and drinks in your school's cafeteria.

A ¿Cómo es la leche?   B La leche es buena.

Estudiante A

1.   2.   3.   4.
5.   6.   7.   8.

Estudiante B

nutritivo(a)
bueno(a)
malo(a)
horrible
rico(a)

Expansión:
Teacher Edition Only
Have students ask each other two more questions about other foods and drinks.

PARA Y PIENSA

Did you get it? Choose the correct interrogative word.
1. ¿(Qué / Quiénes) son las amigas de Rodrigo?
2. ¿(Cuándo / Cuál) llega Trini Salgado?
3. ¿(Quién / Por qué) necesita Rodrigo el autógrafo?

Get Help Online ClassZone.com

Lección 1
ciento sesenta y uno   **161**

Differentiating Instruction

Inclusion

Synthetic/Analytic Support Write these words on separate index cards: **cómo, dónde, quién, por qué, qué, es, está, tiene,** and **Rodrigo.** Display the words on the board at random. Invite volunteers to choose words to build a question. Remind them to start with a question word followed by a verb. They may add additional words, such as adjectives, if necessary.

Heritage Language Learners

Writing Skills Remind students that question words always have an accent. Point out, however, that **como, donde, quien, porque,** and **que** have different meanings. Have students write two sentences using each word, once as a question word, and once as a relative pronoun, adverb, or conjunction.

¿Qué tiene Alicia? Ella tiene la camiseta que tiene el autógrafo.

Communication

Pair Work

Telehistoria Ask students to take on the role of Marisol or Rodrigo in the Telehistoria script. They should read their lines aloud several times. Walk around the room and correct students' pronunciation of words as you hear errors.

✓ Ongoing Assessment

@HomeTutor
More Practice
ClassZone.com

PARA Y PIENSA
Intervention If students have problems completing the sentences in Para y piensa, have them repeat Activity 3. For additional practice, use Reteaching & Practice Copymasters URB 3 pp. 1, 3, 11.

Answers MSRB Transparency 44

Activity 3
1. Qué, c.   4. Por qué, b.
2. Cómo, d.   5. Quién, e.
3. dónde, a.

Activity 4 Answers will vary. Sample answers include:
1. A. ¿Cómo es la pizza? B. La pizza es rica.
2. A. ¿Cómo es el cereal? B. ...es nutritivo.
3. A. ¿Cómo es la sopa? B. ...es buena.
4. A. ¿Cómo es el sándwich de jamón y queso? B. ...es rico.
5. A. ¿Cómo es la banana? B. ...es horrible.
6. A. ¿Cómo es la hamburguesa? B. ...es mala.
7. A. ¿Cómo es el jugo de naranja? B. ...es bueno.
8. A. ¿Cómo es la galleta? B. ...es rica.

Para y piensa
1. ¿Quiénes son las amigas de Rodrigo?
2. ¿Cuándo llega Trini Salgado?
3. ¿Por qué necesita Rodrigo el autógrafo?

162

 Objetives

- Present **gustar** with nouns.
- Practice **gustar** to express what foods you like and don't like.

Core Resource

- *Cuaderno,* pp. 104–106

Presentation Strategies

- Present forms and uses of the verb **gustar** with nouns.
- Remind students that they can use **gustar** with infinitives to talk about things that people like to do.

STANDARDS

4.1 Compare languages

 Warm Up UTB 3 Transparency 17

Interrogative Words Read the following sentence: **José no va al gimnasio los lunes porque tiene que estudiar.** Now write four questions about the sentence using these interrogative words: **¿Quién? ¿Cuándo? ¿Por qué?** and **¿Qué?**

Possible answers: ¿Quién no va al gimnasio? ¿Cuándo no va al gimnasio? ¿Por qué no va al gimnasio José? ¿Qué tiene que hacer José?

Long-term Retention
Connect to Previous Learning

Remind students that they are already familiar with the use of **gustar** with infinitives. Refer them back to **gustar** with infinitives on p. 44 of Unidad 1 to see which pronouns to use.

Communication
Common Error Alert

Tell students to use **gustan** when listing more than one singular noun. For example, **Me gustan la leche y el jugo de naranja.**

 # Presentación de GRAMÁTICA

¡AVANZA! **Goal:** Learn how to use **gustar** with nouns. Then practice using this verb to express what foods you like and don't like. *Actividades 5–11*

English Grammar Connection: In English, the phrase *I like* doesn't change. In Spanish, there are two ways to say it, depending on whether what you like is singular or plural. This is because the Spanish phrase **me gusta** literally means that something *is pleasing to me.*

Gustar with Nouns

Animated Grammar
ClassZone.com

¿Recuerdas? You have already learned to use **gustar** with infinitives to say what people like to do (see p. 44).

To talk about the things that people like, use **gustar** + **noun**.

Here's how:

If what is liked is singular, use the **singular** form **gusta**.

Singular
me gusta **la sopa**
te gusta **la sopa**
le gusta **la sopa**
nos gusta **la sopa**
os gusta **la sopa**
les gusta **la sopa**

matches singular noun
Me gusta **el cereal.**
I like cereal.

If what is liked is plural, use the **plural** form **gustan**.

Plural
me gustan **los jugos**
te gustan **los jugos**
le gustan **los jugos**
nos gustan **los jugos**
os gustan **los jugos**
les gustan **los jugos**

matches plural noun
Me gustan **las uvas.**
I like grapes.

Notice that the singular and plural forms of **gustar** match what is liked, not the person who likes it.

Más práctica
Cuaderno *pp. 104–106*
Cuaderno para hispanohablantes *pp. 105–107*

@HomeTutor
Leveled Grammar Practice
ClassZone.com

Differentiating Instruction

Pre-AP
Relate Opinions Give students a list of food items. Have students circulate around the class and ask their classmates which items they like and dislike. For example: **¿Te gusta la pizza? Sí,/No, no me gusta la pizza.** Have students work in small groups to compile the opinions of their classmates. Have each group report their findings to the class.

Slower-paced Learners
Personalize It Show students a collection of pictures of familiar foods. Then ask them to express their personal preferences using the verb **gustar.** Remind them to focus on whether the food word is singular or plural. **¿Te gustan las uvas? Sí, me gustan las uvas.**

Práctica de GRAMÁTICA

5 | ¿Qué les gusta?

**Hablar
Escribir**

Tell whether the following people like or don't like the following foods and drinks.

modelo: a Luis / el yogur
A Luis **le gusta** el yogur.

1. a los maestros / el café
2. a nosotros / las papas fritas
3. a Adela / las manzanas
4. a mí / las hamburguesas
5. a mis amigos / los sándwiches

6. a ti / las uvas
7. a Jaime y a Rafael / la leche
8. a usted / el cereal
9. a ellos / las bananas
10. a ustedes / el jugo

6 | En el supermercado

**Leer
Escribir**

Indicate what these people like and don't like at the supermarket, according to the description.

modelo: El yogur es horrible. (a Rodrigo)
A Rodrigo no le gusta el yogur.

1. Las uvas son ricas. (a ti)
2. La sopa es buena. (a Marisol)
3. El cereal es malo. (a nosotros)

4. Los huevos son horribles. (a mí)
5. El café es muy bueno. (a usted)
6. Los jugos son nutritivos. (a ellos)

AUDIO

Pronunciación ◆ Las letras r y rr

In Spanish, the letter **r** in the middle or the end of a word is pronounced by a single tap of the tongue against the gum above the upper front teeth. The letter **r** at the beginning of a word or **rr** within a word is pronounced by several rapid taps called a trill.

Listen and repeat.

pa**r**a	ce**r**eal	bebe**r**	yogu**r**
rico	**r**ubio	ho**rr**ible	piza**rr**ón

El ce**r**eal y el yogu**r** son **r**icos; no son ho**rr**ibles.

Lección 1
ciento sesenta y tres **163**

Differentiating Instruction

Inclusion

Alphabetic/Phonetic Awareness Have students write the letter **r** on a card, and the letter **rr** on another card. Then say: **para, horrible, pizarrón, beber, cereal,** and **rico.** Emphasize the trill in the words containing **rr.** Tell students to hold up the appropriate card to show whether they are hearing the **r** or **rr** sound. Then have students repeat each word aloud.

Multiple Intelligences

Logical/Mathematical Ask students to go to the supermarket with whoever in the family buys groceries. Tell them to list the foods they help purchase, and note the prices. Ask them to identify the foods they've learned how to say in Spanish, and make a list of those foods and the prices. Finally, ask them to total the purchases of the foods on their Spanish list.

Objectives
· Practice **gustar** with nouns.
· Pronunciation: the letters **r** and **rr**

Core Resource
· Audio Program: TXT CD 3 track 4

Practice Sequence
· **Activity 5:** Controlled practice: **gustar** with nouns
· **Activity 6:** Controlled practice: **gustar** with nouns

 STANDARDS
1.2 Understand language, Pronunciación
1.3 Present information, Acts. 5–6

Long-term Retention
 Recycle

Ask students to find ads in local newspapers for the food items they know in Spanish. Have them copy the ads, replacing the English food words with the Spanish words. Post all the work on classroom walls, and ask students to choose four food items and tell the class in Spanish whether they do or do not like it. For example: **Me gusta la leche** (name of brand) **porque es rica y muy nutritiva.**

Answers MSRB Transparencies 44–45
Activity 5
1. A los maestros les gusta el café.
2. A nosotros nos gustan las papas fritas.
3. A Adela no le gustan las manzanas.
4. A mí no me gustan las hamburguesas.
5. A mis amigos les gustan los sándwiches.
6. A ti te gustan las uvas.
7. A Jaime y a Rafael no les gusta la leche.
8. A usted le gusta el cereal.
9. A ellos no les gustan las bananas.
10. A ustedes les gusta el jugo.
Activity 6
1. A ti te gustan las uvas.
2. A Marisol le gusta la sopa.
3. A nosotros no nos gusta el cereal.
4. A mí no me gustan los huevos.
5. A usted le gusta el café.
6. A ellos les gustan los jugos.

Objectives

- Practice **gustar** with nouns.
- **Culture:** Compare traditional foods of Puerto Rico and El Salvador.
- Practice using **gustar** to express what foods you like and don't like.

Core Resource

- *Cuaderno*, pp. 104–106

Practice Sequence

- **Activities 7–8:** Transitional practice: **gustar** with nouns
- **Activities 9–11:** Open-ended practice: **gustar** with nouns

STANDARDS

1.1 Engage in conversation, Acts. 7-9
1.3 Present information, Acts. 7-11; PYP
2.2 Products and perspectives, Act. 7
4.2 Compare cultures, Act. 7

Long-term Retention

Critical Thinking

Predict Before students do Activity 8, have them predict what the favorite food and drink of the group will be. After the activity, have students figure out the favorite food and drink of the whole class.

Comparación cultural

Essential Question

Suggested Answer Oftentimes, historical influences affect the types of food we consume and the ways we prepare them. For example, the Spaniards brought olives and garlic to Puerto Rico. People of African descent influenced Puerto Rican cuisine by introducing plantains and coconuts.

Background Information

Many Puerto Rican recipes use **sofrito**, which is a condiment mix based on onions, green bell peppers, red bell peppers, cilantro, and garlic. Meat is usually seasoned with **adobo** (seasoning salt) which is a mix of salt, onion powder, garlic powder, and ground black pepper.

See Activity answers on p. 165.

164

---

7 | Las comidas favoritas

Hablar

Comparación cultural

Tostones

La cocina criolla

How do historical influences affect the food that people eat? Traditional cooking in **Puerto Rico,** known as *la cocina criolla,* combines Spanish, African, and indigenous influences. *Tostones* (fried plantains) are a common side dish. Popular snack foods are *alcapurrias* (fried plantains stuffed with meat) and *bacalaítos* (codfish fritters). In **El Salvador,** traditional cuisine blends indigenous and Spanish influences. A typical food is the *pupusa,* a corn tortilla filled with beans, pork, and cheese. *Pupusas* are often served with *curtido,* a spicy coleslaw. *Semita,* a sweet bread layered with pineapple marmalade, is also popular.

Pupusas

Compara con tu mundo *Which of these dishes would you most like to try and why? What is the most interesting dish that you have ever tried?*

Use the information to talk with a partner about food preferences in Puerto Rico and El Salvador.

A ¿A quiénes les gustan los tostones?

B A los chicos de Puerto Rico les gustan.

Expansión:
Teacher Edition Only
Ask students to mention all the foods they have learned about in this and in previous lessons.

8 | Opiniones

Hablar

Work in a group of three to talk about the foods and drinks you like and don't like.

la pizza   **las uvas**   **la leche**

las manzanas   **el jugo de naranja**   **¿ ?**

A ¿A ustedes les gusta la pizza?

B A mí no me gusta la pizza. No me gusta el queso.

C Sí, a mí me gusta la pizza con jamón.

Expansión:
Teacher Edition Only
Have students extend the dialogue using other foods and beverages.

164 Unidad 3 Puerto Rico
ciento sesenta y cuatro

Differentiating Instruction

English Learners

Build Background Ask students to talk about traditional dishes from their country of origin. What are the main ingredients? Is frying, baking, or boiling the preferred cooking method? How do those dishes compare to the **cocina criolla**? Encourage interested students to research a recipe of one of these dishes and bring it in to share with the group.

Heritage Language Learners

Support What They Know Tell students that in the northern part of Colombia **tostones** are called **patacones.** Also, that in Colombia and Venezuela, the **pupusa** is called **arepa. Arepas** can be mixed with cheese or filled with eggs or meat. Ask students if they know other names or variations of the foods mentioned on p. 164.

9 | El menú

Leer
Hablar

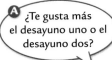

Ask a partner questions about which foods on the menu he or she likes more and why.

A ¿Te gusta más el desayuno uno o el desayuno dos?

B Me gusta más el desayuno dos porque me gusta el cereal y no me gustan los huevos.

Restaurante Boriquen

Desayunos (de 8:00 a 11:00)
1. Huevos fritos o revoltillo con jamón $4.00
2. Cereal frío y fruta $4.00
3. Frutas frescas
   (uvas, guineos, manzanas), yogur $3.50

Bebidas incluidas: jugo de china, café o leche

Almuerzos (de 12:00 a 3:00)
1. Hamburguesa americana, papas fritas $5.50
2. Sándwich de jamón y queso, con fruta $6.50
3. Pizza con jamón y queso $5.50
4. Asopao de vegetales
   (sopa tradicional de Puerto Rico) $4.00

Bebidas incluidas: jugos, refrescos o café
Postres incluidos: helado, flan o pastel del día

Expansión:
Teacher Edition Only
Have students work in groups to create a menu using foods and beverages they know.

10 | ¿Y tú?

Hablar
Escribir

Answer the questions in complete sentences.

1. ¿Qué comida te gusta cuando tienes mucha hambre?
2. ¿Qué bebida te gusta cuando tienes mucha sed?
3. ¿Cuál es una comida nutritiva?
4. ¿Qué comidas nutritivas te gustan y no te gustan?
5. ¿Qué comidas en la cafetería de la escuela te gustan?
6. ¿Qué comidas en la cafetería de la escuela no te gustan?

Expansión:
Teacher Edition Only
Have students generate three more questions about foods.

11 | Le gusta...

Escribir

Think of someone you know who leads an especially healthy lifestyle. Write a short description of that person's favorite activities and the foods he or she likes and doesn't like.

modelo: Mi amigo Javier es muy atlético. Le gusta practicar deportes. Le gustan las frutas, pero no le gusta la pizza porque no es nutritiva...

Expansión:
Teacher Edition Only
Have students write a short description of a person they think leads an unhealthy lifestyle.

Más práctica   Cuaderno *pp. 104–106*   Cuaderno para hispanohablantes *pp. 105–107*

PARA Y PIENSA

Did you get it?
1. Tell a friend you like eggs for breakfast.
2. Say that José likes pizza with ham.
3. Ask a friend why he or she doesn't like fruit.

Get Help Online
ClassZone.com

Differentiating Instruction

Multiple Intelligences

Visual Learners Have students work in small groups to create a menu for a breakfast special. Instruct students to include choices in their special. For example, customers can choose **huevos, huevos con queso,** or **huevos con jamón.** They can choose **jugo de naranja, jugo de manzana,** or **jugo de uva.** Share each menu with the group, and ask volunteers to place their orders.

Slower-paced Learners

Yes/No Questions Ask students to respond to questions about the foods on the menu featured in Activity 9 with **sí** or **no.** For example: **¿Te gustan los huevos fritos con jamón? ¿Te gusta el yogur? ¿Te gusta la pizza con jamón?** Then have them respond with complete sentences. **Sí, me gustan los huevos fritos. No, no me gusta el yogur.**

✓ Ongoing Assessment

PARA Y PIENSA **Peer Assessment** Have student pairs say their sentences aloud and correct each other's pronunciation. For additional practice, use Reteaching & Practice Copymasters URB 3, pp. 4, 5.

Long-term Retention

Critical Thinking

Categorize Before doing Activity 10, ask students to think of categories suggested by the questions. Possible examples: **bebidas, comidas nutritivas, comidas en la cafetería.** Have them list examples of food and beverages under each category.

Answers MSRB Transparency 45

Answers for Activities on pp. 164–165.

Activity 7 Answers will vary. Sample answers should follow the pattern:
¿A quiénes les gustan las...? A los chicos de... les gustan las...

Activity 8 Answers will vary. Sample answers should follow the pattern:
A: ¿A ustedes les gustan las manzanas?
B: No, a mí no me gustan las manzanas.
C: Sí, a mí me gustan las manzanas.

Activity 9 Answers will vary. Sample answers:
A: ¿Te gusta más el desayuno dos o el desayuno tres?
B: Me gusta más el desayuno tres porque me gustan las frutas y no me gusta el cereal...

Activity 10 Answers will vary. Sample answers:
1. Cuando tengo mucha hambre, me gusta comer una hamburguesa.
2. Cuando tengo mucha sed, me gusta beber un jugo de naranja.
3. El cereal es una comida nutritiva.
4. Me gusta el yogur. No me gustan los huevos.
5. Me gusta la sopa.
6. No me gusta el sándwich de jamón y queso.

Activity 11 Answers will vary. Sample answers:

Mi amiga Estela es muy atlética. Le gusta montar en bicicleta y correr todos los días. Le gustan la leche y el jugo de naranja, pero no le gusta el café porque no es nutritivo.

Para y piensa
1. Me gustan los huevos en el desayuno.
2. A José le gusta la pizza con jamón.
3. ¿Por qué no te gusta la fruta?

GRAMÁTICA en contexto

¡AVANZA! **Goal:** Listen to how Marisol and Rodrigo use **gustar** to talk about what they like to eat. Then use **gustar** to talk about likes and dislikes. *Actividades 12–14*

Telehistoria escena 2

@HomeTutor VideoPlus ClassZone.com

STRATEGIES

Cuando lees
Organize with a chart To keep thoughts organized, make a chart listing Rodrigo's and Marisol's likes and dislikes about breakfast foods. Are your preferences more like Rodrigo's or more like Marisol's?

Cuando escuchas
Use mental pictures to remember words Listen for names of foods. For each name you hear, picture the food mentally. Remember these words by repeatedly linking them to the mental pictures.

VIDEO DVD

AUDIO

Marisol: ¿Qué te gusta comer en el desayuno?
Rodrigo: Me gustan el cereal, el yogur, las frutas... Y a ti, Marisol, ¿qué te gusta comer en el desayuno?
Marisol: No me gusta el yogur y no me gustan los huevos.
Rodrigo: ¿Te gustan las frutas? ¿Las uvas, las manzanas?
Marisol: No me gusta comer mucho en el desayuno.
Rodrigo: ¡Tienes que comer bien en el desayuno! ¿Te gusta el pan? ¿O la leche?
Marisol: Me gustan las galletas. Tengo hambre.
Rodrigo: Sí. ¡Porque no te gusta comer mucho en el desayuno!

Continuará... p. 172

¡AVANZA! Objectives
- Understand grammar in context: **gustar** with nouns.
- Practice using **gustar** to express what foods you like and don't like.

Core Resources
- Video Program: DVD 1
- Audio Program: TXT CD 3, track 5

Presentation Strategies
- Have students read the script.
- Ask who the people in the picture are.
- Point out the different breakfast foods mentioned in the script.
- Show the video and/or play the audio.

Practice Sequence
- **Activity 12:** Telehistoria comprehension
- **Activity 13:** Open-ended practice: **gustar** with nouns; foods
  Activity 14: Open-ended practice: **gustar** with nouns; foods

STANDARDS
1.1 Engage in conversation, Act. 14
1.3 Present information, Acts. 12–14, PYP

Warm Up UTB 3 Transparency 17

Gustar with Nouns Complete the sentences with **gusta** or **gustan.**

1. ¿Te _____ las frutas?
2. A mí no me _____ el queso.
3. A Teresa le _____ los helados.
4. ¿Les _____ la leche?
5. ¿A quién no le _____ el jugo de naranja?

Answers: 1. gustan; 2. gusta; 3. gustan; 4. gusta; 5. gusta

Video Summary

@HomeTutor VideoPlus ClassZone.com

Rodrigo and Marisol are at a supermarket. They are talking about the kinds of foods they like for breakfast. Marisol says that she doesn't like to eat much for breakfast, but now she states that she's hungry. Rodrigo concludes that she's hungry because she doesn't eat much for breakfast.

Differentiating Instruction

Inclusion

Metacognitive Support Have students read through the script of the Telehistoria in unison. After each sentence containing the verb **gustar,** ask students to explain why the verb appears as **gusta** or **gustan** in that particular context. For example, why does Marisol say **No me gusta el yogur y no me gustan los huevos.** Elicit that **yogur** is singular, while **huevos** is plural.

Slower-paced Learners

Yes/No Questions Ask students yes/no questions based on the topics discussed in the Telehistoria. Here are a few possibilities:
- **¿Te gustan las frutas?**
- **¿Te gustan los huevos?**
- **¿Te gusta el yogur?**

After answering **sí** or **no,** encourage students to follow up with a complete sentence. **Sí, me gustan las galletas.**

12 ¿Un desayuno grande? *Comprensión del episodio*

Expansión:
Teacher Edition Only
Have students write one more question about the dialog between Rodrigo and Marisol and provide an answer.

Escuchar
Leer

Answer the questions about the episode.

1. ¿Qué le gusta comer a Rodrigo en el desayuno?
2. ¿A quién no le gustan los desayunos grandes?
3. ¿Qué le gusta comer a Marisol?
4. ¿Por qué tiene hambre Marisol?

13 En el desayuno y el almuerzo

Escribir

Write a description of what foods and drinks you like and don't like for breakfast and lunch.

modelo: En el desayuno me gusta el pan. Para beber, me gusta el jugo de naranja. También me gustan las bananas. Es importante comer fruta. No me gustan los huevos. Son horribles. En el almuerzo...

Expansión:
Teacher Edition Only
Ask students to talk about the foods they like and don't like in the school cafeteria.

14 Una entrevista

Hablar
Escribir

Ask another student what he or she likes and doesn't like for lunch. Write the responses. Then compare your likes and dislikes, using a Venn diagram.

modelo: A Nicolás le gustan los sándwiches de queso en el almuerzo. También le gusta la fruta. No le gusta la pizza...

A mí   A Nicolás

Me gustan las hamburguesas. | Nos gusta la fruta. | No le gusta la pizza.

Expansión:
Teacher Edition Only
Ask students to expand the activity by asking other students about their lunch preferences.

PARA Y PIENSA

Did you get it? Complete each sentence based on the Telehistoria with the correct form of **gustar**.

1. A Marisol no le _____ la comida nutritiva.
2. A Rodrigo le _____ el cereal.
3. A Marisol le _____ las galletas.

Get Help Online
ClassZone.com

Differentiating Instruction

Pre-AP

Support Ideas with Details After completing Activity 13, have students copy their descriptions onto a separate piece of paper. Instruct them to leave a few blank lines in between each sentence. Then have students add a phrase of explanation after each sentence using the word **porque. En el desayuno me gusta beber jugo de naranja porque es nutritivo.**

Heritage Language Learners

Writing Skills Have students use their Venn diagrams from Activity 14 for a Compare and Contrast essay. Essays should follow this format: *I. Introduction*—Explain what the essay will be about. *II. Compare*—Describe the foods you have in common. *III. Contrast*—Describe the foods you disagree on. *IV. Conclusion*—Sum up your findings.

Long-term Retention

Critical Thinking

Categorize Before doing Activity 13, ask students to draw a Venn diagram with one oval labeled **el desayuno** and the other **el almuerzo**. Have them write names of breakfast and lunch foods in the appropriate ovals. Use the overlapping area to write in items that fit both categories.

Communication

Role-Playing and Skits

Telehistoria Have students prepare a short dialogue based on the Telehistoria, changing the foods that are mentioned. Encourage them to use humor in their dialogue and gestures. Then have them present the dialogue to the class.

Communication

Common Error Alert

Some students may forget about gender agreement, particularly for nouns not ending in **-a** or **-o**. To avoid this problem, ask students to identify the foods in writing and to include the appropriate article. For example: **la leche, el sándwich, el cereal.**

✓ Ongoing Assessment

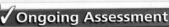
@HomeTutor
More Practice
ClassZone.com

Peer Assessment Have pairs exchange their answers and correct errors. For additional practice, use Reteaching & Practice Copymasters URB 3 pp. 4, 6.

📋 Answers MSRB Transparency 45

Activity 12

1. Le gusta comer el cereal, el yogur y las frutas.
2. A Marisol no le gustan los desayunos grandes.
3. A Marisol le gusta comer galletas.
4. Tiene hambre porque no le gusta comer mucho en el desayuno.

Activity 13 Answers will vary. Answers should include the use of the verb **gustar** + names of foods and drinks.

Activity 14 Answers will vary. Sample answers will follow this outline:
(No) Me gusta(n)...
(No) Nos gusta(n)...
(No) Le gusta(n)...

Para y piensa **1.** gusta; **2.** gusta; **3.** gustan

167

Objective

· Present the present tense of -er and -ir verbs.

Core Resource

· *Cuaderno*, pp. 107–109

Presentation Strategies

· Point out the differences in the endings of -er and -ir verbs.

· Say sentences using -er and -ir verbs, asking students to note the endings in each form.

STANDARDS

4.1 Compare languages

Warm Up   UTB 3 Transparency 18

Gustar with Nouns Write what foods these people like.

1. a Jorge: las papas fritas
2. a mí: el cereal con fruta
3. a Marta y a Estela: los huevos con jamón
4. a nosotros: la pizza
5. a ti: las uvas

Answers: 1. A Jorge le gustan las papas fritas. **2.** A mí me gusta el cereal con fruta. **3.** A Marta y a Estela les gustan los huevos con jamón. **4.** A nosotros nos gusta la pizza. **5.** A ti te gustan las uvas.

Communication
Grammar Activity

Have students write the endings for -er and -ir verbs on index cards. Then have them say a sentence using an -er or -ir verb but leave the verb ending out. For example: **Yo escrib_.** Students should hold up the **-o** card and say in unison **escribo.**

Verbs Students Know

Students have already learned the following -er and -ir verbs. In the next Nota gramatical they will learn that **hacer** has an irregular **yo** form but otherwise follows the pattern for -er verbs.

-er verbs	-ir verbs
aprender	compartir
beber	escribir
comer	
correr	
hacer	
leer	
vender	

168

Presentación de GRAMÁTICA

 ¡AVANZA! **Goal:** Learn how to form -er and -ir verbs. Then use these verbs and **hacer** to talk about school activities and what you and others eat and drink. *Actividades 15–20*

¿Recuerdas? The verb **estar** p. 128

English Grammar Connection: Remember that the **present tense** shows an action happening now (see p. 106).

Present Tense of -er and -ir Verbs

Animated Grammar
ClassZone.com

Regular verbs that end in -er or -ir work a little differently than regular -ar verbs. How do you form the present tense of regular -er and -ir verbs?

Here's how:

The endings for -er and -ir verbs are the same except in the **nosotros(as)** and **vosotros(as)** forms. The letter change in these two forms matches the ending of the infinitive.

vend**er** *to sell*			
yo	vend**o**	nosotros(as)	vend**emos**
tú	vend**es**	vosotros(as)	vend**éis**
usted, él, ella	vend**e**	ustedes, ellos(as)	vend**en**

-er verbs = -emos, -éis

Mario **vend**e comida en la cafetería.
*Mario **sells** food in the cafeteria.*

compart**ir** *to share*			
yo	compart**o**	nosotros(as)	compart**imos**
tú	compart**es**	vosotros(as)	compart**ís**
usted, él, ella	compart**e**	ustedes, ellos(as)	compart**en**

-ir verbs = -imos, -ís

Compartimos las uvas.
*We are **sharing** the grapes.*

Más práctica
Cuaderno *pp. 107–109*
Cuaderno para hispanohablantes *pp. 108–111*

@HomeTutor
Leveled Grammar Practice
ClassZone.com

Differentiating Instruction

Multiple Intelligences

Visual Learners Ask students to illustrate some -er and -ir verbs they know: **beber, comer, compartir, correr, escribir,** and **vender.** Have them write a subject pronoun for each drawing. Ask them to exchange their drawing with another student. He or she should say what the people in the picture are doing.

Inclusion

Metacognitive Support Use Venn diagrams to help students see the similarities and differences between the endings of -ar and -er verbs. Have students recite and compare the endings for two verbs, such as **hablar** and **vender.** When the endings are the same, write the ending in the center of the circles. When the endings are different, write them on the appropriate side. Repeat with -ar and -ir verbs.

Práctica de GRAMÁTICA

15 | ¿Comer o beber?

Hablar
Escribir

Tell what these people eat or drink.

modelo: Rodrigo (cereal)
Rodrigo come cereal.

1. Rodrigo y Marisol (uvas)
2. tú (refrescos)
3. ustedes (pan)
4. Marisol y yo (sopa)
5. Ana (hamburguesas)
6. usted (sándwiches)
7. yo (jugo de naranja)
8. los maestros (café)

> **Expansión:**
> Teacher Edition Only
> Have students make up sentences about what they and their friends eat and drink.

16 | ¿En la cafetería o en clase? ♻ *¿Recuerdas?* The verb **estar** p. 128

Hablar
Escribir

Tell what these people are doing and where they are right now.

modelo: Marisol / vender fruta
Marisol vende fruta. Ahora está **en la cafetería.**

1. yo / beber leche
2. ellas / leer un libro
3. tú / comer yogur
4. Rodrigo / aprender el español
5. ustedes / escribir en el pizarrón
6. tú y yo / compartir una pizza

> **Expansión:**
> Teacher Edition Only
> Have students tell who does these things at their school.

17 | Actividades en el almuerzo

Escuchar
Escribir

Listen to the descriptions of Marisol and her friends, and take notes. Then write sentences saying who does what, using elements from each puzzle piece.

1. Marisol
2. la cafetería
3. Rodrigo y Mateo
4. Carmen
5. Raúl y David
6. Laura y Diana

🎧 **Audio Program**
TXT CD 3 Track 6
Audio Script, TE p. 153b

Differentiating Instruction

Heritage Language Learners

Increase Accuracy Write **Puerto Rico** on the board and read the words aloud. Have students talk about the two **r** sounds: In **Puerto** it sounds soft, and in **Rico** hard. Some Puerto Ricans tend to replace the initial **r** sound with **j**: **Puerto Jico.** Remind them that **r** at the beginning of a word sounds like **rr**. Ask them to find words on p. 169 that have the **r** and **rr** sounds.

Slower-paced Learners

Read Before Listening Before students listen to the descriptions of Marisol and her friends in Activity 17, have them preview the words and pictures presented. Ask volunteers to say aloud each of the items pictured. As other students listen, tell them to point to each item as they hear it.

Objectives

· Practice using the present tense of **-er** and **-ir** verbs.
· Practice lesson vocabulary: breakfast and lunch foods.
· Recycle: **estar.**

Core Resource

· Audio Program: TXT CD 3 track 6

Practice Sequence

· **Activity 15:** Controlled practice: present tense of **-er** and **-ir** verbs
· **Activity 16:** Controlled practice: present tense of **-er** and **-ir** verbs; Recycle: **estar**
· **Activity 17:** Transitional practice: present tense of **-er** and **-ir** verbs

⚙ STANDARDS

1.2 Understand language, Act. 17
1.3 Present information, Acts. 15–17

Long-term Retention

Study Tips

Activity 16 Before doing this activity, prepare an overhead transparency to review the sound of words with **r** and **rr**.

📖 **Answers**   MSRB Transparencies 45–46

Activity 15
1. Rodrigo y Marisol comen uvas.
2. Tú bebes refrescos.
3. Ustedes comen pan.
4. Marisol y yo comemos sopa.
5. Ana come hamburguesas.
6. Usted come sándwiches.
7. Yo bebo jugo de naranja.
8. Los maestros beben café.

Activity 16
1. Yo bebo leche. Ahora estoy en la cafetería.
2. Ellas leen un libro. Ahora están en clase.
3. Tú comes yogur. Ahora estás en la cafetería.
4. Rodrigo aprende el español. Ahora está en clase.
5. Ustedes escriben en el pizarrón. Ahora están en clase.
6. Tú y yo compartimos una pizza. Ahora estamos en la cafetería.

Activity 17
1. Marisol escribe en el cuaderno.
2. La cafetería vende sopa, uvas y bananas.
3. Rodrigo y Mateo comen uvas.
4. Carmen bebe jugo de naranja.
5. Raúl y David leen un libro.
6. Laura y Diana comparten un sándwich.

Objectives
- Practice present tense of **-er** and **-ir** verbs.
- **Culture:** discuss the work of Manuel Hernández Acevedo.
- Introduce the verb **hacer** and connect it to **-er** verbs.

Core Resource
- *Cuaderno*, pp. 107–109

Practice Sequence
- **Activities 18–19:** Transitional practice: present tense of **-er** and **-ir** verbs
- **Activity 20:** Open-ended practice: present tense of **-er** and **-ir** verbs

 ## STANDARDS
1.1 Engage in conversation, Acts. 18, 20
1.3 Present information, Acts. 18–20, PYP
2.2 Products and perspectives, CC
4.2 Compare cultures, CC

Comparación cultural

Essential Question
Suggested Answer Artists depict landmarks in paintings, murals, or prints to make the world aware of their existence.

About the Artist
Manuel Hernández Acevedo was born in 1921 and came from a family of very humble means. His paintings, posters, and prints are described as primitive. His favorite scenes were of streets and houses of Old San Juan.

Nota gramatical
Explain to students the conjugation for **hacer: hago, haces, hace, hacemos, hacéis, hacen.** Ask students to say sentences using **hacer.**

 ### Answers   MSRB Transparency 46

Activity 18 Answers will vary. Sample answers:
1. A. ¿Con quién corres? B. Corro con mis amigos.
2. A. ¿Con quién compartes el almuerzo? B. Comparto el almuerzo con mi hermana.
3. A. ¿Con quién haces la tarea? B. Hago la tarea con mi mamá.

Answers continue on p. 171.

Nota gramatical
The verb **hacer** is irregular in the present tense only in the **yo** form: **hago.** In the other forms, it follows the pattern for **-er** verbs. (See p. R12 for the complete conjugation.)

Hago un sándwich.   Carmen **hace** la tarea.
I am making a sandwich.   *Carmen is doing her homework.*

18 | ¿Con quién?

Hablar   Ask a partner with whom he or she does the following activities.

modelo: comer pizza

A ¿Con quién comes pizza?

B Como pizza con Alicia.

1. correr
2. compartir el almuerzo
3. hacer la tarea

4. comer ¿ ?
5. escribir correos electrónicos
6. beber ¿ ?

Expansión:
Teacher Edition Only
Have pairs of students speak about with whom they do activities at school.

Comparación cultural

La Plaza de Colón
How does an artist's work represent historic landmarks of a country? Many of Manuel Hernández Acevedo's paintings depict scenes of Old San Juan, **Puerto Rico.** In Old San Juan you will find cobblestone streets, Spanish colonial buildings, and many plazas. The Plaza de Colón is popular with both tourists and locals. A statue of Christopher Columbus in the center of the square includes plaques commemorating the explorer's achievements.

Compara con tu mundo *What is a well-known landmark in your area? What does it represent? Why is it important?*

Above: La Plaza de Colón (1986), Manuel Hernández Acevedo; *right: La estatua de Cristóbal Colón*

Differentiating Instruction

Inclusion
Alphabetic/Phonetic Awareness Write the present tense forms of **hacer** on the board. Discuss with students how Spanish and English phonetics differ. How would **hace** be pronounced in English? Remind students that in Spanish, the **h** is silent, the **a** makes an **ah** sound, the **c** is soft, and the **e** makes an **ay** sound.

Multiple Intelligences
Visual Learners Have students work in small groups to create a tourist brochure of Old San Juan. Encourage them to use the Internet to find images and more information. Some possible features might include:
- La Plaza de Colón
- El Morro
- La Plaza de Armas
- La Puerta de San Juan

19 | En el café Buenavida

Hablar
Escribir

Look at the picture below and tell what the people are doing.

Expansión:
Teacher Edition
Only
Have students
describe four of
the people in the
drawing.

20 | Una encuesta

Hablar

Survey your classmates about the following activities.

modelo: leer: en la biblioteca, en la cafetería, en la clase de inglés

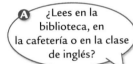 **A** ¿Lees en la biblioteca, en la cafetería o en la clase de inglés?

B Leo en la clase de inglés.

 C Leo en la biblioteca y en la cafetería.

1. beber: leche, refrescos, jugo
2. hacer la tarea: en la clase, en la biblioteca, en la cafetería
3. escribir: en un cuaderno, en el pizarrón, en la computadora
4. comer: sándwiches, pizza, hamburguesas
5. aprender: historia, matemáticas, ciencias
6. compartir: pizza, uvas, papas fritas

Expansión:
Teacher Edition
Only
Ask students what
they do in each of
the places
mentioned.

Más práctica   Cuaderno *pp. 107–109*   Cuaderno para hispanohablantes *pp. 108–111*

PARA Y PIENSA

Did you get it? Complete each sentence with the correct form of the verb in parentheses.

Get Help Online
ClassZone.com

1. ¿Qué _____ ellas? (hacer) Ellas _____ el desayuno. (comer)
2. ¿Qué _____ tú? (hacer) Yo _____ un libro. (leer)
3. ¿Qué _____ Rafael? (hacer) Rafael _____ un refresco. (beber)

Differentiating Instruction

English Learners

Build Background Ask English learners to provide the words in their first languages for the Spanish words. Have groups of students work together to create trilingual mini-dictionaries. Then have groups illustrate their dictionaries to add to their understanding and retention of the new vocabulary.

Slower-paced Learners

Memory Aids Ask students to write the words in Activity 20 on separate index cards. Then ask them to put the words in alphabetical order. Finally, ask students to say the words in order.

Communication
Group Work

Place students in six groups and assign each group one of the numbered surveys in Activity 20. Ask each group to survey their classmates. Then have the group create a chart or table for that survey to illustrate how each student in the class responded.

✓ **Ongoing Assessment**

@HomeTutor
More Practice
ClassZone.com

 PARA Y PIENSA **Intervention** If students have problems completing the Para y piensa have them review p. 168 and repeat Acts. 15, 16 on p. 169. For additional practice, use Reteaching & Practice Copymasters URB 3, pp. 7, 8, 12.

Answers MSRB Transparency 46

Answers continued from p. 170.

4. A. ¿Con quién comes papas fritas? B. Como papas fritas con mi familia.
5. A. ¿Con quién escribes correos electrónicos? B. Escribo correos electrónicos con mi hermano.
6. A. ¿Con quién bebes leche? B. Bebo leche con un amigo.

Activity 19 Answers will vary. Sample answers:
1. El hombre lee un libro.
2. La mujer escribe.
3. Los chicos beben refrescos.
4. La chica y la mujer comparten una pizza.
5. El chico hace la tarea.
6. La chica come una hamburguesa.
7. Las chicas corren.
8. El hombre vende fruta.

Activity 20 Answers will vary. Sample answers:
1. A: ¿Bebes leche, refrescos o jugo? B: Bebo leche. C: Bebo jugo.
2. A: ¿Haces la tarea en la clase, en la biblioteca o en la cafetería? B: Hago la tarea en la cafetería. C: Hago la tarea en la biblioteca.
3. A: ¿Escribes en un cuaderno, en el pizarrón o en la computadora? B: Escribo en un cuaderno. C: Escribo en la computadora.
4. A: ¿Comes sándwiches, pizza o hamburguesas? B: Como sándwiches. C: Como pizza.
5. A: ¿Aprendes historia, matemáticas o ciencias? B: Aprendo ciencias. C: Aprendo historia.
6. A: ¿Compartes pizza, uvas o papas fritas? B: Comparto pizza. C: Comparto uvas.

Para y piensa
1. ¿Qué hacen ellas? Ellas comen el desayuno.
2. ¿Qué haces tú? Yo leo un libro.
3. ¿Qué hace Rafael? Rafael bebe un refresco.

171

Objective
· Integrate lesson content.

Core Resources
· Video Program: DVD 1
· Audio Program: TXT CD 3 tracks 3, 5, 7

Presentation Strategies
· Ask students what they remember about the Telehistoria so far.
· Before showing the video or playing the audio, tell students to watch for the surprise ending and to be ready to talk about it.

Practice Sequence
· **Activities 21–22:** Telehistoria comprehension
· **Activity 23:** Open-ended practice: speaking

STANDARDS
1.1 Engage in conversation, Act. 23
1.3 Present information, Acts. 21–23

Warm Up   UTB 3 Transparency 18

Hacer Match the questions and the answers.
1. ¿Qué haces en   a. Comemos
   la biblioteca?   hamburguesas.
2. ¿Qué hacen ustedes b. Escribo en el
   en la cafetería?   cuaderno.
3. ¿Qué hace Marisa   c. Corre.
   en el gimnasio?

Answers: 1. b; 2. a; 3. c

Video Summary
@HomeTutor VideoPlus ClassZone.com

Marisol wants to buy an ice cream for lunch. Rodrigo continues to stress the importance of eating nourishing foods. Marisol leaves him for a moment, and while she's gone Rodrigo sneaks a taste of her ice cream.

172

Todo junto

¡AVANZA! **Goal:** *Show what you know* Pay attention to the **-er** and **-ir** verbs Rodrigo and Marisol use to talk about eating healthy food. Then practice these verbs and **gustar** to talk about lunchtime in the cafeteria. *Actividades 21–25*

♻ *¿Recuerdas?* Telling time p. 99

Telehistoria completa

@HomeTutor VideoPlus ClassZone.com

STRATEGIES

Cuando lees
Find the twist There is sometimes a "twist," or something unexpected, toward the end of a story or scene. Find the twist in this scene. What is it? Why is it unexpected?

Cuando escuchas
Listen for attitude changes To understand the scene fully, notice people's attitudes. At the beginning of the scene, what are Marisol's and Rodrigo's contrasting attitudes? Whose attitude changes during the scene? Why?

Escena 1 *Resumen*
Rodrigo necesita el autógrafo de Trini Salgado para Alicia. Tiene que estar en la escuela a las cuatro de la tarde.

Escena 2 *Resumen*
Rodrigo compra comida. Le gusta la comida nutritiva. Marisol tiene hambre porque no le gusta comer mucho en el desayuno.

VIDEO DVD

AUDIO

Escena 3

Marisol stops to order an ice cream.
Rodrigo: ¿Helado? ¿En el almuerzo?
Marisol: Sí, tengo ganas de comer helado. ¿Compartimos?
Rodrigo: El helado no es nutritivo.
Marisol: ¡Pero es muy rico!
Rodrigo: ¿Qué comes en la cena? ¿Una hamburguesa con papas fritas?

Marisol: ¿Venden papas fritas?
Rodrigo: Tienes que comer comidas buenas.
Marisol: Sí, sí. Yo como comida nutritiva de vez en cuando.
Rodrigo: ¿Sí? ¿Qué comes?
Marisol: Me gusta la sopa.
Rodrigo: La sopa es muy buena.
Marisol: Necesito una bebida.
Marisol walks away. Rodrigo sneaks a taste of her ice cream.
Rodrigo: El helado es muy rico.

Differentiating Instruction

Pre-AP

Vary Vocabulary As students read Escena 3, have them substitute a different food for each food mentioned in the script. For example, they might say **yogur** in place of **helado,** and **un sándwich de jamón y queso** in place of **una hamburguesa.** Have students read the script with the new food items. Remind them to make necessary changes in articles and adjective endings.

Slower-paced Learners

Personalize It Ask students for their own answers to the questions raised by Rodrigo in the Telehistoria.
· ¿Comes helado en el almuerzo?
· ¿Qué comes en la cena?
· ¿Comes comida nutritiva de vez en cuando?
· ¿Qué comes?

172

21 | ¡A completar! *Comprensión de los episodios*

Expansión:
Teacher Edition Only
Have students make other sentences about Rodrigo and Marisol from the Telehistoria.

Escuchar Leer

Complete the following sentences, based on the episodes.

1. Rodrigo necesita...
2. La amiga de Miami se llama...
3. En el desayuno Rodrigo come...
4. Marisol tiene hambre porque...
5. Marisol tiene ganas de...
6. Cuando Marisol compra una bebida, Rodrigo...

22 | Organiza la información *Comprensión de los episodios*

Escuchar Leer

Write an article about Marisol or Rodrigo. Copy this map on a piece of paper and use it to organize the information.

Expansión:
Teacher Edition Only
Have pairs of students write an article about what they do during lunch time.

23 | ¿Qué hacen en la cafetería? ♻ *¿Recuerdas?* Telling time p. 99

Hablar

> **STRATEGY Hablar**
>
> **Think and practice in advance** First write down words or phrases you want to say. Then practice pronouncing them aloud. Say them in sentences several times and you will be ready for your conversation!

Work in a group of three to talk about what you do in the cafeteria. Include what time you go and what they sell there. Also explain what you eat and drink and why.

A ¿A qué hora van ustedes a la cafetería? ¿Qué hacen?

B Como en la cafetería a la una. Los lunes como pizza y bebo jugo porque no me gusta la leche.

C Yo compro una manzana y leo un libro...

Expansión:
Teacher Edition Only
Ask students to talk about things they do at home and at what time they do each activity.

Ongoing Assessment

Rubric Activity 23

Speaking Criteria	Maximum Credit	Partial Credit	Minimum Credit
Content	Student responds to partners, listens, and asks follow-up questions.	Student provides frequent response or follow-up.	Student provides no conversational response or follow-up.
Communication	Student includes all the information requested and volunteers additional information.	Student provides some of the information requested.	Student provides almost no answers to the information requested.
Accuracy	Few errors in vocabulary and grammar.	Some errors in grammar and/or vocabulary.	Many errors in grammar and vocabulary.

Answers MSRB Transparency 46

Activity 21
1. ...el autógrafo de Trini Salgado para Alicia.
2. ...Alicia.
3. ...cereal, yogur y frutas.
4. ...no le gusta comer mucho en el desayuno.
5. ...comer helado.
6. ...come el helado.

Activity 22 Answers will vary. Sample answers include:
Marisol es simpática. No le gusta comer mucho en el desayuno. Le gustan las galletas y las papas fritas. Come comida nutritiva de vez en cuando.

Activity 23 Answers will vary. Sample answers should follow this outline:
A: ¿A qué hora van a la cafetería? ¿Qué hacen?
B: Como en la cafetería a la(s)... Venden...
C: Como... y bebo... porque...

Differentiating Instruction

Inclusion

Frequent Review/Repetition Have students copy each of the sentence starters in Activity 21 onto a separate index card. Then direct students to reread each of the episodes. When students find the information needed to complete one of the sentences, have them copy the word or phrase onto the card.

Pre-AP

Expand and Elaborate Encourage students to expand their conversations in Activity 23 by adding an anecdote. Ask them to share a story about something that happens often in the school cafeteria. It could be something funny, surprising, or out of the ordinary.

Objective
- Practice using and integrating lesson vocabulary and grammar.

Core Resources
- *Cuaderno*, pp. 110–111
- Audio Program, TXT CD 3 tracks 8, 9

Practice Sequence
- **Activity 24:** Open-ended practice: reading, listening, speaking
- **Activity 25:** Open-ended practice: writing

STANDARDS
1.1 Understand language, Act. 24
1.3 Present information, Acts. 24–25

Long-term Retention
Pre-AP **Integration**

Ask students to write a radio announcement for a supermarket. Have them tape their announcement and play it for the class.

✓ Ongoing Assessment

Rubric Activity 24

Listening/Speaking

Proficient	Not There Yet
Student uses correct forms of **vender** and vocabulary.	Student uses incorrect forms of **vender** and does not use enough vocabulary.

✓ Ongoing Assessment
@HomeTutor
More Practice
ClassZone.com

Intervention If students miss more than one or two of the Para y piensa items, suggest that they review pp. 162 and 168. For additional practice, use Reteaching & Practice Copymasters URB 3, pp. 7, 9, 12.

See Activity answers on p. 175.

174

---

24 | Integración

Leer
Escuchar
Hablar

Read the newspaper ad for Supermercado Grande. Then listen to the radio ad for Supermercado Econo. Say what foods you like and where they sell them.

Fuente 1 Anuncio

Fuente 2 Anuncio de radio

Listen and take notes
- ¿Qué comidas venden en el Supermercado Econo?
- ¿Qué venden en la cafetería?

modelo: A mí me gustan las uvas. Venden uvas en el Supermercado Grande...

Audio Program
TXT CD 3
Tracks 8, 9
Audio Script, TE
p. 153b

Expansión:
Teacher Edition Only
Ask volunteers to read the newspaper ad and other students to correct pronunciation.

25 | La cafetería de la escuela

Escribir

Write a letter to your principal about the school cafeteria. What is good and bad there? Why? Do you have any questions about it?

modelo: Sr. Hogan:
¿Cómo está usted? Me gusta la escuela pero no me gusta mucho la cafetería. No es muy grande y hay muchos estudiantes. ¿Por qué no venden...

Writing Criteria	Excellent	Good	Needs Work
Content	Your letter includes a lot of information.	Your letter includes some information.	Your letter includes little information.
Communication	Most of your letter is organized and easy to follow.	Parts of your letter are organized and easy to follow.	Your letter is disorganized and hard to follow.
Accuracy	Your letter has few mistakes in grammar and vocabulary.	Your letter has some mistakes in grammar and vocabulary.	Your letter has many mistakes in grammar and vocabulary.

Expansión:
Teacher Edition Only
Have students write a reply letter from the principal that responds to their questions and comments.

Más práctica Cuaderno *pp. 110–111*   Cuaderno para hispanohablantes *pp. 112–113*

PARA Y PIENSA

Did you get it? Complete the first sentence with a form of **gustar**, and the second sentence with the correct form of **compartir** or **beber**.
1. A Rodrigo le _____ la fruta. Él _____ jugo de naranja.
2. A Rodrigo y a Ana les _____ los sándwiches. Siempre _____ un sándwich.

Get Help Online
ClassZone.com

Slower-paced Learners

Peer-study Support Remind students of the strategy they learned in Activity 23—to think and practice in advance. Before doing Activity 24, organize them in pairs of differing abilities. Ask them to write the words and phrases they want to use, then to create sentences, and finally, to put the sentences into a story. Ask them to share their story with the class.

Heritage Language Learners

Writing Skills Review the standard form of a business letter with students. Provide a model that shows proper placement of the heading: date, address, and return addresses. Also show the greeting **Estimado Sr. Hogan:** and the closing **Atentamente.** Remind students to tailor the tone of their language to their audience—the principal of their school.

Juegos y diversiones

Review food vocabulary by playing a game of Fly Swatter.

MATAMOSCAS

The Setup

Your teacher will tape a number of picture cards on the board and divide the class into two teams.

Materials

- picture cards representing vocabulary words
- two fly swatters
- tape

Playing the Game

The first player from each team will go up to the board. Your teacher will give each player a fly swatter and then say a vocabulary word represented by one of the pictures. The player who "swats" the correct picture first gets a point.

Play continues with new players from each team.

The Winner!

The team with the most points at the end wins.

Objective
- To review food vocabulary.

 STANDARDS
5.2 Life-long learners

Long-term Retention
Recycle

Use this game to review vocabulary from other units. Suggested topics: after-school activities, weather expressions, numbers, descriptive adjectives, telling time, classroom objects, and so on.

Communication
Group Work

On the board, make three columns with these headings: **Todos los días, De vez en cuando, Nunca.** Ask individual students to call out names of foods and beverages and to come and write them under the appropriate column. Ask students to tally the results in the form of a graph.

Differentiating Instruction

Inclusion

Clear Structure Prepare three groups of index cards with: **a.** subject pronouns, **b.** the verbs **compartir, comprar, comer, beber, c.** names of food. Place the cards in separate boxes. Students will draw a card from each box and create a sentence combining the information on the cards. For example, **María y Felipe comparten las uvas.**

Multiple Intelligences

Intrapersonal Have students keep a journal of what they eat for breakfast and lunch during the school week. For each entry, ask them to give an opinion about the food using adjectives such as **rico(a), bueno(a), malo(a), horrible, nutritivo(a).**

 Answers MSRB Transparency 46
Answers for Activities on p. 174.

Activity 24 Answers will vary. Sample answers: A mí me gusta la pizza de queso. Venden pizza en el Supermercado Grande.

Activity 25 Answers should include the use of lesson vocabulary and grammar.

Para y piensa
1. A Rodrigo le gusta la fruta. Él bebe jugo de naranja.
2. A Rodrigo y a Ana les gustan los sándwiches. Siempre comparten un sándwich.

175

¡AVANZA! **Goal:** Read a fragment from a supermarket circular and then a shopping list. Compare this information with the foods and beverages you eat and drink.

AUDIO

¡A comprar y a comer!

The following is a supermarket circular from Supermercados La Famosa and a shopping list.

STRATEGY Leer
Don't translate; use pictures!
Sketch and label pictures of the foods and beverages on the shopping list. Below each picture, write the brand or type of item you can buy at Supermercados La Famosa.

SUPERMERCADOS LA FAMOSA
TENEMOS BUENOS PRECIOS Y PRODUCTOS SUPERIORES

Hamburguesas El bohío, 1.5 lbs. $1.29

Queso americano de sándwich Vitarroz 12 oz. [1] $1.79

Jamón de sándwich Astor $1.79/LB. [2]

Uvas de California $1.59/LB.

Yogur de mango La Yogurt .59¢

Queso crema La Cremosa 8 oz. $1.29

Leche condensada La Fe 14 oz. .99¢

_____
[1] onzas   [2] libra

Differentiating Instruction

Pre-AP

Self-correct Ask students to add their favorite foods to the grocery list, written by Señora Sánchez, and then work in pairs to read the new lists they've written to a partner. Tell students to think of corrections as they read their lists out loud. Then ask the partners to note points when self-corrections would have been appropriate but did not take place.

Multiple Intelligences

Logical/Mathematical Ask students to create charts organizing the food on the list written by Señora Sánchez. Students should come up with their own categories. Possibilities are dairy products, fruit, beverages, sandwich ingredients, etc. How many categories can each food belong to? Are there foods that only belong to one category?

- Learn about supermarkets in the Spanish-speaking world and the products they sell.
- Compare foods purchased by families in Puerto Rico with food products bought by students' families.
- Read a supermarket shopping list.

Core Resources

- Audio Program: TXT CD 3 track 10

Presentation Strategies

- Ask students to think about the ads they've seen from supermarkets.
- Ask students which items in the ad on pp. 176–177 look familiar.
- Ask which items seem to be typical of a Spanish-speaking country and why.
- Play the audio while students read the circular and shopping list.

STANDARDS

1.1 Engage in conversation
1.2 Understand language
2.1 Products and perspectives
4.2 Compare cultures

Warm Up UTB 3 Transparency 19

Estar and ir + a Complete the following sentences with the correct forms of **estar** and **ir + a.**

1. A las siete yo _____ en el gimnasio.
2. Esteban _____ la biblioteca a las tres.
3. ¿Por qué _____ tú nerviosa?
4. Nosotros _____ en la clase de ciencias.
5. Los estudiantes _____ la cafetería a la una.

Answers: 1. estoy; 2. va a; 3. estás; 4. estamos; 5. van a

Culture

Expanded Information

In Spanish-speaking countries, food flyers are often included in the weekly and Sunday editions of the local paper. Flyers list reduced items on particular days of the week.

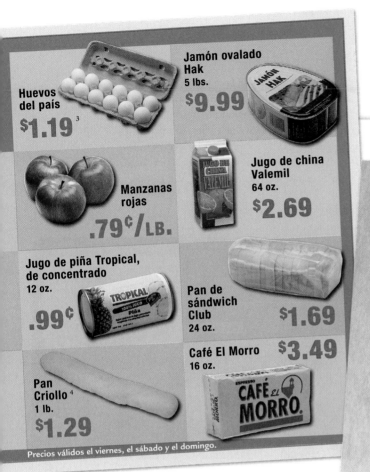

Huevos del país
$1.19 [3]

Jamón ovalado Hak
5 lbs.
$9.99

Manzanas rojas
.79¢/LB.

Jugo de china Valemil
64 oz.
$2.69

Jugo de piña Tropical, de concentrado
12 oz.
.99¢

Pan de sándwich Club
24 oz.
$1.69

Pan Criollo [4]
1 lb.
$1.29

Café El Morro
16 oz.
$3.49

Precios válidos el viernes, el sábado y el domingo.

Lista de compras

café
huevos
leche condensada
jugo de china
pan
yogur
cereal
jamón de sándwich
queso de sándwich
uvas
manzanas

[3] En Puerto Rico usan dólares estadounidenses
[4] bread similar to French bread

PARA Y PIENSA

¿Comprendiste?
1. ¿Qué hay en la lista que no está en la circular?
2. ¿Qué venden en Supermercados La Famosa que no está en la lista?
3. ¿Qué frutas hay en la lista?

¿Y tú?
¿Qué comida en Supermercados La Famosa comes tú? ¿Qué bebes?

Lección 1
ciento setenta y siete **177**

Differentiating Instruction

Multiple Intelligences

Kinesthetic Ask students to role-play a family eating breakfast and lunch. Ask them to take on the characters of different family members and discuss what they would like for the two meals. Students should choose names, decide which family members will ask for the food, and which family members will serve it.

Slower-paced Learners

Yes/No Questions Review names for the foods on Sra. Sánchez's list. Ask students to respond with **sí** or **no** to the question(s): **¿A ti te gusta la leche? ¿el café? ¿el pan? ¿A ti te gustan las uvas? ¿las manzanas?** Then ask students to repeat their classmates' preferences, using **sí** or **no** to questions like **¿A (name) le gustan las uvas?**

Communication
Pair Work

Have student pairs write their own **lista de compras** using items from the supermarket circular on pp. 176–177. They will need to learn the word **libra(s)** to say how many pounds of **jamón, uvas,** and **manzanas** they want. Next to each item, have them write the price indicated in the circular, and ask them to calculate the total cost of the food.

Comparisons
English Language Connection

Cognates Ask students to review all the food items on these pages and list cognates. Tell them to think of similarities in sound as well as spelling and to discuss the relationship between the beginning of words like **jamón** and *ham,* and **jugo** and *juice.*

Communities
Spanish in the Supermarket

Ask students to visit a Spanish market or the section of the supermarket that sells food items from Latin America or Spain. Ask them to make a list of the items they find, including the brand name, and to report their findings back to the class.

Communication
Regionalisms

Explain to students that there are regional variations for some of the words on the supermarket flyer. Fort example, meat and cheese that come in slices can be described as **...de sándwich** (Puerto Rico), **...en fetas** (Argentina), **...en tajadas** (muchos países), **una lonja de...** (España).

Answers

Para y piensa ¿Comprendiste?
1. Cereal está en la lista, pero no está en la circular.
2. Venden hamburguesas, queso crema, jamón ovalado, jugo de piña.
3. Hay uvas y manzanas.

¿Y tú? Answers will vary. Sample answer: Yo como yogur, huevos, pan de sándwich y jamón de sándwich. Bebo jugo de piña y jugo de china.

177

Connections

Las ciencias

The Saffir-Simpson Hurricane Scale is used to categorize hurricanes by the speed of their winds. There are five categories, ranging from 1 (winds from 74–95 mph) to 5 (winds greater than 155 mph). In the West Indies, for several centuries hurricanes were named after the saints on whose day the hurricane hit land. In the mid-twentieth century, hurricanes were given women's names, a practice discontinued in 1978. Today the World Meteorological Association uses a rotating list of names to identify hurricanes.

Answers

Conexiones Have students show their research in writing, in a 3-D model, or in a presentation.

Proyecto 1 The length of Puerto Rico (from Humacao to Mayagüez) is 179 kilometers.
179 km / 24 km per hour = 7.46 hours
Students should write out their calculations using the Spanish words for kilometers (**kilómetros**), hours (**horas**), per hour (**por hora**), divided by (**entre**), equals (**son**).

Answers continue on p. 179.

Conexiones *Las ciencias*

Los huracanes

The Caribbean island of Puerto Rico is located in an area prone to hurricanes (**huracanes**). The word *hurricane* comes from the Taino word *hurákan*, which was used by the pre-Columbian inhabitants of the island to describe these storms (**tormentas**). Hurricanes draw energy from the surface of warm tropical waters and from moisture in the air. The extreme winds of 74 miles per hour or more can create storm surges—domes of water up to 20 feet high and 100 miles wide—and can spawn tornadoes, torrential rain, and floods. Research and write about the most severe weather condition where you live. Create a diagram or drawing to illustrate your report.

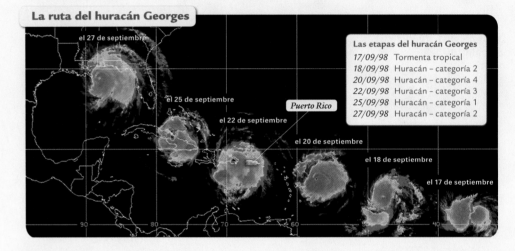

La ruta del huracán Georges

el 27 de septiembre
el 25 de septiembre
el 22 de septiembre
Puerto Rico
el 20 de septiembre
el 18 de septiembre
el 17 de septiembre

Las etapas del huracán Georges	
17/09/98	Tormenta tropical
18/09/98	Huracán – categoría 2
20/09/98	Huracán – categoría 4
22/09/98	Huracán – categoría 3
25/09/98	Huracán – categoría 1
27/09/98	Huracán – categoría 2

Proyecto 1 *Las matemáticas*
Hurricane Georges passed over Puerto Rico at a speed of about 24 kilometers per hour (**kilómetros por hora**). Find the distance from Humacao to Mayagüez in kilometers and calculate the time it took for the storm to move from one city to the other.

Proyecto 2 *La historia*
Research another major hurricane that has hit Puerto Rico in the past century. Draw a map showing the trajectory of the hurricane. Then write a paragraph describing the storm.

Proyecto 3 *La geografía*
Compare this map to the one on page xxxiii to name three other countries that were hit by Hurricane Georges. Make a chart in Spanish showing the three countries, the dates of the storm, and the category of the hurricane at the time it hit.

La playa Ocean Park, Puerto Rico, durante el huracán Georges

Differentiating Instruction

English Learners

Build Background Ask students to read the text about hurricanes. After each line, check for comprehension and clarify any questions that arise. After students finish reading, ask them to explain in their own words how hurricanes form. Personalize the topic by asking them whether they have ever lived through a hurricane in their country of origin. If so, ask them to describe what happened.

Pre-AP

Expand and Elaborate Have students research hurricane-related topics such as: Different terminology for hurricanes in other parts of the world (Typhoon, Severe Tropical Cyclone, etc.); The Saffir-Simpson Hurricane Scale; Hurricane Watches and Forecasts; Hurricane Preparedness Guides; Storm Names. Ask students to give oral reports with visuals such as photos or charts.

Lección 1

En resumen
Vocabulario y gramática

Animated Grammar
Interactive Flashcards
ClassZone.com

Vocabulario

Talk About Foods and Beverages

Meals		For Breakfast			For Lunch	
el almuerzo	lunch	el café	coffee		la hamburguesa	hamburger
la bebida	beverage, drink	el cereal	cereal		el sándwich de	ham and cheese
la cena	dinner	el huevo	egg		jamón y queso	sandwich
compartir	to share	el jugo de naranja	orange juice		la sopa	soup
la comida	food; meal	la leche	milk			
el desayuno	breakfast	el pan	bread		**Fruit**	
vender	to sell	el yogur	yogurt		la banana	banana
					la manzana	apple
					las uvas	grapes

Describe Feelings		Ask Questions		Other Words and Phrases	
tener ganas de...	to feel like . . .	¿Cómo?	How?	ahora	now
tener hambre	to be hungry	¿Cuál(es)?	Which?; What?	Es importante.	It's important.
tener sed	to be thirsty	¿Por qué?	Why?	horrible	horrible
		¿Qué?	What?	nutritivo(a)	nutritious
		¿Quién(es)?	Who?	otro(a)	other
				para	for; in order to
				rico(a)	tasty, delicious

Gramática

Notas gramaticales: Interrogative words *p. 161,* The verb **hacer** *p. 170*

Gustar with Nouns

To talk about the things that people like, use
gustar + **noun.**

Singular		Plural	
me gusta **la sopa**		me gustan **los jugos**	
te gusta **la sopa**		te gustan **los jugos**	
le gusta **la sopa**		le gustan **los jugos**	
nos gusta **la sopa**		nos gustan **los jugos**	
os gusta **la sopa**		os gustan **los jugos**	
les gusta **la sopa**		les gustan **los jugos**	

Present Tense of -er and -ir Verbs

vend**er** *to sell*	
vend**o**	vend**emos**
vend**es**	vend**éis**
vend**e**	vend**en**

compart**ir** *to share*	
compart**o**	compart**imos**
compart**es**	compart**ís**
compart**e**	compart**en**

Lección 1
ciento setenta y nueve **179**

Objective

· Review lesson vocabulary and grammar.

Online SPANISH CLASSZONE.COM

Interactive Flashcards Students can hear every target vocabulary word pronounced in authentic Spanish. Flashcards have Spanish on one side, and a picture or a translation on the other.

Review Games Matching, concentration, hangman, and word search are just a sampling of the fun, interactive games students can play to review for the test.

Featuring...
Cultura INTERACTIVA
Animated Grammar
@HomeTutor

And more...
· Get Help Online
· Interactive Flashcards
· Review Games
· WebQuest
· Self-Check Quiz

Communication
Interpersonal Mode

Ask student pairs to talk about what they like to eat and drink using **gustar** and the food vocabulary listed in En resumen. Responses should include a reason why they like that food item. For example: **¿Te gusta el jugo de naranja? Sí, me gusta porque es muy nutritivo.**

Differentiating Instruction

Inclusion

Frequent Review/Repetition Divide the class into two groups. Ask students to look at the singular and plural columns indicating the use of **gustar** with nouns. Lead one group in calling out **me gusta la sopa**, and the other group in responding **me gustan los jugos.** Then **te gusta la sopa**, and **te gustan los jugos.** Repeat this pattern until both groups have gone through the columns.

Multiple Intelligences

Intrapersonal Have students visualize a time when they are hungry, thirsty, or feel like doing something. Ask them to write a short journal entry, briefly describing the time, and expressing the feeling in Spanish. For example: **A las doce siempre tengo hambre y como una hamburguesa.**

Answers

Answers continued from p. 178.

Proyecto 2 Some major hurricanes include Hugo, Marilyn, Bertha, Hortense, and Lenny.

Proyecto 3 The students' charts should be in Spanish and should include country name, date, and category of the hurricane.

La República Dominicana: el veintidós de septiembre, categoría 3.

Cuba: el veinticinco de septiembre, categoría 1.

Estados Unidos: el veintisiete de septiembre, categoría 2.

Objectives

· Review lesson grammar and vocabulary.

Core Resources

· *Cuaderno*, pp. 112–123
· Audio Program: TXT CD 3 track 11

Presentation Strategies

· Before starting the audio for Activity 1, ask students to listen to it carefully and pay special attention to what Lola eats and drinks for each meal.
· Before doing Activity 2, ask students to identify the foods in the pictures.
· Review question words by giving a statement and asking students to supply a corresponding question. For example: **El helado es rico. ¿Cómo es el helado?**
· Ask students to generate two questions to ask their classmates, based on the Comparación cultural.

✿ STANDARDS

1.2 Understand language, Act. 1
1.3 Present information, Acts. 2–5
4.2 Compare cultures, Act. 5

⬛ Warm Up UTB 3 Transparency 19

Vocabulary Decide whether the following statements are **cierto** or **falso**.

1. Cuando no tengo hambre como una hamburguesa, una pizza, papas fritas y un helado.
2. La manzana es una fruta.
3. La leche es una bebida muy nutritiva.
4. Comemos el desayuno en la noche.
5. Necesito pan para hacer un sándwich.

Answers: 1. falso; 2. cierto; 3. cierto; 4. falso; 5. cierto

See Activity answers on p. 181.

Lección 1

Repaso de la lección

¡LLEGADA!

@HomeTutor ClassZone.com

Now you can
· talk about foods and beverages
· ask questions
· say which foods you like and don't like

Using
· interrogative words
· **gustar** with nouns
· present tense of **-er** and **-ir** verbs
· the verb **hacer**

To review
· **gustar** with nouns p. 162
· present tense of **-er** and **-ir** verbs p. 168

1 | ## Listen and understand

Lola never eats traditional meals. Listen to the radio interview. Write **el desayuno, el almuerzo,** or **la cena,** according to when she eats or drinks each item.

1. huevos
2. café
3. leche
4. hamburguesas
5. banana
6. refresco
7. pan
8. cereal

🎧 **Audio Program**
TXT CD 3 Track 11 Audio Script, TE p. 153b

To review
· present tense of **-er** and **-ir** verbs p. 168
· the verb **hacer** p. 170

2 | ## Talk about foods and beverages

Write what these people are doing in the cafeteria.

modelo: Daniel / comer
Daniel come pan.

1. Irene / beber

5. yo / comer

2. ustedes / compartir

6. tú / hacer

3. yo / hacer

7. los estudiantes / beber

4. nosotros / vender

8. Trinidad y yo / compartir

Differentiating Instruction

Multiple Intelligences

Visual Learners Ask students to make a color code for the endings of **-er** and **-ir** verbs. Tell them to copy the tables showing the present tenses of **vender** and **compartir** on p. 179. Ask them to write the basic verb forms in black, but the endings in one of six colors. They should use the same color for the first person in both verbs, a second color for the second person familiar in both verbs, etc.

Pre-AP

Timed Answer Ask students what food and beverages they like for breakfast and lunch and to explain why they like or dislike them. **Para el desayuno, me gusta el jugo de naranja porque es nutritivo pero no me gusta el café porque es malo.** Tell students they must talk about their likes and dislikes for at least two minutes.

3 | Ask questions

To review
• interrogative words p. 161

Gilberto is a new student. It's lunchtime, and he is in the cafeteria with Julia. Complete the conversation with interrogative words.

modelo: ¿<u>Cuál</u> es el sándwich del día?
Es el sándwich de jamón y queso.

Gilberto: ¿ __1.__ está el yogur?
Julia: Está al lado de las frutas.
Gilberto: ¿ __2.__ no venden pizza?
Julia: Porque hoy no es viernes.
Gilberto: ¿ __3.__ venden los martes?
Julia: Venden hamburguesas.
Gilberto: ¿ __4.__ es la sopa?
Julia: Es muy rica.
Gilberto: ¿ __5.__ prepara la comida?

Julia: La señora Aguirre.
Gilberto: ¿ __6.__ personas trabajan en la cafetería?
Julia: Nueve o diez.
Gilberto: ¿ __7.__ compramos la bebida?
Julia: Ahora, con la comida.
Gilberto: ¿ __8.__ vamos después del almuerzo?
Julia: A la clase de inglés.

4 | Say which foods you like and don't like

To review
• **gustar** with nouns p. 162

These people are in the supermarket and are talking about foods and drinks. Write sentences about what they like and don't like, according to what they say.

modelo: la señora Medina: «El yogur es bueno.»
A la señora Medina le gusta el yogur.

1. ustedes: «No, el yogur es horrible.»
2. Adán y Susana: «Necesitamos manzanas. Son nutritivas.»
3. el señor Chávez: «El café es bueno.»
4. nosotros: «No, el café es malo.»
5. yo: «Tengo ganas de comer uvas.»
6. tú: «Las hamburguesas son ricas.»

5 | Puerto Rico and El Salvador

To review
• El Yunque p. 153
• Comparación cultural pp. 154, 164, 170

Comparación cultural

Answer these culture questions.

1. What is El Yunque and what can you find there?
2. What is a popular cold treat in Puerto Rico?
3. What can you find in Plaza de Colón?
4. Describe some popular foods from Puerto Rico and El Salvador.

Más práctica Cuaderno *pp. 112–123* Cuaderno para hispanohablantes *pp. 114–123*

Get Help Online
ClassZone.com

Lección 1
ciento ochenta y uno **181**

Differentiating Instruction

Slower-paced Learners

Read Before Listening Before playing the audio for Activity 1, distribute copies of the script to the class and read it aloud. Tell them to track your voice by following the words with their index fingers as you say them.

Multiple Intelligences

Interpersonal Have students work with a partner to list the foods served in the school cafeteria that day or the day before. Partners should then take turns asking each other if they like each food or not. They may also emphasize their answers with gestures and facial expressions.

✓ Ongoing Assessment

Alternative Strategy To review the interrogative words in Activity 3, have students generate five questions to ask their classmates using **¿Cómo? ¿Dónde? ¿Por qué? ¿Quién? ¿Cuándo?** and **¿Qué?** Check for correct questions and answers.

✓ Ongoing Assessment

Peer Assessment Have student pairs exchange answers for Activity 4, and correct each other's work.

Answers MSRB Transparencies 46–47

Answers for Activities on p. 180.

Activity 1 **1.** la cena; **2.** la cena; **3.** el almuerzo; **4.** el desayuno; **5.** el almuerzo; **6.** el desayuno; **7.** la cena; **8.** el almuerzo

Activity 2
1. Irene bebe jugo de naranja.
2. Ustedes comparten las uvas.
3. Yo hago un sándwich.
4. Nosotros vendemos manzanas.
5. Yo como cereal.
6. Tú haces sopa.
7. Los estudiantes beben leche.
8. Trinidad y yo compartimos una pizza.

Activity 3 **1.** Dónde; **2.** Por qué; **3.** Qué; **4.** Cómo; **5.** Quién; **6.** Cuántas; **7.** Cuándo; **8.** Adónde

Activity 4
1. A ustedes no les gusta el yogur.
2. A Adán y a Susana les gustan las manzanas.
3. Al señor Chávez le gusta el café.
4. A nosotros no nos gusta el café.
5. A mí me gustan las uvas.
6. A ti te gustan las hamburguesas.

Activity 5
1. **El Yunque** is a tropical rain forest. There you can find many waterfalls and a small frog called **coquí**.
2. A popular cold treat in Puerto Rico is **la piragua**.
3. In Plaza de Colón you can find a statue of Christopher Columbus.
4. Popular foods from Puerto Rico include **tostones** (fried plantains), **alcapurrias** (fried plantains stuffed with meat), and **bacalaítos** (codfish fritters). Typical foods from El Salvador include the **pupusa** (corn tortilla filled with beans, pork, and cheese) and a sweet bread layered with pineapple marmalade called **semita.**

181

Culture at a Glance ❖

Topic & Activity	Essential Question
Mealtime traditions pp. 182–183	Does your family have any traditions or customs involving mealtimes?
Elections in Puerto Rico p. 193	What do elections reveal about a culture?
Portraits by Rafael Tufiño and Fernando Sayán Polo p. 199	How do portraits represent the people in a country?
La quinceañera pp. 204–205	How does a **quinceañera** celebration compare to a Sweet Sixteen celebration?
Instrumentos de Puerto Rico y Perú p. 206	How do certain instruments and music become associated with a particular region?
Culture review, p. 209	What are some cultural traditions in Puerto Rico and Peru?

COMPARISON COUNTRIES 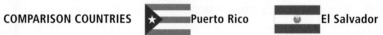 Puerto Rico  El Salvador Perú

Practice at a Glance ❖

	Objective	Activity & Skill
Vocabulary	Family members	1: Speaking/Writing; 2: Reading; 4: Speaking; 5: Reading; 6: Reading/Writing; 8: Speaking; 9: Writing; 10: Listening/Reading; 12: Writing; 21: Speaking; 22: Reading/Listening/Speaking; 23: Writing; Repaso 1: Listening
	Months and numbers	3: Listening/Reading; 4: Speaking; 7: Speaking; 11: Speaking; Repaso 2, Writing; Repaso 4: Writing
Grammar	Using **de** to show possession	2: Reading; 4: Speaking; 6: Reading/Writing; 19: Reading/Listening/Speaking; Repaso 1: Listening; Repaso 4: Writing
	Possessive adjectives	5: Reading; 6: Reading/Writing; 7: Speaking; 8: Speaking; 9: Writing; 11: Speaking; 12: Writing; Repaso 2: Writing
	Comparatives	13: Writing; 14: Speaking/Writing; 15: Writing; 16: Writing; 17: Listening/Writing; 18: Writing; 21: Speaking; 23: Writing; Repaso 3: Writing
Communication	Talk about family Ask and tell ages Express possession	1: Speaking/Writing; 2: Reading; 4: Speaking; 6: Reading/Writing; 8: Speaking; 10: Listening/Reading; 12: Writing; 19: Listening/Reading; 20: Listening/Reading; 21: Speaking; 23: Writing; Repaso 2: Writing
	Give dates	7: Speaking; 9: Writing; 11: Speaking; Repaso 4: Writing
	Make comparisons	13: Writing; 14: Speaking/Writing; 15: Writing; 16: Writing; 17: Listening/Writing; 18: Writing; 21: Speaking; 23: Writing; Repaso 3: Writing
	Pronunciation: The letter **j**	*Pronunciación: La letra **j**,* p. 191: Listening
Recycle	Describing others	8: Speaking
	Numbers from 11 to 100	4: Speaking
	After-school activities	6: Reading/Writing

The following presentations are recorded in the Audio Program for *¡Avancemos!*

- **¡A responder!** *page 186*
- **17: Capitán y Príncipe** *page 199*
- **22: Integración** *page 202*
- **Repaso de la lección** *page 208*
    1: Listen and understand
- **Repaso inclusivo** *page 212*
    1: Listen, understand, and compare

¡A responder! TXT CD 3 track 13

1. María y Cristóbal son los padres de Rodrigo.
2. Camila es la tía de Ana.
3. Rodrigo es el hermano de Ana.
4. Pablo es el hermano de Ester.
5. Camila y Pablo son los padres de Tito.
6. Ana y Ester son hermanas.
7. Tito es el hijo de María.
8. José es el padre de Ana.

17 | Capitán y Príncipe TXT CD 3 track 17

Mi familia y yo tenemos un perro y un gato. Nuestro perro se llama Capitán y nuestro gato se llama Príncipe. Capitán es tan simpático como Príncipe, pero también son diferentes. Príncipe es mucho más pequeño que Capitán. A Príncipe le gusta descansar tanto como comer. Capitán tiene tres años; Príncipe tiene ocho años. Capitán no hace mucho; es más perezoso que Príncipe.

22 | Integración TXT CD 3 tracks 19, 20

Hoy presentamos un perro muy especial. Dino es un bóxer blanco. Él tiene cinco años y es muy bonito. Siempre está tranquilo. Le gusta más descansar que correr. Es un poco perezoso pero muy divertido. La actividad favorita de Dino es mirar la televisión. Es pequeño, inteligente y muy simpático. Si usted vive en San Juan, nuestro número de teléfono es 555-6346.

Repaso de la lección TXT CD 3 track 22

1 Listen and understand

Hola, me llamo Marcos. Tengo una foto de toda mi familia. Mi hermano se llama Pedro y mis hermanas se llaman Elena y Rosa. Detrás de nosotros, están nuestros padres. Nuestro padre se llama Julio y nuestra madre se llama Norma. Mi abuelo se llama Alberto. Al lado de mi abuelo están mis primos. Ellos se llaman Diego y Felipe. Detrás de mis primos está mi tía. Ella se llama Carmen. Mi familia es bonita, ¿no?

Repaso inclusivo TXT CD 3 track 24

1 Listen, understand, and compare

Esperanza: Hola, Diana, ¿qué problema tienes?

Diana: Bueno, yo soy más estudiosa que mi hermano. A él y a sus amigos les gusta tocar la guitarra toda la tarde. A mí me gusta escuchar música tanto como estudiar, pero yo tengo que estudiar mucho. Tengo muchos exámenes en la clase de ciencias.

Esperanza: Hmmm... ¿Óscar es mayor o menor que tú?

Diana: Es menor que yo. Yo tengo catorce años y él tiene diez.

Esperanza: ¡Ah! Diana, tienes que aprender a vivir con tu hermano.

Diana: Pero, ¿qué necesito hacer?

Esperanza: Necesitas hablar con Óscar. Tú estudias de las tres a las cinco de la tarde. Tu hermano y sus amigos tocan la guitarra de las cinco a las siete, y tú escuchas.

Diana: Está bien. ¡Gracias!

Complete Resource List

On your desktop

Everything you need to ...

Plan	Present	Assess
 **easyPlanner** DVD-ROM	**POWER PRESENTATIONS**	**McDOUGAL LITTELL ASSESSMENT SYSTEM** ONLINE
All resources including audio and video	Ready-made PowerPoint™ presentations with  **Animated Grammar**	✓ Assess, score, prescribe, and remediate online ✓ Create customized tests with the Test Generator CD-ROM ✓ Individualized Assessment for on-level, modified, pre-AP, and heritage language learners

 Print

Plan	Present	Practice	Assess
URB 3 • Video Scripts pp. 71–72 • Family Involvement Activity p. 92 • Absent Student Copymasters pp. 101–111 **Lesson Plans** p. 65 **Best Practices Toolkit**	**URB 3** • Video Activities pp. 59–66 **TPRS** pp. 36–42	• *Cuaderno* pp. 124–149 • *Cuaderno para hispanohablantes* pp. 124–149 • *Lecturas para todos* pp. 27–31 • *Lecturas para hispanohablantes* • *¡AvanzaCómics! SúperBruno y Nati, Episodio 2* **URB 3** • Practice Games pp. 39–46 • Audio Scripts pp. 78–82 • Fine Art Activities pp. 88–89	**URB 3** • Did you get it? Reteaching and Practice Copymasters pp. 13–24

Unit Transparency Book 3

Culture	Presentation and Practice	Classroom Management
• Atlas Maps UTB 1 1–6 • Map of Puerto Rico 1 • Fine Art Transparencies 4, 5	• Vocabulary Transparencies 8, 9 • Grammar Presentation Transparencies 12, 13 • Situational Transparencies and label overlay 14, 15 • Situational Student Copymasters pp. 1, 2	• Warm Up Transparencies 20–23 **MSRB** • Student Book Answer Transparencies 48–51

Audio and Video

Audio	Video

• Student Book Audio CD 3 Tracks 12–24
• Workbook Audio CD 2 Tracks 11–20
• Heritage Learners Audio CD 1 Tracks 21–24, CD 3 Tracks 17–20
• Assessment Audio CD 1 Tracks 17–20
• *Lecturas para todos* Audio CD 1 Track 6, CD 2 Tracks 1–6
• *Música del mundo hispano*
• Sing-along Audio CD
	• Vocabulary Video DVD 1
	• *Telehistoria* DVD 1
	  Escena 1
	  Escena 2
	  Escena 3
	  Completa
	• Culture Video DVD 1

Online and CD-ROM Resources

Student	Teacher
Available online and on CD-ROM: • eEdition • @HomeTutor • Animated Grammar **Available online:** • *Cultura interactiva* • Culture Links • WebQuests • Flashcards • Conjuguemos.com • Review Games • Self-check Quiz	**Available online and on CD-ROM:** **EasyPlanner CD-ROM resources:** • Learning Scenarios • Conversation Cards • Family Letters in Spanish • Family Letters in Creole **Available online:** • McDougal Littell Assessment System **Available on CD-ROM:** • Test Generator • Power Presentations

Differentiated Assessment

On-level	Modified	Pre-AP	Heritage Learners
• Vocabulary Recognition Quiz p. 120 • Vocabulary Production Quiz p. 121 • Grammar Quizzes pp. 122–123 • Culture Quiz p. 124 • On-level Lesson Test pp. 125–131 • On-level Unit Test pp. 137–143	• Modified Lesson Test pp. 95–101 • Modified Unit Test pp. 107–113	• Pre-AP Lesson Test pp. 95–101 • Pre-AP Unit Test pp. 107–113	• Heritage Learners Lesson Test pp. 101–107 • Heritage Learners Unit Test pp. 113–119

Core Pacing Guide

50 Minute (9 Day)

	Objectives/Focus	Teach	Practice	Assess/HW Options
DAY 1	**Culture:** learn about Puerto Rican culture **Vocabulary:** family, months, numbers from 200 to 1,000,000 • Warm Up OHT 20 **5 min**	Lesson Opener pp. 182–183 **Presentación de vocabulario** pp. 184–186 • Read A–C • View video DVD 1 • Play Audio TXT CD 3 track 12 • *¡A responder!* TXT CD 3 track 13 **Práctica de vocabulario** p. 187 • *Nota gramatical:* possession with **de** **25 min**	Lesson opener pp. 182–183 **Práctica de vocabulario** p. 187 • Acts. 1, 2 **15 min**	**Assess:** *Para y piensa* p. 187 **5 min** **Homework:** *Cuaderno* pp. 124–126 @HomeTutor
DAY 2	**Communication:** identify family and birthday vocabulary, practice using them to ask and tell a person's age • Warm Up OHT 20 • Check Homework **5 min**	**Vocabulario en contexto** pp. 188–189 • *Telehistoria escena 1* DVD 1 • *Nota gramatical:* use **tener** to talk about age **20 min**	**Vocabulario en contexto** pp. 188–189 • Act. 3 TXT CD 3 track 14 • Act. 4 **20 min**	**Assess:** *Para y piensa* p. 189 **5 min** **Homework:** *Cuaderno* pp. 124–126 @HomeTutor
DAY 3	**Grammar:** possessive adjectives • Warm Up OHT 21 • Check Homework **5 min**	**Presentación de gramática** p. 190 • Possessive adjectives **Práctica de gramática** pp. 191–193 **Culture:** *Las elecciones en Puerto Rico* • *Nota gramatical:* writing the date **20 min**	**Práctica de gramática** pp. 191–193 • Acts. 5, 6, 7, 8, 9 **20 min**	**Assess:** *Para y piensa* p. 193 **5 min** **Homework:** *Cuaderno* pp. 127–129 @HomeTutor
DAY 4	**Communication:** use possessive adjectives to talk about family and people's birthdays • Warm Up OHT 21 • Check Homework **5 min**	**Gramática en contexto** pp. 194–195 • *Telehistoria escena 2* DVD 1 **15 min**	**Gramática en contexto** pp. 194–195 • Act. 10 TXT CD 3 track 15 • Acts. 11, 12 **25 min**	**Assess:** *Para y piensa* p. 195 **5 min** **Homework:** *Cuaderno* pp. 127–129 @HomeTutor
DAY 5	**Grammar:** comparatives • Warm Up OHT 22 • Check Homework **5 min**	**Presentación de gramática** p. 196 • comparatives **Práctica de gramática** pp. 197–199 • *Pronunciación:* TXT CD 3 track 16 **15 min**	**Práctica de gramática** pp. 197–199 • Acts. 13, 14, 15, 16, 18 • Act. 17 TXT CD 3 track 17 **25 min**	**Assess:** *Para y piensa* p. 199 **5 min** **Homework:** *Cuaderno* pp. 130–132 @HomeTutor
DAY 6	**Communication:** Culmination: use comparative words and possessive adjectives to describe your family and friends • Warm Up OHT 22 • Check Homework **5 min**	**Todo junto** pp. 200–202 • *Escenas 1, 2: Resumen* • *Telehistoria completa* DVD 1 **20 min**	**Todo junto** pp. 200–202 • Acts. 19, 20 TXT CD 3 tracks 14, 15, 18 • Act. 22 TXT CD 3 tracks 19, 20 • Acts. 21, 23 **20 min**	**Assess:** *Para y piensa* p. 202 **5 min** **Homework:** *Cuaderno* pp. 133–134 @HomeTutor
DAY 7	**Reading:** The **quinceañera** celebration **Review:** Lesson review • Warm Up OHT 23 • Check Homework **5 min**	**Lectura cultural** pp. 204–205, *La quinceañera* TXT CD 3 track 21 **Repaso de la lección** pp. 208–209 **10 min**	**Lectura cultural** pp. 204–205, *La quinceañera* **Repaso de la lección** pp. 208–209 • Act. 1 TXT CD 3 track 22 • Acts. 2, 3, 4, 5 **25 min**	**Assess:** *Para y piensa* p. 205; *Repaso de la lección* pp. 208–209 **10 min** **Homework:** *En resumen* p. 207; *Cuaderno* pp. 135–146 (optional) Review Games Online @HomeTutor
DAY 8	**Assessment**			**Assess:** Lesson 2 test or Unit 3 test **50 min**
DAY 9	**Unit Culmination** **5 min**	**Comparación cultural** pp. 210–211 TXT CD 3 track 23 **Repaso inclusivo** pp. 212–213 **15 min**	**Comparación cultural** pp. 210–211 **Repaso inclusivo** pp. 212–213 • Act. 1 TXT CD 3 track 24 • Acts. 2, 3, 4, 5, 6 **25 min**	**Homework:** *Cuaderno* pp. 147–149 **5 min**

	Objectives/Focus	Teach	Practice	Assess/HW Options
DAY 1	**Culture:** learn about Puerto Rican culture **Vocabulary:** family, months, numbers from 200 to 1,000,000 • Warm Up OHT 20 **5 min**	Lesson Opener pp. 182–183 **Presentación de vocabulario** pp. 184–186 • Read A–C • View video DVD 1 • Play Audio TXT CD 3 track 12 • *¡A responder!* TXT CD 3 track 13 **Práctica de vocabulario** p. 187 • *Nota gramatical:* showing posession with **de** **25 min**	Lesson Opener pp. 182–183 **Práctica de vocabulario** p. 187 • Acts. 1, 2 **15 min**	**Assess:** *Para y piensa* p. 187 **5 min**
	Communication: identify family and birthday vocabulary, practice using them to ask and tell a person's age **5 min**	**Vocabulario en contexto** pp. 188–189 • *Telehistoria escena 1* DVD 1 • *Nota gramatical:* use **tener** to talk about age **15 min**	**Vocabulario en contexto** pp. 188–189 • Act. 3 TXT CD 3 track 14 • Act. 4 **15 min**	**Assess:** *Para y piensa* p. 189 **5 min** **Homework:** *Cuaderno* pp. 124–126 @HomeTutor
DAY 2	**Grammar:** possessive adjectives • Warm Up OHT 21 • Check Homework **5 min**	**Presentación de gramática** p. 190 • Possessive adjectives **Práctica de gramática** pp. 191–193 **Culture:** *Las elecciones en Puerto Rico* • *Nota gramatical:* writing the date **15 min**	**Práctica de gramática** pp. 191–193 • Acts. 5, 6, 7, 8, 9 **20 min**	**Assess:** *Para y piensa* p. 193 **5 min**
	Communication: use possessive adjectives to talk about family and people's birthdays **5 min**	**Gramática en contexto** pp. 194–195 • *Telehistoria escena 2* DVD 1 **15 min**	**Gramática en contexto** pp. 194–195 • Act. 10 TXT CD 3 track 15 • Acts. 11, 12 **20 min**	**Assess:** *Para y piensa* p. 195 **5 min** **Homework:** *Cuaderno* pp. 127–129 @HomeTutor
DAY 3	**Grammar:** comparatives • Warm Up OHT 22 • Check Homework **5 min**	**Presentación de gramática** p. 196 • comparatives **Práctica de gramática** pp. 197–199 • *Pronunciación:* TXT CD 3 track 16 **15 min**	**Práctica de gramática** pp. 197–199 • Acts. 13, 14, 15, 16, 18 • Act. 17 TXT CD 3 track 17 **20 min**	**Assess:** *Para y piensa* p. 199 **5 min**
	Communication: Culmination: use comparative words and possessive adjectives to describe family and friends **5 min**	**Todo junto** pp. 200–202 • *Escenas 1, 2: Resumen* • *Telehistoria completa* DVD 1 **15 min**	**Todo junto** pp. 200–202 • Acts. 19, 20 TXT CD 3 tracks 14, 15, 18 • Act. 22 TXT CD 3 tracks 19, 20 • Acts. 21, 23 **20 min**	**Assess:** *Para y piensa* p. 202 **5 min** **Homework:** *Cuaderno* pp. 130–134 @HomeTutor
DAY 4	**Reading:** The **quinceañera** celebration • Warm Up OHT 23 • Check Homework **5 min**	**Lectura cultural** pp. 204–205, *La quinceañera* TXT CD 3 track 21 **15 min**	**Lectura cultural** pp. 204–205, *La quinceañera* **20 min**	**Assess:** *Para y piensa* p. 205 **5 min**
	Review: Lesson review **5 min**	**Repaso de la lección** pp. 208–209 **15 min**	**Repaso de la lección** pp. 208–209 • Act. 1 TXT CD 3 track 22 • Acts. 2, 3, 4, 5 **20 min**	**Assess:** *Repaso de la lección* pp. 208–209 **5 min** **Homework:** *En resumen* p. 207; *Cuaderno* pp. 135–146 (optional) Review Games Online @HomeTutor
DAY 5	**Assessment**			**Assess:** Lesson 2 test or Unit 3 test **45 min**
	Unit Culmination **5 min**	**Comparación cultural** pp. 210–211 TXT CD 3 track 23 **Repaso inclusivo** pp. 212–213 **15 min**	**Comparación cultural** pp. 210–211 **Repaso inclusivo** pp. 212–213 • Act. 1 TXT CD 3 track 24 • Acts. 2, 3, 4, 5, 6 **20 min**	**Homework:** *Cuaderno* pp. 147–149 **5 min**

¡AVANZA! Objectives

- Introduce lesson theme: **En mi familia.**
- **Culture:** Learn about **la sobremesa** and compare mealtime traditions.

Presentation Strategies

- Introduce the characters' names: Rodrigo, Marisol, Sra. Vélez, Ana.
- Have students identify the people in the photo and tell what is happening.
- Have students talk about traditions and customs involving mealtime.

STANDARDS

2.1 Practices and perspectives
4.2 Compare cultures

Warm Up   UTB 3 Transparency 20

-er and -ir Verbs Write the correct form of each verb.

1. tú _____ (beber)
2. yo _____ (compartir)
3. ella _____ (escribir)
4. usted _____ (leer)
5. ellos _____ (compartir)

Answers: 1. bebes; 2. comparto; 3. escribe; 4. lee; 5. comparten

Comparación cultural

Exploring the Theme

Ask students the following questions:
1. Is this family eating inside or outside?
2. When do you think is a good time to eat outside the house?
3. What do you think people talk about when they are eating together?
4. Why do you think people in Puerto Rico find it convenient to eat outdoors?

¿Qué ves? Possible answers include:
- Sí, Rodrigo tiene sed.
- Los señores beben café.
- La chica es bonita, joven, seria. La chica tiene pelo castaño.

182

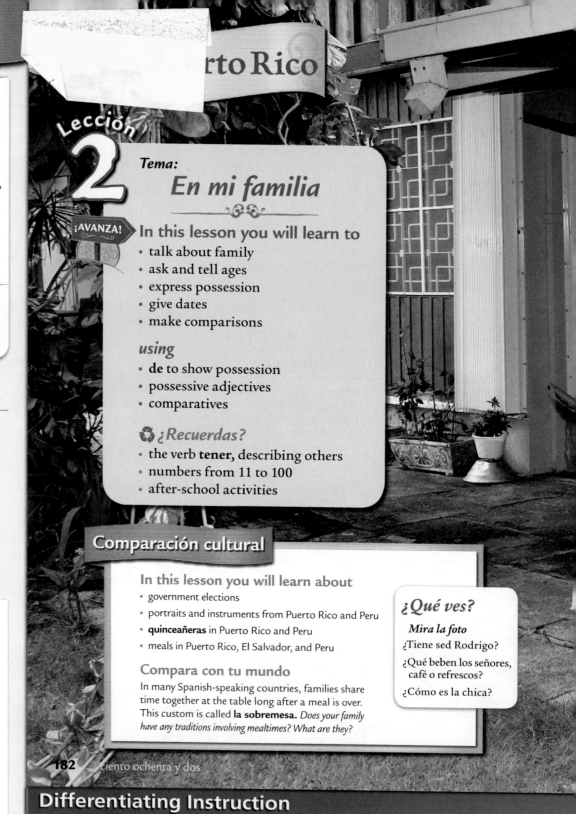

rto Rico

Lección 2

Tema:
En mi familia

¡AVANZA! **In this lesson you will learn to**
- talk about family
- ask and tell ages
- express possession
- give dates
- make comparisons

using
- **de** to show possession
- possessive adjectives
- comparatives

♻ *¿Recuerdas?*
- the verb **tener,** describing others
- numbers from 11 to 100
- after-school activities

Comparación cultural

In this lesson you will learn about
- government elections
- portraits and instruments from Puerto Rico and Peru
- **quinceañeras** in Puerto Rico and Peru
- meals in Puerto Rico, El Salvador, and Peru

Compara con tu mundo

In many Spanish-speaking countries, families share time together at the table long after a meal is over. This custom is called **la sobremesa.** *Does your family have any traditions involving mealtimes? What are they?*

¿Qué ves?

Mira la foto
¿Tiene sed Rodrigo?
¿Qué beben los señores, café o refrescos?
¿Cómo es la chica?

182 ciento ochenta y dos

Differentiating Instruction

Inclusion

Cumulative Instruction Organize students into small groups. Give each group a piece of poster board. Instruct students to write the heading **comer** at the top of their poster. Then have each group brainstorm as many words and phrases related to food and eating as they can remember from previous lessons. Encourage them to add pictures as well. Give each group the opportunity to share their poster.

Slower-paced Learners

Yes/No Questions Ask students yes or no questions about what they see in the photo. Point to the appropriate item in the photo for each question whose answer is yes. **¿Hay un refresco? ¿Hay un café? ¿Hay una chica?** Use vocabulary familiar to students when the answer is no. **¿Hay un cuaderno? ¿Hay un chico triste?**

Online SPANISH CLASSZONE.COM

Featuring...
- Cultura INTERACTIVA
- Animated Grammar
- @HomeTutor

And more...
- Get Help Online
- Interactive Flashcards
- Review Games
- WebQuest
- Self-Check Quiz

¹na familia come en casa
San Juan, Puerto Rico

Puerto Rico
ciento ochenta y tres   **183**

Online SPANISH CLASSZONE.COM

WebQuest Provides step-by-step guidance for your students to help them explore this unit's theme and location online. Students are given a task and a set of pre-approved links to conduct research, answer questions, and submit their findings to the class.

Featuring...
- Cultura INTERACTIVA
- Animated Grammar
- @HomeTutor

And more...
- Get Help Online
- Interactive Flashcards
- Review Games
- WebQuest
- Self-Check Quiz

Using the Photo

Location Information

Puerto Rico is the easternmost island of the Greater Antilles, lying approximately 1,000 miles southeast of Miami. The island itself is slightly smaller than three times the size of Rhode Island. Puerto Rico's interior terrain is mountainous.

Expanded Information

History and Education Puerto Rico was ruled by Spain from 1493 until the end of the Spanish-American War in 1898, when it was ceded to the United States. San Juan is its capital. Puerto Ricans were granted U.S. citizenship in 1917 but have chosen to remain a self-governing commonwealth of the U.S. Puerto Rican students are required to study English as a second language.

Long-term Retention

♻ Recycle

Ask students to look at the photo and answer the following questions in Spanish:
1. ¿Qué tiempo hace?
2. ¿Puerto Rico está en América Central o en el Caribe?
3. ¿De dónde es la familia?
4. ¿Qué bebe Rodrigo?

Possible answers include: 1. Hace calor, sol. 2. Está en el Caribe. 3. La familia es de Puerto Rico (de San Juan). 4. Bebe agua.

Differentiating Instruction

Multiple Intelligences

Visual Learners Have students draw a picture of a typical family meal. Remind them to consider the question words **¿quién?, ¿dónde?, ¿qué?, ¿cuándo?, ¿cómo?** as they draw. Who is at the table? Where do they eat? What are they eating? When do they eat? How do people feel about the meal? Then, ask students to write a short sentence that answers each question.

Heritage Language Learners

Support What They Know Ask students to share expressions that might be heard around their family's table. What do people say when the meal is about to start? How do people in their family ask someone to pass a dish? How do they ask to be excused?

¡AVANZA! **Objective**

- Present vocabulary: family, months of the year.

Core Resources

- Video Program: DVD 1
- Audio Program: TXT CD 3 track 12

Presentation Strategies

- Read the vocabulary words aloud and have students repeat after you. Check students' pronunciation.
- Play the audio as students read A–C.

✿ STANDARDS

1.2 Understand language

Communication

Interpersonal Mode

Based on Rodrigo's family tree, have student pairs ask and answer questions about the names of his family members and pets. For example: **¿Cómo se llama el abuelo? El abuelo se llama Cristóbal. ¿Cómo se llama el perro? El perro se llama Capitán.**

Communication

Common Error Alert

Point out that when a pet is a female, **la perra** and **la gata** may be used in place of **el perro** and **el gato.** Explain to the students that the meanings of the pet names on this page are *Captain* and *Prince.*

Sensitivity

Some students might not be comfortable discussing their family. Always give them the option of describing a fictitious family when answering personal questions.

¡AVANZA! **Goal:** Learn about Rodrigo's family. Then practice what you have learned to talk about families and express possession. *Actividades 1–2*

A Soy Rodrigo. **Vivo** en Puerto Rico con **mis padres.** Ellos tienen dos **hijos.** Yo soy **su hijo** y **mi hermana** Ana es su **hija.** Te presento a las otras personas en **nuestra familia.**

VIDEO DVD

AUDIO

los abuelos — la abuela — el abuelo — María y Cristóbal

los padres — la madre — el padre — Celia y José

los tíos — la tía — el tío — Camila y Pablo

los hermanos — el hermano — la hermana — Rodrigo y Ana

el perro — Capitán

el gato — Príncipe

los primos — el primo — la prima — Tito y Ester

184 Unidad 3 Puerto Rico
ciento ochenta y cuatro

Differentiating Instruction

Heritage Language Learners

Writing Skills Have students write a short paragraph about their family members. Ask them to include names, relationships, ages, and what they like to do. After students complete their writing, have them review it for spelling and grammar.

Pre-AP

Expand and Elaborate Have students create a family tree similar to Rodrigo's on p. 184. Tell them to organize and record the names and relationships of their own family members. Ask for volunteers to share their family trees with the group.

B ¿Cuántos años tienes tú?
Yo **tengo** quince **años.** Ana, mi hermana **menor**, tiene nueve años. Soy su **hermano mayor**.

C ¿Cuál es la fecha? Hoy es el primero de abril. Es mi **cumpleaños.** ¿Cuándo es tu cumpleaños?

¡Feliz cumpleaños!

los meses

enero
febrero
marzo
abril
mayo
junio
julio
agosto
septiembre
octubre
noviembre
diciembre

abril

Continuará...

Lección 2
ciento ochenta y cinco **185**

Communication
Common Error Alert

Months are not capitalized in Spanish, just as days of the week are not capitalized. Be sure to point out that *first* is always expressed as **primero,** but that the cardinal (counting) numbers are used for all other dates.

Communication

Group Work

On the board, write the following chant: **30 días tienen noviembre, abril, junio y septiembre, 31 mayo, julio, agosto, octubre y diciembre, y febrero 28.** Ask students to copy it in their notebooks, then lead them in chanting the words. After two or three group repetitions, ask individual students to recite.

Long-term Retention
Recycle

Have students write a possible weather condition in your area for each date expressed in Spanish.
1. el veinte de julio
2. el primero de enero
3. el cinco de mayo
4. el primero de octubre

Sample answers: 1. hace calor, hace sol; 2. hace frío, nieva; 3. llueve, hace sol, hace viento; 4. hace viento, llueve, hace sol

Differentiating Instruction

Multiple Intelligences

Logical/Mathematical Write the months of the year on the board. Then ask students **¿Cuándo es tu cumpleaños?** Record each response by placing a tally mark under the appropriate month. Instruct students to use this data to create a bar graph. Encourage students to analyze and comment on their graphs. **Cinco estudiantes tienen cumpleaños en abril.**

Slower-paced Learners

Personalize It Ask students to bring in photos of their relatives. Going around the class, ask each student to identify the person and give the person's age. For example: **Es mi hermana menor. Tiene ocho años.**

Objectives
· Present vocabulary: numbers from 200 to 1,000,000.
· Check for vocabulary recognition.

Core Resources
· Video Program: DVD 1
· Audio Program: TXT CD 3 tracks 12, 13

Presentation Strategies
· Say the numbers on p. 186 and have students repeat them after you.
· Play the audio and show the video.

 STANDARDS

1.2 Understand language

Long-term Retention
Connect to Previous Learning

Organize students in pairs, and ask them to take turns dictating these numbers: home phone number, number of students in the class, number of days in the month, the student's year of birth.

 Communication
Common Error Alert

Caution students not to forget the first **s** in **doscientos**, **trescientos**, and **seiscientos**. Another common error occurs with **quinientos**, **setecientos**, and **novecientos**, when students may try to construct a faulty pattern of adding the number to **cientos**.

 Communication
Group Work

Have students write numbers in hundreds from 200 to 1,000 on index cards. Then have them work in small groups and practice saying the numbers out loud.

 Answers MSRB Transparency 48

¡A responder! Audio Script, TE p. 181b
Students will raise their left hand if the statement is true and their right hand if the statement is false.

1. Falsa	5. Cierta
2. Cierta	6. Falsa
3. Cierta	7. Falsa
4. Falsa	8. Cierta

186

Presentación de VOCABULARIO
(continuación)

Los números de 200 a 1.000.000

doscientos(as)   trescientos(as)   cuatrocientos(as)

quinientos(as)   seiscientos(as)   setecientos(as)

ochocientos(as)   novecientos(as)   mil

1,000,000

un millón (de)

Más vocabulario

la madrastra *stepmother*	**la fecha de nacimiento** *birth date*
el padrastro *stepfather*	**ya** *already*

Expansión de vocabulario p. R4

¡A responder! Escuchar

Listen to the sentences about Rodrigo's family. If the sentence is true, raise your left hand. If it is false, raise your right hand.

@HomeTutor VideoPlus
Interactive Flashcards
ClassZone.com

186 Unidad 3 Puerto Rico
ciento ochenta y seis

Differentiating Instruction

Multiple Intelligences

Logical/Mathematical Give students the following number sequences: 100, 200, _____, 400; 250, 350, 450, _____; 500, 525, 550, _____; and 725, 775, _____, 875. Ask them to complete the sequences, then have them read a completed sequence aloud.

Inclusion

Frequent Review/Repetition Lead students in counting from one to ten, forward and backward. Then lead them in counting from 100 to 1000 forward and backward. Repeat this activity counting by 25's (25, 50, 75, 100), by 50's (50, 100, 150, 200), etc., forward and backward, using a strong rhythmic cadence.

Práctica de VOCABULARIO

1 La familia de Rodrigo

Hablar
Escribir

Tell how each person is related to Rodrigo. Use the family tree on page 184 to help you.

modelo: José es el padre.

1.   2.   3.

4.   5.   6.   7.

Expansión:
Teacher Edition Only
Have students create and speak about their own family tree.

Nota gramatical

In Spanish, **'s** is never used. To show possession, use **de** and the **noun** that refers to the owner/possessor.

el gato **de Marisa**   Marisa**'s** cat   los primos **de Juan**   Juan**'s** cousins

2 La familia de Marisol

Leer

Match the columns to describe the relationship between various members of Marisol's family.

1. El padre de mi madre es...   **a.** mi hermana.
2. Las hermanas de mi padre son...   **b.** mi madre.
3. La hija de mi padre es...   **c.** mis tías.
4. Los hijos de mis padres son...   **d.** mi abuelo.
5. Las hijas de mi tía son...   **e.** mis primas.
6. La hermana de mi tía es...   **f.** mis hermanos.

Expansión:
Teacher Edition Only
Have students describe the relationship of two additional family members using **de** to show possession.

Más práctica   Cuaderno *pp. 124–126*   Cuaderno para hispanohablantes *pp. 124–127*

PARA Y PIENSA

Did you get it? Fill in the blank with the correct vocabulary word.

1. El _____ de tus tíos es tu primo.
2. Los _____ de tus padres son tus abuelos.
3. Las _____ de tu madre son tus tías.

Get Help Online
ClassZone.com

Differentiating Instruction

Pre-AP

Circumlocution Remind students they can use words they know to talk around words they don't know. Write the following words on the board: *great-aunt, great-grandfather,* and *second cousins.* Ask students to think about other ways they could express these words using the vocabulary they've already learned. Possible answers: **La hermana de mi abuelo, El abuelo de mi padre, Los hijos del primo de mi madre.**

Heritage Language Learners

Regional Variations Ask students to share any regional terms that people use for family members in their country or region of origin. Do people always say **madre** and **padre,** or are there more familiar words that people use for mother and father? For example: **mamita, papito.** What are some terms of endearment that people use to address other family members?

Objectives
· Practice vocabulary: family members.
· Express possession using **de.**

Core Resource
· *Cuaderno,* pp. 124–126

Practice Sequence
· **Activity 1:** Vocabulary recognition: family members
· **Activity 2:** Vocabulary production: family members; possession using **de**

STANDARDS
1.2 Understand language, Act. 2
1.3 Present information, Acts. 1–2; PYP
4.1 Compare languages, Nota gramatical

✓ **Ongoing Assessment**

@HomeTutor
More Practice
ClassZone.com

PARA Y PIENSA

Peer Assessment Have students compare answers with a classmate. Then call on individuals for the answers. For additional practice, use Reteaching & Practice Copymasters URB 3, pp. 13, 14.

Answers MSRB Transparency 48

Activity 1
1. María es la abuela.
2. Tito es el primo.
3. Camila es la tía.
4. Cristóbal es el abuelo.
5. Celia es la madre.
6. Pablo es el tío.
7. Ana es la hermana.

Activity 2
1. d; 2. c; 3. a; 4. f; 5. e; 6. b

Para y piensa
1. hijo; 2. padres; 3. hermanas

¡AVANZA! Objective

¡AVANZA! Objective

· Understand vocabulary in context.

Core Resources

· Video Program: DVD 1
· Audio Program: TXT CD 3 track 14

Presentation Strategies

· Ask students to provide ideas about creating family trees.
· Show the video with the books closed.
· Play the audio while students follow the script in the text.

Practice Sequence

· **Activity 3:** Telehistoria comprehension
· **Activity 4:** Vocabulary production: family members; Recycle: numbers from 11 to 100

STANDARDS

1.1 Engage in conversation, Act. 4
1.2 Understand language, Act. 3; PYP
1.3 Present information, Act. 4

 Warm Up UTB 3 Transparency 20

Vocabulary Complete the following sentences with the correct word.

abuelos   perro   prima   fecha   cumpleaños

1. La hija de mi tía es mi _____.
2. Mi _____ es el dos de enero.
3. Los padres de mi madre son mis _____.
4. Mi _____ se llama Rover.
5. El 5 de diciembre es mi _____ de nacimiento.

Answers: 1. prima; 2. cumpleaños; 3. abuelos; 4. perro; 5. fecha

Video Summary
@HomeTutor VideoPlus ClassZone.com

Marisol notices a cake and asks if it is Mrs. Vélez's birthday. She learns that the next day, March 1, is Ana's 10th birthday. Marisol informs them that her grandmother's birthday is the same day, and that she'll be 68. Rodrigo asks his mother where the T-shirt is, and says that Trini Salgado is at the school at four.

▶❙ ❙❙

VOCABULARIO en contexto

 ¡AVANZA!

Goal: Identify the words Marisol and Rodrigo use to talk about birthdays and other family members. Then practice the words you have learned to ask and tell a person's age. *Actividades 3–4*

♻ *¿Recuerdas?* The verb **tener** p. 100, numbers from 11 to 100 p. 94

Telehistoria escena 1

@HomeTutor VideoPlus ClassZone.com

STRATEGIES

Cuando lees
Analyze the scene This scene starts out calmly and ends with a problem. What do the characters talk about at the beginning? What is the problem, and whose problem is it?

Cuando escuchas
Remember, listen, and predict Before listening, remember why Rodrigo wanted Alicia's T-shirt. What happens to the T-shirt in this scene? After listening, predict what will happen next.

VIDEO DVD

AUDIO

Rodrigo · Marisol · Sra. Vélez · Ana

Rodrigo and Marisol arrive in Rodrigo's kitchen.

Marisol: Señora Vélez, ¿es su cumpleaños?
Sra. Vélez: No, es el cumpleaños de Ana.
Marisol: ¡Feliz cumpleaños! ¿Cuántos años tienes?
Ana: Hoy tengo nueve años. Mañana, ¡diez!
Marisol: ¿Mañana? ¿El veintiocho de febrero?
Rodrigo: No. El primero de marzo.
Marisol: El cumpleaños de mi abuela es el primero de marzo.
Ana: Ah, ¿sí? ¿Cuántos años tiene?
Marisol: Tiene sesenta y ocho años.
Rodrigo: Mamá, ¿dónde está la camiseta? Trini Salgado está en la escuela a las cuatro.

Continuará... p. 194

También se dice

Puerto Rico Marisol uses the word **abuela** to talk about her grandmother. In other Spanish-speaking countries you might hear:
· **Perú, Argentina** la mamama

Differentiating Instruction

English Learners

Build Background Ask students if they know of any other words used in their country or place of origin to refer to grandparents or great-grandparents. Do they use a diminutive? Do they use special words to refer to the family members they like most? Ask them to say the word in their language or in English, and then repeat the word in Spanish.

Multiple Intelligences

Interpersonal Have students work in pairs to think about what might be causing Ana and Rodrigo to feel certain emotions. **¿Por qué está Ana contenta? ¿Por qué está Rodrigo nervioso?** Encourage students to explain their answers with information from the text.

3 | Un cumpleaños *Comprensión del episodio*

Escuchar Leer

Tell if the sentences are true or false. Correct the false statements to make them true.

1. Es el cumpleaños de la señora Vélez.
2. Mañana es el veintiocho de febrero.
3. El cumpleaños de Ana es en el mes de febrero.
4. El cumpleaños de la abuela de Marisol es el primero de marzo.

Expansión:
Teacher Edition Only
Have students write one additional false statement about the Telehistoria. Then have them switch papers to correct the errors.

Nota gramatical ♻ *¿Recuerdas?* The verb **tener** p. 100

Use the verb **tener** to talk about how old a person is.

¿Cuántos años **tiene** tu amiga?
How old is your friend?

¿Violeta? **Tiene** quince años.
Violeta? She's fifteen years old.

---

4 | ¿Cuántos años tienen? ♻ *¿Recuerdas?* Numbers from 11 to 100 p. 94

Hablar

Talk with a partner about how old the members of Rodrigo's family are. If you need help, look at the family tree on page 184.

45 años

A ¿Cuántos años tiene la madre de Rodrigo?

B Tiene cuarenta y cinco años.

1.
10 años

2.
3 años

3.
66 años

4.
14 años

5.
38 años

6.
47 años

7.
39 años

8.
64 años

Expansión:
Teacher Edition Only
Have students talk about how old their own family members are.

Get Help Online ClassZone.com

PARA Y PIENSA

Did you get it? Give each age, using **tener** and the word for each number in parentheses.
1. Marisol _____ _____ años. (14)
2. El gato de la familia Vélez _____ _____ años. (8)
3. Los padres de Marisol _____ _____ años. (52)

Lección 2
ciento ochenta y nueve **189**

Communication
Pair Work

Have students work in pairs for the game **es posible, es ridículo.** One student makes true or false statements about the ages of people or pets. The other will respond with **es posible** or **es ridículo.** For example, the response to **Mi perro tiene ciento cincuenta años,** would be **es ridículo,** while the response to **Mi abuela tiene sesenta y tres años** would be **es posible.**

Communication
Regionalisms

Many Spanish speakers use the diminutive endings **-ito** and **-ita** to express terms of endearment. For example, **abuelo** becomes **abuelito** and **abuela** becomes **abuelita.**

✓ Ongoing Assessment

@HomeTutor
More Practice
ClassZone.com

PARA Y PIENSA **Quick Check** Have pairs of students talk about the ages of three family members. Check questions and answers. For additional practice, use Reteaching & Practice Copymasters URB 3, pp. 13, 15, 22, 23.

Answers MSRB Transparency 48

Activity 3
1. Falsa. Es el cumpleaños de Ana.
2. Falsa. Mañana es el primero de marzo.
3. Falsa. El cumpleaños de Ana es en el mes de marzo.
4. Cierta.

Activity 4
1. ¿Cuántos años tiene el primo de Rodrigo? Tiene diez años.
2. ¿... el perro de Rodrigo? Tiene tres años.
3. ¿... el abuelo de Rodrigo? Tiene sesenta y seis años.
4. ¿... la prima de Rodrigo? Tiene catorce años.
5. ¿... la tía de Rodrigo? Tiene treinta y ocho años.
6. ¿... el padre de Rodrigo? Tiene cuarenta y siete años.
7. ¿... el tío de Rodrigo? Tiene treinta y nueve años.
8. ¿... la abuela de Rodrigo? Tiene sesenta y cuatro años.

Para y piensa
1. tiene catorce; 2. tiene ocho; 3. tienen cincuenta y dos

189

Differentiating Instruction

Heritage Language Learners

Writing Skills Have students write a short paragraph about a favorite family member. They should include the name of the person, family relationship, physical description, age, date of birth, what he/she likes to do, and why he/she is their favorite relative. Make sure they review their paragraph for correct spelling and punctuation.

Inclusion

Cumulative Instruction Before talking about characters' ages in Activity 4, have students review the present-tense forms of the verb **tener.** If students are keeping verb cards, have them take out and review the card for this verb. Say each pronoun aloud, and ask students to supply the correct form of the verb.

Objective

- Present possessive adjectives.

Core Resource

- *Cuaderno,* pp. 127–129

Presentation Strategies

- Explain when and how possessive adjectives are used.
- Remind students that all possessive adjectives agree in number with the nouns they describe.

STANDARDS

4.1 Compare languages

Warm Up UTB 3 Transparency 21

Vocabulary Write how old each person is using **tener... años.**

1. Luisa: 7
2. mi hermano: 27
3. mis abuelos: 75
4. yo: 14
5. tú: 12
6. mis padres: 35

Answers: 1. Luisa tiene siete años. **2.** Mi hermano tiene veintisiete años. **3.** Mis abuelos tienen setenta y cinco años. **4.** Yo tengo catorce años. **5.** Tú tienes doce años. **6.** Mis padres tienen treinta y cinco años.

Communication
Common Error Alert

Explain to students that possessive adjectives indicate possession, and that they are either singular or plural. Also explain that there should be agreement between the noun and the possessive adjective. For example, **mi hermano/mis hermanos, su prima/sus primas.**

Comparisons
English Grammar Connection

The possessive adjectives **su** and **sus** have multiple meanings. If the meaning is not clear from the context, one can replace the possessive adjective with the definite article and add **de** + a pronoun or the person's name to clarify its meaning. **Margarita estudia con su hermano. Margarita estudia con el hermano de ella.**

190

Presentación de GRAMÁTICA

¡AVANZA! **Goal:** Learn to express possession. Then practice using possessive adjectives to talk about your family members and to give dates. *Actividades 5–9*

¿Recuerdas? After-school activities p. 32, describing others p. 60

English Grammar Connection: Possessive adjectives tell you who owns something or describe a relationship between people or things. The forms of possessive adjectives do not change in English, but they do change in Spanish.

They are **my** cousins.　　　Ellos son **mis** primos.

Possessive Adjectives

Animated Grammar
ClassZone.com

In Spanish, **possessive adjectives** agree in number with the nouns they describe.

Here's how:

Singular Possessive Adjectives	
mi *my*	**nuestro(a)** *our*
tu *your (familiar)*	**vuestro(a)** *your (familiar)*
su *your (formal)*	**su** *your*
su *his, her, its*	**su** *their*

Plural Possessive Adjectives	
mis *my*	**nuestros(as)** *our*
tus *your (familiar)*	**vuestros(as)** *your (familiar)*
sus *your (formal)*	**sus** *your*
sus *his, her, its*	**sus** *their*

Es mi tía.
She is **my** aunt.

Son mis tías.
They are **my** aunts.

Nuestro(a) and vuestro(a) must also agree in gender with the nouns they describe.

agrees
Nuestra abuela tiene 70 años.
Our grandmother is 70 years old.

agrees
Nuestros abuelos viven en San Francisco.
Our grandparents live in San Francisco.

Más práctica
Cuaderno *pp. 127–129*
Cuaderno para hispanohablantes *pp. 128–130*

@HomeTutor
Leveled Grammar Practice
ClassZone.com

190
Unidad 3 Puerto Rico
ciento noventa

Differentiating Instruction

English Learners

Build Background Direct students to the grammar box explaining *Possessive Adjectives* on p. 190. Ask students to describe the facts and patterns they notice within the information presented. For example, they might point out that all plural possessive adjectives end in **s**, or that the word **su** has multiple meanings: *your, his, her, its,* and *their.*

Slower-paced Learners

Personalize It Ask questions about objects in the classroom that belong to different students. If necessary, model the correct possessive adjective. Here are a few examples: **¿Es la mochila de José? ¿Es su mochila? Sí, es su mochila. ¿Es tu cuaderno? Sí, es mi cuaderno. ¿Son los exámenes de ustedes? ¿Son sus exámenes? Sí, son nuestros exámenes.**

Práctica de GRAMÁTICA

5 | Las familias

Leer

Marisol is talking about families and their pets. Choose the correct possessive adjective to express what she says.

1. Nosotros tenemos tres primas. (Nuestros / Nuestras) primas son altas.
2. Ustedes tienen un abuelo. (Su / Nuestro) cumpleaños es el dos de abril.
3. Mi familia y yo tenemos una gata vieja. (Nuestra / Su) gata es Rubí.
4. Yo tengo dos hermanos mayores. (Mi / Mis) hermanos son estudiosos.
5. Mis abuelos tienen un perro. (Su / Mi) perro es perezoso.
6. ¡Feliz cumpleaños! Hoy tienes quince años. Es (tu / su) cumpleaños.

Expansión:
Teacher Edition Only
Have students redo the activity using a different subject in the first sentence and a different possessive adjective in the second.

6 | ¿Qué hacen? ♻ *¿Recuerdas?* After-school activities p. 32

Leer
Escribir

Use a possessive adjective and tell what activities these people do.

modelo: La hermana de Alicia es inteligente. (sacar buenas notas)
Su hermana saca buenas notas.

1. Los abuelos de nosotros no son muy serios. (escuchar música rock)
2. Los tíos de ustedes son trabajadores. (trabajar mucho)
3. La prima de Marisol no es perezosa. (hacer la tarea)
4. La madre de Rodrigo es atlética. (practicar deportes)
5. La hermana de nosotros es muy estudiosa. (leer muchos libros)
6. El padrastro de Luz es simpático. (pasar un rato con la familia)

Expansión:
Teacher Edition Only
Have students write what these people don't do, based on the descriptions.

AUDIO

Pronunciación La letra j

The **j** in Spanish sounds similar to the English *h* in the word *hello*.

Listen and repeat.

jamón   mujer
dibujar   joven
junio   hija

La mujer pelirroja es joven.
El cumpleaños del hijo es en julio.

Soy Javier, el hijo de la mujer pelirroja. Mi cumpleaños es en julio.

Differentiating Instruction

Pre-AP

Self-correct Have students write sentences describing their favorite person. Ask them to use a possessive adjective from p. 190, and subject/adjective agreement. For example, possessive adjective: **Julia es *mi* amiga.** Subject/adjective agreement: ***Ella es simpática.*** Have students read aloud their sentences. Give them a clue when they make a mistake, and allow them time to correct themselves.

Heritage Language Learners

Increase Accuracy Monitor spelling of words with **j** and **h**. Write the word **hijo** on the board. Circle the letter **j**, and ask students to isolate its sound. Point out that the letter **j** in Spanish sounds like the letter **h** in English. Next, circle the letter **h**. Remind students that the **h** in Spanish is silent. Dictate words containing **h** and **j**: **Julio, jamón, hola, mejor, juntos.** Check students' spelling.

Objectives
· Practice possessive adjectives and lesson vocabulary.
· Recycle: after-school activities.
· **Pronunciation:** Practice pronunciation of the letter **j** in Spanish.

Core Resource
· Audio Program: TXT CD 3 track 16

Practice Sequence
· **Activity 5:** Controlled practice: possessive adjectives
· **Activity 6:** Controlled practice: possessive adjectives; Recycle: after-school activities

STANDARDS
1.3 Present information, Acts. 5–6
4.1 Compare languages, Pronunciación

Communication
Grammar Activity

On slips of paper, write the words for different members of one's family: **madre, padre, abuela, abuelos,** etc. Put them in a bag or bowl, and go around the room asking students to draw one. The student will then say a sentence such as: **La abuela de Sara es muy simpática.** The student sitting in the next seat will say: **Su abuela es muy simpática.**

Answers MSRB Transparency 48

Activity 5
1. Nuestras; 2. Su; 3. Nuestra; 4. Mis; 5. Su; 6. tu

Activity 6
1. Nuestros abuelos escuchan música rock.
2. Sus tíos trabajan mucho.
3. Su prima hace la tarea.
4. Su madre practica deportes.
5. Nuestra hermana lee muchos libros.
6. Su padrastro pasa un rato con la familia.

191

GRAMÁTICA

Objectives
- Practice possessive adjectives and lesson vocabulary.
- **Culture:** discuss the election process in Puerto Rico.
- Practice saying and writing dates.
- Recycle: describing others.

Core Resource
- *Cuaderno,* pp. 127–129

Practice Sequence
- **Activity 7:** Transitional practice: possessive adjectives, dates
- **Activity 8:** Open-ended practice: possessive adjectives; Recycle: describing others
- **Activity 9:** Open-ended practice: dates, family members, possessive adjectives

STANDARDS
1.1 Engage in conversation, Acts. 7, 8
1.3 Present information, Act. 9
2.1 Practices and perspectives, CC
4.2 Compare cultures, CC

Nota gramatical

Point out that in Spanish-speaking countries dates are always written with the day first, then the month.

Answers MSRB Transparency 49

Activity 7 Questions and answers should follow the pattern: **¿Cuál es la fecha de nacimiento de...? Su fecha de nacimiento es...**

¿Cuál es la fecha de nacimiento de Francisco Oller? Su fecha de nacimiento es el diecisiete de mayo de mil ochocientos treinta y tres.

¿... de Lola Rodríguez de Tió? ... es el catorce de septiembre de mil ochocientos cuarenta y tres.

¿... de José Enrique Pedreira? ... es el primero de febrero de mil novecientos cuatro.

¿... de Raúl Juliá? ... es el nueve de marzo de mil novecientos cuarenta.

¿... de Sila Calderón? ... es el veintitrés de septiembre de mil novecientos cuarenta y dos.

¿... de Olga Tañón? ... es el trece de abril de mil novecientos sesenta y siete.

Answers continue on p. 193.

192

Nota gramatical

To give the date, use the following phrase: **Es el + number + de + month.**

Hoy **es el diez de** diciembre.   *Today is the **tenth of December.***

Only the first of the month does not follow this pattern.

Es el **primero** de diciembre.   *It is **December first.***

The year is expressed in **thousands** and **hundreds.**

mil cuatrocientos noventa y dos   *1492*

In Spanish-speaking countries, the date is written with the number of the day first, then the number of the month: el dos de mayo = 2/5.

7 | Unos puertorriqueños famosos

Hablar

Work with a partner. Use the timeline to give the birth dates of these famous Puerto Ricans.

A ¿Cuál es la fecha de nacimiento de Carlos Beltrán?

B Su fecha de nacimiento es el veinticuatro de abril de mil novecientos setenta y siete.

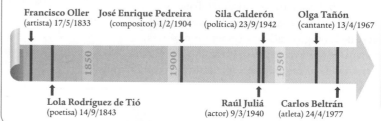

Francisco Oller (artista) 17/5/1833
José Enrique Pedreira (compositor) 1/2/1904
Sila Calderón (política) 23/9/1942
Olga Tañón (cantante) 13/4/1967

1850   1900   1950

Lola Rodríguez de Tió (poetisa) 14/9/1843
Raúl Juliá (actor) 9/3/1940
Carlos Beltrán (atleta) 24/4/1977

> **Expansión:**
> Teacher Edition Only
> Have students write six sentences about the birth dates of their family members and friends.

8 | ¿Cómo son?   ♻ *¿Recuerdas?* Describing others p. 60

Hablar

Talk with another student about the people and pets in your family.

modelo: serio(a)

1. atlético(a)
2. cómico(a)
3. desorganizado(a)
4. inteligente
5. perezoso(a)
6. artístico(a)
7. simpático(a)
8. trabajador(a)
9. ¿?

A ¿Hay una persona seria en tu familia?

B Sí, mi tío David es muy serio.

> **Expansión:**
> Teacher Edition Only
> Have students write a question and its answer, using a possessive adjective.

Differentiating Instruction

Slower-paced Learners

Personalize It Write today's date in numbers on the board, for example, 2/6. Read the date aloud in Spanish and have students repeat **dos de junio.** Then have students write their birth dates in numbers on a separate piece of paper. Invite volunteers to say their birth dates aloud in a sentence. **Mi cumpleaños es el veintiocho de marzo de...**

Inclusion

Frequent Review/Repetition Provide student pairs the opportunity to review the two ways to express possession. Have each student write a list of at least five family members and a possession for each. Students exchange lists and create two sentences, one using possession with **de** and the other one using a possessive adjective. For example: **el primo/el gato: Es el gato de tu primo. Es su gato.**

9 | Las fechas de nacimiento

Escribir Write sentences with the names and birth dates of five of your family members and friends.

madre/madrastra	**abuelo(a)**	**hermano(a)**
padre/padrastro	**amigo(a)**	**¿ ?**

Expansión:
Teacher Edition Only
Ask students to expand the activity by writing the names and birth dates of other family members.

modelo: Mi madre se llama Julia. Su fecha de nacimiento es el veintitrés de marzo de mil novecientos sesenta y dos...

Comparación cultural

Las elecciones en Puerto Rico

What do elections reveal about a culture?
Puerto Rico is a commonwealth of the United States. Puerto Ricans have U.S. citizenship and those living on the mainland can vote in presidential elections. On the island, Puerto Ricans vote for their governor and local legislature. Voter turnout is high, often over 80 percent. Puerto Rico has three main political parties: the *Partido Popular Democrático* favors the current political status, the *Partido Nuevo Progresista* wants Puerto Rico to become the 51st state, and the *Partido Independentista Puertorriqueño* supports independence from the U.S.

Compara con tu mundo *What issues would motivate you to vote when you are 18? Have you ever voted in any school elections?*

Residencia y oficina del gobernador, Viejo San Juan

Más práctica   Cuaderno *pp. 127–129*   Cuaderno para hispanohablantes *pp. 128–130*

PARA Y PIENSA

Did you get it? Fill in the correct possessive adjective and dates.
1. El cumpleaños de _____ *(my)* madrastra es _____ . (6/9)
2. El cumpleaños de _____ *(our)* hermanos es _____ . (25/1)
3. El cumpleaños de _____ *(his)* amigo es _____ . (17/4)

Get Help Online
ClassZone.com

Lección 2
ciento noventa y tres **193**

Differentiating Instruction

Heritage Language Learners
Support What They Know Ask students to describe the political parties in their country of origin.

Multiple Intelligences
Logical/Mathematical Have students create a calendar in Spanish. Record each student's birthday. They should count to see which month has the most birthdays and which has the least. If possible, have the calendar permanently displayed in the classroom.

Comparación cultural

Essential Question
Suggested Answer Elections can reveal the will of the majority of the people and the direction in which they want their country to go.

Expanded Information
Government The formal name in Spanish for Puerto Rico is **Estado Libre Asociado de Puerto Rico** (Free Associated State of Puerto Rico). The executive power of this Commonwealth is exercised by the governor, who leads a cabinet of 15 ministers.

✓ Ongoing Assessment

@HomeTutor
More Practice
ClassZone.com

PARA Y PIENSA **Peer Assessment** Have pairs of students say aloud their sentences in Para y piensa and correct each other. For additional practice, use Reteaching & Practice Copymasters URB 3, pp. 16, 17, 24.

Answers MSRB Transparency 49

Answers continued from p. 192.

Activity 8 Answers will vary. Questions and answers should follow the pattern:
1. ¿Hay una persona atlética en tu familia? Sí, mi abuela Marta es muy atlética.
2. ¿Hay una persona cómica...? Sí mi tío... cómico.
3. ¿Hay una persona desorganizada...? Sí, mi prima... desorganizada.
4. ¿Hay una persona inteligente...? Sí, mi madre... inteligente.
5. ¿Hay una persona perezosa...? Sí, mi gato... perezoso.
6. ¿Hay una persona artística...? Sí, mi abuela... artística.
7. ¿Hay una persona simpática...? Sí, mi hermano... simpático.
8. ¿Hay una persona trabajadora...? Sí, mi abuela... trabajadora.
9. ¿Hay una persona...? Sí, mi padre...

Activity 9 Answers will vary. Sample answer:
Mi madrastra se llama Helen. Su fecha de nacimiento es el tres de marzo de mil novecientos sesenta y ocho.

Para y piensa 1. mi, el seis de septiembre; 2. nuestros, el veinticinco de enero; 3. su, el diecisiete de abril

193

GRAMÁTICA *en contexto*

Goal: Listen to the possessive adjectives Marisol and Rodrigo use to talk about the members of his family. Then use possessive adjectives to talk about your family and the birthdays of people you know. *Actividades 10–12*

Telehistoria escena 2

@HomeTutor VideoPlus
ClassZone.com

STRATEGIES

Cuando lees
List and practice words While reading, list the words for family members, such as **madre.** Then practice! Say these words aloud several times. Say them in sentences and create questions with them.

Cuando escuchas
Track the people and actions While listening, identify the people involved and the actions. What does each one say? Who helps solve the key problem? What new problem arises?

VIDEO
DVD

AUDIO

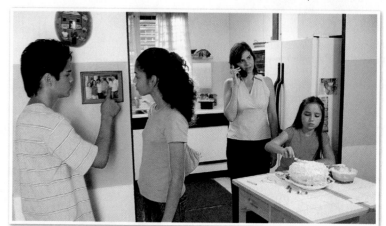

Rodrigo: ¿Dónde está la camiseta?

Sra. Vélez: ¡Ah, tus primos! *(She picks up the phone and dials.)*

Rodrigo: *(explaining to Marisol)* Ellos comen con nosotros todos los viernes. A nuestros primos les gusta jugar al fútbol.

Sra. Vélez: *(on the phone)* ¿Camila? Es Celia. Tengo una pregunta...

Rodrigo: Es mi tía Camila. La tía Camila es la madre de Ester y Tito. Mis primos tienen catorce y diez años.

Marisol: *(pointing to a family portrait)* ¿Es tu familia?

Rodrigo: Mi madre tiene dos hermanas: Inés y Mónica. Mi padre tiene un hermano, Sergio, y una hermana, Camila.

Sra. Vélez: Rodrigo, tu primo Tito tiene la camiseta de tu amiga Alicia.

Rodrigo: *(to Marisol)* Mi primo tiene perros muy grandes. ¡No me gustan los perros de Tito!

Continuará... p. 200

- Practice grammar in context.
- Practice using possessive adjectives, vocabulary for family members, and birth dates.

Core Resources

- Video Program: DVD 1
- Audio Program: TXT CD 3 track 15

Presentation Strategies

- Ask students to name the people in the photo. Ask comprehension questions: **¿Qué hace la señora Vélez? ¿Qué hace Rodrigo?**
- Play the audio and/or show the video.

Practice Sequence

- **Activity 10:** Telehistoria comprehension
- **Activity 11:** Transitional practice: birth dates, months of the year, numbers
- **Activity 12:** Open-ended practice: family members, possessive adjectives, numbers, expressions with **tener**

STANDARDS

1.1 Engage in conversation, Act. 11
1.2 Understand language, Act. 10
1.3 Present information, Act. 11-12; PYP

Warm Up   UTB 3 Transparency 21

Possessive Adjectives Rewrite the phrases with the correct possessive adjective.

1. el amigo de Roberto
2. los tíos de ustedes
3. la prima de nosotros

Answers: 1. su amigo; **2.** sus tíos; **3.** nuestra prima

Video Summary

@HomeTutor
VideoPlus
ClassZone.com

Rodrigo asks where the T-shirt is. Mrs. Vélez calls his cousins and eventually asks if one of them has it. While she is talking, Rodrigo and Marisol look at a family photo. Rodrigo explains to Marisol that his aunt Camila is Ester and Tito's mother. He adds that his mother has two sisters and his father has one brother and one sister. Mrs. Vélez tells them that Tito has Alicia's T-shirt. Rodrigo then tells Marisol that he doesn't like his cousin's big dogs.

▶l ll

Differentiating Instruction

Slower-paced Learners

Read Before Listening Have students preview the Telehistoria in order to create a list of the characters' names mentioned. Then have students search the text to find the relationship of each character to Rodrigo. Write the appropriate word or phrase next to each name. For example: **Camila: la tía de Rodrigo; Celia: la madre de Rodrigo.**

Pre-AP

Draw Conclusions Write the names **Ester** and **Tito** in the center of a concept web. Then have students supply information regarding these characters, based on what they learned in the Telehistoria. For example, **Les gusta jugar al fútbol.** Or **Tito tiene perros grandes.** Then have students draw conclusions to create additional sentences. **Los primos de Rodrigo son atléticos. A Tito le gustan los perros.**

10 Una familia grande *Comprensión del episodio*

Escuchar
Leer

Complete the sentences to describe the episode.

1. La madre de Rodrigo
   a. no tiene la camiseta.
   b. no tiene hermanas.
2. Los primos de Rodrigo
   a. comen en su casa todos los días.
   b. comen en su casa todos los viernes.
3. A los primos de Rodrigo
   a. les gusta jugar al fútbol.
   b. les gusta hablar por teléfono.

4. La tía Camila
   a. es la madre de Tito y Ester.
   b. es la hermana de Inés y Mónica.
5. El padre de Rodrigo
   a. tiene dos hermanas.
   b. tiene una hermana.
6. A Rodrigo
   a. no le gusta la camiseta.
   b. no le gustan los perros.

Expansión:
Teacher Edition Only
Have students write one incomplete statement about the Telehistoria followed by two possible completions. Students exchange statements with a partner and choose the correct completion.

11 ¿Cuál es tu fecha de nacimiento?

Hablar

Find out the birth dates of eight classmates and make a chart. Share the results with the class.

A ¿Cuál es tu fecha de nacimiento?

B Mi fecha de nacimiento es el quince de enero de...

enero	febrero	marzo
Sandy 15/1/...	Lillian 24/2/...	
Doug 21/1/...		

Expansión:
Teacher Edition Only
Have students read aloud their charts to a partner and ask the partner to correct the speaker's pronunciation.

12 Tu familia

Escribir

Write a paragraph about your family. Include the answers to the following questions.

- ¿Es grande o pequeña tu familia?
- ¿Cuántos hermanos y hermanas tienes?
- ¿Cómo son las personas de tu familia?
- ¿Cuántos años tienen las personas de tu familia?

modelo: Mi familia es grande. Tengo tres hermanos y una hermana. Mi madre tiene treinta y siete años. Es...

Expansión:
Teacher Edition Only
Have students say what each family member likes to do on his or her birthday.

PARA Y PIENSA

Did you get it? Using complete sentences, tell the birthdays of the following people.

1. Camila (12/6)   2. Ester (1/10)   3. Tito (28/3)   4. Celia (17/1)

Get Help Online ClassZone.com

Differentiating Instruction

Inclusion

Frequent Review/Repetition Have students say their birthdays aloud in Spanish as they arrange themselves in a line in the order of their birthdays. They will have to say their birthdays repeatedly until the line is formed correctly.

Heritage Language Learners

Support What They Know Have students research and write down the names and dates of three important celebrations in their heritage countries. Give them the opportunity to describe the occasion and the festivities that take place during these celebrations. Check their written work for correct spelling. Allow students to check dates and other facts at a library or on the Internet, if necessary.

Communication
Grammar Activity

Write several dates on the board using numbers and have students tell you the corresponding date in Spanish. For example: **15/4: el quince de abril; 1/2: el primero de febrero.**

Communication
⚠ Common Error Alert

Reiterate to students the difference between English and Spanish when saying or writing dates. In Spanish, **de** is always used to correctly say the month and the year. It is like saying *28 of July of two thousand seven,* which in Spanish is **28 de julio de dos mil siete.** Have students practice verbally saying dates in Spanish.

✓ Ongoing Assessment

@HomeTutor
More Practice
ClassZone.com

PARA Y PIENSA

Dictation **Mis primos vienen a visitarnos el tres de noviembre. El veintisiete de junio tenemos que jugar al fútbol.** For additional practice, use Reteaching & Practice Copymasters URB 3, pp. 16, 18.

📖 Answers MSRB Transparency 49

Activity 10
1. a 2. b 3. a 4. a 5. b 6. b

Activity 11 Answers will vary. Sample answers include: ¿Cuál es tu fecha de nacimiento? Mi fecha de nacimiento es el diez de octubre de...

Activity 12 Answers will vary. Sample answers include: Mi familia es grande. Tengo dos hermanos y una hermana. Mi hermano es inteligente y simpático. Mi hermana es muy desorganizada. Mis padres tienen cuarenta años. Mi hermano mayor tiene diecisiete años, mi hermana tiene seis años y mi hermano menor tiene diez años.

Para y piensa
1. El cumpleaños de Camila es el doce de junio.
2. El cumpleaños de Ester es el primero de octubre.
3. El cumpleaños de Tito es el veintiocho de marzo.
4. El cumpleaños de Celia es el diecisiete de enero.

Objective

· Present comparatives.

Core Resource
· *Cuaderno*, pp. 130–132

Presentation Strategies
· Point out different types of comparatives.
· Explain the use of the irregular comparative words **mayor, menor, mejor,** and **peor**.

STANDARDS
4.1 Compare languages

Warm Up UTB 3 Transparency 22

Dates Write the dates using numerals.
1. el trece de abril
2. el veintiuno de julio
3. el catorce de febrero
4. el primero de diciembre
5. el quince de enero

Answers: 1. 13/4; **2.** 21/7; **3.** 14/2; **4.** 1/12; **5.** 15/1

Comparisons
English Grammar Connection

When saying *more than/less than + number,* **de** is used instead of **que.** For example, **Tengo más de veinte primos.**

Mayor and **menor** are used to compare people's ages. **Yo soy mayor que mi hermano pero menor que mi hermana.**

Mejor and **peor** are the comparative forms of **bueno** and **malo. Ella es mejor estudiante que yo.**

Communication
Grammar Activity

Write a list of adjectives on the board: **viejo, joven, bonito, grande, pequeño, alto, bajo.** Ask students to compare two items in the classroom using the constructions **más... que, menos... que, tan... como.**

196

Presentación de GRAMÁTICA

 ¡AVANZA! **Goal:** Learn to make comparisons. Then use them to describe your family, your friends, and yourself. *Actividades 13–18*

English Grammar Connection: Comparatives are expressions used to compare two people or things. In English, comparative adjectives are formed by adding *-er* to the end of a word or by using *more, less,* and *as.*

Rodrigo is **taller** than his sister. Rodrigo es **más alto** que su hermana.

Comparatives

Animated Grammar
ClassZone.com

There are several phrases in Spanish used to make comparisons.

Here's how: Use the following phrases with an **adjective** to compare two things. The adjectives agree with the first noun.

agrees

más... que *more . . . than*	Mi abuel**a** es m**ás artística** que mi padre. *My grandmother is **more** artistic **than** my father.*
menos... que *less . . . than*	La clase de ciencias es **menos divertida** que la clase de inglés. *Science class is **less fun than** English class.*
tan... como *as . . . as*	Tus hermanas son **tan serias como** la maestra. *Your sisters are **as** serious **as** the teacher.*

When a comparison does not involve an adjective, use these phrases.

más que... *more than . . .*	Me gusta ir a la biblioteca **más que** al gimnasio. *I like to go to the library **more than** to the gym.*
menos que... *less than . . .*	Me gustan las hamburguesas **menos que** los tacos. *I like hamburgers **less than** tacos.*
tanto como... *as much as . . .*	¿Te gusta hablar **tanto como** escuchar? *Do you like to talk **as much as** listen?*

There are a few irregular comparative words. They agree in number with the first noun.

mayor	menor	mejor	peor
older	*younger*	*better*	*worse*

agrees

Mis tí**os** son **mayores** que mi tía.
*My uncles are **older** than my aunt.*

Más práctica
Cuaderno *pp. 130–132*
Cuaderno para hispanohablantes *pp. 131–134*

@HomeTutor
Leveled Grammar Practice
ClassZone.com

Differentiating Instruction

Pre-AP

Expand and Elaborate Have students work in groups to create a fictitious family. Each student in the group will represent a family member. Ask them to select Spanish names, pick ages, and create personalities. Each member should describe himself/herself in complete sentences. For example, **Me llamo Mario. Tengo veintitrés años y soy el tío de Carmen. Soy alto y guapo.**

Multiple Intelligences

Linguistic/Verbal Assign groups of students to become experts in one category of comparisons: **más... que; menos... que; tan... como; más que...; menos que...; tanto como...** Have students say aloud several examples of their category and explain how it works to the rest of the class. **Él es más alto que yo. Yo soy tan grande como él.**

Práctica de GRAMÁTICA

13 | Sus familias

Escribir

Complete the sentences with **que** or **como** to describe the families of Rodrigo and Marisol.

1. Marisol es tan simpática _____ su madrastra.
2. Ana es menor _____ Rodrigo.
3. Marisol corre tanto _____ sus padres.
4. Rodrigo tiene menos hermanos _____ José.
5. El tío Pablo toca la guitarra mejor _____ la tía Camila.
6. Ester es mayor _____ Tito.

Expansión:
Teacher Edition Only
Have students write five sentences with **que** or **como** to describe their own families.

14 | Comparaciones

Hablar
Escribir

Look at the drawings and make comparisons using **más... que, menos... que, tan... como,** or **tanto como.**

modelo: Nicolás / grande / Sara
Nicolás es más grande que Sara.

1. Nora / alto(a) / Patricia

2. Marcos / serio(a) / José

3. Ana / perezoso(a) / Alí

4. Pablo / desorganizado(a) / Pedro

5. María / atlético(a) / David

6. a Elena / gustar / correr / escuchar música

Expansión:
Teacher Edition Only
Have students make additional comparisons reversing the subjects: Sara es más pequeña que Nicolás.

Lección 2
ciento noventa y siete   **197**

Objectives
· Practice comparisons with **más... que, menos... que,** and **tan... como.**
· Practice lesson vocabulary.

Practice Sequence
· Activity 13: Controlled practice: comparatives
· Activity 14: Controlled practice: comparatives

STANDARDS
1.3 Present information, Acts. 13–14

Communication
Pair Work

Bring in photos/clippings of famous people and have students make comparisons. Have students use these adjectives: **alto(a), bajo(a), serio(a), cómico(a).** To practice **mayor que** and **menor que,** ask each pair of students to compare the ages of the famous people.

Differentiating Instruction

Inclusion

Clear Structure Write the words **más, menos, tan,** and **tanto** on the board. Then ask students which word completes each phrase, **que** or **como.** Record their responses on the board. As students complete Activity 13, have them write in their notebooks the comparison word in each sentence. Tell them to refer to the board to choose the correct word to complete each phrase.

English Learners

Provide Comprehensible Input Help students complete Activity 14, by asking them what they are comparing. For example: What are they comparing in question 1? Nora and Patricia. Is there an adjective involved? Yes. Are both girls similar or different? Similar. Then, the comparison requires **tan** + adjective + **como.**

Answers MSRB Transparency 49

Activity 13
1. como   3. como   5. que
2. que   4. que   6. que

Activity 14
1. Nora es tan alta como Patricia.
2. Marcos es más serio que José.
3. Ana es más perezosa que Alí.
4. Pablo es tan desorganizado como Pedro.
5. María es más atlética que David.
6. A Elena le gusta correr tanto como escuchar música.

Objectives

· Practice using comparatives.
· **Culture:** Discuss the portraits of Rafael Tufiño and Fernando Sayán Polo.

Core Resources

· *Cuaderno,* pp. 130–132
· Audio Program: TXT CD 3 track 17

Practice Sequence

· **Activity 15:** Controlled practice: comparatives
· **Activity 16:** Transitional practice: comparatives
· **Activity 17:** Transitional practice: comparatives
· **Activity 18:** Open-ended practice: comparatives

STANDARDS

1.2 Understand language, Act. 17
1.3 Present information, Acts. 15–18
2.2 Products and perspectives, Act. 18
3.1 Knowledge of other disciplines, Act. 18

Communication
Pair Work

Have students work in pairs and write five comparison statements. Statements should include **más/menos... que; tan... como; más/menos que...; mayor, menor, mejor, peor.** Then, on another sheet of paper, have them scramble the words of the sentences. They should then exchange these papers with another pair. Students work together to unscramble the other pair's sentences and then check their work.

Long-term Retention
Personalize It

Ask students to think of something they do better than their friend and another thing the friend does better. For example: **Yo dibujo mejor que mi amigo John. John es más estudioso que yo.** Go around the class, asking students to share the comparisons they've just made.

See Activity answers on p. 199.

198

---

15 | ¿Son diferentes?

Escribir

Marta and her friend Clara have some things in common and some differences. Make comparisons between the two girls.

modelo: Marta estudia todos los días. Clara estudia de vez en cuando.
Marta es más estudiosa que Clara.

1. Marta tiene doce años. Clara tiene trece años.
2. Marta es baja. Clara es alta.
3. Marta trabaja mucho. Clara trabaja mucho también.
4. Marta es muy desorganizada. Clara es un poco desorganizada.
5. Marta tiene dos hermanos. Clara tiene tres hermanos.
6. Marta es cómica. Clara es cómica también.

> **Expansión:**
> Teacher Edition Only
> Ask students to write five sentences to compare two of their friends.

16 | Las diferencias

Escribir

Look at the drawing and write sentences with as many differences and similarities as you can find between the members of each pair.

modelo: La señora Suárez es más baja que Raquel Suárez.

Carlitos · Ramón · Raquel Suárez · la Sra. Suárez · Daniel · Betina

> **Expansión:**
> Teacher Edition Only
> Have students compare their sentences with a partner.

198 Unidad 3 Puerto Rico
ciento noventa y ocho

Differentiating Instruction

Slower-paced Learners

Read Before Listening Before listening to Ana's description in Activity 17, have students copy the sentences on a piece of paper, then have them draw a sketch to represent each sentence. Have students refer to their pictures as they listen to see if the statements are true or false.

Multiple Intelligences

Intrapersonal Ask students to choose a role model, perhaps a relative, and write a journal entry in which they compare themselves to their role models. They should write about five different qualities. For example: **1. Yo tengo trece años. Mi tía Teresa tiene cincuenta. Yo soy menor que ella. 2. Mi tía es muy organizada. Yo no soy tan organizada como ella.**

17 | Capitán y Príncipe

Escuchar
Escribir

Ana is talking about her pets, Capitán and Príncipe. Listen to her description and indicate whether the following sentences are true or false.

1. La familia de Ana tiene más perros que gatos.
2. Príncipe es tan simpático como Capitán.
3. Capitán es más grande que Príncipe.
4. A Príncipe le gusta comer más que descansar.
5. Príncipe es menor que Capitán.
6. Capitán es más perezoso que Príncipe.

🎧 **Audio Program**
TXT CD 3 Track 17
Audio Script, TE
p. 181b

18 | Compara a las personas

Escribir

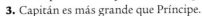
Comparación cultural

Los retratos

How do portraits represent the people in a country? Rafael Tufiño was born in New York and moved to **Puerto Rico,** his parents' homeland, as a child. Much of his work reflects the people and culture of Puerto Rico. He painted many portraits of his mother, giving them the title *Goyita.* These portraits came to represent not just his mother, but Puerto Rican women overall. Fernando Sayán Polo, an artist from **Peru,** also reflects the people of his country through his artwork. His painting *Niña campesina sonriente* depicts a young girl wearing traditional Andean dress.

Compara con tu mundo
If you had to paint a portrait of someone famous, which person would you choose and why? How would you portray him or her? What colors or objects would you include?

Write five sentences comparing the people in the paintings.

modelo: La mujer es mayor que la chica.
La chica es más...

Goyita (1949),
Rafael Tufiño

Expansión:
Teacher Edition Only
Have students exchange their descriptions with a partner and compare them.

Niña campesina sonriente (2005),
Fernando Sayán Polo

Más práctica   Cuaderno *pp. 130–132*   Cuaderno para hispanohablantes *pp. 131–134*

PARA Y PIENSA

Did you get it? 1. Say that your brother is taller than your father.
2. Say that you like apples as much as bananas.
3. Say that math class is better than art class.

🔗 **Get Help Online**
ClassZone.com

Differentiating Instruction

Heritage Language Learners

Literacy Skills Have students use the library or Internet to research the life of painter Rafael Tufiño. Tell them their goal is to find four important events in his life and the respective dates. Have students share their findings to create a group timeline of the artist's life and work.

Multiple Intelligences

Visual Learners Ask students to bring in two photos or illustrations of people. Ask them to compare them, using a Venn diagram. Points of similarities and contrast could include age, facial expression, hair color, and height.

Comparación cultural

Essential Question

Suggested Answer Portraits can reflect the different groups of people of a country in terms of family, relationship, age, gender, ethnicity, and so on.

About the Artists

Rafael Tufiño, born in Brooklyn in 1922, is one of the central figures in the history of twentieth-century Puerto Rican art. **Fernando Sayán Polo** was born in Peru in 1947. The city of Cuzco is the root of his artistic motivation.

✓ **Ongoing Assessment**

@HomeTutor
More Practice
ClassZone.com

PARA Y PIENSA **Quick Check** Call on individual students to read their answers aloud, and correct them if necessary. For additional practice, use Reteaching & Practice Copymasters URB 3, pp. 19, 20.

Answers MSRB Transparency 50

Answers for Activities on pp. 198, 199.

Activity 15
1. Marta es menor que Clara.
2. Marta es más baja que Clara.
3. Marta es tan trabajadora como Clara./ Marta trabaja tanto como Clara.
4. Marta es más desorganizada que Clara.
5. Marta tiene menos hermanos que Clara.
6. Marta es tan cómica como Clara.

Activity 16 Answers will vary. Suggested answers include:
Daniel es más artístico que Betina.
Betina tiene más cuadernos que Daniel.
Ramón lee más que Carlitos.
Carlitos es tan pequeño como Ramón.
La señora Suárez es menos atlética que Raquel.
Raquel es más alta que la señora Suárez.

Activity 17
1. Falsa   3. Cierta   5. Falsa
2. Cierta   4. Falsa   6. Cierta

Activity 18 Sample answers include:
La mujer es tan interesante como la chica.
La chica es más simpática que la mujer.

Para y piensa
1. Mi hermano es más alto que mi padre.
2. Me gustan las manzanas tanto como las bananas.
3. La clase de matemáticas es mejor que la clase de arte.

199

TODO JUNTO

· Integrate lesson content.

Core Resources

· Video Program: DVD 1
· Audio Program: TXT CD 3 tracks 14, 15, 18

Presentation Strategies

· Ask students to identify the people in the photo. Ask: **¿Quién es mayor, Tito o Rodrigo?**
· Have students skim the Telehistoria, paying special attention to comparison words.
· Show the video or play the audio.

Practice Sequence

· **Activity 19:** Telehistoria comprehension
· **Activity 20:** Telehistoria comprehension
· **Activity 21:** Open-ended practice: speaking

STANDARDS

1.1 Engage in conversation, Act. 21
1.2 Understand language, Acts. 19–20
1.3 Present information, Acts. 19–21

Warm Up UTB 3 Transparency 22

Comparisons Unscramble the following sentences.

1. más / Rosa / que / baja / hermano / su / es
2. que / soy / hermano / mi / mayor
3. como / es / nuestra / madre / alto / tan / él

Answers: 1. Rosa es más baja que su hermano. **2.** Soy mayor que mi hermano. **3.** Él es tan alto como nuestra madre.

Video Summary

@HomeTutor VideoPlus ClassZone.com

Marisol and Rodrigo are going to Tito's house to retrieve Alicia's T-shirt. Marisol asks him why he dislikes dogs. Rodrigo says that he likes cats better; they are nicer than dogs. Marisol says that dogs are less lazy than cats, but Rodrigo says that Tito's dogs are lazy and very big. When they arrive, Tito is wearing the T-shirt, which is very dirty. Then the dogs growl, and Rodrigo and Marisol run away.

▶❙ ❙❙

Todo junto

Goal: *Show what you know* Notice the comparative words Marisol and Rodrigo use to talk about why Rodrigo doesn't like Tito's dogs. Then use comparative words and possessive adjectives to describe your family and friends. *Actividades 19–23*

Telehistoria completa

@HomeTutor VideoPlus ClassZone.com

STRATEGIES

Cuando lees
Work with comparisons This scene contains comparisons of animals and of people. How many comparisons do you see? Write down the "comparison words." Practice them in sentences.

Cuando escuchas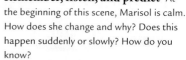
Remember, listen, and predict At the beginning of this scene, Marisol is calm. How does she change and why? Does this happen suddenly or slowly? How do you know?

Escena 1 *Resumen*
Mañana es el cumpleaños de Ana, la hermana de Rodrigo. Rodrigo está nervioso porque no tiene la camiseta de Alicia.

Escena 2 *Resumen*
Tito, el primo de Rodrigo, tiene la camiseta. A Rodrigo no le gustan los perros de Tito.

VIDEO DVD

AUDIO

Escena 3

Tito

Rodrigo and Marisol are walking to Tito's house.

Marisol: ¿No te gustan los perros? Son simpáticos.

Rodrigo: Me gustan más los gatos. Son más simpáticos que los perros.

Marisol: Los perros son menos perezosos que los gatos.

Rodrigo: Los perros de Tito son perezosos y muy grandes. ¡Son tan grandes como tú!

They stop outside the gate and look around. Tito appears, wearing Alicia's T-shirt, which is filthy.

Tito: ¡Hola, Rodrigo! Tu camiseta.

Suddenly the dogs begin growling. Rodrigo and Marisol run away frightened.

Differentiating Instruction

Pre-AP

Expand and Elaborate Invite students to talk about their own pets. Begin by asking if students have a dog or a cat. **¿Tienes un gato? ¿Tienes un perro?** For the students who answer yes, have them share their pets' names. Then ask students to write a short paragraph that answers the questions: **¿Es simpático tu perro? ¿Es perezoso tu gato?**

Multiple Intelligences

Visual Learners Have students select one line from Escena 3 that includes a comparative expression to illustrate. For example, **Los perros son menos perezosos que los gatos.** Students could draw two sleeping cats and two busy dogs. Have students read the scene aloud. Tell them to hold up their drawing when the group comes to the line they have illustrated.

19 | ¿Rodrigo, Marisol o Tito? *Comprensión de los ...*

Escuchar Leer

Expansión:
Teacher Edition Only
Have students write three more statements about the people in the photos.

Tell whether each sentence refers to Rodrigo, Marisol, or Tito.

1. Pasa un rato con su tía Celia.
2. Tiene perros muy grandes.
3. El cumpleaños de su abuela es el primero de marzo.
4. Necesita la camiseta de su amiga Alicia.
5. Come con la familia de Rodrigo todos los viernes.
6. Es menor que Rodrigo.
7. No le gustan los perros.
8. Tiene la camiseta de Alicia.

Rodrigo

Tito

Marisol

20 | ¿Comprendiste? *Comprensión de los episodios*

Escuchar Leer

Answer the questions according to the episodes.

1. ¿Cuándo es el cumpleaños de Ana?
2. ¿A qué hora está Trini Salgado en la escuela?
3. ¿A quién le gustan más los gatos, a Rodrigo o a Marisol?
4. ¿Cuántos años tienen los primos de Rodrigo?
5. ¿Cuántas hermanas tiene la madre de Rodrigo?
6. ¿Quién tiene la camiseta de Alicia?

Expansión:
Teacher Edition Only
Have students write three more questions about the three episodes and then give the answers.

21 | La familia ideal

Hablar

STRATEGY Hablar

Consider your beliefs Before the conversation, consider your beliefs about families. What is an ideal family? Describe it on paper and then aloud. Do you know such a family?

Work in a group of three to express opinions about the ideal family. Include your answers to the following questions.

Para organizarte
• ¿Es grande o pequeña la familia? ¿Dónde vive?
• ¿Cuántas personas hay en la familia?
• ¿Cómo son las personas de la familia? ¿Qué hacen?
• ¿Cuántos años tienen las personas de la familia?

Expansión:
Teacher Edition Only
Have students give a summary of their group's opinions.

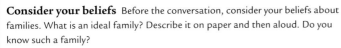

A Una familia pequeña es buena.

B Una familia grande es mejor que una familia pequeña porque es más interesante.

C No, una familia cómica es mejor...

Long-term Retention

Personalize It

Ask students to rewrite the questions in Activity 21 replacing the article **la** with the possessive **tu,** as if they were addressed to his or her family, and then answer them. **¿Es grande o pequeña tu familia? Mi familia es grande.**

Communication

Group Work

Place students in groups of four or five. Ask them to ask each other how many siblings they have. **¿Cuántos hermanos(as) tienes?** Then have them make comparisons. **Carlos tiene más hermanos que yo, pero menos hermanos que Susana.**

✓ Ongoing Assessment

Rubric Activity 21

Speaking Criteria	Maximum Credit	Partial Credit	Minimum Credit
Content	Opinions are well expressed.	Opinions expressed are limited.	Opinions are poorly expressed.
Communication	Pronunciation is correct and easily understood.	Pronunciation is fairly correct and understood.	Difficult to understand.
Accuracy	There are few mistakes in grammar and vocabulary.	There are some mistakes in grammar and vocabulary.	There are many mistakes in grammar and vocabulary.

Answers MSRB Transparency 50

Activity 19
1. Tito
2. Tito
3. Marisol
4. Rodrigo
5. Tito
6. Tito
7. Rodrigo
8. Tito

Activity 20
1. ... es el primero de marzo.
2. ... a las cuatro.
3. A Rodrigo...
4. ... tienen catorce y diez años.
5. ... tiene dos hermanas.
6. Tito...

Activity 21 Answers will vary. Answers should demonstrate correct usage of comparatives: Una familia grande es mejor que una familia pequeña porque siempre hay muchas personas para hablar y jugar.

201

Differentiating Instruction

Inclusion

Synthetic/Analytic Support Before answering the questions in Activity 20, have students write the question words for each in their notebooks. Discuss what kind of answer students should be listening for, based on the question word. For example, the answer to a question starting with **¿cuántos?** will be a number.

English Learners

Increase Interaction Before students discuss their beliefs in Activity 21, create a concept web on the board around the word **familia.** Help students brainstorm as many words and phrases as they can relate to the theme of family. Ask them to write these words on the board. They might include names of family members, adjectives that describe people, or activities that families do together.

Objective

· Practice integrating lesson content.

Core Resources

· *Cuaderno*, pp. 133–134
· Audio Program: TXT CD 3 tracks 19, 20

Presentation Strategies

· **Activity 22:** Open-ended practice: reading, listening, speaking
· **Activity 23:** Open-ended practice: writing

 STANDARDS

1.2 Understand language, Act. 22
1.3 Present information, Acts. 22–23, PYP

Pre-AP Integration
Long-term Retention

Use Activity 22 as a model for writing a short radio announcement about a pet adoption agency. It should include the name of the pet, what it looks like, what it likes to do, and why it would be an ideal pet for a family member.

✓ Ongoing Assessment

Rubric Activity 22

Listening/Speaking

Proficient	Not There Yet
Student takes detailed notes, gives solid reasons, and shows good use of comparisons.	Student takes few notes and gives some good reasons and fair-to-poor use of comparisons.

✓ Ongoing Assessment
@HomeTutor
More Practice
ClassZone.com

 Quick Check If students have difficulties creating the sentences, review pp. 190 and 196 with them. For additional practice, use Reteaching & Practice Copymasters URB 3, pp. 19, 21.

See Activity answers on p. 203.

202

---

22 | Integración

Leer
Escuchar
Hablar

Read the flyer from a family looking for a new home for their dog. Then listen to the radio ad by an animal shelter. Match each dog to someone in your family and explain your choices.

🎧 **Audio Program**
TXT CD 3 Tracks 19, 20
Audio Script, TE p. 181b

Fuente 1 Cartel

Es tan inteligente como su madre y... ¡más activo!

Le gusta correr, nadar y jugar al fútbol. ¡Es más atlético que yo! ☺

Vamos a Nueva York en enero y Rayo no va con nosotros. ☹

Si necesitas un amigo, Rayo necesita una familia.

Rayo
Labrador marrón.
Tiene un año.

Llámanos: 555-8231

Fuente 2 Anuncio de radio

 Listen and take notes
· ¿Cómo es Dino?
· ¿Qué le gusta hacer a Dino?

modelo: Rayo es un buen perro para mi primo Alberto. Rayo es menos tranquilo que Dino y a mi primo le gusta correr...

Expansión:
Teacher Edition Only
Have students match a cat to a family member and explain their decision.

23 | Un amigo nuevo

Escribir

Write a letter to an exchange student from Puerto Rico who is going to stay with your family. Use comparatives to describe the members of your family.

modelo: ¡Hola! Te presento a mi familia. Tengo dos hermanos. Yo soy mayor que mis hermanos. Mi hermano Lance es menor que...

Writing Criteria	Excellent	Good	Needs Work
Content	Your letter includes a lot of information.	Your letter includes some information.	Your letter includes little information.
Communication	Most of your letter is organized and easy to follow.	Parts of your letter are organized and easy to follow.	Your letter is disorganized and hard to follow.
Accuracy	Your letter has few mistakes in grammar and vocabulary.	Your letter has some mistakes in grammar and vocabulary.	Your letter has many mistakes in grammar and vocabulary.

Expansión:
Teacher Edition Only
Have students write descriptions and comparisons of their friends.

Más práctica Cuaderno *pp. 133–134* Cuaderno para hispanohablantes *pp. 135–136*

 PARA Y PIENSA

Did you get it? Create sentences based on the Telehistoria using possessive adjectives and comparatives.

1. los perros (de Tito) / tan grande / Marisol
2. el primo (de Rodrigo) / menor / él
3. los perros (de Tito) / más perezoso(a) / los gatos

🖱 **Get Help Online**
ClassZone.com

Differentiating Instruction

Slower-paced Learners

Sentence Completion If students have difficulty getting their stories started in Activity 22, provide them with two or three sentence starters. Here are a few possibilities:

Rayo es tan inteligente como...
Le gusta correr...
Rayo necesita...

Heritage Language Learners

Support What They Know Ask students to write a short e-mail comparing two of their friends in terms of age, physical characteristics, character, and preferred activities. They should use comparisons and state reasons for their opinion.

Juegos y diversiones

Review possessive adjectives and possession using **de** by playing a game.

¿De quién es?

The Setup

Your teacher will ask you to bring in two items that represent vocabulary words that you have learned. All the items will be put in a box.

Materials
• items collected from students
• box

Playing the Game

You and your classmates will take turns picking an item out of the box and trying to guess who owns it by asking questions using possessive adjectives.

Juan, ¿es tu pluma?

No, no es mi pluma. Es la pluma de Lorena.

The Winner!

The winner is the student who has guessed the owner of the most items.

Lección 2
doscientos tres **203**

Objective
· Review possessive adjectives and possession using **de**.

 STANDARDS
5.2 Life-long learners

Communication
Group Work

You may want to incorporate family vocabulary in this game by having students bring in photos of their family members for the box. For example: **Juan, ¿es tu hermano? No, no es mi hermano, es mi primo.** If you have a large class, you may want to have students play this game in small groups with a box for each group. Appoint a member of each group to be scorekeeper.

Communication
Interpersonal Mode

To make this game more competitive, you may ask students to guess why they think something belongs to a particular person. For example: **Es la calculadora de Luis porque le gustan las matemáticas.**

Differentiating Instruction

Multiple Intelligences

Visual Learners Ask students to draw pictures of objects that can be used in the game. They could draw them on poster board and color them with markers. Then you could laminate them to keep for further use. Ask them to create a minimum of five sentences using the pictures and possessive adjectives. Example: **Son mis plumas. Es tu cuaderno. Son nuestras papas fritas.**

Inclusion

Multisensory Input/Output Before the game starts, review the vocabulary words to be used in the game with students and ask them to copy them in their notebooks. Ask students to repeat the names of the items as they are writing them, and then ask them to repeat them once again as you point to them.

 Answers MSRB Transparency 50

Answers for Activities on p. 202.

Activity 22 Answer will vary. Sample answer should include: Dino es el mejor perro para mi tío Gustavo. Es tan tranquilo como Gustavo y a Gustavo le gusta mirar la televisión.

Activity 23 Answers will vary. Sample answer should include: ¡Hola! Te presento a mi familia. Tengo tres hermanas menores que yo y un hermano mayor.

Para y piensa
1. Sus perros son tan grandes como Marisol.
2. Su primo es menor que él.
3. Sus perros son más perezosos que los gatos.

¡AVANZA! **Objectives**

- Compare **quinceañera** celebrations in Peru and Puerto Rico.
- Compare fifteenth birthday parties in Latin America with similar celebrations in the United States.
- Find out what activities take place at a **quinceañera** celebration.

Core Resource
- Audio Program: TXT CD 3 track 21

Presentation Strategies
- Ask students to predict what **la quinceañera** is, based on what they have learned about birthdays, and the photos on these pages.
- Ask students to describe the activities that take place during a **fiesta de quinceañera**, based on the photos on pp. 204–205.

STANDARDS
1.2 Understand language
1.3 Present information
2.1 Practices and perspectives
4.2 Compare cultures

Warm Up UTB 3 Transparency 23

Comparatives Create sentences using forms of **ser** and comparatives.
1. yo / menor / mi prima.
2. Carla / tan alto(a) / su padre
3. ellas / menos atléticos(as) / yo
4. Ana y Marta / tan perezosos(as) / Alberto
5. nosotros / más serios(as) / el maestro

**Answers: 1. Yo soy menor que mi prima.
2. Carla es tan alta como su padre. 3. Ellas son menos atléticas que yo. 4. Ana y Marta son tan perezosas como Alberto. 5. Nosotros somos más serios que el maestro.**

Comparación cultural

Background Information
The tradition of the **quinceañera** was first established during the years of Spanish colonization in Latin America. When a girl reached the age of fiteen, a party was celebrated where she was "presented to society." In some present-day celebrations, the girl dances a waltz with her father or her godfather.

Lectura cultural

¡AVANZA! **Goal:** Read about the **quinceañera** celebrations in Peru and Puerto Rico. Then compare the parties and talk about the activities at the birthday parties you go to.

Comparación cultural

 AUDIO

La quinceañera

> **STRATEGY Leer**
> **Compare and contrast** Draw a Venn diagram like this one. Use it to compare the **quinceañera** celebrations of Peru and Puerto Rico.
>
>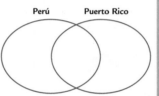
> Perú   Puerto Rico

La fiesta[1] de quinceañera es muy popular en muchos países de Latinoamérica. Es similar al *Sweet Sixteen* de Estados Unidos. Muchas veces hay una ceremonia religiosa y una fiesta con banquete. En la fiesta hacen un brindis[2] en honor a la quinceañera y después todos bailan un vals[3].

La chica que celebra su cumpleaños también se llama la quinceañera. En Perú (y otros países) la quinceañera tiene catorce o quince damas de honor[4]: una por cada[5] año que tiene. No hay un menú especial de banquete, pero en Perú es común comer comida típica del país, bailar y escuchar música tradicional.

---

[1] party   [2] toast   [3] **bailan...** dance a waltz
[4] **damas...** maids of honor   [5] **por...** for each

Perú

Comidas tradicionales: lomo saltado, chupe, mondongo y guiso

Differentiating Instruction

Multiple Intelligences
Linguistic/Verbal Ask students to work in pairs, with each taking turns offering descriptions of a **fiesta de quinceañera.** They should include words and expressions such as **banquete, damas de honor, una fiesta,** and **un vals,** as well as other important elements of the celebration.

Heritage Language Learners
Support What They Know If students have been to a **quinceañera** celebration, ask them to describe it. Where did it take place? Who was there? What food was served? What did people do during the celebration? What did the **quinceañera** wear? What music did they play? What gifts did she receive?

Una quinceañera en Puerto Rico con familia y amigos

En Puerto Rico, la celebración se llama el quinceañero. Muchas veces las chicas tienen la gran fiesta en su cumpleaños número dieciséis (por influencia del *Sweet Sixteen*) y no en el cumpleaños de los quince años.

En el banquete de una quinceañera de Puerto Rico es normal comer comida típica del país, como arroz con pollo[6]. Todos bailan y escuchan música del Caribe: salsa, merengue, reggaetón y el hip-hop cubano.

Puerto Rico

_____
[6] chicken and rice dish

PARA Y PIENSA

¿Comprendiste?
1. ¿Qué fiesta en Estados Unidos es similar a la fiesta de quinceañera?
2. ¿Cuántas damas de honor tiene una quinceañera en Perú?
3. ¿Cuándo tienen la fiesta las chicas de Puerto Rico?

¿Y tú?
¿Te gustan las fiestas de cumpleaños? ¿Qué haces en las fiestas?

Differentiating Instruction

English Learners

Build Background Ask students to describe birthday traditions with their families. How are they similar or different from the **quinceañera** celebrations shown on pp. 204–205?

Pre-AP

Sequence Information Ask students to write about an imaginary **quinceañera** party. Suggest that they brainstorm to generate as many details as they can on such topics as location, date, time and place, guests, type of food served, music, gifts. Ask students to write a short paragraph sequencing the information they have gathered.

Communication
Group Work

Ask students to work in groups to write a short description of the ideal birthday party. They should include where the party takes place, in what month, how many people are going, and the activities. Provide additional vocabulary if needed.

Comparisons
English Language Connection

Cognates Ask students to read the Lectura cultural and list all the cognates they can find. The list should include, but not be limited to, **popular, similar, honor, ceremonia, religiosa, banquete, vals, menú, música, influencia, celebración, tradicional, típica,** and **común.**

Communication
Pair Work

Assign two students the roles of interviewer and **quinceañera.** The interviewer must prepare in advance a minimum of five questions to ask the **quinceañera.** Questions may be based on the reading or on related vocabulary students have learned. Example: **¿Vas a tener una fiesta con banquete? ¿Qué van a bailar? ¿Cuántas damas de honor tienes? ¿Hay un menú especial?**

Answers

Para y piensa
¿Comprendiste?
1. En Estados Unidos el *Sweet Sixteen* es similar a la fiesta de quinceañera.
2. Una quinceañera en Perú tiene catorce o quince damas de honor.
3. Muchas veces las chicas de Puerto Rico tienen la fiesta en su cumpleaños número dieciséis.

¿Y tú? Answers will vary but should follow the model:

A mí me gustan las fiestas de cumpleaños. En las fiestas de cumpleaños yo bailo, escucho música, como comida rica y paso un buen rato con los amigos.

PROYECTOS CULTURALES

Objectives
- Read about musical instruments of Puerto Rico and Peru.
- **Culture:** Learn about percussion instruments in Puerto Rico and the **zampoña** in Peru.
- **Community:** Investigate sources of Andean music in the community.

Presentation Strategies
- Ask students if they have ever heard traditional Andean music.
- Ask if anyone knows how to play a percussion or a wind instrument and ask him/her to identify it.
- If possible, bring CDs of Andean or Puerto Rican music for students to listen to in class.

STANDARDS
1.3 Present information
4.2 Compare cultures
5.1 Spanish in the community

Comparación cultural

Essential Question

Suggested Answer Some instruments played in certain regions have their origins in their history. For example, Andean people inherited a variety of wind instruments of all sizes and shapes, made of materials (such as wood and reeds) that grew in the area.

Communities
Spanish in the Marketplace

Andean music has gained in popularity throughout the world. Performers of this music are easily recognized by their typical Andean attire (ponchos or colorful sweaters). They can be found in squares, fairs, shopping malls, subway stations, and other public areas in the United States. Instruments commonly used in Andean music include the **quena**, a flute, **siku**, panpipes, and a small guitar. Most large music stores have a section dedicated to Andean music. Well-known groups include Inti Illimani, Viento de los Andes and Ecuador Manta.

Proyectos culturales

Comparación cultural

Instrumentos de Puerto Rico y Perú

How do certain instruments and music become associated with a particular region? Percussion instruments that produce strong beats and rhythms are the base of much of the music of **Puerto Rico.** In **Peru,** the **zampoña** is a wind instrument that adds a deep and distinctive sound to traditional Andean music.

Proyecto 1 *Percussion*

Puerto Rico Make your own rhythm on a homemade percussion instrument.

Materials for your own percussion instrument
An object that can be used as a "found" percussion instrument, such as:
- coffee or juice can
- yogurt cup with pebbles, sand or seeds, secured inside with a lid on top
- wooden, plastic, or metal spoons
- pan lid and long-handled brush
- upside-down basket

Instructions
Practice making a rhythm pattern you can repeat on your "found" percussion instrument. Try creating different tones by striking the instrument in different places or with different objects.

Proyecto 2 *Zampoña*

Perú Use these simple materials to create your own **zampoña.**

Materials for zampoña
4 or more plastic or glass bottles, all the same size
Water

Instructions
1. Bring to class four or more bottles (all the same size) and add water so that they all have different amounts, ranging from empty to two thirds full.
2. Put your mouth to the top of each bottle and blow as if playing the flute. Because each bottle contains a different amount of air and water, you should hear various pitches.
3. Add tape so that the bottles are connected in a row. Arrange the bottles according to their pitch, from low to high.

En tu comunidad

You can find Andean music in most large music stores. If there is one in your community, find out what Andean music is sold there and if music from other countries is also available.

Differentiating Instruction

Heritage Language Learners

Support What They Know Ask students for the lyrics to a favorite Spanish-language song, preferably from Peru or Puerto Rico. Ask them to write them on poster board or chart paper. Encourage them to read the lyrics aloud for the class and explain unfamiliar vocabulary. If possible, have them bring a recording of a song so their classmates can listen and read along.

Pre-AP

Expand and Elaborate Ask students to write a short report in English about Andean music. The report should include:
- examples of typical percussion, wind, and string instruments
- origins of instruments
- types of music played

Ask students to share this information with the rest of the class.

En resumen
Vocabulario y gramática

Animated Grammar
Interactive Flashcards
ClassZone.com

Vocabulario

Talk About Family

la abuela	grandmother	la madrastra	stepmother
el abuelo	grandfather	la madre	mother
los abuelos	grandparents	el padrastro	stepfather
la familia	family	el padre	father
la hermana	sister	los padres	parents
el hermano	brother	el (la) primo(a)	cousin
los hermanos	brothers, brother(s) and sister(s)	los primos	cousins
		la tía	aunt
la hija	daughter	el tío	uncle
el hijo	son	los tíos	uncles, uncle(s) and aunt(s)
los hijos	son(s) and daughter(s), children		

Ask, Tell, and Compare Ages

¿Cuántos años tienes?	How old are you?	mayor	older
		menor	younger
Tengo... años.	I am . . . years old.		

Give Dates

¿Cuál es la fecha?	What is the date?
Es el... de...	It's the . . . of . . .
el primero de...	the first of . . .
el cumpleaños	birthday
¡Feliz cumpleaños!	Happy birthday!
la fecha de nacimiento	birth date

Pets

el (la) gato(a)	cat
el (la) perro(a)	dog

Other Words and Phrases

vivir	to live
ya	already

Numbers from 200 to 1,000,000 *p. 186*

Months *p. 185*

Gramática

Notas gramaticales: **de** to express possession *p. 187*, **tener... años** *p. 189*, Giving dates *p. 192*

Possessive Adjectives

In Spanish, **possessive adjectives** agree in number with the nouns they describe. **Nuestro(a)** and **vuestro(a)** must also agree in gender with the nouns they describe.

Singular Possessive Adjectives

mi	nuestro(a)
my	our
tu	vuestro(a)
your (familiar)	your (familiar)
su	su
your (formal)	your
su	su
his, her, its	their

Plural Possessive Adjectives

mis	nuestros(as)
my	our
tus	vuestros(as)
your (familiar)	your (familiar)
sus	sus
your (formal)	your
sus	sus
his, her, its	their

Comparatives

Use the following phrases with an adjective to compare two things.
  más... que
  menos... que
  tan... como

When a comparison does not involve an adjective, use these phrases.
  más que...
  menos que...
  tanto como...

There are a few irregular comparative words.

mayor	menor	mejor	peor
older	younger	better	worse

Lección 2
doscientos siete **207**

Online SPANISH CLASSZONE.COM

Interactive Flashcards Students can hear every target vocabulary word pronounced in authentic Spanish. Flashcards have Spanish on one side, and a picture or translation on the other.

Self-Quiz Students can check their understanding and get instant results with our online multiple-choice quizzes. These quizzes provide immediate feedback, making them a great way to prepare for a quiz or test.

Featuring...

Cultura INTERACTIVA

Animated Grammar

@HomeTutor

And more...
· Get Help Online
· Interactive Flashcards
· Review Games
· WebQuest
· Self-Check Quiz

Long-term Retention
Critical Thinking

Ask students to develop a chant that will emphasize the differences between singular and plural possessive adjectives in Spanish. It could be similar to a sing-song rendition of **Mi perro pero mis perros; mis perros pero mi perro.**

Communication
Group Work

Assign a family member name to each student. Begin by saying **la abuela,** at which point the student who is **la abuela** should say **¡Yo soy la abuela!** and call out another family member, and the student who is that relative should then call out another family member name. Continue until every student has spoken at least once.

Differentiating Instruction

Inclusion

Multisensory Input/Output Ask students to draw a real or imaginary family tree. Tell them to include names, ages, and birthdays. Have students exchange their family trees with a classmate and describe it to the rest of the class. For example: **La familia de Susana es pequeña. Ella tiene un hermano menor. Se llama Jorge y su cumpleaños es el 12 de noviembre. Ella no tiene hermanas.**

Multiple Intelligences

Linguistic/Verbal Divide the class into groups. In three minutes, see how many sentences students can make using at least two vocabulary words per sentence. The team with the largest number of grammatically correct sentences wins.

Objectives

· Review lesson vocabulary and grammar.

Core Resources

· *Cuaderno,* pp. 135–146
· Audio Program: TXT CD 3 track 22

Presentation Strategies

· Before playing the audio for Activity 1, ask students to listen to it carefully, especially to the relationships Marcos describes.
· Monitor correct use of numbers, possessive adjectives, and comparatives.
· Read the Comparación cultural with students and clarify any questions that arise.
· Review may be done in class or given as homework.
· Students can also access the review activities online at ClassZone.com.

 ## STANDARDS

1.2 Understand language, Acts. 1, 3
1.3 Present information, Acts. 1–5
4.2 Compare cultures, Act. 5

Warm Up UTB 3 Transparency 23

Vocabulary Complete the sentences with the correct word.

> **cumpleaños   que   perro   tío   mayor**

1. Jorge tiene un gato, pero ahora quiere un _____.
2. El hermano de mi madre es mi _____.
3. El _____ de mi abuela es el 5 de marzo.
4. Mi hermana es _____ que yo.
5. Nosotros tenemos más primos _____ ellos.

Answers: 1. perro; 2. tío; 3. cumpleaños; 4. mayor; 5. que

Ongoing Assessment

Intervention and Remediation If students achieve less than 90% accuracy with the activities, direct them to review pp. 182, 187, 190, 193, 196, 199, 204–205, and to get help online at ClassZone.com.

See Activity answers on p. 209.

208

 ¡LLEGADA!

@HomeTutor
ClassZone.com

Now you can
· talk about family
· ask and tell ages
· express possession
· give dates
· make comparisons

Using
· **de** to express possession
· possessive adjectives
· comparatives

To review
· **de** to express possession p. 187
· possessive adjectives p. 190

 AUDIO

1 | Listen and understand

Marcos has a family photo and is explaining who everyone is. Listen to Marcos and then indicate each person's relationship to him.

> **modelo:** Pedro
> Pedro es el hermano de Marcos.

🎧 **Audio Prog**
TXT CD 3 Trac
Audio Script, T
p. 181b

1. Elena y Rosa
2. Julio
3. Norma
4. Alberto
5. Diego y Felipe
6. Carmen

To review
· possessive adjectives p. 190

2 | Talk about family

Write sentences describing what family members these people have, and what their ages are. Use possessive adjectives.

> **modelo:** yo / hermano menor (5 años)
> Yo tengo un hermano menor. Mi hermano tiene cinco años.

1. Bárbara / hermana mayor (19 años)
2. tú / dos primos (7 y 11 años)
3. nosotros / abuelo (67 años)
4. Manuel y Óscar / padre (34 años)
5. yo / perro (5 años)
6. ustedes / madre (36 años)
7. tú y yo / dos tíos (48 y 44 años)
8. usted / abuela (81 años)
9. ellas / dos gatos (2 años)
10. yo / tía (30 años)

Differentiating Instruction

Slower-paced Learners

Sentence Completion Review family relationships by asking students to complete sentences with the correct information.
Write on the board:

> El padre de mi padre es mi _____. (abuelo)
> Los hermanos de mi madre son mis _____. (tíos)
> La hija de mi tía es mi _____. (prima)

Pre-AP

Summarize Ask students to explain the way dates are expressed verbally in Spanish, and how they are written numerically. Then ask them to say the dates for the following: **El Día de la Independencia de Estados Unidos; El Día de Año Nuevo; El Día de San Valentín (de los enamorados); el día de Halloween.**

3 | Make comparisons

To review
• comparatives
p. 196

Josefina is describing her cat, Memo, and her dog, Sancho. Read the description and choose the appropriate words.

Memo, mi gato, y Sancho, mi perro, viven con mi familia. Memo tiene diez años y Sancho tiene cinco. Memo es __1.__ (menor / mayor) que Sancho. Pero Sancho es __2.__ (tan / más) grande que Memo y come más __3.__ (como / que) él. Memo come __4.__ (mejor / menor) comida que Sancho porque come buena comida para gatos. Sancho come comida __5.__ (mayor / menos) nutritiva porque muchas veces come pizza y papas fritas. Memo y Sancho son muy perezosos. Memo es __6.__ (tanto / tan) perezoso como Sancho. Descansan mucho. A Memo le gusta descansar __7.__ (tanto / más) como a Sancho. Pero Memo y Sancho no son aburridos. También les gusta jugar un poco todos los días. Jugar con ellos es más divertido __8.__ (como / que) mirar la televisión.

4 | Give dates

To review
• **de** to express possession p. 187

Write sentences giving these people's birthdays.

modelo: el señor Gómez: 13/4
El cumpleaños del señor Gómez es el trece de abril.

1. Berta: 23/12
2. Emilio y Emilia: 1/2
3. la señora Serrano: 14/1
4. Olga: 5/8
5. Germán: 15/10
6. el director: 11/6
7. la maestra: 30/9
8. Luis: 27/3
9. Víctor: 12/11

5 | Puerto Rico and Peru

To review
• Comparación cultural pp. 182, 193, 199
• Lectura cultural pp. 204–205

Comparación cultural

Answer these culture questions.

1. What do people do during **la sobremesa**?
2. Which political positions do people vote for in Puerto Rico?
3. Who does Rafael Tufiño portray in *Goyita*?
4. What are some **quinceañera** traditions? Describe at least three.

Más práctica Cuaderno *pp. 135–146* Cuaderno para hispanohablantes *pp. 137–146*

🔎 **Get Help Online**
ClassZone.com

✓ Ongoing Assessment

@HomeTutor
More Practice
ClassZone.com

Peer Assessment Have students read their completed description from Activity 3 to a partner, who will correct any errors.

Answers MSRB Transparencies 50–51

Answers for Activities on pp. 208, 209.

Activity 1
1. Elena y Rosa son las hermanas de Marcos.
2. Julio es el padre de Marcos.
3. Norma es la madre de Marcos.
4. Alberto es el abuelo de Marcos.
5. Diego y Felipe son los primos de Marcos.
6. Carmen es la tía de Marcos.

Activity 2
1. Bárbara tiene una hermana mayor. Su hermana mayor tiene diecinueve años.
2. Tú tienes dos primos. Tus primos tienen siete y once años.
3. Nosotros tenemos un abuelo. Nuestro abuelo tiene sesenta y siete años.
4. Manuel y Óscar tienen un padre. Su padre tiene treinta y cuatro años.
5. Yo tengo un perro. Mi perro tiene cinco años.
6. Ustedes tienen una madre. Su madre tiene treinta y seis años.
7. Tú y yo tenemos dos tíos. Nuestros tíos tienen cuarenta y ocho y cuarenta y cuatro años.
8. Usted tiene una abuela. Su abuela tiene ochenta y un años.
9. Ellas tienen dos gatos. Sus gatos tienen dos años.
10. Yo tengo una tía. Mi tía tiene treinta años.

Activity 3
1. mayor; 2. más; 3. que; 4. mejor; 5. menos; 6. tan; 7. tanto; 8. que

Activity 4
1. El cumpleaños de Berta es el veintitrés de diciembre.
2. ...de Emilio y Emilia es el primero de febrero.
3. ...de la señora Serrano es el catorce de enero.
4. ...de Olga es el cinco de agosto.
5. ...de Germán es el quince de octubre.
6. ...del director es el once de junio.
7. ...de la maestra es el treinta de septiembre.
8. ...de Luis es el veintisiete de marzo
9. ...de Víctor es el doce de noviembre.

Activity 5
1. During **la sobremesa**, families spend time together at the table long after a meal is over.
2. Puerto Ricans living on the island vote for their governor and local legislators.
3. Rafael Tufiño portrays his mother in *Goyita*.
4. Some **quinceañera** traditions include having a religious ceremony followed by a banquet, having maids of honor, and dancing a waltz.

209

Differentiating Instruction

Inclusion

Frequent Review/Repetition Ask each student to come to the board and write his or her birthday using numbers. When all the birthdays are on the board, lead the class in checking to make sure they are in the Spanish order. Then ask students to say them out loud in Spanish.

Multiple Intelligences

Interpersonal Have students work in pairs and plan a **quinceañera.** Have them create a chart in Spanish and write where and when it will take place, what activities they will do, what food they will eat, and which family members will be there. Students will use their charts and discuss their **quinceañera** with other pairs.

Objectives
· Read three personal accounts about Sunday gatherings written by teens from Puerto Rico, El Salvador, and Peru.
· Compare Sunday meals with one of the three students in the text.
· Write a short essay about your typical Sunday meal.

Core Resources
· *Cuaderno*, pp. 147–149
· Audio Program: CD 3 track 23
· Video Program: DVD 1

Presentation Strategies
· Draw students' attention to the photos on pp. 210–211 and have them predict what the text will be about. Assign a student to list their responses on the board.
· Have students take turns reading each narration as their classmates follow it in the text.
· Play the audio.

STANDARDS
1.2 Understand language
1.3 Present information
2.1 Practices and perspectives
4.2 Compare cultures

Long-term Retention
Personalize It

After students read the three narratives, conduct an informal survey by having students call out the foods they would like to have for their own Sunday meal. Assign one student to write on the board the food items mentioned and have another student read the items to the class. Students can reply with **sí** or **no** after each item is read.

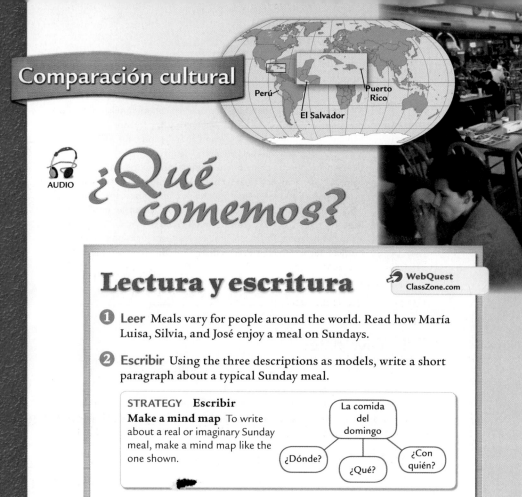

Comparación cultural

¿Qué comemos?

Lectura y escritura

WebQuest ClassZone.com

❶ **Leer** Meals vary for people around the world. Read how María Luisa, Silvia, and José enjoy a meal on Sundays.

❷ **Escribir** Using the three descriptions as models, write a short paragraph about a typical Sunday meal.

> **STRATEGY Escribir**
> **Make a mind map** To write about a real or imaginary Sunday meal, make a mind map like the one shown.
>
> La comida del domingo
> ¿Dónde? ¿Qué? ¿Con quién?

Step 1 Complete the mind map of your Sunday meal by adding details to the categories of place (where you eat), foods (what you eat), and people (with whom you eat).

Step 2 Write your paragraph. Make sure to include all the information from your mind map. Check your writing by yourself or with help from a friend. Make final corrections.

Compara con tu mundo
Use the paragraph you wrote to compare your Sunday meal to a meal described by *one* of the three students. In what ways is your meal similar? In what ways is it different?

Cuaderno *pp. 147–149*   Cuaderno para hispanohablantes *pp. 147–149*

210 Unidad 3
doscientos diez

Differentiating Instruction

English Learners
Provide Comprehensible Input Explain that a mind map consists of a larger oval that contains the main topic and is linked to smaller ovals that contain questions related to the main topic. Ask students what the main topic of the paragraph is: *Sunday Meal.* Go over the meaning of the questions: *Where? What? With whom?* Check comprehension: *Where do you eat on Sundays? With whom do you eat?*`

Heritage Language Learners
Support What They Know Ask students to describe to the class a typical Sunday meal gathering in their country of origin. Where does the meal take place? At what time? Who is invited? Who prepares the meal? What typical dishes are served? What dishes are his or her favorites?

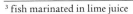
El Salvador — *María Luisa*

Hola, soy María Luisa. Yo soy de El Salvador. Los domingos, voy con mi hermana mayor y mi prima a Metrocentro[1]. Después de pasear unas horas, vamos a un café porque estamos cansadas y tenemos sed y hambre. En el café venden sándwiches, refrescos y jugos de papaya, mango, melón y otras frutas. A mí me gusta más la horchata[2]. Es una bebida muy rica.

[1] popular mall in San Salvador

[2] beverage made of rice, water, and milk

Perú — *Silvia*

Yo soy Silvia y vivo en Lima, Perú. Todos los domingos comemos la cena con mis tíos. Mi tío Ricardo siempre prepara su comida favorita, el ceviche[3]. A mí me gusta más el ají de gallina[4] que hace mi abuela. ¡Es mejor que el ceviche de mi tío! Después de la cena, mis padres y mis tíos beben café y hablan. Mis primos y yo comemos helado y escuchamos música.

[3] fish marinated in lime juice   [4] spicy chicken and potato dish

Puerto Rico — *José*

¿Qué tal? Me llamo José. Vivo en San Juan, Puerto Rico. Todos los domingos, mi familia y yo comemos el almuerzo en un restaurante. Nos gusta comer carne asada[5]. Es muy, muy buena. También me gustan los tostones[6]. ¡Pero los tostones de mi madre son más ricos que los tostones en un restaurante!

[5] barbecued   [6] fried plantains

Puerto Rico
doscientos once **211**

Comparación cultural

Exploring the Theme

Horchata is a beverage made of ground almonds, rice barley, or tigernuts. The name comes from Valencian *orxata*, a barley-based beverage. Eventually the Spanish brought the *orxata* to Latin America, particularly Mexico, Ecuador, and El Salvador. In Mexico, **horchata** is a rice-based beverage that includes blanched almonds, sugar, cinnamon, vanilla, orange, or lime. In El Salvador, **horchata** is typically flavored with ground cocoa and cinnamon as well as sesame seeds.

✓ Ongoing Assessment

Quick Check Ask students quick comprehension questions about each of the three narrations and write their responses on the board. For example: **¿De dónde es María Luisa? ¿Adónde va los domingos? ¿Cuál es la comida favorita de Silvia? ¿Qué le gusta comer a José?**

✓ Ongoing Assessment

Rubric Lectura y escritura

Writing Criteria	Excellent	Good	Needs Work
Content	Paragraph contains a lot of information.	Paragraph contains some information.	Paragraph lacks information.
Communication	Paragraph is organized and easy to follow.	Paragraph is fairly well organized and easy to follow.	Paragraph is disorganized and hard to follow.
Accuracy	Paragraph has few mistakes in vocabulary and grammar.	Paragraph has some mistakes in vocabulary and grammar.	Paragraph has many mistakes in vocabulary and grammar.

Differentiating Instruction

Multiple Intelligences

Kinesthetic Divide the class into three groups, and assign each group to create a skit based on the descriptions José, María Luisa, and Silvia wrote about the time they spend with friends and family. Suggest that students bring in props to create a restaurant scene as well as write a script.

Pre-AP

Communicate Preferences Draw students' attention to the food preferences expressed by José, María Luisa, and Silvia. Ask students to research recipes for these dishes, try them if possible, and then explain why they like or don't like them.

Objective
· Cumulative review.

Core Resource
· Audio Program: TXT CD 3 track 24

Review Options
· **Activity 1:** Listening
· **Activity 2:** Speaking
· **Activity 3:** Speaking
· **Activity 4:** Writing
· **Activity 5:** Speaking and writing
· **Activity 6:** Reading and writing

 STANDARDS

1.1 Engage in conversation, Acts. 2, 3, 5
1.2 Understand language, Act. 1
1.3 Present information, Acts. 2–6

Communication
Presentational Mode

Have students bring a photo of their pet (real or imaginary) to class. Ask them to introduce their pet, talk about its personality traits, favorite activities, and favorite foods. Encourage them to explain why this is the perfect pet for them.

Answers

Activity 1
1. Diana es estudiosa. Su hermano toca la guitarra toda la tarde y ella necesita estudiar.
2. Tiene que estudiar porque tiene muchos exámenes en la clase de ciencias.
3. A Diana le gusta escuchar música y estudiar. A Óscar le gusta tocar la guitarra.
4. Óscar es menor que Diana. Él tiene diez años y Diana tiene catorce.
5. Ella va a estudiar de tres a cinco y él va a tocar la guitarra de cinco a siete.

212

---

1 | Listen, understand, and compare

Escuchar

Listen to this episode from a call-in radio show giving advice to teens. Then answer the questions.

1. ¿Cómo es Diana? ¿Qué problema tiene?
2. ¿Por qué tiene que estudiar Diana?
3. ¿Qué le gusta hacer a Diana? ¿Y a Óscar?
4. ¿Óscar es mayor o menor que Diana? ¿Cuántos años tienen?
5. ¿Qué va a hacer Diana?

Do you have siblings or cousins? Do you have a lot in common or are you very different? Explain.

> 🎧 **Audio Program**
> TXT CD 3 Track 24 Audio Script, TE p. 181b

2 | Present a friend

Hablar

Bring in a photo or drawing of your best friend or a person you admire. Introduce the person to the class and talk about what personality traits, favorite activities, and favorite foods you have in common. Then mention your differences. Prepare to talk for at least two minutes.

3 | Get to know a new student

Hablar

Role-play a conversation in which you are an exchange student from Puerto Rico, and your partner is your host brother or sister. Introduce yourself and ask about his or her classes, likes and dislikes, and what his or her family is like. Then answer his or her questions for you. Your conversation should be at least three minutes long.

¿Cómo es tu familia?

Mi familia es grande.

Differentiating Instruction

Pre-AP

Relate Opinions Have students write a brief paragraph stating some of the possible advantages and disadvantages of living with a large extended family. They should support their opinions with at least three reasons. For example: **Me gusta tener muchos hermanos porque es más divertido. No me gusta tener una familia grande porque siempre tengo que compartir.**

Inclusion

Multisensory Input/Output Ask one student to read aloud the information about Manolo from Activity 6 and another student to read the information about Martín while the class follows in their texts. Draw a Venn diagram on the board with the headings Manolo and Martín. Ask individual students to come to the board and fill in the diagram based on information they have just heard.

4 | Plan a family reunion

Escribir

Your family is hosting a reunion with all of your extended family members. You are in charge of organizing a breakfast for everyone. Create a seating chart, and label each seat with the person's name, age, and relation to you. Write what breakfast foods and drinks each person likes and doesn't like.

5 | Display your family tree

Hablar
Escribir

Work with a partner to create a poster of your family tree or that of a TV family. Use photos or make drawings of each family member. Copy this chart on a piece of paper and use it to organize your information. Label each person's name, age, birthday, favorite activity, and favorite food. Use the family tree to describe your family to your partner, making comparisons between family members. Then present your partner's family to the class.

Nombre	Edad	Cumpleaños	Actividad favorita	Comida favorita

6 | Compare twins

Leer
Escribir

Read this chart from a magazine article about Manolo and Martín Santos, twins that were recently reunited after being separated at birth. Then write a paragraph comparing the two men. Include at least six comparisons.

MUCHAS COINCIDENCIAS

Manolo
Nacimiento: 30/7, a las 2:20 de la tarde
Personalidad: serio, muy artístico
Profesión: Maestro de español. Enseña cuatro clases. Trabaja 45 horas en la semana.
Familia: dos hijos (Enrique y Arturo) y una hija (Rebeca)
Actividades: Le gusta practicar deportes: correr, montar en bicicleta, jugar al fútbol.

Martín
Nacimiento: 30/7, a las 2:22 de la tarde
Personalidad: cómico, muy artístico
Profesión: Maestro de español. Enseña seis clases. Trabaja 52 horas en la semana.
Familia: dos hijos (Eduardo y Ángel) y dos hijas (Rebeca y Rosa)
Actividades: Le gusta practicar deportes: andar en patineta, jugar al fútbol, jugar al golf.

La historia increíble de los hermanos Santos

Correr, montar en bicicleta, jugar al fútbol, andar en patineta, jugar al fútbol...

Integrated Performance Assessment
Rubric Oral Activities 2, 3, 5
**   Written Activities 4, 6**
Use the following rubric to assess the student's progress. The last dimension applies only to the oral performance.

Excellent	Good	Needs Work
The student thoroughly develops all requirements of the task.	The student develops most requirements of the task.	The student does not develop the requirements of the task.
The student demonstrates excellent control of verb forms.	The student demonstrates good to fair control of verb forms.	The student demonstrates poor control of verb forms.
Good variety of appropriate vocabulary.	Adequate variety of appropriate vocabulary.	The vocabulary is not appropriate.
The pronunciation is excellent to very good.	The pronunciation is good to fair.	The pronunciation is poor.

Differentiating Instruction

Slower-paced Learners

Read Before Listening Provide scripts of the audio for Activity 1 before playing it. Ask students to read the questions first, then the script. While they are reading the script, they should look for the answers. After students have read the script, have them put it away. Then play the audio and have students take notes as they listen.

Multiple Intelligences

Linguistic/Verbal Assign student pairs to write an article similar to the one in Activity 6, comparing two people. If possible, have them paste a photo above each description. Have students exchange articles with another pair. Each pair must then make at least five comparisons based on their classmates' article.

Proyectos adicionales

❖ Planning Ahead

Create a city entertainment guide. In small groups, have students create a shopping and entertainment guide for the city of Madrid, or for their own hometown. Each group's guide should include the location and a short description of six different events going on around the city. These may include exhibits at museums, sales at stores, events at parks, concerts, or special menus at restaurants. The guides should also include information about transportation to each event. Advise students to look at examples of entertainment guides on the Internet or in their local newspaper. The events in their guides, however, can be fictional. Also, encourage students to include photos or drawings to show readers what the events will look like. Give each group the opportunity to present their guide to the whole class.

> **PACING SUGGESTION:** Upon completion of **Lección 2** to review vocabulary related to shopping, places and events in town, types of transportation, and restaurants.

❖ Bulletin Board

Create a bulletin board with the title **¡A Madrid!** Provide students with poster board and magic markers. Instruct them to create a poster that might be found on the streets of Madrid. The poster might advertise a museum exhibit, a sale at the shopping center, or a new menu at a restaurant. Remind students that each poster should be attractive and interesting to look at. They should also include information about times, cost, and transportation to get to the place being advertised.

> **PACING SUGGESTION:** After **Lección 1** to reinforce vocabulary related to shopping and prices. After **Lección 2** to reinforce vocabulary related to places around town and transportation.

Get Help Online
ClassZone.com

❖ Web Research

Go online to learn more about interesting places around the city of Madrid. Some examples might include:

- **El Prado**
- **La Plaza Mayor**
- **El Retiro**
- **Teatro de la Zarzuela**
- **Moda** Shopping Center

Begin by having students pick a place or type of place they are interested in learning about. Then have them conduct an Internet search to find more information. A simple search such as "Madrid and shopping" or "Madrid and museums" will yield many results. Once students have focused their research, instruct them to isolate four or five interesting facts or figures about their location. Have them record their information on an index card along with a drawing or photo of their locale. Give students the opportunity to share the information they find with the whole group. Then organize discussions between students who have researched the same type of location, such as theaters or parks. How are their specific places similar and different?

> **PACING SUGGESTION:** Throughout the unit as time allows.

❋ Games

¿Me lo vendes?

Divide the class in half. Give half the students in the class a total of 100 euros each in play money. Give the other half pictures of clothing items to sell. Tell the sellers that they must establish a price for the item they are trying to sell. The sellers should try to get as much money for their items as possible, while the buyers should try to buy as many items as possible. Give students ten minutes to circulate and ask and answer each other's questions about prices. At the end of ten minutes, the seller with the most money, and the buyer with the most clothing items win. Then have students switch roles and play again.

PACING SUGGESTION: After vocabulary is presented in **Lección 1** to reinforce clothing items, colors, and shopping phrases.

Nuestra ciudad

In small groups, have students create a simple board game about their city or hometown. The spaces on the board should offer places or events to go to, such as concerts, stores, parks, restaurants, museums, schools, houses, or streets. The game pieces can be different modes of transportation, such as a car, bus, train, on foot, etc. Students should also prepare game cards that tell each player where to go with a word and picture.

Play the game by choosing a card and moving your vehicle to the place indicated. Once there, you should say something that might be said at that location, such as ordering from the menu at a restaurant, or buying a shirt at the store.

PACING SUGGESTION: Students can work on constructing their games at any time throughout the unit. They can play their games after vocabulary is presented in **Lección 2.**

❋ Recipe

Tortilla española is a popular dish that can be eaten at breakfast, as an appetizer, or as a light supper.

Tortilla española

Ingredientes

4 huevos
3 patatas
1 cebolla pequeña
1/2 taza de aceite de oliva
3/8 cucharadita de sal

Instrucciones

Corte las papas y las cebollas. Póngalas en una sartén y cocine las papas y la cebolla en el aceite de oliva hasta que estén levemente doradas. Bata bien los huevos. Viértalos sobre las papas y la cebolla. Cocínelos a fuego bajo hasta que el huevo esté firme. Ponga un plato encima de la sartén y déle vuelta a la tortilla encima del plato. Deslice nuevamente la tortilla en la sartén para que se cocine por el otro lado.

❋ Music

Have students create their own examples of traditional Spanish instruments, such as the Galician **gaita,** Basque **alboka,** or the rhythm instrument **la zambomba.** Organize students into small groups, and have each group choose one of these, or another traditional Spanish instrument. Advise them to find photos of the instrument, as well as information about its history and how it is played. Then have students use found materials to create their own example of their instrument. For example, to build their own **zambomba,** students might use a pot or box for the base, a piece of plastic to cover the top, and a long stick as the neck.

UNIT THEME
Downtown

✿ UNIT STANDARDS

COMMUNICATION
· Talk about what clothes you want to buy
· Say what you wear in different seasons
· Describe places and events in town
· Talk about types of transportation
· Say what you are going to do
· Order from a menu

CULTURE
· Surrealism and Salvador Dalí
· Climates around the world
· Spanish poet and novelist Antonio Colinas
· Local markets in Spain and Guatemala
· *Las Meninas,* by Velázquez and Picasso

CONNECTIONS
· Art: Designing a courtyard based on the architectural style of La Alhambra
· Music: Researching the musical group *Al-Andalus*
· Health: Learning about the health and beauty benefits of olives and olive oil
· Language: Tracing the Arabic origins of Spanish words that begin with **al-** or **a-**

COMPARISONS
· Shopping in Madrid
· The role of dreams in surrealism
· The Spanish **c** with **a, o, u** and with **e, i**
· Variations in geography and climate in Spain, Chile, and the U.S.
· Teatro de la Comedia and other weekend activities
· Handicrafts and collectibles in different local markets
· Two versions of the painting *Las Meninas:* Velázquez and Picasso
· Weekend activities in Madrid and Santiago de Chile
· Art of Spain and Chile
· Leisure activities in Guatemala, Spain, Chile, and the U.S.

COMMUNITIES
· Art from Spain or a Spanish-speaking country in a nearby museum

España
En el centro

Lección 1
Tema: **¡Vamos de compras!**

Lección 2
Tema: **¿Qué hacemos esta noche?**

Islas Canarias

«**¡Hola!**
Somos Maribel y Enrique.
Vivimos en Madrid, la capital.»

Francia

España

León
Salamanca
Madrid ★
Barcelona
Valencia
Islas Baleares
Portugal
Sevilla
Granada
Océano Atlántico
Ceuta
Melilla
Mar Mediterráneo
Andorra
Argelia
Marruecos

Población: 40.280.780

Área: 194.897 millas cuadradas

Capital: Madrid

Moneda: el euro (comparte con otros 11 países)

Idiomas: castellano (español), catalán, gallego, vasco

Comida típica: tortilla española, paella, gazpacho

Gente famosa: Carmen Amaya (bailaora), Francisco de Goya (artista), Ana María Matute (escritora), Severo Ochoa (bioquímico)

Paella

214 doscientos catorce

Cultural Geography

Setting the Scene
· What is the capital of Spain? (Madrid)
· What is the currency of Spain? (the euro) With how many other countries does it share this currency? (11)
· What other languages besides **castellano** (Spanish) are spoken in Spain? (**catalán, gallego, vasco**)

Teaching with Maps
· Spain has borders with which other countries? (Portugal, Andorra, France)
· Which islands belong to Spain? (Baleares, Canarias)
· Spain has coasts on which bodies of water? (Atlantic Ocean, Mediterranean Sea)

➤ **Cultura INTERACTIVA** *See these pages come alive!*
ClassZone.com

◄ **Aficionados del fútbol** Official songs, or **himnos oficiales,** are an important part of the Spanish soccer experience. Fans of the Real Madrid team sing **¡Hala Madrid!** *(Let's go, Madrid!),* especially during games against rival team FC Barcelona, known as **El Barça.** *What teams have sports rivalries where you live?*

Un jugador de fútbol del Real Madrid

El arte y la literatura Pablo Picasso, one of the 20th century's greatest artists, portrayed traditional Spanish themes in his work. He made this print of fictional characters Don Quijote and Sancho Panza exactly 350 years after Cervantes wrote his famous novel, *El ingenioso hidalgo Don Quijote de la Mancha. What other works of Picasso are you familiar with?* ▶

Don Quijote (1955), Pablo Picasso

◄ **Las costumbres regionales** During the **Feria de Abril** celebration, girls wear Seville's traditional costume, **el traje de sevillana. Sevillanas** are similar to **flamenco,** which involves singing, dance, and guitar as well as rhythmic clapping or foot taps. *What type of music and dress would be considered typically American?*

Bailarinas de flamenco en Sevilla

➤ **Cultura INTERACTIVA**
ClassZone.com

Send your students to www.ClassZone.com to explore authentic Spanish culture. Tell them to click on Cultura interactiva to see these pages come alive!

Comparación cultural

About the Photos

· Real Madrid has been called the best soccer team of the 20th century. Its home games are played at Madrid's Santiago Bernabéu stadium.
· Picasso (1881–1973), who started creating art when he was just a teenager, had a prolific career in which he did more than paint. He was also a sculptor, printmaker, and ceramic artist and is best known for innovating the cubist style.
· Visitors to Seville can enjoy a flamenco show at one of Seville's many theater boats. While the dancers perform with amazing accuracy, grace, and passion, their movements are enhanced by the musicians' guitar playing and voices.

Expanded Information

· Soccer was first played in Spain in the late 1800s. Today, it is a national passion appropriately called **El Deporte Rey,** or *The King of Sports.*
· Much of what Picasso produced in his 75-year career can be seen at the Picasso Museum in Barcelona. Apart from contributing to the evolution of art, Picasso also made many political and social statements through his work.
· Flamenco has its roots in Gypsy culture, but has been evolving for centuries, incorporating Moorish and Spanish influences.

Bridging Cultures

Heritage Language Learners

Support What They Know Ask students if they are familiar with any **himnos** from soccer or other sports. What do they say to cheer for their favorite team? Have students model these chants for the whole group to repeat. Or, have students make up new **himnos** for the sports teams at your school.

English Learners

Build Background Ask students questions to help them report on the information presented on pp. 214 and 215. Follow up each question by asking students to draw a connection to their country of origin. Here are a few examples: *What is the capital city of Spain? What is the capital of your home country? Name one typical Spanish dish. Is it similar to any dish in your culture?*

Video Character Guide

Maribel and Enrique are friends who both love clothes—looking at them, shopping for them, and wearing them. They talk about where to shop and what to buy.

Culture at a Glance ❖

Topic & Activity	Essential Question
Let's go shopping! pp. 216–217	Where do you like to shop for clothes?
Surrealist art in Spain p. 229	How might dreams influence an artist's work?
Different climates p. 233	How does geography affect a country's climate?
Invierno tardío by Antonio Colinas pp. 238–239	How would you describe winter in your area?
Culture review p. 243	What are some elements of Spanish or Chilean culture?

COMPARISON COUNTRIES España Chile  Guatemala

Practice at a Glance ❖

	Objective	Activity & Skill
Vocabulary	Shopping	1: Speaking/Writing; 8: Listening/Writing; 11: Listening/Reading; 19: Listening/Reading; 20: Listening/Reading
	Clothing	2: Speaking; 3: Listening/Reading; 4: Speaking; 6: Writing; 9: Speaking; 12: Speaking; 15: Speaking; 16: Speaking; 18: Speaking; 21: Speaking; 22: Reading/Listening/Speaking; Repaso 1: Listening; Repaso 3: Writing; Repaso 4: Writing
Grammar	**Tener** expressions	4: Speaking; Repaso 3: Writing
	Stem-changing verbs: e → ie	5: Reading; 6: Writing; 7: Reading/Writing; 8: Listening/Writing; 9: Speaking; 10: Speaking/Writing; 12: Speaking; 17: Speaking; 23: Writing; Repaso 2: Writing; Repaso 3: Writing
	Direct object pronouns	13: Reading; 14: Writing; 15: Speaking; 16: Speaking; 17: Speaking; 21: Speaking; Repaso 1: Listening; Repaso 4: Writing
Communication	Talk about what clothes you want to buy	1: Speaking/Writing; 2: Speaking; 6: Writing; 7: Reading/Writing; 9: Speaking; 11: Listening/Reading; 14: Writing; 16: Speaking; 19: Listening/Reading; 20: Listening/Reading; 22: Reading/Listening/Speaking; Repaso 1: Listening; Repaso 2: Writing; Repaso 3: Writing
	Say what you wear in different seasons	3: Listening/Reading; 4: Speaking; 8: Listening/Writing; 12: Speaking; 18: Speaking; 23: Writing; Repaso 4: Writing
	Pronunciation: The letter **c** with **a, o, u**	*Pronunciación: La letra c con a, o, u,* p. 226: Listening/Speaking
Recycle	Numbers from 11 to 100	1: Speaking/Writing
	After-school activities	4: Speaking

The following presentations are recorded in the Audio Program for *¡Avancemos!*

- **¡A responder!** *page 220*
- **8: ¿Tiene suerte en la tienda?** *page 226*
- **22: Integración** *page 236*
- **Repaso de la lección** *page 242*
    1: Listen and understand

¡A responder! TXT CD 4 track 2

1. una camiseta
2. una blusa
3. unos pantalones cortos
4. una camisa
5. unos calcetines
6. unos zapatos
7. unos jeans
8. un vestido

8 | ¿Tiene suerte en la tienda?

TXT CD 4 track 4

Enrique: El invierno empieza. Hoy voy de compras en el centro comercial. Quiero comprar un gorro nuevo. No me gusta tener frío; prefiero tener calor. Mi amiga Micaela también está en el centro comercial porque quiere comprar ropa. Yo prefiero un gorro azul, y Micaela quiere comprar un gorro negro. Pienso que el gorro azul cuesta diez euros. Hablo con la señora.

Vendedora: Cien euros, por favor.

Enrique: ¿Cien euros? ¿No cuesta diez euros? ¡No entiendo! Ah... el precio tiene otro cero. No quiero el gorro azul. Cuesta mucho. A Micaela le gusta el gorro negro; cuesta quince euros. Ella tiene suerte.

22 | Integración TXT CD 4 tracks 8, 9

Buenas tardes. Aquí en Alta Moda tenemos los mejores precios.
Para los chicos, los jeans cuestan 35 euros y los pantalones, 25 euros. Las chaquetas de otoño cuestan 44 euros. También vendemos calcetines que cuestan 8 euros.
Y chicas... tenemos buenos precios para ustedes también. Las blusas cuestan 29 euros y los vestidos cuestan 36. Los zapatos cuestan 60 euros. También vendemos sombreros muy bonitos... ¡18 euros!

Repaso de la lección TXT CD 4 track 11

1 Listen and understand

Hola, soy Paula. Voy de compras en el centro comercial porque necesito ropa nueva. Necesito jeans azules, pero todos los jeans cuestan 70 euros. No quiero pagar 70 euros.

Todos los días llevo una blusa a la escuela. Necesito una blusa nueva. La blusa blanca es muy bonita. ¡Y no cuesta mucho!

En una tienda hay un sombrero amarillo. No es feo, pero prefiero un sombrero negro.

Quiero comprar zapatos nuevos. Tengo suerte porque hay muchos zapatos que me gustan. Pienso que los zapatos negros son bonitos.

Necesito una chaqueta porque el otoño empieza. Me gusta la chaqueta anaranjada más que la chaqueta roja.

En otra tienda hay un vestido amarillo. Tiene un buen precio: 43 euros. Me gusta mucho.

On your desktop

Everything you need to ...

Plan	Present	Assess
 **easyPlanner** DVD-ROM	**POWER PRESENTATIONS**	 **McDOUGAL LITTELL ASSESSMENT SYSTEM** ONLINE
All resources including audio and video	Ready-made PowerPoint™ presentations with **Animated** Grammar	✓ Assess, score, prescribe, and remediate online ✓ Create customized tests with the Test Generator CD-ROM ✓ Individualized Assessment for on-level, modified, pre-AP, and heritage language learners

Print

Plan	Present	Practice	Assess
URB 4 • Video Scripts pp. 69–70 • Family Letter p. 91 • Absent Student Copymasters pp. 93–100 **Lesson Plans** p. 75 **Best Practices Toolkit**	**URB 4** • Video Activities pp. 51–58 **TPRS** pp. 43–49	• *Cuaderno* pp. 151–173 • *Cuaderno para hispanohablantes* pp. 151–173 • *Lecturas para todos* pp. 32–36 • *Lecturas para hispanohablantes* • *¡AvanzaCómics! SuperBruno y Nati*, Episodio 2 **URB 4** • Practice Games pp. 31–38 • Audio Scripts pp. 73–76 • Map/Culture Activities pp. 83–84 • Fine Art Activities pp. 86–87	**URB 4** • Did you get it? Reteaching and Practice Copymasters pp. 1–12

Unit Transparency Book 4

Culture	Presentation and Practice	Classroom Management
• Atlas Maps UTB 1 1–6 • Map of Spain 1 • Fine Art Transparencies 2, 3	• Vocabulary Transparencies 6, 7 • Grammar Presentation Transparencies 10, 11	• Warm Up Transparencies 16–19 **MSRB** • Student Book Answer Transparencies 52–55

Audio and Video

Audio	Video

• Student Book Audio CD 4 Tracks 1–11
• Workbook Audio CD 2 Tracks 21–30
• Heritage Learners Audio CD 1 Tracks 25–28
  CD 3 Tracks 21, 22
• Assessment Audio CD 1 Tracks 21–22
• *Lecturas para todos* CD 1 Track 7, CD 2 Tracks 1–6
• *Música del mundo hispano*
• Sing-along Audio CD
	• Vocabulary Video DVD 1
	• *Telehistoria* DVD 1
	  Escena 1
	  Escena 2
	  Escena 3
	  Completa

Online and CD-ROM Resources

Student	Teacher
Available online and on CD-ROM: • eEdition • @HomeTutor • Animated Grammar **Available online:** • *Cultura interactiva* • Culture Links • WebQuests • Flashcards • Conjuguemos.com • Review Games • Self-check Quiz	**Available online and on CD-ROM:** **EasyPlanner CD-ROM resources:** • Learning Scenarios • Conversation Cards • Family Letters in Spanish • Family Letters in Creole **Available online:** • McDougal Littell Assessment System **Available on CD-ROM:** • Test Generator • Power Presentations

Differentiated Assessment

On-level	Modified	Pre-AP	Heritage Learners
• Vocabulary Recognition Quiz p. 149 • Vocabulary Production Quiz p. 150 • Grammar Quizzes pp. 151–152 • Culture Quiz p. 153 • On-level Lesson Test pp. 154–160	• Modified Lesson Test pp. 119–125	• Pre-AP Lesson Test pp. 119–125	• Heritage Learners Lesson Test pp. 125–131

	Objectives/Focus	Teach	Practice	Assess/HW Options
DAY 1	**Culture:** learn about Spain **Vocabulary:** clothing • Warm Up OHT 16 5 min	Unit Opener pp. 214–215 Lesson Opener pp. 216–217 **Presentación de vocabulario** pp. 218–220 • Read A–E • View video DVD 1 • Play Audio TXT CD 4 track 1 • *¡A responder!* TXT CD 4 track 2 25 min	Lesson Opener pp. 216–217 **Práctica de vocabulario** p. 221 • Acts. 1, 2 15 min	**Assess:** *Para y piensa* p. 221　5 min **Homework:** *Cuaderno* pp. 151–153 @HomeTutor
DAY 2	**Communication:** talking about clothes • Warm Up OHT 16 • Check Homework 5 min	**Vocabulario en contexto** pp. 222–223 • *Telehistoria escena 1* DVD 1 • *Nota gramatical:* **tener** 20 min	**Vocabulario en contexto** pp. 222–223 • Act. 3 TXT CD 4 track 3 • Act. 4 20 min	**Assess:** *Para y piensa* p. 223　5 min **Homework:** *Cuaderno* pp. 151–153 @HomeTutor
DAY 3	**Grammar:** stem-changing verbs: e → ie • Warm Up OHT 17 • Check Homework 5 min	**Presentación de gramática** p. 224 • stem-changing verbs: e → ie **Práctica de gramática** pp. 225–227 *Pronunciación* TXT CD 4 track 6 20 min	**Práctica de gramática** pp. 225–227 • Acts. 5, 6, 7, 9, 10 • Act. 8 TXT CD 4 track 4 20 min	**Assess:** *Para y piensa* p. 227　5 min **Homework:** *Cuaderno* pp. 154–156 @HomeTutor
DAY 4	**Communication:** use stem-changing verbs: e → ie to talk about your clothing preferences • Warm Up OHT 17 • Check Homework 5 min	**Gramática en contexto** pp. 228–229 • *Telehistoria escena 2* DVD 1 **Culture:** *El arte surrealista de España* 15 min	**Gramática en contexto** pp. 228–229 • Act. 11 TXT CD 4 track 5 • Act. 12 25 min	**Assess:** *Para y piensa* p. 229　5 min **Homework:** *Cuaderno* pp. 154–156 @HomeTutor
DAY 5	**Grammar:** direct object pronouns • Warm Up OHT 18 • Check Homework 5 min	**Presentación de gramática** p. 230 • direct object pronouns **Práctica de gramática** pp. 231–233 15 min	**Práctica de gramática** pp. 231–233 • Acts. 13, 14, 15, 16, 17, 18 25 min	**Assess:** *Para y piensa* p. 233　5 min **Homework:** *Cuaderno* pp. 157–159 @HomeTutor
DAY 6	**Communication:** Culmination: stem-changing verbs, direct object pronouns, clothing preference • Warm Up OHT 18 • Check Homework 5 min	**Todo junto** pp. 234–236 • *Escenas 1, 2: Resumen* •*Telehistoria completa* DVD 1 15 min	**Todo junto** pp. 234–236 • Acts. 19, 20 TXT CD 4 tracks, 3, 5, 7 • Act. 22 TXT CD 4 tracks 8, 9 • Acts. 21, 23 25 min	**Assess:** *Para y piensa* p. 236　5 min **Homework:** *Cuaderno* pp. 160–161 @HomeTutor
DAY 7	**Reading:** Winter Memories **Connections:** Art • Warm Up OHT 19 • Check Homework 5 min	**Lectura** pp. 238–239 *Las memorias del invierno* TXT CD 4 track 10 **Conexiones** p. 240 • *El arte* 20 min	**Lectura** pp. 238–239 *Las memorias del invierno* **Conexiones** p. 240 • *Proyectos* 1, 2, 3 20 min	**Assess:** *Para y piensa* p. 239　5 min **Homework:** *Cuaderno* pp. 165–167 @HomeTutor
DAY 8	**Review:** Lesson Review • Warm Up OHT 19 • Check Homework 5 min	**Repaso de la lección** pp. 242–243 15 min	**Repaso de la lección** pp. 242–243 • Act. 1 TXT CD 4 track 11 • Acts. 2, 3, 4, 5 20 min	**Assess:** *Repaso de la lección,* pp. 242–243　10 min **Homework:** *En resumen* p. 241 *Cuaderno* pp. 162–164, 168–173 (optional) 　Review Games Online @HomeTutor
DAY 9	Assessment			**Assess:** Lesson 1 Test　50 min

	Objectives/Focus	Teach	Practice	Assess/HW Options
DAY 1	**Culture:** learn about Spain **Vocabulary:** clothing • Warm Up OHT 16 **5 min**	Unit Opener pp. 214–215 Lesson Opener pp. 216–217 **Presentación de vocabulario** pp. 218–220 • Read A–E • View video DVD 1 • Play audio TXT CD 4 track 1 • *¡A responder!* TXT CD 4 track 2 **20 min**	Lesson Opener pp. 216–217 **Práctica de vocabulario** p. 221 • Acts. 1, 2 **20 min**	**Assess:** *Para y piensa* p. 221 **5 min**
	Communication: talking about clothes **5 min**	**Vocabulario en contexto** pp. 222–223 • *Telehistoria escena 1* DVD 1 • *Nota gramatical:* **tener** **15 min**	**Vocabulario en contexto** pp. 222–223 • Act. 3 TXT CD 4 track 3 • Act. 4 **15 min**	**Assess:** *Para y piensa* p. 223 **5 min** **Homework:** *Cuaderno* pp. 151–153 @HomeTutor
DAY 2	**Grammar:** stem-changing verbs: e → ie • Warm Up OHT 17 • Check Homework **5 min**	**Presentación de gramática** p. 224 • stem-changing verbs: e → ie **Práctica de gramática** pp. 225–227 • *Pronunciación* TXT CD 4 track 6 **20 min**	**Práctica de gramática** pp. 225–227 • Acts. 5, 6, 7, 9, 10 • Act. 8 TXT CD 4 track 4 **15 min**	**Assess:** *Para y piensa* p. 227 **5 min**
	Communication: use stem-changing verbs: e → ie to talk about your clothing preferences **5 min**	**Gramática en contexto** pp. 228–229 • *Telehistoria escena 2* DVD 1 **Culture:** *El arte surrealista de España* **20 min**	**Gramática en contexto** pp. 228–229 • Act. 11 TXT CD 4 track 5 • Act. 12 **15 min**	**Assess:** *Para y piensa* p. 229 **5 min** **Homework:** *Cuaderno* pp. 154–156 @HomeTutor
DAY 3	**Grammar:** direct object pronouns • Warm Up OHT 18 • Check Homework **5 min**	**Presentación de gramática** p. 230 • direct object pronouns **Práctica de gramática** pp. 231–233 **15 min**	**Práctica de gramática** pp. 231–233 • Acts. 13, 14, 15, 16, 17, 18 **20 min**	**Assess:** *Para y piensa* p. 233 **5 min**
	Communication: Culmination: stem-changing verbs, direct object pronouns, clothing preference **5 min**	**Todo junto** pp. 234–236 • *Escenas 1 & 2: Resumen* • *Telehistoria completa* DVD 1 **10 min**	**Todo junto** pp. 234–236 • Acts. 19, 20 TXT CD 4 tracks 3, 5, 7 • Act. 22 TXT CD 4 tracks 8, 9 • Acts. 21, 23 **25 min**	**Assess:** *Para y piensa* p. 236 **5 min** **Homework:** *Cuaderno* pp. 157–161 @HomeTutor
DAY 4	**Reading:** Winter Memories • Warm Up OHT 19 • Check Homework **5 min**	**Lectura** pp. 238–239 *Las memorias del invierno* TXT CD 4 track 10 **15 min**	**Lectura** pp. 238–239 *Las memorias del invierno* **15 min**	**Assess:** *Para y piensa* p. 239 **5 min**
	Review: Lesson Review **5 min**	**Repaso de la lección** pp. 242–243 **15 min**	**Repaso de la lección** pp. 242–243 • Act. 1 TXT CD 4 track 11 • Acts. 2, 3, 4, 5 **25 min**	**Assess:** *Repaso de la lección* pp. 242–243 **5 min** **Homework:** *Cuaderno* pp. 162–173 (optional) Review Games Online @HomeTutor
DAY 5	**Assessment**			**Assess:** Lesson 1 Test **45 min**
	Connections: Art **5 min**	**Conexiones** p. 240 • *El arte* **10 min**	**Conexiones** p. 240 • *Proyectos 1, 2, 3* **30 min**	

¡AVANZA!

Objectives

- Introduce lesson theme: **¡Vamos de compras!**
- **Culture:** Discuss where people like to shop for clothing in different countries.

Presentation Strategies

- Introduce the characters' names: Enrique and Maribel.
- Ask students to compare the clothing in the store window with the type of clothing teens wear in their own community.
- Ask students to talk about shops and department stores in the area where they live.

STANDARDS

2.1 Practices and perspectives
4.2 Compare cultures

Warm Up UTB 4 Transparency 16

Comparatives Complete the sentences with **que** or **como**.

1. Alicia es tan alta _____ su hermana.
2. Mi tío es menos atlético _____ yo.
3. El yogur es tan rico _____ el helado.
4. Patricia es más artística _____ su hermana.
5. Jorge toca la guitarra mejor _____ su padre.

Answers: 1. como; 2. que; 3. como; 4. que; 5. que

Comparación cultural

Exploring the Theme

Ask the following:

1. Is there a difference between the store windows in the photo and the store windows where you live?
2. What kind of clothing is shown in the store window? What season is it for? What clothing do you wear in that season?
3. Who do you see in the picture? Do you ever go clothes shopping with friends of the opposite gender?

¿Qué ves? Possible answers include:
- Sí, la chica está al lado del chico.
- El chico es más alto.
- Ellos están contentos y tranquilos.

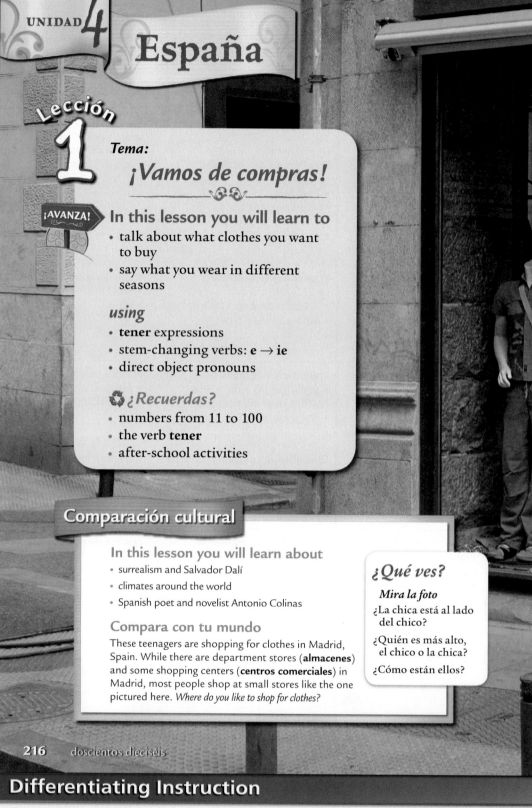

UNIDAD **4**

España

Lección **1**

Tema:

¡Vamos de compras!

¡AVANZA!

In this lesson you will learn to

- talk about what clothes you want to buy
- say what you wear in different seasons

using

- **tener** expressions
- stem-changing verbs: **e → ie**
- direct object pronouns

♻ ¿Recuerdas?

- numbers from 11 to 100
- the verb **tener**
- after-school activities

Comparación cultural

In this lesson you will learn about

- surrealism and Salvador Dalí
- climates around the world
- Spanish poet and novelist Antonio Colinas

Compara con tu mundo

These teenagers are shopping for clothes in Madrid, Spain. While there are department stores (**almacenes**) and some shopping centers (**centros comerciales**) in Madrid, most people shop at small stores like the one pictured here. *Where do you like to shop for clothes?*

¿Qué ves?

Mira la foto

¿La chica está al lado del chico?

¿Quién es más alto, el chico o la chica?

¿Cómo están ellos?

216 doscientos dieciséis

Differentiating Instruction

Heritage Language Learners

Support What They Know Ask students to share experiences or any knowledge they have of shopping customs in other countries. Do people typically shop at **tiendas** or in **un centro comercial**? Ask students if they know some common shopping expressions. How would they ask how much something costs? **¿Cuánto cuesta esto?**

Slower-paced Learners

Yes/No Questions Use yes or no questions about the photograph in the textbook to introduce students to some of the vocabulary related to clothing. You might ask what students see, like, or have themselves. Point to each item in the photo as you ask about it. Here are some possible questions:
¿Hay un vestido? ¿Te gusta la camiseta de la chica? ¿Tienes jeans?

On**line** SPANISH CLASSZONE.COM

Featuring...
Cultura INTERACTIVA
Animated Grammar
@HomeTutor

And more...
• Get Help Online
• Interactive Flashcards
• Review Games
• WebQuest
• Self-Check Quiz

Una tienda de ropa
Madrid, España

España
doscientos diecisiete 217

On**line** SPANISH CLASSZONE.COM

@HomeTutor In this powerful practice tool students have access to vocabulary, grammar, reading, writing, and listening practice at three levels of difficulty. The VideoPlus feature allows students to view the video while following the script, and to check comprehension with follow-up questions.

Featuring...
Cultura INTERACTIVA
Animated Grammar
@HomeTutor

And more...
• Get Help Online
• Interactive Flashcards
• Review Games
• WebQuest
• Self-Check Quiz

Using the Photo

Location Information

Spain In Spain, lunch is the most important meal of the day. It is also the most important time to spend with family and friends, and a time to rest. Most shops, businesses, and schools close for two or three hours during lunchtime. This tradition is called the **siesta.** Due to global influences, however, customs are changing and today some stores remain open during lunchtime, especially in the big cities.

Long-term Retention

Critical Thinking

Predict Have students think about the lesson topics. Have them brainstorm possible vocabulary groups and related items. For example, clothing (pants, shirts, dresses) and colors (blue, green, red).

Differentiating Instruction

Pre-AP

Expand and Elaborate Have students brainstorm a list of questions about the city of Madrid and things to do there. Divide students into pairs or small groups to research one of the questions at the library or on the Internet. Ask each group to share what they learned. If possible, have them download images or maps of the areas they have chosen to accompany their presentation.

Multiple Intelligences

Visual Learners Give students two minutes to memorize the details of the photo on p. 217. Then have them close their books and draw the photo with markers or colored pencils. Ask them to write a brief description of their drawing in Spanish, identifying the people and their characteristics.

VOCABULARIO

¡AVANZA! Objective

- Present vocabulary: stores, clothes, colors.

Core Resources

- Video Program: DVD 1
- Audio Program: TXT CD 4 track 1

Presentation Strategies

- Ask students yes/no questions about what they are wearing: **¿Llevas una blusa? ¿Llevas unos jeans?**
- Ask students to take turns pointing to each of the illustrations on pp. 218–219 and reading the words aloud.
- Play the audio as students read A–D.
- Play the video.

STANDARDS

1.2 Understand language

Communication
Common Error Alert

Monitor correct writing of plural forms of **calcetín, estación, marrón.** Point out that these words do not carry an accent in their plural forms: **calcetines, estaciones, marrones.**

Culture

Expanded Information

The euro is the currency of twelve European Union countries, stretching from the Mediterranean to the Arctic Circle (namely Belgium, Germany, Greece, Spain, France, Ireland, Italy, Luxembourg, the Netherlands, Austria, Portugal, and Finland). Euro bills and coins have been in circulation since January 1, 2002 and are now a part of daily life for over 300 million Europeans living in the euro zone. The Spanish plural of **euro** is **euros.**

218

Presentación de VOCABULARIO

¡AVANZA! **Goal:** Learn about the clothes Enrique and Maribel like to wear. Then practice what you have learned to talk about clothes and how much they cost. **Actividades 1–2**

♻ **¿Recuerdas?** Numbers from 11 to 100 p. 94

VIDEO DVD

AUDIO

A ¡Hola! Me llamo Enrique. **Voy de compras** al **centro comercial** con mi amiga, Maribel. **Queremos** comprar **ropa nueva.** A Maribel le gusta ir a todas **las tiendas.**

la tienda · ir de compras

el centro comercial

B Voy a comprar **una camisa** y **unos jeans. Cuestan** treinta **euros.** El **vestido** de Maribel **cuesta** veinte euros. Es un buen **precio.**

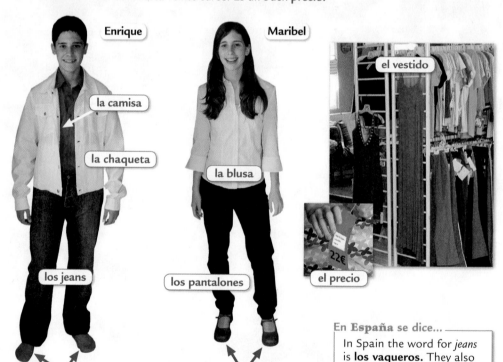

Enrique · la camisa · la chaqueta · los jeans · los calcetines

Maribel · la blusa · los pantalones · los zapatos

el vestido · el precio · 22€

En España se dice...
In Spain the word for *jeans* is **los vaqueros.** They also use **los tejanos.**

Unidad 4 España
218 doscientos dieciocho

Differentiating Instruction

Slower-paced Learners

Memory Aids Provide each student with construction paper and a pair of scissors. Ask them to cut out models of different styles of clothing in different colors. Then have them label each item, for example, **la camisa amarilla, los jeans azules,** etc. Allow students to create and talk about different combinations of clothing.

Multiple Intelligences

Visual Learners Have students brainstorm a description of a person. Encourage them to include personal adjectives, emotion words, clothing and color words. For example: **Es una chica alta. Tiene pelo castaño. Es artística. Tiene una chaqueta verde y un vestido azul.** Then organize students into pairs. As one student reads his or her description, the other student must draw what he or she hears.

C Me gusta llevar ropa **blanca, roja** y **marrón.** A Maribel le gusta llevar **una camiseta verde** y **unos pantalones cortos azules.**

roja · verde · amarilla · anaranjada · **la camiseta**

marrones · azules · blancos · negros · **los pantalones cortos**

D Maribel **piensa** que el **vestido** es un poco **feo.** Ella **tiene razón;** no es muy bonito. Ella compra otro vestido que le gusta más.

pensar

pagar

los euros

el dinero

Continuará...

Lección 1
doscientos diecinueve **219**

Tips for Teaching Vocabulary

I ask students to bring in some of their favorite clothing articles. The items are then classified by seasons and placed in 'booths' around the classroom. Students then follow a shopping plan and select clothes for a particular trip or vacation. Once students have selected their clothes, they describe their choices to the class.

Communication
Interpersonal Mode

Give pages from a clothing catalog to pairs of students. Have one student ask how much an item costs, and a second student answer based on the catalog information. Remind students to use **¿Cuánto cuesta?** for one item and **¿Cuánto cuestan?** for several items.

Communication
Pair Work

Have students describe what they are wearing today, including colors. Tell students that the color words are adjectives that must agree with the nouns they describe in gender and number. Then have them describe what their favorite outfit is to wear.

Long-term Retention
Personalize It

Look at the students in your class and select five to seven students whose clothing is unique from the others. Tell students you will describe what someone is wearing and they will guess that person. You may allow them to volunteer answers or, to involve the entire class, have them write the answer. Go over the correct answers when finished.

Differentiating Instruction

Inclusion

Frequent Review/Repetition Divide the board into two columns: **Sustantivos** and **Adjetivos.** Then have students brainstorm a list of nouns and adjectives based on the new vocabulary. For example, nouns: **blusa;** adjectives: **azul.** Using their lists as a guide, have students create simple sentences like, **La camisa es negra.** Remind them that the adjective's ending must agree with the noun.

Slower-paced Learners

Personalize It Have students use the verbs **tener** and **gustar** to talk about clothing that they have and like. Encourage each student to provide two sentences using the photos on pp. 218–219 as a guide. **Tengo una blusa roja. Me gustan los pantalones cortos.**

Objectives
· Present vocabulary: seasons, expressions with **tener**
· Check for recognition.

Core Resources
· Video Program: DVD 1
· Audio Program: TXT CD 4 tracks 1, 2

Presentation Strategies
· Point to the photos on p. 220, say the words and ask student to repeat after you. Correct pronunciation as needed.
· Ask quick comprehension questions about the photos. For example: **¿Quién lleva un gorro? ¿Quién lleva un sombrero? ¿Cuántas estaciones hay en España?**
· Play the audio as students read E.
· Play the video.

STANDARDS
1.2 Understand language

Long-term Retention
Personalize It

Make a chart with the names of the four seasons. Complete the chart by asking students to write which items of clothing they would wear in each season.

Long-term Retention
Connect to Previous Learning

Review weather expressions with students. Then have them work in pairs to talk about what they are wearing according to the weather. For example: **Hace frío, ¿qué llevas hoy? Llevo una chaqueta, un gorro y pantalones.**

Answers MSRB Transparency 52
¡A responder! Audio Script, TE p. 215b
Answers will vary depending on what students are wearing.

220

Presentación de VOCABULARIO
(continuación)

 En España hay cuatro **estaciones**. Maribel siempre **tiene calor** durante el **verano**. Me gusta el **invierno**, pero siempre **tengo frío**.

las estaciones

la primavera

el verano

el otoño

el invierno

Más vocabulario

cerrar *to close*
¿Cuánto cuesta(n)?
    How much does it (do they) cost?
el dólar *dollar*
empezar *to begin*
entender *to understand*
preferir *to prefer*
tener suerte *to be lucky*
Expansión de vocabulario
    p. R5

---

tener calor

el sombrero

tener frío

el gorro

¡A responder! Escuchar

Listen to the following descriptions of clothes. Raise your hand if you are wearing that item.

@HomeTutor VideoPlus
Interactive Flashcards
ClassZone.com

Unidad 4 España
220 doscientos veinte

Differentiating Instruction

English Learners
Build Background Give students the opportunity to talk about their associations with the four seasons. Also, ask them to share information about seasons in their country of origin. What is the weather like during different parts of the year? When is it mild? When is it extreme? Are there four seasons, or perhaps only two, such as a rainy season and dry season?

Slower-paced Learners
Frequent Review/Repetition Ask students to choose a favorite piece of clothing from the pictures on pages 218 through 220. Then give each student the opportunity to ask how much the item costs using the phrase **¿Cuánto cuesta(n)?** Allow volunteers to respond with a possible price. **¿Cuánto cuesta el sombrero blanco? Cuesta quince euros.**

Práctica de VOCABULARIO

1 | Los precios de la ropa ¿Recuerdas? Numbers from 11 to 100 p. 94

Hablar Escribir

Tell how much the clothing items cost.

modelo: la camisa
La camisa cuesta veintiocho euros.

1. el vestido
2. los jeans
3. los zapatos
4. la chaqueta
5. la camiseta
6. los pantalones cortos
7. la blusa

Expansión:
Teacher Edition Only
Have students rewrite the answers using adjectives to describe the color of the items.

2 | Ropa de muchos colores

Hablar

Ask a partner what color the clothing items are.

Ⓐ ¿De qué color son los zapatos?

Ⓑ Los zapatos son rojos.

 1.   2.   3.   4.

 5.   6.    7.   8.

Expansión:
Teacher Edition Only
Have students make their own price lists. Then have partners ask how much each item costs.

Más práctica   Cuaderno *pp. 151–153*   Cuaderno para hispanohablantes *pp. 151–154*

PARA Y PIENSA

Did you get it? Ask how much the following items cost.
1. the white socks
2. the blue dress
3. the orange jacket
4. the red shorts

Get Help Online
ClassZone.com

Lección 1
doscientos veintiuno **221**

222

Objective

- Understand clothing vocabulary in context.

Core Resources

- Video Program: DVD 1
- Audio Program: TXT CD 4 track 3

Presentation Strategies

- Ask students for what season Maribel and Enrique are dressed.
- Have students scan the dialogue and write the seasons mentioned in it.
- Show the video or play the audio.

Practice Sequence

- **Activity 3:** Telehistoria comprehension
- **Activity 4:** Vocabulary production: clothing, the verb **llevar;** Recycle: after-school activities

STANDARDS

1.1 Engage in conversation, Act. 4
1.2 Understand language, Act. 3
1.3 Present information, Act. 4

Warm Up   UTB 4 Transparency 16

Vocabulary Complete the following sentences with the correct word or expression.

fea	pantalones cortos
ir de compras	estaciones
precio	

1. Es un buen _____.
2. Los _____ son azules.
3. La chaqueta no es bonita. Es _____.
4. En España hay cuatro _____.
5. Me gusta _____ los sábados.

Answers: 1. precio; **2.** pantalones cortos; **3.** fea; **4.** estaciones; **5.** ir de compras

---

VOCABULARIO *en contexto*

Goal: Pay attention to the different articles of clothing Enrique and Maribel talk about. Then practice these words and **tener** expressions to say what you wear in different seasons. *Actividades 3–4*

¿Recuerdas? The verb **tener** p. 100, after-school activities p. 32

Telehistoria escena 1

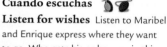
@HomeTutor VideoPlus
ClassZone.com

STRATEGIES

Cuando lees

Scan for details Before reading, quickly scan the scene to discover basic details: Who's in the scene? What are they doing? Where are they? What time is it? What's the season?

Cuando escuchas

Listen for wishes Listen to Maribel and Enrique express where they want to go. Who gets his or her way in this scene? How does this happen?

VIDEO
DVD

AUDIO

Enrique
Maribel

Maribel is opening a package from Alicia.

Enrique: ¿Es una camiseta?

Maribel: *(reading a flyer from the package)* Sí. Y Trini está en el centro comercial del Parque de las Avenidas de las doce a la una de la tarde.

Enrique: ¿Dónde está el Parque de las Avenidas?

Maribel: Necesito un mapa. ¿Vamos?

They start walking. Enrique stops and points at a store.

Enrique: ¡Una tienda de ropa! ¡Y yo necesito comprar una chaqueta! ¡Tengo frío!

Maribel: ¡Eres muy cómico! En el verano, cuando hace calor, ¿necesitas una chaqueta?

Enrique: ¿Hace calor? Yo no tengo calor.

Maribel: En el invierno, cuando hace frío, llevas pantalones cortos. Y durante la primavera, ¡nunca llevas calcetines!

Enrique: ¡Me gusta ser diferente! ¿No necesitas unos zapatos nuevos?

Maribel: *(reluctantly)* ¡Vale! Diez minutos. **Continuará...** p. 228

También se dice

España Maribel uses the word **vale** to say *OK.* In other Spanish-speaking countries you might hear:
- **México** órale, sale, ándale
- **Cuba** dale

Differentiating Instruction

Slower-paced Learners

Read Before Listening Before listening to the Telehistoria, have students preview the text silently. Tell them to look specifically for clothing words, and to create a list of the words that they find. Then have students draw a quick sketch next to each clothing word to represent its meaning.

Pre-AP

Support Ideas with Details Write Enrique's line **¡Me gusta ser diferente!** on the board. Then ask for volunteers to add information from the text that supports this idea. For example: **Lleva pantalones cortos cuando hace frío.** Ask students to imagine other things Enrique might do. For example: **Lleva un gorro en el verano.**

3 | La ropa apropiada *Comprensión del episodio*

Escuchar
Leer

Complete the sentences by choosing the correct word or phrase, according to the episode.

1. Maribel tiene _____ .
2. Trini está en _____ .
3. Enrique necesita comprar _____ .
4. Enrique lleva _____ en el invierno.
5. Enrique nunca lleva _____ en la primavera.
6. A Enrique le gusta ser _____ .

a. pantalones cortos
b. diferente
c. calcetines
d. una camiseta
e. el centro comercial
f. una chaqueta

Expansión:
Teacher Edition Only
Have students work in pairs. Each student writes two false statements about the episode and exchanges them with his/her partner to correct them.

Nota gramatical ¿*Recuerdas?* The verb **tener** p. 100

Tener is used to form many expressions that in English would use the verb *to be*.

tener **calor**	*to be hot*	tener **razón**	*to be right*
tener **frío**	*to be cold*	tener **suerte**	*to be lucky*

En el invierno **tengo frío,** y en el verano **tengo calor.**
In winter, I'm cold, and in summer, I'm hot.

4 | ¿Qué ropa llevas? ¿*Recuerdas?* After-school activities p. 32

Hablar

Ask a partner what he or she wears in these situations.

Ⓐ ¿Qué ropa llevas cuando paseas?

Ⓑ Llevo pantalones, una camiseta y un sombrero.

Estudiante Ⓐ
1. montar en bicicleta
2. tener calor
3. practicar deportes
4. tener frío
5. ir a la escuela
6. ¿ ?

Estudiante Ⓑ
gorro
pantalones cortos
chaqueta
camiseta
vestido
¿ ?

Expansión:
Teacher Edition Only
Have students choose three activities they like to do with friends and say what they wear.

PARA
Y
PIENSA

Did you get it? Enrique likes to be different. Complete each sentence with the correct form of **tener calor** or **tener frío.**
1. En el verano, Enrique _____ y lleva una chaqueta.
2. En el invierno, él lleva pantalones cortos porque _____ .
3. Cuando Maribel tiene calor, Enrique _____ .

Get Help Online
ClassZone.com

Differentiating Instruction

Pre-AP

Expand and Elaborate Once students have chosen the correct ending in Activity 3, encourage them to expand each sentence by providing details or an explanation, based on the Telehistoria. For example:
Enrique necesita comprar una chaqueta porque tiene frío.

Multiple Intelligences

Kinesthetic Ask students to write one expression with the **yo** form of the verb **tener** on a piece of paper and to keep the papers out of sight from other students: **Tengo hambre, tengo sed, tengo calor, tengo frío, tengo suerte,** etc. Ask volunteers to pantomime their phrases and have the class guess by saying the phrase aloud. Continue until all students have participated.

Nota gramatical

Students have learned the following expressions with the verb **tener: tener que** in Unidad 1, Lección 2; **tener ganas de...**, **tener sed, tener hambre** in Unidad 3, Lección 1, and **tener... años** in Unidad 3, Lección 2.

✓ **Ongoing Assessment**

@HomeTutor
More Practice
ClassZone.com

PARA Y PIENSA **Quick Check** Ask students to write three sentences explaining what they would wear to be different from other students. For additional practice, use Reteaching & Practice Copymasters URB 4, pp. 1, 3, 11, 12.

Video Summary

@HomeTutor
VideoPlus
ClassZone.com

Maribel has just received a package from her friend Alicia. The package contains a t-shirt and a flyer indicating that Trini will be at the Parque de las Avenidas mall between noon and 1:00 PM. Neither Enrique nor Maribel knows where the mall is. On their way, Enrique says he is cold and needs to buy a jacket. Maribel thinks it funny that Enrique needs a jacket when it's warm in summer. Enrique says he likes to be different. Maribel agrees to go into the store with Enrique for ten minutes.

▶ ❙❙

 Answers MSRB Transparency 52

Activity 3 **1.** d; **2.** e; **3.** f; **4.** a; **5.** c; **6.** b

Activity 4 Answers will vary. Sample answers:
1. ¿Qué ropa llevas cuando montas en bicicleta? Llevo jeans y un gorro.
2. ... tienes calor? Llevo pantalones cortos y una camiseta.
3. ... practicas deportes? Llevo una camiseta y pantalones.
4. ... tienes frío? Llevo un gorro y una chaqueta.
5. ... vas a la escuela? Llevo pantalones cortos y una camisa.
6. ... en verano? Llevo un vestido y zapatos blancos.

Para y piensa **1.** tiene frío; **2.** tiene calor; **3.** tiene frío

223

Objetives

- Present stem-changing verbs: **e → ie.**
- Practice using stem-changing verbs to talk about clothes you and your friends want to buy.

Core Resource

- *Cuaderno,* pp. 154–156

Presentation Strategies

- Present forms and uses of stem-changing verbs: **e → ie.**
- Remind students that stem-changing verbs have regular **-ar, -er,** and **-ir** present-tense endings.

STANDARDS

4.1 Compare languages

Warm Up UTB 4 Transparency 17

Expressions with tener Complete each sentence with the appropriate expression.

a. tenemos suerte   **c.** tienes razón

b. tienes calor   **d.** tiene frío

1. Liliana lleva un gorro porque _____.
2. Dos y dos son cinco, ¿verdad? No, no _____.
3. Compramos los pantalones más bonitos. _____.
4. Tú llevas pantalones cortos porque _____.

Answers: 1. d; 2. c; 3. a; 4. b

Communication
TPR Activity

Prepare in advance a list of ten sentences, some with regular verbs and some with **e → ie** stem-changing verbs and read them aloud. Have students clap once when they hear a sentence with a regular verb form. Have students clap twice when they hear a sentence with an **e → ie** verb. For example:
Hoy llevo zapatos negros. (Clap once.)
Hoy quiero comprar zapatos marrones. (Clap twice.)

224

Presentación de GRAMÁTICA

¡AVANZA! **Goal:** Learn how to form **e → ie** stem-changing verbs. Then use these verbs to talk about clothes you and others want to buy. *Actividades 5–10*

English Grammar Connection: There are no stem-changing verbs in the present tense of English.

Stem-Changing Verbs: e → ie

Animated Grammar
ClassZone.com

In Spanish, some verbs have a stem change in the present tense. How do you form the present tense of **e → ie** stem-changing verbs?

Here's how:

Stem-changing verbs have regular **-ar, -er,** and **-ir** present-tense endings. For **e → ie** stem-changing verbs, the **e** of the stem changes to **ie** in all forms except **nosotros(as)** and **vosotros(as).**

stem changes to

qu**e**rer   qu**ie**ro

qu**e**rer	*to want*
qu**ie**ro	qu**e**remos
qu**ie**res	qu**e**réis
qu**ie**re	qu**ie**ren

Other **e → ie** stem-changing verbs you have learned are **c**errar, **emp**ezar, **ent**ender, **p**ensar, and **pref**erir. In stem-changing verbs, it is the next-to-last syllable that changes.

Paula **prefi**ere el vestido azul.
*Paula **prefers** the blue dress.*

Notice that when one verb follows another, the **first verb** is conjugated and the second is in its **infinitive** form.

¿**Qui**eres mirar la televisión o leer un libro?
***Do you want** to watch television or read a book?*

Más práctica
   Cuaderno *pp. 154–156*
   Cuaderno para hispanohablantes *pp. 155–157*

@HomeTutor
Leveled Grammar Practice
ClassZone.com

Differentiating Instruction

Slower-paced Learners

Memory Aids Point out that **e → ie** stem-changing verbs are called boot verbs because if you outline the verb forms that have a stem change, the resulting shape forms a boot. Show an example on the board using **querer.** Ask: Which verb forms are outside the boot? Students should answer: **queremos, queréis.** Have students write a similar chart with the forms of **pensar.**

Inclusion

Metacognitive Support Ask a volunteer to read aloud the stem-changing verbs: **e → ie** on p. 224 while you write on the board: **Mario _____ (querer) _____ (leer) un libro.** Ask students to say the missing verbs: **Mario quiere leer un libro.** Ask them to write other sentences using **querer, preferir,** and **pensar** followed by another verb.

Práctica de GRAMÁTICA

5 | Después de las clases

Leer Enrique is talking to his parents after school. Match the sentences that he would logically say together.

1. La clase de matemáticas es difícil.
2. Tengo hambre.
3. No me gusta andar en patineta.
4. Tenemos sed.
5. Hace calor.
6. Queremos unos zapatos nuevos.

a. Prefiero montar en bicicleta.
b. Preferimos llevar pantalones cortos.
c. Quiero un sándwich.
d. No cuestan mucho dinero.
e. Queremos un refresco.
f. No entiendo la tarea.

Expansión:
Teacher Edition Only
Have students choose three sentences and write three other logical follow-ups.

6 | Todos quieren ropa

Escribir Enrique and Maribel are looking at a clothes catalog. Use the pictures to write sentences about what clothing items they and other people want.

modelo: la madre de Enrique
La madre de Enrique quiere la blusa anaranjada.

1. Maribel
2. tú
3. vosotros
4. usted
5. yo
6. los amigos de Maribel
7. mis amigos y yo
8. ustedes

Terráqueo - Ropa para este planeta

ROPA DE TEMPORADA

49 €
13,05 €
24 €
13,95 €
12 €
6 €
69 €
44 €

LLAME AL 555 22 13 40 O VISÍTENOS EN WWW.TERRAQUEO.ES 23

Expansión:
Teacher Edition Only
Have students say how much each item costs.

Lección 1
doscientos veinticinco **225**

Objective
· Practice e → ie stem-changing verbs and lesson vocabulary.

Practice Sequence
· **Activity 5:** Controlled practice: e → ie stem-changing verbs
· **Activity 6:** Transitional practice: e → ie stem-changing verbs, clothes, colors

STANDARDS
1.3 Present information, Acts. 5–6

Communication
Pair Work

Have students create five questions asking **¿Quieres...?** followed by different activities. They will then ask a partner the questions and record the answers. If the partner answers **no,** they will then supply what they prefer to do.
Example: A: **¿Quieres hacer la tarea?**
B: **No, prefiero mirar la televisión.**

Long-term Retention
Recycle

Bring pictures cut out from magazines or a catalog depicting various types of clothing. Place around the classroom. Have students walk around the room and select four outfits they like and four that they do not like. They will then write four sentences beginning with **No quiero (a particular outfit); prefiero (another outfit.)** Have a class recorder log the results to find out which outfits were liked the least and the most.

Differentiating Instruction

Inclusion

Cumulative Instruction Before beginning Activity 6, help students review the verb forms and vocabulary they will need. Elicit the present tense forms of the verb **querer** and write them on the board. Then ask students to supply clothing and color words that they see in the catalog. Create a list of each on the board. Encourage students to refer to these lists as they craft their responses.

Multiple Intelligences

Visual Learners Ask students to bring in clothing catalogs from home. Then have them repeat Activity 6 using the names of their friends and family, and pictures from the catalogs they have brought in. Instruct students to cut out pictures of clothing they like, and glue them onto a separate page. They should then write a sentence below each picture explaining who wants that item.

Answers MSRB Transparencies 52–53
Activity 5 **1.** f; **2.** c; **3.** a; **4.** e; **5.** b; **6.** d
Activity 6
1. Maribel quiere el vestido rojo.
2. Tú quieres la camiseta blanca.
3. Vosotros queréis la camisa amarilla.
4. Usted quiere el sombrero negro.
5. Yo quiero los jeans azules.
6. Los amigos de Maribel quieren los pantalones cortos verdes.
7. Mis amigos y yo queremos los zapatos marrones.
8. Ustedes quieren los calcetines anaranjados.

225

Objectives

- Practice **e → ie** stem-changing verbs and lesson vocabulary.
- **Pronunciation:** Practice pronunciation of the letter **c** with **a, o, u.**

Core Resources

- *Cuaderno,* pp. 154–156
- Audio Program: TXT CD 4 tracks 4, 6

Practice Sequence

- **Activities 7 and 8:** Transitional practice: **e → ie** stem-changing verbs, clothes, seasons
- **Activity 9:** Open-ended practice: **e → ie** stem-changing verbs, clothes, colors
- **Activity 10:** Open-ended practice: **e → ie** stem-changing verbs, clothes, seasons, activities, classes

 STANDARDS

1.1 Engage in conversation, Acts. 7, 9–10
1.2 Understand language, Act. 8, Pronunciación
1.3 Present information, Act. 7–10

Long-term Retention
Study Tips

Before doing Activity 7, have students skim the paragraph before completing it with forms of the appropriate verb.

Communication
Presentational Mode

Have students create posters related to the topics studied so far in this unit. They should draw pictures or cut them from magazines and include phrases, not just words, as part of the art work. Display the posters in thematic groupings if possible.

✓ Ongoing Assessment

Dictation Have students write the following dictation with the letter combinations **ca, co,** and **cu: Carolina Camacho es de Cúcuta, Colombia, pero ahora está en Cuenca, Ecuador.**

See Activity answers on p. 227.

226

---

7 | El regalo de cumpleaños

Leer
Escribir

Maribel wants to buy a present for her sister. Complete what she says with the correct form of the appropriate verb.

querer	cerrar	preferir
entender	pensar	empezar

Mañana celebramos el cumpleaños de mi hermana mayor. Voy a la tienda de ropa porque ella __1.__ una chaqueta nueva. Ya tiene dos chaquetas, pero ella __2.__ que las otras chaquetas son feas. Mis padres no __3.__ por qué necesita tres chaquetas. Pero ahora el otoño __4.__ y a ella no le gusta tener frío. Mis hermanos y yo vamos a la tienda Moda 16. Yo __5.__ otra tienda pero ellos tienen el dinero. Tenemos que llegar antes de las ocho porque la tienda __6.__ a las ocho.

> **Expansión:**
> Teacher Edition Only
> Have students add two more sentences to the paragraph.

8 | ¿Tiene suerte en la tienda?

Escuchar
Escribir

Enrique is at the mall. Listen to what he says, and answer the questions.

1. ¿Qué estación empieza?
2. ¿Qué quiere comprar Enrique?
3. ¿Prefiere tener frío o calor él?
4. ¿Qué quiere comprar Micaela?
5. ¿Qué no entiende Enrique?
6. ¿Quién tiene suerte?

> **Audio Program**
> TXT CD 4 Track 4
> Audio Script, TE
> p. 215b

AUDIO

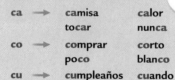 **Pronunciación** **La letra c con a, o, u**

Before **a, o,** or **u,** the Spanish **c** is pronounced like the /k/ sound in the English word *call.* Listen and repeat.

> Soy Carlos.
> Compro una camiseta.

ca →	camisa	calor
	tocar	nunca
co →	comprar	corto
	poco	blanco
cu →	cumpleaños	cuando
	cuaderno	escuela

Carmen compra pantalones **cortos.**
Carlos tiene **calor;** quiere una **camiseta.**

Before a consonant other than **h,** it has the same sound: **clase, octubre.**

Unidad 4 España
226 doscientos veintiséis

Differentiating Instruction

Slower-paced Learners

Read Before Listening Have students preview each question before listening to Activity 8. Ask them to write down a key word or phrase in each, and then brainstorm possible answers. For example:

¿Qué estación empieza? (circle **estación**)
Possible Answers: **invierno/primavera/verano/otoño**

Inclusion

Alphabetic/Phonetic Awareness Inform students that the hard /k/ sound in Spanish is almost always spelled with the letter **c.** One exception would be words in the metric system that start with the prefix **kilo.** Write **ca co cu** on the board. Have them brainstorm words they have learned that have these sound combinations. Have them come to the board and write these words.

9 | ¿Qué piensas de la ropa?

Hablar

Talk with a classmate about your opinions on clothes.

A ¿Quieres comprar un sombrero marrón?

B No, pienso que los sombreros marrones son feos. Prefiero los sombreros negros. (Sí, quiero comprar un sombrero marrón.)

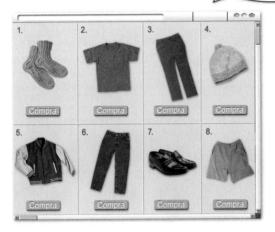

1. 2. 3. 4.
Compra Compra Compra Compra

5. 6. 7. 8.
Compra Compra Compra Compra

Expansión:
Teacher Edition Only
Have students make a list of the clothes both they and their partner want to buy. Have them share their results with the class.

10 | ¿Y tú?

Hablar
Escribir

Answer the following questions in complete sentences.

modelo: ¿Qué piensas hacer este fin de semana?
Pienso montar en bicicleta y leer un libro.

1. ¿A qué hora empieza tu clase de español?
2. ¿Qué entiendes mejor, las matemáticas o las ciencias?
3. ¿Qué quieres hacer después de las clases hoy?
4. ¿Qué colores prefieren tú y tus amigos?
5. ¿Piensas que ir de compras es divertido o aburrido?
6. ¿Qué estación prefieres? ¿Por qué?

Expansión:
Teacher Edition Only
Have students use these questions to interview a partner.

Más práctica   Cuaderno *pp. 154–156*   Cuaderno para hispanohablantes *pp. 155–157*

PARA Y PIENSA

Did you get it? Complete each sentence with the correct form of the appropriate verb: **empezar, cerrar,** or **pensar.**

1. Yo _____ que la blusa amarilla es bonita.
2. Ya hace frío cuando _____ el invierno.
3. El centro comercial _____ a las nueve de la noche.

Get Help Online
ClassZone.com

Differentiating Instruction

Inclusion

Synthetic/Analytic Support Have students copy each question from Activity 10 onto a sentence strip. Then instruct them to cut the strip so that each word is on a different piece. Next, have students rearrange the words to form their answer. If they need to change a word, such as from **tu** to **mi,** they should turn the piece over and write the new word on the back.

Pre-AP

Relate Opinions Show an illustration of clothing, such as a green T-shirt. Review with students the different strategies they now have for expressing opinions about the item. They might begin with **Prefiero..., Quiero..., (No) Me gusta...,** or **Pienso que...** For example: **Quiero otro color de camiseta. Pienso que las camisetas verdes son feas.** Repeat the discussion with other clothing items.

Communication
Role-Playing and Skits

Bring in catalogs from well-known clothing stores. Assign student pairs the role of customer and telephone operator taking orders. For example: **A: Quiero comprar una camisa verde. El número del catálogo es 123 y el precio es $23.00. B: No tenemos más camisas verdes. ¿No quiere comprar una camisa azul? A: No, gracias, prefiero una camisa verde.**

✓ Ongoing Assessment

@HomeTutor
More Practice
ClassZone.com

PARA Y PIENSA

Intervention If students have difficulties completing the Para y piensa, have them review p. 224. For additional practice, use Reteaching & Practice Copymasters URB 4, pp. 4, 5.

Answers MSRB Transparency 53

Answers for Activities on pp. 226, 227.

Activity 7
1. quiere   3. entienden   5. prefiero
2. piensa   4. empieza   6. cierra

Activity 8
1. El invierno empieza.
2. Enrique quiere comprar un gorro nuevo.
3. Enrique prefiere tener calor.
4. Micaela quiere comprar un gorro negro.
5. Enrique no entiende el precio del gorro azul.
6. Micaela tiene suerte.

Activity 9
Answers will vary. Sample answers include:
1. ¿Quieres comprar unos calcetines azules? Sí, quiero (No, no quiero) comprar unos calcetines azules.
2. ¿... una camiseta roja?
3. ¿... unos pantalones marrones?
4. ¿... un gorro anaranjado?
5. ¿... una chaqueta roja?
6. ¿... unos jeans azules?
7. ¿... unos zapatos negros?
8. ¿... unos pantalones cortos verdes?

Activity 10
Answers will vary. Sample answers include:
1. Mi clase de español empieza a las diez y cuarto.
2. Entiendo mejor las ciencias.
3. Después de las clases hoy quiero pasar un rato con los amigos.
4. Mis amigos y yo preferimos los colores azul y rojo.
5. Pienso que ir de compras es divertido.
6. Prefiero el verano porque hace calor.

Para y piensa 1. pienso; 2. empieza; 3. cierra

228

Objectives
- Practice **e → ie** stem-changing verbs and new vocabulary in context.
- **Culture:** Surrealist art in Spain.

Core Resources
- Video Program: DVD 1
- Audio Program: TXT CD 4 track 5

Presentation Strategies
- Ask students to identify the characters in the photo, tell where they are, and describe what they are doing.
- Have students preview the video activities before watching the video.
- Show the video and/or play the audio.

Practice Sequence
- **Activity 11:** Telehistoria comprehension
- **Activity 12:** Transitional practice: **e → ie** verbs, clothes, seasons

STANDARDS
1.1 Engage in conversation, Act. 12
1.2 Understand language, Act. 11
2.2 Products and perspectives, CC
4.2 Compare cultures, CC

Warm Up   UTB 4 Transparency 17

e → ie Stem-changing Verbs Complete each sentence with the correct verb form.
1. La tienda _____ a las ocho de la noche. (cerrar)
2. Los estudiantes no _____ ir de compras. (querer)
3. ¿ _____ Jaime la camisa blanca o la camisa amarilla? (preferir)

Answers: 1. cierra; 2. quieren; 3. prefiere

Video Summary   @HomeTutor VideoPlus ClassZone.com

Maribel is eager to get to the shopping center at noon, but Enrique is busy shopping in the clothing store. Maribel wonders if Enrique wouldn't prefer to go shopping in the mall, but Enrique says the prices there are not good. To hurry Enrique along, Maribel points out items in the store she likes, but Enrique says he doesn't like those things.

▶❙ ❙❙

228

GRAMÁTICA *en contexto*

¡AVANZA!   **Goal:** Listen to the **e → ie** stem-changing verbs that Enrique and Maribel use while they are shopping for clothes. Then use the stem-changing verbs to talk about your clothing preferences. *Actividades 11–12*

Telehistoria escena 2
    @HomeTutor VideoPlus ClassZone.com

STRATEGIES

Cuando lees
Look for color words In this scene, Enrique and Maribel discuss colors and types of clothing. Which color words do you find?

Cuando escuchas
Disregard stereotypes Who wants to keep looking at clothes and who is worried about being late? Is this expected? Why or why not?

VIDEO DVD

AUDIO

Maribel: Tenemos que estar en el centro comercial a las doce, ¿entiendes?

Enrique: Sí, entiendo. Dos minutos más. ¿Prefieres los vaqueros negros o los pantalones verdes?

Maribel: Prefiero ir al centro comercial, ¡ahora!

Enrique: Quiero la camisa blanca.

Vendedora: Tenemos camisas en color azul y en verde. ¿Queréis ver?

Maribel: *(to the clerk)* No, gracias. *(to Enrique, frustrated)* Pero Enrique, ¿una tienda de ropa? ¿No prefieres ir de compras al centro comercial?

Enrique: No. No quiero comprar la ropa en el centro comercial. Los precios no son buenos. *(still shopping)* ¿Te gustan los pantalones cortos azules?

Maribel: *(rushing him)* Sí, sí. Y me gustan los calcetines rojos, la camisa amarilla y los zapatos marrones...

Enrique: No, no, no. ¿Rojo, amarillo y marrón? No, no me gustan.

Continuará... p. 234

Differentiating Instruction

Heritage Language Learners

Regional Variations Ask students to comment on ways to say **los jeans.** Point out that the word **vaqueros** is used in Uruguay, Spain, and Argentina. Spaniards also use **los tejanos** for jeans. In recent years, **los jeans** seems to be the preferred term used in much of Latin America. In Puerto Rico, however, the preferred term is **los mahones.**

Slower-paced Learners

Memory Aids Have students create a drawing of each piece of clothing mentioned in the Telehistoria to help them remember vocabulary. Have students sketch each item on the same piece of paper. Then have students use their drawings to ask questions of their peers. **¿Prefieres la camisa blanca o los pantalones verdes? ¿Te gustan los zapatos marrones?**

11 | En la tienda de ropa *Comprensión del episodio*

 Escuchar
Leer

Who prefers the following things: Maribel or Enrique?

1. ir de compras en una tienda de ropa
2. la camisa amarilla
3. la camisa blanca
4. los calcetines rojos
5. los zapatos marrones
6. ir al centro comercial temprano

 Maribel   **Enrique**

Expansión:
Teacher Edition Only

Have students write a statement that refers to either Maribel or Enrique and have their peers guess who the statement refers to.

12 | La ropa y las estaciones

Hablar

Talk with a partner about what you prefer to wear and not wear during each season.

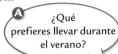

A ¿Qué prefieres llevar durante el verano?

B Prefiero llevar pantalones cortos. Nunca llevo chaqueta durante el verano.

Expansión:
Teacher Edition Only
Have students describe what their partner is wearing.

Comparación cultural

El arte surrealista de España

How might dreams influence an artist's work? Artist Salvador Dalí from **Spain** is well known for his surrealist paintings. In surrealist art, the imagery reflects an artist's imagination and is often inspired by dreams. *La persistencia de la memoria,* considered one of Dalí's masterpieces, shows pocket watches that appear to be melting. Many interpret this painting as a commentary about the nature of time. What do you think Dalí's message is?

Compara con tu mundo *Can you think of a dream you had that would make an interesting painting? What would your painting look like?*

La persistencia de la memoria (1931), Salvador Dalí

 PARA Y PIENSA

Did you get it? Complete each sentence based on the Telehistoria with the correct form of the verb in parentheses.
1. Enrique _____ que van al centro comercial. (entender)
2. Maribel _____ ir al centro comercial. (preferir)
3. Enrique _____ comprar la camisa blanca. (querer)

 Get Help Online ClassZone.com

Communication

Interpersonal Mode

Ask each student in the class to write a description of what another student in the class is wearing. Collect the descriptions, then ask a student to read one description aloud. Ask another student to guess who is being described. Students should begin their descriptions with **La persona lleva...** so as not to reveal the gender.

Comparación cultural

Essential Question

Suggested Answer Dreams are part of the artist's subconscious imagination and can come out in an artist's work unintentionally. Some artists strive to depict images they have seen in dreams.

About the Artist

Salvador Dalí This painting is considered one of Salvador Dalí's masterpieces. The background of the painting shows Cape Creus, in the Catalonian region of Spain where Dalí grew up. The images in Dalí's surrealist paintings are confusing and startling, like those in dreams.

✓ Ongoing Assessment

@*HomeTutor* More Practice ClassZone.com

PARA Y PIENSA   **Intervention** If students miss more than one item in the Para y piensa, have them review p. 224 and repeat Activities 5 and 6 on p. 225. For additional practice, use Reteaching & Practice Copymasters URB 4, pp. 4, 6.

Answers MSRB Transparency 53

Activity 11
1. Enrique 3. Enrique 5. Maribel
2. Maribel 4. Maribel 6. Maribel

Activity 12 Answers will vary. Sample answers include:
¿Qué prefieres llevar durante el otoño? Prefiero llevar unos pantalones y una camisa durante el otoño.

¿Qué prefieres llevar durante el invierno? Prefiero llevar unos jeans y un gorro durante el invierno.

Para y piensa
1. entiende; 2. prefiere; 3. quiere

229

Differentiating Instruction

Pre-AP

Expand and Elaborate Ask students to research information about a well-known Spanish or Latin American surrealist painter using the encyclopedia or the Internet. Key words for research: Roberto Matta (Chile), Remedios Varos (Mexico), Óscar Domínguez (Spain), Joan Miró (Spain). Have students share their findings.

Multiple Intelligences

Visual Learners Have students create a drawing that illustrates different clothing items using surrealist techniques. Students present their drawings to the class and describe it in terms of items depicted, colors and techniques.

Presentación de **GRAMÁTICA**

¡AVANZA! **Goal:** Learn how to use direct object pronouns. Then practice using them to talk about the clothes you wear and those you want to buy. *Actividades 13–18*

English Grammar Connection: Direct objects receive the action of the verb in a sentence. They answer the question *whom?* or *what?* about the verb. The direct object can be a **noun** or a **pronoun.**

Luisa is buying the **blouse.** Luisa is buying **it.** Luisa compra la **blusa.** Luisa **la** compra.

| noun | pronoun | | noun | pronoun |

Direct Object Pronouns

Animated Grammar
ClassZone.com

Direct object **pronouns** can be used to replace **direct object nouns.**

Here's how:

	Singular			Plural	
	me	me		nos	us
	te	you (familiar)		os	you (familiar)
masculine	lo	you (formal), him, it		los	you, them	masculine
feminine	la	you (formal), her, it		las	you, them	feminine

The **direct object noun** is placed *after* the **conjugated verb.**

The **direct object pronoun** is placed directly *before* the **conjugated verb.**

replaced by

Quiero la **camisa** azul. **La quiero.**
I want the blue **shirt.** *I want* **it.**

When an **infinitive** follows the **conjugated verb,** the **direct object pronoun** can be placed *before* the **conjugated verb** or be *attached* to the **infinitive.**

replaced by

Quiero comprar **zapatos** negros. Y **los quiero** comprar hoy.
I want to buy black **shoes.** *or* Y **quiero comprarlos** hoy.
And I want to buy **them** *today.*

Más práctica
Cuaderno *pp. 157–159*
Cuaderno para hispanohablantes *pp. 158–161*

@HomeTutor
Leveled Grammar Practice
ClassZone.com

· Present direct object pronouns.

Core Resource
· *Cuaderno,* pp. 157–159

Presentation Strategies
· Explain how direct object pronouns are used.
· Explain that when an infinitive follows the conjugated verb, the direct object pronoun can be placed before the conjugated verb or be attached to the infinitive.

STANDARDS
4.1 Compare languages

Warm Up   UTB 4 Transparency 18

Noun/Adjective Agreement Complete each sentence with the appropriate adjective.

| amarilla | blancos | rojas | negro |

1. Eduardo lleva unos calcetines _____.
2. Gloria lleva un vestido _____.
3. Los niños llevan unas chaquetas _____.
4. Yo quiero comprar una camiseta _____.

Answers: 1. blancos; 2. negro; 3.rojas; 4. amarilla

Comparisons
English Grammar Connection

Note that unlike English, direct object pronouns are usually placed before the conjugated verb in Spanish.
I buy them. **Yo los compro.**
In Spanish, a direct object pronoun must reflect the number and gender of the noun it replaces.
Quiero la camisa. La quiero. Quiero los zapatos. Los quiero.

Communication
Common Error Alert

If the direct object pronoun comes before a conjugated verb, add **no** before the pronoun to make the sentence negative. **No la quiero. No la quiero comprar.** If the direct object pronoun is attached to an infinitive, add **no** before the conjugated verb to make the sentence negative. **No quiero comprarlos.**

Differentiating Instruction

Multiple Intelligences

Kinesthetic Write on index cards each word of the following sentence: **Prefiero los zapatos negros, pero no los venden en la tienda.** Distribute the cards to different students and ask them to come to the front of the class and hold up the cards in scrambled order. Ask volunteers to arrange the students/cards in the correct order. Ask students to identify the direct object pronoun.

Slower-paced Learners

Yes/No Questions Use yes or no questions to provide students practice using direct object pronouns. Write each question and answer on the board. Circle each noun and pronoun, and draw a line connecting the two. **¿Quieres la blusa? Sí, la quiero. ¿Compras los jeans azules? Sí, los compro. ¿Prefieres las camisetas verdes? Sí, las prefiero.** Continue the activity using other questions.

Práctica de GRAMÁTICA

13 | Ropa para una fiesta

Leer | Maribel and her friend are talking about the clothes they want to buy for a party on Saturday. Complete their instant messages with the correct direct object pronouns.

> **mensajero instantáneo**
>
> **pelirroja16:** Quiero comprar un vestido azul pero no tengo mucho dinero. ¿ __1.__ (Lo/La) compro?
>
> **busco_rebaja:** Mmm... __2.__ (me/te) entiendo. Bueno, ¿cuánto cuesta el vestido?
>
> **pelirroja16:** Veintinueve euros. Y tú, ¿qué necesitas comprar? ¿Una blusa blanca?
>
> **busco_rebaja:** Ya __3.__ (la/los) tengo. Necesito unos zapatos. Los zapatos negros son más elegantes. ¿ __4.__ (Me/Os) entiendes?
>
> **pelirroja16:** Sí, tienes razón. Si quieres zapatos negros, __5.__ (nos/los) venden en la Tienda Betún.
>
> **busco_rebaja:** ¡Vale! También venden vestidos azules. __6.__ (Nos/Los) tienen por veinte euros.

Expansión:
Teacher Edition Only
Have students write what they and their friends prefer to wear to a party.

14 | Lo que Enrique quiere

Escribir | Use direct object pronouns to tell what Enrique wants or doesn't want to buy.

> **modelo:** No le gustan **los zapatos anaranjados.**
> No **los** quiere comprar. (No quiere comprar**los.**)

1. Los pantalones son feos.
2. No le gusta la camiseta.
3. Le gustan mucho las camisas.
4. Prefiere los calcetines verdes.
5. El sombrero es horrible.
6. Prefiere los zapatos azules.
7. No necesita pantalones cortos.
8. Prefiere la chaqueta blanca.
9. Le gusta el gorro rojo.
10. Los jeans son feos.

Expansión:
Teacher Edition Only
Have students rewrite each answer, changing the placement of the direct object pronoun.

Objectives
- Practice direct object pronouns.
- Practice lesson vocabulary.

Practice Sequence
- **Activity 13:** Controlled practice: direct object pronouns
- **Activity 14:** Transitional practice: direct object pronouns

 STANDARDS

1.3 Present information, Acts. 13–14

✓ Ongoing Assessment

Dictation Have students write the following as they are read aloud. Tell them to underline the direct object pronoun used in each sentence. Have students write sentences on the board when you are finished.
1. Marta va a comprarlos. 2. Yo la quiero comprar. 3 Los chicos prefieren jugarlo.
4. Tú las vas a escribir.

Answers MSRB Transparency 53

Activity 13

1. Lo	**3.** la	**5.** los
2. te	**4.** Me	**6.** Los

Activity 14
1. No los quiere comprar. (No quiere comprarlos.)
2. No la quiere comprar. (No quiere comprarla.)
3. Las quiere comprar. (Quiere comprarlas.)
4. Los quiere comprar. (Quiere comprarlos.)
5. No lo quiere comprar. (No quiere comprarlo.)
6. Los quiere comprar. (Quiere comprarlos.)
7. No los quiere comprar. (No quiere comprarlos.)
8. La quiere comprar. (Quiere comprarla.)
9. Lo quiere comprar. (Quiere comprarlo.)
10. No los quiere comprar. (No quiere comprarlos.)

Differentiating Instruction

Pre-AP

Self-correct As students choose the correct direct object pronoun in Activity 13, encourage them to read both of the possible choices aloud. Advise students to listen for the pronoun that agrees with the noun being replaced, and also makes sense in the context of the sentence.

Inclusion

Metacognitive Support After completing Activity 13, ask students to explain why they chose the direct object pronouns that they chose. Have them name the noun each pronoun refers to. Possible answer:
*I chose **lo** because the noun is **vestido,** which is masculine. **La** is incorrect because it is feminine.*

Objectives

· Practice direct object pronouns.
· **Culture:** Compare different climates.

Core Resource

· *Cuaderno,* pp. 157–159

Practice Sequence

· **Activity 15:** Transitional practice: direct object pronouns
· **Activities 16, 17:** Transitional practice: direct object pronouns, clothing
· **Activity 18:** Open-ended practice: direct object pronouns, seasons

STANDARDS

1.1 Engage in conversation, Acts. 15–18
1.3 Present information, Acts. 15–18
2.1 Practices and perspectives, Act. 18
4.2 Compare cultures, Act. 18

Answers MSRB Transparency 54

Activity 15

1. ¿Quién lleva unos zapatos marrones? Enrique los lleva.
2. ¿... una camisa roja? Enrique la lleva.
3. ¿... una chaqueta blanca? Enrique la lleva.
4. ¿... unos pantalones cortos azules? Maribel los lleva.
5. ¿... unos jeans negros? Enrique los lleva.
6. ¿Quién lleva ...?

Activity16

A: ¿Compra Martina la blusa (la camisa) verde?
B: Sí, Martina la compra.
A: ¿Compra Daniel los calcetines rojos y la chaqueta azul?
B: Sí, Daniel los compra.
A: ¿Compran Adriana y Andrea los gorros verdes?
B: No, Adriana y Andrea no los compran.
A: ¿Lleva el Sr. Costa el sombrero rojo?
B: Sí, el Sr. Costa lo lleva.
A: ¿Compra la Sra. Oliva los pantalones marrones?
B: Sí, la Sra. Oliva los compra.

232

---

15 | Unos modelos cómicos

Hablar

Enrique and Maribel are trying on all kinds of clothes at the store. Ask a partner about what they are wearing.

modelo: gorro

A ¿Quién lleva un **gorro verde**?

B Enrique **lo** lleva.

1. zapatos
2. camisa
3. chaqueta
4. pantalones cortos
5. jeans
6. ¿ ?

Expansión:
Teacher Edition Only
Have students write a paragraph about going shopping for clothing.

16 | En la tienda de ropa

Hablar

Ask a partner about what people are buying or wearing in the picture. Your partner will use direct object pronouns to answer.

A ¿Compra el señor Costa un sombrero rojo?

B Sí, el señor Costa lo compra.

la Sra. Oliva
el Sr. Costa
Martina
Daniel
Adriana
Andrea
Leonardo

Expansión:
Teacher Edition Only
Have student pairs talk about which items they would like to buy.

Differentiating Instruction

Slower-paced Learners

Yes/No Questions Before students ask and answer questions with a partner in Activity 15, give them this warm up. Ask a series of yes or no questions to help familiarize students with who is wearing what. **¿Lleva Enrique pantalones blancos? ¿Lleva Maribel un gorro negro?** Encourage students to correct the information when the answer is no. **No, Enrique lleva pantalones negros. Maribel lleva un sombrero negro.**

Heritage Language Learners

Support What They Know Encourage students to expand on their responses in Activity 16. Ask them to talk about why each person is purchasing the item shown. Why does Daniel need a new jacket? Why does Martina need a new blouse? Encourage students to be creative in their explanations.

17 | ¿Cuándo lo usas?

Hablar

Work with a partner to name as many situations as you can in which you use the following items.

modelo: un lápiz

A ¿Cuándo usas un lápiz?

B Lo uso cuando hago la tarea y cuando escribo.

Expansión:
Teacher Edition Only
Have student pairs talk about situations in which they do not use these items.

1. una chaqueta
2. el dinero
3. los pantalones cortos
4. un sombrero
5. una computadora
6. un gorro
7. el teléfono
8. un libro
9. una calculadora
10. un cuaderno

18 | ¿Qué llevas en julio?

Hablar

Comparación cultural

Climas diferentes

How does geography affect a country's climate? Countries near the equator have rainy and dry seasons, but have warm temperatures year-round. Countries in the northern and southern hemispheres have opposite seasons. For example, in **Spain,** July is a summer month and the weather is often hot, but in **Chile** it is a winter month. Chile's varied terrain, from beaches to mountains, and length (over 2,600 miles) create many different climates.

Compara con tu mundo
How does the geography of your area affect the climate? Is there a large body of water or a mountain range that influences the weather?

Ask a partner about the clothing items he or she wears in the following places in July: Chile, Mexico, Spain, Puerto Rico, Argentina, and New York.

Barcelona, España

Los Andes en Chile

A ¿Llevas una camiseta en Chile en julio?

B No, no la llevo. Llevo una chaqueta y...

Más práctica Cuaderno pp. 157–159 Cuaderno para hispanohablantes pp. 158–161

PARA Y PIENSA

Did you get it? In each sentence, use the correct direct object pronoun.
1. Luisa quiere los pantalones blancos. Ella _____ compra.
2. No quiero la blusa nueva. ¿ _____ quieres tú?
3. Nosotros preferimos las camisas azules. _____ compramos.

Get Help Online ClassZone.com

Lección 1
doscientos treinta y tres **233**

Differentiating Instruction

Multiple Intelligences

Naturalist Organize students into small groups, and assign each group one of the countries listed in Activity 18. Tell students to use their prior knowledge, information from the text, or other research to create a depiction of an outdoor scene in their country in the month of July. Have them write labels and captions in Spanish to describe the climate and what people wear.

Pre-AP

Expand and Elaborate Have students research the climate and geography of one of the countries mentioned in Activity 18 using an encyclopedia or the Internet. Students should include specific information such as the name of the continent where the country is located, longitude, latitude, topographical information, average annual temperatures, and average precipitation.

Comparación cultural

Essential Question

Suggested Answer The physical features of our planet such as mountains, valleys, rivers, lakes, oceans, desert, rain forests, etc., have a great impact on weather patterns.

Expanded Information

Spain is surrounded by the Atlantic Ocean and the Mediterranean Sea, while the country's interior is high and mountainous. These factors give Spain the most varied climate in Europe. **Chile** also has a varied climate. The country stretches 1,800 miles from north to south. It rises from the Pacific Ocean to the Andes mountains, which cover one third of the country.

✓ Ongoing Assessment

@HomeTutor
More Practice
ClassZone.com

PARA Y PIENSA **Quick Check** Say five sentences starting with **Quiero...** followed by an item of clothing and have students repeat them replacing the direct object with a corresponding object pronoun. Example: **Quiero las camisetas. Las quiero.** For additional practice, use Reteaching & Practice Copymasters URB 4, pp. 7, 8.

Answers MSRB Transparency 54

Activity 17
1. ¿Cuándo usas una chaqueta?
   La uso cuando hace frío.
2. ¿Cuándo usas el dinero?
   Lo uso cuando voy de compras.
3. ¿Cuándo usas los pantalones cortos?
   Los uso en el verano o cuando hace calor.
4. ¿Cuándo usas un sombrero?
   Lo uso cuando hace sol.
5. ¿Cuándo usas la computadora?
   La uso cuando hago la tarea.
6. ¿Cuándo usas un gorro?
   Lo uso cuando hace frío o en el invierno.
7. ¿Cuándo usas el teléfono?
   Lo uso cuando hablo con mis amigos.
8. ¿Cuándo usas un libro?
   Lo uso cuando quiero leer.
9. ¿Cuándo usas la calculadora?
   La uso en la clase de matemáticas.
10. ¿Cuándo usas un cuaderno?
    Lo uso cuando tomo apuntes.

Activity 18 Answers will vary. Sample answers:
¿Llevas pantalones cortos en Argentina en julio? No, llevo una chaqueta y un gorro.

Para y piensa 1. los; 2. La; 3. Las

233

¡AVANZA! Objective

· Integrate lesson content.

Core Resources

· Video Program: DVD 1
· Audio Program: TXT CD 4 tracks 3, 5, 7

Presentation Strategies

· Have students read the Resumen from Escena 1 and Escena 2 to review background information.
· Ask a few quick comprehension questions about the Escena 3 photo. ¿Quiénes están en la foto? ¿Qué tiene la vendedora?
· Show the video or play the audio.

Practice Sequence

· **Activities 19–20:** Telehistoria comprehension
· **Activity 21:** Open-ended practice: speaking

STANDARDS

1.1 Engage in conversation, Act. 21
1.2 Understand language, Acts. 19–20
1.3 Present information, Act. 21

 Warm Up UTB 4 Transparency 18

Direct Object Pronouns Complete each sentence with **lo, la, los** or **las.**

1. ¿La chaqueta azul? _____ quiero comprar.
2. ¿Unos jeans negros? No _____ compro.
3. ¿El vestido rojo? No _____ tengo.

Answers: 1. La; 2. los; 3. lo

Video Summary

@HomeTutor VideoPlus ClassZone.com

Although Maribel has her eye on the time and is eager to leave the clothing store, Enrique continues to look at different items and ask how much they cost. When it finally comes time to pay, Enrique realizes he has neither his money nor his backpack and asks Maribel if she has any money.

234

 ¡AVANZA!

Goal: *Show what you know* Listen to Maribel and Enrique talk to the salesclerk about what Enrique wants to buy. Then use **e → ie** stem-changing verbs and direct object pronouns to talk about clothing preferences. ***Actividades 19–23***

Todo junto

Telehistoria completa

@HomeTutor VideoPlus ClassZone.com

STRATEGIES

Cuando lees
Discover what's forgotten Enrique forgets something in this scene. Find out what he forgot. How does this create a problem?

Cuando escuchas
Take the "emotional temperature" Find out who has the greatest intensity of feeling by listening to voices. Who is the most upset and why?

Escena 1 *Resumen*
Maribel tiene que ir al centro comercial porque necesita el autógrafo de Trini. Pero Enrique quiere ir de compras en una tienda.

Escena 2 *Resumen*
Enrique y Maribel están en una tienda, y Enrique quiere comprar mucha ropa. Maribel prefiere ir al centro comercial.

VIDEO DVD

AUDIO

Escena 3

Maribel: Enrique, tienes que pagar. Son las once y media.
Enrique: Un gorro verde. ¡Lo quiero comprar! ¡Tengo que comprarlo!
Maribel: Enrique, ¡pero tú ya tienes un gorro verde!
Enrique: Sí, pero nunca lo llevo.
Maribel: Quieres una chaqueta, ¿no?

Enrique: Tienes razón. La chaqueta... la necesito. *(to the salesclerk)* ¿Vende chaquetas?
Vendedora: ¿En verano? No. Las vendo en el otoño.
Enrique: ¿Cuánto cuesta todo?
Vendedora: Los pantalones cuestan treinta euros, la camisa cuesta veinticinco, y el gorro, quince. Son setenta euros.
Enrique: ¡Mi dinero! ¡No lo tengo!

Maribel: ¡No te entiendo! ¿Quieres ir de compras y no tienes dinero?
Enrique: Está en mi mochila. ¿Dónde está mi mochila? ¿Tienes dinero? En el centro comercial yo compro la comida.
Maribel: ¿Con qué piensas pagar? No tienes dinero.

Unidad 4 España
234 doscientos treinta y cuatro

Differentiating Instruction

Heritage Language Learners

Support What They Know Ask students to recall the problem Enrique has at the end of the Telehistoria. Then encourage them to share an experience they've had in which they lost something important. Have them explain what they lost, why it was important, and what they did to resolve the situation.

Multiple Intelligences

Interpersonal Have students read through the Telehistoria twice silently. The first time, instruct them to read the script for meaning. The second time, tell them to read the script for emotion. Then have volunteers take turns reading lines aloud, emphasizing the emotional tone. Have students name the emotion expressed in each line.

19 | ¿Cierto o falso? *Comprensión de los episodios*

Escuchar
Leer

Read the sentences and say whether they are true or false. Correct the false statements.

1. Enrique piensa que los precios son buenos en el centro comercial.
2. Maribel prefiere llegar al centro comercial a las doce.
3. Maribel necesita comprar una chaqueta.
4. Enrique tiene setenta euros para comprar su ropa.
5. A Maribel le gusta ser diferente.
6. Enrique prefiere llevar una chaqueta en el invierno.
7. Enrique compra una chaqueta en la tienda de ropa.

Expansión:
Teacher Edition Only
Have students write two additional false statements about the three scenes, exchange them with their partners and have each other correct them.

20 | Analizar la historia *Comprensión de los episodios*

Escuchar
Leer

Answer the questions about the episodes in complete sentences.

1. ¿Qué estación es?
2. ¿Dónde quiere comprar ropa Enrique?
3. ¿De qué color es el gorro?
4. ¿Cuánto cuestan los pantalones? ¿La camisa? ¿El gorro?
5. ¿Qué problema tiene Enrique?

Expansión:
Teacher Edition Only
Have students write a summary of what happens in the Telehistoria.

21 | ¡A jugar! Un juego de quién

Hablar

STRATEGY Hablar

Prepare and don't stress out Create a list of useful questions and possible answers. Include various types of clothes. Review your verb endings. Then just talk!

Work in a group of three. Give a clue about someone in your Spanish class. The other members of your group will ask you yes/no questions to identify who it is. Follow the model.

Expansión:
Teacher Edition Only
Ask students to write about the color and type of clothing they are wearing.

Rubric Activity 21

Speaking Criteria	Maximum Credit	Partial Credit	Minimum Credit
Content	Questions and answers include a variety of vocabulary. Clues are clear.	Questions and answers do not include enough vocabulary. Clues are somewhat clear.	Questions and answers are not complete. Clues are not clear.
Communi-cation	Easy to follow.	Somewhat easy to follow.	Hard to follow.
Accuracy	Few mistakes in grammar and vocabulary.	Some mistakes in grammar and vocabulary.	Many mistakes in grammar and vocabulary.

Answers MSRB Transparency 54

Activity 19
1. Falso. ... los precios no son buenos en el....
2. Cierto.
3. Falso. Enrique....
4. Falso. Enrique no tiene dinero.
5. Falso. A Enrique le gusta ser diferente.
6. Falso. ... una chaqueta en el verano.
7. Falso. Enrique compra unos pantalones...

Activity 20
1. Es el verano.
2. Enrique quiere comprar ropa en una tienda.
3. El gorro es verde.
4. Los pantalones cuestan treinta euros. La camisa cuesta veinticinco euros. El gorro cuesta quince euros.
5. Enrique no tiene dinero.

Activity 21 Answers will vary. Sample answers:
Estudiante A: Lleva unos jeans azules.
Estudiante B: ¿Tiene una camiseta blanca?
Estudiante A: Sí, la tiene. (No, no la tiene.)
Estudiante C: ¿Lleva unos calcetines rojos?
Estudiante A: Sí, los lleva. (No, no los lleva.)
Estudiante B: ¿Es Justin?
Estudiante A: ¡Sí, tienes razón! (No, no tienes razón.)

Differentiating Instruction

Slower-paced Learners

Sentence Completion Before students complete Activity 20, help them convert each question into the beginning of a sentence. Then have them find the information to complete the sentence. Here are a few examples:
¿Qué estación es? La estación es _____.
¿Dónde quiere comprar ropa Enrique?
Enrique quiere comprar ropa en _____.

Pre-AP

Expand and Elaborate Once students guess the correct person in Activity 21, ask them to take turns creating a descriptive sentence about the person in question. Remind students to use vocabulary related to clothing, as well as personal traits, favorite activities, and emotions. The goal is to keep the description going as long as possible.

Objective

· Practice using and integrating lesson vocabulary and grammar.

Core Resources

· *Cuaderno*, pp. 160–161
· Audio Program: TXT CD 4 tracks 8, 9

Practice Sequence

· **Activity 22:** Open-ended practice: reading, listening, speaking
· **Activity 23:** Open-ended practice: writing

 STANDARD

1.3 Present information, Acts. 22, 23

Long-term Retention

Pre-AP Integration

Assign students to create an ad for clothing similar to the one in Activity 22. Ask them to provide prices in euros for each item. Have them exchange the ad with a partner. Each student will describe the items he or she wants to buy, for whom and how much each item costs.

✓ **Ongoing Assessment**

Rubric Activity 22 Listening/Speaking

Proficient	Not There Yet
Student takes detailed notes and correctly describes the items and how much they cost.	Student takes few notes and cannot describe the items and how much they cost.

✓ **Ongoing Assessment**

@HomeTutor
More Practice
ClassZone.com

PARA Y PIENSA **Remediation** If students have difficulty answering the Para y piensa questions, ask them to review the Telehistoria on p. 234. For additional practice, use Reteaching & Practice Copymasters URB 4, pp. 7, 9.

See Activity answers on p. 237.

236

---

22 | Integración

Leer
Escuchar
Hablar

Read the discount coupon and listen to the store ad. Describe four items you want to buy for your friends and how much each item costs.

🎧 **Audio Program**
TXT CD 4 Tracks 8, 9
Audio Script, TE p. 215b

Fuente 1 Cupón

ALTA MODA
¡Descuentos de otoño!

Ropa de chicos
· pantalones
· chaquetas
· jeans
Descuento de 5€

Ropa de chicas
· zapatos
· blusas
· vestidos
Descuento de 10€

Calle Toro, 38 · Avenida de las Américas, 440 · Madrid

Fuente 2 Anuncio

Listen and take notes
· ¿Qué venden en la tienda?
· ¿Cuánto cuesta la ropa?

modelo: Quiero comprar un vestido verde para Emily. Cuesta...

Expansión:
Teacher Edition Only
Have students talk about three items in the ad or the coupon that they don't want to buy.

---

23 | Un poema de la estación

Escribir

Write a poem about one of the seasons. Include the following elements.

Para organizarte:

· *el nombre de la estación* ——→ verano
· *dos colores que describen la estación* ——→ verde, azul
· *tres cosas que quieres* ——→ quiero zapatos, helado, camisetas
· *cuatro actividades que prefieres hacer* ——→ prefiero jugar, pasear, leer, descansar
· *una descripción de cómo estás* ——→ tengo calor

modelo:

Writing Criteria	Excellent	Good	Needs Work
Content	Your poem includes all of the elements.	Your poem includes some of the elements.	Your poem includes a few of the elements.
Communication	Most of your poem is easy to follow.	Parts of your poem are easy to follow.	Your poem is hard to follow.
Accuracy	Your poem has very few mistakes in grammar and vocabulary.	Your poem has some mistakes in grammar and vocabulary.	Your poem has many mistakes in grammar and vocabulary.

Expansión:
Teacher Edition Only
Have students display their poems on visuals that reflect what they have expressed.

Más práctica Cuaderno *pp. 160–161* Cuaderno para hispanohablantes *pp. 162–163*

 PARA Y PIENSA

Did you get it? Answer each question based on the Telehistoria with **sí,** using direct object pronouns.
1. ¿Necesita Enrique la chaqueta?
2. ¿Prefiere Enrique el gorro verde?
3. ¿Quiere comprar Enrique la comida?

Get Help Online
ClassZone.com

Differentiating Instruction

Inclusion

Multisensory Input/Output Before doing Activity 22, have them read the script as they listen to the announcement. Help them take notes by listing first the items on sale for boys and next the items on sale for girls. Ask comprehension questions about what they have written. For example: **¿Qué ropa venden para chicos? ¿Qué ropa venden para chicas?** Use these same questions for the coupon.

Multiple Intelligences

Musical/Rhythmic As students compose their poems, remind them to consider the sound and rhythm of the words they choose. They might focus on similar beginning sounds: **verano, verde.** Or they might create a pattern with endings: **quiero jugar, pasear, descansar.** Perhaps they want to create contrast with the sounds and rhythms they choose. Allow them to read their poetry aloud.

Juegos y diversiones

Review vocabulary by playing a game.

Pasa la bola

The Setup

Everyone should stand up and form a circle.

Materials
- small foam ball
- stopwatch or clock

Playing the Game

First: One of you will start by saying a vocabulary word from this lesson and tossing a small foam ball to another player. The player catching the ball will have five seconds to think of a word in the same category as the one just said (another color, clothing item, shopping word, or season). Your teacher will be the timekeeper and judge.

Then: Once the player has thought of a word and said it correctly, he or she will toss the ball to another player. That player then has to come up with another word in the same category as the first player's word. Players who cannot think of a valid answer in the allotted time must sit down.

The Winner!

The winner is the last person standing.

dinero

precio

Lección 1
doscientos treinta y siete **237**

Objective
· To review vocabulary by playing a game.

STANDARD
5.2 Life-long learners

Communication
Group Work

Game If your class is too big to have one big circle, try having smaller circles of seven or eight students. Appoint a student to be judge and timekeeper for each circle. The student who catches the ball can't throw it back to the same person.

You could also have one smaller circle at a time. The winner of each first-round game would go on to the finals. You may want to expand the rules to allow any related word. For example, **invierno** could lead to **gorro**.

Long-term Retention
Recycle

Have students brainstorm various categories of vocabulary from previous units: after-school activities, foods, family members, and so on; then play the game with these words.

Communication
Humor/Creativity

Game Write a phrase vertically on each side of the board, such as **tienda de ropa.** Divide students into two teams and line up each team in front of the phrase they will be using. Beginning with the top letter, students should go to the board and write any Spanish word that begins with the letter. For example, the first student writes a word containing the letter **t.** The next person writes a word containing **i.** The first team to complete the relay with all words spelled correctly wins.

Answers MSRB Transparency 54

Answers for Activities on p. 236.
Activity 22 Answers will vary.
Activity 23 Answers will vary.
Para y piensa
1. Sí, Enrique la necesita. 2. Sí, lo prefiere.
3. Sí, la quiere comprar. / Sí, Enrique quiere comprarla.

237

Differentiating Instruction

Pre-AP

Timed Response Add excitement to **Pasa la bola** by decreasing the time limit with each round. Give students five seconds to think of a word in the first round. In the second round of play, limit their response time to four seconds. Decrease the time limit by one second with each round.

Multiple Intelligences

Interpersonal Give individual volunteers the opportunity to play the part of the timekeeper and judge in **Pasa la bola.** Remind leaders that they must listen carefully in order to judge whether words do or do not fit into the category. Tell leaders they are also responsible for respectfully telling their classmates when they are out of the game and must sit down.

¡AVANZA! **Goal:** Read a poem by a Spanish poet. Then talk about what you have read and describe winter in your region.

¡AVANZA! Objectives

· Learn about Spanish poet Antonio Colinas.
· Discuss the poet's feelings about winter.
· Compare a description of winter in a poem with winter in your own region.

Core Resource

· Audio Program: TXT CD 4 track 10

Presentation Strategies

· Play the audio as students read and listen to the poem.
· Ask students to take turns reading the poem lines. Correct pronunciation as needed.
· Ask students to think about how Colinas uses nature (animals, plants, weather) to express his thoughts.

STANDARDS

1.2 Understand language
2.1 Practices and perspectives
4.1 Compare languages
4.2 Compare cultures

Warm Up UTB 4 Transparency 19

Direct Object Pronouns Complete the sentences by choosing the correct direct object pronoun.
1. Quiero la camiseta verde. ¿(Lo / La) compro?
2. ¿Quieres calcetines rojos? (Las / Los) venden en la Tienda Ramón.
3. No quiero el gorro. ¿(Me / Lo) quieres tú?
4. No (te / nos) entiendo. ¿No tienes el dinero?

Answers: 1. La; 2. Los; 3. Lo; 4. te

Culture

Background Information

El Premio Nacional de Literatura en la modalidad de Poesía is awarded annually in Spain to a poet whose work has been published in Spain in the year preceding the award. A panel of distinguished judges selects the winner, who receives 15,000 euros in addition to being honored with this prestigious title. It is comparable to the Pulitzer Prize in the U.S.

AUDIO

Las memorias del invierno

Antonio Colinas is a poet and novelist from León, in northern Spain. He published the following poem in 1988.

STRATEGY Leer
Find the feelings Find phrases that show the poet's feelings and write them in a chart like the one below. Write the feeling after each phrase.

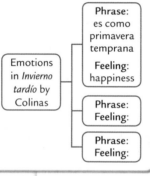

Emotions in *Invierno tardío* by Colinas

Phrase: es como primavera temprana
Feeling: happiness

Phrase:
Feeling:

Phrase:
Feeling:

Antonio Colinas nació[1] en 1946 en La Bañeza, en la provincia de León, España. Escribe poesía, novelas, ensayos[2] y crítica. También estudia literatura italiana y la adapta al español. Su poesía ha ganado[3] muchos premios[4] en España, como el Premio Nacional de Literatura, en 1982. Ahora vive en Salamanca, España.

[1] was born   [2] essays   [3] has won   [4] awards

238   Unidad 4 España
doscientos treinta y ocho

Differentiating Instruction

English Learners

Increase Interaction Ask English learners to work on the strategy with native English speakers. Have them create a chart together and write the name of each feeling or emotion in English and the English learner's native language.

Heritage Language Learners

Literacy Skills Encourage students to expand their vocabulary by asking them to search in a Spanish dictionary for examples of words that belong to the same family as words in the poem. Ask: **¿Qué palabra es similar a tardío? (tarde) ¿A nieve o nieva? (nevar, nevada) ¿A florido? (flor) ¿A humanidad? (humano)**

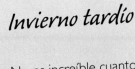

Invierno tardío

No es increíble cuanto ven mis ojos [5]:

nieva sobre el almendro florido [6],

nieva sobre la nieve.

Este invierno mi ánimo [7]

es como primavera temprana,

es como almendro florido

bajo la nieve.

Hay demasiado [8] frío

esta tarde en el mundo [9].

Pero abro la puerta a mi perro

y con él entra en casa [10] calor,

entra la humanidad.

---

[5] **ven...** my eyes see
[6] **sobre...** on the flowery almond tree
[7] spirit   [8] too much   [9] world   [10] house

~56~

PARA Y PIENSA

¿Comprendiste?

1. ¿De dónde es Antonio Colinas? ¿Qué escribe? ¿Dónde vive ahora?
2. ¿Dónde está la persona en el poema? ¿Qué mira? En tu opinión, ¿está triste o contenta la persona?
3. ¿Piensas que el perro es un buen amigo? ¿Por qué?

¿Y tú?
¿Cómo es el invierno en tu región? ¿Qué te gusta hacer?

Lección 1
doscientos treinta y nueve   **239**

Differentiating Instruction

Pre-AP

Summarize Ask students to write a brief summary of *Invierno tardío*. Encourage them to include as many details as possible, including what the poem is about, how the author feels, and how it makes them feel.

Multiple Intelligences

Naturalist Give students the following questions about flowering almond trees and ask them to research the answers. **¿Dónde hay almendros? ¿De qué color son?** Then ask them to choose a plant or flower in their region and describe what happens to it in winter.

Cognates Ask students to search the poem for words that have English cognates, and to list the cognate pairs on the board. They should include: **increíble, humanidad.**

Communication
Pair Work

Cut the poem into separate lines. Present the poem in this fashion to pairs of students and ask them to order the lines. After they have finished and presented their work, ask them to read the original version. Discuss the differences with the class.

Long-term Retention
Personalize It

Present to the class the concept of simile, a figure of speech expressing comparison by the use of the terms *like* or *as*. Point to the word **como** in the poem and explain that without the accent this word means *like*. Ask students to find examples of similes in the poem. Then have them compose their own simile about winter starting with the following phrase. **Este invierno mi ánimo es como...**

Answers

Para y piensa
¿Comprendiste?
1. Antonio Colinas es de la provincia de León, España. Él escribe poesía, novelas, ensayos y crítica. Vive en Salamanca, España.
2. Está en casa. Mira el almendro y la nieve. Está contenta.
3. Sí, el perro es un buen amigo porque con él entra la humanidad en casa.

¿Y tú? Answers will vary. Sample answer: Hace mucho frío en el invierno en mi región. Me gusta estar en casa, descansar y mirar la televisión.

239

Objectives
- Learn about the history of the Moors in Spain.
- Read about the distinctive decorative styles of the Alhambra.
- Use perspectives from music, health, and language to better understand the Arab legacy in Spain.

Presentation Strategies
- Ask if students are aware of the relationship between Arab Muslims and Spain.
- Draw students' attention to the pictures, and ask them to reflect on the architectural style.

STANDARDS
1.3 Present information
3.1 Knowledge of other disciplines
3.2 Acquire information

Connections

La historia

The *oud*, ancestor of the guitar, has an ancient history, and has been traced to 1600 B.C. in Mesopotamia. In the 9th century A.D., the instrument was used in healing, and it is believed that it was used this way in Arab Spain during the 11th century. It was thought to be invigorating, at the same time bringing harmony to the body and the heart.

Answers

Conexiones Students can create their design by drawing, building a model, or using computer software.

Proyecto 1 At the core of the group Al-Andalus are Tarik Banzi and Julia Banzi. Their music is inspired by the music of Moorish Spain from the 8th to 15th centuries. They play in various locations, including museums, concert halls, international festivals, embassies, and colleges. Examples: 1991 Portland Classical Guitar Festival, Smithsonian Institute, Embassy of Egypt in Washington, D.C.

Proyecto 2 Olive oil is used as a moisturizer by many. It is also considered a healthy cooking oil.

Proyecto 3
almohada – pillow; **álgebra** – algebra; **algodón** – cotton; **ajedrez** – chess; **alcachofa** – artichoke; **azúcar** – sugar.

240

Conexiones *El arte*

Los árabes en España

For almost 800 years, from 711 to 1492, the Moors, Arab Muslims from northern Africa, occupied an area in southern Spain called **Al-Andalus,** now known as **Andalucía.** This was a period of rich cultural exchange in the arts, sciences, mathematics, agriculture, and architecture.

The Alhambra palace in Granada is a notable example of Moorish architecture in Spain. The interior is exquisitely detailed, bright, and airy. Ornately carved pillars and arches open onto sunny courtyards. The walls and ceilings are decorated with intricate geometric designs.

Design a courtyard based on the architectural styles illustrated in these pictures of the Alhambra. Create a drawing or model to show your design.

El patio de los leones

La Alhambra

Un arco musulmán

Los jardines del Generalife

Proyecto 1 *La música*

Moorish civilization had a lasting influence on the music of Spain. The guitar may be derived from the oud, a type of lute and a classic Arab instrument. The word **guitarra** comes from the Arabic *qithara.* Some contemporary music is similar to the music played during the Moorish rule. Research and write about the musical group *Al-Andalus.* Include the members of the group, the places where they perform, and a description of their music.

Proyecto 2 *La salud*

Olives have always been a part of Spanish tradition. Olive seeds that date back 8,000 years have been found in Spain. The majority of olive trees grown in the country are found in **Andalucía.** Spain is also one of the world's foremost producers of olive oil. Research and write about the health and beauty benefits of olives and olive oil. Describe how they are used on a daily basis.

Proyecto 3 *El lenguaje*

The Moors brought many concepts and inventions to Spain. The Arabic words for many of these things still exist in Spanish. Often these words begin with **al-** or **a-.** Some examples are **almohada, álgebra, algodón,** and **ajedrez.** Using a Spanish-English dictionary, write the meanings of these words. Then find three more Spanish words that begin with **al-,** write their English definitions, and use the Internet or the library to find out if they have Arabic origin.

Differentiating Instruction

English Learners

Increase Interaction Have students take turns reading the Conexiones aloud. After each paragraph, ask them to list any words that they don't understand and clarify their meaning. Then ask brief questions to check comprehension. For example: For how many years did the Moors occupy Spain? Where is **Andalucía?** Where is the Alhambra?

Pre-AP

Expand and Elaborate Ask students to work in groups to research on the Internet additional information about the Moors and their occupation of Spain and to construct a timeline starting with the year 711 and ending in 1492, listing additional important dates and significant events. Have them provide a brief description of what happened on each date. Search Key Words: Moors + Spain.

LECCIÓN 1

En resumen
Vocabulario y gramática

Animated Grammar

Interactive Flashcards
ClassZone.com

Vocabulario

Talk About Shopping			
el centro comercial	shopping center, mall	el dólar	dollar
¿Cuánto cuesta(n)?	How much does it (do they) cost?	el euro	euro
		ir de compras	to go shopping
Cuesta(n)...	It costs . . . (They cost . . .)	pagar	to pay
		el precio	price
el dinero	money	la tienda	store

Describe Clothing			
la blusa	blouse	nuevo(a)	new
los calcetines	socks	los pantalones	pants
la camisa	shirt	los pantalones cortos	shorts
la camiseta	T-shirt		
la chaqueta	jacket	la ropa	clothing
feo(a)	ugly	el sombrero	hat
el gorro	winter hat	el vestido	dress
los jeans	jeans	los zapatos	shoes
llevar	to wear		

Colors

amarillo(a)	yellow	marrón (pl. marrones)	brown
anaranjado(a)	orange		
azul	blue	negro(a)	black
blanco(a)	white	rojo(a)	red
		verde	green

Expressions with tener	
tener calor	to be hot
tener frío	to be cold
tener razón	to be right
tener suerte	to be lucky

Discuss Seasons	
la estación (pl. las estaciones)	season
el invierno	winter
el otoño	autumn, fall
la primavera	spring
el verano	summer

Other Words and Phrases	
durante	during
cerrar (ie)	to close
empezar (ie)	to begin
entender (ie)	to understand
pensar (ie)	to think, to plan
preferir (ie)	to prefer
querer (ie)	to want

Gramática

Nota gramatical: tener expressions p. 223

Stem-Changing Verbs: e → ie

For e → ie stem-changing verbs, the e of the stem changes to **ie** in all forms except **nosotros(as)** and **vosotros(as)**.

querer	to want
quiero	queremos
quieres	queréis
quiere	quieren

Direct Object Pronouns

Direct object **pronouns** can be used to replace direct object nouns.

	Singular		Plural
me	me	nos	us
te	you (familiar)	os	you (familiar)
lo	you (formal), him, it	los	you, them
la	you (formal), her, it	las	you, them

Lección 1
doscientos cuarenta y uno **241**

Objective
· Review lesson grammar and vocabulary.

Core Resources
· *Cuaderno*, pp. 162–173
· Audio Program: TXT CD 4 track 11

Presentation Strategies
· Before playing the audio for Activity 1, ask students to listen to it carefully and pay special attention to the articles of clothing Paula mentions.
· Before doing Activities 2–4 review stem-changing **e → ie** verbs by saying a subject followed by an infinitive and asking students to supply the correct verb form. For example: **tú: empezar → tú empiezas.**
· For Activity 3, remind students that the season often determines what you wear.
· Ask students to generate two questions to ask their classmates, based on the Comparación cultural.

STANDARDS
1.2 Understand language, Act. 1
1.3 Present information, Acts. 2–5
4.2 Compare cultures, Act. 5

Warm Up UTB 4 Transparency 19

Querer Fill in the blanks with the appropriate forms of **querer.**
1. Nosotros _____ los pantalones cortos.
2. Yo _____ el gorro rojo.
3. Tú _____ la camiseta amarilla.
4. María _____ la chaqueta azul.
5. Ustedes _____ los calcetines verdes.

Answers: 1. queremos; 2. quiero; 3. quieres; 4. quiere; 5. quieren

√ **Ongoing Assessment**
@HomeTutor More Practice ClassZone.com

Remediation If students achieve less than 80% accuracy with the activities, direct them to review pp. 215, 223–224, 229–230, 233, 238–239 and to get help online at ClassZone.com.

See Activity answers on p. 243.

242

Lección **1**
Repaso de la lección

¡LLEGADA!

@HomeTutor
ClassZone.com

Now you can
· talk about what clothes you want to buy
· say what you wear in different seasons

Using
· **tener** expressions
· stem-changing verbs: **e → ie**
· direct object pronouns

To review
· stem-changing verbs: **e → ie** p. 224
· direct object pronouns p. 230

1 Listen and understand

AUDIO

Listen to Paula talk about clothes. Tell whether she wants to buy each article of clothing or not. Use direct object pronouns.

1.
2.
3.
4.
5.
6.

Audio Program
TXT CD 4 Track 11 Audio Script, TE p. 215b

To review
· stem-changing verbs: **e → ie** p. 224

2 Talk about what clothes you want to buy

Fernando is going shopping with his parents. What does he say?

preferir cerrar entender
empezar pensar querer

Las clases __1.__ el lunes y necesito ropa. Yo __2.__ comprar unas camisetas y unos pantalones pero no tengo mucho dinero. Yo __3.__ las camisetas a las camisas. Yo no __4.__ por qué una camiseta cuesta más en el centro comercial que en otras tiendas. Mi amiga Carla __5.__ que hay ropa más bonita y menos cara en la tienda Moda Zaragoza. Necesito ir hoy porque la tienda __6.__ los domingos.

Differentiating Instruction

Slower-paced Learners

Personalize It Ask students to adapt and rewrite Activity 2 by adding the names of people and stores they know, by using the name of their favorite mall, and by talking about clothing they have recently bought or plan to buy soon.

Pre-AP

Circumlocution Ask students to look up additional items of clothing in a Spanish-English dictionary. For example: **suéter** (sweater), **sandalias** (sandals), **tenis** (sneakers), etc. Ask them to describe the clothing in Spanish so that their classmates understand, and then refer to those items with pronouns. For example: **Las sandalias son zapatos. Las llevo en el verano.**

3 | Talk about what clothes you want to buy

To review
• **tener** expressions p. 223
• stem-changing verbs: **e → ie** p. 224

Tell whether these people are hot or cold, based on what they are thinking about buying.

modelo: Ana / blusa de verano

Ana piensa comprar una blusa de verano porque tiene calor.

1. Juan y yo / gorros
2. yo / pantalones cortos
3. tú / chaqueta
4. Laura y Carlos / camisetas de verano
5. ustedes / calcetines de invierno
6. Pilar / vestido de primavera

4 | Say what you wear in different seasons

To review
• direct object pronouns p. 230

Write sentences telling who prefers to wear these clothing items.

modelo: los zapatos negros (Juan)

Juan los prefiere llevar. (Juan prefiere llevarlos.)

1. los pantalones cortos (Rosa)
2. las camisas azules (ellas)
3. el sombrero rojo (yo)
4. la camiseta anaranjada (Carlos)
5. el gorro negro (ellos)
6. la blusa amarilla (nosotras)
7. los calcetines blancos (ustedes)
8. la chaqueta marrón (tú)
9. los zapatos marrones (usted)
10. el vestido verde (Amanda)

5 | Spain and Chile

To review
• **Sevillanas** p. 215
• Comparación cultural pp. 229, 233
• Lectura pp. 238–239

Comparación cultural

Answer these culture questions.

1. What are the characteristics of **sevillanas**?
2. How do the climates of Spain and Chile differ in July and why?
3. What are some characteristics of surrealist art?
4. What season is represented in Antonio Colinas' poem? How does the speaker of the poem feel and why?

Más práctica Cuaderno *pp. 162–173* Cuaderno para hispanohablantes *pp. 164–173*

 **Get Help Online** ClassZone.com

✔ Ongoing Assessment

Alternative Strategy Have students redo Activity 4, replacing the verb **preferir** with **pensar** or **querer** and using different clothing items. For example: **los pantalones verdes (Juan)—Juan los piensa llevar. (Juan piensa llevarlos.)**

Answers MSRB Transparencies 54–55

Answers for Activities on pp. 242, 243.

Activity 1
1. Ella no quiere comprarlos.
2. Ella quiere comprarla.
3. Ella no quiere comprarlo.
4. Ella quiere comprarlos.
5. Ella no quiere comprarla.
6. Ella quiere comprarlo.

Activity 2
1. empiezan
2. quiero
3. prefiero
4. entiendo
5. piensa
6. cierra

Activity 3
1. Juan y yo pensamos comprar unos gorros porque tenemos frío.
2. Yo pienso comprar unos... porque tengo calor.
3. Tú piensas comprar una... porque tienes frío.
4. ...piensan comprar unas... porque tienen calor.
5. ...piensan comprar unos... porque tienen frío.
6. ...piensa comprar un... porque tiene calor.

Activity 4
1. Rosa los prefiere llevar.
2. Ellas las prefieren llevar.
3. Yo lo prefiero llevar.
4. Carlos la prefiere llevar.
5. Ellos lo prefieren llevar.
6. Nosotras la preferimos llevar.
7. Ustedes los prefieren llevar.
8. Tú la prefieres llevar.
9. Usted los prefiere llevar.
10. Amanda lo prefiere llevar.

Activity 5
1. **Sevillanas** are similar to **flamenco**, which involves singing, dance, and guitar as well as rhythmic clapping or foot taps.
2. The climates of Spain and Chile differ in July because these countries are located in different hemispheres. In Spain July is a summer month, but in Chile it is a winter month.
3. In surrealist art, the imagery reflects an artist's imagination and is often inspired by dreams.
4. The season represented in Antonio Colinas' poem is winter. The speaker of the poem feels happy because it feels like early spring.

Differentiating Instruction

Heritage Language Learners

Support What They Know Ask students which fashion magazines in Spanish are popular among teens in their country of origin. If possible, ask them to bring magazines to share with their classmates and to use as a starting point to discuss fashion's latest trends.

Multiple Intelligences

Kinesthetic Tell students that they are going to have a fashion show. Bring to class several large-sized, colorful clothing items (or ask students to bring them). Students will put on these items over their clothes and model them for their classmates. Assign one student to be the presenter and describe the clothes being modeled.

Culture at a Glance ❈

Topic & Activity	Essential Question
Madrid's Teatro de la Comedia pp. 244–245	What do you like to do on weekends?
The local markets p. 255	How do local markets reflect the culture of an area?
Las meninas p. 261	Why might an artist create a version of another artist's masterpiece?
Weekends in Spain and Chile pp. 266–267	What are some of the weekend activities that people enjoy in Spain and Chile?
Paintings from Spain and Chile p. 268	What messages can an artist communicate through a painting?
Culture review p. 271	What are some aspects of culture in Spain, Guatemala, and Chile?

COMPARISON COUNTRIES  España   Chile  Guatemala

Practice at a Glance ❈

	Objective	Activity & Skill
Vocabulary	In town	1: Reading; 3: Listening/Reading; 7: Writing; 8: Speaking; 9: Speaking; 11: Listening/Reading; 12: Speaking; 19: Listening/Reading; 20: Listening/Reading; 22: Reading/Listening/Speaking; Repaso 3: Writing
	In a restaurant	2: Speaking; 4: Speaking; 13: Speaking/Writing; 14: Speaking/Writing; 15: Speaking/Writing; 16: Listening/Writing; 17: Speaking/Writing; 18: Speaking; 21: Speaking; 23: Writing; Repaso 1: Listening; Repaso 4: Writing
Grammar	Stem-changing verbs: **o → ue**	5: Reading/Writing; 6: Reading/Writing; 8: Writing; 9: Speaking; 12: Speaking; 22: Reading/Listening/Speaking; Repaso 3: Writing
	Ir a + infinitive	4: Speaking; 8: Speaking; 22: Reading/Listening/Speaking; Repaso 2: Writing
	Stem-changing verbs: **e → i**	13: Speaking/Writing; 14: Speaking/Writing; 15: Speaking/Writing; 16: Listening/Writing; 17: Speaking/Writing; 18: Writing; 23: Writing; Repaso 4: Writing
Communication	Describe places and events in town	1: Reading; 2: Speaking; 7: Writing; 11: Listening/Reading; 12: Speaking; 22: Reading/Listening/Speaking; Repaso 3: Writing
	Say what you are going to do	4: Speaking; 8: Speaking; 22: Reading/Listening/Speaking; Repaso 2: Writing
	Order from a menu	13: Speaking/Writing; 15: Speaking/Writing; 18: Speaking; 21: Speaking; Repaso 1: Listening; Repaso 4: Writing
	Pronunciation: The letter **c** with **e, i**	*La letra **c** con **e, i** p. 259: Listening
Recycle	Present tense of **-er** verbs	2: Speaking
	Tener expressions	18: Speaking
	Direct object pronouns	14: Speaking/Writing
	The verb **ir**	4: Speaking

The following presentations are recorded in the Audio Program for *¡Avancemos!*

- **¡A responder!** *page 248*
- **16: ¿Qué sirven en el café?** *page 260*
- **22: Integración** *page 264*
- **Repaso de la lección** *page 270*
  - **1: Listen and understand**
- **Repaso inclusivo** *page 274*
  - **1: Listen, understand, and compare**

¡A responder! TXT CD 4 track 13

1. la ensalada
2. el pescado
3. las patatas
4. el bistec
5. el pollo
6. las verduras
7. el arroz
8. el pastel

16 | ¿Qué sirven en el café?

TXT CD 4 track 17

Enrique:	Hola, soy Enrique. Estoy en el Café Moderno. ¡Los camareros trabajan mucho hoy! Ahora sirven pollo y arroz. Señor Fuentes, ¿qué sirve usted?
Sr. Fuentes:	Sirvo bistec y patatas.
Enrique:	Camarero, ¿vas a servir brócoli?
Camarero:	Sí, lo sirvo ahora.
Camarera:	Hola. Soy camarera. Ahora sirvo un pescado. Es muy rico.
Enrique:	Luis y José, ¿qué servís vosotros?
Luis:	Servimos verduras. Son muy nutritivas.
Enrique:	Hola, Ana. ¿Qué sirves después de los platos principales?
Ana:	De postre, sirvo un pastel de frutas. Es más nutritivo que un pastel de chocolate.

22 | Integración TXT CD 4 tracks 19, 20

Hay muchas actividades hoy en el centro. Si quieres ver una película en inglés, hay películas de Estados Unidos en el Cine Ábaco. Pero, si te gustan las películas de España, puedes ir a la Biblioteca Nacional. Hoy en el Restaurante Oberón sirven paella y pescado. En el Café Almagro hay pasteles y café. También puedes pasear en el Parque del Buen Retiro. O, si prefieres escuchar música rock, hay un concierto en la Plaza de la Moncloa. Hay otro concierto, de música clásica, en el Teatro Marquina. ¡Ah! Otra actividad... puedes ir de compras en el centro comercial. Pero necesitan volver al hotel a las seis, ¿vale?

Repaso de la lección TXT CD 4 track 22

1 Listen and understand

Raúl:	Una mesa para dos.
Camarero:	¿Para dos? Por aquí, por favor. En el menú ustedes van a ver los platos principales. Todos son ricos.
Raúl:	Mmmm. Me gusta mucho el bistec. Voy a pedir el bistec con arroz. Y para beber, quiero un refresco.
Camarero:	Muy bien. ¿Y para usted, señorita?
Tere:	Prefiero el pescado con una ensalada. Y para beber, un jugo, por favor.
Camarero:	¿Van a pedir postre después?
Raúl:	Sí, pero no encuentro los postres en el menú... Ah, aquí están. De postre quiero el pastel de manzana.
Tere:	Yo prefiero el helado.
Camarero:	El pastel para el señor y el helado para la señorita. Vuelvo en un minuto.

Repaso inclusivo TXT CD 4 track 24

1 Listen, understand, and compare

Camarero:	Buenas tardes. ¿Ustedes van a pedir ahora?
Carlitos:	Sí. Tengo ganas de comer papas fritas.
Sra. Estrada:	No, no. Hoy no vas a comerlas.
Camarero:	¿Quieren empezar con sopa? También servimos unas ensaladas muy ricas.
Carlitos:	Bueno... Empiezo con sopa, y de plato principal, pollo con papas fritas.
Sra. Estrada:	Está bien. Yo tengo mucha hambre. Quiero empezar con una ensalada de tomates. Y de plato principal... el pescado.
Camarero:	Perdón, señora, hoy no lo servimos. ¿Prefiere otro plato?
Sra. Estrada:	Bueno... yo también pido el pollo, pero con frijoles.
Camarero:	¿Y para beber?
Carlitos:	Un refresco.
Sra. Estrada:	Y yo voy a beber agua.
Camarero:	Muy bien. Vuelvo en un minuto con las bebidas.

On your desktop

Everything you need to ...

Plan	Present	Assess
**easyPlanner** DVD-ROM	**POWER PRESENTATIONS**	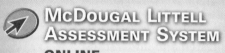**MCDOUGAL LITTELL ASSESSMENT SYSTEM** ONLINE
All resources including audio and video	Ready-made PowerPoint™ presentations with **Animated Grammar**	✓ Assess, score, prescribe, and remediate online ✓ Create customized tests with the Test Generator CD-ROM ✓ Individualized Assessment for on-level, modified, pre-AP, and heritage language learners

 Print

Plan	Present	Practice	Assess
URB 4 • Video Scripts pp. 71–72 • Family Involvement Activity p. 92 • Absent Student Copymasters pp. 101–111 **Lesson Plans** p. 83 **Best Practices Toolkit**	**URB 4** • Video Activities pp. 59–66 **TPRS** pp. 50–56	• *Cuaderno* pp. 174–199 • *Cuaderno para hispanohablantes* pp. 174–199 • *Lecturas para todos* pp. 37–41 • *Lecturas para hispanohablantes* • *¡AvanzaCómics! SuperBruno y Nati*, Episodio 2 **URB 4** • Practice Games pp. 39–46 • Audio Scripts pp. 77–82 • Fine Art Activities pp. 88–89	**URB 4** • Did you get it? Reteaching and Practice Copymasters pp. 13–24

 Unit Transparency Book 4

Culture	Presentation and Practice	Classroom Management
• Atlas Maps UTB 1 1–6 • Map of Spain 1 • Fine Art Transparencies 4, 5	• Vocabulary Transparencies 8, 9 • Grammar Presentation Transparencies 12, 13 • Situational Transparencies and label overlay 14, 15 • Situational Student Copymasters pp. 1, 2	• Warm Up Transparencies 20–23 **MSRB** • Student Book Answer Transparencies 56–59

Audio and Video

Audio	Video
• Student Book Audio CD 4 Tracks 12–24 • Workbook Audio CD 2 Tracks 31–40 • Heritage Learners Audio CD 1 Tracks 29–32, CD 3 Tracks 23–28 • Assessment Audio CD 1 Tracks 23–28 • *Lecturas para todos* Audio CD 1 Track 8, CD 2 Tracks 1–6 • *Música del mundo hispano* • Sing-along Audio CD	• Vocabulary Video DVD 1 • *Telehistoria* DVD 1 Escena 1 Escena 2 Escena 3 Completa • Culture Video DVD 1

 ## Online and CD-ROM Resources

Student	Teacher
Available online and on CD-ROM: • eEdition • @HomeTutor • Animated Grammar **Available online:** • *Cultura interactiva* • Culture Links • WebQuests • Flashcards • Conjuguemos.com • Review Games • Self-check Quiz	**Available online and on CD-ROM:** **EasyPlanner CD-ROM resources:** • Learning Scenarios • Conversation Cards • Family Letters in Spanish • Family Letters in Creole **Available online:** • McDougal Littell Assessment System **Available on CD-ROM:** • Test Generator • Power Presentations

Differentiated Assessment

On-level	Modified	Pre-AP	Heritage Learners
• Vocabulary Recognition Quiz p. 166 • Vocabulary Production Quiz p. 167 • Grammar Quizzes pp. 168–169 • Culture Quiz p. 170 • On-level Lesson Test pp. 171–177 • On-level Unit Test pp. 183–189 • On-level Midterm pp. 195–204	• Modified Lesson Test pp. 131–137 • Modified Unit Test pp. 143–149 • Modified Midterm pp. 155–164	• Pre-AP Lesson Test pp.131–137 • Pre-AP Unit Test pp. 143–149 • Pre-AP Midterm pp. 155–164	• Heritage Learners Lesson Test pp. 137–143 • Heritage Learners Unit Test pp. 149–155 • Heritage Learners Midterm pp. 161–170

Core Pacing Guide

50 Minute (9 Day)

	Objectives/Focus	Teach	Practice	Assess/HW Options
DAY 1	**Culture:** learn about Spain **Vocabulary:** places and events in town • Warm Up OHT 20 **5 min**	Lesson Opener pp. 244–245 **Presentación de vocabulario** pp. 246–248 • Read A–F • View video DVD 1 • Play audio TXT CD 4 track 12 • *¡A responder!* TXT CD 4 track 13 **25 min**	Lesson Opener pp. 244–245 **Práctica de vocabulario** p. 249 • Acts. 1, 2 **15 min**	**Assess:** *Para y piensa* p. 249　**5 min** **Homework:** *Cuaderno* pp. 174–176 @HomeTutor
DAY 2	**Communication:** talking about transportation • Warm Up OHT 20 • Check Homework **5 min**	**Vocabulario en contexto** pp. 250–251 • *Telehistoria escena 1* DVD 1 • *Nota gramatical:* **ir a** + infinitive **20 min**	**Vocabulario en contexto** pp. 250–251 • Act. 3 TXT CD 4 track 14 • Act. 4 **20 min**	**Assess:** *Para y piensa* p. 251　**5 min** **Homework:** *Cuaderno* pp. 174–176 @HomeTutor
DAY 3	**Grammar:** stem-changing verbs: **o → ue** • Warm Up OHT 21 • Check Homework **5 min**	**Presentación de gramática** p. 252 • stem-changing verbs: **o → ue** **Práctica de gramática** pp. 253–255 **20 min**	**Práctica de gramática** pp. 253–255 • Acts. 5, 6, 7, 8, 9, 10 **20 min**	**Assess:** *Para y piensa* p. 255　**5 min** **Homework:** *Cuaderno* pp. 177–179 @HomeTutor
DAY 4	**Communication:** use stem-changing verbs: **o → ue** to talk about things to do in the city • Warm Up OHT 21 • Check Homework **5 min**	**Gramática en contexto** pp. 256–257 • *Telehistoria escena 2* DVD 1 **15 min**	**Gramática en contexto** pp. 256–257 • Act. 11 TXT CD 4 track 15 • Act. 12 **25 min**	**Assess:** *Para y piensa* p. 257　**5 min** **Homework:** *Cuaderno* pp. 177–179 @HomeTutor
DAY 5	**Grammar:** stem-changing verbs: **e → i** • Warm Up OHT 22 • Check Homework **5 min**	**Presentación de gramática** p. 258 • stem-changing verbs: **e → i** **Práctica de gramática** pp. 259–261 **Pronunciación** CD 4 track 16 **Culture:** *Las meninas* **15 min**	**Práctica de gramática** pp. 259–261 • Acts. 13, 14, 15, 17, 18 • Act. 16 TXT CD 4 track 17 **25 min**	**Assess:** *Para y piensa* p. 261　**5 min** **Homework:** *Cuaderno* pp. 180–182 @HomeTutor
DAY 6	**Communication:** Culmination: stem-changing verbs, order food • Warm Up OHT 22 • Check Homework **5 min**	**Todo junto** pp. 262–264 • *Escenas 1, 2: Resumen* • *Telehistoria completa* DVD 1 **15 min**	**Todo junto** pp. 262–264 • Acts. 19, 20 TXT CD 4 tracks 14, 15, 18 • Acts. 21, 23 • Act. 22 TXT CD 4 tracks 19, 20 **25 min**	**Assess:** *Para y piensa* p. 264　**5 min** **Homework:** *Cuaderno* pp. 183–184 @HomeTutor
DAY 7	**Reading:** Weekends in Spain and Chile • Warm Up OHT 23 • Check Homework **Review:** Lesson Review **5 min**	**Lectura cultural** pp. 266–267 *El fin de semana en España y Chile* TXT CD 4 track 21 **Repaso de la lección** pp. 270–271 **20 min**	**Lectura cultural** pp. 266–267 *El fin de semana en España y Chile* **Repaso de la lección** pp. 270–271 • Act. 1 TXT CD 4 track 22 • Acts. 2, 3, 4, 5 **20 min**	**Assess:** *Para y piensa* p. 267　**5 min** **Repaso de la lección** pp. 270–271 **Homework:** *En resumen* p. 269, *Cuaderno* pp. 185–196 (optional) Review Games Online @HomeTutor
DAY 8	**Assessment**			**Assess:** Lesson 2 Test or Unit 4 Test **50 min**
DAY 9	**Unit Culmination**	**Comparación cultural** pp. 272–273 • TXT CD 4 track 23 **Repaso inclusivo** pp. 274–275 **20 min**	**Comparación cultural** pp. 272–273 **Repaso inclusivo** pp. 274–275 • Act. 1 TXT CD 4 track 24 • Acts. 2, 3, 4, 5, 6　**30 min**	**Homework:** *Cuaderno* pp. 197–199

	Objectives/Focus	Teach	Practice	Assess/HW Options
DAY 1	**Culture:** learn about Spain **Vocabulary:** places and events in town • Warm Up OHT 20 **5 min**	Lesson Opener pp. 244–245 **Presentación de vocabulario** pp. 246–248 • Read A–F • View video DVD 1 • Play audio TXT CD 4 track 12 • *¡A responder!* CD 4 track 13 **20 min**	Lesson Opener pp. 244–245 **Práctica de vocabulario** p. 249 • Acts. 1, 2 **20 min**	**Assess:** *Para y piensa* p. 249 **5 min**
	Communication: talking about transportation **5 min**	**Vocabulario en contexto** pp. 250–251 • *Telehistoria escena 1* DVD 1 • *Nota gramatical:* **ir a** + infinitive **15 min**	**Vocabulario en contexto** pp. 250–251 • Act. 3 TXT CD 4 track 14 • Act. 4 **15min**	**Assess:** *Para y piensa* p. 251 **5 min** **Homework:** *Cuaderno* pp. 174–176 @HomeTutor
DAY 2	**Grammar:** stem-changing verbs: **o → ue** • Warm Up OHT 21 • Check Homework **5 min**	**Presentación de gramática** p. 252 • stem-changing verbs: **o → ue** **Práctica de gramática** pp. 253–255 **20 min**	**Práctica de gramática** pp. 253–255 • Acts. 5, 6, 7, 8, 9, 10 **15 min**	**Assess:** *Para y piensa* p. 255 **5 min**
	Communication: use stem-changing verbs: **o → ue** to talk about things to do in the city **5 min**	**Gramática en contexto** pp. 256–257 • *Telehistoria escena 2* DVD 1 **20 min**	**Gramática en contexto** pp. 256–257 • Act. 11 TXT CD 4 track 15 • Act. 12 **15 min**	**Assess:** *Para y piensa* p. 257 **5 min** **Homework:** *Cuaderno* pp. 177–179 @HomeTutor
DAY 3	**Grammar:** stem-changing verbs: **e → i** • Warm Up OHT 22 • Check Homework **5 min**	**Presentación de gramática** p. 258 • stem-changing verbs: **e → i** **Práctica de gramática** pp. 259–261 **Pronunciación** TXT CD 4 track 16 **Culture:** *Las meninas* **15 min**	**Práctica de gramática** pp. 259–261 • Acts. 13, 14, 15, 17, 18 • Act. 16 TXT CD 4 track 17 **20 min**	**Assess:** *Para y piensa* p. 261 **5 min**
	Communication: Culmination: stem-changing verbs, order food **5 min**	**Todo junto** pp. 262–264 • *Escenas 1, 2: Resumen* • *Telehistoria completa* DVD 1 **10 min**	**Todo junto** pp. 262–264 • Acts. 19, 20 TXT CD 4 tracks 14, 15, 18 • Acts. 21, 23 • Act. 22 TXT CD 4 tracks 19, 20 **25 min**	**Assess:** *Para y piensa* p. 264 **5 min** **Homework:** *Cuaderno* pp. 180–184 @HomeTutor
DAY 4	**Reading:** Weekends in Spain and Chile • Warm Up OHT 23 • Check Homework **5 min**	**Lectura cultural** pp. 266–267 *El fin de semana en España y Chile* TXT CD 4 track 21 **15 min**	**Lectura cultural** pp. 266–267 *El fin de semana en España y Chile* **15 min**	**Assess:** *Para y piensa* p. 267 **5 min**
	Review: Lesson Review **5 min**	**Repaso de la lección** pp. 270–271 **15 min**	**Repaso de la lección** pp. 270–271 • Act. 1 TXT CD 4 track 22 • Acts. 2, 3, 4, 5 **25 min**	**Assess:** *Repaso de la lección* pp. 270–271 **5 min** **Homework:** *En resumen* p. 269; *Cuaderno* pp. 185–196 (optional) Review Games Online @HomeTutor
DAY 5	**Assessment**			**Assess:** Lesson 2 Test, Unit 4 Test, or Midterm **45 min**
	Unit Culmination	**Comparación cultural** pp. 272–273 • TXT CD 4 track 23 **Repaso inclusivo** pp. 274–275 **15 min**	**Comparación cultural** pp. 272–273 **Repaso inclusivo** pp. 274–275 • Act. 1 TXT CD 4 track 24 • Acts 2, 3, 4, 5, 6 **30 min**	**Homework:** *Cuaderno* pp. 197–199

¡AVANZA! Objectives

- Introduce lesson theme: **¿Qué hacemos esta noche?**
- **Culture:** Discuss activities teens do on the weekend in different countries.

Presentation Strategies

- Introduce characters' names: Maribel and Enrique.
- Have students make a list of their favorite places and events in town.
- Have students talk about their favorite weekend activities and the foods they like to eat.

STANDARDS

2.2 Products and perspectives
4.2 Compare cultures

Warm Up UTB 4 Transparency 20

Direct Object Pronouns Complete the following sentences with the correct direct object pronoun attached to the infinitive.

1. ¿El vestido? No quiero llevar _____.
2. ¿Los pantalones? ¿Vas a comprar _____ mañana?
3. ¿La camiseta? Voy a comprar _____ en la tienda de ropa.
4. ¿El gorro? Voy a necesitar _____ para practicar el béisbol.
5. ¿Las blusas? Quiero comprar _____ en el centro comercial.

Answers: 1. llevarlo; **2.** comprarlos; **3.** comprarla; **4.** necesitarlo; **5.** comprarlas

Comparación cultural

Ask the following:

1. Are there theaters in or near your town or city? What productions can you see there?
2. Are there historic buildings in your community?
3. What places do you like to visit in your spare time?

¿Qué ves? Possible answers include:

- Sí, el teatro es viejo.
- Maribel lleva un vestido.
- La camisa de Enrique es roja.

244

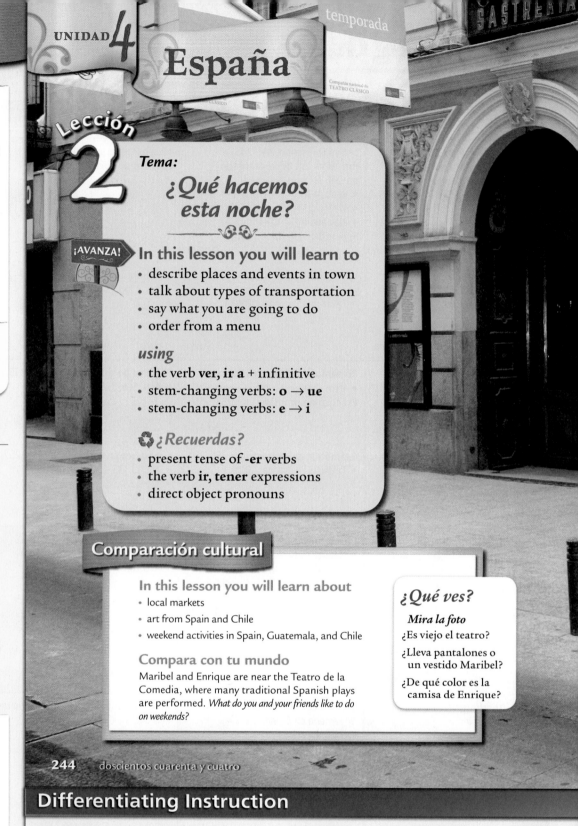

UNIDAD **4**
España

Lección **2**

Tema:

¿Qué hacemos esta noche?

¡AVANZA!

In this lesson you will learn to

- describe places and events in town
- talk about types of transportation
- say what you are going to do
- order from a menu

using

- the verb **ver, ir a** + infinitive
- stem-changing verbs: **o → ue**
- stem-changing verbs: **e → i**

♻¿Recuerdas?

- present tense of **-er** verbs
- the verb **ir, tener** expressions
- direct object pronouns

Comparación cultural

In this lesson you will learn about

- local markets
- art from Spain and Chile
- weekend activities in Spain, Guatemala, and Chile

Compara con tu mundo

Maribel and Enrique are near the Teatro de la Comedia, where many traditional Spanish plays are performed. *What do you and your friends like to do on weekends?*

¿Qué ves?

Mira la foto
¿Es viejo el teatro?
¿Lleva pantalones o un vestido Maribel?
¿De qué color es la camisa de Enrique?

244 doscientos cuarenta y cuatro

Differentiating Instruction

English Learners

Build Background Ask students if they have been to a concert, play, or movie. What did they see? Did they like it? Ask them to describe the event and the building where it took place. Ask them how to say *concert, theatre,* or *movies* in their language. Give them time to share experiences and say what they know.

Multiple Intelligences

Kinesthetic Collect an assortment of funny clothes to use as costumes. Write a number of expressions related to emotions and activities on separate index cards, like **triste, contento, ir de compras, jugar al fútbol.** Invite a volunteer to choose a costume and a card to act out. The group needs to describe the costume, as well as guess the activity or emotion being portrayed.

El Teatro de la Comedia
en la calle Príncipe
Madrid, España

España
doscientos cuarenta y cinco   245

Online SPANISH CLASSZONE.COM

Featuring...
- Cultura INTERACTIVA
- Animated Grammar
- @HomeTutor

And more...
- Get Help Online
- Interactive Flashcards
- Review Games
- WebQuest
- Self-Check Quiz

Online SPANISH CLASSZONE.COM

Animated Grammar This entertaining animated tutor helps students learn Spanish grammar in a fun and lively way. Verbs are conjugated before students' eyes, and direct and indirect object pronouns pop into place! Animated characters walk students through every explanation, adding a special zing to Spanish grammar that students won't forget!

Featuring...
- Cultura INTERACTIVA
- Animated Grammar
- @HomeTutor

And more...
- Get Help Online
- Interactive Flashcards
- Review Games
- WebQuest
- Self-Check Quiz

Using the Photo

Location Information

Teatro de la Comedia is located in downtown Madrid. It was inaugurated on September 18, 1875 by King Alfonso XII and his sister Princess Isabel. At that time it was able to seat 1,000 spectators. Each season (September to June) includes three to four performances of the Spanish classical repertoire by playwrights such as Calderón de la Barca and Lope de Vega, to name a couple.

Expanded Information

Teatro Español is another well-known theater that performs works by both classic and modern Spanish playwrights, among them Federico García Lorca and Jardiel Poncela. It is located in the **Plaza de Santa Ana,** not too far from the **Puerta del Sol.**

Long-term Retention
Recycle

Ask students **¿Qué llevan Maribel y Enrique?** to see how many items of clothing they can identify.

Differentiating Instruction

Inclusion

Cumulative Instruction Use limited choice questions about the photo to help students review vocabulary related to clothing, colors, and emotions. Here are a few possibilities:
¿Lleva Maribel un vestido o unos jeans?
¿Tiene Enrique zapatos blancos o zapatos marrones?
¿Está contenta o está triste Maribel?

Heritage Language Learners

Support What They Know Have students watch a Spanish-language comedy. It might be a television show or a movie. Have them describe the characters involved, their names, what they look like, their personalities, and what they wear.

- Present vocabulary: places to go in town, means of transportation, ordering a meal.

Core Resources

- Video Program: DVD 1
- Audio Program TXT CD 4 track 12

Presentation Strategies

- Point to the items illustrated on pp. 246–247, say each word and have students repeat it after you.
- Play the audio as students read A–E.
- Play the video.

STANDARDS

1.2 Understand language
4.1 Compare languages

Communication
Group Work

Prepare props in advance and have students work in pairs or small groups to pantomime scenes that take place in various locations in the city: **el restaurante, el parque, el teatro, el concierto**. The class guesses the location.

Communication
Common Error Alert

Point out that the adjective **bueno** becomes **buen** when it comes before a masculine noun: **Un buen restaurante.** However, it does not change when the noun is feminine: **Una buena película.**

Long-term Retention
Recycle

Review food vocabulary from Unidad 3, Lección 1. Ask the following questions: **¿Qué te gusta comer en la mañana? ¿Qué te gusta comer en el almuerzo? ¿Qué te gusta comer en la noche?**

246

Presentación de VOCABULARIO

¡AVANZA! **Goal:** Learn about what Enrique and Maribel do when they go out. Then practice what you have learned to describe places and events in town. *Actividades 1–2*

 ¿*Recuerdas?* Present tense of **-er** verbs p. 168

VIDEO DVD

AUDIO

A En **el centro** de Madrid hay muchos **lugares** para comer. Maribel y yo queremos ir a **la calle** de Alcalá para **encontrar** un buen **restaurante.** ¿Vamos **a pie, en coche** o **en autobús**?

a pie

en coche

en autobús

B En **el menú** hay muchos **platos principales.** Si te gusta **la carne,** hay **bistec.** Si no, también hay **pescado.**

el camarero
el brócoli
las patatas
el bistec
el pollo
el menú
el arroz
el pescado
la ensalada
las verduras
el tomate

Unidad 4 España
doscientos cuarenta y seis

Differentiating Instruction

Slower-paced Learners

Yes/No Questions Check students' comprehension by pointing to the photos on pp. 246–247. For example, point to the fish and ask, **¿Es el pescado?** Then point to the salad and ask, **¿Es el pollo?**

Multiple Intelligences

Visual Learners Organize students into small groups, and provide each group with a piece of poster board. Instruct each group to create a city plan for an ideal city center. Have them label each location in their city center, and provide as much detail as possible. Encourage students to review vocabulary from previous lessons to include perhaps a school, a shopping center, or a store.

C La **cuenta** es veinticinco euros. ¿Cuánto dinero necesitamos para **la propina**?

la cuenta

D **Tomamos** el autobús para ir al **cine.** Vamos al Cine Ideal para ver una película.

el cine

la ventanilla

las entradas

E **Aquí** en Madrid también hay **teatros** y **parques** pero yo prefiero ir a **un concierto** para escuchar música.

el teatro

el parque

el concierto

Continuará...

Lección 2
doscientos cuarenta y siete **247**

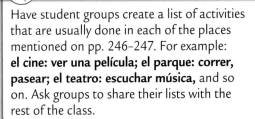

TEACHER to TEACHER

Elizabeth Parks
Dover, NJ

Tips for Presenting Vocabulary

Whenever I teach vocabulary for places in the city, I use a map transparency with street names and names of various places in the city (stores, museums, theaters, parks, restaurants, etc.). I also include vocabulary terms for different types of transportation. In addition to teaching vocabulary, the map can also be used to teach the verb ir, prepositions of locations and for giving directions.

Long-term Retention

Recycle

Have student groups create a list of activities that are usually done in each of the places mentioned on pp. 246–247. For example: **el cine: ver una película; el parque: correr, pasear; el teatro: escuchar música,** and so on. Ask groups to share their lists with the rest of the class.

Long-term Retention

Critical Thinking

Categorize Have students arrange the vocabulary on pp. 246–247 in the following category groups: **Comidas, Lugares, Transporte.** Have them write their lists and exchange them with a partner to correct and add items as needed.

Differentiating Instruction

Heritage Language Learners

Regional Variations Ask students if they know different ways to say any other words on pp. 246–247. Mention a few other variations of how Spanish words are said throughout Latin America, for example, **coche** is **carro, auto, automóvil.** Also, the word **patatas** is **papas,** and **entradas** is **boletos.**

Pre-AP

Relate Opinions Ask students to share their opinions about the foods and places presented on pp. 246 and 247. Encourage them to use the phrase **porque** to provide more detail. **Me gusta el cine porque me gusta ver películas. No como bistec porque no me gusta comer carne.** Have students continue providing other phrases.

Objectives
· Present vocabulary: places to go in town.
· Discuss regional variations in vocabulary

Core Resources
· Video Program: DVD 1
· Audio Program: TXT CD 4 tracks 12, 13

Presentation Strategies
· Have students look at the photos and scan the text on p. 248 and ask: **¿Dónde están las personas? ¿Qué hay en el café? ¿Qué van a pedir de postre? ¿Quién necesita dormir?**
· Play the audio as students read the text.
· Show the video.

STANDARDS
1.2 Understand language
4.1 Compare languages

Long-term Retention
Critical Thinking

Categorize Have students categorize the vocabulary under these headings, **el café, el restaurante, el cine, el teatro, el concierto** writing all related new words. Tell them some new words may be listed more than once and some new words will not be used at all.

Communication
Humor/Creativity

Have students create a menu of a café of their own creation. They should give their café a name in Spanish and give the prices in euros. They may enjoy displaying their menus in the classroom.

Long-term Retention
Personalize It

Have students describe how they would go to various places in your city or town—**a pie, en coche, en autobús.** You may designate specific places or allow them to select their own.

Answers MSRB Transparency 56

¡A responder! Audio Script, TE p. 243b

Students should point to the following photos:
1. salad	**2.** fish	**3.** potatoes
4. steak	**5.** chicken	**6.** vegetables
7. rice	**8.** cake	

248

Presentación de VOCABULARIO
(continuación)

F Vamos a **un café. De postre** nos gusta **pedir un pastel.** Después, Maribel está muy cansada. Es la hora de **dormir.**

el café

la mesa

el pastel

En España se dice...
In Spain the word for *cake* is **la tarta.** The word for *beans* is **las alubias.**

dormir

Más vocabulario
allí *there*
almorzar *to eat lunch*
costar *to cost*
los frijoles *beans*
la música rock *rock music*
poder *to be able, can*
servir *to serve*
tal vez *perhaps, maybe*
volver *to return, to come back*
Expansión de vocabulario p. R5

¡A responder! Escuchar
Listen to the waiter. Point to the photo with the food that he mentions.

@HomeTutor VideoPlus
Interactive Flashcards
ClassZone.com

Differentiating Instruction

Heritage Language Learners

Regional Variations Direct students to the **En España se dice** box at the right of the page. Ask students to comment on the different ways to say *cake* and *beans.* Which of these words is most familiar to them? What are some of the names for other popular foods in their region or country of origin?

Slower-paced Learners

Yes/No Questions Ask yes or no questions to help students with the words presented under **Más vocabulario.** When asking a question using a stem-changing verb, write the infinitive of the verb on the board to help students find its meaning. Use gestures to make the meaning of the questions clear.
¿Puedes estudiar conmigo?
¿Almuerzas en la cafetería?

Práctica de VOCABULARIO

1 | Diversiones en el centro

Leer Read each description and look for the matching word.

1. Es una persona que trabaja en un café.
2. Es el lugar adonde vas para comer.
3. Vas aquí para ver una película.
4. La necesitas para ir a un concierto.
5. Lo comes después del plato principal.
6. Compras entradas aquí.

a. la ventanilla
b. el restaurante
c. la camarera
d. la entrada
e. el cine
f. el postre

Expansión:
Teacher Edition Only
Ask students to write two additional descriptions of new vocabulary words.

Nota gramatical ♻ **¿Recuerdas?** Present tense of **-er** verbs p. 168

Ver has an irregular **yo** form in the present tense: **veo.**

Veo muchos autobuses en el centro. *I see a lot of buses downtown.*

---

2 | ¿Qué ves en el restaurante?

Hablar Señor and Señora Ortiz are at the restaurant Los Reyes. Ask a partner what he or she sees.

 ¿Qué ves en el restaurante?

 Allí veo una silla.

Expansión:
Teacher Edition Only
Have students create menus for their own cafés, including prices.

Más práctica Cuaderno *pp. 174–176* Cuaderno para hispanohablantes *pp. 174–177*

Did you get it?
1. Name three things you would find in a restaurant.
2. Name three places where you and your friends might go to have fun.

🔄 **Get Help Online** ClassZone.com

Lección 2
doscientos cuarenta y nueve **249**

Differentiating Instruction

Multiple Intelligences

Kinesthetic Ask the class to play a charade game with the questions in Activity 1. For example, have a volunteer mimic a place where you go to see a movie, and other students guess it is **el cine.** Once all six questions have been done, have students continue playing charades with other vocabulary words.

Inclusion

Frequent Review/Repetition Before doing Activity 2, help students write a list of the people and items they see in the illustration. Go over their list to correct and add words as needed. Check pronunciation before starting the activity.

Objectives
· Practice vocabulary: places in town and items in a restaurant.
· Recycle: present tense of **-er** verbs.

Core Resource
· *Cuaderno,* pp. 174–176

Practice Sequence
· **Activity 1:** Vocabulary recognition: places in town, food
· **Activity 2:** Vocabulary production: the verb **ver,** restaurant-related vocabulary

---

STANDARDS
1.1 Engage in conversation, Act. 2, PYP
1.3 Present information, Acts. 1–2, PYP

 @HomeTutor
More Practice
ClassZone.com

✓ **Ongoing Assessment**

PARA Y PIENSA **Quick Check** If students have difficulties supplying answers in the Para y piensa, have them review the vocabulary on pp. 246–248. For additional practice, use Reteaching & Practice Copymasters URB 4, pp. 13, 14, 22.

Communication
⚠ **Common Error Alert**

Students may try to use **ver** with a direct object that is a person or a pet. Tell students that when doing this, they must use an **a** after the verb. They will learn the personal **a** in Unit 6, Lesson 1.

 Answers MSRB Transparency 56

Activity 1 1. c; 2. b; 3. e; 4. d; 5. f; 6. a
Activity 2 Answers should follow the format:
1. A. ¿Qué ves en el restaurante? B. Veo un postre.
2. A. ¿Qué ves... ? B. Veo el menú.
3. A. ¿Qué ves... ? B. Veo la propina.
4. A. ¿Qué ves... ? B. Veo la cuenta.
5. A. ¿Qué ves... ? B. Veo una mesa.
6. A. ¿Qué ves... ? B. Veo agua.

Para y piensa Answers will vary. Answers may include:
1. el camarero, el menú, la propina
2. el teatro, el parque, el cine

249

VOCABULARIO

· Understand activity vocabulary in context.

Core Resources

· Video Program: DVD 1
· Audio Program: TXT CD 4 track 14

Presentation Strategies

· Have students look at the photo and ask them either/or questions: **¿Quién lleva la mochila, Enrique o Maribel? ¿Dónde están los chicos, en la calle o en el restaurante?**
· Have students scan the dialog to find how many means of transportation are mentioned.
· Play audio or video while students follow the script in their text.

Practice Sequence

· **Activity 3:** Telehistoria comprehension
· **Activity 4:** Vocabulary production: **ir a** + infinitive, foods

STANDARDS

1.1 Engage in conversation, Act. 4
1.2 Understand language, Act. 3
1.3 Present information, Act. 4, PYP

Warm Up UTB 4 Transparency 20

Vocabulary Complete each sentence.

    mesas   pastel   cuenta   coche

1. La _____ es treinta euros.
2. El _____ es un postre.
3. Hay muchas _____ en el café.
4. No voy en autobús, voy en _____.

Answers: 1. cuenta; **2.** pastel; **3.** mesas;
4. coche

Video Summary

@HomeTutor
VideoPlus
ClassZone.com

Maribel is eager to get to the shopping center to see Trini by twelve o'clock. Enrique wonders how they will get there. He suggests they take a bus into town, walk to the library, and from there get a ride to the shopping center with his mother. When Maribel worries they will arrive late, Enrique discovers that a number 74 bus will soon go to the shopping center, arriving at 12:30 P.M. Maribel agrees with Enrique's plan.

▶❙ ❙❙

250

VOCABULARIO *en contexto*

¡AVANZA! **Goal:** Focus on how Maribel and Enrique talk about where they go and how they get there. Then practice these words and **ir a** + infinitive to talk about types of transportation and what you are going to do.
Actividades 3–4

♻ *¿Recuerdas?* The verb **ir** p. 134

Telehistoria escena 1

@HomeTutor VideoPlus
ClassZone.com

VIDEO
DVD

AUDIO

STRATEGIES

Cuando lees 📖

Think about timing Consider timing while reading. How long will Enrique's plan take? Will they see Trini? Why or why not?

Cuando escuchas 🎧

Enter the scene As you listen to Enrique's travel plan, enter the scene. If you were Maribel, would you feel calm or nervous about Enrique's ideas? Why?

Enrique

Maribel

Enrique: ¿Trini Salgado está en el centro comercial del Parque de las Avenidas a las doce?

Maribel: Sí. Y ya es tarde. Enrique, ¡por favor!

Enrique: ¡Vale! ¿Y cómo vamos a llegar allí? ¿En autobús?

Enrique puts the T-shirt in his bag so that Maribel can open the map.

Maribel: Podemos empezar aquí en el parque. El centro comercial está allí. ¿Cuál es la calle?

Enrique: Calle Poveda. ¡Es fácil! Tomamos el autobús al centro. Vamos a pie a la biblioteca —aquí. Mi madre está allí. Ella tiene coche. ¡Llegamos al centro comercial en coche!

Maribel: ¡Pero, Enrique! Son las once y cuarenta y cinco. Vamos a llegar tarde. ¿Qué voy a hacer?

Enrique: ¡Ah! El autobús setenta y cuatro va al centro comercial. Llega aquí a las doce y llega al centro comercial a las doce y media.

Maribel: ¡Vale!   Continuará... p. 256

También se dice

España Enrique says **el autobús** to talk about taking the bus. In other Spanish-speaking countries you might hear:
· **Puerto Rico, República Dominicana, Cuba** **la guagua**
· **México el camión**
· **muchos países el colectivo, el micro**

Differentiating Instruction

Slower-paced Learners

Read Before Listening Have students preview the Telehistoria silently, paying particular attention to information about locations. Then divide the group into two teams to read the parts of Maribel and Enrique. Tell students to raise their hand each time they say or hear the name of a specific place.

Pre-AP

Sequence Information Ask students to write on index cards, in sequential order, Enrique's initial transportation plan to the **centro comercial.**
Tomamos el autobús al centro.
Vamos a pie a la biblioteca.
Llegamos al centro comercial en coche.

3 | ¿Cómo piensan llegar? *Comprensión del episodio*

Escuchar
Leer

Read the sentences and tell whether they are true or false.

1. Maribel y Enrique no tienen mapa.
2. La madre de Enrique está en la biblioteca.
3. El centro comercial está en la calle Poveda.
4. Enrique quiere ir a pie al centro comercial.
5. El autobús llega al centro comercial a las doce.

Expansión:
Teacher Edition Only
Have students write two additional true/false statements.

Nota gramatical ♻ ¿*Recuerdas?* The verb **ir** p. 134

To talk about what you are going to do, use a form of **ir a** + **infinitive.**

¿Qué van a **hacer** ustedes?   Vamos a **mirar** una película.
*What **are you going to do**?*   ***We're going to watch** a movie.*

Vamos a can also mean *Let's.*

4 | ¿Qué vas a comer?

Hablar

Ask a partner what he or she is going to eat this week. Your partner should explain his or her answers.

A ¿Vas a comer carne?

B Sí, voy a comer carne. Es rica. (No, no voy a comer carne. Es horrible.)

 1.

2.

3.

4.

5.

6.

7.

8.

Expansión:
Teacher Edition Only
Have students list these foods in order from their favorite to their least favorite and compare lists with a partner.

PARA Y PIENSA

Did you get it? Complete each sentence with the correct phrase to tell what form of transportation is used.

1. Maribel va a la escuela _____ ; va a tomar el cuarenta y dos.
2. Enrique y su hermano van a ir _____ al parque; les gusta pasear.
3. Maribel y su mamá van al concierto _____ porque no quieren llegar tarde.

🔲 **Get Help Online**
ClassZone.com

Differentiating Instruction

Multiple Intelligences

Interpersonal Review the forms of **ir.** Then have students brainstorm a list of activities while a volunteer writes them on the board. Encourage them to review previous lessons to refresh their memories. Then have students work in pairs to ask and answer the question **¿Qué vas a hacer mañana?** using the ideas on the board for reference.

Heritage Language Learners

Writing Skills Invite students to develop the question **¿Qué vas a hacer el sábado?** into a full paragraph. Have them make a list to use as a graphic organizer. Encourage them to use time and sequence words, such as **antes** and **después** to link their sentences together.

Nota gramatical

Make sure students can make the distinction between **ir a** + place to tell where someone is going and **ir a** + infinitive to tell what someone is going to do. Ask questions starting with **¿Adónde vas?** and **¿Qué vas a hacer?** to elicit correct responses.

Long-term Retention

♻ **Recycle**

Before doing Activity 4 review forms of **ir** with students by saying a subject and asking them to provide the corresponding form of **ir.** For example: **nosotros: vamos.** You might remind them of the adjectives learned in Unidad 3 Lección 1 to describe food: **nutritivo(a), rico(a), horrible.**

✓ **Ongoing Assessment**   @HomeTutor
More Practice
ClassZone.com

PARA Y PIENSA   **Quick Check** Show illustrations of each mode of transportation and have students say the corresponding words. For additional practice, use Reteaching & Practice Copymasters URB 4, pp. 13, 15, 22.

Answers MSRB Transparency 56

Activity 3
1. Falso   2. Cierto   3. Cierto
4. Falso   5. Falso

Activity 4
1. ¿Vas a comer frijoles? Sí, voy (No, no voy) a comer frijoles.
2. ... Sí, voy (No, no voy) a comer bistec.
3. ... Sí, voy (No, no voy) a comer pescado y arroz.
4. ... Sí, voy (No, no voy) a comer verduras.
5. ... Sí, voy (No, no voy) a comer pastel.
6. ... Sí, voy (No, no voy) a comer brócoli.
7. ... Sí, voy (No, no voy) a comer tomates.
8. ... Sí, voy (No, no voy) a comer pollo.

Para y piensa
1. en autobús; 2. a pie; 3. en coche

251

Objective

· Present stem-changing verbs: **o → ue**.

Core Resource

· *Cuaderno,* pp. 177–179

Presentation Strategies

· Write the forms of the verb **poder** on the board. Call on a student to underline the **o → ue** stem changes. Ask students which forms don't undergo a stem change.

· Monitor correct usage of forms by saying a pronoun followed by an infinitive and asking students to provide you with the correct form. For example **él: almorzar → él almuerza.**

· Remind students that only two forms of **costar** are used: **cuesta** and **cuestan.**

STANDARD

4.1 Compare languages

Warm Up   UTB 4 Transparency 21

ir a + infinitive   Complete the sentences with an appropriate phrase.

  a. vamos a pedir   **b.** van a dormir
  c. vas a comer   **d.** voy a pagar

1. Yo _____ la cuenta.
2. Nosotros _____ pastel y café.
3. Los chicos _____ a las ocho.
4. Tú _____ carne.

Answers: 1. d; 2. a; 3. b; 4. c

Communication

Interpersonal Mode

Point out that when **poder** is followed by another verb, the second verb is in the infinitive: **Puedo ir al cine.** Ask students whether they can do certain activities or not. Example: **¿Puedes dibujar bien? Sí, puedo dibujar bien** or **No, no puedo dibujar bien.**

Verbs Students Know

Students have learned the following **o → ue** stem-changing verbs in this lesson:

almorzar	encontrar
costar	poder
dormir	volver

252

Presentación de GRAMÁTICA

 Goal: Learn how to form **o → ue** stem-changing verbs. Then practice using these verbs to talk about going out with friends. *Actividades 5–10*

English Grammar Connection: Remember that there are no stem-changing verbs in the present tense of English (see p. 224). In Spanish, **o → ue** stem changes happen in all three classes of verbs: **-ar, -er,** and **-ir.**

Stem-Changing Verbs: o → ue

Animated Grammar
ClassZone.com

Some verbs have an **o → ue** stem change in the present tense. How do you form the present tense of these verbs?

Here's how:

Remember that stem-changing verbs have regular **-ar, -er,** and **-ir** endings. For **o → ue** stem-changing verbs, the last **o** of the stem changes to **ue** in all forms except **nosotros(as)** and **vosotros(as).**

poder	*to be able, can*
p**ue**do	p**o**demos
p**ue**des	p**o**déis
p**ue**de	p**ue**den

Carmen p**ue**de ir al concierto.
*Carmen **can** go to the concert.*

Other verbs you know that have this stem change are **alm**o**rzar, c**o**star, d**o**rmir, enc**o**ntrar,** and **v**o**lver.**

    Almue**rzo** a la una.
    ***I eat lunch** at one o'clock.*

    Antonio, ¿cuándo **vue**lves?
    *Antonio, when **are you coming back**?*

Más práctica
  Cuaderno *pp. 177–179*
  Cuaderno para hispanohablantes *pp. 178–180*

@HomeTutor
Leveled Grammar Practice
ClassZone.com

Differentiating Instruction

Pre-AP

Self-correct Allow students to hear and say the different forms of stem-changing verbs. Have them ask and answer everyday classroom questions using **poder, almorzar,** and **encontrar.** It may be easier to recognize that **puedo** sounds right, while **podo** doesn't, rather than always remembering to change the **o** to **ue** before adding the appropriate ending.

Slower-paced Learners

Memory Aids Organize students into small groups. Provide each group with six pieces of paper. Have the groups create a chart of the forms for each stem-changing verb: **almorzar, costar, dormir, encontrar,** and **volver.** Tell students to model their charts on the one for **poder** on p. 252.

Práctica de GRAMÁTICA

5 | Un concierto de música rock

Leer
Escribir

Maribel is talking with her friend Toni about when they can go to a concert. Complete what she says with forms of **poder,** and use the poster to answer her question.

Presenta

Los Rebeldes

en el Centro Cívico, Madrid
Entrada: 18€ en la ventanilla
Fecha: 22–23 de abril
Hora: el viernes por la tarde
(19:00) y por la noche (22:00)
el sábado por la tarde
(14:00) y por la noche (21:00)

Nosotros queremos ir a un concierto el viernes o el sábado, pero ¿cuándo? Yo no __1.__ ir el viernes en la noche porque tengo que trabajar. Manolo no __2.__ ir el sábado en la noche. Ana y Miguel no __3.__ ir el viernes en la noche y el sábado en la tarde no van a estar aquí. Enrique y su hermano no __4.__ ir el sábado en la tarde porque van a un restaurante con su primo. Y Toni, tú no __5.__ ir el sábado en la noche. ¿Cuándo __6.__ ir todos nosotros?

6 | ¿Quieres ir?

Leer
Escribir

Complete the conversation between Enrique and Maribel by choosing the correct verb and conjugating it in the appropriate form.

Enrique: Yo __1.__ (dormir / almorzar) en el café Mariposa hoy. La comida es muy rica y no __2.__ (volver / costar) mucho. ¿Quieres ir?

Maribel: Gracias, pero yo no __3.__ (encontrar / poder) comer ahora. Mis padres __4.__ (volver / dormir) de sus vacaciones en México. Necesito ir a la tienda ahora para comprar comida.

Enrique: Tú __5.__ (poder / dormir) ir a pie porque la tienda está cerca de aquí.

Maribel: Mis padres quieren comer unas verduras y nosotros siempre __6.__ (costar / encontrar) buenas verduras allí.

Enrique: ¿Tú y tus padres __7.__ (poder / volver) ir al cine esta noche? Yo voy a las siete y media.

Maribel: Gracias, Enrique, pero mis padres siempre están muy cansados después de sus vacaciones y __8.__ (dormir / almorzar) mucho.

Expansión:
Teacher Edition Only
Have students rewrite Maribel's part of the conversation, giving different reasons for not going to the café or the movies with Enrique.

Lección 2
doscientos cincuenta y tres **253**

Differentiating Instruction

Inclusion

Clear Structure Before students complete Activity 5, have them preview the text noting on a separate piece of paper the noun or pronoun associated with the verb in each sentence. Based on what they write, have students choose the correct form of the verb to complete the sentence.

Multiple Intelligences

Visual Learners Working in small groups, have students design a poster for a concert they would like to attend. Their poster should contain the name of the musical group, the location, ticket price information, and the dates and times. Have students use their posters to talk about which concerts they can and cannot attend.

Objective
· Practice using o → ue stem-changing verbs and lesson vocabulary.

Practice Sequence
· **Activity 5:** Controlled practice: poder
· **Activity 6:** Controlled practice: o → ue

STANDARD
1.3 Present information, Acts. 5–6

Long-term Retention

Recycle

Review **e → ie** stem-changing verbs by having a race to see who can conjugate the following verbs correctly in the fastest time. Write these verbs on the board or overhead, but keep them hidden until time for the race to begin: **querer, preferir, entender, cerrar.**

Communication

Pair Work

Have students create five questions to ask a partner, using the o → ue stem-changing verbs. Remind them that infinitives follow **poder.** They will then ask their partner the questions and record the answers.

Comparisons

English Grammar Connection

When doing Activity 5, have students notice the date and time in the poster. Remind them that in Spanish-speaking countries the day goes before the month as shown in the poster: **22-23 de abril.** Also remind students that in many countries the official time is written using the 24-hour clock, as in **19:00** (7:00 P.M.), **22:00** (10:00 P.M.), **14:00** (2:00 P.M.), and **21:00** (9:00 P.M.).

Answers MSRB Transparency 56

Activity 5
1. puedo; **2.** puede; **3.** pueden; **4.** pueden; **5.** puedes; **6.** podemos

Activity 6
1. almuerzo; **2.** cuesta; **3.** puedo; **4.** vuelven; **5.** puedes; **6.** encontramos; **7.** pueden; **8.** duermen

Objectives

- Practice using **o → ue** stem-changing verbs and lesson vocabulary.
- **Culture:** the local markets of **El Rastro** and **Chichicastenango.**
- Write about activities in town.
- Give excuses for things one cannot do.

Core Resource

- *Cuaderno,* pp. 177–179

Practice Sequence

- **Activity 7:** Transitional practice: **o → ue** stem-changing verbs
- **Activity 8:** Transitional practice: **ir a** + infinitive; **o → ue** stem-changing verbs
- **Activity 9:** Open-ended practice: **o → ue** stem-changing verbs.
- **Activity 10:** Open-ended practice: **ir a** + infinitive; **o → ue** stem-changing verbs.

 STANDARDS

1.1 Engage in conversation, Acts. 8–10
1.3 Present information, Acts. 7–10, PYP
2.2 Products and perspectives, Act. 9
4.2 Compare cultures, Act. 9

Communication
Group Work

Game Divide the class into two teams and have them stand in a line facing the board. Write **dormir, almorzar** on the left side of the board; write **encontrar, poder** on the right side. The first person in each line will go to his/her respective side of the board and write the **yo** form of the first verb listed. The next person will go to the board and write the **tú** form. The first team to conjugate their verbs correctly is the winner.

 Answers MSRB Transparency 56

Activity 7

1. Las entradas para el concierto cuestan quince euros.
2. Yo almuerzo en el café con mi familia.
3. Vosotros encontráis la calle en el mapa.
4. Tú puedes jugar al fútbol con amigos en el parque.
5. Usted duerme bien después de comer mucho.
6. Nosotros volvemos al centro en autobús.

Answers continue on p. 255.

254

---

7 | Las actividades en el centro

Escribir

Combine phrases from the three puzzle pieces to describe activities downtown. Use the correct verb forms to write your sentences.

modelo: el camarero / no poder trabajar / en el restaurante
El camarero no puede trabajar en el restaurante.

las entradas para el concierto
yo
vosotros
tú
usted
nosotros

almorzar
costar
encontrar la calle
poder jugar al fútbol
dormir bien
volver al centro

en el mapa
con amigos en el parque
después de comer mucho
quince euros
en el café con mi familia
en autobús

Expansión:
Teacher Edition Only
Have students choose three verbs from this activity and write three sentences about themselves.

8 | Todos tienen excusas

Hablar

Talk with another student about the activities that you can't do this weekend. Say that you can't do something and make up an excuse.

modelo: ir a un concierto

A ¿Vas a ir a un concierto?

B No, no puedo ir a un concierto. Voy a ir al cine con mi hermano.

1. ir al teatro
2. dormir diez horas
3. practicar deportes
4. almorzar en un café
5. pasar un rato con los amigos
6. ver una película en el cine
7. ir al centro
8. comprar ropa
9. montar en bicicleta
10. preparar la comida

Expansión:
Teacher Edition Only
Have students compare with a classmate which of the activities they are going to do this weekend.

Differentiating Instruction

Inclusion

Synthetic/Analytic Support Provide students with small pieces of paper in three different colors. Then instruct them to copy the words and phrases from Activity 7 on separate papers. Remind students to keep all of the words and phrases from one group on the same color. Then have students rearrange their papers to find the best combination to form a sentence.

Pre-AP

Vary Vocabulary Before students converse with a partner in Activity 8, invite five students to form a line or sit in a circle. Ask these students one of the questions from the activity. **¿Vas a ir al teatro?** Then have each student present a different excuse explaining why he or she cannot go. Tell students they may not repeat an excuse already given.

9 | ¡Vamos a ir de compras!

Hablar | **Comparación cultural**

Los mercados

How do local markets reflect the culture of an area? Every Sunday, tourists and locals head to El Rastro, one of the oldest flea markets in Madrid, **Spain,** to search for bargains amid the hundreds of stalls. Vendors offer a wide variety of items such as antiques, secondhand clothing, CDs, books, maps, and art.

In **Guatemala,** the town of Chichicastenango hosts a popular market in which you can find handicrafts from the Maya-Quiché culture. Many vendors wear the traditional dress of their region and sell colorful textiles including Mayan blouses called *huipiles*. Other common items include fruits and vegetables, masks, baskets, candles, and flowers.

Chichicastenango, Guatemala

El Rastro en Madrid, España

Compara con tu mundo *What type of souvenir might a visitor to your community purchase? Why is it popular?*

Ask a partner where you can find books, CDs, fruit, art, vegetables, maps, and **huipiles.**

A ¿Dónde puedo encontrar libros?

B Encuentras libros en El Rastro.

Expansión:
Teacher Edition Only
Have students think of other souvenirs to add to the list of items.

10 | ¿Y tú?

Hablar Escribir

Answer the following questions in complete sentences.

1. ¿A qué hora almuerzas?
2. ¿Cuánto cuesta el almuerzo en la cafetería de tu escuela?
3. ¿A qué hora vuelves de la escuela?
4. ¿Cuándo puedes pasar un rato con los amigos?
5. ¿Cuántas horas duermes los sábados?
6. ¿En qué tiendas encuentras tu ropa?

Expansión:
Teacher Edition Only
Have students write three questions they would like to ask a teacher using o → ue verbs.

Más práctica Cuaderno *pp. 177–179* Cuaderno para hispanohablantes *pp. 178–180*

PARA Y PIENSA

Did you get it? Complete each sentence with the correct form of the appropriate verb: **poder, costar, almorzar,** or **dormir.**

Get Help Online ClassZone.com

1. El pescado _____ diez dólares.
2. Nosotros _____ a la una en el café.
3. Yo _____ ocho horas.
4. Ellos no _____ contestar.

Lección 2
doscientos cincuenta y cinco **255**

255

¡AVANZA! **Objectives**

- Identify **o → ue** stem-changing verbs in context.
- Talk about places around town and what you find there.

Core Resources

- Video Program: DVD 1
- Audio Program: TXT CD 4 track 15

Presentation Strategies

- Have students read the Telehistoria and discuss Enrique's behavior.
- Play the audio.
- Show the video. Point to the Spanish intonation and the use of the word **¡Vale!**

Practice Sequence

- **Activity 11:** Telehistoria comprehension
- **Activity 12:** Transitional practice: **o → ue** verbs

STANDARDS

1.1 Engage in conversation, Act. 12
1.2 Understand language, Telehistoria, Act. 11
1.3 Present information, Act. 12, PYP

Warm Up UTB 4 Transparency 21

o → ue Stem-changing Verbs Complete the following sentences with the correct verb form.

1. Los chicos _____ a casa a las siete de la noche. (volver)
2. La entrada _____ veinte euros. (costar)
3. Nosotros _____ en la cafetería. (almorzar)
4. Susana _____ hablar bien el español. (poder)
5. Yo _____ en la noche. (dormir)

Answers: 1. vuelven; 2. cuesta; 3. almorzamos; 4. puede; 5. duermo

Video Summary

@HomeTutor VideoPlus ClassZone.com

Enrique and Maribel discuss what to do in the afternoon after going shopping. Maribel says she wants to return to town to hear a rock concert, to go to the movies, or to the theater. After some discussion, they decide to go to the concert. Enrique offers to go quickly to the ticket window to buy the tickets; the bus arrives while he is gone. Maribel is about to board the bus alone, but realizes that she does not have the T-shirt.

256

GRAMÁTICA *en contexto*

¡AVANZA! **Goal:** Identify the **o → ue** stem-changing verbs Enrique and Maribel use to talk about things to do in the city. Then practice using these verbs to talk about where you go. *Actividades 11–12*

Telehistoria escena 2

@**HomeTutor** VideoPlus
ClassZone.com

STRATEGIES

Cuando lees
Compare scenes As you read this scene, compare it to Scene 1. How are these scenes alike in terms of Enrique's promises and his behavior? What trends do you find?

Cuando escuchas
Identify causes A negative feeling can have more than one cause. Listen for the causes of Maribel's anxiety and concerns. How many causes are there? What are they?

VIDEO DVD
AUDIO

Enrique: ¿Qué vas a hacer hoy por la tarde?

Maribel: Después de ir de compras, quiero volver al centro. Hay un concierto de música rock, o puedo ir al cine a ver una película... ¡o puedo ir al teatro!

Enrique: ¡Un concierto de rock! ¿Puedo ir?

Maribel: Mmm... ¡quiero ir al teatro! Vamos al teatro.

Enrique: ¿Al teatro? Pero las entradas cuestan mucho, y...

After the trouble he caused, Enrique decides to go along with Maribel's idea.

Enrique: ¡Vale! Vamos al teatro.

Maribel: *(amused)* No, vamos al concierto.

Enrique: ¡Muy bien! Voy a comprar las entradas.

Maribel: ¡Pero, Enrique! El autobús...

Enrique: La ventanilla está allí, cerca del café. Vuelvo en dos minutos.

As he runs to buy the tickets, Maribel sees the bus approaching. She decides to go alone, but realizes she no longer has the T-shirt.

Maribel: ¡La camiseta! ¡No encuentro la camiseta! ¡Enrique!

Continuará... p. 262

Differentiating Instruction

Slower-paced Learners

Sentence Completion Write the following sentence starters on the board.

Después de _____, quiero _____.
Después de _____, puedo _____.
Después de _____, voy a _____.

Then ask students to complete the sentences based on their own interests and their own daily schedule.

Inclusion

Frequent Review/Repetition Ask pairs of students to read the Telehistoria and write in their notebooks forms of **poder, volver,** and **encontrar.** Have each pair read aloud the sentences containing the verb forms. Check students' pronunciation. **Hay un concierto de música rock, o puedo ir al cine. ¿Puedo ir? Vuelvo en dos minutos. ¡No encuentro la camiseta!**

11 | Planes para la tarde *Comprensión del episodio*

Escuchar
Leer

Match phrases to complete the sentences.

1. Después de ir de compras, Maribel quiere...

2. Enrique no quiere ir al teatro porque...

3. Maribel y Enrique van...

4. El autobús llega...

5. Enrique va a comprar las entradas...

a. cuando Enrique va a comprar las entradas.

b. volver al centro.

c. a un concierto de música rock en la tarde.

d. y tiene la camiseta.

e. las entradas cuestan mucho.

Expansión:
Teacher Edition Only
Ask students to write one additional incomplete statement followed by three possible phrases.

12 | ¿Qué encuentras?

Hablar
Talk with a partner about what you find in these places.

A ¿Qué encuentras en una biblioteca?

B Encuentro libros y computadoras allí.

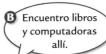

1.
2.
3.

4.
5.
6.

Expansión:
Teacher Edition Only
Have students write a description of what people can do in each of these places.

PARA Y PIENSA

Did you get it? Complete each sentence based on the Telehistoria with the correct form of the verb in parentheses.

Get Help Online
ClassZone.com

1. Maribel _____ ir al cine o al teatro. (poder)

2. Maribel no _____ la camiseta. (encontrar)

3. Enrique _____ tarde y los dos no van al centro comercial. (volver)

Differentiating Instruction

Slower-paced Learners

Memory Aids Before students begin Activity 12, give them this pre-speaking activity. Draw six circles on the board. Elicit from students the name of each location presented, and write one location in the center of each circle. Then have students brainstorm words and phrases associated with each place. Write these words around the appropriate circle.

Pre-AP

Expand and Elaborate After choosing the correct answers in Activity 11, have students brainstorm a follow-up sentence. The second sentence should provide an explanation of the first or tell what will happen next. Here is a possible elaboration for sentence 1.

Ella quiere ir a un concierto, al cine o al teatro.

Communication
Role-Playing and Skits

Have students act out a scene at the ticket window of a movie theater. Encourage students to ask questions about movie times and the cost of the tickets. For example:
¿A qué hora empieza la película? La película empieza a las tres de la tarde. ¿Cuánto cuestan las entradas? Las entradas cuestan cinco euros.

Communication
Pair Work

Have students complete answers to Activity 12 in writing. Have students correct each other's work in pairs or small groups.

✓ **Ongoing Assessment**

@HomeTutor
More Practice
ClassZone.com

PARA Y PIENSA **Quick Check** If students have difficulty completing the sentences, practice with them the conjugation of the verbs. For additional practice, use Reteaching & Practice Copymasters URB 4, pp. 16, 18.

257

¡AVANZA! Objective
· Present e → i stem-changing verbs

Core Resource
· *Cuaderno,* pp. 180–182

Presentation Strategy
· Write the full conjugation of the verb **servir** on the board. Ask students to say what the stem change is and in what forms it occurs.

STANDARD
4.1 Compare languages

⬆ Warm Up UTB 4 Transparency 22

Vocabulary Complete the sentences with the appropriate location.

**la ventanilla   el autobús   el cine
el restaurante   el parque**

1. Vamos a comer pollo en _____.
2. Queremos ver una película en _____.
3. ¿Por qué no paseamos en _____?
4. Puedes comprar entradas en _____.
5. Tomamos _____ para ir al teatro.

**Answers: 1. el restaurante; 2. el cine;
3. el parque; 4. la ventanilla; 5. el autobús**

Communication
⚠ Common Error Alert

Remind students of the Spanish pronunciation of the vowels **e** and **i**. The **e** has an *ay* sound and the **i** has an *ee* sound. This may help them correctly spell forms of the verb **servir**.

Verbs Students Know

Students have learned the following **e → i** stem-changing verbs in this lesson: **pedir** and **servir**. They will learn another one in Unit 8: **vestirse**. Remind students that stem-changing verbs are also called boot verbs.

258

Presentación de GRAMÁTICA

¡AVANZA! **Goal:** Learn how to form **e → i** stem-changing verbs. Then practice using these verbs to order from a menu. *Actividades 13–18*

♻ *¿Recuerdas?* Direct object pronouns p. 230, **tener** expressions p. 223

English Grammar Connection: Remember that there are no stem-changing verbs in the present tense of English (see p. 224). There are, however, a number of stem-changing verbs in Spanish.

Stem-Changing Verbs: e → i

**Animated Grammar
ClassZone.com**

Some **-ir** verbs have an **e → i** stem change in the present tense. How do you form the present tense of these verbs?

Here's how:

For **e → i** stem-changing verbs, the last **e** of the stem changes to **i** in all forms except **nosotros(as)** and **vosotros(as)**.

servir	to serve
s**i**rvo	s**e**rvimos
s**i**rves	serv**í**s
s**i**rve	s**i**rven

El camarero s**i**rve la comida.
The waiter serves the food.

Another verb you know with this stem change is **pedir**.

¿**Pi**des una ensalada?
Are you ordering a salad?

Siempre p**e**dimos pollo.
We always order chicken.

Más práctica
Cuaderno pp. 180–182
Cuaderno para hispanohablantes pp. 181–184

@HomeTutor
Leveled Grammar Practice
ClassZone.com

Differentiating Instruction

Heritage Language Learners

Support What They Know Ask students to model the present-tense forms of the verbs **servir** and **pedir** by using each form in a sentence. **Tú pides pollo. Nosotros pedimos pollo.** Then ask students to discuss what they notice about the stem change in each case. It changes from **e** to **i** in all conjugated forms except for **nosotros** and **vosotros**.

Multiple Intelligences

Musical/Rhythmic Have students join in a call-and-response chant to help practice the forms of stem-changing verbs. This will provide them with opportunities to hear the vowel change from **e** to **i**, for example.

Maestro(a)	Estudiantes
¡Yo sirvo!	¡Yo sirvo!
¡Tú sirves!	¡Tú sirves!
¡Nosotros servimos!	¡Nosotros servimos!

Práctica de GRAMÁTICA

13 | ¿Qué piden?

Hablar
Escribir

Tell what these people are ordering.

modelo: yo
Yo pido carne.

1. tú

2. mis amigas

3. yo

4. vosotros

5. mi madre

6. Maribel

7. mis abuelos y yo

8. ustedes

> **Expansión:**
> Teacher Edition Only
> Ask students to say what their family's favorite foods are.

14 | ¿Quién sirve la comida? ¿Recuerdas? Direct object pronouns p. 230

Hablar
Escribir

Tell what these people ask for and who serves it.

modelo: Maribel: bebida (la camarera)
Maribel pide una bebida y la camarera la sirve.

1. yo: ensalada (Enrique)

2. mi amigo: pollo (sus padres)

3. tú: pescado (yo)

4. mis amigas y yo: verduras (vosotros)

5. usted: patatas (nosotros)

6. vosotros: postre (el camarero)

> **Expansión:**
> Teacher Edition Only
> Have students talk about what they ask for and what their family serves for breakfast, lunch, and dinner.

Pronunciación   La letra c con e, i

AUDIO

Before **e** and **i**, the Spanish **c** is pronounced like the *c* in *city*.

Listen and repeat.

ce → cero   centro
      cerrar   quince

ci → cien   cine
      precio   estación

In many regions of Spain, the **c** before **e** and **i** is pronounced like the *th* of the English word *think*.

Necesitamos cinco lápices para hacer la tarea de ciencias.

Differentiating Instruction

Pre-AP

Expand and Elaborate Ask students to write a note to a friend who is coming to visit him or her. The e-mail should mention what time to arrive, a description of what they will eat, and what they will do. **Llegas el sábado a las doce. Vamos a almorzar pescado con ensalada y un buen postre. Después vamos al cine.**

Inclusion

Clear Structure Have students work in groups to create restaurant menus including pictures and prices in euros. Allow them to use their imagination in creating the menu. Then ask each group to read aloud their menus and prices. **En nuestro restaurante el pollo cuesta nueve euros. El pescado cuesta quince euros.** Have students compete for the best menu and presentation.

Objectives

· Practice the present tense of **e → i** stem-changing verbs.
· **Culture:** Compare Velázquez's *Las meninas* to a re-creation of it by Picasso.
· Practice food-related vocabulary.
· Recycle: **tener** expressions.

Core Resources

· *Cuaderno,* pp. 180–182
· Audio Program: TXT CD 4, track 17

Practice Sequence

· **Activity 15:** Controlled practice: **e → ie** stem-changing verbs
· **Activity 16:** Transitional practice: **e → ie** stem-changing verbs
· **Activity 17:** Open-ended practice: **e → ie** stem-changing verbs; food vocabulary
· **Activity 18:** Transitional practice: **e → ie** stem-changing verbs, food vocabulary; Recycle: **tener** expressions.

STANDARDS

1.1 Engage in conversation, Acts. 17–18
1.2 Understand language, Act. 16
1.3 Present information, Acts. 15–18, PYP
2.2 Products and perspectives, CC
4.2 Compare cultures, CC

 Answers MSRB Transparency 57

Activity 15
1. pide; **2.** piden; **3.** pido; **4.** sirven; **5.** pedimos; **6.** sirve

Activity 16
1. Sirven pollo y arroz. **2.** Sirve bistec y patatas. **3.** Sirve brócoli. **4.** Sirve pescado. **5.** Sirven verduras. **6.** Sirve pastel de frutas.

Activity 17
Diana pide pescado y ensalada.
Tomás pide pollo y una patata.
Las chicas piden un refresco.
Gabriel pide un jugo de naranja.
El Sr. Rivera pide café.
El camarero sirve una pizza.
Los dos camareros sirven pasteles.
Un camarero sirve bistec y brócoli.

260

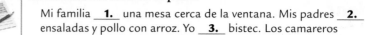

15 | Una cena especial

Hablar Escribir

Enrique and his family are going out to dinner. Complete what he says with the correct form of **servir** or **pedir**.

Mi familia __1.__ una mesa cerca de la ventana. Mis padres __2.__ ensaladas y pollo con arroz. Yo __3.__ bistec. Los camareros __4.__ las ensaladas y los platos principales. Todos nosotros __5.__ helado. El camarero __6.__ los postres.

Expansión:
Teacher Edition Only
Have students rewrite the paragraph using different subjects; then have them exchange with partners.

16 | ¿Qué sirven en el café?

Escuchar Escribir

Enrique is in a café and is talking to the waiters and waitresses. Write sentences to tell what these people are serving.

1. los camareros   **3.** el camarero   **5.** Luis y José
2. el señor Fuentes   **4.** la camarera   **6.** Ana

⌂ Audio Program
TXT CD 4 Track 17
Audio Script, TE p. 243b

17 | En el restaurante

Hablar Escribir

Look at the restaurant scene below. Tell what the people are ordering or serving.

Tomás

Diana

Gabriel

el Sr. Rivera

Expansión:
Teacher Edition Only
Have students tell why the customers are ordering these foods and beverages.

Differentiating Instruction

Inclusion

Alphabetic/Phonetic Awareness Help students practice the stem-changing verbs **pedir** and **servir** by playing this spelling game. Say a form of one of the verbs aloud slowly, such as **pido.** Isolate each sound as you come to it. Have students repeat. Then ask for a volunteer to come spell the word on the board. Have all students judge whether the form is spelled correctly.

Slower-paced Learners

Personalize It Ask students to imagine they are in the restaurant shown in the scene at the bottom of the page. Have students talk about what they would order. **Yo pido pastel y café. Nosotros pedimos pizza.**

18 ¿Qué pides del menú?  ¿Recuerdas? tener expressions p. 223

Hablar Ask a partner what he or she orders in a restaurant in the following situations.

modelo: bebida / en el almuerzo

> **A** ¿Qué bebida pides en el almuerzo?
>
> **B** Pido leche o un refresco.

1. comida / en el almuerzo
2. bebida / cuando tienes frío
3. bebida / en el desayuno
4. comida / cuando tienes calor
5. comida / cuando tienes hambre
6. bebida / cuando tienes mucha sed

Expansión:
Teacher Edition Only
Have students write about other things that they ask for at home and at school.

Comparación cultural

Las meninas

Why might an artist create a version of another artist's masterpiece? Diego Velázquez served as the official painter for King Philip IV of **Spain** and painted many portraits of the royal family. *Las meninas* shows the *Infanta* (princess) and her attendants. Velázquez included himself in the painting. Three centuries later, Pablo Picasso, also from Spain, completed 58 interpretations of this painting. What similarities and differences do you notice?

Las meninas (1656), Diego Velázquez

Las meninas (Infanta Margarita) (1957), Pablo Picasso

Compara con tu mundo

What famous artwork would you like to try to re-create and why? How would your version be different from the original?

Más práctica Cuaderno *pp. 180–182* Cuaderno para hispanohablantes *pp. 181–184*

PARA Y PIENSA

Did you get it? Complete each sentence with the correct form of **pedir** or **servir**.
1. En la cena los camareros _____ arroz con pollo.
2. Mi madre hace un pastel y lo _____ de postre.
3. Nosotros no _____ mucho porque no tenemos mucha hambre.

Get Help Online ClassZone.com

Lección 2
doscientos sesenta y uno **261**

Differentiating Instruction

Multiple Intelligences

Interpersonal Have students practice ordering food. Have a few advanced students act as **camareros** writing the orders from other students acting as **clientes.** Be ready to correct pronunciation. Student A: **Tengo calor. Yo pido una ensalada.** Student B: **Yo quiero pollo y ensalada.** When all students have ordered, have the **camareros** show what they wrote and correct if necessary.

Heritage Language Learners

Writing Skills Have students create a Venn diagram with the heading **Las meninas, Diego Velázquez** on one side, and **Las meninas, Pablo Picasso** on the other. Have them record details describing how the two works are similar and different. Allow them to share their observations, and then develop their organizers into a brief compare/contrast paragraph.

Have students stand in a circle. Tell the students that you will be reviewing all three types of stem-changing verbs. You may want to review the forms before beginning this activity. Toss a soft ball to a student and say a stem-changing verb and a subject. That student will respond with the correct form and toss the ball back to you. Continue until you have heard each student give at least one correct response. Use as many of the stem-changing verbs as possible.

Comparación cultural

Essential Question

Suggested Answer An artist might recreate a famous painting to honor the work of the artist who created the original work or to continue a particular art or historical tradition.

About the Artist

Diego Velázquez (1599–1660), born in Seville, Spain, was a noted portrait artist. He created many portraits of the Spanish royal family, other notable European figures, and commoners, culminating in the production of his masterpiece, **Las Meninas.**

✓ Ongoing Assessment

@HomeTutor More Practice ClassZone.com

PARA Y PIENSA
Remediation If students have problems completing the Para y piensa, have them review p. 258 and repeat Activities 13 and 14 on p. 259. For additional practice, use Reteaching & Practice Copymasters URB 4, pp. 19, 20, 23, 24.

Answers MSRB Transparency 57

Activity 18 Answers will vary. Sample answers include:
1. **A.** ¿Qué comida pides en el almuerzo?
   B. Pido una ensalada.
2. **A.** ¿... cuando tienes frío? **B.** Pido un café.
3. **A.** ¿... en el desayuno? **B.** Pido leche.
4. **A.** ¿... cuando tienes calor? **B.** Pido una ensalada.
5. **A.** ¿... cuando tienes hambre? **B.** Pido carne.
6. **A.** ¿... cuando tienes mucha sed? **B.** Pido un refresco.

Para y piensa 1. sirven; 2. sirve; 3. pedimos

261

Objectives

· Integrate lesson content.

Core Resources
· Video Program: DVD 1
· Audio Program: TXT CD 4 tracks 14, 15, 18

Presentation Strategies
· Ask students to describe the photo for Escena 3 by asking: **¿Dónde están Enrique y Maribel ahora? ¿Quién más está en la foto?**
· Show the video and/or play the audio.

Practice Sequence
· **Activities 19, 20:** Telehistoria comprehension
· **Activity 21:** Open-ended practice: speaking

STANDARDS
1.1 Engage in conversation, Act. 21
1.2 Understand language, Acts. 19–20
1.3 Present infomation, Acts. 19–20

Warm Up UTB 4 Transparency 22

e → i Stem-changing Verbs Complete the sentences with appropriate forms of **pedir** or **servir.**

1. El camarero _____ la comida.
2. Ana Luisa _____ una ensalada porque no tiene mucha hambre.
3. Nosotros preparamos un pastel y lo _____.

Answers: 1. sirve; 2. pide; 3. servimos

Video Summary @HomeTutor VideoPlus ClassZone.com

Later, at a café, Maribel is disappointed not to have Trini's autograph. Enrique offers to pay for the meal. When the waiter arrives, Maribel orders a big meal. Enrique is alarmed. He then realizes his backpack (and money) are still missing. Maribel offers to pay.

▶❚ ❚❚

262

Todo junto

¡AVANZA! **Goal:** *Show what you know* Pay attention to how Maribel and Enrique tell the waiter what they would like to eat. Then practice using **o → ue** and **e → i** stem-changing verbs to order food and give your opinion on restaurants. *Actividades 19–23*

Telehistoria completa

@*HomeTutor* VideoPlus ClassZone.com

STRATEGIES

Cuando lees

Analyze the communication Analyze this scene's communication by answering these questions: Why does Maribel order so much food? What is the effect?

Cuando escuchar

Listen for contrasts Listen for contrasts during the scene. Examples: What do Maribel and Enrique order? Who promises to pay, and who actually pays?

 **Escena 1** *Resumen*
Enrique y Maribel pueden tomar el autobús setenta y cuatro al centro comercial. Piensan llegar a las doce y media.

 **Escena 2** *Resumen*
Enrique va a comprar las entradas para un concierto. El autobús llega pero Enrique no está. Maribel no tiene la camiseta.

VIDEO DVD

AUDIO

Escena 3

They arrive at an outdoor restaurant.

Enrique: Es un restaurante muy bonito.

Maribel: Pero no tengo el autógrafo de Trini.

Enrique: Vamos a pedir la comida. ¡Yo pago!

Maribel: Ah, ¿pagas tú? Ahora pido toda la comida del menú.

The waiter arrives.

Maribel: Señor, ¿sirven pescado hoy?

Camarero: No, hoy no tenemos pescado.

Maribel: Quiero empezar con una ensalada. De plato principal quiero el pollo con verduras y... Sí, y filete con patatas.

Camarero: ¿Dos platos principales? ¿Filete y pollo?

Enrique: Es mucho, ¿no?

Maribel: Sí. Y de postre quiero un arroz con leche.

Enrique: *(nervously)* Pan y agua, por favor.

Maribel: Él va a pagar la cuenta.

Enrique: *(nods, then remembers)* ¡Maribel! ¡Mi mochila! ¡No tengo dinero!

Maribel: *(smiling)* Ay, Enrique, yo sí tengo dinero.

Unidad 4 España
262 doscientos sesenta y dos

Differentiating Instruction

Pre-AP

Sequence Information Have students make a written summary of what happened in the **Escena 3.** For example: 1. **Enrique y Maribel llegan al restaurante.** 2. **Ellos piden la comida.** 3. **Enrique no puede pagar porque no tiene su mochila.** 4. **Maribel paga. Ella sí tiene dinero.** Have students read aloud their summaries. Check for misspellings and pronunciation.

Inclusion

Frequent Review/Repetition Assign students one line from the Telehistoria to focus on. Give them time to interpret the line's meaning, and rehearse saying it aloud. Remind students to read with intonation when they see exclamation points and question marks. **¡Yo pago!** and **Ah, ¿pagas tú?** After students are prepared, read through the script, pointing to each reader in turn.

19 | ¿Quién lo hace? *Comprensión de los episodios*

Escuchar Leer

Read these sentences and tell whether they are about Enrique or Maribel.

1. Quiere volver al centro después de ir de compras.
2. Piensa que las entradas cuestan mucho.
3. No encuentra la camiseta.
4. Piensa que el restaurante es muy bonito.
5. Pide mucha comida.

> **Expansión:**
> Teacher Edition Only
> Ask students to create two sentences that refer to both Enrique and Maribel.

20 | Problemas en el centro *Comprensión de los episodios*

Escuchar Leer

Answer the questions according to the episodes.

1. ¿Cómo quieren ir Maribel y Enrique al centro comercial?
2. ¿Adónde va el autobús setenta y cuatro?
3. ¿Por qué no quiere ir al teatro Enrique?
4. ¿Por qué está enojada Maribel?
5. ¿Qué pide Maribel en el restaurante?

> **Expansión:**
> Teacher Edition Only
> Ask students to summarize what has happened in the Telehistoria so far.

21 | Clientes y camareros

Hablar

> **STRATEGY**
>
> **Plan the whole scene** Plan the whole scene from start to finish. What would the waiter or waitress say before, during, and after the meal? What would the customers say at each stage?

Work in a group of three. Prepare a scene in a café with customers and a waiter or waitress. Present your scene to the class.

Para organizarte:
- qué comidas y bebidas piden
- qué sirve el (la) camarero(a)
- cuánto cuesta la comida (la cuenta y la propina)

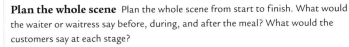

Camarero(a) Buenas tardes. ¿Quieren ver el menú?

Cliente 1 Buenas tardes. Sí, por favor. Tenemos mucha hambre.

Ustedes pueden pedir el pollo con patatas. Es mucha comida.

Cliente 2 Tal vez, pero hoy tengo ganas de comer...

> **Expansión:**
> Teacher Edition Only
> Ask students to write what they would order at a restaurant.

Lección 2
doscientos sesenta y tres **263**

Pre-AP

Expand and Elaborate Read aloud the sentences in the Telehistoria where **servir** and **pedir** are used: **Vamos a pedir la comida.** and **¿Sirven pescado?** Ask each student to expand those two sentences by using other verb forms. For example, **Yo pido ensalada, nosotros pedimos pollo.** Continue with **Nosotros servimos. Tú sirves frutas.** Continue until all students have participated.

Heritage Language Learners

Support What They Know Encourage students to add a complication to their scene in Activity 21. Have them create a problem at the restaurant that needs to be resolved. Perhaps the kitchen has run out of a certain dish. Perhaps the client has forgotten his or her wallet. As students plan their scenes, have them brainstorm how the problem will be resolved.

Rubric Activity 21

Speaking Criteria	Maximum Credit	Partial Credit	Minimum Credit
Content	Dialogue includes all the information.	Dialogue includes some of the information.	Dialogue includes little information.
Communication	Easy to understand. Good pronunciation.	Can be understood. Some errors in pronunciation.	Hard to understand. Many errors in pronunciation.
Accuracy	Few mistakes in grammar and vocabulary.	Some mistakes in grammar and vocabulary.	Many mistakes in grammar and vocabulary.

Answers MSRB Transparency 58

Activity 19
1. Maribel
2. Enrique
3. Maribel
4. Enrique
5. Maribel

Activity 20
1. Maribel y Enrique quieren ir al centro comercial en autobús.
2. El autobús setenta y cuatro va al centro comercial.
3. Enrique no quiere ir al teatro porque las entradas cuestan mucho.
4. Maribel está enojada porque no tiene la camiseta. Enrique la tiene en su mochila.
5. Maribel pide una ensalada, pollo con verduras, filete con patatas, y arroz con leche.

Activity 21 Answers should follow this pattern:

Camarero(a): Buenas tardes (noches). ¿Quieren ver el menú? Pueden pedir...

Cliente(s): Yo quiero... or Tengo ganas de comer... or Tengo hambre, voy a pedir...

263

Objective

· Practice using and integrating lesson vocabulary and grammar.

Core Resources

· *Cuaderno*, pp. 183–184
· Audio Program: TXT CD 4 tracks 19, 20

Practice Sequence

· **Activity 22:** Open-ended practice: reading, listening, speaking
· **Activity 23:** Open-ended practice: writing

STANDARDS

1.2 Understand language, Act. 22
1.3 Present information, Acts. 22–23, PYP

Long-term Retention

 Pre-AP Integration

Activity 22 can be used as a model for a short writing assignment. Have students write a paragraph in which they describe five activities they are going to do, where, and how they are going to get there.

 Ongoing Assessment

Rubric Activity 22
Listening/Speaking

Proficient	Not There Yet
Students' notes and oral description reflect comprehension of the materials.	Students' notes and oral description do not reflect comprehension of the materials.

Ongoing Assessment

@HomeTutor More Practice ClassZone.com

PARA Y PIENSA **Quick Check** If students have difficulties choosing the correct verb form, review pp. 252, 258. For additional practice, use Reteaching & Practice Copymasters URB 4, pp. 19, 21.

See Activity answers on p. 265.

---

22 | Integración

Leer
Escuchar
Hablar

Read the pamphlet and listen to the guide. Describe five activities you are going to do, where, and how you can get there.

Fuente 1 Folleto del hotel

Fuente 2 Anuncio del guía turístico

Listen and take notes

· ¿Qué actividades menciona el guía?
· ¿En qué lugares puedes hacer las actividades?

modelo: Voy a comer pescado. Voy al Restaurante Oberón. Puedo ir a pie o en coche...

Audio Program
TXT CD 4 Tracks 19, 20
Audio Script, TE p. 243b

23 | Una crítica culinaria

Escribir

You are a newspaper food critic. Write a short review of your favorite restaurant. Explain what the waiters are like, what they serve, what you order, what the food is like, and how much it costs.

modelo: El restaurante Salazar es muy bueno. Los camareros son trabajadores. De plato principal sirven...

Writing Criteria	Excellent	Good	Needs Work
Content	Your review includes a lot of information.	Your review includes some information.	Your review includes little information.
Communication	Most of your review is organized and easy to follow.	Parts of your review are organized and easy to follow.	Your review is disorganized and hard to follow.
Accuracy	Your review has few mistakes in grammar and vocabulary.	Your review has some mistakes in grammar and vocabulary.	Your review has many mistakes in grammar and vocabulary.

Expansión:
Teacher Edition Only
Ask students to read aloud their critiques, and then ask the class to select the best critique.

Más práctica   Cuaderno *pp. 183–184*   Cuaderno para hispanohablantes *pp. 185–186*

 PARA Y PIENSA

Did you get it? Choose the correct verb to make each sentence logical according to the Telehistoria.
1. Maribel y Enrique (almuerzan / encuentran) en un restaurante bonito.
2. Maribel (sirve / pide) mucha comida.
3. Enrique no (puede / vuelve) pagar.

Get Help Online ClassZone.com

Differentiating Instruction

Multiple Intelligences

Interpersonal Organize students into pairs. Then have them perform Activity 22 in the form of a role-play. One student is the tour guide, and the other is the traveler. Encourage students to think about how their characters would feel at each stage of the situation.

Slower-paced Learners

Peer-study Support Make copies of the Writing Criteria Rubric for each student. Have them exchange their restaurant reviews with a partner. Instruct students to read their partner's work, and circle what they feel is the appropriate box for each criterion. Require students to justify their evaluations with concrete examples, as well as provide advice for improvement.

Juegos y diversiones

Review vocabulary by playing a game.

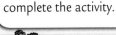

CUATRO RINCONES

The Setup

Your teacher will label a poster for each corner of the room: **el restaurante, el cine, el parque,** and **el centro.** Form two teams.

Playing the Game

Your teacher will give each of you in turn an index card with a Spanish word or phrase on it. Go to the corner of the room for the place related to the word or phrase on your card. Then use the word(s) on your card and the location name in a sentence.

Your team will receive one point for each player who goes to the correct corner and a second point for each player to use the words correctly in a sentence.

The Winner!

The team with the most points at the end wins.

Materials

- index cards with Spanish words and phrases
- four posters representing places in a city

Hay tiendas en el centro.

EL CENTRO

Lección 2
doscientos sesenta y cinco **265**

Objective
- Review vocabulary by playing a game.

 STANDARDS
5.2 Life-long learners

Communication
Pair Work

Have students create a word search (using graph paper) or a word scramble using vocabulary related to **el restaurante, el cine, el parque,** and **el centro.** Limit the number of words that they are to use. Have them exchange their puzzles with a partner and complete the activity.

Communication
Group Work

You may want to have students make posters representing the restaurant, the movie theater, the park, and downtown. Here are suggestions for words to go with the four places:
el restaurante: **almorzar, camarero(a), cena, cuenta, desayuno, menú, plato principal, postre, propina, servir,** and other food vocabulary students have learned
el cine: **entradas, película, ventanilla**
el parque: **correr, montar en bicicleta, practicar deportes**
el centro: **calles, ir de compras, teatro, tiendas**

Long-term Retention
Recycle

To make the game more challenging, you may want to use words from other units that could logically go with more than one of the places. Some examples are: **concierto, comprar, dinero, pagar, pasar un rato con los amigos, pasear, vender.**

Answers MSRB Transparency 58

Answers for Activities on p. 264.

Activity 22 Answers will vary. Sample answers include: Voy a buscar libros. Voy a la Biblioteca Nacional. Puedo ir a pie o en autobús.

Activity 23 Answers will vary. Sample answers include: Mi restaurante favorito se llama Sevilla. Allí sirven pollo con arroz y ensalada, y postres muy ricos. Siempre pido pollo y una ensalada y de postre arroz con leche...

Para y piensa 1. almuerzan; **2.** pide; **3.** puede

265

Differentiating Instruction

Inclusion

Cumulative Instruction Before students play **Cuatro rincones,** give them the opportunity to review what they know about the four locations mentioned. Create four concept webs on the board with the name of one location in the center of each. Then have volunteers add words and phrases around each web. Encourage students to use each word or phrase in a sentence.

Heritage Language Learners

Support What They Know Challenge students to play the game using different places. For example: **el estadio, el centro comercial, el teatro, el café.** Encourage them to say at least three sentences about each place. **Me gusta ir al centro comercial. Allí hay muchas tiendas, cafés y restaurantes. Mi tienda favorita se llama...**

¡AVANZA! Objectives
- Read about weekend activities in Spain and Chile.
- Compare weekend activities in Spain, Chile, and the U.S.
- Find out about popular places and attractions in Madrid and Santiago de Chile.

Core Resources
- Audio Program: TXT CD 4 track 21

Presentation Strategies
- Ask a volunteer to read the ¡Avanza! out loud to the class
- Discuss students' favorite weekend activities briefly before listening to the audio or reading the text.

STANDARDS
1.2 Understand language
1.3 Present information
3.2 Acquire information
4.2 Compare cultures

Warm Up UTB 4 Transparency 23

e → i Verbs Complete each sentence with the correct form of **pedir.**
1. Jorge _____ carne.
2. Yo _____ verduras.
3. Carlos y José _____ patatas.
4. Emilia y yo _____ pollo.
5. Vosotros _____ postre.

Answers: 1. pide; 2. pido; 3. piden; 4. pedimos; 5. pedís

Comparación cultural

Background Information
El Parque del Buen Retiro was originally the site of a royal palace built in 1632 for King Philip IV. Most of the palace was destroyed during the Napoleonic Wars, but its site was opened to the public in 1868. Within the park is the **Estanque del Retiro**, a large artificial lake. Next to it is the Mausoleum of King Alfonso XII, which features a statue of the king on horseback. King Alfonso XII reigned between 1874 and 1885.

266

Lectura cultural

¡AVANZA! **Goal:** Read about weekend activities in Spain and Chile. Then talk about what each city offers and compare these activities with what you do on weekends.

Comparación cultural

AUDIO

El fin de semana en España y Chile

STRATEGY Leer
List attractions and places
Use a table like the one below to list attractions and the places where they can be found.

	conciertos	zoológico	botes
Madrid	Parque del Buen Retiro		
Santiago de Chile			

Los habitantes de Madrid, España, y Santiago de Chile hacen muchas actividades en el fin de semana. Van a parques, restaurantes, teatros, cines y otros lugares divertidos. También van de compras.

En Madrid hay muchos lugares interesantes para pasar los fines de semana. La Plaza Mayor tiene muchos cafés y restaurantes. Hay un mercado de sellos[1] los domingos. El Parque del Buen Retiro es un lugar perfecto para descansar y pasear. En este parque hay jardines[2], cafés y un lago[3] donde las personas pueden alquilar botes. Hay conciertos allí en el verano. Otro parque popular es la Casa de Campo. Hay un zoológico, una piscina[4], un parque de diversiones[5] y un lago para botes.

Hay muchas tiendas en el centro. El almacén[6] más grande es El Corte Inglés: allí los madrileños[7] pueden comprar ropa, comida y mucho más.

---

[1] **mercado...** stamp market [2] gardens [3] lake
[4] swimming pool [5] **parque...** amusement park
[6] department store [7] people of Madrid

Unidad 4 España
266 doscientos sesenta y seis

El Parque del Buen Retiro en Madrid

Differentiating Instruction

Pre-AP
Sequence Information Ask students to work in pairs, telling each other about favorite weekend activities. Ask them to put them in chronological order. **For example: Los sábados a las once practico básquetbol. A la una voy a un restaurante.**

Multiple Intelligences
Interpersonal Divide the class into groups of four. Ask each group to decide on a weekend activity they all like, and where they like to take part in this activity. Have them work collaboratively to create a collage that illustrates what they want to do, where they want to do it, how they will get there, and what they will wear. Their collages should include sentences and phrases in Spanish.

La Plaza de Armas

En Santiago de Chile las personas pasan los fines de semana en muchos lugares. Siempre hay mucha actividad en la Plaza de Armas, la parte histórica de Santiago. Hay conciertos allí los domingos.

El parque del Cerro Santa Lucía es perfecto para pasear. Los santiaguinos[8] pueden ver jardines y el panorama de Santiago. El Cerro San Cristóbal en el Parque Metropolitano es un lugar favorito para comer, correr y montar en bicicleta. Hay jardines, piscinas, un zoológico, cafés y restaurantes en el parque.

Los santiaguinos van a tiendas en el centro y a centros comerciales como Alto Las Condes. En el Mercado Central pueden comprar pescado y frutas y comer en restaurantes con precios baratos[9].

---

[8] people of Santiago, Chile   [9] inexpensive

Chile

Cerro San Cristóbal

PARA Y PIENSA

¿Comprendiste?

1. ¿Qué hay en la Plaza Mayor y la Plaza de Armas los domingos?
2. ¿A qué parques van los madrileños y los santiaguinos?
3. ¿Dónde pueden ir de compras los habitantes de Madrid y Santiago?

¿Y tú?

¿Cuál(es) de estos lugares en Madrid y Santiago quieres visitar? ¿Adónde vas los fines de semana donde vives? ¿Qué haces allí?

Lección 2
doscientos sesenta y siete **267**

Differentiating Instruction

Multiple Intelligences

Logical/Mathematical Ask students to list three of their favorite weekend activities, and think about how much time they need to take part in them. Ask them to create a schedule that will show whether they can do all three activities in a Saturday or Sunday afternoon. They should be sure to include time to get ready and transportation time.

Slower-Paced Learners

Yes/No Questions Ask students yes/no questions to evaluate their understanding of the readings. Examples: **¿Hay muchos cafés y restaurantes en la Plaza Mayor? ¿Hay un lago en el Parque del Buen Retiro? ¿Hay conciertos en la Plaza de Armas? ¿Está el Cerro San Cristóbal en el Parque Metropolitano?**

Communication

Pair Work

Assign student pairs to talk about a weekend at one of the parks mentioned in the reading. Their conversation should include a place, mode of transportation, what to wear, when to go, and what to do there. For example: **A: ¿Vamos al Parque del Buen Retiro? B: Vale. ¿Vamos a pie o en autobús? A: Vamos en autobús. ¿Qué vas a llevar? B: Jeans y una camiseta porque hace calor. A: ¿Quieres montar en bicicleta? B: No, prefiero...** Ask them to rehearse the conversation before presenting it to the class.

Comparisons

English Language Connections

Call students' attention to the construction: **pasar los fines de semana.** Ask them to compare the grammar and word order to the English: *to spend the weekends*.

Long-term Retention

Personalize It

Ask students to choose a place they would like to visit in Madrid or Santiago. Ask them to imagine themselves in that place and write a short description of it. What time of day is it? What are the people doing? What are they wearing? Encourage them to add as many details as possible.

Answers

Para y piensa ¿Comprendiste?
1. Hay un mercado de sellos en la Plaza Mayor y hay conciertos en la Plaza de Armas.
2. Los madrileños van al Parque del Buen Retiro y a la Casa de Campo. Los santiaguinos van al parque del Cerro Santa Lucía y al Parque Metropolitano.
3. Los habitantes de Madrid pueden ir a El Corte Inglés y los habitantes de Santiago pueden ir a centros comerciales como Alto Las Condes.

¿Y tú? Answers will vary but should follow the model: Quiero visitar... Yo voy a... Voy a las tiendas. Como en restaurantes. Escucho conciertos.

267

Proyectos culturales

Objectives

- Read about paintings from Spain and from Chile.
- **Culture:** Discuss how to interpret an artist's painting.
- **Community:** Investigate sources of Spanish or Latin American art in the community.
- Create an original landscape painting.

Presentation Strategies

- Draw students' attention to the two paintings and to the essential question.
- Ask students to think of the subjects and the colors of the paintings.

STANDARDS

1.3 Present information
2.1 Practices and perspectives
2.2 Products and perspectives
4.2 Compare cultures
5.1 Spanish in the community

Comparación cultural

Essential Question

Suggested Answer An artist can communicate a wide range of messages through a work of art. Artists can express many emotions, from anger to sadness, from love to hatred. They can express the harmony or fury of nature, and they can communicate their opinions of historical events.

Expanded Information

Juan Francisco González studied in Europe and traveled widely; he was one of the most accomplished Chilean painters of his era.
Ignacio Zuloaga y Zabaleta also traveled widely, returning to Spain to create a personal vision of his country.

Communities

Spanish in the Marketplace

Visit a museum or a poster store in your area. Can you find works of art from Spanish-speaking countries? If so, which artists are represented and what are the titles of their paintings?

268

Comparación cultural

Pinturas de España y Chile

What messages can an artist communicate through a painting? When you look at a painting, you might see something different than what the artist originally intended when he or she painted it. In fact, a single work of art can have a number of different interpretations.

España *Landscape near El Escorial (1932), Ignacio Zuloaga y Zabaleta*

Chile *Calle de Melipilla (sin fecha), Juan Francisco González*

Proyecto 1 *Interpret and investigate*

Interpreting the two paintings above from **Spain** and **Chile.**

Instructions

1. After looking at each painting, describe it to yourself. What message do you get from it? As you scan the painting, does any particular point draw your attention?
2. Use the Internet or your school's library to learn more about the two paintings. You might look up information about the artists and whether the paintings reflect personal events in their lives.

Proyecto 2 *Your own painting*

Now try your hand at being an artist.

Materials for your own painting
Construction paper
Charcoal pencil, colored pencils or pens, watercolor paint, paintbrushes

Instructions
Create a landscape scene on construction paper. Use the paintings above as an inspiration.

En tu comunidad

Visit a museum in your community or area that contains works of art from a Spanish-speaking country. What can you learn about that country by examining the artwork? Record your impressions in a journal.

268 Unidad 4 España
doscientos sesenta y ocho

Differentiating Instruction

Multiple Intelligences

Naturalist Ask students to look at the two paintings for clues to the time of year and the climate of the environment. Ask: **¿Qué estación es? ¿Qué tiempo hace?** What can they tell about the trees? Can they identify the species? In what climates do these trees grow?

English Learners

Build Background Look for landscapes depicting the countryside in the home countries of English learners. Using gestures and simple directions, ask students to find similarities between the paintings of their first countries with those of González and Zuloaga.

Lección 2

En resumen
Vocabulario y gramática

Animated Grammar
Interactive Flashcards
ClassZone.com

Vocabulario

Describe Places in Town

el café	café
el centro	center, downtown
el cine	movie theater; the movies
el parque	park
el restaurante	restaurant
el teatro	theater

Describe Events in Town

el concierto	concert
las entradas	tickets
la música rock	rock music
la película	movie
la ventanilla	ticket window

Getting Around Town

a pie	by foot
la calle	street
en autobús	by bus
en coche	by car
encontrar (ue)	to find
tomar	to take

In a Restaurant

el (la) camarero(a)	(food) server
costar (ue)	to cost
la cuenta	bill
de postre	for dessert
el menú	menu
la mesa	table
el plato principal	main course
la propina	tip

For Dinner

el arroz	rice
el bistec	beef
el brócoli	broccoli
la carne	meat
la ensalada	salad
los frijoles	beans
el pastel	cake
la patata	potato
el pescado	fish
el pollo	chicken
el tomate	tomato
las verduras	vegetables

Ordering from a Menu

pedir (i)	to order, to ask for
servir (i)	to serve

Other Words and Phrases

allí	there
almorzar (ue)	to eat lunch
aquí	here
dormir (ue)	to sleep
el lugar	place
poder (ue)	to be able, can
tal vez	perhaps, maybe
ver	to see
volver (ue)	to return, to come back

Gramática

Notas gramaticales: The verb **ver** *p. 249,* **ir a** + infinitive *p. 251*

Stem-Changing Verbs: o → ue

For o → ue stem-changing verbs, the last o of the stem changes to ue in all forms except **nosotros(as)** and **vosotros(as).**

poder	*to be able, can*
puedo	**po**demos
puedes	**po**déis
puede	**pue**den

Stem-Changing Verbs: e → i

For e → i stem-changing verbs, the last e of the stem changes to i in all forms except **nosotros(as)** and **vosotros(as).**

se**rvir**	*to serve*
si**rvo**	se**rvimos**
si**rves**	se**rvís**
si**rve**	si**rven**

Objective
· Review lesson vocabulary and grammar.

Online SPANISH CLASSZONE.COM

Interactive Flashcards Students can hear every target vocabulary word pronounced in authentic Spanish. Flashcards have Spanish on one side, and a picture or a translation on the other.

Self-Quiz Students can check their understanding and get instant results with our online multiple-choice quizzes. These quizzes provide immediate feedback, making them a great way to prepare for a quiz or test.

Featuring...
- Cultura INTERACTIVA
- Animated Grammar
- @HomeTutor

And more...
· Get Help Online
· Interactive Flashcards
· Review Games
· WebQuest
· Self-Check Quiz

Long-term Retention
Study Tips

Encourage students to list new vocabulary in groups that will help them remember the words later. For example, they could list food vocabulary under meats and vegetables. They could list places and events in town in order of preference.

Communication
Pair Work

Ask students to take turns practicing stem-changing verbs. One student starts a pattern sentence like **Yo puedo ir a la escuela,** and takes turns with his or her partner repeating it using other subject pronouns.

Communication
Humor and Creativity

Ask students to draw cartoons illustrating a visit to a restaurant. They should also create a dialog between waiter (waitress) and client(s), using the vocabulary words, and write it in balloons over the characters' heads.

Differentiating Instruction

Inclusion

Multisensory Input/Output Ask students to act out going to a concert, and to narrate what they're doing. For example: **Vamos en coche al concierto. Voy a la ventanilla para comprar las entradas. Escuchamos música rock.**

Slower-paced Learners

Memory Aids Ask students to work in groups to create murals on butcher paper. One mural should show a group of friends going out to dinner at a restaurant. The other should show a group of friends going to a concert. The murals should show as much of the activity as possible, and each part should be labeled with the appropriate vocabulary words.

Objective
· Review lesson grammar and vocabulary.

Core Resources
· *Cuaderno*, pp. 185–196
· Audio Program: TXT CD 4 track 22

Presentation Strategies
· Before playing the audio for Activity 1, ask students to listen carefully to the dishes that are mentioned.
· Before doing Activity 2, have students identify the modes of transportation in the photos.
· Monitor use of correct forms of **o → ue** and **e → i** stem-changing verbs in Activities 3–4.
· Read the Comparación cultural with students and clarify any questions that arise.
· Review may be done in class or given as homework.
· Students can access additional review activities online at ClassZone.com.

STANDARDS
1.2 Understand language, Acts. 1, 3
1.3 Present information, Acts. 2, 4
4.2 Compare cultures, Act. 5

Warm Up UTB 4 Transparency 23

Vocabulary Identify the following as either **carne** or **verdura**.

1. el bistec
2. el brócoli
3. el pescado
4. los frijoles
5. el pollo

Answers: 1. carne; 2. verdura; 3. carne; 4. verdura; 5. carne

✓ Ongoing Assessment
@HomeTutor More Practice ClassZone.com

Remediation If students achieve less than 85% accuracy with the activities, direct them to pp. 244, 251–252, 255, 258, 261, 266–267 and to get help online at ClassZone.com.

See Activity answers on p. 271.

Lección 2

Repaso de la lección

¡LLEGADA!

@HomeTutor
ClassZone.com

Now you can
· describe places and events in town
· talk about types of transportation
· say what you are going to do
· order from a menu

Using
· **ir a** + infinitive
· stem-changing verbs: **o → ue**
· stem-changing verbs: **e → i**

Audio Program
TXT CD 4 Track 22
Audio Script, TE
p. 243b

To review
· stem-changing verbs: **o → ue** p. 252
· **ir a** + infinitive p. 251
· stem-changing verbs: **e → i** p. 258

1 | Listen and understand

AUDIO

Listen to the conversation in a restaurant. Then answer the questions.

1. ¿Cuántas personas van a comer?
2. ¿Cómo son los platos principales?
3. ¿Qué pide Raúl con el bistec?
4. ¿Qué pide Raúl para beber?
5. ¿Qué pide Tere de plato principal?
6. ¿Quién pide el pastel de postre?

To review
· **ir a** + infinitive p. 251

2 | Say what you are going to do

Tell what people are going to do on Saturday and how they plan to get there.

modelo: Angélica / almorzar en un restaurante
Angélica va a almorzar en un restaurante.
Va a ir en autobús.

1. Gilberto / correr en el parque

2. yo / volver al centro

3. las chicas / beber refrescos en un café

4. tú / ver una película en el cine

5. nosotros / escuchar música rock

6. vosotros / ir al teatro

Differentiating Instruction

Slower-paced Learners

Read Before Listening Before listening to the audio for Activity 1, provide students with the script. Ask student pairs to identify the main characters. Then ask them to read the roles of Raúl and the waiter. Check comprehension as students read: **¿Es la mesa para dos personas?** (Sí.) **¿Ven los platos principales en el pizarrón?** (No.)

Pre-AP

Circumlocution Ask students to use an English-Spanish dictionary to find as many different kinds of vegetables as they can and to write them in Spanish and English in their notebooks. Ask them to name the vegetables to the class and to describe them using terms they know. For example: **Las espinacas son verduras verdes. A Popeye le gustan mucho.**

3 | Describe places and events in town

To review
- stem-changing verbs: o → ue p. 252

Tomás is describing his activities. Complete his e-mail message with the correct form of the appropriate verb.

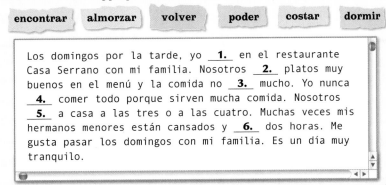

| encontrar | almorzar | volver | poder | costar | dormir |

Los domingos por la tarde, yo __1.__ en el restaurante Casa Serrano con mi familia. Nosotros __2.__ platos muy buenos en el menú y la comida no __3.__ mucho. Yo nunca __4.__ comer todo porque sirven mucha comida. Nosotros __5.__ a casa a las tres o a las cuatro. Muchas veces mis hermanos menores están cansados y __6.__ dos horas. Me gusta pasar los domingos con mi familia. Es un día muy tranquilo.

4 | Order from a menu

To review
- stem-changing verbs: e → i p. 258

Describe the problems in the restaurant.

modelo: Leonor: carne / el camarero: pescado
Leonor pide carne, pero el camarero sirve pescado.

1. tú: agua / la camarera: leche
2. yo: brócoli / el camarero: patatas
3. ustedes: bistec / los camareros: pollo
4. Nicolás: ensalada / el camarero: tomates
5. nosotros: arroz / los camareros: verduras
6. vosotros: pastel / la camarera: helado

5 | Spain, Guatemala, and Chile

To review
- Comparación cultural pp. 244, 255, 261
- Lectura cultural pp. 266–267

Comparación cultural

Answer these culture questions.

1. What is featured at Madrid's Teatro de la Comedia?
2. What can you find at Madrid's Rastro and Chichicastenango's market?
3. Who is depicted in *Las meninas*?
4. What can you see and do in Madrid's Parque del Buen Retiro and Santiago's Parque Metropolitano?

Más práctica Cuaderno *pp. 185–196* Cuaderno para hispanohablantes *pp. 187–196*

Get Help Online
ClassZone.com

Differentiating Instruction

Multiple Intelligences

Visual Learners Ask students to work in groups to make a brochure of a park, real or imaginary. The brochure should include the park's location, days open, opening and closing times, main attractions, and activities for each place. It should include a map of the park with the sites labeled as well as pictures with captions of main attractions.

Heritage Language Learners

Support What They Know Elicit recommendations from students about traditional restaurants and/or foods one would try when visiting their home communities. What do the restaurants look like? When do they open for lunch and for dinner? What items would be found on the menu?

✓ Ongoing Assessment

Peer Assessment Have students read their completed e-mail from Activity 3 to a partner, who will correct any errors.

Answers MSRB Transparencies 58–59

Answers for Activities on pp. 270, 271.

Activity 1
1. Dos personas van a comer.
2. Los platos principales son ricos.
3. Raúl pide arroz con el bistec.
4. Raúl pide un refresco para beber.
5. Tere pide el pescado con una ensalada.
6. Raúl pide el pastel.

Activity 2
1. Gilberto va a correr.... Va a ir a pie.
2. Yo voy a volver al centro. Voy a ir en coche.
3. Las chicas van a beber refrescos en un café. Van a ir en autobús.
4. Tú vas a ver.... Vas a ir a pie.
5. Nosotros vamos a escuchar música rock. Vamos a ir en autobús.
6. Vosotros vais a ir.... Vais a ir en coche.

Activity 3
1. almuerzo
2. encontramos
3. cuesta
4. puedo
5. volvemos
6. duermen

Activity 4
1. Tú pides agua, pero la camarera sirve leche.
2. Yo pido brócoli, pero el camerero sirve patatas.
3. Ustedes piden bistec, pero los camareros sirven pollo.
4. Nicolás pide ensalada, pero el camarero sirve tomates.
5. Nosotros pedimos arroz, pero los camareros sirven verduras.
6. Vosotros pedís pastel, pero la camarera sirve helado.

Activity 5
1. Many traditional Spanish plays are featured at Madrid's Teatro de la Comedia.
2. At El Rastro fleamarket in Madrid one can find antiques, secondhand clothing, CDs, books, maps and art. In Chichicastenango's market one can find handicrafts from the Maya-Quiché culture, such as traditional dresses, colorful textiles, *huipiles* and other items such as fruits, vegetables, masks, baskets, candles, and flowers.
3. *Las Meninas* shows the *Infanta* (princess) and her attendants.
4. In Madrid's Parque del Buen Retiro there are gardens, cafés, and a lake. You can go there for walks, row on the lake, have refreshments at a café, or listen to concerts during the summer. Santiago's Parque Metropolitano has gardens, swimming pools, a zoo, cafés, and restaurants. You can eat, run, ride bikes, swim, look at the animals in the zoo, and take walks in the gardens.

Objectives
- Read three personal narratives about weekend activities in three different countries.
- Have students compare their favorite activities with one of the three students in the text.
- Write a paragraph about favorite Saturday activities.

Core Resources
- *Cuaderno,* pp. 197–199
- Audio Program: TXT CD 4 track 23
- Video Program: DVD 1

Presentation Strategies
- Ask students to look at the photos on pp. 272 and 273 and describe what they see.
- Instruct students to follow the text in the book as they listen to the audio.
- Tell students to think about their own favorite activities while they are reading about those of Anita, Rodrigo, and Armando.

STANDARDS
1.2 Understand language
1.3 Present information
2.1 Practices and perspectives
2.2 Products and perspectives
4.2 Compare cultures

Long-term Retention
Personalize It

Ask students to respond to a student on p. 273, as if they were pen pals. Have them include a brief description of themselves, where they go on weekends, what activities they do, and what type of clothes they wear.

Comparación cultural

Exploring the Theme

In many towns and cities, young people like to spend leisure time at local shopping malls. Whether they visit a two-story mall with 100 shops and a food court or a place like Xanadú in Madrid, where they can not only shop, but take ski lessons and practice with artificial snow, **centros comerciales** are a favorite for teens. They can be found in nearly every corner of the world.

272

Guatemala
España
Chile

AUDIO

¿Adónde vamos el sábado?

Lectura y escritura

WebQuest
ClassZone.com

1 Leer Activities that young people do vary around the world. Read what Anita, Rodrigo, and Armando do for fun on Saturdays.

2 Escribir Using the three descriptions as models, write a short paragraph about what you like to do on Saturdays.

STRATEGY Escribir
Create an activity chart
To write about what you do for fun on Saturdays, use an activity chart like the one shown.

Categoría	Detalles
lugares	
ropa	
actividades	

Step 1 Complete the chart with details about where you go, what you wear, and what you do for fun on Saturdays.

Step 2 Write your paragraph. Make sure to include all the information from your chart. Check your writing by yourself or with help from a friend. Make final corrections.

Compara con tu mundo
Use the paragraph you wrote to compare the activities you do for fun to the activities described by *one* of the three students. How are the activities similar? How are they different?

Cuaderno *pp. 197–199*   Cuaderno para hispanohablantes *pp. 197–199*

Unidad 4
272 doscientos setenta y dos

Differentiating Instruction

Slower-paced Learners
Read Before Listening Prepare a list of statements related to each of the people in the narratives. After students read the narratives, read the statements and have them say the name of the person to which it refers. For example: **Necesito comprar camisetas y calcetines. (Rodrigo) Quiero llevar un sombrero de vaquero. (Armando)**

Multiple Intelligences
Logical/Mathematical Have students calculate the distance between: their town/city and Madrid; Madrid and Santiago; and Santiago and Guatemala. Also have them figure out the flight time between these countries. Have them write out the statistics they find in Spanish. Example: **De Madrid a Santiago de Chile–diez mil kilómetros. Llegas en trece horas y media en avión** (plane).

Cultura INTERACTIVA *See these pages come alive!*
ClassZone.com

Guatemala

Anita

¿Qué tal? Soy Anita y me gusta escuchar música folklórica. El sábado mis amigos y yo pensamos ir a un concierto de marimba[1] en el centro. Las entradas no cuestan mucho y los conciertos son muy buenos. ¿Qué ropa voy a llevar? Quiero llevar un vestido porque es primavera y hace calor. Mis amigos prefieren llevar camisetas y jeans.

[1] musical instrument resembling a xylophone

España

Rodrigo

¡Hola! Me llamo Rodrigo y vivo en Madrid. El sábado quiero ir de compras con mi hermano. Siempre necesito comprar camisetas y calcetines. Muchas veces los encuentro en el centro comercial. Se llama Xanadú y tiene tiendas, restaurantes y ¡un parque de nieve! Allí puedes practicar deportes de invierno durante todo el año. A mi hermano le gusta la nieve en el verano, pero a mí no. En el verano ¡prefiero tener calor!

Chile

Armando

¡Hola! Me llamo Armando y soy de Santiago, Chile. En septiembre puedes ir a muchos rodeos porque hay muchas fiestas nacionales en Chile. El sábado voy a ir a un rodeo con mis amigos para ver a los huasos[2]. Pienso llevar unos jeans nuevos y una chaqueta porque no quiero tener frío. Quiero llevar un sombrero de vaquero[3], pero no puedo. ¡Cuestan mucho!

[2] Chilean cowboys   [3] cowboy

España
doscientos setenta y tres **273**

Communication

Group Work

Divide the class into groups of three. One student plays the role of Anita, Rodrigo, or Armando and the other two are students from the U.S. The students from the U.S. write a list of questions in Spanish based on the narratives. They use these questions to conduct an interview with one of the three teenagers and report the results to the class. Sample questions to Anita: **¿Qué te gusta escuchar? ¿Adónde piensas ir el sábado? ¿Qué ropa vas a llevar?**

✓ Ongoing Assessment

Quick Check Ask students yes/no questions to assess comprehension about each of the three narrations, and write their responses on the board. **¿Quiere Armando llevar un sombrero de vaquero? ¿A Rodrigo le gusta tener frío? ¿Piensa Anita llevar un vestido?**

✓ Ongoing Assessment

Rubric Lectura y escritura

Writing Criteria	Excellent	Good	Needs Work
Content	Paragraph contains a lot of information.	Paragraph contains some information.	Paragraph lacks information.
Communication	Paragraph is organized and easy to follow.	Paragraph is fairly well organized and easy to follow.	Paragraph is disorganized and hard to follow.
Accuracy	Paragraph has few mistakes in vocabulary and grammar.	Paragraph has some mistakes in vocabulary and grammar.	Paragraph has many mistakes in vocabulary and grammar.

Differentiating Instruction

Pre-AP

Draw Conclusions Ask students to write a short paragraph in which they explain why shopping malls have become so popular. For example: **A muchas personas les gustan los centros comerciales. Pueden hacer muchas cosas allí: pueden comprar ropa, comer y pasar un rato con los amigos.** After they've written their paragraphs, ask them to share their thoughts with the class.

Heritage Language Learners

Writing Skills Ask students to choose Anita, Rodrigo, or Armando as the subject of a fictional story they will write. The story should be at least two paragraphs long and should describe in greater detail the activities they discuss here. Students should be creative.

UNIDADES
1-4

Repaso inclusivo
♻ Options for Review

Objective
· Cumulative review

Core Resource
· Audio Program: TXT CD 4 track 24

Review Options
· **Activity 1:** Listening
· **Activities 2, 3:** Speaking
· **Activity 4:** Speaking
· **Activity 5:** Speaking and writing
· **Activity 6:** Reading and writing

 STANDARDS

1.1 Engage in conversation, Acts. 2–5
1.2 Understand language, Act. 1
1.3 Present information, Acts. 2–6

Long-term Retention
Study Tips

Have students review the vocabulary for Unidad 4. Ask them to list the cognates. Then tell students to make a second list for words that are not cognates. Discuss the best ways for them to organize this list.

1 | Listen, understand, and compare

Escuchar

Listen to Mrs. Estrada and her son, Carlitos, order a meal at a restaurant. Then answer the questions.

1. ¿Qué tiene ganas de comer Carlitos?
2. ¿Qué pide para empezar? ¿Y de plato principal?
3. ¿Qué plato pide la señora Estrada para empezar?
4. ¿Qué no sirven hoy en el restaurante?
5. ¿Qué van a beber ellos?

> 🎧 **Audio Program**
> TXT CD 4 Track 24
> Audio Script, TE
> p. 243b

Which order most resembles what you like to eat? What foods and drinks do you order when you go to restaurants?

2 | Present a family outing

Hablar

Prepare a presentation about a family outing to a restaurant. Bring in a photo of your own or one from a magazine. Talk about the clothes each person is wearing, what food the restaurant serves, what each person orders, and how much it costs. You should talk for at least two minutes.

3 | Compare school days

Hablar

Interview a partner about his or her day at school. Ask about the classes your partner prefers, what he or she eats for lunch and at what time, and what he or she is going to do after school today. Finish by comparing your days. Your conversation should be at least three minutes long.

¿A qué hora almuerzas?

Almuerzo a las doce.

Differentiating Instruction

Multiple Intelligences

Kinesthetic Ask students to help set up stations around the room at which they will find a variety of props they might want to use to do the activities. For example, they might want to put mirrors, fashion show costumes, and makeup in one area for Activity 5.

Pre-AP

Main Idea Ask students to review pp. 274 and 275. Give them the following questions to guide their review: What are the common themes in all the activities? How will these activities help them learn more successfully? In other words, what is the main idea? Have them write their answers in Spanish.

Answers

Activity 1
1. Carlitos tiene ganas de comer papas fritas.
2. Para empezar, pide sopa y de plato principal pollo con papas fritas.
3. Para empezar, la señora Estrada pide una ensalada de tomates.
4. Hoy no sirven pescado en el restaurante.
5. Carlitos va a beber un refresco y la señora Estrada va a beber agua.

274

4 | Help find a lost child

Hablar

Role-play a situation in which you are a mall employee in customer service. Your partner is at the mall with a younger cousin, but can't find him or her. Ask your partner about age, physical characteristics, and clothing. Copy this chart on a piece of paper and use it to organize your information. Your conversation should be at least two minutes long.

Edad	
Características físicas	
Ropa	

5 | Create a fashion show

Hablar
Escribir

Work in a group of five. Individually, write a description of the clothes you are wearing. Include color, where you can buy each item, how much they cost, and in what season(s) you can wear them. Your description should have at least eight sentences. Then perform the fashion show for the class, reading each other's descriptions as each "model" walks down the runway.

6 | Plan a weekend with family

Leer
Escribir

You are studying in Barcelona, Spain, for the summer and your parents are coming to visit. Read this newspaper supplement to find out about the weekend's events. Then write an e-mail to your parents, and suggest what you can do and where you can go together or separately during the weekend. Keep in mind everyone's likes and dislikes. Your e-mail should have at least six suggestions.

Suplemento especial – fin de semana

GUÍA DEL OCIO - BARCELONA

VIERNES
Cena especial
Comida española típica, con música de flamenco.
Restaurante Casals (de las 21.30 a las 23.30 h)
Concierto
Los hermanos Pujols tocan música rock.
Plaza Cataluña (a las 14.30 h)
SÁBADO
Películas
Terror en el centro Hollywood. Película de terror. Dos chicos de Nueva York van en autobús cuando llegan

unos extraterrestres horribles.
Cines Maremagnum (a las 16.00 y 18.30 h)
Mi tía loca
España. Película cómica. La historia de una chica y su tía favorita.
Cine Diagonal Mar (a las 13.30 y 21.00 h)
Comprar y pasear
La calle que lo tiene todo: libros, ropa, comida ¡y más!
Las Ramblas (todo el día)
DOMINGO
Eliminar el cáncer
Puedes pasear y donar

dinero para combatir el cáncer.
Parque Güell (a las 10.00 h)
Compras
Los mejores precios del verano en las tiendas de ropa.
Centro Comercial Barcelona Glorias (de las 10.30 a las 20.30 h)
Concierto de Beethoven
La orquesta de Barcelona toca música clásica. Un concierto para toda la familia.
Teatro Liceu (a las 20.00 h)

Communication

Group Work

Assign students to work in groups to create summaries of each section in Unit 4. When the summaries are all completed, make multiple copies and have students bind them into booklets for each class member.

✓ Ongoing Assessment

Integrated Performance Assessment Rubric **Oral Activities 2, 3, 4, 5**
Written Activities 5, 6

Very Good	Proficient	Not There Yet
The student thoroughly develops all requirements of the task.	The student develops most requirements of the task.	The student does not develop the requirements of the task.
The student demonstrates excellent control of verb forms.	The student demonstrates good to fair control of verb forms.	The student demonstrates poor control of verb forms.
Good variety of appropriate vocabulary.	Adequate variety of appropriate vocabulary.	The vocabulary is not appropriate.
The pronunciation is very good to excellent.	The pronunciation is fair to good.	The pronunciation is poor.

Differentiating Instruction

Inclusion

Metacognitive Support For Activity 4, students will need to review descriptive information including age, physical characteristics and clothing. Refer them to the En resumen, pp. 83, 207, and 241 and ask them to copy the vocabulary for each topic in their notebooks, using different colored pencils or markers and saying the words as they write them.

Heritage Language Learners

Writing Skills Have students write an e-mail to a friend from another state or country making suggestions about what to do on the weekend in their own city or town. Suggestions should include going to a restaurant, going to a movie, play or concert, and going shopping. Students should check their work for correct spelling, punctuation, and grammar.

Recursos

Lección 1
¿Qué te gusta hacer?

Talk About Activities

cuidar niños	to baby-sit
pintar	to paint
la reunión	meeting
el club	club
manejar	to drive
trabajar a tiempo parcial	to work part-time
trabajar de voluntario	to volunteer
tocar un instrumento	to play an instrument

Instruments	
el piano	piano
el clarinete	clarinet
la flauta	flute
el saxofón	saxophone
el tambor	drum
la trompeta	trumpet
la viola	viola
el violín	violin

Snack Foods and Beverages

la merienda	snack
las papitas	chips
las galletas saladas	crackers
las galletitas	cookies
el chicle	chewing gum
los dulces	candy
la limonada	lemonade

Lección 2
Mis amigos y yo

Describe Yourself and Others

Personality	
listo(a)	clever / smart
callado(a)	quiet
extrovertido(a)	outgoing
tímido(a)	shy
sincero(a)	sincere
tonto(a)	silly
travieso(a)	mischievous
paciente	patient
talentoso(a)	talented
creativo(a)	creative
ambicioso(a)	ambitious

Appearance	
el pelo oscuro	dark hair
el pelo rizado	curly hair
el pelo lacio	straight hair
calvo(a)	bald
los frenillos	braces

People

el (la) policía	police officer
el actor	actor
la actriz	actress
el (la) compañero(a) de clase	classmate
el (la) bombero(a)	firefighter
el (la) secretario(a)	secretary
el jefe, la jefa	boss

Unidad 2 — Expansión de vocabulario

Lección 1
Somos estudiantes

Tell Time and Discuss Daily Schedules

la medianoche	midnight
el mediodía	noon

Describing Classes

School Subjects	
la asignatura	school subject
la educación física	physical education
las ciencias sociales	social studies
la geometría	geometry
la geografía	geography
el álgebra	algebra
la lengua, el idioma	language
la literatura	literature
la biología	biology
la química	chemistry
la banda	band
el coro	choir
la orquesta	orchestra
la hora de estudio	study hall

In School	
la asamblea	assembly
el recreo	recess, break

Classroom Activities	
preguntar	to ask
la respuesta	answer
la prueba	test, quiz

Describe Frequency

cada	each
a veces	sometimes
¿Con qué frecuencia...?	How often. . . ?
rara vez	rarely

Other Words and Phrases

terminar	to finish
esperar	to wait (for)
mientras	while
otra vez	again

Lección 2
En la escuela

Describe Classroom Objects

la carpeta	folder
las tijeras	scissors
la regla	ruler
el diccionario	dictionary
la impresora	printer
la bandera	flag
el globo	globe

Places in School

la sala de clase	classroom
el casillero	locker
el auditorio	auditorium

Say Where Things Are Located

entre	between
fuera (de)	out / outside (of)
(a la) derecha (de)	(to the) right (of)
(a la) izquierda (de)	(to the) left (of)
aquí	here
allí	there
enfrente (de)	across from, facing

Talk About How You Feel

feliz, alegre	happy
preocupado(a)	worried
listo(a)	ready
Estoy de acuerdo.	I agree.

Other Words and Phrases

mismo(a)	same
según	according to
creer	to think, to believe
especialmente	especially
olvidar	to forget
sobre	about
además	besides, further
suficiente, bastante	enough
sin	without

Lección 1
Mi comida favorita

Talk About Foods and Beverages

For Breakfast	
desayunar	to have breakfast
la mantequilla	butter
la miel	honey
el pan tostado	toast
el batido	milkshake, smoothie
For Lunch	
la bolsa	bag
la mantequilla de cacahuate	peanut butter
la jalea	jelly
el atún	tuna
la ensalada	salad
Fruit	
el plátano	banana; plantain
la toronja	grapefruit
la piña	pineapple
el durazno	peach
el limón	lemon
la sandía	watermelon

Lección 2
En mi familia

Talk About Family

el esposo	husband
la esposa	wife
la hermanastra	stepsister
el hermanastro	stepbrother
la media hermana	half-sister
el medio hermano	half-brother
el nieto	grandson
la nieta	granddaughter
el sobrino	nephew
la sobrina	niece
el (la) bebé	baby

Pets

el pájaro	bird
el pez (*pl.* **los peces**)	fish
el conejo	rabbit
el lagarto	lizard
la rana	frog
el hámster	hamster

Unidad 4

Expansión de vocabulario

Lección 1
¡Vamos de compras!

Describe Clothing

las botas	boots
el impermeable	raincoat
la falda	skirt
el suéter	sweater
la sudadera (con capucha)	(hooded) sweatshirt
los pantalones deportivos	sweatpants
el abrigo	coat
los zapatos de tenis	tennis shoes, sneakers
el pijama	pajamas
las sandalias	sandals
la gorra	baseball cap
las gafas de sol	sunglasses
los guantes	gloves
la bufanda	scarf
el paraguas	umbrella
la bolsa	bag, purse
Colors	
morado(a)	purple
rosado(a)	pink
gris	gray

Discuss Seasons

el norte	north
el sur	south
el este	east
el oeste	west

Lección 2
¿Qué hacemos esta noche?

Describe Places In Town

la iglesia	church
el edificio	building
el centro de videojuegos	arcade
la piscina	pool
la acera	sidewalk
el correo	post office
la librería	bookstore
la zapatería	shoe store
el templo	temple
la tienda de discos	music store
Music	
el rap	rap
alternativa	alternative
la música electrónica	electronic music, techno
la canción	song
la letra	lyrics

In a Restaurant

la cuchara	spoon
el cuchillo	knife
el tenedor	fork
el vaso	glass
la servilleta	napkin
el tazón	bowl
la taza	cup
For Dinner	
el puerco	pork
el pavo	turkey
los fideos	noodles
la salsa	sauce
la pimienta	pepper
la sal	salt
los mariscos	seafood
Vegetables	
la zanahoria	carrot
la lechuga	lettuce
el maíz	corn

Para y piensa
Self-Check Answers

Lección preliminar

p. 5
1. Buenos días.
2. ¿Cómo estás?
Answers may vary but can include:
3. Adiós, hasta mañana, hasta luego.

p. 9
1. c.
2. a.
3. b.

p. 11
1. See p. 10

p. 15
1. b.
2. a.
3. c.

p. 17
1. seis - dos - cinco - uno - cuatro -
   dos - cero - nueve
2. tres - siete - cero - ocho - nueve -
   dos - seis - tres
3. cuatro - uno - ocho - cinco - dos -
   siete - seis - cero

p. 19
1. lunes
2. mañana

p. 21
1. b.
2. a.
3. c.

p. 24
1. ¿Cómo se dice *please*?
2. ¿Comprendes?

Unidad 1 Estados Unidos

Lección 1

p. 35 Práctica de vocabulario
1. escuchar música
2. hacer la tarea

p. 37 Vocabulario en contexto
1. jugar
2. música
3. comer

p. 41 Práctica de gramática
1. Cristóbal y yo somos de Honduras.
2. Tomás es de la República
   Dominicana.
3. Yo soy de México.

p. 43 Gramática en contexto
1. El Sr. Costas es de la Florida.
2. Alicia es de Miami.
3. Teresa y Miguel son de Honduras y
   Cuba.

p. 47 Práctica de gramática
1. Le gusta
2. Te gusta
3. Nos gusta

p. 50 Todo junto
1. Teresa es de Honduras.
   Le gusta tocar la guitarra.
2. Alicia es de Miami.
   Le gusta comer.
3. Miguel es de Cuba.
   Le gusta mirar la televisión.

Lección 2

p. 63 Práctica de vocabulario
1. Juan es bajo.
2. David es artístico.
3. Carlos es serio.

p. 65 Vocabulario en contexto
1. perezoso
2. atlético
3. estudioso

p. 69 Práctica de gramática
1. la televisión
2. unas frutas
3. el libro
4. unos hombres

p. 71 Gramática en contexto
1. Ricardo es un amigo de Alberto.
2. Marta y Carla son unas chicas de
   una clase de Juan.
3. Ana es una chica muy inteligente.

p. 75 Práctica de gramática
1. una estudiante desorganizada
2. unos chicos simpáticos
3. unas mujeres trabajadoras
4. un hombre grande

p. 78 Todo junto
1. Alberto es un chico simpático.
2. Ricardo es un estudiante trabajador.
3. Sandra es una persona organizada.

Unidad 2 México

Lección 1

p. 97 Práctica de vocabulario
1. Me gusta dibujar en la clase de arte.
2. Hay veintitrés chicos en la clase de matemáticas.

p. 99 Vocabulario en contexto
1. a las diez y cuarto (a las diez y quince)
2. las ocho y veinte
3. a las siete

p. 103 Práctica de gramática
1. Juan nunca tiene que preparar la comida.
2. Tenemos la clase de inglés todos los días.
3. Siempre tengo que usar la computadora.

p. 105 Gramática en contexto
1. tienen
2. tiene que
3. tienen

p. 109 Práctica de gramática
1. usamos
2. preparo
3. dibujan
4. Necesitas

p. 112 Todo junto
1. toma
2. practicar
3. estudian

Lección 2

p. 125 Práctica de vocabulario
Answers may vary but can include:
1. el baño, el gimnasio, la cafetería, la biblioteca, etc.
2. el mapa, el escritorio, la silla, el reloj, etc.

p. 127 Vocabulario en contexto
1. la biblioteca
2. el gimnasio
3. la biblioteca

p. 131 Práctica de gramática
1. Estoy cerca de las ventanas.
2. Pablo, ¿estás nervioso?

p. 133 Gramática en contexto
Answers may vary but can include:
1. Pablo y Claudia están en la biblioteca.
2. Pablo está nervioso.
3. Pablo tiene que estar en el gimnasio a las cinco.

p. 137 Práctica de gramática
1. Teresa va a la cafetería.
2. Los estudiantes van a la oficina del director.
3. Nosotros vamos al gimnasio.
4. Yo voy a la clase de matemáticas.

p. 140 Todo junto
1. está; va a
2. están; van a
3. está; va a

Unidad 3 Puerto Rico

Lección 1

p. 159 Práctica de vocabulario
Answers may vary but can include:
1. los huevos, el cereal, el yogur, la fruta
2. el sándwich, la sopa, la hamburguesa

p. 161 Vocabulario en contexto
1. Quiénes
2. Cuándo
3. Por qué

p. 165 Práctica de gramática
1. Me gustan los huevos en el desayuno.
2. A José le gusta la pizza con jamón.
3. ¿Por qué no te gusta la fruta?

p. 167 Gramática en contexto
1. gusta
2. gusta
3. gustan

p. 171 Práctica de gramática
1. hacen; comen   3. hace; bebe
2. haces; leo

p. 174 Todo junto
1. gusta; come
2. gustan; comparten

Lección 2

p. 187 Práctica de vocabulario
1. hijo   3. hermanas
2. padres

p. 189 Vocabulario en contexto
1. Marisol tiene catorce años.
2. El gato de la familia Vélez tiene ocho años.
3. Los padres de Marisol tienen cincuenta y dos años.

p. 193 Práctica de gramática
1. mi; el seis de septiembre
2. nuestros; el veinticinco de enero.
3. su; el diecisiete de abril.

p. 195 Gramática en contexto
1. El cumpleaños de Camila es el doce de junio.
2. El cumpleaños de Ester es el primero de octubre.
3. El cumpleaños de Tito es el veintiocho de marzo.
4. El cumpleaños de Celia es el diecisiete de enero.

p. 199 Práctica de gramática
1. Mi hermano es más alto que mi padre.
2. Me gustan las manzanas tanto como las bananas.
3. La clase de matemáticas es mejor que la clase de arte.

p. 202 Todo junto
1. Sus perros son tan grandes como Marisol.
2. Su primo es menor que él.
3. Sus perros son más perezosos que los gatos.

Unidad 4 España

Lección 1

p. 221 Práctica de vocabulario
1. ¿Cuánto cuestan los calcetines blancos?
2. ¿Cuánto cuesta el vestido azul?
3. ¿Cuánto cuesta la chaqueta anaranjada?
4. ¿Cuánto cuestan los pantalones cortos rojos?

p. 223 Vocabulario en contexto
1. tiene frío
2. tiene calor
3. tiene frío

p. 227 Práctica de gramática
1. pienso
2. empieza
3. cierra

p. 229 Gramática en contexto
1. entiende
2. prefiere
3. quiere

p. 233 Práctica de gramática
1. los
2. La
3. Las

p. 236 Todo junto
1. Sí, Enrique la necesita.
2. Sí, Enrique lo prefiere.
3. Sí, Enrique la quiere comprar. (Sí, Enrique quiere comprarla.)

Lección 2

p. 249 Práctica de vocabulario
Answers may vary but can include:
1. El menú, el (la) camarero(a), la cuenta, los platos principales, etc.
2. El teatro, el parque, el cine, etc.

p. 251 Vocabulario en contexto
1. en autobús
2. a pie
3. en coche

p. 255 Práctica de gramática
1. cuesta
2. almorzamos
3. duermo
4. pueden

p. 257 Gramática en contexto
1. puede
2. encuentra
3. vuelve

p. 261 Práctica de gramática
1. sirven
2. sirve
3. pedimos

p. 264 Todo junto
1. almuerzan
2. pide
3. puede

Resumen de gramática

Nouns, Articles, and Pronouns

Nouns

Nouns identify people, animals, places, and things. All Spanish nouns, even if they refer to objects, are either **masculine** or **feminine**. They are also either **singular** or **plural**.

Nouns ending in **-o** are usually masculine; nouns ending in **-a** are usually feminine.

To form the **plural** of a noun, add **-s** if the noun ends in a vowel; add **-es** if it ends in a consonant.

<table>
<tr><th colspan="2">Singular Nouns</th><th colspan="2">Plural Nouns</th></tr>
<tr><th>Masculine</th><th>Feminine</th><th>Masculine</th><th>Feminine</th></tr>
<tr><td>abuelo</td><td>abuela</td><td>abuelos</td><td>abuelas</td></tr>
<tr><td>chico</td><td>chica</td><td>chicos</td><td>chicas</td></tr>
<tr><td>hombre</td><td>mujer</td><td>hombres</td><td>mujeres</td></tr>
<tr><td>papel</td><td>pluma</td><td>papeles</td><td>plumas</td></tr>
<tr><td>zapato</td><td>blusa</td><td>zapatos</td><td>blusas</td></tr>
</table>

Articles

Articles identify the class of a noun: masculine or feminine, singular or plural. **Definite articles** are the equivalent of the English word *the*. **Indefinite articles** are the equivalent of *a, an,* or *some*.

Definite Articles

	Masculine	Feminine
Singular	**el** chico	**la** chica
Plural	**los** chicos	**las** chicas

Indefinite Articles

	Masculine	Feminine
Singular	**un** chico	**una** chica
Plural	**unos** chicos	**unas** chicas

Pronouns

Pronouns take the place of nouns. The pronoun used is determined by its function or purpose in a sentence.

Subject Pronouns	
yo	nosotros(as)
tú	vosotros(as)
usted	ustedes
él, ella	ellos(as)

Direct Object Pronouns	
me	nos
te	os
lo, la	los, las

Adjectives

Adjectives describe nouns. In Spanish, adjectives match the **gender** and **number** of the nouns they describe. To make an adjective plural, add **-s** if it ends in a vowel; add **-es** if it ends in a consonant. The adjective usually comes after the noun in Spanish.

Adjectives

	Masculine	Feminine
Singular	el chico alt**o**	la chica alt**a**
	el chico inteligente	la chica inteligente
	el chico joven	la chica joven
	el chico trabajador	la chica trabajador**a**
Plural	los chicos alto**s**	las chicas alta**s**
	los chicos inteligente**s**	las chicas inteligente**s**
	los chicos jóven**es**	las chicas jóven**es**
	los chicos trabajador**es**	las chicas trabajador**as**

Sometimes adjectives are shortened when they are placed in front of a masculine singular noun.

Shortened Forms	
bueno	**buen** chico
malo	**mal** chico

Adjectives (continued)

Possessive adjectives indicate who owns something or describe a relationship between people or things. They agree in number with the nouns they describe. **Nuestro(a)** and **vuestro(a)** must also agree in gender with the nouns they describe.

Possessive Adjectives

	Masculine		Feminine	
Singular	**mi** amigo	**nuestro** amigo	**mi** amiga	**nuestra** amiga
	tu amigo	**vuestro** amigo	**tu** amiga	**vuestra** amiga
	su amigo	**su** amigo	**su** amiga	**su** amiga
Plural	**mis** amigos	**nuestros** amigos	**mis** amigas	**nuestras** amigas
	tus amigos	**vuestros** amigos	**tus** amigas	**vuestras** amigas
	sus amigos	**sus** amigos	**sus** amigas	**sus** amigas

Comparatives

Comparatives are used to compare two people or things.

Comparatives

más (+)	menos (–)	tan, tanto (=)
más serio **que...**	**menos** serio **que...**	**tan** serio **como...**
Me gusta leer **más que** pasear.	Me gusta pasear **menos que** leer.	Me gusta hablar **tanto como** escuchar.

There are a few irregular comparative words. When talking about the age of people, use **mayor** and **menor.** When talking about qualities, use **mejor** and **peor.**

Age	Quality
mayor	mejor
menor	peor

Verbs: Present Tense

Regular Verbs

Regular verbs ending in **-ar, -er,** or **-ir** always have regular endings in the present tense.

-ar Verbs

habl**o**	habl**amos**
habl**as**	habl**áis**
habl**a**	habl**an**

-er Verbs

vend**o**	vend**emos**
vend**es**	vend**éis**
vend**e**	vend**en**

-ir Verbs

compart**o**	compart**imos**
compart**es**	compart**ís**
compart**e**	compart**en**

Verbs with Irregular yo Forms

Some verbs have regular forms in the present tense except for the **yo** form.

hacer

ha**go**	hacemos
haces	hacéis
hace	hacen

ver

v**eo**	vemos
ves	veis
ve	ven

Stem-Changing Verbs

e → ie

quiero	queremos
quieres	queréis
quiere	quieren

Other **e → ie** stem-changing verbs are **cerrar, comenzar, despertarse, empezar, entender, pensar,** and **preferir.**

e → i

sirvo	servimos
sirves	servís
sirve	sirven

Another **e → i** stem-changing verb is **pedir.**

o → ue

puedo	podemos
puedes	podéis
puede	pueden

Other **o → ue** stem-changing verbs are **almorzar, costar, dormir, encontrar,** and **volver.**

Irregular Verbs

The following verbs are irregular in the present tense.

estar

estoy	estamos
estás	estáis
está	están

ir

voy	vamos
vas	vais
va	van

ser

soy	somos
eres	sois
es	son

tener

tengo	tenemos
tienes	tenéis
tiene	tienen

Glosario español-inglés

This Spanish-English glossary contains all the active vocabulary words that appear in the text as well as passive vocabulary lists. **LP** refers to the Lección preliminar.

A

a to, at
  A la(s)... At... o'clock. **2.1**
  a pie on foot **4.2**
  ¿A qué hora es/son...? At what time is/are...? **2.1**
abril April **3.2**
la abuela grandmother **3.2**
el abuelo grandfather **3.2**
los abuelos grandparents **3.2**
aburrido(a) boring **2.2**
acabar de... to have just... **5.2**
la actividad activity **1.1**
Adiós. Goodbye. **LP**
adónde (to) where **2.2**
  ¿Adónde vas? Where are you going? **2.2**
agosto August **3.2**
el agua (fem.) water **1.1**
ahora now **3.1**
al to the **2.2**
  al lado (de) next to **2.2**
allí there **4.2**
el almacén (*pl.* los almacenes) department store
almorzar (ue) to eat lunch **4.2**
el almuerzo lunch **3.1**
alquilar to rent **1.1**
  alquilar un DVD to rent a DVD **1.1**
alto(a) tall **1.2**
amarillo(a) yellow **4.1**
el (la) amigo(a) friend **1.2**
anaranjado(a) orange (color) **4.1**
andar en patineta to skateboard **1.1**
el ánimo spirit
antes (de) before **1.1**
la antorcha torch
el anuncio advertisement; announcement

el año year **3.2**
  el Año Nuevo New Year
  ¿Cuántos años tienes? How old are you? **3.2**
  tener... años to be... years old **3.2**
aprender to learn **1.1**
  aprender el español to learn Spanish **1.1**
los apuntes notes **2.1**
  tomar apuntes to take notes **2.1**
aquí here **4.2**
el arrecife de coral coral reef
el arroz rice **4.2**
el arte art **2.1**
el artículo article
artístico(a) artistic **1.2**
atlético(a) athletic **1.2**
el autobús (*pl.* los autobuses) bus **4.2**
  en autobús by bus **4.2**
avanzar to advance, to move ahead
  ¡Avanza! Advance!, Move ahead!
  avancemos let's advance, let's move ahead
el aymara indigenous language of Bolivia and Peru
azul blue **4.1**

B

bailar to dance
el (la) bailarín(ina) (*pl.* los bailarines) dancer
el baile dance
bajo(a) short (height) **1.2**
la banana banana **3.1**
la banda musical band
el baño bathroom **2.2**
la batalla battle
beber to drink **1.1**
la bebida beverage, drink **3.1**
la biblioteca library **2.2**
la bicicleta bicycle **1.1**

bien well, fine **LP**
  Bien. ¿Y tú/usted? Fine. And you? (familiar/formal) **LP**
  Muy bien. ¿Y tú/usted? Very well. And you? (familiar/formal) **LP**
el bistec beef **4.2**
blanco(a) white **4.1**
la blusa blouse **4.1**
bonito(a) pretty **1.2**
el borrador eraser **2.2**
el brindis celebratory toast
el brócoli broccoli **4.2**
bueno(a) good **1.2**
  Buenos días. Good morning. **LP**
  Buenas noches. Good evening; Good night. **LP**
  Buenas tardes. Good afternoon. **LP**

C

cada each; every
el café coffee; café **3.1, 4.2**
la cafetería cafeteria **2.2**
la calavera skull
el calcetín (*pl.* los calcetines) sock **4.1**
la calculadora calculator **2.2**
caliente hot
la calle street **4.2**
el (la) camarero(a) (food) server **4.2**
el cambio change
la camisa shirt **4.1**
la camiseta T-shirt **4.1**
cansado(a) tired **2.2**
Carnaval Carnival
la carne meat **4.2**
la carreta horse-drawn carriage
la casa house
el cascarón (*pl.* los cascarones) confetti-filled egg

la caseta small house or tent
casi almost **2.1**
castaño(a) brown (hair) **1.2**
catorce fourteen **2.1**
el cementerio cemetery
la cena dinner **3.1**
el centro center, downtown **4.2**
   el centro comercial shopping center, mall **4.1**
cerca (de) near (to) **2.2**
el cereal cereal **3.1**
cero zero **LP**
cerrar (ie) to close **4.1**
la chaqueta jacket **4.1**
la chica girl **1.2**
el chico boy **1.2**
cien one hundred **2.1**
las ciencias science **2.1**
cierto(a) true
cinco five **LP**
cincuenta fifty **2.1**
el cine movie theater; the movies **4.2**
la clase class, classroom **LP**; kind, type
el coche car **4.2**
   en coche by car **4.2**
el colegio high school
comer to eat **1.1**
cómico(a) funny **1.2**
la comida meal; food **1.1, 3.1**
como as, like
¿Cómo...? How...? **3.1**
   ¿Cómo eres? What are you like? **1.2**
   ¿Cómo estás? How are you? (familiar) **LP**
   ¿Cómo está usted? How are you? (formal) **LP**
   ¿Cómo se llama? What's his/her/your (formal) name? **LP**
   ¿Cómo te llamas? What's your name? (familiar) **LP**
comparar to compare
compartir to share **3.1**
comprar to buy **1.1**
¿Comprendiste? Did you understand?
la computadora computer **2.1**
común common
el concierto concert **4.2**
contento(a) happy **2.2**
contestar to answer **2.1**
el correo electrónico e-mail **1.1**
correr to run **1.1**

costar (ue) to cost **4.2**
   ¿Cuánto cuesta(n)? How much does it (do they) cost? **4.1**
   Cuesta(n)... It (They) cost... **4.1**
la Cremà burning of papier-mâché figures during Las Fallas
el cuaderno notebook **2.2**
el cuadro painting
¿Cuál(es)? Which?; What? **3.1**
   ¿Cuál es la fecha? What is the date? **3.2**
   ¿Cuál es tu/su número de teléfono? What is your phone number? (familiar/formal) **LP**
cuando when **2.2**
¿Cuándo? When? **2.2**
cuánto(a) how much **3.2**
   ¿Cuánto cuesta(n)? How much does it (do they) cost? **4.1**
cuántos(as) how many **3.2**
   ¿Cuántos(as)...? How many...? **2.1**
   ¿Cuántos años tienes? How old are you? **3.2**
cuarenta forty **2.1**
cuatro four **LP**
cuatrocientos(as) four hundred **3.2**
la cuenta bill (in a restaurant) **4.2**
el cumpleaños birthday **3.2**
   ¡Feliz cumpleaños! Happy birthday! **3.2**

de of, from **1.1**
   de la mañana in the morning (with a time) **2.1**
   De nada. You're welcome. **LP**
   de la noche at night (with a time) **2.1**
   ¿De qué color es/son...? What color is/are...?
   de la tarde in the afternoon (with a time) **2.1**
   de vez en cuando once in a while **2.1**
debajo (de) underneath, under **2.2**
del (de la) of *or* from the **2.2**
delante (de) in front (of) **2.2**
demasiado too much
dentro (de) inside (of) **2.2**
los deportes sports **1.1**
deprimido(a) depressed **2.2**
el desayuno breakfast **3.1**

descansar to rest **1.1**
desear to wish, to want
el desfile parade
desorganizado(a) disorganized **1.2**
después (de) afterward; after **1.1**
detrás (de) behind **2.2**
el día day **LP**
   Buenos días. Good morning. **LP**
   ¿Qué día es hoy? What day is today? **LP**
   todos los días every day **2.1**
dibujar to draw **1.1**
el dibujo drawing
diciembre December **3.2**
diecinueve nineteen **2.1**
dieciocho eighteen **2.1**
dieciséis sixteen **2.1**
diecisiete seventeen **2.1**
diez ten **LP**
diferente different
difícil difficult **2.1**
el difunto deceased
el dinero money **4.1**
el (la) director(a) principal **2.2**
el disfraz (*pl.* los disfraces) costume
divertido(a) fun **2.2**
doce twelve **2.1**
el dólar dollar **4.1**
domingo Sunday **LP**
donde where
¿Dónde? Where? **2.2**
   ¿De dónde eres? Where are you from? (familiar) **LP**
   ¿De dónde es? Where is he/she from? **LP**
   ¿De dónde es usted? Where are you from? (formal) **LP**
dormir (ue) to sleep **4.2**
dos two **LP**
doscientos(as) two hundred **3.2**
durante during **4.1**
el DVD DVD **1.1**

el ejército army
él he **1.1**
ella she **1.1**
ellos(as) they **1.1**
emocionado(a) excited **2.2**
empezar (ie) to begin **4.1**
en in **2.1**; on
   en autobús by bus **4.2**
   en coche by car **4.2**

Encantado(a). Delighted; Pleased to meet you. **LP**

encima (de) on top (of) **2.2**

encontrar (ue) to find **4.2**

la encuesta survey

enero January **3.2**

enojado(a) angry **2.2**

la ensalada salad **4.2**

enseñar to teach **2.1**

entender (ie) to understand **4.1**

la entrada ticket **4.2**

entrar to enter

el equipo team

la escena scene

escribir to write **1.1**

    escribir correos electrónicos to write e-mails **1.1**

el escritorio desk **2.2**

la escritura writing

escuchar to listen (to) **1.1**

    escuchar música to listen to music **1.1**

la escuela school **1.1**

    la escuela secundaria high school

el español Spanish **2.1**

especial special

el esqueleto skeleton

la estación (pl. las estaciones) season **4.1**

estar to be **2.2**

    ¿Está bien? OK?

el (la) estudiante student **1.2**

estudiar to study **1.1**

estudioso(a) studious **1.2**

el euro euro **4.1**

el examen (pl. los exámenes) test, exam **2.1**

fácil easy **2.1**

las fallas displays of large papier-mâché figures

el (la) fallero(a) celebrant of Las Fallas

falso(a) false

la familia family **3.2**

febrero February **3.2**

la fecha date **3.2**

    ¿Cuál es la fecha? What is the date? **3.2**

    la fecha de nacimiento birth date **3.2**

feo(a) ugly **4.1**

la fiesta party; holiday

    la fiesta nacional national holiday

    la fiesta patria patriotic holiday

el fin de semana weekend

el (la) francés(esa) (pl. los franceses) French

los frijoles beans **4.2**

la fruta fruit **1.1**

los fuegos artificiales fireworks

la fuente source; fountain

el fútbol soccer (the sport) **1.1**

la galleta cookie **1.1**

el (la) gato(a) cat **3.2**

el gimnasio gymnasium **2.2**

el gorro winter hat **4.1**

Gracias. Thank you. **LP**

    Muchas gracias. Thank you very much. **LP**

la gramática grammar

grande big, large; great **1.2**

el grito shout

guapo(a) good-looking **1.2**

la guitarra guitar **1.1**

gustar

    Me gusta... I like... **1.1**

    No me gusta... I don't like... **1.1**

    ¿Qué te gusta hacer? What do you like to do? **1.1**

    ¿Te gusta...? Do you like...? **1.1**

el gusto pleasure

    El gusto es mío. The pleasure is mine. **LP**

    Mucho gusto. Nice to meet you. **LP**

hablar to talk, to speak **1.1**

    hablar por teléfono to talk on the phone **1.1**

hacer (hago) to make, to do **3.1**

    Hace calor. It is hot. **LP**

    Hace frío. It is cold. **LP**

    Hace sol. It is sunny. **LP**

    Hace viento. It is windy. **LP**

    hacer la tarea to do homework **1.1**

¿Qué tiempo hace? What is the weather like? **LP**

la hamburguesa hamburger **3.1**

hasta until

    Hasta luego. See you later. **LP**

    Hasta mañana. See you tomorrow. **LP**

hay... there is/are... **2.1**

el helado ice cream **1.1**

la hermana sister **3.2**

el hermano brother **3.2**

los hermanos brothers, brother(s) and sister(s) **3.2**

la hija daughter **3.2**

el hijo son **3.2**

los hijos children, son(s) and daughter(s) **3.2**

la hispanidad cultural community of Spanish speakers

la historia history **2.1**

Hola. Hello; Hi. **LP**

el hombre man **1.2**

la hora hour; time **2.1**

    ¿A qué hora es/son...? At what time is/are...? **2.1**

    ¿Qué hora es? What time is it? **2.1**

el horario schedule **2.1**

horrible horrible **3.1**

hoy today **LP**

    ¿Qué día es hoy? What day is today? **LP**

    Hoy es... Today is... **LP**

el huevo egg **3.1**

el idioma language

Igualmente. Same here; Likewise. **LP**

importante important **3.1**

    Es importante. It's important. **3.1**

los incas Incas, an indigenous South American people

la independencia independence

la información information

el inglés English **2.1**

inteligente intelligent **1.2**

interesante interesting **2.2**

el invierno winter **4.1**

ir to go **2.2**
   ir a... to be going to... **4.2**
   ir de compras to go shopping **4.1**
   Vamos a... Let's... **4.2**

el jamón (*pl.* **los jamones**) ham **3.1**
el jardín (*pl.* **los jardines**) garden
los jeans jeans **4.1**
joven (*pl.* **jóvenes**) young **1.2**
jueves Thursday **LP**
jugar (ue) to play (sports or games)
   jugar al fútbol to play soccer **1.1**
el jugo juice **1.1**
   el jugo de naranja orange
    juice **3.1**
julio July **3.2**
junio June **3.2**

el lado side
   al lado (de) next to **2.2**
el lago lake
el lápiz (*pl.* **los lápices**) pencil **2.2**
la lección (*pl.* **las lecciones**) lesson
la leche milk **3.1**
la lectura reading
leer to read **1.1**
   leer un libro to read a book **1.1**
lejos (de) far (from) **2.2**
las lentejas lentils
el libertador liberator
el libro book **1.1**
llamarse to be called
   ¿Cómo se llama? What's his/her/
    your (formal) name? **LP**
   ¿Cómo te llamas? What's your
    name? (familiar) **LP**
   Me llamo... My name is... **LP**
   Se llama... His/Her name is... **LP**
la llegada arrival
llegar to arrive **2.1**
llevar to wear **4.1**
llover (ue) to rain
   Llueve. It is raining. **LP**
el lugar place **4.2**
lunes Monday **LP**

la madrastra stepmother **3.2**
la madre mother **3.2**
el (la) maestro(a) teacher **LP**
malo(a) bad **1.2**
   Mal. ¿Y tú/usted? Bad. And you?
    (familiar/formal) **LP**
la manzana apple **3.1**
mañana tomorrow **LP**
   Hasta mañana. See you
    tomorrow. **LP**
   Mañana es... Tomorrow is... **LP**
la mañana morning **2.1**
   de la mañana in the morning
    (with a time) **2.1**
el mapa map **2.2**
marrón (*pl.* **marrones**) brown **4.1**
martes Tuesday **LP**
marzo March **3.2**
más more **1.1**
   Más o menos. ¿Y tú/usted? So-
    so. And you? (familiar/
    formal) **LP**
   más que... more than... **3.2**
   más... que more... than **3.2**
la máscara mask
la mascleta firecracker explosions
   during Las Fallas
las matemáticas math **2.1**
mayo May **3.2**
mayor older **3.2**
la medianoche midnight
medio(a) half
   ...y media half past... (the
    hour) **2.1**
mejor better **3.2**
menor younger **3.2**
menos less
   ...menos (diez) (ten) to/before...
    (the hour) **2.1**
   menos que... less than... **3.2**
   menos... que less... than **3.2**
el mensaje instantáneo instant
   message
el menú menu **4.2**
el mercado market
   el mercado al aire libre open-air
    market
el mes month **3.2**
la mesa table **4.2**
mi my **3.2**
miércoles Wednesday **LP**
mil thousand, one thousand **3.2**

un millón (de) million, one
   million **3.2**
el minuto minute **2.1**
mirar to watch **1.1**; to look at
   mirar la televisión to watch
    television **1.1**
mismo(a) same
la mochila backpack **2.2**
montar to ride **1.1**
   montar en bicicleta to ride a
    bike **1.1**
mucho a lot **2.1**
   Mucho gusto. Nice to meet
    you. **LP**
muchos(as) many **2.1**
   muchas veces often, many
    times **2.1**
la mujer woman **1.2**
el mundo world
el museo museum
la música music **1.1**
   la música folklórica folk music
   la música rock rock music **4.2**
el (la) músico(a) musician
muy very **1.2**
   Muy bien. ¿Y tú/usted? Very well.
    And you? (familiar/formal) **LP**

nacer to be born
nada nothing
   De nada. You're welcome. **LP**
la naranja orange (fruit) **3.1**
necesitar to need **2.1**
negro(a) black **4.1**
nervioso(a) nervous **2.2**
nevar (ie) to snow
   Nieva. It is snowing. **LP**
la nieve snow
el ninot (*pl.* **los ninots**) large papier-
   mâché figure
no no **LP**
la noche night **2.1**; evening **LP**
   Buenas noches. Good evening;
    Good night. **LP**
   de la noche at night (with a
    time) **2.1**
la Nochebuena Christmas Eve
la Nochevieja New Year's Eve
el nombre name
nosotros(as) we **1.1**

la nota grade (on a test) **2.1**
   sacar una buena/mala nota to get a good/bad grade **2.1**
novecientos(as) nine hundred **3.2**
noventa ninety **2.1**
noviembre November **3.2**
nuestro(a) our **3.2**
nueve nine **LP**
nuevo(a) new **4.1**
el número number **LP**
   el número de teléfono phone number **LP**
nunca never **2.1**
nutritivo(a) nutritious **3.1**

o or **1.1**
ocho eight **LP**
ochocientos(as) eight hundred **3.2**
octubre October **3.2**
ocupado(a) busy **2.2**
la oficina office **2.2**
   la oficina del (de la) director(a) principal's office **2.2**
el ojo eye
once eleven **2.1**
la oración (*pl.* **las oraciones**) sentence
organizado(a) organized **1.2**
el otoño autumn, fall **4.1**
otro(a) other **3.1**

el padrastro stepfather **3.2**
el padre father **3.2**
los padres parents **3.2**
pagar to pay **4.1**
la página page
el país country, nation **LP**
el pan bread **3.1**
   el pan de muertos special bread made for Día de los Muertos
los pantalones pants **4.1**
   los pantalones cortos shorts **4.1**
la papa potato **1.1**
   las papas fritas French fries **1.1**
el papel paper **2.2**
   el papel picado paper cutouts
para for; in order to **3.1**

parar to stop
   Para y piensa. Stop and think.
la pareja pair
el párrafo paragraph
el parque park **4.2**
   el parque de diversiones amusement park
la parte part
el pasado the past
pasar to happen
   pasar un rato con los amigos to spend time with friends **1.1**
   ¿Qué pasa? What's happening? **LP**
   ¿Qué te pasa (a ti)? What's the matter (with you)?
pasear to go for a walk **1.1**
el paseo walk, stroll; ride
el pasillo hall **2.2**
el pastel cake **4.2**
la patata potato **4.2**
pedir (i) to order, to ask for **4.2**
la película movie **4.2**
pelirrojo(a) red-haired **1.2**
el pelo hair **1.2**
   el pelo castaño/rubio brown/blond hair **1.2**
pensar (ie) to think; to plan **4.1**
peor worse **3.2**
pequeño(a) little, small **1.2**
Perdón. Excuse me. **LP**
perezoso(a) lazy **1.2**
el periódico newspaper
   el periódico escolar student newspaper
pero but **1.1**
el (la) perro(a) dog **3.2**
la persona person **1.2**
el pescado fish (as food) **4.2**
el pie foot
   a pie on foot **4.2**
la piscina swimming pool
la pista clue
el pizarrón (*pl.* **los pizarrones**) chalkboard, board **2.2**
la pizza pizza **1.1**
la planta plant
el plato plate; dish; course
   el plato principal main course **4.2**
la playa beach
la pluma pen **2.2**
un poco a little **1.2**
pocos(as) few
poder (ue) to be able, can **4.2**

el pollo chicken **4.2**
por for, per
   Por favor. Please. **LP**
   ¿Por qué? Why? **3.1**
porque because **1.2**
el postre dessert **4.2**
   de postre for dessert **4.2**
practicar to practice **1.1**
   practicar deportes to play or practice sports **1.1**
el precio price **4.1**
preferir (ie) to prefer **4.1**
la pregunta question
el premio award
preparar to prepare **1.1**
   preparar la comida to prepare food, to make a meal **1.1**
presentar to introduce **LP**
   Te/Le presento a... Let me introduce you to... (familiar/formal) **LP**
la primavera spring **4.1**
primero(a) first
   el primero de... the first of... (date) **3.2**
el (la) primo(a) cousin **3.2**
los primos cousins **3.2**
el problema problem **2.2**
la procesión (*pl.* **las procesiones**) procession
proclamar to declare
la propina tip (in a restaurant) **4.2**
el pueblo town
la puerta door **2.2**

¿Qué? What? **3.1**
   ¿De qué color es/son...? What color is/are...?
   ¿Qué día es hoy? What day is today? **LP**
   ¿Qué hora es? What time is it? **2.1**
   ¿Qué pasa? What's happening? **LP**
   ¿Qué tal? How's it going? **LP**
   ¿Qué te gusta hacer? What do you like to do? **1.1**
   ¿Qué tiempo hace? What is the weather like? **LP**
el quechua indigenous language from South America
querer (ie) to want **4.1**

el queso cheese 3.1
  el queso crema cream cheese
¿Quién(es)? Who? 3.1
  ¿Quién es? Who is he/she/it? LP
quince fifteen 2.1
quinientos(as) five hundred 3.2

un rato a while, a short time
la raza (human) race
la razón (pl. las razones) reason
  tener razón to be right 4.1
la reconstrucción (pl. las
  reconstrucciones) reenactment
recordar (ue) to remember
  ¿Recuerdas? Do you remember?
el recorrido run, journey
el recreo recess
el refresco soft drink 1.1
regular OK LP
  Regular. ¿Y tú/usted? OK. And
    you? (familiar/formal) LP
el reloj watch; clock 2.2
el repaso review
responder to reply
el restaurante restaurant 4.2
el resultado result
el resumen summary
  en resumen in summary
los Reyes Magos Three Kings
rico(a) tasty, delicious 3.1
rojo(a) red 4.1
la rosca de reyes sweet bread eaten
  on January 6
la ropa clothing 4.1
rubio(a) blond 1.2

sábado Saturday LP
sacar una buena/mala nota to get a
  good/bad grade 2.1
¡Saludos! Greetings!
  Saludos desde... Greetings from...
el sándwich sandwich 3.1
  el sándwich de jamón y queso
    ham and cheese sandwich 3.1
el santo saint
seis six LP
seiscientos(as) six hundred 3.2

la semana week LP
  el fin de semana weekend
  Semana Santa Holy Week
Señor (Sr.) Mr. LP
Señora (Sra.) Mrs. LP
Señorita (Srta.) Miss LP
septiembre September 3.2
ser to be 1.1
  Es de... He/She is from... LP
  Es el... de... It's the... of... (day and
    month) 3.2
  Es la.../Son las... It is...
    o'clock. 2.1
  Soy de... I'm from... LP
serio(a) serious 1.2
servir (i) to serve 4.2
sesenta sixty 2.1
setecientos(as) seven hundred 3.2
setenta seventy 2.1
si if
sí yes LP
siempre always 2.1
siete seven LP
la silla chair 2.2
simpático(a) nice, friendly 1.2
sobre about; on
el sombrero hat 4.1
la sopa soup 3.1
su his, her, its, their, your
  (formal) 3.2
el supermercado supermarket

tal vez perhaps, maybe 4.2
también also, too 1.1
  también se dice... you can
    also say...
tan... como as... as 3.2
tanto como... as much as... 3.2
tanto(a) so much
tantos(as) so many
tarde late 2.1
la tarde afternoon 2.1
  Buenas tardes. Good
    afternoon. LP
  de la tarde in the afternoon
    (with a time) 2.1
la tarea homework 1.1
la tarjeta postal postcard
el teatro theater 4.2

el teléfono telephone
  ¿Cuál es tu/su número de
    teléfono? What is your phone
    number? (familiar/formal) LP
  Mi número de teléfono es... My
    phone number is... LP
el tema theme
temprano early 2.1
tener to have 2.1
  ¿Cuántos años tienes? How old
    are you? 3.2
  tener... años to be... years old 3.2
  tener calor to be hot 4.1
  tener frío to be cold 4.1
  tener ganas de... to to feel
    like... 3.1
  tener hambre to be hungry 3.1
  tener que... to have to... 2.1
  tener razón to be right 4.1
  tener sed to be thirsty 3.1
  tener suerte to be lucky 4.1
la tía aunt 3.2
el tiempo weather LP
  ¿Qué tiempo hace? What is the
    weather like? LP
la tienda store 4.1
el tío uncle 3.2
los tíos uncles, uncle(s) and
  aunt(s) 3.2
típico(a) typical
el tipo type
la tiza chalk 2.2
tocar to play (an instrument) 1.1
  tocar la guitarra to play the
    guitar 1.1
todo junto all together
todos(as) all 1.2
  todos los días every day 2.1
tomar to take 4.2
  tomar apuntes to take notes 2.1
el tomate tomato 4.2
trabajador(a) hard-working 1.2
trabajar to work 1.1
tranquilo(a) calm 2.2
trece thirteen 2.1
treinta thirty 2.1
treinta y uno thirty-one 2.1
tres three LP
trescientos(as) three hundred 3.2
triste sad 2.2
tu your (sing., familiar) 3.2
tú you (sing., familiar) 1.1
el turismo tourism
el turrón (pl. los turrones) almond
  nougat candy

último(a) last
la unidad unit
uno one **LP**
usar to use **2.1**
    usar la computadora to use the
    computer **2.1**
usted you (sing., formal) **1.1**
ustedes you (pl.) **1.1**
la uva grape **3.1**
    las doce uvas twelve grapes
    eaten on New Year's Eve

¡Vale! OK!
varios(as) various
veinte twenty **2.1**
veintiuno twenty-one **2.1**
el (la) vendedor(a) salesclerk
vender to sell **3.1**
la ventana window **2.2**
la ventanilla ticket window **4.2**
ver (veo) to see **4.2**

el verano summer **4.1**
la verdad truth
    ¿Verdad? Really?; Right? **LP**
verde green **4.1**
las verduras vegetables **4.2**
el vestido dress **4.1**
la vez (*pl.* **las veces**) time
    a veces sometimes
    de vez en cuando once in a
    while **2.1**
    muchas veces often, many
    times **2.1**
    tal vez maybe **4.2**
la vida life
el videojuego video game
viejo(a) old **1.2**
el viento wind
    Hace viento. It is windy. **LP**
viernes Friday **LP**
el villancico seasonal children's
    song
visitar to visit
vivir to live **3.2**
el vocabulario vocabulary
volver (ue) to return, to come
    back **4.2**
vosotros(as) you (pl. familiar) **1.1**
vuestro(a) your (pl. familiar) **3.2**

y and
    ...y (diez) (ten) past... (the
    hour) **2.1**
    ...y cuarto quarter past... (the
    hour) **2.1**
    ...y media half past... (the
    hour) **2.1**
    ¿Y tú? And you? (familiar) **LP**
    ¿Y usted? And you? (formal) **LP**
ya already **3.2**
yo I **1.1**
el yogur yogurt **3.1**

el zapato shoe **4.1**

Glosario
inglés-español

This English-Spanish glossary contains all the active vocabulary words that appear in the text as well as passive vocabulary lists. **LP** refers to Lección preliminar.

A

about sobre
activity la actividad **1.1**
to advance avanzar
advertisement el anuncio
after después (de) **1.1**
afternoon la tarde **2.1**
  Good afternoon. Buenas tardes. **LP**
  in the afternoon de la tarde **2.1**
afterward después **1.1**
all todos(as) **1.2**
all together todo junto
almost casi **2.1**
already ya **3.2**
also también **1.1**
always siempre **2.1**
and y
angry enojado(a) **2.2**
announcement el anuncio
answer la respuesta
to answer contestar **2.1**
apple la manzana **3.1**
April abril **3.2**
arrival la llegada
to arrive llegar **2.1**
art el arte **2.1**
article el artículo
artistic artístico(a) **1.2**
as como
  as... as tan... como **3.2**
  as much as... tanto como... **3.2**
to ask for pedir (i) **4.2**
at a
  at night de la noche **2.1**
  At... o'clock. A la(s)... **2.1**
  At what time is/are...? ¿A qué hora es/son...? **2.1**
athletic atlético(a) **1.2**
August agosto **3.2**
aunt la tía **3.2**
autumn el otoño **4.1**
award el premio

B

backpack la mochila **2.2**
bad malo(a) **1.2**
  Bad. And you? (familiar/formal) Mal. ¿Y tú/usted? **LP**
banana la banana **3.1**
bathroom el baño **2.2**
to be ser **1.1**; estar **2.2**
  to be able poder (ue) **4.2**
  to be called llamarse
  to be cold tener frío **4.1**
  to be hot tener calor **4.1**
  to be hungry tener hambre **3.1**
  to be lucky tener suerte **4.1**
  to be right tener razón **4.1**
  to be thirsty tener sed **3.1**
  to be... years old tener... años **3.2**
beach la playa
beans los frijoles **4.2**
because porque **1.2**
beef el bistec **4.2**
before antes (de) **1.1**; menos (with a time) **2.1**
to begin empezar (ie) **4.1**
behind detrás (de) **2.2**
better mejor **3.2**
beverage la bebida **3.1**
bicycle la bicicleta **1.1**
big grande **1.2**
bill (in a restaurant) la cuenta **4.2**
birth date la fecha de nacimiento **3.2**
birthday el cumpleaños **3.2**
  Happy birthday! ¡Feliz cumpleaños! **3.2**
black negro(a) **4.1**
blond rubio(a) **1.2**
blouse la blusa **4.1**
blue azul **4.1**
board el pizarrón (*pl.* los pizarrones) **2.2**
boat el bote
book el libro **1.1**
boring aburrido(a) **2.2**

boy el chico **1.2**
bread el pan **3.1**
breakfast el desayuno **3.1**
broccoli el brócoli **4.2**
brother el hermano **3.2**
brown marrón (*pl.* marrones) **4.1**
  brown hair el pelo castaño **1.2**
bus el autobús (*pl.* los autobuses) **4.2**
  by bus en autobús **4.2**
busy ocupado(a) **2.2**
but pero **1.1**
to buy comprar **1.1**

C

café el café **4.2**
cafeteria la cafetería **2.2**
cake el pastel **4.2**
calculator la calculadora **2.2**
calm tranquilo(a) **2.2**
can (to be able) poder (ue) **4.2**
car el coche **4.2**
  by car en coche **4.2**
cat el (la) gato(a) **3.2**
center el centro **4.2**
cereal el cereal **3.1**
chair la silla **2.2**
chalk la tiza **2.2**
chalkboard el pizarrón (*pl.* los pizarrones) **2.2**
change el cambio
cheese el queso **3.1**
  cream cheese el queso crema
chicken el pollo **4.2**
children los hijos **3.2**
class la clase **LP**
classroom la clase **LP**
clock el reloj **2.2**
to close cerrar (ie) **4.1**
clothing la ropa **4.1**
clue la pista
coffee el café **3.1**

cold el frío
   It is cold. Hace frío. **LP**
   to be cold tener frío **4.1**
color el color
   What color is/are...? ¿De qué color es/son...?
to come back volver (ue) **4.2**
common común
to compare comparar
computer la computadora **2.1**
concert el concierto **4.2**
cookie la galleta **1.1**
coral reef el arrecife de coral
to correct corregir
to cost costar (ue) **4.2**
   How much does it (do they) cost? ¿Cuánto cuesta(n)? **4.1**
   It (They) cost... Cuesta(n)... **4.1**
costume el disfraz (*pl.* los disfraces)
country el país **LP**
course el plato
   main course el plato principal **4.2**
cousin el (la) primo(a) **3.2**

dance el baile
to dance bailar
date la fecha **3.2**
   birth date la fecha de nacimiento **3.2**
   What is the date? ¿Cuál es la fecha? **3.2**
daughter la hija **3.2**
day el día **LP**
   every day todos los días **2.1**
   What day is today? ¿Qué día es hoy? **LP**
December diciembre **3.2**
delicious rico(a) **3.1**
Delighted. Encantado(a). **LP**
department store el almacén (*pl.* los almacenes)
depressed deprimido(a) **2.2**
desk el escritorio **2.2**
dessert el postre **4.2**
   for dessert de postre **4.2**
different diferente
difficult difícil **2.1**
dinner la cena **3.1**
dish el plato
   main dish el plato principal **4.2**

disorganized desorganizado(a) **1.2**
to do hacer (hago) **3.1**
dog el (la) perro(a) **3.2**
dollar el dólar **4.1**
door la puerta **2.2**
downtown el centro **4.2**
to draw dibujar **1.1**
drawing el dibujo
dress el vestido **4.1**
drink la bebida **3.1**
to drink beber **1.1**
during durante **4.1**
DVD el DVD **1.1**

each cada
early temprano **2.1**
easy fácil **2.1**
to eat comer **1.1**
   to eat lunch almorzar (ue) **4.2**
egg el huevo **3.1**
eight ocho **LP**
eight hundred ochocientos(as) **3.2**
eighteen dieciocho **2.1**
eleven once **2.1**
e-mail el correo electrónico **1.1**
English el inglés **2.1**
to enter entrar
eraser el borrador **2.2**
euro el euro **4.1**
evening la noche **LP**
   Good evening. Buenas noches. **LP**
every cada
   every day todos los días **2.1**
exam el examen (*pl.* los exámenes) **2.1**
excited emocionado(a) **2.2**
Excuse me. Perdón. **LP**
eye el ojo

fall el otoño **4.1**
false falso(a)
family la familia **3.2**
far (from) lejos (de) **2.2**
father el padre **3.2**
February febrero **3.2**
to feel like... tener ganas de... **3.1**

few pocos(as)
fifteen quince **2.1**
fifty cincuenta **2.1**
to find encontrar (ue) **4.2**
fine bien **LP**
   Fine. And you? (familiar/ Bien. ¿Y tú/usted? formal) **LP**
fireworks los fuegos artificiales
first primero(a)
   the first of... el primero de... **3.2**
fish el pescado **4.2**
five cinco **LP**
five hundred quinientos(as) **3.2**
food la comida **1.1, 3.1**
food server el (la) camarero(a) **4.2**
foot el pie
   on foot a pie **4.2**
for para **3.1**; por
forty cuarenta **2.1**
fountain la fuente
four cuatro **LP**
four hundred cuatrocientos(as) **3.2**
fourteen catorce **2.1**
French fries las papas fritas **1.1**
Friday viernes **LP**
friend el (la) amigo(a) **1.2**
   to spend time with friends pasar un rato con los amigos **1.1**
from de **1.1**
fruit la fruta **1.1**
fun divertido(a) **2.2**
funny cómico(a) **1.2**

garden el jardín (*pl.* los jardines)
girl la chica **1.2**
to go ir **2.2**
   to be going to... ir a... **4.2**
   to go for a walk pasear **1.1**
   to go shopping ir de compras **4.1**
good bueno(a) **1.2**
   Good afternoon. Buenas tardes. **LP**
   Good evening. Buenas noches. **LP**
   Good morning. Buenos días. **LP**
   Good night. Buenas noches. **LP**
Goodbye. Adiós. **LP**
good-looking guapo(a) **1.2**

grade la nota **2.1**
    to get a good/bad grade sacar una buena/mala nota **2.1**
grammar la grámatica
grandfather el abuelo **3.2**
grandmother la abuela **3.2**
grandparents los abuelos **3.2**
grape la uva **3.1**
green verde **4.1**
Greetings! ¡Saludos!
    Greetings from... Saludos desde...
guitar la guitarra **1.1**
gymnasium el gimnasio **2.2**

hair el pelo **1.2**
    blond hair pelo rubio **1.2**
    brown hair pelo castaño **1.2**
half medio(a)
    half past... ... y media **2.1**
hall el pasillo **2.2**
ham el jamón (*pl.* los jamones) **3.1**
hamburger la hamburguesa **3.1**
to happen pasar
    What's happening? ¿Qué pasa? **LP**
happy contento(a) **2.2**
hard-working trabajador(a) **1.2**
hat el sombrero **4.1**
    winter hat el gorro **4.1**
to have tener **2.1**
    to have to... tener que... **2.1**
he él **1.1**
Hello. Hola. **LP**
her su **3.2**
here aquí **4.2**
Hi. Hola. **LP**
high school el colegio, la escuela secundaria
his su **3.2**
history la historia **2.1**
homework la tarea **1.1**
    to do homework hacer la tarea **1.1**
horrible horrible **3.1**
hot caliente
    It is hot. Hace calor. **LP**
    to be hot tener calor **4.1**
hour la hora **2.1**

How...? ¿Cómo...? **3.1**
    How are you? ¿Cómo estás? (familiar); ¿Cómo está usted? (formal) **LP**
    How many...? ¿Cuántos(as)...? **2.1**
    How old are you? ¿Cuántos años tienes? **3.2**
    How's it going? ¿Qué tal? **LP**
how many cuántos(as) **3.2**
how much cuánto(a) **3.2**
    How much does it (do they) cost? ¿Cuánto cuesta(n)? **4.1**
hungry: to be hungry tener hambre **3.1**

I yo **1.1**
ice cream el helado **1.1**
if si
important importante **3.1**
    It's important. Es importante. **3.1**
in en **2.1**
    in front (of) delante (de) **2.2**
    in order to para **3.1**
    in the afternoon de la tarde **2.1**
    in the morning de la mañana **2.1**
inexpensive barato(a)
information la información
inside (of) dentro (de) **2.2**
intelligent inteligente **1.2**
interesting interesante **2.2**
to introduce presentar **LP**
    Let me introduce you to... Te/Le presento a... (familiar/formal) **LP**
its su **3.2**

jacket la chaqueta **4.1**
January enero **3.2**
jeans los jeans **4.1**
juice el jugo **1.1**
    orange juice el jugo de naranja **3.1**
July julio **3.2**
June junio **3.2**

kind la clase

lake el lago
language el idioma, el lenguaje
large grande **1.2**
late tarde **2.1**
later
    See you later. Hasta luego. **LP**
lazy perezoso(a) **1.2**
to learn aprender **1.1**
    to learn Spanish aprender el español **1.1**
less menos
    less than... menos que... **3.2**
    less... than menos... que **3.2**
lesson la lección
Let's... Vamos a... **4.2**
library la biblioteca **2.2**
life la vida
like como
to like
    Do you like...? ¿Te gusta...? **1.1**
    I don't like... No me gusta... **1.1**
    I like... Me gusta... **1.1**
    What do you like to do? ¿Qué te gusta hacer? **1.1**
Likewise. Igualmente. **LP**
to listen (to) escuchar **1.1**
    to listen to music escuchar música **1.1**
little pequeño(a) **1.2**
    a little un poco **1.2**
to live vivir **3.2**
to look (at) mirar
a lot mucho **2.1**
lunch el almuerzo **3.1**
    to eat lunch almorzar (ue) **4.2**

to make hacer (hago) **3.1**
mall el centro comercial **4.1**
man el hombre **1.2**
many muchos(as) **2.1**
    many times muchas veces **2.1**
map el mapa **2.2**

March marzo **3.2**
market el mercado
   open-air market el mercado al aire libre
math las matemáticas **2.1**
May mayo **3.2**
maybe tal vez **4.2**
meal la comida **1.1, 3.1**
meat la carne **4.2**
to meet
   Nice to meet you. Mucho gusto. **LP**
menu el menú **4.2**
milk la leche **3.1**
million un millón (de) **3.2**
minute el minuto **2.1**
Miss Señorita (Srta.) **LP**
Monday lunes **LP**
money el dinero **4.1**
month el mes **3.2**
more más **1.1**
   more than... más que... **3.2**
   more... than más... que **3.2**
morning la mañana **2.1**
   Good morning. Buenos días. **LP**
   in the morning de la mañana **2.1**
mother la madre **3.2**
movie la película **4.2**
movie theater el cine **4.2**
the movies el cine **4.2**
Mr. Señor (Sr.) **LP**
Mrs. Señora (Sra.) **LP**
museum el museo
music la música **1.1**
   folk music la música folklórica
   rock music la música rock **4.2**
my mi **3.2**

name el nombre
   His/Her name is... Se llama... **LP**
   My name is... Me llamo... **LP**
   What's his/her/your (formal) name? ¿Cómo se llama? **LP**
   What's your (familiar) name? ¿Cómo te llamas? **LP**
near (to) cerca (de) **2.2**
to need necesitar **2.1**
nervous nervioso(a) **2.2**
never nunca **2.1**

new nuevo(a) **4.1**
   New Year el Año Nuevo
newspaper el periódico
   student newspaper el periódico escolar
next to al lado (de) **2.2**
nice simpático(a) **1.2**
   Nice to meet you. Mucho gusto. **LP**
night la noche **2.1**
   at night de la noche **2.1**
   Good night. Buenas noches. **LP**
nine nueve **LP**
nine hundred novecientos(as) **3.2**
nineteen diecinueve **2.1**
ninety noventa **2.1**
no no **LP**
notebook el cuaderno **2.2**
notes los apuntes **2.1**
   to take notes tomar apuntes **2.1**
November noviembre **3.2**
now ahora **3.1**
number el número **LP**
   phone number el número de teléfono **LP**
nutritious nutritivo(a) **3.1**

o'clock: It is... o'clock. Es la.../Son las... **2.1**
October octubre **3.2**
of de **1.1**
office la oficina **2.2**
   principal's office la oficina del (de la) director(a) **2.2**
often muchas veces **2.1**
OK
   OK! ¡Vale!
   OK? ¿Está bien?
   OK. And you? Regular. ¿Y tú/ usted? (familiar/formal) **LP**
old viejo(a) **1.2**
   How old are you? ¿Cuántos años tienes? **3.2**
   to be... years old tener... años **3.2**
older mayor **3.2**
on en; sobre
   on foot a pie **4.2**
   on top (of) encima (de) **2.2**
once: once in a while de vez en cuando **2.1**
one uno **LP**
one hundred cien **2.1**

one thousand mil **3.2**
or o **1.1**
orange (color) anaranjado(a) **4.1**
orange (fruit) la naranja **3.1**
to order pedir (i) **4.2**
organized organizado(a) **1.2**
other otro(a) **3.1**
our nuestro(a) **3.2**

page la página
painting el cuadro
pair la pareja
pants los pantalones **4.1**
paper el papel **2.2**
parade el desfile
paragraph el párrafo
parents los padres **3.2**
park el parque **4.2**
   amusement park el parque de diversiones
part la parte
party la fiesta
past
   half past... ...y media **2.1**
   quarter past... ...y cuarto **2.1**
the past el pasado
to pay pagar **4.1**
pen la pluma **2.2**
pencil el lápiz (*pl.* los lápices) **2.2**
perhaps tal vez **4.2**
person la persona **1.2**
phone el teléfono **LP**
   What is your phone number? ¿Cuál es tu/su número de teléfono? (familiar/formal) **LP**
   My phone number is... Mi número de teléfono es... **LP**
pizza la pizza **1.1**
place el lugar **4.2**
to plan pensar (ie) **4.1**
plant la planta
plate el plato
to play
   (an instrument) tocar **1.1**
   (games) jugar (ue) **1.1**
   (sports) jugar (ue), practicar **1.1**
Please. Por favor. **LP**
   Pleased to meet you. Encantado(a). **LP**
pleasure el gusto
   The pleasure is mine. El gusto es mío. **LP**
postcard la tarjeta postal

potato la papa **1.1**; la patata **4.2**
to practice practicar **1.1**
to prefer preferir (ie) **4.1**
to prepare preparar **1.1**
  to prepare food/a meal preparar la comida **1.1**
pretty bonito(a) **1.2**
price el precio **4.1**
principal el (la) director(a) **2.2**
problem el problema **2.2**

quarter (to) (menos) cuarto **2.1**
quarter past ...y cuarto **2.1**

to rain llover (ue)
  It is raining. Llueve. **LP**
to read leer **1.1**
  to read a book leer un libro **1.1**
reading la lectura
Really? ¿Verdad?
recess el recreo
red rojo(a) **4.1**
red-haired pelirrojo(a) **1.2**
to rent alquilar **1.1**
  to rent a DVD alquilar un DVD **1.1**
to reply responder
to rest descansar **1.1**
restaurant el restaurante **4.2**
result el resultado
to return volver (ue) **4.2**
review el repaso
rice el arroz **4.2**
to ride a bike montar en bicicleta **1.1**
right derecho(a)
  Right? ¿Verdad? **LP**
  to be right tener razón **4.1**
to run correr **1.1**

S

sad triste **2.2**
salad la ensalada **4.2**
salesclerk el (la) vendedor(a)
same mismo(a)
  Same here. Igualmente. **LP**

sandwich el sándwich **3.1**
  ham and cheese sandwich el sándwich de jamón y queso **3.1**
Saturday sábado **LP**
scene la escena
schedule el horario **2.1**
school la escuela **1.1**
  high school el colegio, la escuela secundaria
science las ciencias **2.1**
season la estación (*pl.* las estaciones) **4.1**
to see ver (veo) **4.2**
  See you later. Hasta luego. **LP**
  See you tomorrow. Hasta mañana. **LP**
to sell vender **3.1**
sentence la oración (*pl.* las oraciones)
September septiembre **3.2**
serious serio(a) **1.2**
to serve servir (i) **4.2**
seven siete **LP**
seven hundred setecientos(as) **3.2**
seventeen diecisiete **2.1**
seventy setenta **2.1**
to share compartir **3.1**
she ella **1.1**
shirt la camisa **4.1**
shoe el zapato **4.1**
shop: to go shopping ir de compras **4.1**
shopping center el centro comercial **4.1**
short (height) bajo(a) **1.2**
shorts los pantalones cortos **4.1**
sister la hermana **3.2**
six seis **LP**
six hundred seiscientos(as) **3.2**
sixteen dieciséis **2.1**
sixty sesenta **2.1**
to skateboard andar en patineta **1.1**
to sleep dormir (ue) **4.2**
small pequeño(a) **1.2**
snow la nieve
to snow nevar (ie)
  It is snowing. Nieva. **LP**
so
  so many tantos(as)
  so much tanto(a)
soccer el fútbol **1.1**
sock el calcetín (*pl.* los calcetines) **4.1**
soft drink el refresco **1.1**
sometimes a veces
son el hijo **3.2**
So-so. And you? Más o menos. ¿Y tú/usted? (familiar/formal) **LP**

soup la sopa **3.1**
source la fuente
Spanish el español **2.1**
to speak hablar **1.1**
special especial
to spend: to spend time with friends pasar un rato con los amigos **1.1**
spirit el ánimo
sports los deportes **1.1**
spring la primavera **4.1**
stepfather el padrastro **3.2**
stepmother la madrastra **3.2**
to stop parar
store la tienda **4.1**
street la calle **4.2**
student el (la) estudiante **1.2**
studious estudioso(a) **1.2**
to study estudiar **1.1**
summary el resumen
  in summary en resumen
summer el verano **4.1**
sun el sol
  It is sunny. Hace sol. **LP**
Sunday domingo **LP**
supermarket el supermercado
survey la encuesta
swimming pool la piscina

table la mesa **4.2**
to take tomar **4.2**
  to take notes tomar apuntes **2.1**
to talk hablar **1.1**
  to talk on the phone hablar por teléfono **1.1**
tall alto(a) **1.2**
tasty rico(a) **3.1**
to teach enseñar **2.1**
teacher el (la) maestro(a) **LP**
team el equipo
ten diez **LP**
test el examen (*pl.* los exámenes) **2.1**
Thank you. Gracias. **LP**
  Thank you very much. Muchas gracias. **LP**
theater el teatro **4.2**
their su **3.2**
them ellos(as) **7.2**
theme el tema
there allí **4.2**
  there is/are... hay... **2.1**
they ellos(as) **1.1**

to think pensar (ie) **4.1**
thirst la sed
  to be thirsty tener sed **3.1**
thirteen trece **2.1**
thirty treinta **2.1**
thirty-one treinta y uno **2.1**
thousand mil **3.2**
three tres **LP**
three hundred trescientos(as) **3.2**
Thursday jueves **LP**
ticket la entrada **4.2**
time la hora **2.1**; la vez
  At what time is/are...? ¿A qué
    hora es/son...? **2.1**
  What time is it? ¿Qué hora
    es? **2.1**
tip la propina **4.2**
tired cansado(a) **2.2**
to menos (with a time) **2.1**; a
today hoy **LP**
  Today is... Hoy es... **LP**
  What day is today? ¿Qué día es
    hoy? **LP**
tomato el tomate **4.2**
tomorrow mañana **LP**
  See you tomorrow. Hasta
    mañana. **LP**
  Tomorrow is... Mañana es... **LP**
too también **1.1**
too much demasiado
tourism el turismo
town el pueblo
true cierto(a)
T-shirt la camiseta **4.1**
Tuesday martes **LP**
twelve doce **2.1**
twenty veinte **2.1**
twenty-one veintiuno **2.1**
two dos **LP**
two hundred doscientos(as) **3.2**
type el tipo; la clase
typical típico(a)

ugly feo(a) **4.1**
uncle el tío **3.2**
under debajo (de) **2.2**
underneath debajo (de) **2.2**
to understand entender (ie) **4.1**
  Did you understand?
    ¿Comprendiste?
unit la unidad

to use usar **2.1**
  to use the computer usar la
    computadora **2.1**

various varios(as)
vegetables las verduras **4.2**
very muy **1.2**
  Very well. And you? Muy bien.
    ¿Y tú/usted? (familiar/formal)
    LP
video game el videojuego
to visit visitar
vocabulary vocabulario

waiter el camarero **4.2**
waitress la camarera **4.2**
to walk caminar **6.2**
  to go for a walk pasear **1.1**
to want querer (ie) **4.1**; desear
watch el reloj **2.2**
to watch mirar **1.1**
  to watch television mirar la
    televisión **1.1**
water el agua (fem.) **1.1**
we nosotros(as) **1.1**
to wear llevar **4.1**
weather el tiempo **LP**
  What is the weather like? ¿Qué
    tiempo hace? **LP**
Wednesday miércoles **LP**
week la semana **LP**
welcome: You're welcome. De
  nada. **LP**
well bien **LP**
  Very well. And you? Muy bien.
    ¿Y tú/usted? (familiar/formal)
    LP
what qué
  What? ¿Qué?; ¿Cuál? **3.1**
  What are you like? ¿Cómo
    eres? **1.2**
  What color is/are...? ¿De qué
    color es/son...?
  What day is today? ¿Qué día es
    hoy? **LP**
  What do you like to do? ¿Qué
    te gusta hacer? **1.1**
  What is the date? ¿Cuál es la
    fecha? **3.2**

What is the weather like? ¿Qué
  tiempo hace? **LP**
What is your phone number?
  ¿Cuál es tu/su número de
  teléfono? (familiar/formal) **LP**
What time is it? ¿Qué hora
  es? **2.1**
What's happening? ¿Qué
  pasa? **LP**
What's his/her/your (formal)
  name? ¿Cómo se llama? **LP**
What's your (familiar)
  name? ¿Cómo te llamas? **LP**
when cuando **2.2**
  When? ¿Cuándo? **2.2**
where donde
  Where? ¿Dónde? **2.2**
  (To) Where? ¿Adónde? **2.2**
  Where are you from? ¿De
    dónde eres es usted
    (familiar)/(formal)? **LP**
  Where are you going? ¿Adónde
    vas? **2.2**
  Where is he/she from? ¿De
    dónde es? **LP**
Which? ¿Cuál(es)? **3.1**
a while un rato
  once in a while de vez en
    cuando **2.1**
white blanco(a) **4.1**
Who? ¿Quién(es)? **3.1**
  Who is he/she/it?
    ¿Quién es? **LP**
Why? ¿Por qué? **3.1**
wind el viento
  It is windy. Hace viento. **LP**
window la ventana **2.2**
  ticket window la ventanilla **4.2**
winter el invierno **4.1**
to wish desear
woman la mujer **1.2**
to work trabajar **1.1**
world el mundo
worse peor **3.2**
to write escribir **1.1**
  to write e-mails escribir correos
    electrónicos **1.1**
writing la escritura

year el año **3.2**
  New Year el Año Nuevo
  to be... years old tener...
    años **3.2**

yellow amarillo(a) **4.1**
yes sí **LP**
yogurt el yogur **3.1**
you
    (sing., familiar) tú **1.1**
    (sing., formal) usted **1.1**
    (pl., familiar) vosotros(as) **1.1**
    (pl.) ustedes **1.1**
young joven (*pl.* jóvenes) **1.2**
younger menor **3.2**
your
    (sing., familiar) tu **3.2**
    (pl., familiar) vuestro(a) **3.2**
    (formal) su **3.2**

zero cero **LP**

✤ Índice

ÍNDICE

Créditos

Acknowledgment

"Invierno tardío" by Antonio Colinas. Reprinted by permission of the author.

Photography

Cover *center* Steve Dunwell/The Image Bank/Getty Images; *inset* Marc Bacon/LatinFocus.com; **i** *Title Page* Steve Dunwell/The Image Bank/Getty Images; *Half Title Page* Marc Bacon/LatinFocus.com; **iii** Marc Bacon/LatinFocus.com; **Back Cover** *top left* Steve Dunwell/The Image Bank/Getty Images; *top center* Rodriguez Joseph/Gallery Stock Limited; *top right* Panoramic Images/Getty Images; *bottom left* Doug Armand/Getty Images; *bottom center* David Noton/Masterfile; *bottom right* P. Pet/zefa/Corbis; **iv** *top* Guy Jarvis/School Division/Houghton Mifflin Co.; *bottom left* Jaime Puebla/AP Images; *bottom right* Alberto Martin/Agencia EFE; **v** *bottom left* Gregory Bull/AP Images; *bottom right* Jennifer Szymaszek/AP Images; **vi** Ann Summa/McDougal Littell/Houghton Mifflin Co.; **vii** *left, right* Ann Summa/McDougal Littell/Houghton Mifflin Co.; **xxii** *top* Erich Lessing/Art Resource, New York; **xxiii** *top* Ann Summa/McDougal Littell/Houghton Mifflin Co.; *center, bottom* Ken Karp/McDougal Littell/Houghton Mifflin Co.; **xxv** *top* Jay Penni/McDougal Littell/Houghton Mifflin Co.; **xxvii** *left, right* Michael Goss/McDougal Littell/Houghton Mifflin Co.; **xxviii** *top left* Robert Galbraith/Reuters Pictures; *top right* McDougal Littell/Houghton Mifflin Co.; **xxix** *top left* Richard Wareham Fotografie/Alamy; *top right* Ann Summa Stock; *center* Edward Hernandez/Edward H. Photos; *bottom* Philip Coblentz/Brand X Pictures/Getty Images; **C2** *banner, left to right 1* Jesus Dominguez/Agencia EFE; *2-4* Rafael Diaz/Agencia EFE; *all others* Rafael Diaz/Agencia EFE; **C3** *top left, top right* Rafael Diaz/Agencia EFE; *bottom right* Jesus Dominguez/Agencia EFE; **C4** *banner, left to right* Juan Carlos Ulate/Reuters Pictures; The Brownsville Herald/Anthony Padilla/AP Images; Jose Luis Magana/AP Images; Agencia EFE; *bottom left* Hector Lopez/Agencia EFE; *bottom right* Marco Ugarte/AP Images; **C5** *top right* Kent Gilbert/AP Images; *top left* Daniel LeClair/Reuters Pictures; *bottom right* Juan Carlos Ulate/Reuters Pictures; **C6** *banner, left to right* Greg Smith/Corbis; Eduardo Verdugo/AP Images; Claudia Daut/Landov/Reuters Pictures; Les Stone/NewsCom/Zuma Press; *left* Laura Cano/NewsCom/Agence France Presse; *bottom right* Jacqueline Castellon/NewsCom/Notimex; **C7** *center left* Dennis Callahan/NewsCom/Notimex; *bottom right* Susana Vera/Reuters Pictures; *top right* Claudia Daut/Reuters/Landov LLC; **C8** *banner, left to right* Ann Summa; © 2007 Robert Frerck/Odyssey/Chicago; Denis Defibaugh; Rodrigo Abd/AP Images; *bottom left* Juan Barreto/Getty Images; *bottom left, inset* Ann Summa; *center left* Charles Bennett/AP Images; *top right* Marco Ugarte/AP Images; **C9** *top left* Glen Allison/Alamy; *top right* Eduardo Verdugo/AP Images; *bottom left* Jaime Puebla/AP Images; **C10** *banner, left to right* Marcelo Del Pozo/NewsCom/Reuters; Enrique Marcarian/Reuters Pictures; Juan Martin/Agencia EFE; Blake Sell/NewsCom/Reuters; *top left* Alberto Lowe/NewsCom/Reuters; *bottom left* Viesti Associates, Inc.; *bottom right* Leo La Valle/Agencia EFE; **C11** *top* Silvia Izquierdo/AP Images; *bottom* Desmond Boylan/NewsCom/Reuters; **C12** *banner, left to right* Dolores Ochoa R./AP Images; Marcou/Sipa Press; Denis Doyle/AP Images; Eric L. Weather/Lonely Planet Images; Luis Nereo Bueno Martinez/NewsCom/Reforma; *top left* Silvia Izquierdo/AP Images; *bottom right* Alberto Martin/Agencia EFE; *bottom center* Juanjo Martin/Agencia EFE; *bottom left* Olga Vasilkova/ShutterStock; **C13** *top right* Kryzsztof Dydynki/Lonely Planet Images; *left* Richard I'Anson/Lonely Planet Images; **C14** *banner, left to right* Miguel Vidal/Reuters/Corbis; Pablo Aneli/EPA/Sipa Press; Miguel Menendez V./EPA/Sipa Press; Andres Leighton/AP Images; *left* Elvira Urquijo A./EPA/Sipa Press; *bottom right* Martin Crespo/EPA/Sipa Press; **C15** *top left* Juan Barreto/Staff/Getty Images; *right* David Mercado/Reuters Pictures; *bottom left* Javier Galeano/AP Images; *bottom right* Guy Jarvis/McDougal Littell/Houghton Mifflin Co.; **C16** *banner, left to right 1* Kai Forsterling/Agencia EFE; *2* Hannah Levy/Lonely Planet Images; *3-5* Manuel Bruque/Agencia EFE; *bottom* Hannah Levy/Lonely Planet Images; *left* J.C. Cardenas/Agencia EFE; **C17** *right* Heino Kalis/Reuters/Corbis; *left* Kai Forsterling/Agencia EFE; **C18** *banner, left to right* Jack Kurtz/NewsCom/Zuma Press; Viesti Associates, Inc.; Viesti Associates, Inc.; Jack Kurtz/NewsCom/Zuma Press; *bottom right* Viesti Associates, Inc.; *left* Ann Summa; **C19** *top left* Pilar Olivares/Reuters Pictures; *bottom right* Viesti Associates, Inc.; *right* Brian Doben/BA-REPS.com; **C20** *banner, left to right* Tyler Hicks/New York Times; Joe Raedle/Getty Images; Jorge Uzon/Getty Images; Damian Dovarganes/AP Images; *right, bottom left* Robert Galbraith/Reuters Pictures; **C21** *top right* Jose Luis Magana/AP Images; *center* Michael Springer/Zuma Press; **C22** *banner, left to right 1-2* Paolo Aguilar/Agencia EFE; Paolo Aguilar/Agencia EFE; *bottom right, left* Paolo Aguilar/Agencia EFE; **C23** *right* Guillermo Legaria/Agencia EFE; *left* Christian Lombardi/Agencia EFE; **C24** *banner, left to right* Dado Galdieri/AP Images; Tony Morrison/South American Pictures; Stuart Franklin/Magnum Photos; *left* Daniel Munoz/Reuters/Corbis; *bottom right* Jupiter Images/Comstock; **C25** *bottom* Pablo Corral V/Corbis; *top left* Stuart Franklin/Magnum Photos; *top right* *Simón Bolívar* (1830), José Gil de Castro. Oil on canvas, 237cm x 167cm (93 5/16" x 65 3/4"). Museo Nacional de